4.2 Identify the categories of RAM (Random Access Memory) terminology, their locations, and physical characteristics.

Content may include the following:
- Terminology:
  - EDO RAM (Extended Data Output RAM)
  - DRAM (Dynamic Random Access Memory)
  - SRAM (Static RAM)
  - VRAM (Video RAM)
  - WRAM (Windows Accelerator Card RAM)
- Locations and physical characteristics:
  - Memory bank
  - Memory chips (8-bit, 16-bit, and 32-bit)
  - SIMMS (Single In-line Memory Module)
  - DIMMS (Dual In-line Memory Module)
  - Parity chips versus non-parity chips

4.3 Identify the most popular type of motherboards, their components, and their architecture (for example, bus structures and power supplies).

Content may include the following:
- Types of motherboards:
  - AT (Full and Baby)
  - ATX
- Components:
  - Communication ports
  - SIMM and DIMM
  - Processor sockets
  - External cache memory (Level 2)
- Bus Architecture
  - ISA
  - EISA
  - PCI
  - USB (Universal Serial Bus)
  - VESA local bus (VL-Bus)
  - PC Card (PCMCIA)
- Basic compatibility guidelines

4.4 Identify the purpose of CMOS (Complementary Metal-Oxide Semiconductor), what it contains and how to change its basic parameters.

Examples of Basic CMOS Settings:
- Printer parallel portUni., bi-directional, disable/enable, ECP, EPP

- COM/serial portmemory address, interrupt request, disable
- Floppy drive enable/disable drive or boot, speed, density
- Hard drive size and drive type
- Memory parity, non-parity
- Boot sequence
- Date/Time
- Passwords

DOMAIN 5.0 PRINTERS

5.1 Identify basic concepts, printer operations, and printer components.

Content may include the following:
- Types of Printers
  - Laser
  - Inkjet
  - Dot Matrix
  - Paper feeder mechanisms

5.2 Identify care and service techniques and common problems with primary printer types.

Content may include the following:
- Feed and output
- Errors
- Paper jam
- Print quality
- Safety precautions
- Preventive maintenance

5.3 Identify the types of printer connections and configurations.

Content may include the following:
- Parallel
- Serial
- Network

DOMAIN 6.0 PORTABLE SYSTEMS

6.1 Identify the unique components of portable systems and their unique problems.

Content may include the following:
- Battery
- LCD
- AC adapter
- Docking stations
- Hard Drive
- Type I, II, and III cards
- Network cards
- Memory

DOMAIN 7.0 BASIC NETWORKING

7.1 Identify basic networking concepts, how a network works.
the following:

7.2 Identify proc... and configuring netw... ...ce cards.

7.3 Identify the ramifications of repairs on the network.

Content may include the following:
- Reduced bandwidth
- Loss of data
- Network slowdown

DOMAIN 8.0 CUSTOMER SATISFACTION

8.1 Differentiate effective from ineffective behaviors as these contribute to the maintenance or achievement of customer satisfaction.

Content may include the following:
- Communicating and listening (face-to-face or over the phone)
- Interpreting verbal and nonverbal cues
- Responding appropriately to the customer's technical level
- Establishing personal rapport with the customer
- Professional conduct, for example, punctuality and accountability
- Helping and guiding a customer with problem descriptions
- Responding to and closing a service call
- Handling complaints and upset customers, conflict avoidance, and resolution
- Showing empathy and flexibility
- Sharing the customer's sense of urgency

A+ DOS/WINDOWS EXAM

DOMAIN 1.0 FUNCTION, STRUCTURE OPERATION, AND FILE MANAGEMENT

1.1 Identify the operating system's functions, structure, and major system files.

Content may include the following:
- Functions of DOS, Windows 3.x, and Windows 95
- Major components of DOS, Windows 3.x, and Windows 95
- Contrasts between Windows 3.x and Windows 95
- Major system files: what they are, where they are located, how they are used, and what they contain:
  - System, Configuration, and User Interface files
  - **DOS**
    Autoexec.bat
    Config.sys
    Io.sys
    Ansi.sys
    Msdos.sys
    Emm386.exe
    HIMEM.SYS

Command.com (internal DOS commands)
- **Windows 3.x**
  Win.ini
  System.ini
  User.exe
  Gdi.exe
  win.ini
  Win.com
  Progman.ini
  progMAN.exe
  Krnlxxx.exe

- **Windows 95**
  Io.sys
  Msdos.sys
  Command.com
  regedit.exe
  System.dat
  User.dat

CompTIA OFFICIAL A+ EXAM OBJECTIVES

1.2 Identify ways to navigate the operating system and how to get to needed technical information.

Content may include the following:
- Procedures (e.g., menu or icon -driven) for navigating through DOS to perform such things as locating, accessing, and retrieving information
- Procedures for navigating through the Windows 3.x/Windows 95 operating system, accessing, and retrieving information

1.3 Identify basic concepts and procedures for creating, viewing and managing files and directories, including procedures for changing file attributes and the ramifications of those changes (for example, security issues).

Content may include the following:
- File attributes
- File naming conventions
- Command syntax
- Read Only, Hidden, System, and Archive attributes

1.4 Identify the procedures for basic disk management.

Content may include the following:
- Using disk management utilities
- Backing up
- Formatting
- Partitioning
- Defragmenting
- ScanDisk
- FAT32
- File allocation tables (FAT)
- Virtual file allocation tables (VFAT)

DOMAIN 2.0 MEMORY MANAGEMENT

2.1 Differentiate between types of memory.

Content may include the following:
- Conventional
- Extended/upper memory
- High memory
- Expanded memory
- Virtual memory

2.2 Identify typical memory conflict problems and how to optimize memory use.

Content may include the following:
- What a memory conflict is
- How it happens
- When to employ utilities
- System Monitor
- General Protection Fault
- Illegal operations occurrences
- MemMaker or other optimization utilities
- Himem.sys
- SMARTDRV
- Use of expanded memory blocks (using Emm386.exe)

DOMAIN 3.0 INSTALLATION, CONFIGURATION AND UPGRADING

3.1 Identify the procedures for installing DOS, Windows 3.x, and Windows 95, and for bringing the software to a basic operational level.

Content may include the following:
- Partition
- Format drive
- Running appropriate setup utility
- Loading drivers

3.2 Identify steps to perform an operating system upgrade.

Content may include the following:
- Upgrading from DOS to Windows 95
- Upgrading from Windows 3.x to Windows 95

3.3 Identify the basic system boot sequences and alternative ways to boot the system software, including the steps to create an emergency boot disk with utilities installed.

Content may include the following:
- Files required to boot
- Creating emergency boot disk
- Startup disk
- Safe Mode
- DOS mode

3.4 Identify procedures for loading/adding device drivers and the necessary software for certain devices.

Content may include the following:
- Windows 3.x procedures
- Windows 95 Plug and Play

DOMAIN 4.0 DIAGNOSING AND TROUBLESHOOTING

This domain requires the ability to apply knowledge to diagnose and troubleshoot common problems relating to DOS, Windows 3.x, and Windows 95. This includes understanding normal operation and symptoms relating to common problems.

4.1 Recognize and interpret the meaning of common error codes and startup messages from the boot sequence, and identify steps to correct the problems.

Content may include the following:
- Safe Mode
- Incorrect DOS version
- No operating system found
- Error in CONFIG.SYS line XX
- Bad or missing Command.com
- Himem.sys not loaded
- Missing or corrupt Himem.sys
- Swap file
- A device referenced in SYSTEM.INI could not be found

4.2 Recognize Windows-specific printing problems and identify the procedures for correcting them.

Content may include the following:
- Print spool is stalled
- Incorrect/incompatible driver for printer

4.3 Recognize common problems and determine how to resolve them.

Content may include the following:
- Common problems
  - General Protection Faults
  - Illegal operation
  - Invalid working directory
  - System lockup
  - Option will not function
  - Application will not start or load
  - Cannot log on to network
- DOS and Windows-based utilities
  - ScanDisk
  - Device manager
  - ATTRIB.EXE
  - EXTRACT.EXE
  - Defrag.exe
  - Edit.com
  - Fdisk.exe
  - MSD.EXE
  - Mem.exe
  - SYSEDIT.EXE

4.4 Identify concepts relating to viruses and virus types, their danger, their symptoms, sources of viruses, how they infect, how to protect against them, and how to identify and remove them.

Content may include the following:
- What they are
- Sources
- How to determine presence

DOMAIN 5.0 NETWORKS

5.1 Identify the networking capabilities of DOS and Windows including procedures for connecting to the network.

Content may include the following:
- Sharing disk drives
- Sharing print and file services
- Network type and network card

5.2 Identify concepts and capabilities relating to the Internet and basic procedures for setting up a system for Internet access.

Content may include the following:
- TCP/IP
- E-mail
- HTML
- HTTP://
- FTP
- Domain Names (web sites)
- ISP
- Dial-up access

A+ Certification
Study Guide

Second Edition

A+ Certification
Study Guide

Second Edition

Syngress Media, Inc.

Osborne McGraw-Hill

Berkeley New York St. Louis San Francisco Auckland Bogotá Hamburg London Madrid Mexico City
Milan Montreal New Delhi Panama City Paris São Paulo Singapore Sydney Tokyo Toronto

Osborne/**McGraw-Hill**
2600 Tenth Street
Berkeley, California 94710
U.S.A.

For information on translations or book distributors outside the U.S.A.,
or to arrange bulk purchase discounts for sales promotions, premiums, or
fund-raisers, please contact Osborne/**McGraw-Hill** at the above address.

A+ Certification Study Guide, Second Edition

4567890 DOC DOC   019876543210

ISBN 0-07-212130-0

Publisher Brandon A. Nordin	**Editorial Assistant** Tara Davis	**Indexer** Jack Lewis
Associate Publisher and Editor-in-Chief Scott Rogers	**Series Editor** D. Lynn White	**Computer Designers** Gary Corrigan Roberta Steele
Senior Acquisitions Editor Gareth Hancock	**Technical Editor** Amy Thomson	Jani Beckwith
Editorial Management Syngress Media, Inc.	**Copy Editor** Eileen Kramer	**Illustrators** Brian Wells Beth Young
Project Editor Jody McKenzie	**Proofreader** Carroll Proffitt	Robert Hansen
		Series Design Roberta Steele

This book has been composed in Corel VENTURA.

From Global Knowledge

At Global Knowledge we strive to support the multiplicity of learning styles required by our students to achieve success as technical professionals. In this series of books, it is our intention to offer the reader a valuable tool for successful completion of the A+ Certification Exam.

As the world's largest IT training company, Global Knowledge is uniquely positioned to offer these books. The expertise gained each year from providing instructor-led training to hundreds of thousands of students worldwide has been captured in book form to enhance your learning experience. We hope that the quality of these books demonstrates our commitment to your lifelong learning success. Whether you choose to learn through the written word, computer-based training, Web delivery, or instructor-led training, Global Knowledge is committed to providing you the very best in each of those categories. For those of you who know Global Knowledge, or those of you who have just found us for the first time, our goal is to be your lifelong competency partner.

Thank you for the opportunity to serve you. We look forward to serving your needs again in the future.

Warmest regards,

Duncan Anderson
President and Chief Operating Officer, Global Knowledge

The Global Knowledge Advantage

Global Knowledge has a global delivery system for its products and services. The company has 28 subsidiaries, and offers its programs through a total of 60+ locations. No other vendor can provide consistent services across a geographic area this large. Global Knowledge is the largest independent information technology education provider, offering programs on a variety of platforms. This enables our multi-platform and multi-national customers to obtain all of their programs from a single vendor. The company has developed the unique CompetusTM Framework software tool and methodology which can quickly reconfigure courseware to the proficiency level of a student on an interactive basis. Combined with self-paced and on-line programs, this technology can reduce the time required for training by prescribing content in only the deficient skills areas. The company has fully automated every aspect of the education process, from registration and follow-up, to "just-in-time" production of courseware. Global Knowledge, through its Enterprise Services Consultancy, can customize programs and products to suit the needs of an individual customer.

Global Knowledge Classroom Education Programs

The backbone of our delivery options is classroom-based education. Our modern, well-equipped facilities staffed with the finest instructors offer programs in a wide variety of information technology topics, many of which lead to professional certifications.

Custom Learning Solutions

This delivery option has been created for companies and governments that value customized learning solutions. For them, our consultancy-based approach of developing targeted education solutions is most effective at helping them meet specific objectives.

Self-Paced and Multimedia Products

This delivery option offers self-paced program titles in interactive CD-ROM, videotape and audio tape programs. In addition, we offer custom development of interactive multimedia courseware to customers and partners. Call us at 1 (888) 427-4228.

Electronic Delivery of Training

Our network-based training service delivers efficient competency-based, interactive training via the World Wide Web and organizational intranets. This leading-edge delivery option provides a custom learning path and "just-in-time" training for maximum convenience to students.

ARG

American Research Group (ARG), a wholly-owned subsidiary of Global Knowledge, one of the largest worldwide training partners of Cisco Systems, offers a wide range of internetworking, LAN/WAN, Bay Networks, FORE Systems, IBM, and UNIX courses. ARG offers hands on network training in both instructor-led classes and self-paced PC-based training.

Global Knowledge Courses Available

Network Fundamentals
- Understanding Computer Networks
- Telecommunications Fundamentals I
- Telecommunications Fundamentals II
- Understanding Networking Fundamentals
- Implementing Computer Telephony Integration
- Introduction to Voice Over IP
- Introduction to Wide Area Networking
- Cabling Voice and Data Networks
- Introduction to LAN/WAN protocols
- Virtual Private Networks
- ATM Essentials

Network Security & Management
- Troubleshooting TCP/IP Networks
- Network Management
- Network Troubleshooting
- IP Address Management
- Network Security Administration
- Web Security
- Implementing UNIX Security
- Managing Cisco Network Security
- Windows NT 4.0 Security

IT Professional Skills
- Project Management for IT Professionals
- Advanced Project Management for IT Professionals
- Survival Skills for the New IT Manager
- Making IT Teams Work

LAN/WAN Internetworking
- Frame Relay Internetworking
- Implementing T1/T3 Services
- Understanding Digital Subscriber Line (xDSL)
- Internetworking with Routers and Switches
- Advanced Routing and Switching
- Multi-Layer Switching and Wire-Speed Routing
- Internetworking with TCP/IP
- ATM Internetworking
- OSPF Design and Configuration
- Border Gateway Protocol (BGP) Configuration

Authorized Vendor Training
Cisco Systems
- Introduction to Cisco Router Configuration
- Advanced Cisco Router Configuration
- Installation and Maintenance of Cisco Routers
- Cisco Internetwork Troubleshooting
- Cisco Internetwork Design
- Cisco Routers and LAN Switches
- Catalyst 5000 Series Configuration
- Cisco LAN Switch Configuration
- Managing Cisco Switched Internetworks
- Configuring, Monitoring, and Troubleshooting Dial-Up Services
- Cisco AS5200 Installation and Configuration
- Cisco Campus ATM Solutions

Bay Networks
- Bay Networks Accelerated Router Configuration
- Bay Networks Advanced IP Routing
- Bay Networks Hub Connectivity
- Bay Networks Accelar 1xxx Installation and Basic Configuration
- Bay Networks Centillion Switching

FORE Systems
- FORE ATM Enterprise Core Products
- FORE ATM Enterprise Edge Products
- FORE ATM Theory
- FORE LAN Certification

Operating Systems & Programming
Microsoft
- Introduction to Windows NT
- Microsoft Networking Essentials
- Windows NT 4.0 Workstation
- Windows NT 4.0 Server
- Advanced Windows NT 4.0 Server
- Windows NT Networking with TCP/IP
- Introduction to Microsoft Web Tools
- Windows NT Troubleshooting
- Windows Registry Configuration

UNIX
- UNIX Level I
- UNIX Level II
- Essentials of UNIX and NT Integration

Programming
- Introduction to JavaScript
- Java Programming
- PERL Programming
- Advanced PERL with CGI for the Web

Web Site Management & Development
- Building a Web Site
- Web Site Management and Performance
- Web Development Fundamentals

High Speed Networking
- Essentials of Wide Area Networking
- Integrating ISDN
- Fiber Optic Network Design
- Fiber Optic Network Installation
- Migrating to High Performance Ethernet

DIGITAL UNIX
- UNIX Utilities and Commands
- DIGITAL UNIX v4.0 System Administration
- DIGITAL UNIX v4.0 (TCP/IP) Network Management
- AdvFS, LSM, and RAID Configuration and Management
- DIGITAL UNIX TruCluster Software Configuration and Management
- UNIX Shell Programming Featuring Kornshell
- DIGITAL UNIX v4.0 Security Management
- DIGITAL UNIX v4.0 Performance Management
- DIGITAL UNIX v4.0 Intervals Overview

DIGITAL OpenVMS
- OpenVMS Skills for Users
- OpenVMS System and Network Node Management I
- OpenVMS System and Network Node Management II
- OpenVMS System and Network Node Management III
- OpenVMS System and Network Node Operations
- OpenVMS for Programmers
- OpenVMS System Troubleshooting for Systems Managers
- Configuring and Managing Complex VMScluster Systems
- Utilizing OpenVMS Features from C
- OpenVMS Performance Management
- Managing DEC TCP/IP Services for OpenVMS
- Programming in C

Hardware Courses
- AlphaServer 1000/1000A Installation, Configuration and Maintenance
- AlphaServer 2100 Server Maintenance
- AlphaServer 4100, Troubleshooting Techniques and Problem Solving

ABOUT THE CONTRIBUTORS

Syngress Media

Syngress Media creates books and software for Information Technology professionals seeking skill enhancement and career advancement. Its products are designed to comply with vendor and industry standard course curricula and are optimized for certification exam preparation. You can contact Syngress via the Web at www.syngress.com.

Contributors

Cameron Brandon (MCSE, CNE, CNA, MCSE +Internet, A+, Network+) is a Network Engineer/Administrator in the greater Portland, Oregon, area. His specialty is Windows NT with BackOffice Integration. Cameron participated in the Intel migration to Windows NT in Oregon, the largest migration of its kind in history. He completed his MCSE, CNE, CNA, MCPS:Internet Systems, and A+ certifications in five months, which shows what you can do if you set your mind to it.

Robert Aschermann (MCP, MCSE, MCT, MBA) has been involved with information systems as an IS professional for nearly 10 years. During his career he has worked in technical support, systems design, consulting, and training. Robert has been an MCSE for almost five years and has passed more than 15 Microsoft certification exams. Currently Robert works for a large computer manufacturer based in Austin, Texas. His job responsibilities include systems engineering, project management, and business analysis. As a project manager he has lead large Windows NT and Windows 95 operating system migrations and many small to medium size client/server development projects. As a systems engineer and architect his responsibilities include identifying business processes that need improvement, drafting design specifications for solutions, and building systems that meet those design specifications. He routinely works with Microsoft development tools such as SQL Server 7.0, Access, IIS 4.0, Visual InterDev, Visual Basic, and the Microsoft Solutions Framework.

Jeffrey A. Ferris (MCSE) works as Systems Engineer for Dell Computer Corporation in Austin, Texas, where his responsibilities include technical development for emerging technologies, such as implementation recommendations for the Microsoft Windows 2000 operating system. Jeffrey has been working with computers since just after learning to walk, focusing on TCP/IP technologies, network security, and Windows NT for the past five years. Prior to moving to Texas, Jeffrey was an associate consultant with Celeritas Technologies, LLC, a prominent consulting firm in the Kansas City area. While in Kansas, Jeffrey fulfilled a major role in the development of the first nationwide rollout of a Windows NT 4.0 domain architecture for the Call Center Services division of Sprint Communications Company, L.P. After growing up in—and as an interesting side note, this may well be the first time the town's name has ever appeared in print—Beaufort, Missouri, Jeffrey moved to Springfield, Missouri, where he worked as a network support technician for City Utilities of Springfield while completing his BS in Computer Information Systems at Southwest Missouri State University. Jeffrey can be reached online at trackzero@track-zero.com. Jeffrey would like to extend thanks to his family and friends for all of their support over the years, and to Barb Coleman and Dangerous Dave, who helped him find his way through those first few levels.

Kyle L. Rhynerson (MCSE, MCT, A+, MBA) is a Systems Engineer for Dell Computer Corporation. Prior to working for Dell, Kyle was the Director of Technical Training for PC University teaching A+ and Microsoft certification classes. Kyle resides in Austin, Texas, with his loving wife, Delores, and two beautiful daughters, Emily and Audrey.

Dorothy L. McGee has worked in the computer industry for more than 12 years and currently holds A+, CNA, CNE, 2 MCNEs, MCP, MCP+Internet, and MCSE certifications.

Tim First began his computer experiences at the age of 10 with a Zenith Z-100. Since then he has gained the credentials of MCSE and MCP+Internet. Tim is presently preparing for the MCSE+Internet and Oracle DBA certifications. Tim can be reached by email at first64bus.msu.edu.

Catherine Masterson is a LAN Administrator in Toronto and has worked in the technical support field since 1988. She has a bachelor's degree in Physical and Health Education, is A+ certified, and holds several CNE certifications.

John Barnes has been working with PC hardware for more than 14 years. John currently works as a Systems Engineer for Cylink Corp. and lives in the Washington, DC area. John is currently the lead field engineer for two Cylink product lines. Beside supporting Cylink customers nationwide, he currently supports a nationwide Windows NT network. John holds MCSE and CNE certifications.

David Yorke is a Systems Support Engineer in Phoenix, Arizona. An A+ certified technician with a specialty in DOS/Windows, he is also certified as an MCP in Windows 95 and Networking Essentials and is pursuing MCSE status. His experience with different computer hardware and software platforms has spanned over 10 years.

Ted Hamilton (MCSE, MCP + I) is a system administrator for EDS. He has been involved with computers since 1979. He graduated from the College of Wooster with a bachelor's degree in Business Economics. He also completed some work in graduate-level accounting. Ted is now working toward completing his MCSE + I. You can reach Ted by e-mail at Tjhtjhtjh64aol.com, or reach him on the Web at http://homepage.usr.com/h/hamilton/.

Cary Stotland is currently engaged as a Networking Consultant for a Midwest-based systems integration firm. He has worked with microcomputers since their inception, and continues to study their underpinnings. He may be reached at carys64usa.net.

Melissa Craft is a Senior Consulting Engineer for MicroAge. MicroAge is a global systems integrator headquartered in Tempe, Arizona. MicroAge provides IT design, project management, and support for distributed computing systems. Melissa develops enterprise-wide technology solutions and methodologies for client organizations. These technology solutions touch every part of a system's lifecycle—from network design, testing and implementation to operational management and strategic planning. Aside from earning a bachelor's degree from the University of Michigan, Melissa has several technical certifications including Microsoft's MCSE, Cisco's CCNA, Novell's Master CNE, and Citrix's CCP. Melissa is a member of the IEEE, the Society of Women Engineers, and American MENSA, Ltd.

Melissa currently resides in Phoenix, Arizona, with her family, Dan, Justine and Taylor, and her two dogs, Marmaduke and Pooka. She can be contacted at mmcraft@compuserve.com.

Mark Larma is a Senior Systems Engineer for MicroAge in Phoenix, Arizona. He has an MCSE in both the 3.51 and 4.0 track, with an emphasis on messaging. He currently has certifications on Exchange, versions 4.0, 5.0, and 5.5. Mark taught himself to program in BASIC at the age of 11 and hasn't stopped using the technology since. Mark dedicates his writing to his patient family: his wife Mary Ann, daughters Alexis and Veronica, and newborn son Hunter.

Series Editor

D. Lynn White (MCPS, MCSE, MCT, MCP+Internet) is president of Independent Network Consultants, Inc. Lynn has more than 14 years of programming and networking experience. She has been a system manager in the mainframe environment as well as a software developer for a process control company. She is a technical author, editor, trainer, and consultant in the field of networking and computer-related technologies. Lynn has been delivering mainframe, Microsoft-official curriculum and other networking courses in and outside the United States for more than 12 years.

Technical Review by:

Amy Thomson (A+ certified technician) is a software and A+ instructor in Halifax, Nova Scotia, and she has more than 10 years of experience in dealing with computer hardware and applications. Amy has taught computer classes from one end of Canada to the other and back again. She holds an Honours B.Sc. in Psychology and is currently preparing for certification as an MCP in Windows 95 and as a Network+ certified technician.

CONTENTS AT A GLANCE

CONTENTS

Part I
A+ Core Examination

ACKNOWLEDGMENTS

We would like to thank the following people:

- Richard Kristof of Global Knowledge for championing the series and providing us access to some great people and information. And to Patrick Von Schlag, for his help with this book.

- To all the incredibly hard-working folks at Osborne/McGraw-Hill: Brandon Nordin, Scott Rogers, and Gareth Hancock for their help in launching a great series and being solid team players. In addition, Tara Davis and Jody McKenzie for their help in fine-tuning the book.

This book's primary objective is to help you prepare for and pass the required A+ exam so you can begin to reap the career benefits of certification. We believe that the only way to do this is to help you increase your knowledge and build your skills. After completing this book, you should feel confident that you have thoroughly reviewed all of the objectives that CompTIA has established for the exam.

In This Book

This book is organized around the actual structure of the A+ exam administered at Sylvan Testing Centers. CompTIA has let us know all the topics we need to cover for the exam. We've followed their list carefully, so you can be assured you're not missing anything.

In Every Chapter

We've created a set of chapter components that call your attention to important items, reinforce important points, and provide helpful exam-taking hints. Take a look at what you'll find in every chapter:

- Each chapter begins with the **Certification Objectives**—what you need to know in order to pass the section on the exam dealing with the chapter topic. The Certification Objective headings identify the objectives within the chapter, so you'll always know an objective when you see it!

- **Exam Watch** notes call attention to information about, and potential pitfalls in, the exam. These helpful hints are written by authors who have taken the exams and received their certification—who better to tell you what to worry about? They know what you're about to go through!

EXERCISE
- **Certification Exercises** are interspersed throughout the chapters. These are step-by-step exercises that mirror vendor-recommended labs. They help you master skills that are likely to be an area of focus on the exam. Don't just read through the exercises; they are hands-on practice that you should be comfortable completing. Learning by doing is an effective way to increase your competency with a product.

- **From the Field** sidebars describe the issues that come up most often in real world settings. These sidebars give you a valuable perspective into certification- and product-related topics. They point out common mistakes and address questions that have arisen from on-the-job discussions and experience.

- **Q & A** sections lay out problems and solutions in a quick-read format:

QUESTIONS AND ANSWERS

The computer lost its BIOS settings. What should I do?	This is commonly caused by a low CMOS battery. Replace the battery and reconfigure the CMOS.

- The **Certification Summary** is a succinct review of the chapter and a re-statement of salient points regarding the exam.

- The **Two-Minute Drill** at the end of every chapter is a checklist of the main points of the chapter. It can be used for last-minute review.

- The **Self Test** offers questions similar to those found on the certification exams, including multiple choice, true/false questions, and fill-in-the-blank. The answers to these questions, as well as explanations of the answers, can be found in Appendix A. By taking the Self Test after completing each chapter, you'll reinforce what you've learned from that chapter, while becoming familiar with the structure of the exam questions.

Some Pointers

Once you've finished reading this book, set aside some time to do a thorough review. You might want to return to the book several times and make use of all the methods it offers for reviewing the material:

1. *Re-read all the Two-Minute Drills,* or have someone quiz you. You also can use the drills as a way to do a quick cram before the exam.

2. *Re-read all the Exam Watch notes.* Remember that these are written by authors who have taken the exam and passed. They know what you should expect—and what you should be careful about.

3. *Review all the Q & A scenarios* for quick problem solving.

4. *Re-take the Self Tests.* Taking the tests right after you've read the chapter is a good idea, because it helps reinforce what you've just learned. However, it's an even better idea to go back later and do all the questions in the book in one sitting. Pretend you're taking the exam. (For this reason, you should mark your answers on a separate piece of paper when you go through the questions the first time.)

5. *Complete the exercises.* Did you do the exercises when you read through each chapter? If not, do them! These exercises are designed to cover exam topics, and there's no better way to get to know this material than by practicing.

6. *Check out the Web site.* Global Knowledge invites you to become an active member of the Access Global Web site. This site is an online mall and an information repository that you'll find invaluable. You can access many types of products to assist you in your preparation for the exams, and you'll be able to participate in forums, on-line discussions, and threaded discussions. No other book brings you unlimited access to such a resource. You'll find more information about this site in Appendix C.

A+ Certification

Although you've obviously picked up this book to study for a specific exam, we'd like to spend some time covering what you need in order to attain A+ certification status. Because this information can be found on the CompTIA Web site, http://www.comptia.org/index.asp?ContentPage= certification/certification.htm, we've repeated only some of the more important information in the Introduction of this book, "How to Take an A+ Certification Exam." Read ahead to the introduction.

The CD-ROM Resource

This book comes with a CD-ROM holding test preparation software and providing you with another method for studying. You will find more information on the testing software in Appendix C.

How to Take an A+ Certification Exam

This chapter covers the importance of your A+ certification as well as prepares you for taking the actual examinations. It gives you a few pointers on methods of preparing for the exam, including how to study, register, what to expect, and what to do on exam day.

Importance of A+ Certification

The Computing Technology Industry Association (CompTIA) created the A+ certification to provide technicians with an industry recognized and valued credential. Due to its acceptance as an industry-wide credential, it offers technicians an edge in a highly competitive computer job market. Additionally, it lets others know your achievement level and that you have the ability to do the job right. Prospective employers may use the A+ certification as a condition of employment or as a means of a bonus or job promotion.

Earning A+ certification means that you have the knowledge, the technical skills, and now, the customer relations skills necessary to be a successful computer service technician. Computer experts in the industry establish the standards of certification. Although the test covers a broad range of computer software and hardware, it is not vendor-specific. In fact, more than 45 organizations contributed and budgeted the resources to develop the A+ examination.

To become A+ certified you must pass two examinations: the Core exam and a DOS/Windows specialty exam. The core exam measures essential competencies for a break/fix microcomputer hardware service technician with six months of experience. The exam covers basic knowledge of desktop and portable systems, basic networking concepts, and printers. Also included on the exam is safety and common preventive maintenance procedures.

With this new revision of the A+ certification, released in July of 1998, you now have only one choice for the specialty exam: DOS/Windows. The previous version of the A+ exam also offered Macintosh OS as a specialty, but since our world is becoming more and more PC-driven, the new exam also reflects this change. The DOS/Windows module covers basic knowledge of DOS, Windows 3.*x*, and Windows 95 operating systems for installing, upgrading, troubleshooting, and repairing microcomputer systems.

Computerized Testing

As with Microsoft, Novell, Lotus, and various other companies, the most practical way to administer tests on a global level is through Sylvan Prometric testing centers. Sylvan Prometric provides proctored testing services for Microsoft, Oracle, Novell, Lotus, and the A+ computer technician certification. In addition to administering the tests, Sylvan Prometric also scores the exam and provides statistical feedback on each section of the exam to the companies and organizations that use their services.

Typically, several hundred questions are developed for a new exam. The questions are reviewed for technical accuracy by subject matter experts and are then presented in the form of a beta test. The beta test consists of many more questions than the actual test and provides for statistical feedback to CompTIA to check the performance of each question.

Based on the performance of the beta examination, questions are discarded based on how good or bad the examinees performed on them. If a question is answered correctly by most of the test-takers, it is discarded as too easy. The same goes for questions that are too difficult. After analyzing the data from the beta test, CompTIA has a good idea of which questions to include in the question pool to be used on the actual exam.

Test Structure

Currently the A+ exam consists of a *form* type test. This type of test draws from a question pool of some set value and randomly selects questions to generate the exam you will take. We will discuss the various question types in greater detail later in this chapter.

Some certifications are using *adaptive* type tests. This interactive test weights all of the questions based on their level of difficulty. For example, the questions in the form might be divided into levels one through five, with level one questions being the easiest and level five being the hardest. Every time you answer a question correctly you are asked a question of a higher level of difficulty, and vice versa when you answer incorrectly. After answering about 15–20 questions in this manner, the scoring algorithm is able to determine whether or not you would pass or fail the exam if all the questions were answered. The scoring method is pass or fail. You won't find this type of exam for A+ certification as of yet. Currently Novell is employing the adaptive test format.

The exam questions for the A+ test are all equally weighted. This means that they all count the same when the test is scored. An interesting and useful characteristic of the form test is that questions may be marked and returned to later. This helps you manage your time while taking the test so that you don't spend too much time on any one question. Remember, unanswered questions are counted against you. Assuming you have time left when you finish the questions, you can return to the marked questions for further evaluation.

The form test also marks the questions that are incomplete with a letter "I" once you've finished all the questions. You'll see the whole list of questions after you finish the last question. The screen allows you to go back and finish incomplete items, finish unmarked items, and go to particular question numbers that you may want to look at again.

Question Types

The computerized test questions you will see on the examination can be presented in a number of ways. Some of the possible formats you may see on the A+ test, and some you may not, are described below.

True/False

We are all familiar with True/False type questions, but due to the inherent 50 percent chance of guessing the right answer, you will probably not see any of these on the A+ exam. Sample questions on CompTIA's web site and on the beta exam did not include any True/False type questions.

Multiple Choice

The majority of the A+ exam questions are of the multiple choice variety. Some questions require a single answer, whereas some require multiple answers. The easiest way to differentiate between the number of answers required is the use of a radio button or a checkbox in front of possible answers. The radio button will only allow you to select one item from the given choices. The checkbox allows you to select any or all of the given answers in response to the question.

One interesting variation of multiple choice questions with multiple answers is whether or not the examinee is told how many answers are correct.

EXAMPLE:

Which files are processed immediately upon the completion of POST? (Choose two.)

OR

Which files are processed immediately upon the completion of POST? (Choose all that apply.)

You may see both variations of the multiple answer questions on the exam, but the trend seems to be towards the first type, where examinees are told explicitly how many answers are correct. Questions of the "choose all that apply" variety are more difficult and can be very confusing to the test taker. The majority of questions on the A+ exam are multiple choice with single answers.

Graphical Questions

Some questions incorporate a graphical element to the question in the form of an exhibit either to aid the examinee in a visual representation of the problem or to present the question itself. These questions are easy to identify because they refer to the exhibit in the question and there is also an "Exhibit" button on the bottom of the question window. An example of a graphical question might be to identify a component on a drawing of a motherboard.

Test questions known as hotspots actually incorporate graphics as part of the answer. These types of questions ask the examinee to click on a location or graphical element to answer the question. As a variation of the above exhibit example, instead of selecting A, B, C, or D as your answer, you would simply click on the portion of the motherboard drawing where the component exists.

Free Response Questions

Another type of question that can be presented on the form test requires a *free response* or type-in answer. This is basically a fill-in-the-blank type question where a list of possible choices is not given. More than likely you will not see this type of question on the exam.

Study Strategies

There are appropriate ways to study for the different types of questions you will see on an A+ certification exam. The amount of study time needed to pass the exam will vary with the candidate's level of experience as a computer technician. Someone with several years experience might only need a quick review of materials and terms when preparing for the exam.

For the rest of us, several hours may be needed to identify weaknesses in knowledge and skill level and working on those areas to bring them up to par. If you know that you are weak in an area, work on it until you feel comfortable talking about it. You don't want to be surprised with a question knowing it was your weak area.

Knowledge-Based Questions

Knowledge-based questions require that you memorize facts. The questions may not cover knowledge material that you use on a daily basis, but they do cover material that CompTIA thinks a computer technician should be able to answer. Here are some keys to memorizing facts:

- **Repetition** The more times you expose your brain to a fact, the more it "sinks in" and increases your ability to remember it.

- **Association** Connecting facts within a logical framework makes them easier to remember.

- **Motor Association** It is easier to remember something if you write it down or perform another physical act, like clicking on the practice test answer.

Performance-Based Questions

Although the majority of the questions on the A+ exam are knowledge-based, some questions are performance-based scenario questions. In other words, the performance-based questions on the exam actually measure the candidate's ability to apply one's knowledge in a given scenario.

The first step in preparing for these scenario type questions is to absorb as many facts relating to the exam content areas as you can. Of course, any actual hands-on experience will greatly help you in this area. For example, knowing how to discharge a CRT is greatly enhanced by having actually done the procedure at least once. Some of the questions will place you in a scenario and ask for the best solution to the problem at hand. It is in these scenarios that having a good knowledge level and some experience will help you.

The second step is to familiarize yourself with the format of the questions you are likely to see on the exam. The questions in this study guide are a good step in that direction. The more you're familiar with the types of questions that can be asked, the better prepared you will be on the day of the test.

The Exam Makeup

To receive the A+ certification, you must pass both the Core and the DOS/Windows exams within 90 calendar days of each other. There are 69 questions on the Core exam and 70 questions on the DOS/Windows exam. You will have one hour to complete the Core portion and one hour and 15 minutes for the DOS/Windows portion. CompTIA has established the passing rate of the Core exam at 65 percent and the passing rate for the DOS/Windows exam at 66 percent. This information could be subject to change—check the CompTIA site at www.comptia.org for the most recent information, or call the CompTIA Certification Area: (630) 269-1818 extension 359.

The Core Exam

The Core exam is broken down into eight categories. Note that the final category, customer satisfaction, will be tested but will not count towards the passing or failing of the exam. The score on those particular questions will be posted on your score card, though, so your employer can see how you did on these types of questions. CompTIA lists the percentages as the following:

Installation, configuration, upgrading	30%
Diagnosing and troubleshooting	20%
Safety and preventive maintenance	10%
Motherboard, processors, memory	10%
Printers	10%
Portable systems	5%
Basic networking	5%
Customer satisfaction	10%

The DOS/Windows Exam

The majority of the DOS/Windows exam will focus on Windows 95 (a whopping 75%), with the rest of the coverage divided between DOS and Windows 3.*x*. CompTIA's breakdown of this portion is as follows:

Function, structure, operation, and file management	30%
Memory management	10%
Installation, configuration, and upgrading	30%
Diagnosing and troubleshooting	20%
Networks	10%

Signing Up

After all the hard work preparing for the exam, signing up is a very easy process. Sylvan operators in each country can schedule tests at any authorized Sylvan Prometric Test center. To talk to a Sylvan registrar, call

1-800-77 MICRO (1-800-776-4276). There are a few things to keep in mind when you call:

1. If you call Sylvan during a busy period, you might be in for a bit of a wait. Their busiest days tend to be Mondays, so avoid scheduling a test on Monday if at all possible.

2. Make sure that you have your social security number handy. Sylvan needs this number as a unique identifier for their records.

3. Payment can be made by credit card, which is usually the easiest payment method. If your employer is a member of CompTIA you may be able to get a discount, or even obtain a voucher from your employer that will pay for the exam. Check with your employer before you dish out the money. The fee for one exam is $78 for members and $128 for non-members.

4. You may take one or both of the exams on the same day. However, if you only take one exam, you have 90 calendar days to complete the second exam. If more than 90 days elapse between tests, you must retake the first exam.

Taking the Test

The best method of preparing for the exam is to create a study schedule and stick to it. Although teachers have told you time and time again not to cram for tests, there just may be some information that just doesn't quite stick in your memory. It's this type of information that you want to look at right before you take the exam so that it remains fresh in your mind. Most testing centers provide you with a writing utensil and some scratch paper that you can utilize after the exam starts. You can brush up on good study techniques from any quality study book from the library, but some things to keep in mind when preparing and taking the test are:

1. Get a good night's sleep. Don't stay up all night cramming for this one. If you don't know the material by the time you go to sleep, your head won't be clear enough to remember it in the morning.

2. The test center needs two forms of identification, one of which must have your picture on it (e.g., a driver's license). A social security card or credit card are also acceptable forms of identification.

3. Arrive at the test center a few minutes early. There's no reason to feel rushed right before taking an exam.

4. Don't spend too much time on one question. If you think you're spending too much time on it, just mark it and go back to it later if you have time. Unanswered questions are counted wrong whether you knew the answer to them or not.

5. If you don't know the answer to a question, think about it logically. Look at the answers and eliminate the ones that you know can't possibly be the answer. This may leave with you with only two possible answers. Give it your best guess if you have to, but most of the answers to the questions can be resolved by process of elimination.

6. Books, calculators, laptop computers, or any other reference materials are not allowed inside the testing center. The tests are computer based and do not require pens, pencils, or paper, although as mentioned above, some test centers provide scratch paper to aid you while taking the exam.

After the Test

As soon as you complete the test, your results will show up in the form of a bar graph on the screen. As long as your score is greater than the required score, you pass! Also a hard copy of the report is printed and embossed by the testing center to indicate that it's an official report. Don't lose this copy; it's the only hard copy of the report that is made. The results are sent electronically to CompTIA.

The printed report will also indicate how well you did in each section. You will be able to see the percentage of questions you got right in each section, but you will not be able to tell which questions you got wrong.

After you pass the Core exam and the DOS/Windows exam, an A+ certificate will be mailed to you within a few weeks. You'll also receive a lapel pin and a credit card–sized credential that shows your new status: A+ Certified Technician. You're also authorized to use the A+ logo on your business cards as long as you stay within the guidelines specified by CompTIA. If you don't pass the exam, don't fret. Take a look at the areas you didn't do so well in and work on those areas for the next time you register. Just remember that the Core and DOS/Windows exams must be taken within 90 days of each other to count toward certification.

Once you pass the exam and earn the title of A+ Certified Technician, your value and status in the IT industry increases. A+ certification carries along an important proof of skills and knowledge level that is valued by customers, employers, and professionals in the computer industry.

Part I

A+ Core
Examination

I

Installation, Configuration, and Upgrading

I n order to pass the A+ Certification Core Module, you need to study the function, installation, and configuration procedures for all systems' components, from the devices themselves to the connectors and cables they use. You also need to know the common tools of the trade and how they are used. This chapter describes the terms and concepts that relate to each of the components and informs you of the industry-standard procedures used in installation and configuration. Knowing the concepts involved and procedures for installation and configuration of devices will not only ensure you pass the A+ exam, but will also ensure that you are a successful computer technician in the real world.

CERTIFICATION OBJECTIVE 1.01

Functions of System Modules

When you think of a computer, you generally picture a monitor and keyboard hooked up to a box. However, there are many components, called *Field Replaceable Modules (FRMs)* or *Field Replaceable Units (FRUs)*, that make up a computer system. Each FRU has a specific function to perform, whether it accepts data from a user or produces data for a user. As a technician, you need to familiarize yourself with the various modules that are available on the market because you will be required to upgrade or replace these units in the field. The following subsections describe each FRU's function and explain the basic terms and concepts related to each module.

System Board

The most important module of every computer system is the *system board*, also referred to as the *main board*, the *motherboard*, or the *planar board*. The system board is made from a fiberglass sheet interlaid with electronic circuitry. This circuitry provides the pathways for electrical signals, referred to as the *bus*, to travel across the board. Each module that makes up a computer system attaches to the motherboard and is able to communicate with other modules through the bus. Also found on the system board are the central processing unit (CPU), memory slots, cache, various connectors, and expansion slots.

Expansion slots come in several varieties, and are labeled according to the type of bus architecture that is used. Examples of bus architecture are Industry Standard Architecture (ISA), Extended Industry Standard Architecture (EISA), Peripheral Component Interconnect (PCI), and Micro Channel Architecture (MCA), just to name a few. Each bus architecture is responsible for distributing signals back and forth from the expansion slot to the system board, and typically only one or two types are available on any given motherboard (see Figure 1-1). For a more detailed description of bus architectures and available types, please refer to Chapter 4.

FIGURE 1-1   A typical motherboard and its components

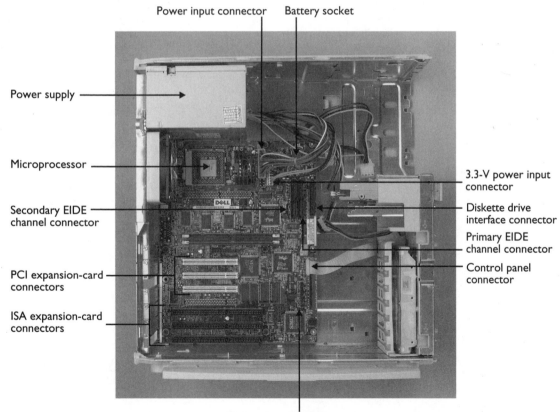

It is very important that you can identify which type of bus architecture an expansion card uses just by looking at it.

Power Supply

Because computers use electrical signals to communicate between the various system modules, a reliable source of power is required for a computer to function. Electrical power comes in two forms: *alternating current (AC)*, which is the type that comes out of a wall outlet, and *direct current (DC)*, which is the type that your computer uses. The power supply provides your computer with the electricity it needs by converting AC, or *volts alternating current (Vac)* into DC, also known as *volts direct current (Vdc)*. This current is fed to your computer in each of several forms: +5 Vdc (used to power nearly all chips), +12 Vdc (used to power motors and some communications circuits), –5 and –12 Vdc (required for compatibility, but rarely used in today's PCs). The latest ATX standard also calls for a 3.3 Vdc supply line, used by some of the newest motherboards.

Conventional (linear) power supplies use a diode bridge to convert between current types. All PC power supplies, known as *switching mode* power supplies, add switching transistors to the design, which enables the power supply to be lighter, more compact and more efficient at converting power than a conventional power supply. However, they still generate quite a bit of heat. As a result, power supplies have a built-in fan that is used to prevent them from overheating. An overheated power supply will not only fail, but can damage other components inside the computer.

exam
ⓦatch

Most people have a tendency to glance over these details. However, it is important that you know the voltages generated by the power supply.

Processor/CPU

With all of these electrical signals racing around the system board, a method of directing and controlling these signals becomes necessary. A device, known as the *central processing unit (CPU)*, or merely the *processor*, fulfills this task. CPUs come in different shapes, pin structures, architectures, and speeds.

Generally, the CPU is a square or rectangular chip that attaches to the motherboard through legs, called *pins*, located on the bottom of the chip. Rectangular chips were common in personal computers that predate the early 1980s as well as the original IBM-PC and XT. Since the 80286 CPU was first used in the AT in 1983, all chips through the Pentium have come in a square shape. The newest chips in the PC line-up have returned to a rectangular shape, in two different ways: the PentiumPro is two chips with two sets of connections, in one large rectangular chip; and the Pentium II is a rectangular cartridge that fits into a slot and connects to the motherboard through gold fingers, rather than using pins inserted into a socket. The chip itself contains millions of transistors on a silicon base structure like a tiny circuit board. These transistors perform the work of directing electrical signals to their destinations and performing calculations.

The pins that attach the chip to the motherboard come in two forms: the *Dual In-Line Package (DIP)* and the *Pin Grid Array (PGA)*. DIP pins are identified as two rows, located on opposing sides of the chip. PCs using either the 8088 or 8086 processor used 40-pin DIPs. The PGA chip has pins arranged in rows on each of the four sides, and was used in PCs using the 80286, 80386, 486 and the first Pentium CPUs (60 MHz and 66 MHz). Later Pentiums (75 MHz and up) used a slightly different form factor called the Staggered PGA, and the Pentium II dispensed with sockets entirely by going to a cartridge type mounting method called "slot-1."

Memory

Just as you need a work surface, whether it is a desk in an office or a countertop in your kitchen, your computer also needs a work area. This area, called *memory*, is used by the computer to store the instructions from your applications and manipulate data. Memory is comprised of *integrated circuits (ICs)* that reside on a chip. ICs work in a manner similar to a light switch in that each circuit can have only one of two states: on or off. Your computer recognizes an off switch as a numerical 0, whereas an on switch is translated as a numerical 1. This *binary* pattern of 0s and 1s is how your computer stores, retrieves, and communicates data. Memory is broken up into several types: *Random-Access Memory (RAM), Read-Only Memory (ROM),* and *cache memory.*

RAM is the most common type of memory chips used for the CPU's main memory: the CPU loads your programs into RAM, runs the program's instructions from RAM, loads data into RAM, and manipulates the data while it is in RAM. RAM is sometimes called by its more specific name, *DRAM (Dynamic RAM),* which is the basis for all main memory chips in all PC systems.

ROM is a memory chip that is also part of main memory, except that its contents are written only once, usually at the factory, and when used in a PC system can only be read, hence the name Read-Only. ROM usually stores only the *Basic Input Output System (BIOS),* which is the set of instructions that your computer uses to boot.

Cache memory is made up of much faster memory called *SRAM (Static RAM).* Starting with the 80386 CPU, DRAM could not work as fast as the CPU and therefore created a bottleneck that slowed down the CPU. SRAM, which runs up to ten times as fast, could not practically replace DRAM since it also costs ten times as much. However, it was discovered that a small, relatively inexpensive cache of SRAM memory chips could keep copies of the most frequently used main memory locations, and enable the main memory to keep up with the CPU 90% of the time. The faster the CPU, the more cache is needed to maintain that 90% edge. Early 386 systems typically used 64KB or 128KB of cache memory on the motherboard. 486 and Pentium CPUs have added a primary SRAM cache on the CPU chip itself, using a secondary memory cache on the motherboard of 128KB to 1MB in size. The Pentium-II CPU includes a 512KB or 1MB cache built into the processor cartridge (in addition to an on-chip primary cache of 32KB) and therefore needs no memory cache on the motherboard. All of these design combinations result in an overall memory system performance of 85% to 95% of the theoretical maximum performance, for thousands of dollars less.

Storage Devices

Information has become one of the most important commodities to individuals and businesses today. In the past, data was kept in the form of paper documents held in rows of file cabinets. Storing that information for any length of time became an almost impossible task due to space limitations. When personal computers began populating offices, their storage potential began to be explored. The first computers used floppy disks and hard drives, but today's computers have a wider variety of storage media available, such as CD-ROMs, tape drives, optical drives, Zip drives, and Jaz drives. Do not expect any questions on your exam on Jaz and Zip drives, as these are not standard hardware devices found on all computers. However, many leading computer manufacturers are including Jaz and Zip drives with their computers.

Tape Drives

Shortly after the first computers were invented, it was discovered that magnetic tape could store information as a series of 1s and 0s. However, magnetic tape can only store data sequentially, and is most commonly used as a backup medium. As tape drives are not covered on the A+ Certification exam, they get only a brief mention here.

Floppy Drives

Floppy drives write data on disks that are inserted and removed from the drive. The actual disk is encased in an envelope, which has a small opening to allow a read/write head to access the disk. The read/write head passes over the disk, reading data from or writing data to the disk itself. Floppy drives, and the disks used by them, come in two sizes: 5.25" or 3.5".

The 5.25" drives are the older of the two, and are seldom used today. The original single-sided drives had a capacity of only 180 kilobytes. Double-sided drives and disks were later introduced, which increased the storage to 360KB. The 5.25" disks eventually reached a capacity of 1.2MB as technology refined both the accuracy of the drives and the surface of the disk.

As programs began to take up more space, the demand for higher capacity floppy disks increased. 3.5" drives emerged to fill this requirement, and added the extra bonus of using smaller disks encased in a more rigid medium. These floppy disks also have a spring-loaded metal casing that protects the surface of the magnetic media, unlike their 5.25" counterparts. The first 3.5" disks held only 720KB, but capacity increased as technology progressed. A newer design allowing 2.88MB was created several years ago, but did not catch on. Today's systems still support the 1.44MB format, while the 720KB and 2.88MB sizes have fallen by the wayside. All of these floppy disk specifications should be memorized for the exam, and are summarized in Table 1-1.

Hard Drives

Hard drives work in a manner similar to a floppy drive, but actually contain multiple disks stacked on top of each other inside the drive itself. The disks reside on a rotating pole, called the *spindle*, and are in constant motion. Several read/write heads pass over the disk, allowing for a more rapid retrieval of data than the floppy drive. While the original hard drives stored only around 10MB or 20MB, today's personal computer drive capacities currently reach above 30GB.

TABLE 1-1   Characteristics of Each Floppy Disk Type

Size	Type	Tracks Per Inch	Tracks Per Side	Sectors Per Track	Storage
5 1/4"	DSDD (Double-sided Double-Density)	48	40	9	360KB
5 1/4"	DSHD (Double-sided High-Density)	96	80	15	1.2MB
3 1/2"	DSDD (Double-sided Double-Density)	135	80	9	720KB
3 1/2"	DSHD (Double-sided High-Density)	135	80	18	1.44MB
3 1/2"	DSED (Double-sided Extra-Density)	135	80	36	2.88MB

Your computer's central processing unit (CPU) has to spend a lot of time waiting for the much slower hard drive to catch up. While operations inside the CPU are timed in nanoseconds (one billionth of a second), your hard drive operations are limited to milliseconds. Although milliseconds are very fast, a millisecond is one million times slower than a nanosecond. Comparing the speed of your CPU to the speed of your hard drive is like comparing a Porsche to a snail.

So when you're loading a program your CPU will have to wait until your hard drive can access all of the necessary data and load it into RAM (which also operates in nanoseconds). As you can see, the hard drive is currently the bottleneck in most computer operations. For this reason, many computer users are going with SCSI hard drives, which have much faster data transfer rates and seek times. SCSI hard drives also generally have a faster spin rate, and we will learn later how the spin rate of a drive can increase disk transfer rates.

The *average seek time* of the drive is the amount of time it takes for the heads to move from one cylinder on the drive to any other cylinder.

The *average access time* takes into account the drive's latency. Latency is defined as the average time (in milliseconds) that it takes for a sector to be available after the heads have reached a track. This figure is generally half the time it would take for the disk to fully rotate once. The average access time of the drive is the sum of its average seek time and latency. This gives us the average amount of time that is needed before a sector (chosen at random) can be accessed.

The *disk transfer rate* represents the speed at which data is moved to and from the drive. This is the number most often reported by benchmarking software because it gives the actual number of kilobytes that can be transferred in a given amount of time. The disk transfer rate of a drive depends on the spin rate of the drive. A drive that can spin at 9000 RPMs will outperform a similar drive at 5400 RPMs. The *host transfer rate* represents the speed at which the CPU can access information from the disk controller. Most computers manufactured as of last year will support PIO (Processor Input/Output) Mode 3 and Mode 4. The maximum theoretical transfer rate for PIO Mode 3 is 11.1 MBps and 16.6 MBps. for PIO Mode 4.

Every file you store on a hard drive relies on some kind of file addressing system to organize the data. The most common file system is known as *File Allocation System (FAT),* native to the DOS operating system. Windows 95 uses a modified version of FAT called *virtual FAT (VFAT),* which adds support for long filenames. Windows NT supports both FAT and its own NTFS format. *NTFS* is a more advanced file system that allows access to much larger partitions. Each file system must organize data into segments called clusters. Under the FAT file system, the maximum size of any one cluster is 32KB (32,768 bytes). The maximum number of these clusters is limited to 65,536. When you multiply these two numbers, you come up with what has come to be termed the 2GB barrier, which refers to the maximum number of bytes that can be allocated on the drive.

Under the FAT system, the cluster size is determined by your partition size. By dividing the partition size by the maximum number of clusters the drive can hold, we get the individual cluster size. The larger the partition size, the larger the cluster size. For example, a 2GB partition will give you a 32KB cluster size. Keep in mind that every file on your hard drive must occupy at least one cluster. This means that if you have a tiny text file that is only 214 bytes long, the FAT system will automatically allocate an entire cluster to that file, despite the fact that it's so small. This has caused great concern for computer enthusiasts who worry about the amount of wasted space on their hard drive. To remedy this, you can partition your disk into a few smaller partitions, such as four 512MB partitions to lower the cluster size, and therefore reduce the amount of wasted space for each cluster. However, some operating system vendors will have a limit beyond which any increase in partition size will not generate an increase in cluster size.

You may be wondering whether you should choose a SCSI hard drive over an EIDE hard drive. In the past, SCSI was the obvious choice if you wanted capacity and speed. Some EIDE drives have a larger capacity than SCSI drives, and are almost as fast. In addition, EIDE drives are much less expensive than SCSI drives. It may be easier for you to go with an EIDE drive because you will not have to add a SCSI controller to your system, which consumes some of the cost of upgrading to a SCSI system. If you plan on adding multiple drives to your system in the future, you should choose the SCSI path, which has much more flexibility for numerous devices in a system. With a SCSI controller, not only can you attach multiple hard drives, you can attach scanners and CD-ROMS.

CD-ROMs

Compact Disc Read Only Memory (CD-ROM drives), have become increasingly popular and are now a standard component of today's computers. CD-ROMs are used more as a distribution medium than as a true storage medium, but this will change as CD-R writers (CD-Recordable, a writable standard that is compatible with most CD-ROM readers) become more affordable. This drive uses a laser instead of a read/write head to read data off a compact disc, which is similar to the audio compact discs available at any music store.

As applications increased in size, it became cost-ineffective for vendors to package software on floppy disks. CD-ROMs offer an average capacity of 650MB and allow software manufacturers to store their applications on a single CD-ROM as opposed to multiple disks. This saves the manufacturers quite a bit of money in postage and handling costs. In turn, it saves the customer time by not having to wait around the computer to swap disks. Also, reading data from a CD-ROM is much faster than reading from a floppy disk. As a result, floppy disks have become the dinosaur of distribution medium.

Monitor

Monitors are an integral part of any computer system, and you must become extremely familiar with them. Monitors come in a wide variety of types, ranging from the original *monochrome display adapter (MDA)*, which only permitted text-based characters, to today's high-resolution *super video graphics adapter (SVGA)*.

Depending on the type of monitor you are working with, the number of colors and screen resolution varies. However, all monitors function basically the same way. The back of the display screen, called a *cathode ray tube (CRT)*, is coated with special chemicals, called phosphors, that glow when electrons strike them. An electron gun, controlled by the monitor's electronics, resides inside the monitor and continuously shoots electrons at the CRT, panning across the monitor from left to right and top to bottom. In a color monitor, each position on the screen, called a *pixel* (or picture element), has a group of three cells—red, green, and blue. The adapter receives a character to be displayed from the computer and converts it into a synchronized series of signals sent to the video monitor, which then uses those signals to light up the correct pixels at the right time, to produce the text and graphics we see on the screen.

Different monitors have the ability to produce a different number of colors and resolution. The original monochrome monitor supported only one color and no graphics. The Hercules monitor was developed to include graphics, but it still supported only one color. Both of these monitors used digital adapters, which limited the output to a form of 0s and 1s.

Color Graphics Adapters (CGA) provided four types of digital output. This output was defined with the red, green, and blue colors plus an intensity bit (RGBI). This meant that by combining all three colors, and changing the intensity of those colors, you could get a total of 16 different colors on the display (remember, digital output). However, the display could show only 640 pixels horizontally and 200 pixels vertically, referred to as 640 × 200, on the screen at any time in monochrome, or 160 × 100 in 16 colors.

The next improvement on the monitor was dubbed *Enhanced Graphics Adapter (EGA)* and added an intensity bit (RGB) to each of the primary colors (RGB) to give a palette of 64 colors. However, while it could display only 16 colors at a time, it improved resolution by enhancing the maximum pixel resolution to 720 × 350 in text mode and 640 × 350 in graphics mode, even though it still used the old digital output technology.

Monitors were ready for a revolution in technology, and the *Virtual Graphics Array (VGA)* gave it to us in 1987. It allowed for analog output, meaning that the adapter could control each RGB line incrementally. Each wire was no longer restricted to the digital binary value of ON or OFF, but could instead use a whole range of analog voltages. Therefore, the monitor was able to display an unlimited range of colors for each individual pixel. The very first VGA adapter cards were limited to only 16 colors, but competitors quickly designed video adapters to display up to 256 different colors at any given time from a virtually unlimited palette. Resolution was improved to 720 × 400 in text mode and 640 × 480 in graphics mode.

Still, there was one more step in monitor technology to be explored, and it was probably the final step. *Super Virtual Graphics Array (SVGAs)* hit the market and brought us higher resolution standards of 800 × 600, 1024 × 768 (sometimes known as *XGA*, or *eXtended Graphics Array*), 1280 × 1024, and even higher. Depending on the amount of RAM included on the video adapter, the number of colors could be 256 or more. 32KB or 64KB colors are sometimes known as *High-Color* which is very good, but not quite as good as 16-million color combinations, known as *True-Color*. The human eye can distinguish approximately 4 million different colors throughout the entire spectrum, so there is no need for any higher color definition. Table 1-2 summarizes the characteristics of each video type.

Monitors are used with *adapters*, or video cards. As stated before, the adapter used must match the type of monitor that is connecting to it. This is because the adapter translates digital information from your computer into the appropriate signal type used by the monitor to generate the picture. If an incorrect adapter is used, the monitor will not work and can result in severe damage to the monitor.

Modem

Today's society has come to rely heavily upon computer systems to facilitate the exchange of information. As a direct result, computers must also have the ability to communicate with other computers in order to send or receive information, regardless of the distance involved. Modems are not only one

TABLE 1-2	Video Type	Maximum Color Depth	Maximum Resolution
Characteristics of Each Video Type	CGA	Monochrome	640 × 200
	CGA	16 colors	160 × 100
	EGA	64 colors	720 × 350 (text mode)
	EGA	64 colors	640 × 350 (graphics mode)
	VGA	256 colors	720 × 400 (text mode)
	VGA	256 colors	640 × 480 (graphics mode)
	SVGA	16 million colors	1280 × 1024 and higher

of the many devices that permit two separate computers to talk to each other, but they're also one of the most common peripherals a technician will work with.

Modems work by translating signals between a computer and a standard telephone line. A computer utilizes binary signals to read, process, store, and communicate data. However, the standard telephone line uses analog signals to carry sound waves, and therefore requires a much wider range of data than a computer. A modem takes data from the sending computer and translates it from digital signals into analog signals before transmitting it across a telephone line, a process called *modulation*. When a modem receives analog signals from a telephone line, it converts the data back into digital signals, a process called *demodulation*. As you've probably guessed, the word *modem* is merely an acronym for MOdulator/DEModulator.

Internal modems are notorius for being more difficult to configure than their external couterparts. The internal modem acts as another COM port, so you do not have to assign the internal modem a COM port. You do have to disable the COM port in BIOS for the corresponding COM port that the internal modem will be using. For example, if you have jumpered your internal modem as COM2, you will need to enter your computer's BIOS setup program and disable COM2, so the internal modem can act as COM2 without any conflicts. This has caused many technicians trouble when it comes to configuring internal modems. Add that to the fact that some operating systems will have code that will share the port with a modem and another device without the need to modify the BIOS system settings. Consult the operating system documentation for more information on this feature.

External modems are much easier to configure than internal modems. They require a serial port, but do not have the hassle of disabling COM ports as internal modems do. External modems are also easier to transport to another computer, and it is easier to determine the status of the modem with the blinking LED lights on its face.

Input Devices

Computers exist to handle data, which means they must have a way to accept input. Input devices take data from a user, such as the click of a mouse or keystrokes, and convert that data into electrical signals used by your computer. Several devices that provide input are keyboards, mice, trackballs, pointer devices, digitized tablets, and touch screens.

FROM THE FIELD

Use That Screen Saver

There are many misperceptions and rumors regarding screen savers. In recent years, they have come to be regarded as just something fun to look at. People think that the monitors of today will not get any image burned into them. These people are wrong. In the field, I have seen monitors that have been turned on with the same desktop pattern for 24 hours and they have the image of the desktop burned into them rather deeply. These have been high-quality monitors that were less than a year old.

Choose your screen saver carefully. I'm sure you have seen the veritable plethora of available screen savers for your PC. Some are simple and some are quite complex. The complex ones usually have 3-D graphics and may contain animation or even have an interactive mode for the user to play a game or whatnot. Remember though that this comes at a price in terms of system resources. As you know, some system resources are very limited. If you are maxing out your system with a screen saver, you may be thrashing on the hard drive as your system is desperately swapping out memory to the disk just to keep this thing running. In the long run, this causes wear on the hard drive.

It has been rumored that the Windows OpenGL screen savers have one option that rarely, but every so often, renders a teapot instead of the tubes, which has been known to bring down systems. This can be tragic on a server. These OpenGL screen savers, and they are not alone, have been the culprit for many systems crashing. When troubleshooting a PC, especially in memory-related freezes and crashes after people come in after lunch, always look at the screen saver they are using as a possible cause. If you think it is their screen saver, change the saver back to the standard ones that don't take up that much memory. It is truly amazing how many times this is overlooked.

—*Ted Hamilton, MCSE, MCP, A+ Certified*

Output Devices

In order for your computer to be useful, it must provide data to you in some form, called *output*. Output devices take electronic signals from a computer and convert it into a format that the user can use. Examples of output devices include monitors and printers.

Printers produce paper output, called *hardcopy* or *printouts*. Printouts can include text, graphical images, or both on the same page. Printers come in a variety of types, and many printers now include color. The most common printer types are dot-matrix, ink jet, bubble jet, and laser printers. For a more detailed description of the various printers available, please refer to Chapter 5.

BIOS

As difficult as it is for you to keep up with all the peripheral devices available in the marketplace, not to mention the different models available from any given vendor, it is even more complex for your computer. And, as if things weren't already rough enough, your computer needs to know how to communicate with each device attached to it, regardless of the operating system software used. The *Basic Input/Output System (BIOS)* is the mechanism used by your computer to keep track of all this information and still remain independent of the operating system.

The system BIOS is stored in ROM. When an application needs to perform an input-output (I/O) operation on a computer, the operating system makes the request to the system BIOS. The BIOS then translates the request into the appropriate instruction set used by the hardware device. Most system BIOS programs can run only in DOS mode, and are therefore, essentially, DOS-mode device drivers for standard devices. Only DOS, early Windows versions, and parts of Windows 95/98 use the system BIOS to communicate with the basic devices. Parts of Windows 95/98, Windows/NT, and many other operating systems (such as UNIX) cannot use the system BIOS and must include their own device drivers for even the basic system devices that are recognized industry-wide.

CMOS

Different FRUs require different settings, such as interrupts, memory address ranges, and input-output ports. To inform the computer of all the necessary operating parameters every time the computer boots up would be inefficient. The *Complementary Metal-Oxide Semiconductor (CMOS)*, contained in the *Real-Time Clock/Calendar (RTCC)* chip, allows the computer to store this information even after the computer has been turned off.

CMOS is an integrated circuit manufacturing method using metal-oxide as an insulator between contacts that allows for very low-power operation—the Real-Time Clock/Calendar chip used in your PC can run for two to ten years on the small battery included on every motherboard! Along with keeping track of the date and time even when the system is turned off and unplugged, there are a few extra storage locations (from approximately 50 bytes for older systems, to 2000 for the latest) where data can be written to the chip. While it is commonly identified as CMOS memory, it is really a battery-backed device that is written to only when a new component is installed, such as a hard disk drive or an internal peripheral card that requires component-specific information to be available before the boot process.

CERTIFICATION OBJECTIVE 1.02

Adding and Removing Field Replaceable Modules

As technology increases (often at an exponential rate), new forms of components come into being. These components have to be added to the computer or must replace, or upgrade, an existing component. In addition, some parts will fail as a result of being defective or worn out through use. Therefore, one of the most common tasks every technician has to perform is adding or replacing a system module.

The first, and most important, step that you must take is to power off the computer and disconnect the power cord from the wall outlet. Powering off the computer ensures that no computer activity is occurring while you are working on it, which could cause data loss or worse. And, of course, no circuit boards or devices should be installed or removed while powered up. To do so will likely cause permanent electrical damage. By removing the power cord from the wall outlet, you are ensuring that if you mistakenly hit the power switch while working on the computer, no damage will occur. There may be times when you need to have the power on while inspecting the unit, or testing for voltages; in such cases, be sure the power is turned off while removing the case, as you may cause damage to the system (particularly the hard drive) if it were to receive any sharp jolts while operating. Be careful while performing tests on "live" circuits, as a misplaced probe or static charges can cause damage to the system. Also, *never open up the power supply* for any reason, as there are dangerous voltages inside that can be lethal. If you believe the power supply is failing, simply replace it.

Before the cover can be removed from the computer, called the *chassis*, you must ground both the PC and yourself together. This is due to the possibility of an *ElectroStatic Discharge (ESD)* that could damage the computer. ESD occurs when there is a difference in charge between one object and another, resulting in an exchange of electrons that equalize the potential between the two. In order to properly ground yourself to the computer, you must place the chassis on an ESD mat and connect one of the two wires to the computer. The second wire is connected to a ground pin that can be found on any electrical outlet. To ground yourself, wear an ESD wrist strap and attach the wire from the strap to the mat, or to a common ground. ESD and related procedures are more closely explained in Chapter 3.

After you have followed the ESD procedures, the cover can be safely removed. First, remove the screws that hold the cover in place. Some chassis also employ an operating latch to hold the cover in place. Disengage any latches that are present. Then, slide or lift the cover from the chassis. Place the cover in a location that is out of everyone's way.

At times, it will be necessary to remove expansion cards from the computer as they tend to get in your way. Note their locations and any connectors that attach to them before removal to ensure that you will be able to put everything back in its appropriate spot. To remove cables and power connectors, simply grasp the connector and pull away from the component.

Adapter cards are held in place along the back plane of the computer by screws. Remove all screws holding the card in place and then get a firm grasp on both ends of the board. While using a gentle pulling motion, slightly rock the card from end to end. Some cards may need a bit more effort than others to get out of the expansion slot, but be careful not to exert too much force or you can damage the card and/or the system board. Repeat this procedure for all of the remaining cards that you need to remove.

The following subsections will assume that you have already completed the preceding procedures before continuing.

System Board

Prior to removing the system board, you need to remove all expansion cards, cables, and power connectors attached to the motherboard. You might even have to remove the hard drive bays that interfere with the removal of the motherboard. Once this has been completed, you need to locate and remove any screws or plastic clips that attach the board to the computer. Once all fasteners have been removed, the system board can then be removed from the chassis.

It is also helpful to take a look in the system BIOS setup program and note the existing settings before disassembling the computer. Once the system board is free of the case, take note of any jumper settings and/or DIP switch settings on the old system board and configure the new board in the same fashion. It is also helpful to take a look in the system BIOS setup program and note the existing settings. It's a good idea to consult the manufacturer's instruction manual to ensure that none of the settings have changed. At this point, you can move the CPU and memory chips to the new board. You must make sure the CPU and the memory chips use the same type of sockets between the two motherboards, or you will have to replace your CPU and/or memory chips. Reverse the procedure used to install the replacement system board.

Power Supply

Power supplies are one of the easiest components to replace because they do not require any jumper or DIP switch settings. However, every power supply will not fit in every chassis. Some companies use a proprietary chassis that makes it difficult to use a standard power supply. Fortunately, these types of systems are usually older, and not encountered much today. The power supply is attached to the system board and the disk drives by power connectors. Follow the procedure in Exercise 1-1 to remove the power supply from your system.

| EXERCISE 1-1 |

Removing a Power Supply

1. Mark the positions of the power connectors so that you can hook up the new power supply properly. Note that both of the power connectors are identical, with the exception of the stamp, usually marked as J8 and J9.

2. Next, firmly grasp the connector and gently pull it from the socket. Never pull on the wires, as they are very easily damaged.

3. Some power supplies have a cable or plastic rod that runs from the power supply to the power switch that must be disconnected as well.

4. After all of the connectors have been detached, the final stage is to remove the mounting hardware used to hold the power supply in place. Depending on the power supply and mounting hardware, you may need to remove the four screws that hold it in place. With others, you can simply pull or slide the power supply out of the computer.

To install a new power supply, simply reverse the procedures used to remove it, as shown in Figure 1-2. However, you must remember that when

FIGURE 1-2

Installing a power supply

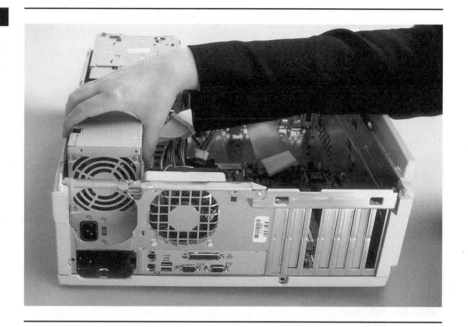

you reattach the two power connectors to the motherboard, the black wires that are located on each connector must be facing each other. Failure to connect the proper connectors could result in burning up the motherboard.

Processor/CPU

Some processors are attached to the motherboard by a *Zero Insertion Force (ZIF),* socket. If your motherboard has one of these, you operate a lever to remove the chip. In other cases, you use a chip puller to gently grasp the corners or sides of the processor. Use a gentle upward motion to remove the chip from its socket. A slight rocking of the chip is often needed to remove it; make sure you do not rock the chip more than 5 degrees in each direction as you remove it because this can damage the pins that attach the processor to the circuit board.

If you are inserting a different speed or type of processor, you must reconfigure the system board. The settings that will need to be configured are for the internal clock speed of the processor, and the external processor bus speed. This is done through a series of jumpers or DIP switches that are located on the motherboard. As the board settings differ between the type of board and manufacturer's specifications, refer to the manual provided with the board and configure it appropriately. If the documentation is unavailable, you may be able to consult the manufacturer's Web site for the correct settings.

Once the system board has been reconfigured, the manner in which you install the new processor differs depending on whether you have a ZIF socket. If so, simply place the new processor over the socket and operate the lever, or position the processor over the socket and gently push down until the chip is seated. Reinstall any expansion cards or connectors that you removed previously and the installation is complete. A typical processor installation is outlined in Figure 1-3.

FIGURE 1-3

Installing a processor

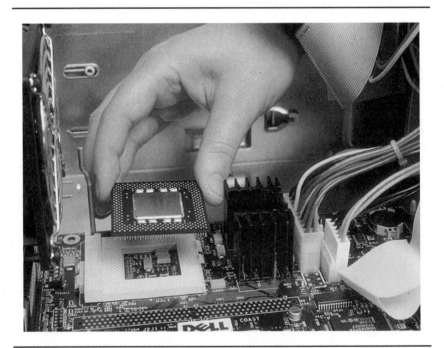

Once you have powered on your computer after the processor upgrade, the system BIOS will most likely tell you the speed of the processor. If the reported processor speed is not identical to the actual speed of the processor, you have misconfigured the processor and/or bus settings. Be aware that overclocking a processor can cause system instability and can actually overheat and burn the processor, rendering it useless.

Memory

Memory is one of the most common upgrades you will do as a computer technician; therefore you must be very familiar with the process. To install memory, follow the procedure outlined in Exercise 1-2 and Figure 1-4.

FIGURE 1-4

Installing SIMM memory

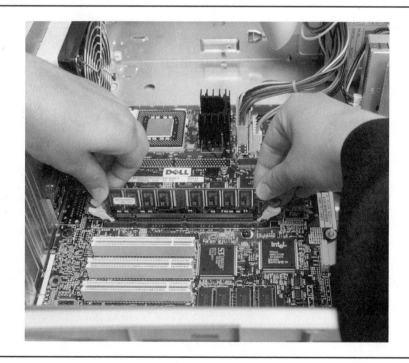

EXERCISE 1-2	### Installing SIMM Memory

1. Place the SIMM memory module over the slot at a 45-degree angle.

2. Gently work the module into the bottom of the socket, and move it to an upright position until it clicks into place.

3. SIMM memory modules are keyed so that they can fit into the slot only one way. If the SIMM module will not go all the way into the socket, then it is probably reversed. Do not force the chip if you are meeting with resistance when installing it.

To remove a SIMM memory module, first disengage the clips from the module. Then, tilt the chip in the reverse direction from installation and slide it out. If you try to pull directly up on the module, you may damage the clips or the electrical contacts in the bottom of the socket.

Nearly all of the latest Pentium and Pentium-II motherboards have a newer kind of memory module called the *Dual-Inline Memory Module (DIMM)*. Whereas the SIMM had a single row of 72 connecting fingers, each making contact on both sides, the DIMM has two rows of connecting fingers, one row on each side, for a total of 168 connections. The DIMM design and installation method was changed to help eliminate the common problem of broken clips on SIMM sockets. DIMM memory is also much easier to install, and does not require you to place the memory module at a 45-degree angle. Adding or removing SIMM sockets often required removing system components to make room for your hands to install the chips at a 45-degree angle. Many times you have to remove all of the SIMM chips just to upgrade one or two chips.

EXERCISE 1-3	### Installing DIMM Memory

1. Place the DIMM memory module directly over the slot, so that the notches in the bottom of the module match up with the keys in the socket.

2. Press down carefully on the top of the DIMM module, making sure that the notches are positioned directly over the socket's plastic keys.

3. As the module moves into place, you may notice the side-mounted retention clips moving towards the locked position—you may need to guide them into the locking notches on the side of the DIMM module.

4. When the board is in all the way, the retention clips on the side should be lined up with the notches on the side of the DIMM module—press them into place to lock the module and prevent it from coming out.

To remove a DIMM memory module, simply move the locking retention clips away from the DIMM module. The bottom of the clip will cause the DIMM module to automatically eject.

Some older DIMM sockets do not have the locking retention clips—these motherboards should be avoided, as the DIMM memory modules can come loose and cause memory problems. Also, be careful that the slots on the bottom of the DIMM socket correspond with the slots on the DIMM socket. Before DIMM chips became standardized, some companies were manufacturing DIMM chips for their computers with the slots in different places from the standard slots.

There are usually no CMOS settings to be concerned about, as memory is auto-sensed by most recent BIOS programs. Even so, you may be required to enter the BIOS Setup program and simply choose the Save Changes option. Some older systems may require you to input the actual amount of memory before saving your changes. However, older systems will most likely not have DIMM sockets available on their motherboards.

Storage Devices

There are several types of storage devices that are available for computers today, and that number is growing as technology improves. However, the most common peripherals that you will see are floppy drives, hard drives, tape drives, and CD-ROM drives. Hard drives are discussed in later sections under IDE/EIDE and SCSI.

Floppy Drives

To remove a floppy drive, follow the procedure outlined in Exercise 1-4.

Removing a Floppy Drive

1. Remove the chassis cover from the PC or the front faceplate if you have a proprietary chassis that utilizes rails to mount the drive.

2. Remove the four restraining screws on the sides of the drive or the two screws in the front that fasten the rails to the chassis.

3. Remove the power connector located in the back of the drive that runs from the power supply to the floppy drive. When you remove this connector, ensure that you grasp the connector and *not* the wires, as you could damage the electrical connections either in the cable connector or in the drive's receptacle.

4. Remove the floppy drive cable, which is a flat ribbon cable with a small twist in the wires located in the back of the drive that connects the drive to the floppy controller. In some cases, the floppy controller is on the motherboard.

5. After all of the connectors are free, simply slide the drive out of the computer.

When you install a floppy drive, simply reverse this procedure, as shown in Figure 1-5.

Tape Drives

Tape drives come in two forms, internal or external. To add or remove external tape drives, plug or unplug the connector from the adapter located in the back of the computer. External tape drives usually use SCSI or parallel interfaces. With internal drives, you need to remove the power connector and the tape drive cable. After the connectors have been removed, simply slide the drive out of the computer. To install, you reverse this procedure and add one more step. Some tape drives require a device driver installation. This is accomplished through the operating system software. Consult the manufacturer's documentation for more specific details.

FIGURE 1-5

Installing a floppy drive

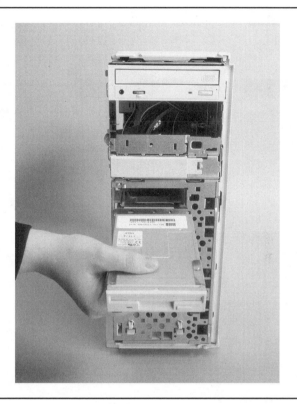

CD-ROM Drives

CD-ROM drive removal and installation is similar to a tape drive with two exceptions. The first is an extra cable that connects the CD-ROM drive to either the controller or the sound board. This cable is used to transmit audio signals from the CD-ROM drive to the controller/sound board. The second difference is that a CD-ROM drive usually requires a device driver installation through the system software, while the tape drive's device driver is usually contained within the application program accompanying the tape drive and usually cannot be used by any other software. Again, consult the product documentation to obtain more details on the particular model you are installing. A typical installation is outlined in Figure 1-6.

Installing a CD-ROM drive

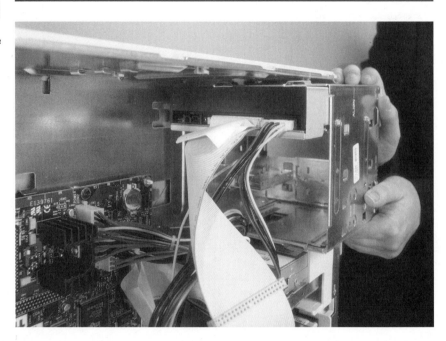

Monitor

Although most of the equipment you will deal with isn't too out of date, monitors are the exception. Monitors of all types are still in use today, including the old monochrome monitor. When you remove a monitor, you simply unplug it from the back of the computer. If it is a monochrome, Hercules, CGA, or EGA monitor, it is a digital monitor and will have a male DB-9 connector that plugs into a digital adapter. If it is a VGA or SVGA monitor, it will have a male high-density DB-15 connector that plugs into an analog adapter also located in the back of the computer. *Never plug a digital monitor into an analog adapter, or vice versa, as severe damage will result.*

If you need to remove the graphics adapter card, make sure that you note any cable connections to the adapter before removing them. The adapter card itself is held to the chassis by a single screw that must also be removed. Then, gently pull the card out of its socket. To install, simply reverse the procedure.

If you are installing a different model of VGA or SVGA video monitor, be aware that if it is not as capable as the previous monitor, the image on the screen may not be readable. In this case, change the video resolution to Standard VGA before installing the new monitor. You may then experiment with choosing the best resolution for the new monitor. However, if you are installing a different type of VGA or SVGA video adapter, ensure that you install the video adapter's device drivers into the operating system. Without changing device drivers, the video adapter will not work correctly, if at all. (Note: If you do not have the drivers for that specific video adapter and operating system available, you can usually specify Generic VGA and most adapters will work—you can then often download the necessary drivers from the video adapter manufacturer's Web site).

Modem

If you are removing an internal modem, detach the phone cord from the back of the computer before removing the modem card. You can then remove the single screw that holds the modem in place and gently pull upward on the card until it is free from its socket. If it is an external modem, you simply unplug the device from the back of the computer.

To install a modem, you merely reverse the procedure for removing it.

Input Devices

Several forms of input devices are available, such as keyboards and mice. Keyboards are the easiest component to install, as you simply plug them into an available port in the back of the computer. There are two types of keyboard connectors in use, the DIN-5 connector and the Mini DIN-6 connector. DIN-5s are generally found on AT style keyboards and have a round port with five pins. The Mini DIN-6 came out with the release of IBM's PS/2 machine, and also has a round port but differs in that it has six pins with one square plastic positioning pin.

There are several kinds of mice available, and thus several connectors in use. If you have a serial mouse, it will have a male DB-9 connector and requires a free COM port. A PS/2-type mouse will use a DIN-6 connector and require a free IRQ, almost always IRQ 12. The last type of mouse is the bus-mouse, which is similar to the PS/2-type except that it requires the installation of an expansion card. The bus-mouse type is now considered obsolete. Once you have connected the mouse, you have to install the device driver in the operating system software.

While there are a variety of other input devices available, you will not need to know about them for the A+ Certification exam, and thus they are not explained here.

Output Devices

Output devices come in various forms, but the standard devices tested on the A+ exam are monitors and printers. As we have already discussed monitor installation in an earlier section, we will discuss printers in this section.

Printer installation usually requires a cable, a power outlet, and device drivers. The printer cable, which is a flat ribbon type or a round shielded cable, attaches to a parallel port in the back of the computer. Printers have their own power supply inside the unit and must be connected to a power outlet. Once this has been completed, the device driver that shipped with the printer must be installed in the operating system software. To remove a printer, simply reverse the procedure.

IRQs, DMAs, and I/O Addresses

In order to ensure that information is passed between the system modules and the CPU in a timely fashion, devices must be able to directly communicate with the CPU. Because the processor is a busy device, system components must first get the CPU's attention. This is accomplished through a special set of lines, called *interrupt request lines (IRQs)*, in the bus. IRQs are given a number, ranging from 0 through 15, to identify them. In turn, devices are given an IRQ to use. However, with most BIOSs, no two devices in the computer can use the same IRQ because the processor wouldn't know who is calling it. Some of the newer BIOSs support IRQ sharing, but you need to consult with the vendor's documentation to see if this feature is supported.

Once the CPU receives an interrupt from a device, it can directly communicate with that device through *I/O addresses*, also known as *I/O ports*. I/O ports are assigned a range of numbers that are in turn assigned to specific devices. As with IRQs, no two devices can use the same I/O address.

There are times when some components need to write information directly into main memory. When a device has to do this, it uses a channel called a *Direct Memory Access (DMA) Channel*. This method can be used to improve the module's performance, by removing the overhead of having the processor move the information from the device to main memory.

Standard IRQ Settings

The computer industry has come up with a set of standard IRQ settings, listed in Table 1-3. These settings should be used whenever you are

TABLE 1-3	**IRQ Number**	**Standard Device Assignment**
Standard IRQ settings	NMI (nonmaskable interrupt)	Memory parity error
	0	System timer
	1	Keyboard
	2	On motherboard, cascaded from IRQs 8-15. From device IRQ 2, is re-directed to IRQ 9
	3	Serial port (COM2)
	4	Serial port (COM1)
	5	Parallel port (LPT2)
	6	Floppy controller
	7	Parallel port (LPT1)
	8	Real-time clock
	9	Unassigned (also redirected from IRQ 2)
	10	Unassigned
	11	Unassigned
	12	Mouse and touch pads
	13	Math co-processor
	14	Hard disk controller
	15	Secondary hard disk controller

installing a device. IRQ 2 is the subject of a good bit of confusion. This results from the fact that the original PC had only eight interrupt lines, numbered 0 to 7. When the AT computer was designed, a second interrupt controller was added to provide eight more interrupt lines (numbered 8 to 15). This second interrupt controller had to deliver its signal through the primary controller on the motherboard, and IRQ 2 was chosen for this task ("cascade" from second controller). Unfortunately, some earlier cards had already made plans to hook into the IRQ 2 signal wire, so on newer machines with the second controller, that signal wire now leads to IRQ 9 on the second controller. The bottom line: For hardware purposes, IRQ 2 and IRQ 9 should be considered the same interrupt signal, and should not be used together in the same system.

Know your IRQs cold. There are several questions on interrupt assignments on the exam.

Standard I/O Address Settings

In addition to standard IRQ settings, you need to know the standard I/O address settings. Table 1-4 lists the more frequently used port addresses.

Know your I/O addresses like the back of your hand. You will encounter several questions on the exam pertaining to I/O addresses.

Differences Between Jumpers and Switches

Interrupts, I/O addresses, DMA channels, and some additional features have to be configured in the hardware. Jumpers and *Dual In-Line Package (DIP)* switches are used to accomplish configuration.

Jumpers are actually made of two separate components. The first component is a row of metal pins on the hardware itself. The second component is a small plastic cap with a metal insert inside. Each jumper has two positions, either on or off, sometimes described as closed or open, respectively. The particular setting, or combination of settings you choose, determines the configuration according to the hardware design, which

TABLE 1-4	Port Address (hex range)	Device
Standard I/O Addresses	1F0–1F8	Hard drive controller, 16-bit ISA
	200–20F	Game control
	201	Game I/O
	278–27F	Parallel port (LPT2)
	2F8–2FF	Serial port (COM2)
	320–32F	Hard drive controller, 8-bit ISA
	378–37F	Parallel port (LPT1)
	3B0–3BF	Monochrome graphics adapter
	3D0–3DF	Color graphics adapter
	3F0–3F7	Floppy controller
	3F8–3FF	Serial port (COM1)

should be described in the device manual. *DIP switches* are tiny boxes with switches embedded in them and work exactly the same as jumpers. Each switch is set to on or off, and is sometimes referred to in the manual as 0 or 1, depending on how they are set. You will see two forms of DIP switches in use, but the only difference between the two is the method by which you set the switch. One type of switch is a miniature flip-toggle type switch and the second type is a slide type switch.

Locating and Setting Switches/Jumpers

Regardless of the type of configuration device used, you must locate and set them according to the directions found in the component's documentation. On hard drives, these switches are generally found near the connectors. However, on system boards or expansion cards, you must look around the card. There is no hard and fast rule used to locate them, but setting these devices can be a bit difficult. To make things a bit easier on yourself when installing a jumper, use a pair of tweezers or the small parts-grabber device found in some toolkits. Never use a pen or pencil point to set DIP switches, as any stray ink or graphite particles can eventually find their way inside the switch and cause intermittent failure. Instead, use a tweezer or the tip of a small screwdriver to press or slide each DIP switch. Always be sure to follow the manufacturer's guidelines for installing. Figure 1-7 shows a typical jumper installation.

Modems

Modems may or may not need to be configured with an IRQ and I/O address depending on what type they are. If they are external devices, they will use an existing serial port on your computer and therefore do not need a separate IRQ or I/O address. However, if they are internal devices, you will definitely have to configure these values. Computers today often have four COM ports, labeled COM1 through COM4. You must choose an unused COM port and I/O address in order to get the modem to function correctly, but most modems are now configured to use either COM3 with an I/O setting of 3E8-3EF or COM4 with an I/O setting of 2E8-2EF. In

FIGURE 1-7   Installing a jumper

Jumper

addition, you need to select a free IRQ. To be sure that these settings will work with your modem, consult the manufacturer's documentation.

If you have a modem that is Plug-and-Play compatible with a Plug-and-Play operating system such as Windows 95, then most likely Windows 95 will detect the internal modem and configure it accordingly. Some modems have a jumper to toggle between Plug-and-Play mode and manual configuration. Many experienced technicians force the modem into non-Plug-and-Play mode so they have full control over allocating resources for the modem, rather than having the computer assign these resources dynamically.

Sound Cards

Sound cards have become popular, thanks to the video game industry. Imagine trying to shoot the bad guys with your space ship without having sound to hear those marvelous explosions! Creative Labs has been the industry leader in the sound card business, and has set the standard. Typically, sound cards have the following configuration: IRQ 5, DMA 1, and I/O Address 220. These are standard numbers used with SoundBlasters, but as always, consult the manufacturer's documentation in case you have one of the esoteric kinds.

Network Cards

Network cards are becoming more common as networks have proven to be a cost-effective method of sharing information. Network cards need to have an IRQ, I/O address, and a memory address configured both on the card and in the device driver. Different forms of network cards, such as Ethernet or Token Ring, have different configuration standards. Figure 1-8 shows the correct procedure for seating an adapter card, but consult the manufacturer's documentation for the appropriate settings.

FIGURE 1-8

Seating an adapter card

Peripheral Ports, Cabling, and Connectors

As a computer technician, your clients expect you to be extremely knowledgeable about *every* facet of a computer's operation. Unless you have been blessed with a photographic memory, this is an almost impossible task. However, you can use a combination of documentation, knowledge, observation, and deductive reasoning to figure out an unfamiliar component's operation, installation, and configuration. In this respect, you become a computer detective, and like any good investigator, you must at least learn the basics of your trade. As you will be working with many different types of FRMs, you need to have a good working knowledge of the various kinds of cables, peripheral ports, and connectors associated with them.

Cable Types

The function of a cable is to transmit electronic signals from one device to another. It does this by sending the signal over some form of medium, such as copper wire or fiber-optics. The medium is enclosed in a tube or a ribbon sheathing in order to protect it from damage. Cables come in two different forms, *shielded* cables and *unshielded* cables, as shown in Figure 1-9. Shielded cables have a wire mesh or Mylar layer added between the medium and the sheathing that protects the cables from interference. Signals normally follow the medium through the line, but sometimes a signal will stray into the atmosphere producing electrical noise, which is known as *Electro-Magnetic Interference (EMI)* or, more specifically, *Radio Frequency Interference (RFI)*. Unshielded cables do not have this kind of protection.

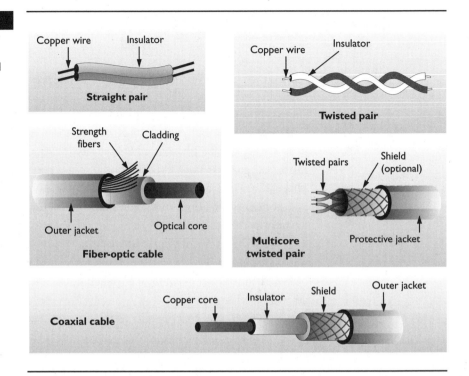

FIGURE 1-9

Common cable types: shielded and unshielded

Cable and Connector Location—Internal/External

Cables are used to connect peripherals to adapters. Peripherals generally have the connector located in the back of the device while adapters typically have the connector located on the side of the card. Some adapter cards have the connector extending out of the computer in order to enable connection with external devices, while others have it on the side of the card for internal devices.

Serial Versus Parallel

Serial and parallel communications are defined by their transmission characteristics and primary control signals. We explore these forms of communication in the following subsections.

Serial Communication

Serial ports are used for serial communications. PC serial communications ports follow an RS-232C standard. When a device transmits data serially, it is actually transmitting the bits of information sequentially over a single conductor. These bits travel one at a time down the wire. However, there are two methods used to transmit the data: synchronous and asynchronous.

Synchronous communication uses a single clock circuit in the transmitting device to synchronize the data transfer and set the rate of transmission. This synchronization defines the start and end of each and every bit. With *asynchronous communications*, both the sending and receiving devices have their own clock circuits. Synchronization is established by inserting a start bit in front of the data to be transmitted, then either seven or eight data bits, an optional parity bit, and finally one or two stop bits. When the receiver sees the first start bit, it begins its own clocking sequence. As long as the transmitting clock and the receiving clock are approximately the same, the receiver should be able to decode the following bits through the stop bits correctly. Because of the uncertainty of how closely the two different clocks correspond, asynchronous serial communications is usually limited to a maximum of 115,200 bps (bits per second). In fact, some devices will have problems at anything above approximately 50,000 bps.

The primary control signals are summarized in Table 1-5.

TABLE 1-5	Control Signal	Description
Primary Control Signals Used in Synchronous Communication	Serial Data Out (TxD)	Used to transmit data. Output from the computer to the device
	Serial Data Receive (RxD)	Used to transmit data. Input to the computer from the device
	Data Terminal Ready (DTR)	Used to tell the receiver that the data terminal (computer) is ready
	Data Set Ready (DSR)	Used to tell the receiver that the data communications equipment (usually a modem) is ready
	System Ground	Ground reference voltage between the two devices

Parallel Communication

Parallel communications transmit data over eight parallel conductors. The signals are broken down into two types, data signals and control signals. Control signals are used to control functions or synchronize the devices, called *handshaking*, while data signals contain the actual information. When data is sent out using parallel communications, it transmits one byte at a time by transferring 8 bits on eight separate wires simultaneously (in parallel), versus 8 bits transferred one after another on one wire in serial communication.

The primary control signals used in parallel communications are summarized in Table 1-6.

exam
Watch

Memorize the primary control signals for the exam. There are several questions that refer to both parallel and serial communications.

TABLE 1-6	Control Signal	Description
Primary Control Signals Used by Parallel Communications	Acknowledgment	Used to inform the transmitting device that data was received
	AutoFeed	Used by the processor to inform a printer to generate an automatic line feed
	Busy	Used to inform the processor that the receiving device cannot receive data
	Error	Used by the receiving device to indicate an error condition
	Init	Used by the processor device to initialize the receiving device
	Slct	Used by the receiving device to acknowledge a Slctin
	SlctIn	Used by the processor to select the device
	Strobe-Asserted	Used by the receiving device to inform it that valid data is present on the data lines

Pin Connections

Each pin on a connector is used to carry control signals back and forth from the device. For a listing of the control signals used in serial and parallel communications, please refer back to Tables 1-5 and 1-6, respectively.

Cable Handling/Routing

When you handle cables, you must be careful with them as they are more easily damaged than you may think. Never place cables near any sharp corners, as any movement or vibration can eventually wear through the insulation. A common source of cable damage is from excessive bending of a cable, the cable being crushed by a desk or table, or a chair running over the cable. Also, interference with the signals that travel along the cable from high-voltage equipment could cause problems with the proper function of devices that will still try to interpret corrupted signals. A common source of interference is florescent lighting or power supplies.

Types of Connectors

Connectors come in two standard flavors, male (pins) or female (sockets). The names in parentheses are due to a new wave of political correctness sweeping through the computer industry that has decided to rename the connectors. Male connectors are distinguished by possessing rows of pins, while female connectors are characterized by having sockets. When you attach a connector to a device, you are actually attaching it to another connector. For example, if you are connecting a keyboard to a computer, you are using a male connector to link up with a female connector on your motherboard. You must be very careful to not use excessive force when resistance is met trying to connect two connectors. A pin may be bent, and continued force could bend it beyond repair, or break it.

In addition, there are several categories of connectors in use. While there are too many to define here, we discuss the connectors most commonly found on the exam.

DB-9

DB-9 connectors are distinguished by their trapezoid appearance. There are nine pins in the connector, five pins in the bottom row and four pins in the top row. This type of connector is most commonly used for video display devices and serial ports. Joystick connectors are also trapezoidal in their appearance; however, these connectors are 15-pin DB-15 connectors.

DB-25

DB-25 connectors are similar to DB-9s in that they are trapezoidal in shape. There are 25 pins set in two rows on the connector. This type of connector is used for parallel and serial ports.

RJ-11

RJ-11 connectors are the same connectors that are used to attach a phone line to a phone. They are also used to link a modem to a phone line. These connectors have only two pins that clip into the modem.

RJ-14

RJ-14 connectors are dual-line phone jacks that can handle up to two phone lines. These types of connectors are not very common in the industry.

RJ-45

RJ-45 connectors are most commonly used to attach an unshielded twisted pair (UTP) cable with a network card. These connectors have eight pins, and are similar to the RJ-11 connector. This is the most common connector used on an Ethernet network.

PS2/Mini-DIN

PS2/Mini-Din connectors are most commonly used for mice and keyboards. These connectors have six pin positions (sometimes with only five pins), plus one square positioning key.

Installing and Configuring IDE/EIDE Devices

The earliest hard drives, the ST-506 and the *Enhanced Small Device Interface (ESDI)* drives, had to utilize a device known as a *controller* in order for the drive to function. The controller's job was to interpret commands from the CPU into the instructions needed by the hard drive. For example, if the CPU was told to write data to the hard disk, it would send the proper software instructions to the controller. The controller would create a set of hardware instructions that would tell the hard drive how to position the read/write heads over the disk, and then actually read the data. Once the drive got to the data, it would send it back to the controller, which would then pass it back to the CPU.

Controllers complicated the installation of hard drives because they were an additional circuit board that had to be configured and installed in the computer. *Integrated Drive Electronics (IDE)* drives simplified hard drive installation and improved reliability by integrating the controller into the drive itself. It is because of this that IDE drives gained popularity in the computer industry. However, IDE drives are limited by the fact that they are restricted to about 504MB(about 528 million bytes). The *Enhanced IDE (EIDE)* drives were created to overcome this limitation, and can be found in a variety of sizes in the gigabyte range.

Before installing an IDE or EIDE drive, you must have a hard drive adapter connected to the motherboard. Most of the more recent system boards already have an IDE/EIDE adapter built-in, but if it is an older board, you merely plug the adapter into the system board, and then plug the drive into the adapter. Once the adapter is in place, you can install the drive into the computer, as outlined in Figure 1-10. The drive is attached to the adapter using a 40-pin cable, which is similar to the floppy drive cable we discussed earlier except that it doesn't have a twist, and it has 40 pins instead of the floppy's 34 pins.

FIGURE 1-10

Installing a hard drive

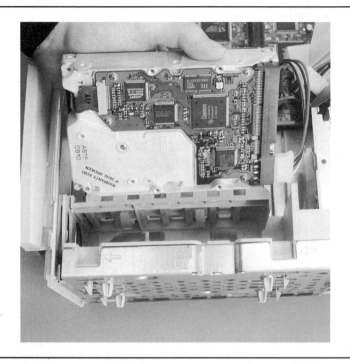

The last phase of your installation is to run the computer's CMOS (Complementary Metal-Oxide Semiconductor) Setup program. Without completing this step, many computers won't even know that the hard drive is there. When you turn on the computer, you should see a message on the screen that states to press a key, or keys, for SETUP. On some of the newer computers, you have to pay strict attention to the monitor or you may miss this message. When you press the key combination that brings up the Setup program, enter the Fixed Disk section and complete the appropriate information needed by the Setup program to identify the drive. This information generally includes items such as the number of sectors, cylinders, and heads that the hard drive has. You can usually find all of the correct configuration information imprinted on the drive itself or in the accompanying manufacturer's documentation. If you still have not found the information, the hard disk manufacturer's Web site is guaranteed to have the information you are looking for.

Master/Slave

The preceding installation information works if you have only one drive to install, but what if there is an existing drive in the computer or you have to install multiple drives at once? Because the IDE interface was designed to emulate the original Western Digital hard drive controller used in the IBM PCs, it has retained the same limit of two drives per controller. To install a second IDE drive, the installation is performed the same way as previously discussed up to the point where you actually install the drive itself. At this point, installation becomes slightly more complex due to the fact that each drive has a controller built into the device itself. When two IDE drives (and two built-in controllers) are attached to the same cable (or channel) at the same time, the adapter that is attached to the cable would get confused as to which controller was "in charge." This problem is resolved through the *master/slave* relationship.

Basically, one drive on each IDE/EIDE channel becomes the *master* drive. All commands that direct the slave drive's operations are passed through the master's controller. Configuring the master/slave drives is accomplished by setting the appropriate jumpers on the individual drives before you install them. First, consult the manufacturer's documentation for the correct jumper setting, set the jumpers accordingly, and install the drives. The rest of the installation is completed as before.

Devices per Channel

With either IDE or EIDE drives, you can have up to four drives installed but you will be able to put only two drives on a single cable (or channel). In order to have three or four drives, you need a separate cable that is connected to the second IDE/EIDE interface. Each connector on the IDE/EIDE controller is given a channel number. The first channel is Channel 0 (primary) and the second is Channel 1 (secondary). Think of this as the master drive on the primary controller, and the master drive on the secondary controller. The primary controller can also have a slave drive, just as the secondary controller can also have a slave drive, for a total of four IDE/EIDE devices in your system.

Installing and Configuring SCSI Devices

Small Computer Systems Interface (SCSI), pronounced "scuzzy" in the computer industry, has become more popular in the PC field recently. This interface permits you to connect multiple devices to one cable or SCSI channel in configurations of up to 8, 16, or 32 devices (including the adapter as one device) on a single channel, depending on the SCSI implementation that you are using. In order to properly install or upgrade SCSI devices, there are several things that must be taken into consideration and these are discussed in the following sections. We will first discuss the types of SCSI devices that are available.

Types of SCSI Devices

As technology advances, new forms of devices and standards become available. The organization that defines the SCSI standard is the American National Standards Institute (ANSI), which was responsible for releasing the first SCSI standard in 1986. Since then, SCSI has gone through several evolutions. The types of SCSI devices that you may encounter are the topics of the following subsections.

SCSI-1

The original SCSI device had an 8-bit bus that was attached to the devices using either female DB-25 or Centronics-50 connectors for external SCSI devices. Internally, SCSI devices were attached with a 50-pin ribbon cable. Its data transfer rate was a maximum of 5 megabytes-per-second (MBps), and was the fastest drive on the market. However, vendors did not adhere to the standard and made a few small changes in their implementation. As a result, some SCSI devices would interfere with the correct operation of other SCSI devices. This made them a major headache to install and configure when those differences made themselves known.

SCSI-2

In 1994, ANSI released a new standard that was aptly named SCSI-2. This standard allowed for backward compatibility with the original SCSI-1 devices. However, three different variants of the device have been released because of the different options that the standard permitted. One of the variants, named *Wide SCSI-2*, included a 16-bit bus that enabled large data transfers to be more efficient (a 32-bit version is also available, but is rarely implemented). *Fast SCSI-2* was another option that increased the data transfer rate to 10 MBps. However, the final variant combined the features of both options to create *Fast-Wide SCSI-2*. This combination yielded a 16-bit bus with a total transfer rate of 20 MBps.

SCSI-3

Because the SCSI-3 standard is so new, relative to the A+ Certification exam, there really isn't anything about it that you need to study for the exam. However, the information is included here as a reference point for real-world situations.

SCSI-3 is the latest SCSI standard issued by ANSI. Like SCSI-2, SCSI-3 also provides for extra options, and at the time of this writing there are only two additional variants on the market. The first one goes by the names *Fast-20 SCSI* or *Ultra SCSI*. It was developed for high-performance SCSI devices and comes on an 8-bit bus with a 20 MBps transfer rate. The second variation on a 16-bit bus goes by the label *Wide Fast-20 SCSI* and more currently *Wide Ultra SCSI*. Its characteristics are a 16-bit bus with transfer speeds at a maximum of 40 MBps.

Address Conflicts

Like IDE drives, there can be more than one SCSI device per channel. Unlike IDE drives, SCSI can have more than two devices on one interface, so it is important that you be aware of the SCSI ID address used for each device on a particular adapter, and the rules that govern them. Keep in mind the following rules when identifying and setting the SCSI ID for each SCSI device:

■ **SCSI ID Address (8-bit)** For SCSI-1 or SCSI-2 using a standard 25 or 50-pin cable, the ID can be only 0 through 7. The adapter uses one ID, which is usually 7. In some rare cases the adapter may use ID 0. Although SCSI ID 7 has the highest priority, this has very little importance since it is only a means of arbitrating which device goes first in the rare situation when two devices try to activate the bus at the very same time (within 2.4 microseconds of each other).

■ **SCSI ID Address (Wide SCSI)** For 16-bit Wide SCSI, there are 16 possible SCSI IDs, 0-15. The additional SCSI ID numbers 8-15 have a lower priority than 0-7, with 8 being the lowest. For 32-bit Wide SCSI, the additional ID numbers 16-23 have the next lower priorities (with ID 16 being the lowest) and ID addresses have priorities that are lower still, with ID 24 having the lowest priority of absolutely all device ID addresses. In a SCSI system with a mixed bus (some 8-bit, some 16-bit for instance), the entire ID addressing for the entire SCSI bus on that adapter will be limited to the smallest limit—in this case, even the Wide-SCSI devices would be limited to ID addresses 0-7. As stated earlier, although the ID addressing limitations are very important, the priority is essentially unimportant.

■ **SCSI ID Address (All)** No two SCSI devices can use the same SCSI ID address on one particular SCSI Channel. If a PC has two or more SCSI adapters with separate cables (channels), then these rules apply only to each channel independently. Adaptec, for instance, has the capability in most of their SCSI adapters to have up to 4 separate SCSI adapters (and therefore 4 SCSI channels) operating in the same PC at the same time. The SCSI adapter itself is usually ID 7, although a few have been designed as ID 0. For those that can be set to any number, 0-7 must be chosen in order to work with all SCSI devices, and generally 7 should be chosen to help avoid confusion.

■ **Bootable SCSI devices**   SCSI devices were not assumed to be boot-type devices such as floppy or hard drives. For this reason, in order to boot to a SCSI device, a supplemental BIOS chip must usually be present on the SCSI adapter. In the most recent motherboard designs, a SCSI adapter may be included on the motherboard and, if so, the SCSI boot code is then likely to be included in the system BIOS. Please check your SCSI adapter (motherboard or not) for actual instructions for activating a SCSI device for boot purposes. In most cases, the SCSI boot device will need to be assigned either ID 0 or 1.

Switch and Jumper Settings

SCSI devices must be manually set to a SCSI ID address prior to their installation, according to the addressing rules just discussed. This is accomplished through a series of jumpers or DIP switches located on the back of the device. In order to correctly configure the address, consult the manufacturer's documentation for the appropriate settings. If the documentation is unavailable, configuration information may be found at the manufacturer's Web site.

Cabling

The kind of cable used to connect SCSI devices is dependent upon whether it is an internal or external device, and the speed and width of the SCSI device it is attaching. Internal 8-bit devices use a single, unshielded 50-pin ribbon cable, while external 8-bit devices use either a DB-25 or Centronics-50 cable. For external Fast-SCSI connections, SCSI-2 and SCSI-3 specified a new mini-Sub-D connector, approximately half the dimensions of the Centronics-50 cable but still containing 50 pins. These are all considered the *A-cable* in SCSI-2 definitions, and are for 8-bit operation.

16-bit Wide-SCSI requires new cabling; either a second 68-pin cable called *the B-cable* to be used in conjunction with the A-cable, or a newer single cabling method with 68 pins called the *P-cable*. Internally, the P-cable is a 68-pin ribbon cable with half the pitch (.025-inch conductor spacing and .05-inch contact spacing) of the original internal 8-bit A-cable. Externally, a 68-pin mini-Sub-D is defined in SCSI-2 for Wide SCSI operation, which is the same as the 50-pin mini-Sub-D, with the exception of 18 extra pins.

32-bit Wide SCSI is defined in SCSI-3 as using yet another cable, the *Q-cable*, another separate 68-pin cable used in conjunction with the P-cable. Internally or externally, the two cables are used together where the lower 16 bits are transferred on the P-cable while the upper 16 bits are transferred along the Q-cable.

It is imperative that you identify each type of SCSI connector by its appearance, as illustrated in Figure 1-11.

Termination Conflicts

Armed with a unique address and attached to the bus, the circuitry on the SCSI device takes over. When a signal is sent out on the bus, only the

FIGURE 1-11

The various SCSI connectors available

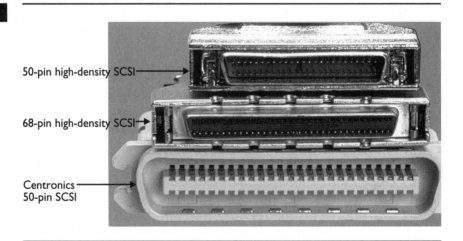

50-pin high-density SCSI

68-pin high-density SCSI

Centronics 50-pin SCSI

device that corresponds to the correct address responds to the initiator. However, that signal doesn't stop at the device but instead continues traveling along the bus. To prevent these signals from hitting the end of the bus and being reflected back down the cable, a *terminator* must be attached on both ends of the bus. Some devices and adapters have the terminator incorporated into the device, in which case you can enable or disable the terminator using a jumper or a DIP switch. Termination on any device in the middle of the bus must be removed or disabled. Keep in mind that if an adapter has both internal devices and external devices attached to their respective cables, the adapter itself must have its own termination removed or disabled, as it is sitting in the middle of one SCSI bus containing both internal and external devices.

If termination is not set up correctly, any SCSI device on the bus may function intermittently, or not at all. Typically, if no termination is installed anywhere on the SCSI bus, nothing will work. If only one terminator is installed, all SCSI devices may work, but occasionally hang. If two terminators are installed, but not at the end of the cable, any devices located on the unterminated portion of the cable will be subject to failure or hanging. If excessive termination is installed (three or more terminators), the devices may work intermittently, or fail completely.

When running SCSI devices, it is recommended that passive terminators be used on systems with a short bus, or systems that have only a few devices connected. In many applications, passive terminators have been used successfully. However, as clock rates and signal transition speeds increase, and noise margins decrease, the SCSI passive terminator can no longer ensure a reliable signal.

Active terminators provide optimum termination for SCSI II applications to create a reliable signal with longer cable runs of up to six meters and higher data rates.

Termination Power (TERMPWR)

If *Active Termination* is used on any SCSI device (to find this out, consult your SCSI device documentation), termination power must be enabled on one and only one SCSI device.

Installation Steps

For the installation of SCSI devices, you will need to configure up to three settings: the SCSI ID addresses, SCSI bus width, and termination. You will find that almost all SCSI problems stem from improperly configuring one or more of these three settings.

1. **SCSI ID addresses**   For each SCSI channel, make sure each SCSI device, both internal and external, has a unique SCSI ID address. Check the ID address for the adapter itself, and make sure no other device is assigned that ID. If you have a choice, you should usually set the adapter to ID 7. If you have a SCSI device that you want to be bootable, you will probably need to set it to ID 0, or possibly ID 1. Check your system documentation to be sure.

2. **SCSI bus width**   If using a mixture of 8-, 16-, and/or 32-bit SCSI devices on one channel, be sure to place the smaller-width devices closer to the end of each cable (internal or external) than the larger-width devices. For example, if installing one 8-bit and two Wide SCSI (16-bit) devices internally, connect both 16-bit devices to the P-cable coming from the adapter, then use a 16-to-8-bit transition adapter to connect the 8-bit device.

3. **Termination**   Remove or disable termination from all devices, except the device at the end of each cable. If only one cable is used (either internal or external), the terminator on the adapter itself must be enabled or installed. If both cables are in use, the adapter terminator must be removed or disabled.

Configuration

With all of your SCSI devices addressed, installed, terminated, and cabled together, it is time to tell the computer about them. The procedure used depends on whether you have a bootable SCSI device installed. If there is a bootable device, you must enable the BIOS on the adapter card. This is performed through a jumper or DIP switch setting that should be listed in the adapter's documentation. Once the BIOS is enabled, you configure the adapter to use a memory area located in reserved memory. Again, you must consult the documentation for the appropriate address and setting information.

If your device is not bootable, such as a SCSI scanner or CD-ROM drive, you must load a device driver in the operating system software. The driver itself should have come on a floppy disk with the SCSI adapter card, but in some cases you may need to visit the manufacturer's Web site to get it. Be aware that sometimes there might be problems with the drivers themselves, as problems have a tendency to show up after the adapters have hit the market. If you encounter problems, try visiting the manufacturer's Web site for an updated driver or a small piece of software, called a *patch*, that will resolve the difficulty.

Installing and Configuring Peripheral Devices

As peripheral devices are the most frequent modules that need to be installed or replaced, it is critical that you understand how to install the many common components available. The following subsections describe how to install and configure common devices that you should be familiar with.

Remember that when you work with any computer, you must follow ESD procedures. This requires you to ensure that the computer itself is on an electrostatic mat and attached properly, as well as guaranteeing that your electrostatic wrist band is properly secured on your person. The only time that you would not wear the wrist strap is when you are working with monitors. *Never wear a wrist strap when working on monitors because the high voltage section, even with the power turned off or unplugged, may contain a residual charge that can harm you, or possibly even kill you.*

Once you have your ESD procedures completed, you need to remove the screws in the back of the computer to remove the case. These screws are located around the edges of the computer. Some cases must be unlatched before you slide them out, but usually you just have to slide the cover up and away from the computer. Make sure that you place the cover out of everyone's way, including yourself, to avoid unnecessary injury.

With some components, you may be required to remove various expansion cards or connectors that may be in your way. If there are any such cards or connectors, remove them only after marking their placement and connections. This will save you some grief during the installation process.

Monitor/Video Card

Before installing a new monitor, you must note whether this is a different type of monitor than was previously installed, for example, upgrading from an EGA to an SVGA. If so, you will require a new video adapter as well. If you are only replacing a monitor of the same type, take note of the models, as different model monitors may not work with some features or modes of your video card.

Either way, follow the procedures in Exercise 1-5 when installing the card.

<table>
<tr><td>**EXERCISE 1-5**</td><td></td></tr>
</table>

Installing a Monitor/Video Card

1. Power off the monitor and unplug it from the back of the computer.

2. If you are replacing the adapter card, make sure that you note the connectors that attach to the card as the new card will probably have the same connector setup, then remove the connectors.

3. Remove the single screw that holds the card to the chassis, then gently pull upwards and away from the computer. If you apply too much force, you may damage the card.

4. Once it is free, replace the card with a new one by reversing the procedures.

5. After replacing any adapter cards, you can now plug the new monitor into the computer.

6. When you boot the computer, you must install the appropriate device drivers if it is a new type of video card or a different brand. Make sure that you follow the manufacturer's documentation when installing new monitors. If you are working with a Windows 95 machine, it will probably detect the new component and step you through the installation.

If there were problems during the installation of a new adapter card, it will have paid off to have the case off the computer during the testing phase. Once you have ensured that all the components are working correctly, power off the monitor and the computer to replace the case. Simply slide the case back onto the chassis and reinstall the screws. You can reattach the monitor to the computer at this point.

Modem

Most of today's modems use either COM3 or COM4 for the port. When you install a modem, check the back of the computer for any other connections going in.

You may need to move an expansion card to another slot in order to position a modem so it's easy to access later for troubleshooting purposes, or to change phone lines going into the computer. Modems come in two forms, internal or external. External modems need only a free COM port, and can plug into an existing serial port in the back of the computer with an RS232-compliant cable. However, with an internal modem, you must make sure that you already have a free IRQ, I/O address, and COM port prior to installation. To install an internal modem, you must insert it into one of the expansion slots inside the computer and install the screw that holds it in place. The IRQ, I/O address, and COM port information will also need to be configured in the operating system software or using device drivers.

Please be aware that many computers have a mouse or other pointing device that uses a COM port and not a PS/2 mouse port. During the installation of the modem you will have to avoid the port that is in use by the serial mouse, which will most likely be COM1. Since COM1 and COM3 share the same IRQ, your modem cannot use COM3, as a conflict between the pointing device and the modem will occur. Before you install the modem, make a note of the current COM port settings, including which COM ports are available for use by the modem. Also determine if the serial devices have deviated from the standard COM port resource assignments. Many times technicians will have to use an IRQ other than the standard IRQ for a COM port in order to successfully configure a device.

If you are upgrading a modem, make sure you note the existing modem's configuration, and use those settings if possible with the new modem to avoid having to spend additional time reconfiguring devices in your system.

Storage Devices

Installation and configuration of the various storage devices have already been discussed in previous sections. For floppy drives, tape drives, and CD-ROM drives, please refer back to the section on Adding and Removing Peripheral Devices. If you need to reference information on hard drives, please refer to either the Installing and Configuring IDE/EIDE or Installing and Configuring SCSI Devices sections for the appropriate type of drive.

Associated Drivers

Various peripherals require that a device driver be installed into the operating system. With MS-DOS systems, the information is placed in the AUTOEXEC.BAT or CONFIG.SYS files. With Microsoft Windows 95, the operating system will detect the new component upon boot and step you through the process of installing the driver if there isn't already one available to the system. Depending on the operating system, consult the documentation provided by the manufacturer to ensure that you install the driver correctly.

CERTIFICATION OBJECTIVE 1.08

Functions and Use of Common Hand Tools

In order to install or upgrade computer hardware, you must have a good set of tools. Nothing is more frustrating than going to a customer site and not having the proper equipment with you. Worse yet, the customer will get the impression that you may not know what you're doing. There are several items that should be included in any toolkit, and they are discussed in the following sections.

Screwdrivers

The most common tool found in every technician's toolkit is the screwdriver. Screwdrivers come in various sizes and types. The usual assortment of screwdrivers include flat-blade, Phillips, and Torx, all discussed in the following subsections.

Flat-Blade

Flat-blade screwdrivers are common and easily recognizable by their flat blade or flat head. The screws have a single slot that runs dead center across its head. While older computers may still use these types of screws, more modern ones seldom do. The reason is that the metal around the slot has a tendency to be easily damaged by the force used to turn the screw, causing the need to replace the screws more often. If you've ever had to remove a case from a computer, you'll know how stubborn some screws are to remove, especially if it hasn't been used in awhile. Phillips, and more recently Torx, screws are more commonly used. Hex drivers are also common today.

Phillips

The Phillips screwdriver provides more protection against damaging the head of the screw, and is used more frequently in the computer industry. The blade of the screwdriver is in a cross shape, tapering down to a point. The screw itself has two slots that form an X or a cross. The extra slot allows the screwdriver to more evenly distribute the force exerted on the screw itself, reducing the potential for the screwdriver to slip off the screw head. Unfortunately, if a screw has been over-torqued or otherwise damaged, during your attempt to remove it, you can easily cause damage to the screw. With either type of screw, any slippage can cause bits of metal to flake off, possibly causing short circuits in the system later on. When buying bits or screwdrivers, note that Phillips uses a number system, such as #2, to denote the size of the blade. Be sure to get several different sizes into your toolkit, to minimize the chance of slippage and subsequent damage.

Torx

The Torx screwdriver looks somewhat similar to the Phillips screwdriver with its cross shape, except that it has two extra points of contact, and goes vertically into the screw head (instead of angled) to eliminate the chance of slippage and damage. This type of screw and driver is sometimes called a *star* tip or head. This gives even more protection from damage to the screw itself. Currently, you will usually need this type of screwdriver only to work on Apple Macintosh or Compaq systems, but the popularity of this type is increasing. Torx screwdrivers also use a numbering system to denote the size of the blade, but are given a *T* instead of the pound (#) sign.

Hex Driver

IBM, among others, uses hex-head (1/4-inch or 3/16-inch six-sided) type screws, which are nearly as good as Torx for reliable assembly and disassembly of PC components. Although they are very common with the generic computer chassis and components supplied out of Korea and Taiwan, unfortunately the screws are of very low quality and often are not sized accurately for either English (SAE) or metric hex-head tools. It's a good idea to stock your lab with a bulk supply of case, motherboard, and component screws with high-quality hex-head or Torx-head screws in the three or four common threads used by PC components.

Chip Puller

In order to remove integrated circuits, a special type of tool called the *chip puller* or *integrated circuit (IC) puller*, is used. The standard IC puller is U-shaped, and has small fingers on the ends that slip between the socket and the chip itself. These fingers ensure that the force used to pull the chip from the socket is spread equally between the two sides to reduce the possibility of damage to the chip. Once you have the puller on the chip, gently pull until the chip comes out of the socket. Some techs find it easier to pull straight up on the tool when removing a chip; others find they cannot modulate the upward force closely enough, and find it easier to hold the tool lower and rock the chip slightly (less than 5 degrees each way) while applying moderate upward pressure.

Never try to remove an integrated circuit with your fingers. For one thing, you could damage the pins that attach the chip to the board. Another reason is that static electricity on yourself (and therefore, your fingers) can discharge to the pins on the chip and damage the internal circuitry. Another no-no is to use a pair of pliers or tweezers on chips. These tools magnify the force that you apply to them, risking an overexertion of force and hence damage to the chip.

You will find yourself using the chip puller for integrated circuit upgrades such as a BIOS chip upgrade and the addition or removal of a boot-PROM chip on a network adapter card.

Multimeter

Computers work by utilizing electricity in their operations. As such, you can use a measuring device, called a *multimeter*, to determine whether certain components are functioning correctly. Most common multimeters enable you to measure current, resistance, or voltage using the same unit. Switching between these functions is accomplished through a button or dial. The measurements are made through two probes, one colored red for positive (+) and one colored black for negative (-), that are touched on the component that is to be checked. A built-in display shows you the values obtained by the probes.

A multimeter is most commonly used for two situations, either using the resistance (Ohms) position to make a continuity test of switches or cables, or using the DC (volts) position to verify that the supply voltages from the power supply are operating correctly.

To test *continuity* of a switch, the leads are placed on both sides of any switch, and then the switch is operated. When the switch is off, the resistance should read *infinite* (open-circuit). However, if the switch is in-circuit at the time, there will be other circuitry that will conduct some amount of electricity, so you should simply see some value of resistance, at least 1000 ohms or more. When you move the switch to the off position, you should then read less than 2 ohms. On some multimeters, any resistance less than 10 ohms or so will cause it to emit a tone signal.

Testing cables is even easier: after removing the cable, placing the test leads across two neighboring contacts should show *open circuit* resistance of at least 20 megohms (million ohms) or more; otherwise the two pins have some kind of defect between them. Placing the two probe leads at the same pin number at opposite ends of the cable should show continuity, less than 5 Ohms. If not, that wire or contact is broken and defective.

Testing for proper positive output voltages of the power supply is easy— switch the multimeter to a range that will allow the correct voltage to be displayed without going over full-scale (for instance, if your choices for full-scale are 2, 20, or 200 volts, for measuring +12 or +5 volts, use the 20-volt range). Then, place the black lead on the ground wire (always black coming from the power supply) and the red lead on the point to be tested. You should then be able to read the voltage from the display. Check the system documentation for allowable value of that supply line.

Testing the negative supply voltages is exactly the same if using a digital multimeter—the display will simply show a minus sign in front of the number. If using an analog (needle-type) multimeter, just reverse the black and red leads, and read the voltage from the meter as a negative number.

Testing the AC supply voltage from the outlet or inside the power supply is strongly discouraged, as the voltage and current together present a lethal combination that can kill. Fortunately, the only dangerous voltages (other than the video monitor mentioned earlier) are inside the power supply itself. All voltages found anywhere else in the PC case are as safe to work around as the voltages found in a flashlight.

Current cannot be measured in any computer circuit without actually breaking the circuit, and so is rarely performed. To check the correct operation of most integrated circuits would require a detailed schematic and either an oscilloscope or logic analyzer, and so that level of troubleshooting is left to the manufacturer.

Flashlight

Many times it is difficult to look into a computer to find jumper markings, DIP switches, or a lost screw. A flashlight can come in quite handy, saving you from having to remove adapter cards, floppy drives, or hard drives in order to look down into the chassis. A flashlight is also especially handy when computers are placed in darker locations, such as a warehouse, or in tight corners or within enclosed casings to protect the computer from the elements. With a flashlight you can check for connectors and ports on the back of the computer without having to remove all the cables and pulling the computer into a better lit area.

CERTIFICATION OBJECTIVE 1.09

Upgrading BIOS

The Basic Input-Output System (BIOS) contains the program to start the system, and will read various settings from the battery-backed CMOS storage on the Real-Time Clock/Calendar chip located on the motherboard. Most BIOS chips also contain the Setup program (accessed by pressing a special key combination shortly after powering up) to choose the settings from a menu and save them in the CMOS Clock/Calendar chip for use during the boot-up process. Other systems require the use of a special disk program to change the BIOS boot-up settings.

System BIOS (Flash or Replace)

Occasionally, a system manufacturer may make a BIOS upgrade available to fix a bug or add a feature. For older systems with the BIOS chip installed in a socket on the motherboard, you simply remove the old chip and replace it with the new one. Newer systems use something called *Electrically-Erasable, Programmable, Read-Only Memory (EEPROM)*, also known as *Flash-ROM*. In those cases, a special program can reprogram the Flash-ROM chip without removing it, from a file either supplied on disk or possibly downloaded from the manufacturer's Web site.

EXERCISE 1-6 ### Replacing BIOS

1. Follow the ESD procedures prior to removing the case.

2. When the case has been removed, mark and remove any expansion cards or connectors that may be in the way.

3. It is at this point that you can use a chip puller to gently remove the chip from its socket.

4. To install a new BIOS chip, position the chip over the socket, ensuring that the pins are properly in place, and gently push down on the chip until it is seated.

System Hardware

The BIOS boot-up settings contain information on the system hardware and may need to be updated when a new component has been added to the computer. To access the BIOS, you must enter the SETUP program when the computer is booting. Some systems use the DEL or F1 key to enter the program, while others may use an ALT-ESC key combination. To ensure that you hit the appropriate key(s), carefully watch the computer as it powers up for a message that tells you how to access the SETUP program. In some older computers, it is common to not see a message during the boot process. You will have to refer to the manufacturer's documentation in order to determine the correct key, or key combination to enter the SETUP program. If documentation is not available, the information should be found on the manufacturer's Web site.

CERTIFICATION OBJECTIVE 1.10

System Optimization

Sometimes you are required to *optimize* a computer system. This basically involves improving the performance of the equipment. While there is only so much you can do, there are various devices that can be optimized, such as memory, hard drives, and cache memory. System optimization can either be software-based, as in disk defragmenting utilities or through the use of memory management utilities, or the computer can be optimized by the addition of a hardware device, such as memory. You can also optimize a system by modifying system parameters, such as those found in the Registry of the current Microsoft operating systems such as Windows 95, Windows 98, and Windows NT. The following sections describe each in detail.

Memory

Optimizing memory usually means that you free up conventional memory, which is the memory address range between 0K and 640K, if you are using DOS, basic Windows, or even in some cases, Windows 95 or 98. One of the things you can do to free conventional memory is to load MS-DOS into the *High Memory Area (HMA)* by adding the following line to the CONFIG.SYS file:

```
DOS = HIGH
```

You should always specify DOS = HIGH in your CONFIG.SYS file if your computer supports it. This can easily free up to 55K of conventional memory and there is no drawback.

In addition to specifying DOS = HIGH in your CONFIG.SYS, you should also add the UMB parameter to allow DOS to load resident programs into upper memory blocks with the DEVICEHIGH and LOADHIGH commands:

```
DOS = HIGH,UMB
```

Another way to free up conventional memory is to load device drivers or *terminate-and-stay resident (TSR)* programs into upper memory. TSRs are just programs that remain in memory and do not do anything until a special condition takes place, such as a screen saver program. The first step is to check the system memory configuration by using a special program called MEM.EXE with the /C switch. The /C tells the memory program to *classify*, or individually list the programs that use up memory and what type of memory is being used, as shown in Figure 1-12. In the Conventional column, any number over 0K means that something is using conventional memory.

FIGURE 1-12

Output of the MEM /C command

```
Modules using memory below 1 MB:

Name          Total              Conventional         Upper Memory
--------   ----------------   ----------------      ----------------
MSDOS       17,648   (17K)      17,648   (17K)           0    (0K)
SETVER         848    (1K)         848    (1K)           0    (0K)
HIMEM        1,168    (1K)       1,168    (1K)           0    (0K)
SMS_10X     27,808   (27K)      27,808   (27K)           0    (0K)
IFSHLP       2,864    (3K)       2,864    (3K)           0    (0K)
WIN          3,648    (4K)       3,648    (4K)           0    (0K)
vmm32        3,424    (3K)       3,424    (3K)           0    (0K)
COMMAND      7,504    (7K)       7,504    (7K)           0    (0K)
Free       590,176  (576K)     590,176  (576K)           0    (0K)

Memory Summary:

Type of Memory      Total          Used           Free
----------------  ------------  ------------   ------------
Conventional          655,360        65,184        590,176
Upper                       0             0              0
Reserved              393,216       393,216              0
Extended (XMS)     66,060,288       188,416     65,871,872
                  ------------  ------------   ------------
Total memory       67,108,864       646,816     66,462,048

Total under 1 MB      655,360        65,184        590,176

Total Expanded (EMS)               66,584,576       (64M)
Free Expanded (EMS)                16,777,216       (16M)
Largest executable program size       590,160      (576K)
Largest free upper memory block             0        (0K)
MS-DOS is resident in the high memory area.
```

To move a device driver or TSR to upper memory, you must first load the EMM386.EXE program from the CONFIG.SYS file if it is not already loaded. For device drivers, use a DEVICEHIGH=<<*drivername*>> line in the CONFIG.SYS file to load the driver into upper memory. With TSRs, you need to use a LOADHIGH <<*TSR_name*>> line in the AUTOEXEC.BAT file instead. The following illustrates the lines needed by the CONFIG.SYS file and the AUTOEXEC.BAT file:

```
In the CONFIG.SYS file:

DEVICEHIGH=C:\<drivername>
```

In the AUTOEXEC.BAT file:

```
LOADHIGH <tsr_name>
```

Or

```
LH <tsr_name>
```

on the job

It would appear as if the days of DOS are over, because operating systems like Windows 95 and Windows 98 do not rely on DOS as much, and Windows NT does not contain any DOS. However, you will be surprised at how often you will use your DOS skills in the workplace. Every Windows NT networking position I have ever had required working with DOS computers, or working with batch files and commands that are derived from the days of DOS. You will find yourself creating batch files that contain tons of valid DOS commands. These batch files will make your administrative duties easier by attaching to network drives, automatically deleting, copying, or moving some files, setting environment variables, and even calling other programs or batch files. If your company has older computers, such as those running Windows 3.x, you will have to deal with not only DOS commands, you will have to work with the actual DOS operating system itself. This may involve streamlining the CONFIG.SYS and AUTOEXEC.BAT files to increase conventional memory.

If you are not familiar with DOS memory management, you may have to find an old DOS book and spend some time configuring a DOS-based computer. You will be surprised at the amount of knowledge you will gain and how useful it will be in the future. It's also nice to have a DOS expert help you with problems. At my last job there were a few DOS experts and they would give me assignments to create complicated batch files. We were both challenging each other to improve our batch file that would scan the entire hard disk twice, and tell you which files have changed since the first scan. The results would then be printed with which files were added, deleted, or modified, and the date and time each of these files was modified. The batch file was much more complicated than we had anticipated, but it worked very well and we all learned a lot more DOS commands. It brought back some old memories of working with DOS and assured me that DOS isn't dead.

Hard Drives

Hard drives have a tendency to become *fragmented*. By fragmented, we are talking about the way in which they store files and file locations. When you save a file to a hard disk, it is not necessarily stored in consecutive areas on the disk. Instead, the drive locates the first areas available and dumps whatever will fit there, then moves on to the next location, and so on until the file is stored. A *pointer* is used to tell the drive where the next piece of data that constitutes the file is located. Sometimes the pointers become *corrupt*, or the data itself may be damaged. Also, as the drive has to search in different locations just to retrieve a single file, the speed at which the drive can retrieve the information is slowed down. To *defragment* the drive, you must run a utility, such as Microsoft's Defragmenter (DEFRAG.EXE).

There are also some software packages on the market that are used to optimize hard drives, such as Norton's SpeedDisk, which you can purchase at any computer software store.

Windows NT helps alleviate fragmentation by determining the size of the data that needs to be written, and rather than finding the first available block to begin writing the data, it will find an area of contiguous free space on the hard disk that will fit the entire amount of data. This will make retrieval time quicker because the data is in one contiguous section of the hard drive. If Windows NT cannot find an area of contiguous free space on the hard drive to fit the entire amount of data, it will then write to the first available block of space and continue the write process in the next area of free space as necessary. For this reason, Windows NT version 4.0 does not ship with a disk defragmenting utility.

Compression

With Windows 95/98 you have the option of compressing drives, which can create a very significant amount of space. However, this increase in space comes at a price: a decrease in system performance. With very fast computers, this performance hit may be negligible. However, on 486 systems, you will see a drop in performance opening files, as they need to be uncompressed on the fly. Windows NT users who format their partitions with the NTFS file system can now take advantage of compressing individual files or folders without having to compress the entire drive or partition.

Many experienced technicians shy away from disk compression, due to the large capacity and low cost of hard drives today. If you or a client is considering disk compression, you should evaluate your needs, and whether a slight degredation in system performance is desired or not.

Cache Memory

The only way to improve the performance of cache memory is to add more. By adding more cache memory, you enable the computer to store more of the frequently accessed instructions and information. Generally, any cache beyond 1MB will not show much additional improvement. Most motherboards come equipped with 512KB of cache memory, with the option of upgrading to 1MB at an additional cost. Whenever you have the option of purchasing a motherboard, make sure you choose one with at least 512KB cache. It may be possible to upgrade an older motherboard from 256KB to 512KB of cache.

CERTIFICATION SUMMARY

This chapter has provided you with the knowledge of what each system module does and how it works. Understanding this material provides you with the insight necessary to proceed with installing, removing, and configuring the various components that are used by a computer system. Also discussed were the various addressing methods and communications aspects of system components. Armed with this knowledge, you should be able to identify unfamiliar devices by the manner in which they connect to the system, as well as by their function. And if that wasn't enough information, you were presented with system optimization techniques to improve the performance of the equipment.

 # TWO-MINUTE DRILL

❑ When installing a new power supply, remember that when you re-attach the two power connectors to the motherboard, the black wires that are located on each connector must be facing each other.

❑ Always wear an electrostatic wrist band to ground yourself when removing the computer's chassis.

❑ Never wear an electrostatic wrist band when working near a monitor, as the high-voltage circuits may contain residual charge, that even when unplugged can hurt you, or possibly even kill you.

❑ Every module that makes up a computer system attaches to the motherboard (also called the *system board, main board,* or *planar board*) and is able to communicate with other modules through the bus.

❑ Electrical power comes in two forms: *alternating current (AC)*, which is the type that comes out of a wall outlet, and *direct current (DC)*, which is the type that your computer uses.

❑ The DC current is fed to your computer in one of several forms: +5 volts, +12 volts, −5 volts, and −12 volts. The newer ATX and NLX standards provide for an optional +3.3 volt supply voltage as well.

❑ All PC-compatible power supplies, known as *switching-mode* power supplies, use transistors in addition to diodes to convert current and are much more efficient at converting the AC power from the wall outlet to the DC power needed inside the PC.

❑ An overheated power supply will not only fail, but can damage other components inside the computer.

❑ Memory, of which there are several types (cache memory, random access memory (RAM), and read only memory (ROM)), is comprised of *integrated circuits (ICs)* that reside on a chip.

❑ Monitors come in a wide variety of types, ranging from the original monochrome display adapter (MDA), which only permitted text-based characters, to today's high-resolution super video graphics adapter (SVGA). Other types are CGA, EGA, and VGA.

❑ A modem takes data from the sending computer and translates it from digital to analog signals before transmitting it across a telephone line, a process called modulation. When a modem receives analog signals from a telephone line, it converts the data back into digital signals, a process called demodulation.

❑ The *Basic Input/Output System (BIOS),* is the mechanism used by your computer to essentially provide device drivers for basic system devices for the DOS/Windows operating system, and also contains the program to initially perform a basic test and boot up of the system.

❑ The *Complementary Metal-Oxide Semiconductor (CMOS),* an integrated circuit containing the Real-Time Clock/Calendar circuitry and related battery-backed storage, allows the computer to store this information even after the computer has been turned off.

❑ The first, and most important, step that you must take before adding or replacing a system module is to power off the computer and disconnect the power cord from the wall outlet.

❑ Always note the locations and any connectors that attach to expansion cards before removal to ensure that you will be able to put everything back into its appropriate spot. Make it a habit to mark such things when removing and installing modules.

❑ To install most SIMM memory modules, place the SIMM over the slot at a 45-degree angle and gently push the chip into place by moving it to an upright position until it clicks into place.

❑ Never plug a digital monitor into an analog adapter, or vice versa, as severe damage will result.

❑ There are two types of keyboard connectors in use, the DIN-5 connector and the Mini DIN-6 connector. DIN-5s are generally found on AT style keyboards and have a round port with five pins. The Mini DIN-6 also has a round port but differs in that it has six pins plus one square plastic positioning pin.

❑ Devices request attention from the CPU through a special set of lines, called *interrupt request lines (IRQs)*, in the bus.

❑ Once the CPU receives an IRQ from a device, it can directly communicate with that device through *I/O addresses* or *I/O ports*.

❑ Refer back to Table 1-1 and review the standard IRQ settings.

❑ Refer back to Table 1-2 and review the more frequently used I/O addresses.

❑ Interrupts, I/O addresses, DMA channels, and some additional features have to be configured in the hardware. Jumpers and Dual In-Line Package (DIP) switches are used to accomplish configuration.

❑ Cables come in two different forms, *shielded* cables and *unshielded* cables. Shielded cables have a wire mesh or Mylar layer added between the medium and the sheathing that protects the cables from interference.

❑ Refer back to Tables 1-3 and 1-4 and memorize the primary control signals for serial and parallel communication.

❑ IDE/EIDE drives can have up to four drives installed, but you will be able to put only two drives on a single cable.

❑ *Small Computer Systems Interface (SCSI)* devices permit you to connect multiple devices to one cable, or "chain" them, in configurations of up to seven to fifteen devices on a single cable depending on the SCSI implementation that you are using. 32-bit Wide SCSI is rarely available at present, but will allow 31 devices plus the adapter to work together on one 32-bit SCSI channel.

❑ Common tools in every computer technician's toolkit include each variety of screwdriver, a chip puller, and a multimeter.

❑ BIOS boot-up settings contain information on the system hardware and may need to be updated when a new component has been added to the computer.

❑ Flash BIOS means that the BIOS chip can be reprogrammed with new settings. This type of BIOS requires special software, called a *flash program*, and a special data file in order to replace the instructions that drive the BIOS.

❑ One of the things you can do to free conventional memory is to load MS-DOS into the High Memory Area (HMA) by adding a simple line to the CONFIG.SYS file.

❑ To defragment a fragmented hard drive, you must run a utility, such as Microsoft's Defragmenter (DEFRAG.EXE).

SELF TEST

The following Self Test questions will help you measure your understanding of the material presented in this chapter. Read all the choices carefully, as there may be more than one correct answer. Choose all correct answers for each question.

1. Which of the following types of system memory is the fastest?

    A. DRAM

    B. ROM

    C. SRAM

    D. WRAM

2. Which type of floppy disk supported a 1.2MB capacity?

    A. DSDD 3 1/2"

    B. DSDD 5 1/4"

    C. DSHD 3.1/2"

    D. DSHD 5 1/4"

3. You have been instructed to install a computer in the library for the new multimedia-based book inventory system. This computer will need to support 256 colors in graphics mode. Which of the following monitor specifications could you use to achieve this? (Choose all that apply.)

    A. SVGA

    B. CGA

    C. EGA

    D. VGA

4. You are watching a junior technician as he prepares to upgrade the modem and video card in a customer's computer. In order to protect the computer from ESD, he places the computer on the rubber mat and connects one of the two wires to the computer. He then takes the second wire and connects it to the ground pin on the electrical outlet. Next, he puts on his ESD wrist strap and attaches a wire from his strap to the mat. Where did this technician go wrong in protecting the computer from ESD?

    A. He should have connected both wires to the ground pin found on any electrical outlet.

    B. He should have connected his wrist strap directly to the computer chassis.

    C. He should have connected the second wire from the chassis to the ground pin on the power supply.

    D. He obeyed all of the recommended ESD prevention practices.

5. After you have upgraded the processor in a client's computer from a Pentium 75 to a Pentium 166, you notice that the BIOS reports the processor as a Pentium 133. Which of the following are possible reasons for this? (Choose all that apply.)

    A. Misconfigured external speed jumper

    B. Improper setting in the SETUP program for the processor

C. Misconfigured CPU clock speed jumper

D. Misconfigured CPU DMA

6. What is the physical difference between a SIMM and a DIMM module?

A. A SIMM has 45 pins, whereas a DIMM has 72 pins.

B. A SIMM has two rows of 45 pins, whereas a DIMM has one row of 168 pins.

C. A SIMM has one slot on the bottom, whereas a DIMM has two slots on the bottom.

D. A SIMM has 72 pins, whereas a DIMM has 168 pins.

7. What type of connector will a VGA or SVGA monitor have?

A. A male DB-9 connector

B. A male DB-15 connector

C. A female DB-9 connector

D. A female DB-15 connector

8. DIN-5 connectors are generally found where?

A. On serial ports

B. On AT keyboards

C. On parallel ports

D. On SCSI ports

9. What is the Standard Device Assignment for IRQ 6?

A. Floppy controller

B. Hard disk controller

C. COM port 1

D. Math Co-Processor

10. What is the standard IRQ for Serial port (COM2)?

A. IRQ 2

B. IRQ 3

C. IRQ 4

D. IRQ 7

11. Which of the following IRQs are cascaded? (Choose all that apply.)

A. 1

B. 2

C. 8

D. 9

E. 11

12. Which of the following is the port address (hex range) for serial port COM2?

A. 3F8-3FF

B. 2E8-2FF

C. 2F8-2FF

D. 378-37F

13. Which device uses the port address (hex range) of 378-37F?

A. Serial port COM1

B. Serial port COM2

C. Parallel port LPT1

D. Parallel port LPT2

14. You have been called out to investigate why a user's game can no longer play sounds. The sound card was configured at

the factory with standard settings. You are configuring the game to use these same settings. You configure the I/O address of 320, the IRQ of 5, and the DMA channel of 1. Will these settings work correctly?

A. No, because the I/O address is not the standard sound card I/O address assignment.

B. No, because the IRQ is not the standard sound card IRQ assignment.

C. No, because the DMA channel is not the standard sound card DMA channel assignment.

D. Yes, the sound card should work correctly now.

15. Which control signal in serial communications tells the receiver that the data terminal (computer) is ready?

A. TxD

B. RxD

C. DSR

D. DTR

16. Which type of connector does a video adapter card have?

A. A socket DB-9 connector

B. A socket DB-15 connector

C. A pin DB-9 connector

D. A pin DB-15 connector

17. Which type of connector is commonly used to attach an unshielded twisted pair (UTP) cable with a network card?

A. RJ-11

B. RJ-14

C. RJ-45

D. RJ-10

18. What are the characteristics of Wide Fast-20 SCSI? (Choose all that apply.)

A. Transfer speeds at a maximum of 40 MBps

B. 16-bit bus

C. Transfer speeds at a maximum of 20 MBps

D. 32-bit bus

19. How many pins are there on a 16-bit Wide-SCSI connector?

A. 72 pins

B. 50 pins

C. 68 pins

D. 42 pins

20. What do you have to remember when dealing with SCSI termination?

A. Always terminate the SCSI adapter.

B. Remove termination from all devices, except the device at the end of the cable.

C. Terminate the device closest to the SCSI adapter.

D. Place a terminator at the end of the cable, and a backup terminator on the first device in the chain.

21. What do you need to do if you have a bootable SCSI device?

A. Disable the BIOS on the SCSI adapter.

B. Disable your system BIOS.

C. Enable SCSI BIOS shadowing in your system's SETUP utility.

D. Enable SCSI BIOS on your SCSI adapter.

22. When is the only time you should not wear an ESD wrist strap?

A. When replacing the power supply

B. When working on a monitor

C. When replacing a sensitive IC chip, such as a CPU

D. When using a multimeter

23. Which of the following is a numbering system to denote the size of the blade on a Torx screwdriver?

A. #2

B. R2

C. T2

D. *2

24. Which of the following are common voltages that you will find when testing a computer with a multimeter?

A. +2

B. +5

C. +10

D. +12

25. What switch is used with the MEM.EXE command to individually list the programs that use up memory and what type of memory is being used?

A. /L

B. /C

C. /list

D. /A

2

Diagnosing and Troubleshooting

W hen diagnosing any component connected to a computer system, it helps to know some of the basic troubleshooting procedures. In addition, if you are armed with the knowledge of common symptoms and problems that relate to each device, the time spent locating and repairing the problem is significantly reduced. In this chapter, we explore basic troubleshooting techniques along with the common trouble spots that afflict individual devices.

CERTIFICATION OBJECTIVE 2.01

Symptoms and Problems

When troubleshooting a problem, it helps if you understand how the various symptoms relate to common problems. Many field replaceable modules have several parts to them, and some of these parts may be the cause of the problem. It is recommended to isolate the components in the subsystem for troubleshooting. In the next subsections, we look at each module and the common causes of problems.

Processor/Memory

When the processor has a problem, it may be related to the Complementary Metal-Oxide Semiconductor (CMOS). For example, if you notice that the time is constantly incorrect, then the CMOS battery is running low on power and needs to be replaced. However, other problems usually show themselves during the Power On Self Test (POST) that occurs during boot time. These errors usually are preceded by a 1**, where the ** can be any set of numbers. The descriptive messages inform you of what type of problem is discovered and you can act accordingly. If the computer displays an error code, before replacing the processor, see if the chip has become slightly loose in the socket, a phenomenon called *chip creep*.

Memory problems are also detected when POST runs at boot time. These types of errors are usually preceded by a 2**, again where the ** can be any set of numbers. Check the descriptive message that comes with the error code and proceed accordingly.

Input Devices

Input devices are the easiest components to check, as there are few things that can go wrong with them. We discuss the various types of input devices in the next subsections.

Keyboards

When troubleshooting a keyboard, there are only a few symptoms that you have to worry about. These items include the following:

- Non-functional keyboard
- Sporadic keys
- Sticking keys

The first item, the non-functional keyboard, usually leads to an error message from the computer at boot that reads:

```
KEYBOARD ERROR
PRESS <F1> TO CONTINUE
```

You can check that the keyboard connector is snugly secure in the socket, but if it is, then you may need to replace the keyboard itself.

exam
*W*atch

Keyboard errors usually generate a 3** error code when POST runs at boot time.

With sporadically functioning keys or sticking keys, you need to give the keyboard a good cleaning. This type of problem is fairly obvious, as many customers have a nasty habit of eating and drinking over keyboards. You can purchase a keyboard cleaning kit at any computer or electronics store, but if the problem isn't resolved after a cleaning, you will have to replace the keyboard. The good news is that keyboards are relatively inexpensive items and that any replacement takes less than one minute.

Mice

Diagnosing problems with mice is similar to keyboards, with just a few exceptions. The items to consider in mouse troubleshooting are as follows:

- Dirty mouse
- Conflicting address
- Device driver
- Adapter card, if any

A dirty mouse is the most common problem reported. The roller bars inside the mouse tend to pick up dust and dirt from the mouse ball when it rolls over a mouse pad. A symptom of a dirty mouse is when you attempt to move it across the mouse pad and get little, sometimes jerky, response. You can remove the screws from the bottom of the mouse or spin the plastic cover off and physically check these rollers. If needed, clean them with alcohol, reassemble the mouse, and try again. Using a mouse pad that does not have a glossy surface can also increase traction with a mouse and improve response.

If another device is using the same IRQ or I/O address as the mouse, then it probably won't work at all. This is because the results are being returned to the conflicting device. Try checking IRQs and I/O addresses with diagnostic software to ensure that there is not another device using either of these. Most computers have four available COM ports but only two can be used at the same time. Therefore the most common configuration in a system with a serial mouse is the serial mouse on COM1 and the modem on COM2.

Device drivers control how the mouse communicates with the processor. If the driver is configured incorrectly, such as a wrong address or an incorrect sensitivity setting, the mouse will have slow to non-functional response. In addition, if the device uses an adapter card, there may be a problem with the card itself. If you suspect that this is the case, you can try to replace the adapter card and see if the problem is resolved.

Trackball

Most of the time that you will encounter a trackball is with a laptop computer. With laptops, the trackball is integrated into the keyboard and the repair process becomes a bit more difficult. However, trackballs work in the same manner as a mouse and the problems have the same symptoms and causes as mice. If the device is unresponsive, you have to replace it. On many laptop machines, this also requires that you replace the entire keyboard unit. However, if the response is slow or sporadic, you probably can give it a good cleaning to resolve the problem. Check with your local computer or electronics store for the appropriate cleaning kit, as well as the manufacturer's recommendations listed in the documentation.

If you are working on a personal computer, the trackball is a peripheral device and is not integrated into the keyboard. If the device is non-responsive, check the connection to the computer to ensure that it has not come loose. Also, check any adapter cards and device drivers that are associated with the trackball. Usually, there is a device driver configuration error or driver corruption that causes the problem. You can also check these items for a sporadic problem, but most likely you will need to clean the device to resolve the problem.

Pen/Stylus

With the increased graphical capabilities of today's computers, the stylus is becoming very popular with graphics-oriented shops. These tools look similar to a pen that is attached to a drawing tablet via a cable. Most of the time, the stylus is not the problem but the drawing tablet is. If the tablet is dirty, try cleaning it with a damp cloth. Also look for device driver problems, such as in the configuration or driver corruption, as well as any cable connection from the tablet into the computer. Be sure to check the preferences or configuration to verify that settings such as speed and sensitivity are appropriate. These settings work in the same way as the settings for the mouse in the Control Panel.

Scanners

There are two types of scanners that you will come into contact with: the flat-bed scanner and the hand-held scanner. Both work in a similar fashion, except that the flat-bed can scan a full sheet at a time while the hand-held works primarily with smaller images. When troubleshooting these devices, take the following into consideration:

- Dirty scanner surface
- Cable and power connections
- Adapter card, if used
- Device drivers

A dirty scanner surface usually results in smudged or poor-quality images. With flat-bed scanners, it is merely a matter of cleaning the glass surface with a good glass cleaner. However, with hand-held scanners, you need to consult the manufacturer's documentation for the recommended method of cleaning.

Always ensure that the cable connection from the scanner to the computer is properly attached. A loose connection usually results in a non-responsive scanner. If you are diagnosing a flat-bed scanner, you also need to check the power connection if the device does not power up.

Adapter cards do the work of translating signals between the scanner and the computer. They are good suspects when you encounter communication-related errors. However, most problems with scanners that are not resolved by cleaning the unit are device-driver related. The driver is the software interface between the computer and the adapter card, and may have been inadvertently modified by the customer. If not, ensure that the driver is not corrupted. If you have determined that the device driver is corrupted, you can reinstall it from the original floppy or floppies that came with the scanner.

Scanners can also use a SCSI adapter card. This involves a whole new level of diagnostics and troubleshooting by introducing problems normally associated with SCSI devices, such as termination and SCSI IDs. Make sure you have followed all SCSI guidelines if you are using a SCSI scanner.

Microphones

Microphones are being utilized more and more with computers these days. These devices enable the user to control the computer through speech recognition software, and some software packages even interact with word processing applications to accept dictation. And even though the technology is still in its infancy, microphones pick up your voice in the form of audio signals for video conferencing. However, there is not much that you can do to clean or repair a microphone. You can check the device driver configuration for conflicts and the application software for a correct configuration. The manufacturer's documentation should specify these items. However, if one goes bad, you have to replace the device.

Touch Pad

Touch pads are relative newcomers to the computer industry, but have a wide variety of applications. If you have stopped at a fast food restaurant or visited the mini-market at a gas station, you will notice that the cash registers have plastic sheets that the cashier presses rather than depressing buttons, to ring up your order. These registers are early forms of touch pads, and work by having a dollar amount associated to each square on the pad. When the cashier presses the square, a small button or a sensor is triggered that rings up the price. Computer touch pads work the same way. They are pads that have either thin wires running through them, or specialized surfaces that can sense the pressure of your finger on them.

If touch pads need repair, usually a good cleaning with a damp cloth (no detergents) will resolve the problem. You can verify that any device driver or application software has a correct configuration, but beyond this you may need to replace the device.

Floppy Drive Failures

When troubleshooting floppy drive failures, there is a myriad of components that you must take into consideration as the true point of failure. These items include the following:

- Media errors
- Drive incompatibilities

- Dirty read/write heads
- Cabling or connection errors
- Floppy controller card
- Device driver errors
- Drive failure

Commonly, what seems to be a floppy drive error is not actually a drive problem but a media error. Floppy disks are susceptible to physical and magnetic corruption, giving the appearance of a bad drive with "Error reading disk" or "Error writing to disk" messages. At other times, there are drive incompatibilities so that when one drive writes to a disk, another drive can't read it. This is common, for example, when you copy files from one PC and try to read them on another PC that has an incompatible drive. If you encounter this problem, try reading from another disk, preferably one that was written to by the suspect drive, or writing to a second disk. If the drive can perform the operation on a different disk, it probably is a media error. It is also quite common for a floppy disk to be defective from the manufacturer. In this case, formatting the floppy won't help; you will have to throw the disk away.

Media errors can also be caused by dirty read/write heads on the floppy drive. Dirt can get into a computer through the vents used to pull in fresh air, and will stick to the read/write heads. Also, while floppies have less chance of getting dirty from the plastic encasement, there is still some dirt deposited on the media when it is in use by the drive. Floppy drive cleaning kits can be purchased rather cheaply at any computer store, and you should follow the manufacturer's instructions for using them. If you continue to use floppy disks in a computer that is in a dusty environment, you may risk ruining floppies by using them. Dust particles can be dragged across the surface of the floppy disk and destroy data, rendering the floppy useless.

Another thing to check for is that there is nothing stuck in the drive itself. Sometimes, people put items in the drive that do not belong there, such as the wrong type of media. Small children are also notorious for placing items into a floppy drive just as they do with VCRs. When troubleshooting a floppy drive, first check that no foreign objects have been placed into the drive.

Cabling can also lead to drive problems. If you have just installed a floppy drive and are experiencing a problem with the drive, such as the drive light not going out, you probably have the cable on backwards. The red stripe on the floppy cable must be connected to pin 1 on the adapter and on the drive. Also, there will be times when you think that a cable is firmly seated on the drive, or on the adapter, and it might be a hair off. This can cause communication problems between the drive and the adapter. Try pressing on both connections to see if they move at all. However, do not force a cable if you meet resistance when making the connection. You could bend or break a pin. If you break a pin on a hard drive, the drive will be useless.

If the drive isn't getting power, it won't work. Sometimes the power cable isn't properly seated in the drive's power connector. You can attempt to push the power connector to see if it moves or visually inspect the connection. If it doesn't move, and the drive still isn't getting any power, then you have to replace the drive, or inspect the power supply and cables to determine if you are experiencing another problem not related to the floppy disk.

An improperly seated controller card may also cause communication problems between the drive and the adapter. Try gently, but firmly, pressing down on the adapter card. If it hasn't moved, then you may want to check the contacts. Contacts can get dirty and may require cleaning with isopropyl alcohol. If you suspect that the contact might be defective, you can attempt to check it using a multimeter. However, if you believe that you have a problem controller card, you can test it by installing a second floppy drive. If you can successfully use the second drive, then the controller probably isn't the problem. Remember that the components of the floppy disk drive subsystem are the floppy drive itself, the cable, and the disk controller. Replace each component one at a time with known good components to determine where the fault lies.

If the problem doesn't fit into any of the previously mentioned categories, you must check for possible software problems. The device driver used by the operating system software may have become corrupt, in which case you can try reinstalling the driver. However, if the computer has been losing its BIOS (Basic Input Output System) settings from a dying CMOS battery, you have to enter the SETUP program to re-enter the settings. With newer computers, this shouldn't be a concern as the BIOS can usually autodetect the drive. Unfortunately, older computers require you to re-enter these settings manually.

At this point, if you are still encountering problems, then the drive itself is at fault and must be replaced. The good news is that floppy drives are relatively inexpensive items, and they only take around 15 minutes to replace.

Hard Drives

Hard drives can be tricky to diagnose or relatively simple, depending on the source of the problem. The following are some areas to consider when troubleshooting a hard drive problem:

- Power connection
- Cabling
- Addressing conflicts
- Hard drive controller or SCSI interface
- BIOS settings
- Fragmented or corrupt drives

Without power, the hard drive is useless. One of the first things to try is listening to the hard drive itself. If you cannot hear it, it probably has no power. Verify that the power connection is snugly in the socket and that the power supply is working. This is a common problem with newly installed drives.

Communication takes place between the hard drive and the controller via a flat data ribbon cable. This cable could be loose or may have gone bad. This is common with newly installed drives rather than those that have already been functioning properly. Check the cable connection to ensure that it is connected properly, and if it is, try swapping cables. The stripe on the edge of one side of the cable is for PIN1, and should correspond with the PIN1 designation on the hard disk controller.

If you have more than one hard drive in the computer, verify that the master/slave configuration is correct. You will need to ensure that both hard drives are configured correctly. One hard drive should be set for master, and the other hard drive should be set for slave. This is the case only for hard drives that are chained to the same controller. If you have two hard drive controllers and two hard drives, each hard drive could be a master on their own controller.

The controller card may also be a problem for the hard drive. Verify the address settings for the controller and ensure that there are no conflicts with another device. If another hard drive is attached to the controller and is functioning properly, you probably do not have a controller problem.

If you feel that you have file corruption or bad sectors on the disk, you can use a utility such as Microsoft's ScanDisk or Norton Disk Utilities to repair or remove damaged files, as well as check and mark any bad sectors on the disk. File corruption or bad sectors can be caused by several things: faulty cables, physical damage to the hard drive data surface, incorrectly configured controller, or even a computer shutdown while the file is in use. A scanning utility can be used to check each sector on the disk and allow you several repair options, depending on the software. If the utility finds a bad sector on the disk, it flags the spot as bad so that it is not used by the drive. Remember, running some disk utilities can destroy long filenames and, in some cases, even destroy the data contained on the disk. Check with the disk utility vendor to verify which operating systems the disk utility is certified to work with.

Remember that the hard disk subsystem consists of the drive itself, the controller, and the cable. When you are experiencing a disk problem, one of these devices will be at fault. Replace each component one at a time with known good components to determine where the fault lies.

exam
Watch

Be prepared for a few questions on troubleshooting floppy and hard disk drives on the A+ exam. These are common topics because nearly every computer has both a floppy and hard disk drive, and they are common components for replacement, especially hard disk drives.

Tape Drives

Tape drives, similar to hard and floppy disk drives can have both hardware and software problems. The tape drive subsystem also consists of the drive itself, the controller, and the cable. The media is susceptible to manufacturing defects and continual wear and tear. Problem areas that are encountered with tape drive systems include the following:

- Media problems
- Dirty read/write heads
- Cabling and power connections
- Controller card
- Device drivers

When diagnosing tape drive problems, it is a good idea to rule out the possibility of media problems first. As with floppy drives, tape cartridges wear out with use and can become corrupted. In addition, if the cartridge has been written to by another device, you might have an incompatibility problem arising between the two devices. A media problem could be caused by the software. Most available backup software, such as ArcServe or Legato, put an expiration date on the tape's internal label. The standard expiration date is one year, and if the cartridge has been in use longer than that, it is probably time to dispose of it. Try using another cartridge to determine if there is a media problem.

If you are able to rule out the cartridge, the next step is to inspect the power connection. If the device is not getting power, it will not work. Try checking the power cable and ensuring that the power connector is firmly seated. If the connector is not properly seated, it may be slightly shaken as the drive motors are in operation, and thus cause sporadic power problems. Also check to see if a power strip is in use, as surges or lapses in power can "trip" the power strip, causing it to require a reset.

Another connection to check is the cabling from the drive to the adapter card. If the cables are not connected properly, then the drive will experience communication problems. Try to push down on all the connections, as well as on the adapter card itself, to see if there is any perceptible movement. If there is, you have probably found the problem, although sometimes the cable itself may be defective. In this case, replace the cable to see if the problem goes away.

Because device driver software resides on the computer's hard disk, there is also the potential for the driver to become corrupted. There are two ways that you can check this angle. The first method is to verify the software configuration; the second method is to reinstall the driver. Always check the software configuration first, as it is also possible that the customer may have inadvertently made a configuration change, referred to as *operator error*. If you see any garbage characters in the configuration, then you definitely have a corrupt driver and must reinstall it. However, if the values have been slightly altered, you probably have an operator error.

Tape drives require cleaning based on the number of hours the drive is used. A cleaning cartridge should be used after the recommended number of hours the drive has been in use. Consult the tape drive manufacturer's recommendations for the amount of time between routine cleanings.

CD-ROMs

When troubleshooting CD-ROM drives, there are several things that should be checked:

- Media problems
- Cable and/or connectors
- Address conflicts
- Controller board
- Device drivers

One good troubleshooting tool that comes in handy is a diagnostic program that came with the CD-ROM drive or the controller board. While not all manufacturers package diagnostic software with the hardware, you may be able to check their Web site for any of these aids. If you have access to a diagnostic utility, try running it against the equipment and view the results. Often, these programs are able to pinpoint the problem and save you some time.

When dealing with CD-ROM problems, as with many problems relating to computers, you need to ask yourself when the last time the device was working properly. This can give you a good indication as to the nature of the problem. With a CD-ROM that is not working correctly, knowing when the device was last functioning can make all the difference in your troubleshooting methodology. If the CD-ROM does not work after installation, chances are you have a device driver problem, bad CD-ROM drive, or a cabling error. The next sections will discuss these in detail. If the CD-ROM drive has been working for weeks, then you can begin looking for problems such as operator error or device failure.

One of the most common problems reported to the technician with regard to CD-ROMs is that the customer cannot read a CD-ROM disk. There are several things that can cause this, but usually having the customer verify that there is, in fact, a compact disk in the tray or that it was not inadvertently inserted upside down commonly solves this problem. In addition, if the customer is using a CD-ROM tower or a disk changer, they may have forgotten to perform a software mount on the CD, which is usually performed with a MOUNT command. When there is still a problem accessing the disk, try having the customer read from another disk to ensure that there is not a media problem. If the drive can successfully read a second CD, there may be a problem with the original disk through an incompatible CD-ROM format or a corrupted disk.

When you cannot successfully access a second disk, verify that you can hear the motor on the drive. This is usually a high-pitched whirring sound that is easily heard. If you cannot detect the noise, there may be a problem with the drive itself or its power connections. However, if you do hear the drive, try checking the cabling to ensure that there is not a loose connection. Also, do an I/O address check to ensure that there isn't an address conflict going on with another device.

If none of these measures solve the problem, verify that the proper device driver for the CD-ROM and/or the controller card has been installed and that it is configured correctly. Ensure that the driver hasn't become corrupted as a result of a bad spot on the hard disk. If necessary, try to reinstall the driver and see if the problem is resolved before replacing the CD-ROM drive.

If the computer doesn't boot after you have installed a CD-ROM, you may have an address problem, a cable problem, or a connector problem. First, make sure that the address has been configured properly and that there are no address conflicts with another device. Next, check the cable between the controller board and the drive itself, ensuring that it is properly attached with the red stripe facing PIN1. Verify that the power connector is snugly in the socket. Finally, ensure that the proper device drivers have been installed for the drive and the controller board.

When the computer will boot, but the CD-ROM drive isn't being recognized, you may have a communication error between the computer and the drive. If you have diagnostic software with you, it is easier to pinpoint the problem. If not, the first things to check for are the device drivers and their configurations. Ensure that you do not have any conflicts with another device, such as an incorrectly addressed drive. Also, verify that the controller board does not have a problem, whether it is the cabling, addressing, or the board itself.

Another commonly reported error with a CD-ROM drive no longer functioning after an installation of Windows 95 was the result of the drivers not being loaded after Windows 95 has been installed. For a CD-ROM drive to work, you need the device driver to be loaded from the CONFIG.SYS file, and you also need MSCDEX.EXE to be loaded from the AUTOEXEC.BAT file. Windows 95 would put a remark (REM) at the beginning of the line that contained the instructions for loading the MSCDEX.EXE (Microsoft Compact Disc Extension) file in the AUTOEXEC.BAT. This would cause the CD-ROM drive to not appear in Windows Explorer, or from DOS. Simply removing the REM at the beginning of the line would remedy this situation. MSCDEX.EXE allows a CD-ROM to be accessed from the command prompt with a drive designator, just as a partition on a hard drive is capable of being accessed.

Parallel Ports/Serial Ports

Parallel and serial ports rarely fail, unlike the peripherals that connect to them. Therefore, they are usually the last item to be considered. To diagnose parallel or serial port problems, you need special diagnostic software in order to verify that the ports are working. If you find that you are having a port problem, you need to replace the Input/Output (I/O) adapter card that contains the port.

A hardware loopback adapter is a way to test the serial and parallel ports on a system without having to connect to an external device. For example, you can use a serial loopback adapter to verify that a transmitted signal is leaving your serial port and returning through the loopback adapter, verifying that your serial port is working correctly.

Sound Card/Audio

The most common problem with sound cards is related to configuration problems with the software driver configuration. This is in the form of IRQ, I/O Address, or direct memory access (DMA) channel conflicts. The standard settings for a SoundBlaster compatible sound card are an I/O address of 220, an IRQ of 5, and a DMA channel of 1. The first thing that you can do to check for these types of conflicts is to run software diagnostics, such as Windows Diagnostics or Norton Utilities, that show where the conflict is occurring. If there is no conflict found, then you should check the speakers used in conjunction with the card. Often, the customer turns the sound down and doesn't realize it, or battery-operated speakers have run out of power. The power adapter for the speakers may have come unplugged from the wall or power strip.

You can also ensure that the device driver is not corrupted, and whether it has to be reinstalled from the original disk. If you are working with an older card, you may want to check the manufacturer's Web site to see if the driver has been updated. However, do not rule out the possibility that the card is defective, even if it is a new card.

Sound cards require an environment setting in the AUTOEXEC.BAT file to work correctly. This variable is set with the SET command. The sound card configuration line will be preceded with the following:

```
SET BLASTER=
```

If your sound card does not work, you should verify that this line is present in your AUTOEXEC.BAT file.

Remember that you need to ask yourself when the audio system was last working correctly. If the audio system was working fine before you went to lunch, this is very different from the audio system not working correctly after you have installed Windows NT.

Printers

Printers are one of the most complex systems that you will diagnose. Many technicians have not had experience troubleshooting printers before their first major technical job. This leads to on-the-job training in printer installation, configuration, and troubleshooting. As an onsite support specialist, you will no doubt be expected to troubleshoot printers, as they are such a vital ingredient in every business and office. Some items to consider when you troubleshoot a malfunctioning printer are the following:

- Paper faults
- Toner cartridges or ink ribbon
- Mechanical parts
- Cabling
- Interface cards
- Device drivers
- Application software configuration

A paper fault can be a symptom of the use of poor quality paper, such as recycled paper, or an impeded pathway. While we are all environmentalists at heart and we should recycle everything we can, recycled paper and printers do not mix.

An impeded pathway can also cause paper jams, but usually the jam occurs in the same location every time. It only takes a small bit of paper to cause the problem, and usually you have to take the printer apart to find it. If you open the printer and find a lot of paper dust, you need to clean the whole unit to ensure that the dust isn't the cause of the problem as well, as dust and dirt can carry a small charge and cause the paper to stick to metal parts just enough to cause a jam.

When you encounter a printer that produces blank pages, the usual suspect for dot-matrix printers is the ribbon or the print head. The print head is made up of pins that strike the ribbon onto the paper to form text or graphics. These pins can get dirty and stick, and if the characters are missing spots, you should clean or replace the head.

Printers are basically mechanical devices, whether you are working with a dot matrix or a laser printer. As with any mechanical device, parts become worn out with time and heavy use. It is important that you check for any signs of wear on all internal components and replace any that exhibit symptoms of deterioration, as worn-out parts can also cause an excessive amount of paper jams. In addition, ensure that all mechanical parts are properly lubricated. Care and maintenance of the printer and internal components is sometimes reserved for the printer specialist, usually a contractor who routinely visits the site for regular printer maintenance. This is not to say you won't be expected to maintain printers as a computer technician. You will not, however, be expected to repair printers without adequate training. Opening printers and replacing major components, especially on laser printers, requires trained technicians.

Cabling can be a problem when you are faced with a non-responsive printer. The connectors between the printer and the computer may have been jostled loose enough that the signals are not being transmitted or received properly. This includes the power connectors to the printer and the parallel cable from the printer to the computer or print server.

Interface cards are also responsible for proper communication between the computer and the printer. Check the card to see if it has failed. If a printer has an internal or external network interface, incorrect configuration of the network interface can disable it from communicating on the network. These settings can be changed with the printer's control panel or from a PC with software designed to manage network printers. This area is complex, and often requires knowledge of the TCP/IP and DLC protocols. When using TCP/IP, you must configure the IP address, subnet mask, and default gateway; and improper settings could render the printer unable to communicate on the network. The network adapter card in the printer can also experience hardware failure, which can result in either intermittent or consistent problems.

When troubleshooting printer problems, don't rule out the possibility of a print server problem. A print job stuck in the print queue will halt all printing on that specific printer. A downed print server will affect every printer on that print server. Basically, any problem that can affect the print server's ability to communicate on the network can cause printing problems. Unfortunately, when troubleshooting a printer, you may spend too much time debating whether the printer itself is the problem before you realize you are having a print server problem. A print server that has run out of hard disk space will no longer have the ability to queue print jobs for every printer and could crash the server until more hard disk space is free. This can be catastrophic, affecting the entire department or company that depends on this print server. To determine if it is the printer or the print server, try printing from another printer that uses the same print server, verify the contents of the print queue, or visually inspect the print server for possible problems, such as a print job stuck in the print queue. Many times you will see a print job that is quite large, such as 250MB, that someone is trying to print. The date and timestamp on the print job will tell you if the print job has recently been submitted, or if it has been sitting in the queue for hours, even days.

Software applications also have printer settings. Most of the newer software packages use the operating system information to enable a user to choose between various printers to which they may be connected. However, some of the older packages may require that you specify these settings. Verify all software applications that have a problem interfacing with a printer.

In Windows 95/98 and Windows NT, the user has the ability to change details for their specific print job, such as the orientation and size. This may last for only a single printing, or numerous printings. However, a user cannot alter the default settings that are configured at the print server without permissions. This is to deter users from changing the color, orientation, resolution, and paper size for the entire department or company; this is reserved for administrators or print administrators.

exam
ⓦatch

Diagnosing and troubleshooting printer problems are likely to be on the A+ exam, especially the phases for laser printing. These questions are very challenging because many technicians are unaware of the components involved with the laser printer.

on the
ⓙob

It is imperative that you learn how to diagnose and troubleshoot many types of printers if you plan on becoming a computer technician. Every company requires the ability to print, and users are not tolerant when they cannot print. You will most likely gain experience troubleshooting ink jet, laser printers, print servers, and the software configuration of these printers. If you are like most technicians, you won't have much experience with printers, but you will have the necessary troubleshooting skills to effectively diagnose printer problems. You will be surprised how quickly you can accumulate printer-troubleshooting techniques and begin fixing problems for your company. It just takes knowledge of the various types of printers and some practice in troubleshooting them.

Monitor/Video

Monitors do not last forever. Some items that you should check for when diagnosing monitors include the following:

- Power and power connections
- Brightness and/or contrast controls
- Sync frequencies
- Cables
- Video adapter card
- Device drivers

One of the most common complaints you will encounter is the "dead" monitor, one that has no picture at all. One of the first things to check, and one of the most forgotten, is to see if the monitor is turned on. You hear jokes about it, but it's true: Technicians receive countless calls from frantic customers who can't make a transmission by the deadline because of a dead monitor, and it turns out that they have forgotten to turn the monitor on.

With the newer power-saver monitors, it may take a couple of keystrokes or clicks of a mouse to turn the monitor back on when the power saver has kicked in.

Another possibility is that the customer has the brightness and/or contrast controls turned all the way down. This is another common problem with video displays. Readjusting these controls may revive the display and save quite a bit of time and money on the repair. If the monitor still does not work, try replacing it with one of the same type. If another monitor works, then the original monitor needs repair. Note that you must check with the customer as to whether or not it is under warranty. To get a replacement, most manufacturers require the client to ship the original monitor back. Never try to repair the monitor yourself unless you have experience in monitor repair, as monitors are high-voltage equipment and you could accidentally injure or kill yourself.

Monitors use a *sync frequency* to control the refresh rate, which is the rate at which the display device is repainted. If this setting is incorrect, you get symptoms such as: a dead monitor, lines running through the display, a blank screen, and a reduced or enlarged image. This setting is configured through the device driver. In order to ensure that you are using the correct frequency, consult the vendor's documentation.

If a monitor swap doesn't do the trick, you may have a problem with the cables or the adapter card. First, check that all of the cables are properly seated before attempting to replace them. This includes the power cable, as the power cord probably connects to a power strip. Make sure that the power strip is on and that it hasn't been "tripped" by a momentary power lapse.

If you suspect that there is a video adapter problem, check that the card has been correctly configured. This requires you to consult with the manufacturer's documentation to ensure that all jumpers and/or DIP switches are properly set. You may also want to check that any memory installed on the card hasn't suffered from chip creep, and gently press on the memory chips to ensure that they are seated correctly. When you have determined that the card's configuration is accurate and that any onboard memory is seated, proceed to swap video cards. This should solve the problem of a dead monitor. A computer's POST will emit a beep code if the video adapter has failed. The beep code for adapter malfunction varies from vendor to vendor. If you are experiencing a video problem, and when you cold-boot the computer you receive a beep code, there is no sense looking up the code because it will most likely be an adapter error unless your system has encountered other fatal errors, such as a bad motherboard.

Sometimes you will be called on to diagnose a monitor that has poor image quality. As stated earlier, monitors do not last forever. You can still check for such problems as brightness/contrast change and cable problems, but most likely the problem lies in either a defective adapter card or a configuration error. To ensure that the adapter card is not the problem, follow the procedures discussed in the previous paragraph. However, when there is a configuration error, it is usually found in the device driver. Check the configuration of the device driver. Remember, if you spot any garbage characters in the configuration information, you probably have a corrupted driver and must reinstall it. However, the most common cause of configuration problems after a monitor has been working properly for awhile is operator error.

Modems

Complaints with modems are frequent, and diagnosing them can become difficult. Some of the things that you should check for include the following:

- Power connection
- Cabling
- Phone line
- Communication software
- Device driver

When diagnosing a modem, it is important to first determine if the modem is an internal modem or an external one. External modems are easier to diagnose, as you can see the signals from the display panel. If you have an internal modem, there isn't a display panel for you to look at, making troubleshooting more difficult. You also have to determine if the problem stems from a nonfunctioning modem or a sporadic problem.

With a modem that is not functioning, the first thing to check is the power connection. If it is an external modem, you can power on the modem and see if any of the lights on the control panel are lit. If none of the lights come on, the modem isn't getting power and you must check both the power connector leading into the modem and the connection to the power outlet. Sometimes the power outlet may have a problem and you can move the connector to another outlet. If there has been a momentary lapse or surge in power, the power strip may need to be reset. If the modem still has no lights, then you have to replace the modem. However, if you have an internal modem, you have to open the case and gently push down on the power connection. At this stage, try using the modem to make a connection and see if the problem is resolved.

The next phase in modem diagnosis is to check on the cabling. Sometimes the cable connections between the modem and the computer become loose, especially if the computer is moved around. This includes the phone line leading into the modem as well as the wall socket. A common problem with phone lines is that the locking tab on the cable itself breaks off, resulting in a loose connection. In both cases, you need to replace the problem cable and test the modem again.

Besides the phone-line cable, there may be another problem stemming from the phone line itself. Call-waiting should be disabled, as it is a common cause of modem communication interruptions. With a sporadic problem, it could be that the modem and the office fax are hooked up to the same phone line, which is commonplace in the office environment. If a fax machine is in use when the problem occurs, you may be encountering this type of situation. Another possibility is that the modem could be sharing a phone line with a regular phone, as is typical in home/office environments, which may explain some sporadic problems. If either one is the case, you may want to recommend that the customer lease a separate line for the modem. However, if this isn't the case, you should physically check the phone line itself. To do so, simply unplug the phone line from the modem and plug it into a regular telephone, then pick up the handset. If you do not get a dial tone, the line is dead and you need to turn over the problem to the phone company.

Connection problems are the most common problem you will encounter when diagnosing a modem. Some of these problems are caused by static, or *noise*, on the phone line itself, particularly on the Hayes 14.4 Optima modems. When you connect to another modem, both of the modems have to agree on the method of communication used, called *handshaking*. When noise is present on the line, the analog signals that are transmitted back and forth between the modems may be misinterpreted and result in a failed connection. Static can also cause problems in the transmission of data for the same reason, leading to bad data transmissions, dropped connections, and garbage characters appearing at random intervals. Check the phone line for noise by plugging the phone cable into a regular phone and picking up the handset. Listen for a minute and see if you can hear any noise on the line. If there is, you must get the phone company to look into the problem.

If none of these solutions resolve the problem, you need to check the COM port used. In order to do so, you can use diagnostic software designed specifically to test COM ports. On an internal modem, the COM port is located on the modem card. You can often determine which COM ports (serial ports) your machine is using by running the DOS MSD (Microsoft Diagnostic Utility) program. The MSD program comes with DOS 6.0 and later versions of DOS and with Microsoft Windows 3.1. So, if you have DOS 6.0 or later and/or Windows 3.1, you will have MSD.

If you are in Windows, you must first exit out to the DOS prompt. In Program Manager, select File and Exit.

To run the MSD program, at the DOS prompt type:

msd

When the MSD menu is shown on your screen, press the highlighted letter C for COM port information:

C

You will then be placed in a screen that displays which COM ports are being used. It will not specifically state what is in each but it will narrow your choices down from 4 to 1 or 2.

Use F3 to quit out of MSD.

You can also use the DOS MODE command that comes with DOS to determine which COM port your modem is on. If you have an older system and don't have the MSD program, you can often use the MODE command to see which COM ports are being used.

To test for COM1, issue the following command at the DOS prompt:

```
mode com1
```

If COM1 is being used you should get a report like this:

```
STATUS FOR DEVICE COM1:
-----------------------
RETRY=NONE
```

If you get a report like the above, it means that the COM port is being used. Just follow the MODE command with the COM port that you want to test.

However, if you get a report like this:

```
ILLEGAL DEVICE NAME - COM2
```

the COM port is not being used. If you have an internal modem, you may wish to set your modem to use that unused COM port.

Another way to determine which COM ports are active on an MS-DOS computer is to use a utility that comes with DOS called DEBUG. This technique works with most machines.

At the DOS prompt, type the following:

```
debug
```

Then, when you have the hyphen prompt, type this:

```
d40:00
```

The screen will show rows and columns with numbers. On the first line, there are four sets of paired numbers that appear to the right of 0040:0000. These represent COM1, COM2, COM3, and COM4. You do not need to be concerned with the other seven rows of numbers. A zeroed pair of numbers indicates that the COM port is not being used.

For example, suppose you see:

```
-d40:00
0040:0000 F8 03 F8 02 00 00 00 00 -78 03 00 00 00 00 00 00
```

Look to the right of the numbers 0040:0000. The F8 03 indicates that COM1 is being used. The next set of F8 02 shows that COM2 is being used. Because the next pair of numbers indicates four zeros, that tells us that COM3 is not being used. The following pair (four zeros) also indicates that COM4 is not being used and is available for a serial device such as a modem.

To exit DEBUG and go back to the DOS prompt type:

```
q
```

Since most computers use a Windows-based operating system, you can use the graphical-based utilities to determine which COM ports your modem is using, along with much more information. Device Manager, located in the System applet of the Control Panel on Windows 95 and Windows 98 machines, can be used to diagnose and troubleshoot resource conflicts. This is also a great central repository for system configuration information. Unfortunately, Windows NT does not have Device Manager, so diagnosing and troubleshooting is more difficult under this operating system.

The Modems applet in the Control Panel is important for configuring a modem. By opening the Modems applet and selecting the Diagnostics tab, you determine which COM port your modem is located on, as illustrated in Figure 2-1.

By highlighting the selected modem port and clicking the More Info button, you can determine if the computer is able to properly communicate with the modem. This will bring up a window with port information and the response received when the computer attempted to communicate and send commands to the modem, as illustrated in Figure 2-2.

Most port testing software can be more thorough if you have a loopback adapter, a small inexpensive device that exists for this sole purpose.

Another consideration with modem problems is the communication software itself. Ensure that the baud rate, stop bits, parity bits, and communication protocol used are correct for the session that the customer

FIGURE 2-1

Using the Diagnostics tab
to determine the COM
port on which your modem
is located

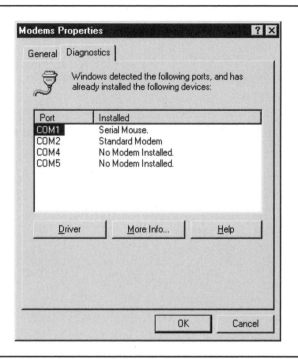

is attempting to establish. The most common symptom for an incorrect
configuration is receiving garbage characters after making a connection.
For example, if the software is configured to use an Even Parity and the
connecting modem expects the parity to be set to None, you will see a
steady stream of garbage coming across the screen right after connection.
Try different configuration settings if the customer is unsure of the
communication parameters, but only after you have noted the current
configuration somewhere.

An important item that should be checked is the device driver installed
in the operating system software. A corrupt, or improperly configured driver
causes many of the symptoms that have been discussed. Also ensure that
you check the IRQ and I/O address of the modem as it is possible that there
is a conflict with another device configured in the system. Sometimes a
reinstall of the driver solves the problem, but be prepared to replace the
modem if it doesn't.

Receiving a response from
the modem

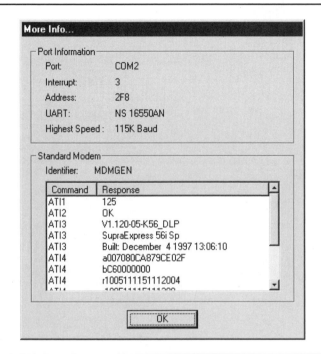

POST Audible/Visual Error Codes

The *Power On Self Test (POST)* happens every time you cold-boot the
computer. A warm boot (pressing the reset button or using CTRL-ALT-DEL
is not a cold boot, and will not perform the POST test). The POST is used
to diagnose system-related problems, such as errors found in memory or
BIOS settings, and is a two-fold alert system: the audible series of beeps,
which alerts the operator to a problem, and the on-screen error
code/message combination, which specifies the exact error encountered.
Typically, anything other than a single beep during this time indicates an
error. The most common errors are a keyboard error and a CMOS low, or
battery failure, error.

The error codes that you see on the screen fall into a particular range that
can be associated with a specific component. Table 2-1 lists these ranges
and their associated devices.

	Error Range	Component
TABLE 2-1 Common POST Error Code Ranges and Related Components	100–199	System board problem
	200–299	Memory error
	300–399	Keyboard problem
	400–499	Video problems, monochrome
	500–599	Video problems, color
	600–699	Floppy disk errors
	1700–1799	Hard disk problems

exam
ⓦatch

The preceding list of error ranges are helpful to know not only for real-life troubleshooting experiences, but for the A+ exam too. Expect one or two questions during your exam on the subsystem involved when you receive a POST error code on system startup.

BIOS

The most common problem with the BIOS is when the Complementary Metallic-Oxide Semiconductor (CMOS) battery begins to run low on power. Usually, a message is displayed at boot time that states "CMOS battery low." If this is the case, you need to replace the battery and reconfigure the BIOS. However, there are times when the BIOS goes bad and must be replaced. Usually, this is indicated by an obvious message during the POST that occurs when you boot the computer.

Power Supply

Because the power supply is the computer's source of power, problems with the power supply usually exhibit themselves as a computer that does not boot or an overheated system that constantly reboots itself. Power supplies include a fan in the unit to cool it down, thus preventing overheating. If the fan is not moving on the power supply while the computer is running, it is a good bet that it is time to clean it with compressed air or replace it entirely. However, if the system does not boot at all, then the power supply is shot and must be replaced.

Device Drivers

Device drivers are the computer's translators with the various devices installed on them. If they are to perform their job, they must be configured correctly. Always check the configuration against the manufacturer's documentation, as customers have a tendency to attempt to improve upon a device's performance and forget to mention their modifications.

Because device drivers are stored on a hard disk, you want to ensure that the driver has not become corrupted. This occurs when the hard disk has begun to fail or is experiencing problems, and sometimes when a computer has had a power surge. If you see garbage characters appearing in the device driver description or in its configuration, then it is definitely a corruption problem. Try reinstalling the driver according to the vendor's instructions.

If you are installing a new device, make sure you are installing the correct drivers for the device. Sometimes it can be difficult to determine which drivers to install. For example, a printer driver comes with PCL and Postscript drivers. Most technicians do not know the difference, and guess during the installation process.

Slot Covers

Most people do not think that a missing slot cover can cause a problem, but your computer knows better. Computers are designed to allow for proper airflow going into and out of the case. Should the airflow become impeded or its route modified, you run the risk of overheating a component in the computer case. If you are experiencing sporadic problems or symptoms of overheating on one or more of the computer's components, be sure that you have all of the slots in the back of the computer covered. Without slot covers you could be causing unintentional damage to the computer components. Slot covers also inhibit dust from entering the computer.

Troubleshooting Tools

Several types of troubleshooting tools are available, ranging from hardware to software solutions. For software, there are several excellent diagnostic tools such as Microsoft Windows Diagnostics and PC Medic, Check-It Pro, and Norton Utilities, just to name a few. These software programs can do everything from verifying the status of the hard drive to ensuring that there are no conflicts with interrupts, I/O addresses, or DMA channels.

Hardware tools are used to verify the status of hardware, and can range from a network analyzer, which displays data about the packets of information traveling over your network, to a multimeter that checks for a variety of things. The multimeter is a favorite topic on the A+ exam, and it is prudent to understand its function. Remember from the discussion in Chapter 1 that the multimeter is actually a multi-measuring tool that measures current, resistance, and voltage. If you suspect that a device is not getting current, you can turn the multimeter to the Amperes, or amps, and measure the current that flows through the device. However, if you need to check a component, such as a battery, any voltage you set the multimeter to will measure volts. The most common use of a multimeter is the resistance measurement, which is measured in ohms. This feature is used to locate the breaking point in a wire by determining if there is resistance on the wire, which is indicated by an infinite reading.

CERTIFICATION OBJECTIVE 2.02

Basic Troubleshooting

When troubleshooting computer-related problems, you are putting on your detective's hat and searching for clues that identify the problem. In your search, you need to gather all the information that you can from the customer, scrutinize the environment, use your observational skills on the equipment and software, and attempt to re-create the problem itself. By combining these steps, you should be able to isolate the problem and complete the repair.

Information Gathering

The first step in diagnosing the problem is to gather as much information on the problem as you can. These are your "clues" that help point you in the right direction. As with any good mystery, you need to question the customer about the problem. Items that you want to include in your information gathering constitute the computer's environment as well as the symptoms exhibited before, during, and after the problem. We discuss both of these in detail in the following subsections, and round it off with some of the more common problem situations in which you might find yourself.

Customer Environment

Observation is an important skill to have. Your audio, visual, touch, and olfactory senses all play a part in observation. When you walk into the customer's office, take note of the environment around you for possible environmental causes to the problem. Is there excessive heat in the office? Computers absolutely hate heat, and an overly warm office could be the cause of some sporadic problems. Is the computer near high-voltage equipment? Computers are susceptible to interference caused by high-voltage equipment.

FROM THE FIELD

How To Prepare a Good Repair Arsenal; Pack Your Bags

PC technicians should always try to pack into a case as many repair tools as they can carry comfortably. They should always have most of the equipment to deal with any situation. What exactly goes in this case depends on the types of repairs that you plan to do and the operating system and hardware that you expect to encounter.

I prefer to have a sturdy briefcase, which is about 1 ½' by 2' by 6". Do not pick a flimsy material for this case, because it will most likely be used a lot. Do not buy tools haphazardly. Stick with the kits that you can find in a computer store. Try and get the most tools that you can afford. These kits range from simple to quite elaborate. You'll do well in the $30 to $50 range.

You also need your array of disks. Get startup disks for all the operating systems that you are using. Also, get disks with drivers for all the hardware that you think you'll encounter. Get disk holders for these disks. If you are working on systems with CD-ROMs, get a CD-ROM holder and pack it with ten of the best CDs for repairs. Pack your bag with compressed air, anti-static wrist guards, and books. Why books? Because there are some indispensable books out there that will save you a lot of time when you are in the field. Try to get a small book that lists all the manufacturers' settings for computers, hard drives, error codes, company phone numbers, and so forth. These can be found for under $10. Most operating systems have good books that can be used as reference. Find a good one and keep it in your case. Also, include miscellaneous items that you will always need. Converters, networks cables, computer cables, bolts, adapters, extenders, phone lines, and the like will all prove handy and will save you a trip to go back and get what you need.

Also in this case keep plenty of pens and a notepad. I've seen some techs even carry a sandwich in their repair cases. This is nice if you happen to have a really big repair around lunchtime. Always keep your eyes on what other people carry around in their cases. Just make sure you can carry all that you put in it, or you may end up having to move equipment as well as carrying your case.

—*Ted Hamilton MCSE, MCP, A+ Certified*

If the physical environment is not a problem, you need to verify the computer environment. One of the first things you can check is if there were any changes made to the system of which you might not have been informed. This enables you to verify that any modifications that may have been made aren't the source of the problem. This could be in the form of hardware or software upgrades, including any changes that might have been made to a network to which the customer connects.

If the customer is on a network, find out if software applications are loading from the network. Sometimes, a software upgrade may have put the newer application in a different directory and the new drive mappings haven't been properly implemented. If their operating system loads directly from the network, it is also possible that a device driver has been moved or deleted. Ask the customer if it is a constantly recurring problem or if it is a sporadic problem. Sporadic problems are harder to isolate as they are difficult to re-create.

Verify device drivers and their configurations. Does the customer load their operating system, such as Windows 95, from the network? If so, the device driver may not be in the root directory of the operating system or possibly a different version has overwritten the original one. The customer may have inadvertently made changes to the driver configuration. These are all things that you should check on.

Symptoms/Error Codes

When examining the symptoms, it helps to get any information on error messages or codes received by the customer when the error occurred. Oftentimes, the customer may not have noted the exact message and is unable to supply you with this information. If this has happened, you have to try to re-create the error if the symptoms do not lead you directly to the problem itself.

Most error codes occur during the POST diagnostic routing that is performed during boot time. These codes are listed later in the chapter, but a few of the more common ones are listed in Table 2-2.

Problem Situations

When working in the computer industry, it is surprising how the same problems occur over and over again. Patience with users, who usually know

TABLE 2-2	Error Code	Error Message	Description
Common Error Codes, Messages, and Their Descriptions	161	CMOS battery failure	CMOS battery needs to be replaced.
	164	Memory size error	Occurs after a memory upgrade. Run the SETUP program and the error should disappear.
	201	Memory test failed	One or more of the RAM chips failed the test. May need to try replacing them one at a time to find the defective chip.
	301	Keyboard did not respond	Indication that the keyboard probably needs cleaning.
	303	Keyboard or system unit error	Indicates a bad keyboard that needs to be replaced.
	423	Parallel port test failed	Reported with monochrome adapters. Will need to replace the adapter.

little or nothing about how a computer operates, is not just a virtue but a necessity. Some of the more common problems and their resolutions are discussed in the following subsections.

Isolation of Problems and Procedures

When you are faced with a problem, you have to use the information that you have gathered and come up with a plausible cause of the problem. Start with the easiest item to test and work your way upward. This type of method is known as the "bottom-up" method. For example, if you have a floppy drive error, start with the media used and work your way up to the drive.

If you have encountered a problem similar to the reported problem, then use that knowledge to isolate the cause. Once you have encountered a similar problem, you can apply that knowledge to the situation at hand, resulting in a faster diagnosis and repair. Some technicians even keep a notebook with them to log problems and their resolutions to reference when a situation is unusual or infrequent. Keeping a log that references specific sites can also be useful, as you may be called on to troubleshoot the same problem you resolved before.

QUESTIONS AND ANSWERS

My computer is getting a keyboard error.	The keyboard needs cleaning, the connection has worked its way loose, or the keyboard must be replaced.
The computer lost its BIOS settings.	This is commonly caused by a low CMOS battery. Replace the battery and reconfigure the CMOS.
My monitor is dead.	Several issues revolve around this one. If it is a power-saver monitor, try hitting a few keys and see if it comes on. Check that the monitor is actually powered on and that the cable connection is secure.
The mouse moves sporadically.	This is a symptom of either a dirty mouse or an incorrectly configured mouse. If it is a configuration problem, you probably have to raise the mouse-sensitivity property higher than it currently is.
My printer won't print.	Run the printer's diagnostic routine, or self-test, and see if there is any problem. If it passes, the printer is not at fault and you need to check that the cable is correctly attached. Verify the device driver configuration, and if necessary, the software application's configuration. If the printer has a network adapter card, the printer may have lost its configuration and you have to use the configuration utility and ensure that the settings are still intact.
The output on the page from my printer is fuzzy.	If you are working with a dot-matrix printer, check the print head for stuck pins. If you are using a laser printer, then it probably needs a good cleaning.

Hardware/Software Problems

Determining if you are faced with a hardware or software problem can be easy, such as with a completely dead component, or complex, as with configuration problems. Most of the time, the customer is absolutely sure that the problem resides in the hardware itself. Use any error codes from the POST diagnostic routine to isolate hardware problems, as well as any diagnostic software that can be applied to the device and its adapter cards.

With software problems, you need to check for device driver problems, such as configuration errors or corrupted software. Also, verify any application settings that relate to the device itself. If you suspect that an application is at fault, you may have to reinstall the software to resolve the situation.

CERTIFICATION SUMMARY

In this chapter, we have discussed the basic procedures used to troubleshoot hardware and software problems. This background forms the basis for diagnosing hardware and/or software errors, even when you encounter an uncommon error. We have also discussed some common items to look for when working on specific hardware devices. Armed with this knowledge, you are pointed in the right direction for isolating the offending component and speeding the repair time.

TWO-MINUTE DRILL

- ❑ CMOS (Complementary Metal-Oxide Semiconductor) is an integrated circuit composed of a metal oxide that is located directly on the system board.

- ❑ Chip creep is a phenomenon whereby a computer chip becomes loose within its socket.

- ❑ Input devices are the easiest types of components to check, as there are fewer things that can go wrong with them.

- ❑ Keyboard errors usually generate a 3** error code when POST runs at boot time.

❑ With sporadically functioning keys or sticking keys, you need to give the keyboard a good cleaning.

❑ A dirty mouse is the most common mouse-related problem reported.

❑ If another device is using the same IRQ or I/O address as the mouse, it probably won't work at all.

❑ If a trackball on a laptop is unresponsive, you have to replace it, which on many laptop machines also requires that you replace the entire keyboard unit.

❑ A dirty scanner surface usually results in smudged or poor-quality images.

❑ Most problems with scanners that are not resolved by cleaning the unit are device-driver related.

❑ Sometimes the most obvious solution will solve your problem. With most components, the first thing to do is check that the power is turned on or that the power supply is snugly in place.

❑ Floppy disks are susceptible to physical and magnetic corruption, giving the customer the appearance of a bad drive with "Error reading disk" or "Error writing to disk" messages.

❑ File corruption or bad sectors can be caused by several things: corrupted or invalid device driver, faulty controller cable, an incorrectly configured controller, or even a computer shutdown while the file is in use.

❑ Problems that are encountered with tape drive systems include media problems, dirty read/write heads, cable and power connections, controller card, and device drivers.

❑ For CD-ROM problems, one good troubleshooting tool that comes in handy is any diagnostic program that may have come with the CD-ROM drive or the controller board.

❑ One of the most common problems reported to the technician with regard to CD-ROMs is that the computer cannot read a CD-ROM disk.

❏ If the computer doesn't boot after you have installed a CD-ROM drive, you have an address problem, a cable problem, or a connector problem.

❏ To diagnose parallel or serial port problems, you need special diagnostic software in order to verify that they are working.

❏ The most common problem with sound cards is related to configuration problems with the software driver configuration, which are in the form of IRQ, I/O address, or DMA channel conflicts.

❏ A paper fault can be a symptom of the use of poor quality paper, such as recycled paper, or an impeded pathway.

❏ Printers are one of the most complex systems that you will diagnose.

❏ When you get a complaint of a "dead" monitor, one of the first things to check (and one of the most forgotten) is to see if the monitor is turned on.

❏ Monitors use a sync frequency to control the refresh rate, which is the rate at which the display device is repainted.

❏ External modem problems are easier to diagnose than internal modem problems because you can see the signals from the display panel.

❏ When one modem connects to another modem, both of the modems have to agree on the method of communication used, called handshaking.

❏ A null modem cable is a special cable that has the send and receive lines reversed on the connector.

❏ A Power On Self Test (POST) is a self test performed by the computer that occurs during boot time. It is used to diagnose system-related problems.

❏ Refer back to Table 2-1 and review the error code ranges and components they relate to.

❏ The most common problem with the BIOS is when the CMOS battery begins to run low on power.

❑ Power supplies include a fan in the unit to cool it down, thus preventing overheating.

❑ Device drivers are programs that translate necessary information between the operating system and the specific peripheral device for which they are configured, such as a printer.

❑ When troubleshooting computer-related problems, you need to gather all the information that you can from the customer: scrutinize the environment, use your observational skills on the equipment and software, and attempt to re-create the problem itself.

❑ Refer back to Table 2-2 and review error codes and their meanings.

❑ Patience with users, who usually know little or nothing about how a computer operates, is not just a virtue but a necessity.

❑ When you are faced with a computer problem, start with the easiest item to test and work your way upward.

SELF TEST

The following Self Test questions will help you measure your understanding of the material presented in this chapter. Read all the choices carefully, as there may be more than one correct answer. Choose all correct answers for each question.

1. Which of the following would indicate a memory error on the POST?

   A. 1**

   B. 2**

   C. 3**

   D. 4**

2. You have been called out to diagnose a problem with a user's computer. Whenever they attempt to go online, the mouse no longer functions. What is most likely the cause of this problem?

   A. Conflicting DMA channels

   B. Incorrect DMA channel

   C. Conflicting IRQs

   D. Memory error

3. What is the most common floppy disk drive-related problem reported?

   A. Bad cable

   B. Loose cable

   C. Media problems

   D. Resource conflicts

4. You have been called to help a customer who has an important report on a floppy disk that cannot be read. You try reading the floppy disk and discover that Windows 95 is asking to format the floppy disk. The user cannot lose the data and warns you not to format the floppy because it already contains data. What should you do in this case?

   A. The floppy is bad. Format it and start again.

   B. Throw away the floppy disk.

   C. Try the floppy in another computer.

   D. Run ScanDisk on the floppy.

5. A junior technician was sent out to replace a floppy disk drive on a customer's computer. The technician has called and cannot figure out why the floppy drive does not work correctly. He tells you the floppy drive activity light stays lit the entire time when the computer is booting. What would you tell him is the problem?

   A. This is normal.

   B. Insert a floppy to begin the boot process. The floppy drive is waiting for a disk to be inserted.

   C. The floppy drive cable is not connected.

   D. The floppy drive cable is on backwards.

6. You have been trying to fix a problem with a floppy disk drive on a user's computer. What is the easiest way to determine if the floppy disk controller is the problem?

A. Install the floppy disk controller on another computer.

B. Replace the floppy disk controller in the same computer.

C. Try another floppy disk drive to determine if the problem continues.

D. Run MS-DOS MSD to determine if the controller is having errors.

7. How often should you clean the heads of a tape drive?

A. Every day

B. Every week

C. Every month

D. Depends on how many hours the device is in use

8. Which of the following are required to make a CD-ROM drive accessible in DOS? (Choose all that apply.)

A. A device driver

B. A DMA channel

C. A SET entry in the AUTOEXEC.BAT

D. An MSCDEX.EXE entry in the AUTOEXEC.BAT

9. You think that one of your serial ports is not working correctly because it cannot pass information to a serial port-based device. What is the best way to verify this?

A. Call the manufacturer of the device.

B. Use MSD to determine if there are any resource conflicts.

C. Use a loopback adapter to test.

D. Try opening HyperTerminal and typing ATA to verify connectivity.

10. Which of the following is the standard configuration for a SoundBlaster compatible sound card?

A. I/O address 220, IRQ 7, DMA 1

B. I/O address 320, IRQ 4, DMA 0

C. I/O address 220, IRQ 5, DMA 1

D. I/O address 240, IRQ 3, DMA 1

11. Which of the following will most likely be found in an AUTOEXEC.BAT file when a sound card is present?

A. SET SOUND=

B. SET TYPE=

C. SET BLASTER=

D. SET AUTO=

12. If you have a network printer that uses the TCP/IP protocol, what will you have to configure? (Choose all that apply.)

A. DNS name

B. IP address

C. Default gateway

D. Subnet mask

13. Which of the following can you use to determine the COM port an internal modem is using?

A. MSD

B. The MODE command

C. The DEBUG command

D. The Modems applet in the Control Panel

14. Which of the following methods will cause a POST?

A. A warm reboot

B. A cold reboot

C. Using CTRL-ALT-DEL

D. Holding the shift key down during a warm reboot

15. Which of the following errors would correspond with the 3** error code during a POST test?

A. Memory error

B. Keyboard error

C. Motherboard error

D. Video error

16. Which of the following can cause problems for more than one printer at the same time?

A. Running out of toner

B. Print server running out of hard disk space

C. Misconfigured printer

D. Slow printer

17. Where is the best place to look for more information on a Windows 95 computer if you feel you have a device conflict with your mouse and another device?

A. System Admin

B. WinMSD

C. Device Manager

D. Mouse applet in the Control Panel

18. If you have two hard drives and two hard disk controllers in a system, how could you configure them? (Choose all that apply.)

A. One drive as master on the primary controller, and the other drive as a master on the secondary controller.

B. One drive as the slave on the secondary controller, and the other drive as a slave on the primary controller.

C. One drive as a slave on the primary controller, and the other drive as a master on the primary controller.

D. You cannot have two hard disk controllers in the same system because of IRQ conflicts.

19. Which of the following can reduce the number of paper jams in a printer?

A. Adjusting the brightness/contrast for the computer

B. Cleaning the printer often

C. Replacing the ink cartridge

D. Adjusting the print quality

20. What should you do when you arrive on the scene and notice a monitor that has a distorted flickering image on the screen?

A. Restart the computer.

B. Swap video cards with a known good card.

C. Try the monitor on another computer.

D. Replace the monitor cable with a known good cable.

21. What is most likely the cause when you see garbled characters across the screen during data communication with another computer?

A. An incorrect video driver

B. Incorrect start or stop bits

C. Incorrect error control

D. Resource conflict

22. Which of the following are ways to determine if a power supply has gone bad?

A. The computer will not boot.

B. The POST will give you an error.

C. Windows 95 will give you an error.

D. The fan will stop spinning.

23. What can slot covers protect a computer from? (Choose all that apply.)

A. Dust

B. Fluorescent interference

C. Heat

D. Magnetic interference

24. How do you get a POST memory size error to disappear?

A. Restart the computer.

B. Cold-boot the computer.

C. Enter the SETUP program.

D. Hold down the SHIFT key while restarting the computer.

25. What is most likely the cause if a mouse moves sporadically? (Choose all that apply.)

A. Incorrect driver

B. Incorrectly configured mouse

C. Dirty mouse

D. Memory problem

3

Safety and Preventive Maintenance

I n the previous chapter, we discussed troubleshooting and repair procedures. In this chapter, we discuss the products and procedures used for preventive maintenance of computer systems and associated peripherals. Following this, we discuss safety issues that you should become familiar with to ensure that you do not injure or kill yourself during the repair or upgrade process.

CERTIFICATION OBJECTIVE 3.01

Preventive Maintenance Products and Procedures

Preventive maintenance is something that customers often forget or do not believe is necessary. However, nothing could be further from the truth. For example, suppose you have a customer who frequently reschedules their preventive maintenance time. Because you are unable to perform the maintenance, neither of you would be aware that the fan in the power supply had stopped working. As a result, instead of just having to replace the power supply, the processor and some of the memory failed due to excessive heat. In addition, the unscheduled downtime may result in a loss of productivity and a larger bill from you. This is exactly the case with automobiles; the longer you put off your regular maintenance, the greater the risk you put on the automobile, and the more likely you will end up paying more in the long run for repairs due to the neglect.

By performing regular maintenance on computer equipment, you can extend the life of the components themselves as well as locating potential problems. In the long run, this will save the customer time and money. In the following subsections, we discuss the various products available on the market along with the proper procedures for using them.

Manufacturer's Suggested Guidelines

Before beginning any preventive maintenance procedures, it is critical that you consult the manufacturer's documentation. Vendors include the information on the proper cleaning materials to use when cleaning or maintaining their components. Failure to follow these guidelines could result in component degradation, complete failure, or a voided warranty. Never assume that you already know what you can use with what device; instead, take the time to review the documentation. Remember that customer service involves not only solving problems, but also ensuring that you do not generate them.

Components that require special attention are tape drives, floppy drives, and printers. These mechanical devices are used often and require cleaning in order to perform at their peak performance. A floppy drive that is not cleaned regularly can destroy floppy disks by contaminating the surface of the disk with debris and scratches. A tape drive can not only damage the media; it can also damage the tape drive itself, resulting in a costly replacement. The tape drive, unlike the floppy drive, can inform you when it needs to be cleaned. However, you should not wait for the blinking LED on the tape drive to clean the device; you should be cleaning the device on a regular basis based on the manufacturer's suggested guidelines. Printers can produce smudged and speckled images if the print heads are not cleaned often. Ink jet printers are notorious for this. Also, any ink on rollers can be transferred to the paper during the printing process. Replacing ink cartridges based on the manufacturer's suggested guidelines will ensure that your printer performs better.

Liquid Cleaning Compounds

There are several liquid cleaning compounds that are used when you perform preventive maintenance. However, it is important to keep in mind that you should always refer to the manufacturer's documentation prior to using any cleaning compound on a component. This is because each vendor may use different materials in the component itself. In addition, some vendors require specialized cleaning compounds that can be purchased from them.

Various forms of alcohol are frequently used in cleaning computer components, such as isopropyl alcohol and denatured alcohol. These items are generally used to clean contacts and are applied to special disks used for cleaning floppy drive read/write heads. Mild detergent can be used on the outside of the monitor, the computer case, and on keyboards. A sponge dampened with mild soapy water will clean most dirt from the outside of your case, monitor, keyboard, and other peripherals. Rinse well and allow to dry thoroughly before you turn it back on.

Cleaning Contacts and Connectors

Few people realize, or remember, that contacts and connectors require cleaning. The reason people forget is because connectors are seldom removed from their respective sockets. Nevertheless, these items do get dirty over time and do require cleaning. Most components can be cleaned with a cotton swab that has been coated with isopropyl alcohol. However, many manufacturers recommend that you use a pencil eraser to clean the contacts on expansion cards. As with most computer components, it is important that you consult the vendor's documentation to ensure that the equipment will not be damaged by the cleaning materials that you use.

Cleaning Tools

There are several cleaning tools that you should keep in your maintenance kit. One nice item to have is a rubber knife. When you are called upon to remove hardened residue from metal components, you can use a rubber knife to dislodge particles that the vacuum or dust-free cloth could not remove. Never use a metal knife or other metallic object when cleaning the computer or its components, as you can either damage them or cause injury to yourself through electrostatic discharge (ESD). ESD occurs when two charged objects come into contact with each other, such as your hand against a doorknob. The charge is transferred between the two objects until both objects have an equal charge.

Compressed air comes in handy when you are cleaning components, such as a keyboard, or areas that a vacuum cannot get to (or shouldn't get to!). Compressed air is distributed in an aerosol can and is available at any computer or electronics store. The air is compressed in the can, hence its name, by extreme pressure and dispelled through a nozzle that is similar to the old aerosol cans. You would use compressed air when you need to blow dust, dirt, or other unwanted debris out and away from a component.

Dust-free, lint-free disposable cloths or wipes are inexpensive and should be used whenever you need to wipe the surface of a component. Normal cloths naturally attract lint and dust, while dust-free or lint-free cloths do not. This helps to ensure that you are not contributing harmful materials to sensitive components.

Mouse Cleaning

Is your mouse movement irregular? Does your mouse cursor jump around the screen? If so, then your mouse is most likely dirty. The rubber-coated ball found in most mice is designed for traction, but it has the side effect of picking up dirt from your workplace and depositing it on the rollers inside the mouse. A mouse pad is an excellent way to slow this process (but only if the pad itself is kept clean), but with time, almost all mice get dirty rollers. Follow the procedure in Exercise 3-1 to clean the mouse.

| EXERCISE 3-1 |

Cleaning a Mouse

Before cleaning your mouse, disconnect it from your computer to eliminate the chance of electric shock.

1. On the bottom of the mouse, there is a removable ring around the ball. Generally there are arrows showing how to remove it. Usually it either turns or slides. Remove this ring, then turn the mouse right-side up to remove the ball.

2. Wash the ball with soapy water, rinse well, then let dry.

3. Wash the rollers inside the mouse with a cotton swab dipped in alcohol. For best results, rub the rollers from side to side. When all the rollers (there are usually three) are clean, let them dry thoroughly before reconnecting the mouse.

4. Return the ball and the ring. If the mouse requires screws in order to remove the rubber ball, return them at this time.

Floppy Drive and Tape-Head Cleaning

When you've determined that the read/write heads on a floppy drive need cleaning, you need to obtain a floppy-drive cleaning kit. The kits contain a special cleaning disk that looks like a normal floppy and a small bottle of isopropyl alcohol. These kits are relatively inexpensive and can be found at most computer and electronics stores. Over time, the heads, which read and write information to the disk, become dirty, causing slow disks, errors, and possibly even ruining disks. The cleaning disk has an access hole, similar to a regular disk, on which you place a few drops of the isopropyl alcohol. Insert the cleaning disk into the drive and the drive will spin up. When the read/write heads attempt to read it, the disk will spin over the heads and clean them. By cleaning your drive, you can avoid many problems and prolong the life of your floppy drive.

When you clean a tape drive, you are performing the same function as with a floppy drive. The only difference is that you would use a special tape-cleaning cartridge instead of a cleaning disk with isopropyl alcohol. The cleaning cartridge looks exactly like a normal tape cartridge, although some manufacturers use a different color casing (usually white or beige) around a cleaning cartridge to help differentiate it from a normal cartridge.

Much like floppy drives, the lens on your CD-ROM reader can become dirty. This has much to do with how clean you keep your CDs. There are several products that will clean your CD-ROM lens, and many that will clean CDs. Though these are not really must-have items, if your CDs are dirty or scratched, or you start having problems reading your disks, they might be a good investment.

on the **！**ob

When it comes to cleaning the heads on a tape drive, it is imperative that you clean the heads on a regular basis. The tape backup has the critical job of backing up very important data. You must do everything you can to ensure that the backup process is working correctly. At one company where I worked, we had two tape drives fail for mysterious reasons. The only thing we could attribute this to was the lack of cleaning on a regular basis. The cleaning light would continue to stay lit, even after we cleaned the heads. We were cleaning the tape heads after we received the cleaning light, not on a regular basis. This was a costly lesson, because we had to replace two very expensive tape drives.

Hard Drive Maintenance

Because hard drives are sealed units that can be opened only in a "clean room," there is nothing you can do to clean the read/write heads. However, hard drives have a tendency to become fragmented over a period of time or with excessive use and should be defragmented as part of normal preventive maintenance. To perform a *defragmentation*, you can use a special software program that was designed specifically for this purpose, such as Norton Utilities or Microsoft Disk Defragmenter.

Another problem with hard drives is that the disk surface can become corrupted over time. If the drive attempts to read or write to these corrupted sections, the computer could crash or exhibit strange symptoms that are difficult to pin down. Some software utilities, such as the Microsoft ScanDisk utility, are designed to locate and mark corrupted sections on the disk. The mark tells the hard drive to ignore this section of the hard drive. This process should be performed on a regular basis in conjunction with a disk defragmentation.

Follow the procedure in Exercise 3-2 to check your disk drive for errors.

EXERCISE 3-2

Checking a Hard Disk For Errors
For Windows 95 or Windows 98:

1. Click the Start menu, select Programs | Accessories | System Tools | ScanDisk.

2. Select the drive you wish to check. (generally C:).

3. Ensure that the type of test is Standard, and that the Automatically fix errors box is checked.

4. Press the start button. If the program asks you what to do when an error is found, always choose the default.
   The program will notify you when it is complete.

For DOS (and Windows 3.x):

1. If you are running Windows, exit completely out of windows to the DOS prompt.

2. Type **SCANDISK** followed by the drive letter and press ENTER (for example, **SCANDISK C:**). If the program asks you what to do when an error is found, always choose the default.
   The program will notify you when it is complete.

Follow the procedure in Exercise 3-3 to check your disk drive for errors.

EXERCISE 3-3 ### Defragmenting a Hard Disk

For Windows 95 and Windows 98:

1. Always run ScanDisk first.

2. Click the Start menu, select Programs | Accessories | System Tools | Disk Defragmenter.

3. Select the drive to defragment (generally C:).

4. Click OK.
   The program will notify you when it is complete.

For DOS (and Windows 3.x):

1. Always run ScanDisk first.

2. If you are running Windows, exit completely out of Windows to the DOS prompt.

3. Type **DEFRAG** followed by the drive letter and press ENTER (for example, **DEFRAG C:**). The program will notify you when it is complete.

   Be sure you consult the vendor documentation when using disk utilities, as there is the potential to corrupt long filenames and possibly even corrupt data on the disk.

Now that you have seen the methods for cleaning computers and components, here is a quick reference of possible questions and the appropriate answers:

QUESTIONS AND ANSWERS

How do I clean a mouse?	Use soapy water for the ball and a cotton swab that has been coated with isopropyl alcohol for the rollers.
How do I clean the connectors on an adapter card?	Use a pencil eraser or a cotton swab that has been coated with isopropyl alcohol.
How do I clean my floppy drive?	Purchase a floppy-drive cleaning kit.
How do I clean my CD-ROM drive?	Purchase a CD-ROM-drive cleaning kit, and clean your dirty CDs to avoid possible debris from entering the CD-ROM drive in the future.
How do I clean my tape drive?	Purchase a tape-drive-cleaning cartridge.
How do I clean the inside of my computer?	Use a vacuum or compressed air.
How do I clean the outside of my computer case?	Use a light cleaning compound or soapy water.

Determining Wear and Tear

Computer peripherals are not only electrical components; they are also mechanical components. These components wear out over time and eventually fail. As a service technician, you should inspect peripherals for signs of deterioration and replace any components that are about to expire. By doing so, you will save the customer time and money from downtime when the component finally fails. Signs of wear can include thin spots on belts, bends or tears in cables, and moving parts that are functioning only sporadically.

Media, such as floppy disks are also susceptible to wear and tear. Continual use of the same floppy disks, tapes, or zip disks will increase your chances of physically wearing out the media. Often you will not get a warning and the next time you need to access the data, it could be gone. If you use floppy disks, tapes, or zip disks for nightly backups, be sure to rotate or retire your media on a regular basis to avoid media wear and tear.

Hard disks are also subject to extreme wear and tear, especially on a very disk-intensive server, such as a database or Web server. You most likely will not receive early warning when a hard disk drive is showing signs of fatigue;

therefore, you should make sure you back up data regularly. If you notice your hard disk making unusual sounds, power the computer off immediately, if possible. If you have important data on the disk that cannot be lost, you risk the chance of damaging the disk even more if the heads are crashing against the surface of the disk. If you must send the disk out for data recovery, the chances are greater that you can retrieve more data from the disk if you minimize the amount of activity the disk was making during the head crash.

Vacuuming

Most people do not realize it, but it is important to vacuum the inside of a computer case whenever you open it. Dust and dirt particles get sucked into the case through the air ducts and deposit themselves anywhere they can. These particles can conduct an electrical charge, resulting in possible damage to the delicate electronic components inside. Any air holes in the case should be vacuumed out to remove dust. This will allow for proper air circulation and will extend your computer's life. Most offices do not have a vacuum that you will be able to use, as there are usually cleaning crews who carry their own equipment with them. However, small, portable vacuums are available for as little as $20 and are well worth the investment. Just be careful that you don't damage the components inside the computer by coming into direct contact with the vacuum nozzle.

Whenever you have to open a printer for repair, it is important that you vacuum out the interior. Bits of paper and dust have a tendency to accumulate on the inside of a printer at a faster rate than the interior of a computer. This happens because of the nature of the printer—that is, producing output on paper medium. Small bits of paper can tear off and become lodged inside the printer from clearing a paper jam. The dust produced during the printing process itself also contributes to the mess. As stated earlier, dirt and dust can carry an electrical charge. This small charge can be enough to damage the electrical components inside a computer, as well as causing excess wear and tear on mechanical components that will have to work a bit harder against the dirt.

CERTIFICATION OBJECTIVE 3.02

Environmental Hazard Protection

Computers must have a reliable source of power in order to function. However, there are many problems with the power supply that have the potential to damage computer systems and their individual components. The Uninterruptible Power Supply (UPS) is designed to protect your computer and its components from possible injury from the problems that are inherent with today's existing power supply structure.

Power Issues

With society's increasing demand for power comes a price. The power utility companies have been hard-pressed to keep up with the present demand, leading to problems in dealing with future increases. As a result, brownouts, which are momentary lapses in power supply, have become more common than they used to. Brownouts can cause problems with computer components that are not designed to withstand these events. Blackouts are long-term power outages.

When there is a power spike, there is a sudden, huge increase in power that lasts for a split second. Power spikes can literally fry computer components. A power surge is similar to a spike, except that a power surge may not have the intensity of a spike.

As stated previously, noise creeps into a power line and is transmitted to the computer. This noise is almost impossible to keep out of the power line due to the vast distances involved and the technology used to transmit power. Noise is one of the most prevalent problems with the power supply today.

Uninterruptible Power Supply (UPS)

Sudden changes in the main power supply can create havoc with a computer system leaving users and your customers without their essential computer systems. Without an Uninterruptible Power Supply (UPS), your business is at risk from corrupt or inaccurate data, and valuable work time is lost while the system is down. Even with battery backup, where critical data is protected by a controlled power down, it can still take time to re-establish the service to users. A typical UPS provides power during a main failure from between 5 minutes to 3–4 hours. Every key business support system should have a UPS because the main power supply is not 100 percent reliable and a power surge or power failure could cause software problems, a system crash, and loss of data at any time. A UPS provides power to the system when the main power fails, as well as smoothing and conditioning the supply during normal operation. This is accomplished by several components in the UPS, such as suppressors, noise filters, and surge protectors. Each of these items is discussed in the following subsections.

Suppressors

At times, your power outlet will experience momentary surges of current, called *spikes*. Spikes can harm computers and their components much in the same way as ESD damage. However, the damage that results is usually on a much greater, even catastrophic, level. A suppressor is designed to absorb or block the excess power and thus save computer components from damage.

Noise Filters

When someone refers to *dirty current*, they are talking about the noise present on the power line itself. This noise is caused by *electromagnetic interference (EMI)* that can stray, or leak, from the current into nearby components. When EMI leaks from power current, it is called a magnetic field and can easily damage computer components. A UPS contains a special filter, called a *noise filter*, that reduces the amount of noise present in electrical current and eliminates magnetic fields caused by noise, thus providing some protection to the components that utilize the current or are nearby.

Storage of Components

A UPS is essentially a battery that is designed to take over when there is a power loss, in addition to ensuring that only the proper type and form of current are passed on to the computer. When you need to store a UPS, you must ensure that it has not been discharged. A discharged UPS that is stored for a long period of time may lose some of its capacity to store power or may become unable to accept a charge at all. To ensure that your UPS is stored in the proper manner, review the manufacturer's documentation for recommended storage procedures.

You need to protect other computer components from damage resulting from electrostatic discharge (ESD). ESD occurs when two charged objects come into contact with each other and energy is transferred between them. This transference of energy occurs to equalize the charge between these two objects. A good example of ESD is when you grab a doorknob, or other metal object, and get a little shock. Computer components are very sensitive to ESD and can even be rendered useless. Whenever you store computer components, you must place them in an anti-static bag to ensure their safety from ESD. Anti-static bags are designed so that static build-up is contained on the outside of the bag rather than on the inside, thus protecting the delicate components.

UPS Features

Most modern UPS systems are capable of performing the following functions:

- Absorb relatively small power surges
- Smooth out noisy power sources
- Continue to provide power to equipment during line sags
- Provide power for some time after a blackout has occurred

In addition, some UPS or UPS/software combinations provide the following functions:

- Automatic shutdown of equipment during long powers outages

- Monitoring and logging of the status of the power supply
- Display the Voltage/Current draw of the equipment
- Restart equipment after a long power outage
- Display the voltage currently on the line
- Provide alarms on certain error conditions
- Provide short-circuit protection

on the job

You need to use extreme caution when dealing with a live UPS system that is currently providing protection to servers or workstations. At one company where I worked, we had a UPS with a warning LED that remained lit. We didn't know much about the UPS, because most technicians just turn the UPS on and forget about it. We pressed the wrong button and it dropped the power to one of the servers. The server was up in a few minutes, but all the connections were broken and data may have been lost. Either work on UPS systems off hours, or schedule a time for downing the server to avoid costly accidents.

CERTIFICATION OBJECTIVE 3.03

Lasers and High-Voltage Equipment

Whenever you work around lasers or high-voltage equipment, you must be extremely careful not to injure yourself. These forms of equipment can cause burns, eye-related problems including blindness, and even death. There are procedures that should be followed whenever working with high-voltage equipment and lasers. These procedures are discussed in the following subsections.

Lasers

Lasers employ a high-intensity light beam that can cause severe damage to your eyes, including blindness. *Never look directly into a laser beam.* Some lasers can cause severe burns when they come into contact with skin, or even death, depending on the intensity of the beam and the location on you. However, the lasers employed in CD-ROM drives are Level 3 laser beams and are of a significantly lower intensity than those employed in construction or scientific applications. As a result, you will not get a severe burn from them but should nevertheless be cautious when working with them.

The laser that is employed in laser printers is also a Level 3 type of beam. However, laser printers do generate an excessive amount of heat, and components that reside inside these printers *can* cause severe burns. It is for this reason that you should be extremely cautious when working inside a laser printer.

High-Voltage Equipment

You should exercise extreme caution when working around any high-voltage equipment, including any equipment near the computer itself. You can spot these items from one of two types of labels on the equipment itself. The first type of label is a Warning label that usually informs you of the potential of equipment damage as well as personal injury. The second type of label is a Caution that tells you of possible personal injuries that can occur. Most labels refer to a procedure or set of guidelines to be performed whenever you work on the equipment, although some refer you to the equipment's documentation for more information. It is always important to follow the manufacturer's guidelines when working on or around high-voltage equipment. Failure to follow these instructions to the letter can result in severe burns or electrocution.

There are a few considerations that you should keep in mind whenever you are working on or around high-voltage equipment. First, never wear an ESD strap around this form of equipment, as the electrical charge could kill you. Second, be especially aware of the electrical pathways on your person. This means that you should never use both hands on the equipment itself. If you do, you are forming a "live" circuit between you and the equipment, resulting in an electrical pathway that leads from one hand and passes through your body to the other hand. The first sensation is one of extreme pain as your skin is cooked where you have come into contact with it. The second is the acrid odor of burning flesh. When electric current passes through your heart, the end result is death as your heart cooks and your blood boils from being heated by the electricity. It cannot be stressed enough how important it is for you to be extremely cautious around any high-voltage equipment and to be aware of the environment around you.

FROM THE FIELD

Common Sense May Not Be So Common

In the years that I have been doing PC repairs, I think I've seen it all. Many techs (who of course are not A+ certified) make big mistakes that can ruin hardware and jeopardize data. One would think that a tech would not plug a monitor in after carrying it in a downpour of rain. The result: lots of smoke, and an expensive monitor that needs to be replaced.

Or how about the tech who tries to "hot dock" hardware accessories on a system that does not support this method. (Hot docking is the ability of a system to accept new accessories while it is plugged in.) I'll tell you from first-hand experience that a hard drive cannot be plugged into the system while the power is on. If you try it, the result is a hard drive that is completely erased.

Never force anything. This is how RAM sockets get broken, causing replacement of the motherboard. If the processor does not fit right, do not try to force it in. The result will be spending the next hour with needle-nosed pliers trying to get all the pins straight again,

or worse—a broken pin and a fun time explaining to your supervisor what happened.

If you drop a screw in the machine, never just leave it there. It could end up against two contact points and really mess things up. Take the time to find and remove the screw. Plug a power cord in backwards and you will see smoke. Turn the power switch on the back of the machine from 120 volts to 240 volts and you might as well grab some marshmallows. Start trying to repair the monitor when you don't fully understand the voltage involved, and I'll say a prayer for you.

Be careful in what you do. Fires, lost data, personal injury, and damaged hardware can be prevented. Your best protection is to know exactly what you are doing at all times and be careful. If you are in doubt about anything that you are doing, do not be afraid to ask someone who knows. No one is supposed to be able to fix everything. If you are in over your head, do not proceed.

—Ted Hamilton, MCSE, MCP,
A+ Certified

Power Supply

A power supply is the perfect example of high-voltage equipment. As discussed in Chapter 1, these devices convert the alternating current (AC) that comes from your regular power outlet into the direct current (DC) that your computer uses. Therefore, when troubleshooting, you want to ensure that the computer is turned off and that the power cord has been disconnected from the power supply.

When the power supply performs the power conversion process, some of that energy is lost and converted into another form of energy: heat. The heat generated by a power supply can cause severe burns. Therefore, it is important for you to ensure that the power supply has had sufficient time to cool down before coming into contact with it.

If you ever open a power supply, you risk severe shock or even electrocution from the electrical charge stored in the capacitors located within the power supply itself. This is true even if the power supply has been off for a long time, as the static electricity that builds up over time can get into deadly ranges. As a result, *never remove the case from a power supply*. Remember, while a power supply is a replaceable component, you aren't.

CRT

Monitors are high-voltage components that should be repaired only by experienced personnel. When working on monitors, it is important to remember that extreme caution should be taken at all times, as any built-up charge can be lethal. However, the first thing to remember is *never wear an ESD wrist strap when handling monitors*. After you have removed your wrist strap, ensure that the monitor is powered off and disconnected from the power outlet. This is an important step because you have to discharge the monitor.

To discharge a monitor, you need to have a jumper wire and a screwdriver with a non-conductive handle. First, connect one end of the jumper wire to a ground such as the screw on an electrical outlet. Next, wrap the free end of the wire around the metal shaft of the screwdriver. When you do this, make sure that the wire is as far away from the handle of the screwdriver as possible. This helps to prevent any accidental contact between you and the wire.

Assuming that you have already removed the casing from the monitor, locate the anode lead that is attached to the glass inside the monitor. An anode lead looks like a small suction cup with a wire connected to it. *Do not touch the anode lead or the wire!* Using the tip of the screwdriver against the underside of the anode lead, gently pry the lead away from the monitor until you hear a small "pop" or the lead is free of the glass. The small "pop" sound is any built-up charge that has accumulated on the glass. This charge will pass into the screwdriver and follow the jumper wire into the ground. At this point, the monitor has been safely discharged.

If you should come into contact with either the shaft of the screwdriver or the jumper wire while the monitor is being discharged, part of that charge will enter your body and can cause severe injury.

Know the procedure for properly discharging the monitor. Not only for your own safety, but because most people who take the exam get two or three questions on this procedure.

CERTIFICATION OBJECTIVE 3.04

Disposal Procedures

Once you have replaced a component, the next question is what to do with it. Landfills used to be the answer, but these areas have proven to be only a short-term solution. Environmental concerns have become an issue because harmful chemicals have a tendency to leak into the water table and contaminate our drinking water supply. As a result, most states have enacted stringent rules and regulations regarding the disposal of any item deemed harmful to the environment. Recycling of these hazardous substances has become a more viable, long-term solution. As a service technician, you need to dispose of the various computer components and chemicals that you use in an environmentally-responsible manner.

For more information regarding hazardous waste and proper disposal procedures not discussed in the following subsections, you can visit the

EPA's Hazardous Waste Resource Conservation and Recovery Act Web site at http://www.epa.gov/epaoswer/osw/hazwaste.htm.

Batteries

Batteries contain environmentally harmful substances and should *not* be disposed of through a convenient trashcan. The Battery Act passed by Congress on May 13th, 1996 was designed to phase out the use of mercury in batteries and to provide for the recycling or proper disposal of nickel-cadmium batteries. However, each state has different rules and regulations regarding the proper reclamation and disposal of batteries. To ensure that you follow the appropriate procedures for your location, check with your state's environmental regulatory office before disposing of used batteries.

For more information on The Battery Act, obtain the document from the United States Environmental Protection Agency Web site at http://www.epa.gov/epaoswer/hazwaste/state/policy/pl104.txt.

exam
Ⓦatch

Every A+ Certification Exam will have at least one question on battery disposal.

Toner Kits/Cartridges

Toner cartridges are recyclable items. Normally, the vendor will take your old toner cartridges when you order new ones, and will even give you a small credit for doing so (who says recycling doesn't pay?). However, if you are unable to exchange the cartridge, ask the vendor if they have any information or suggestions on the proper disposal method. If, for some reason, they cannot assist you, contact your state's environmental regulatory office for the appropriate disposal measures.

Computers

Computers and monitors contain hazardous waste. Since 1988 it has been against the law to put these items in landfills. If your equipment is found in a dumpster or landfill you can be fined and made to pay for a SuperFund cleanup, which could cost millions of dollars. Computers and monitors contain lead and mercury. These heavy metals damage the central nervous systems of humans and animals.

It has been estimated that with an install base of over 100 million computers, every month about one million computers are trashed, which equals about fifty million pounds of waste. Old computers need not be thrown away if they are still usable. There are many churches and public schools in dire need of computers, who will accept them as a donation. By doing so, you receive a write-off on your taxes for a charitable contribution. However, if the computer is so antiquated as to be useless or the computer is beyond repair, there are many companies that will buy them for spare parts or demanufacture them for scrap metal.

Chemical Solvents

Chemical solvents are materials that are considered hazardous waste. The reason for this is that the liquid gets absorbed in the ground and eventually makes its way into the water table. *Never dispose of chemical solvents by emptying them into a sink or toilet.* The Environmental Protection Agency and your local state government regulate proper disposal of chemical solvents. As each state's rules and regulations are different concerning the disposal of these materials, you need to check with your state's environmental regulatory office for the proper procedure.

CRTs

If a monitor still functions, it is a good idea to keep one around for testing purposes. However, if you have enough monitors on hand, you can donate them to any church or public school for a tax break. If the monitor is useless, check to see if the manufacturer included disposal instructions with the monitor or contact the manufacturer directly. Some manufacturers will accept the monitor and give you a small credit when you purchase a new one. However, if neither of these options is available, you need to check with your state's environmental regulatory agency for proper disposal procedures, as monitors are no longer acceptable to landfills.

MSDS (Material Safety Data Sheet)

Material Safety Data Sheets (MSDS) are white pages that contain information on any substance that is deemed hazardous, most notably cleaning solvents. MSDS is required by the United States Department of Occupational Safety and Health Administration, and must be posted in obvious locations. The purpose of MSDS is to inform employees about the dangers inherent in hazardous materials and the proper use of these items to prevent potential injuries from occurring. For more information on MSDS, please consult their Web site at http://www.osha.gov.

CERTIFICATION OBJECTIVE 3.05

Electrostatic Discharge (ESD)

A computer is not just a valuable resource; it is a costly one. As we become more dependent on them in our everyday lives, the most expensive feature is the time wasted by a malfunctioning computer, called *downtime*. As an example, suppose you have over 600 people on a network server that goes down for four days. While they wait for the server to be repaired, they are not only unable to perform any work, but you still must pay them. Once the server is operational again, it could take an entire week's worth of overtime for them to catch up with the workload, costing you even more money and many missed deadlines. It is because of these types of expenses that you must ensure that the computer is repaired as soon as possible. Another cost is that of lost business due to customer dissatisfaction.

One of the things that can cause downtime is damage to delicate computer components through a common phenomenon called *electrostatic discharge (ESD)*. Everyone has been shocked at least a dozen times when grabbing a doorknob or other metal object, and you may even see a spark when it happens. When an object can conduct electricity, such as a computer component or the human body, it has a tendency to retain some of that energy. That energy, known as *static electricity* because it doesn't move, builds up in an object over time, and is said to be *charged*.

When two objects come into contact with each other, electrons are transferred between them until they both have an equal charge. This electron transfer is an electrostatic discharge.

What ESD Can Do

While ESD may not hurt you, it can damage a computer component. Most devices operate between the 3- to 5-volt range, and can be damaged by ESD charges as low as 30 volts. When you actually feel the shock caused by ESD, that energy transfer is over 3,000 volts. Even worse, if you can see a spark when ESD occurs, that discharge is in the vicinity of 20,000 volts. Unless precautions are taken, you can actually destroy a device without even realizing it. This type of damage is called *catastrophic damage* because the device is rendered inoperable.

Another type of ESD damage is *degradation*. A component that suffers from degradation may continue to operate for days, or even months, before failing entirely and could damage other components while it is functioning. Depending on the severity of the damage, a device may even pass a diagnostic test. However, the components can cause intermittent problems in the computer that are extremely difficult to pinpoint, causing frustration to both the client and the technician and extending the downtime required to repair the computer.

Hidden ESD

The term *hidden ESD* refers to a couple of things. A static discharge that you do not feel can be considered hidden ESD because you will not even realize that it has occurred. Remember that when you feel ESD, you are receiving a charge around 3,000 volts. Charges that are below 3,000 volts can still damage electronic components.

Another form of hidden ESD is dust and dirt. As discussed in an earlier section, dust and dirt particles are capable of carrying an electrical charge. This charge can destroy computer components over time, as the particles can pick up a charge and transfer it to a component several times. Unless you can keep your computer in a *clean room*, which is a special sealed room that contains almost no dust or dirt, you will have to schedule regular cleanings for your computer system to reduce the chances of catastrophic damage to computer components.

One last item to consider is the humidity level in the room. A humidity level below 50 percent may lead to static electricity. You will notice this especially in the winter months, when humidity levels are naturally low. Check any air-handling equipment in the room for a properly set humidity level. However, ensure that the humidity is not set too high, as high levels condense the water particles in the air and these particles stick to computer components. Remember that water is a natural conductor of electricity as well!

Common ESD Protection Devices and Procedures

There are several forms of ESD protection devices, such as mats, wrist straps, and bags. These items should be used whenever you are working with computer components to prevent ESD damage.

ESD mats are made of an insulate material that is designed to slowly bleed away any excess charge from whatever comes into contact with it. There are two wires with alligator clips, one clip connected on the end of each wire, that are attached to the mat. When you use an ESD mat, you should first lay out the mat on a flat surface, such as a desk or workbench that is near an electrical ground. Next, attach the first wire to an electrical ground, such as the screw on an electrical outlet, using the alligator clip. *Never attach the clip to the electrical socket itself as you can electrocute yourself!* Place the computer, or component, on the mat and connect the second wire to the computer. This safely transfers any static electricity that has stored up in the computer or the device and directs the charge into the ground. However, if you are working on a monitor, do not connect the second wire, as you need to discharge the monitor according to the procedures discussed earlier in the chapter.

ESD wrist straps are also made of an insulate material and are worn on your wrist to safely bleed off any excessive charge stored in your body. The strap commonly has a Velcro fastener on it and a metal button that has a wire attached to it. To properly use an ESD wrist strap, you need to put it on and connect the wire to an electrical ground. The wire connects to the ground using an alligator clip that is attached to the end of the wire. Make sure that the ground is close to the work area and that you are aware of where the wire is at all times. Some ESD straps have a long wire that can be tripped over as you move around the work area.

ESD bags are the anti-static bags in which computer components are shipped. These bags are designed to collect stray electrical charges on the outside of the bag as opposed to the inside. Thus, the component stored inside the bag is kept safe from ESD damage. Always store computer components in ESD bags to ensure that they are kept as free as possible from dust and dirt as well as from ESD damage. As these bags are handy items to keep around, you should have a good supply of them for storing old, but still functional, computer components. You can do this by keeping the bags that new components were shipped in rather than throwing them away. This saves you money, as you need not purchase them at an electronics store, and it helps protect the environment by keeping them out of landfills.

You can also purchase anti-static sprays to use on carpets and fabrics to reduce the build-up of static electricity. It is a good idea to spray surfaces that are anywhere near your work area. Wear shoes that contain a rubber sole so that you do not build up any static electricity between yourself and the carpet as you walk around.

Education is absolutely necessary for a successful ESD protection program. As with all quality functions, ESD prevention depends upon the understanding and commitment of every person working with sensitive components. From the moment components are installed in a computer until the completed product is shipped, everyone must understand the danger of ESD and know the part each individual plays in preventing ESD failures.

Hazardous Situations

Because there are many hands that touch the electronic components, from the people who manufactured the equipment to the packaging plant, ESD is not something that you can entirely eliminate. However, there are things that you can do to control the potential for harm to electronic devices and injury to yourself. The first thing is to ensure that you are not wearing any jewelry while working on a computer system. Watches, rings, necklaces, bracelets, and earrings all contain metal parts that conduct electricity. In addition, these items themselves can cause damage to components, as well as you, if the jewelry gets caught on anything inside the chassis. If you still don't believe it, imagine an earring getting caught on a cable as you lift your head out of the chassis!

Another thing that you can do to minimize the possibility of injury to yourself and computer components are to always follow the ESD procedures discussed earlier in this section. Always place components on an ESD mat and, unless you are working on a monitor or a high-voltage device, always wear your ESD wrist strap. *It cannot be emphasized enough that you must remember to take off the wrist strap when working around monitors or high-voltage devices.* The charge that builds up in monitors, even after they have been powered off for a long period of time, can prove lethal. And never pack computer components in anything other than ESD bags. You can place the bags in boxes or packing peanuts, but only after the bag has been properly sealed with the component inside.

While the newer computer operating systems, especially network servers, enable you to repair them while the computer is still running, it is extremely important that you follow the manufacturer's guidelines to the letter. When live current is running through a computer, you are faced with the possibility of severe burns or even death. All it takes is a moment's contact with the wrong component and you could become history. Always take the extra time to review the vendor's guidelines before performing the repair.

CERTIFICATION SUMMARY

Preventive maintenance is one of the most important aspects in ensuring a healthy computer system. The tools and materials that are used during this process are equally important, because using improper equipment or cleaning products can result in harm to the delicate components. In addition, it is important to remember that the computer can become dangerous if you are not careful when working on it. Hazards can include anything from high-voltage equipment to electrostatic discharge, and preventive measures must be taken to ensure that you and the computer are not damaged. This chapter has discussed all of this in detail in order to arm you with the knowledge to prevent severe injury, or even death.

TWO-MINUTE DRILL

❏ A discharged UPS that is stored for a long period of time may lose some of its capacity to store power or may become unable to accept a charge at all.

❏ As a service technician, you should inspect all computer peripherals for signs of deterioration and replace any components that are about to expire.

❏ The lasers employed in CD-ROM drives are Level 3 laser beams and are of a significantly lower intensity than those employed in construction or scientific applications.

❏ Batteries contain environmentally harmful substances and should *not* be disposed of in a convenient trashcan.

❏ Electrostatic discharge (ESD) occurs when two charged objects come into contact with each other, such as your hand against a doorknob. The charge is transferred between the two objects until both objects have an equal charge.

❏ It cannot be emphasized enough that you must remember to take off the ESD wrist strap when working around monitors or high-voltage devices.

❏ A component that suffers from degradation may continue to operate for days, or even months, before failing entirely and could damage other components while it is functioning.

❏ It is important to keep in mind that you should always refer to the manufacturer's documentation prior to using any cleaning compound on a component.

❏ Never use a metal knife or other metallic object when cleaning the computer or its components, as you can either damage them or cause injury to yourself through ESD.

❑ ESD mats are made of an insulate material that is designed to slowly bleed away any excess charge from whatever comes into contact with it.

❑ Always take the extra time to review the vendor's guidelines before performing any repair.

❑ Noise is one of the most prevalent problems with the power supply.

❑ One of the things that can cause downtime is damage to delicate computer components through the common phenomenon called ESD.

❑ Power spikes can literally fry computer components.

❑ When you are called upon to remove hardened residue from metal components, you can use a rubber knife to dislodge particles that the vacuum or dust-free cloth could not remove.

❑ Signs of wear on peripherals can include thin spots on belts, bends or tears in cables, and moving parts that are functioning only sporadically.

❑ The laser that is employed in laser printers is also a Level 3 type of beam.

❑ Never remove the case from a power supply—you risk severe shock or even electrocution from the electrical charge stored in the capacitors located within the power supply itself.

❑ To discharge a monitor, you need to have a jumper wire and a screwdriver with a non-conductive handle.

❑ Various forms of alcohol are frequently used in cleaning computer components, such as isopropyl alcohol and denatured alcohol.

❑ When a power supply performs the power conversion process, some of the energy is lost and converted into another form of energy: heat.

SELF TEST

The following Self Test questions will help you measure your understanding of the material presented in this chapter. Read all the choices carefully, as there may be more than one correct answer. Choose all correct answers for each question.

1. What should be your first source for determining which cleaning products to use on a device?

    A. The Internet

    B. Phone technical support

    C. Manufacturer's documentation

    D. Lead technician

2. Which of the following needs to be cleaned regularly? (Choose all that apply.)

    A. Hard drives

    B. Floppy drives

    C. Printers

    D. Tape drives

3. When should you clean the heads in a tape drive?

    A. Every ten hours of use

    B. Based on the manufacturer's suggested guidelines

    C. When the software program informs you

    D. When the cleaning LED on the face of the unit illuminates

4. Which of the following is not a recommended liquid cleaning compound for use with computers and components?

    A. Isopropyl alcohol

    B. Ammonia

    C. Denatured alcohol

    D. Mild detergent

5. Which of the following are recommended methods for cleaning contacts and connectors? (Choose all that apply.)

    A. A pencil eraser

    B. A cotton swab that has been coated with isopropyl alcohol

    C. Tweezers

    D. A plastic knife

6. When should you use a metal knife when working on a computer?

    A. When working on a monitor

    B. When working on a power supply

    C. When removing chips or adapters

    D. You should never use a metal knife when working on a computer.

7. What two cleaning products should be used when cleaning a mouse?

    A. Ammonia and water

    B. Isopropyl alcohol and water

    C. Soapy water and isopropyl alcohol

    D. Soapy water and Windex

8. How can you tell the difference between a tape-drive-cleaning cartridge and a regular cartridge?

   A. Cleaning cartridges are white.

   B. Cleaning cartridges are beige.

   C. Cleaning cartridges are dark brown.

   D. You cannot tell the difference between some cleaning cartridges and regular cartridges.

9. What is the difference between brownouts and blackouts?

   A. Brownouts cause more damage.

   B. Brownouts are for DC current, and blackouts are for AC current.

   C. Brownouts are decreases in power, and blackouts are huge surges of power.

   D. Blackouts are long-term outages.

10. How can you completely eliminate noise from a power line?

    A. Use a surge suppressor.

    B. Use a line conditioner.

    C. Use a noise filter.

    D. You cannot completely eliminate noise from a power line.

11. You are moving a set of servers from one room to another. The new server has a UPS unit that can protect every server in the room from line disturbances and power outages. You need to store the individual UPS units that were in the old server room. What should you do with each UPS before you store it?

    A. Discharge the unit.

    B. Do not discharge the unit.

    C. Remove the battery from the unit.

    D. Remove the charging portion of the unit.

12. What is the best way to protect individual computer components from ESD?

    A. Vacuum them regularly.

    B. Use compressed air on them.

    C. Keep them on a low shelf.

    D. Store them in an anti-static bag.

13. What level are the lasers employed in CD-ROM drives?

    A. Level 1

    B. Level 2

    C. Level 3

    D. Level 4

14. What are the two types of high-voltage equipment labels? (Choose all that apply.)

    A. Warning

    B. Attention

    C. Danger

    D. Caution

15. When discharging a monitor, what two parts do you need to make contact with?

    A. The power supply and the electron gun

    B. The anode lead and a jumper wire

    C. The jumper wire and the electron gun

    D. The anode lead and the power supply

16. What does MSDS stand for?

    A. Maintaining Standards Developing Safety

    B. Material Standard Disposal Sheet

    C. Material Safety Data Sheets

    D. Maintaining Standard Disposal Safety

17. Which of the following are results of ESD? (Choose all that apply.)

    A. Downtime

    B. Customer dissatisfaction

    C. Line noise

    D. Damaged components

18. You have just walked into your shop across the carpet and as you sit in your chair, you feel a shock, but don't see it as you reach for your desk drawer. What is the amount of voltage that caused this shocking sensation you just felt?

    A. Around 30 volts

    B. Around 500 volts

    C. Around 3000 volts

    D. Around 20,000 volts

19. What is another possible result of ESD on a component?

    A. Degradation

    B. Contamination

    C. Transformation

    D. Polarization

20. A humidity level below what percent tends to lead to static electricity?

    A. Below 50 percent

    B. Below 20 percent

    C. Below 30 percent

    D. Below 65 percent

21. Which of the following will not help minimize the amount of ESD in your work area?

    A. Wear steel-toed shoes.

    B. Use an anti-static spray for the carpet.

    C. Wear a wrist strap.

    D. Use anti-static bags.

22. Which of the following is not recommended for maintaining a hard disk drive? (Choose all that apply.)

    A. Running a utility such as ScanDisk on a regular basis

    B. Low-level formatting the drive once a year

    C. Defragmenting the hard disk often

    D. Partitioning the drive often

23. You have been called out to help a small company streamline their computer processes. You are especially interested in their backup routine, which consists of copying their data to a floppy disk and storing this floppy underneath the counter. The information on this disk is critical, and cannot be lost. The information contained on the floppy is only a few kilobytes worth of service records. How can you help them with their backup process?

A. Have them back up their data to a different area of the hard disk to avoid floppy disk wear and tear.

B. Have them copy their data to numerous floppy disks for each day of the week to avoid wear and tear on the same floppy. Store this floppy somewhere other than underneath the counter, preferably where it is free from dust and debris. Use a cleaning disk several times a month to keep the floppy drive heads clean.

C. Purchase a Zip drive and five disks, one for each day of the week. Have them back up the data to the disks and store them somewhere other than underneath the counter, preferably where it is free from dust and debris.

D. Purchase a tape drive, one cleaning cartridge and five cartridges, one for each day of the week. Have them back up the data to the tape and store them somewhere other than underneath the counter, preferably where it is free from dust and debris.

24. Why is it important to vacuum a computer on a regular basis? (Choose all that apply.)

A. Because dust and debris can cause components to fail

B. Because it looks more professional

C. Because dust and debris can create excessive heat inside the computer

D. Because you should never use compressed air on the inside of a computer

25. You have a brand new network server that supports hot-swappable components. Which devices can you remove without damaging the computer?

A. Hard drives

B. Hard drives and floppy drives

C. Hard drives and 16-bit ISA cards

D. You do not know which devices are hot-swappable without referring to the vendor's documentation.

4

Motherboard/ Processors/ Memory

I n the computer industry technology increases at an exponential rate. Yesterday's technology has already become outdated as soon as it hits your desk. Although it can seem overwhelming at times, if you understand the basics behind each current component, you will form the foundation necessary to understand new technologies as they are developed. This chapter focuses on the most important components of every computer: processors, memory, motherboards, and the CMOS.

CERTIFICATION OBJECTIVE 4.01

CPU Chips

The *Central Processing Unit (CPU)*, or simply the processor, is the operations center of a computer. It provides the devices attached to the computer with directives that retrieve, display, manipulate, and store information. Therefore, the rate at which the CPU can process electronic signals is a determinant factor in the speed of the computer.

CPU chips are integrated circuits that contain thousands to millions of transistors. These *transistors* are used to process information in the form of electronic signals. The more transistors a CPU has, the faster it can process data. Several evolutions of CPUs have allowed for the chips to hold more transistors than their predecessors, and therefore process information at increasing speeds. As a technician, you will encounter several different types of processors in operation and must familiarize yourself with their various characteristics and features. The following subsections describe each chip in detail.

Popular CPU Chips

As with everything in the computer industry, chip architectures change rapidly. Chip architectures are defined by the number of transistors in the chip and the size of the bus. One of the earliest IBM PCs contained an Intel 8088 chip, which contained only 29,000 transistors and an 8-bit bus. Today's Intel

Pentium II processors contain 7.5 million transistors and support a 64-bit bus. As discussed in the previous paragraph, the number of transistors inside a chip is one of the determining factors in the rate at which a chip can process information. For example, the 8088 chip processed data at approximately 4.77 MHz, while the Pentium II is reported to run at speeds of 233 MHz to 450 MHz. Although the Pentium III chips are currently on the market, the A+ exam will not cover them.

386

The leading processor manufacturer of the time, Intel Corporation, released the 80386 chip in 1985. This chip featured a 32-bit register size, a 32-bit data bus, and a 32-bit address bus and could handle up to 16MB of memory. However, the 386 did not have an internal math coprocessor and users who required heavy calculations had to purchase one separately.

Prior to the 386 chip, Intel would license its technology to its competitors. But the competition found ways to make cheaper, and in some cases faster, processors. Consumers were buying these less expensive chips at an increasing rate, which cut into Intel's market share and reduced its status as the leading manufacturer. Eventually, Intel's competitors came out with their own version of the 386 chip.

The 386 processor was also the first instance where there were two versions of the same basic processor: the SX version and the DX version. The 386SX processor came with a 16-bit data bus, a 24-bit address bus, and a 32-bit register size. The 386DX processor's data bus, address bus, and register size were all 32 bits. Both the SX and DX chips operated at 16 MHz, 20 MHz, 25 MHz, and 33 MHz.

486

The 486 processor is also broken down into four types: 486SX, 486DX, 486DX2, and 486DX4. The 486SX chip did not increase the processor speed, which remained at 33 MHz, nor did it enlarge the bus size from 32-bit. It did introduce an on-board cache to the processor, which was an 8-bit cache, along with an on-chip math coprocessor. Unfortunately, the math coprocessor was disabled at the factory and a secondary chip had to be purchased to obtain the benefits.

When the 486DX was released, it had the same characteristics as the SX version, only the math coprocessor was enabled. A later version of the chip, the 486DX2, was still able to run at 33 MHz externally, but doubled the processor speed, or clock speed, internally and brought it up to 66 MHz. Following that, the 486DX4 chip was released, which increased the clock speed even more and brought it up to 133 MHz.

586 or Pentium Class

Intel decided that it wanted to break away from the standard naming convention when it couldn't trademark the 80 x 86 name. With the 586 chip, Intel named its chip the *Pentium chip* and introduced several new features and improvements. The first improvement was in the register size and the data bus size, which were doubled to 64-bit. It also doubled the on-board cache size from 8-bit to 16-bit and increased speeds to a range of 60 MHz up to 200 MHz.

Along with the improvements came a significant change in processor architecture and capabilities. The chip combined two 486DX chips into one, called the *Dual Independent Bus Architecture*, which allowed each processor inside the chip to execute instructions simultaneously and independently from each other, called *parallel processing*. The end result was a faster chip, but it required a special motherboard that was able to withstand the enormous amount of heat generated by the chip. Heat sinks also had to be employed to help remove the excess heat from the chip or it would burn itself out.

686 or Pentium II Class

Intel's Pentium II chip outpaced the other chips by offering speeds ranging between 233 MHz and 450 MHz. (Top speed is always increasing for processors, which are always being replaced by newer versions). Another improvement was the integration of Intel's MMX technology, which speeds up the processing of video, audio, and graphical data. MMX does this by employing an enhanced instruction set and the *Single Instruction Multiple Data (SIMD)* technique. According to Intel, SIMD works by allowing a single instruction to operate on multiple pieces of data when an application is performing a repetitive loop.

Chip Characteristics

Table 4-1 provides an overview of the different varieties of chips and their respective characteristics.

Table 4-2 provides an overview of the different varieties of processors along with their bus sizes.

TABLE 4-1   Characteristics of Different Types of Chips

Processor	Physical Size	Voltage	Speed (MHz)	Heat Sink	Cooling Fan	On Board Cache	Sockets	Pins
8088		5	4.77 10	No	No	No	DIP	40
80286		5	6 10 12	No	No	No	LLC PGA PLCC	68
80386SX		5	16 20 25 33	No	No	No	PGA	100
80386DX		5	16 20 25 33	No	No	No	PGA	100
80486SX		5	16 20 25 33	No	Yes on 33 MHz	Write-Through	PGA	100
80486DX	345 square	5	25 33 50	No	Yes on 33 MHz	Write-Through	PGA SQFP	168 208
Pentium	1.95 x 1.95	2.9 3.3 5	60-233	Yes	Yes	Write-Back	PGA	296
Pentium Pro	2.46 x 2.66	2.9	233-266	Yes	Yes	Write-Back	PGA	387

TABLE 4-2		Bus Sizes of Different Processors	

Processor	Register	Data Bus	Address Bus
8088	16-bit	8-bit	20-bit
80286	16-bit	16-bit	24-bit
80386SX	32-bit	16-bit	24-bit
80386DX	32-bit	32-bit	32-bit
80486SX	32-bit	32-bit	32-bit
80486DX	32-bit	32-bit	32-bit
Pentium	64-bit	64-bit	32-bit

exam
⍟atch

Know Table 4-2 cold for the exam, as there are several questions that will test your knowledge of the different processors' bus size.

CERTIFICATION OBJECTIVE 4.02

Random Access Memory (RAM)

When the processor needs to perform calculations or store data, it needs a temporary storage area to hold the information. As discussed in Chapter 1, memory is your computer's work area. Memory is composed of integrated circuits that connect to the system board, or to an expansion card, located inside the computer. These circuits can be either on or off, and therefore represent data as a series of 1s and 0s, respectively. This *binary* representation is the language that your computer understands.

RAM is much faster to write to than the other kinds of storage in a computer, such as the hard disk, floppy disk, and CD-ROM. However, the data in RAM stays there only as long as your computer is running. When you turn the computer off, RAM loses its data. When you turn your computer on again, your operating system and other files are once again loaded into RAM, usually from your hard disk.

In order to understand memory, you need to know some of the terms related to memory, beginning with terms describing memory sizes. Each individual 0 or 1 is called a *bit*, which is written as a lowercase "b." To keep track of the millions and billions of bits would prove a laborious task, so bits are grouped into sets of eight, called a *byte*, which is written as an uppercase "B". Since computers work with large numbers of bytes, it would still get a bit tedious listing file sizes of 500,000 bytes or 5,000,000 bytes. Instead, we use a form of shorthand that cuts the numbers down to a more manageable size. There are three common denotations that are used to represent computer numbers: a *kilobyte (KB)* is 1,024 bytes, a *megabyte (MB)* denotes 1,048,576 bytes, and a *gigabyte (GB)* means 1,073,741,824 bytes! So, if you had 16MB of memory in your computer, you actually have 16,777,216 bytes of memory available. If you are wondering why a kilobyte, for example, isn't equal to 1,000 bytes it is because the computer works on powers of 2 rather than 10. Thus, when we calculate 2^{10}, we get 1,024 bytes instead of 1,000 bytes. If we were trying to get a megabyte, we would calculate 2^{20}.

Memory comes in several forms, but generally the processor accesses *Random Access Memory (RAM)*. RAM gets its name from how the memory is physically accessed. Data can be accessed by one of two methods, either sequentially or randomly. When you store data sequentially, you cannot get immediate access to the data that you need. Instead, you must go through all of the information that has been stored before actually getting to the data that you need, which is the way that magnetic tape stores and retrieves data. However, with random access, you can bypass the data that you don't need and go directly to the location where the information is stored. RAM allows your computer to store and retrieve data in *random* locations in memory.

In addition to hard disk, floppy disk, and CD-ROM storage, another important form of storage is *Read-Only Memory (ROM),* a more expensive kind of memory that retains data even when the computer is turned off. Every computer comes with a small amount of ROM that holds just enough programming so that the operating system can be loaded into RAM each time the computer is turned on.

There are several forms of RAM available, each with its own method of random access and differing physical characteristics. We discuss each in the following subsections.

Terminology

As we mentioned in the preceding paragraphs, memory stores data as a series of 0s and 1s. These 0s and 1s are stored electronically, but signals on memory chips can degrade unless power is constantly fed to them. To ensure that those signals are correct, memory chips are constantly updated, by a process called *refresh*. The rate at which the chips are refreshed is called the *refresh rate* and usually occurs around 60 or 70 nanoseconds, or about 60 to 70 billionths of a second. Although fewer nanoseconds is better, user-perceived performance is based on coordinating access times with the computer's clock cycles.

RAM can be divided into two general areas: main system RAM and video RAM (VRAM). Main system RAM stores every kind of data and makes it quickly accessible to the CPU. Video RAM stores data intended for your display, enabling images to load faster.

Main RAM

Main RAM can be divided into *static RAM (SRAM)* and *dynamic RAM (DRAM)*. Every computer on the market today uses both SRAM for high-speed Level 2 cache and DRAM for main system memory. There are many types of DRAM, which are discussed in the following subsection.

Static RAM (SRAM)

Static Random Access Memory (SRAM) does not need to be constantly refreshed; hence it is *static*. However, while it doesn't need a constant update, it does require a periodic update and tends to use excessive amounts of power when it does update. SRAM chips were used in the original IBM PC and XT computers and employed transistors to store information, leading to a large chip size. SRAM is used for a computer's fast cache memory and is also used as part of the RAMDAC on a video card.

Unfortunately, an SRAM chip can only hold approximately 256KB of data per chip and is relatively expensive.

Dynamic Random Access Memory (DRAM)

Dynamic Random Access Memory (DRAM) chips abandoned the idea of using the unwieldy transistors and switched in favor of using the smaller capacitors that could represent 0s and 1s as an electronic charge. This resulted in the ability to store more information on a single chip, but also meant that the chip needed a constant refresh and hence more power. DRAM is the least expensive kind of RAM.

Windows Accelerator Card RAM (WRAM)

Microsoft Windows has become one of the most popular client operating systems (OS) in use today due to its graphical nature and ease of use. However, in some environments, Windows can be slow. To help speed up the OS without purchasing a new processor, and in some cases a new motherboard to go with it, the *Windows Accelerator Card RAM (WRAM)* was introduced. This card utilizes memory that resides on the card itself to perform the Windows-specific functions, and therefore speeds up the OS. WRAM, compared to VRAM, is *dual-ported* and has about 25% more bandwidth than VRAM but costs less. It has features that make it more efficient to read data for use in block fills and text drawing. It can be used for very high resolution (such as 1600 by 1200 pixels) projection using true color.

Video RAM (VRAM)

Video RAM means in general all forms of RAM used to store image data for the video display monitor. All types of video RAM are special arrangements of dynamic RAM (DRAM). Video RAM is really a buffer between the processor and the display monitor. When images are to be sent to the display, they are first read by the processor as data from some form of main storage RAM and then written to video RAM. From video RAM, the data is converted by a *RAM digital-to-analog converter (RAMDAC)* into analog signals that are sent to the display, such as a cathode ray tube (CRT). Usually, video RAM comes in a 1- or 2-megabyte package and is located on the video or graphics card in the computer. Most forms of video RAM are *dual-ported.* While the processor is writing a new image to video RAM, the display is reading from video to refresh its current display content. The dual-port design is the main difference between main storage RAM and video RAM.

Extended Data Output RAM (EDO RAM)

Extended Data Output RAM (EDO RAM) is a DRAM memory chip designed for processor access speeds of approximately 10 to 15 percent above fast-page mode processors and reduces the need for Level 2 cache memory. This requires both a motherboard and processor that is capable of supporting EDO RAM. EDO RAM is the most common type of main system RAM in Pentium computers and later.

Table 4-3 provides an overview of the different varieties of RAM along with their characteristics.

TABLE 4-3   Characteristics of Each RAM Type

RAM Technology	Application and Computer Location	Access Speed	Characteristics
SRAM	Level 1 and Level 2 cache. Also used in the video RAMDAC	Fast	Continually charged RAM. More expensive than DRAM.
DRAM	Main memory and low-cost video memory	Slow	A generic term for any kind of dynamic RAM.
WRAM	Less expensive video memory used to speed up Windows performance on older machines	50% faster than VRAM	Dual-ported, and supports true color at very high resolutions.
VRAM	Higher-cost video memory	Twice the speed of DRAM	Dual-ported, meaning a new image can be stored in RAM while a previous image is being sent to the display.
EDO RAM	Main memory and low-cost video memory	Faster than DRAM	Most common type of DRAM.

RAM Locations and Physical Characteristics

Random Access Memory (RAM) is where your computer temporarily stores the instructions that make up an application, as well as the actual data it manipulates. As mentioned in the previous section, RAM comes in several physical forms.

Memory Bank

A *memory bank* is the actual slot that memory goes into. The original memory chips were installed individually in sockets designed to hold only one chip at a time. These chips were soldered into place on the motherboard, and were susceptible to a condition known as *chip creep*, where the chips would occasionally become unseated from their sockets over time, due to normal thermal expansion and contraction. Newer memory components are installed in special slots designed to hold one card that contains multiple memory chips to relieve the condition of chip creep. With both types of memory, the socket or slot is located on the motherboard and uses the system board's circuitry to communicate directly with the processor. In cases where a device uses a DMA channel, such as with sound cards, the component itself can communicate directly with RAM.

To add memory to your computer, you simply add more RAM modules in a prescribed configuration. These are single in-line memory modules (SIMMs) or dual in-line memory modules (DIMMs). Since DIMMs have a 64-bit pin connection, they can replace two 36-bit (32-bits plus 4 parity bits) SIMMs when synchronous DRAM is used. Laptop and notebook computers contain smaller 32-bit DIMMs known as small outline DIMMs (SO DIMMs).

Parity versus Non-Parity Chips

Parity is an error-checking mechanism that enables the device to recognize single-bit errors. Parity comes in two forms: even parity and odd parity. With odd parity, the number of ones in a byte are added up and checked to see if it is an odd number. If it is, an extra bit set to zero (0) is added to the byte, thus ensuring that the total number of ones results in an odd number. However, if the number of ones adds up to an even number, the extra bit added on is set to one (1), thus ensuring that the total number of ones results in an odd number.

Even parity works in the same manner, except that the total number of ones must add up to an even number. Therefore, if the sum of ones equals an even number, the extra bit is set to zero. However, if the sum of ones equals an odd number, the extra bit is set to one. Should one of the data bits switch, say from a one to a zero, the total number of ones will not result in the correct odd number (for odd parity) or even number (for even parity). The problem with this is that if two of the bits were switched, the data would still pass the parity test.

Parity is not just used with memory, but is utilized in hard drives and communications. While it is not a 100-percent guaranteed method of ensuring that your data is intact, it is still better than having no parity at all. With a non-parity chip, you have no guarantee that the data that is stored on the chip is what was truly sent.

Memory Chips (8-bit, 16-bit, and 32-bit)

Memory chips communicate with the processor or peripherals through the bus. As stated in Chapter 1, the bus is the actual pathway used to transmit electronic signals from one device to another. The number of bits that can be transmitted or received simultaneously is one of the determining factors of bus architecture. Bus configurations come in 8-bit, 16-bit, 32-bit, and 64-bit.

SIMMs (Single In-Line Memory Module)

Before the Single In-Line Memory Module, or SIMM, memory chips were purchased individually and placed on the motherboard in separate sockets. With SIMMs, you get a card that has several DIP chips embedded typically on one side of the card. Each SIMM module is given a pin designation, such as a 30-pin SIMM card, and is called the SIMM type. The "30-pin" refers to the number of fingers, or pins, that are on the connector.

SIMMs come as either 30-pin or 72-pin cards, but each card has a different format. The format is broken down as follows:

```
Capacity of the Chip x Data Bits
```

The capacity is the amount of data the card can hold, usually denoted in megabytes. However, the data bits determine if the SIMM utilizes parity. If the data bits equal 8 or 32, the SIMM does not use a parity bit, but a 9 or 36 indicates that parity is in use (8 + 1 parity bit or 32 + 4 parity bits).

DIMMs (Dual In-Line Memory Module)

Dual In-Line Memory Modules (DIMMs) are similar to SIMMs except that they have memory chips embedded in both sides of the chip. Thus, the memory card can hold twice as many chips and twice as much memory as a SIMM. DIMMs come in 32-bit or 64-bit configurations, as well as a variety of pin types. However, as 64-bit motherboards are more common, the DIMM is becoming the memory type of choice. Because the Pentium processor requires a 64-bit path to memory, you need to install SIMMs two at a time. With DIMMs, you can install memory one DIMM at a time.

CERTIFICATION OBJECTIVE 4.03

Motherboards

The most important component of any computer is the motherboard. The motherboard is made of a fiberglass sheet that has miniature electronic circuitry embedded in it. This circuitry provides the pathways for electronic signals to flow between devices. However, not all motherboards are created equal. In the next sections, we will discuss different types of motherboards, their components, and give you some basic compatibility guidelines.

Types of Motherboards

Motherboards come in various shapes and sizes, but there are two basic types: AT and ATX. Both motherboards provide the same basic services to the computer, but they are not interchangeable. In the next sections, we take a brief look at both forms of system boards.

AT (Full and Baby)

The AT motherboard actually comes in two different types: Full and Baby. The primary difference between the two types is a matter of size, with the Full form at approximately 12" wide and the Baby at about 8.5" wide. The Full form is usually found with 386 or earlier computers and fits in a wider case. However, most AT-type motherboards manufactured until 1998 in today's computer systems are usually Baby ATs.

Regardless of which type of AT motherboard you are working with, the characteristics are basically the same. The processor is normally located in the front of the board, which has been an annoyance to many technicians attempting to install a new expansion card. The serial and parallel ports are actually located on the back of the case, and attach to the motherboard by headers.

ATX

The ATX motherboard specification was introduced by Intel and has become an industry-accepted standard. The ATX system board is approximately the same size as the Baby AT. However, the motherboard has been rotated 90 degrees, and the processor is now at the back of the board and out of the way of expansion cards. In addition, the ATX form integrates the serial and parallel ports on the motherboard. The disk drive cable connectors are also closer to the drive bays, and the CPU is closer to the power supply and cooling fan.

Components

A motherboard is composed of several components that work together as a unit. As a service technician, you should familiarize yourself with each of these components and their functions. By understanding each component's job and how it works, you will be able to troubleshoot problems with these components more quickly. The following subsections discuss each component.

Communication Ports

The computer was developed to process information of all kinds, but in order to receive that data, it has to have a method of communicating with peripheral devices. Internal components attach directly to the motherboard through expansion slots. However, for external devices to connect to the motherboard in this fashion would require the computer's case to be removed. Instead, the communication ports on the system board allow external devices to attach directly to the processor without having to remove the case.

There are two types of communication ports found on a motherboard: serial and parallel. *Serial ports* transmit data sequentially, bit by bit over a single conductor. This type of communication is usually found with modems and mice. A *parallel port* allows transmission of data over eight conductors at one time. An example of a device that utilizes a parallel port is a printer.

CMOS

The Complementary Metallic-Oxide Semiconductor (CMOS) stores the settings used by the Basic Input/Output System (BIOS). When the computer is rebooted or has lost power, the BIOS is incapable of retaining its settings. To avoid having to reenter these settings, a task that can prove tedious to say the least, the CMOS uses a battery to store the settings and then provide them to the computer's BIOS upon reboot.

SIMM AND DIMM

Single In-Line Memory Modules (SIMM) and Dual In-Line Memory Modules (DIMM) are the memory types used on the motherboard. These types of memory were discussed in depth earlier in the chapter.

Processor Sockets

The processor socket is the actual socket used to attach the processor to the motherboard. In earlier computers, the processor was actually soldered onto the motherboard. When it came time for an upgrade, you would usually have to purchase a new motherboard. With today's computers, the processor is not soldered onto the motherboard and can be removed when necessary.

All Intel Pentium processors except the Pentium Pro and Pentium II and III conform to socket 7 specifications. Intel's competitors, AMD and Cyrix, also conform to socket 7 specifications. The Pentium Pro uses socket 8 specifications. Pentium II and III processors use a slot rather than socket 7 or 8.

External Cache Memory (Level 2)

Cache memory is used to store frequently used instructions and data so that they can be accessed quickly by the computer. The system cache is responsible for a great deal of the system performance improvement of today's PCs. The cache is a buffer of sorts between the very fast processor and the relatively slow memory that serves it. While many processors offer an integrated cache (Level 1 cache, integrated into the processor), it is useful to increase the capacity of the cache memory to speed up the computer's performance. The motherboard contains cache memory slots, or external cache memory slots, that allow you to put additional cache memory onboard the system board.

ROM

Read-Only Memory (ROM) is a form of memory that is only read from, rather than written to. This is because the memory chips were permanently written to by the manufacturer. Types of ROM include the Basic Input/Output System (BIOS) chip, and Complementary Metal-Oxide Semiconductor (CMOS). It is possible to reprogram ROM, using different techniques with a few different types of ROM chips:

- **Programmable ROM (PROM)** This is a type of ROM that can be programmed using special equipment. It can be written to, but only once. This is useful for companies that make their own ROMs from software they write, because when they change their code, they can create new PROMs without requiring expensive equipment.

- **Erasable Programmable ROM (EPROM)** An *EPROM* is a ROM that can be erased and reprogrammed. A little glass window is installed in the top of the ROM package, through which you can actually see the chip that holds the memory. Ultraviolet light of a specific frequency can be directed through this window for a specified period of time, which will erase the EPROM and allow it to be reprogrammed again.

■ **Electrically Erasable Programmable ROM (EEPROM)**   The next level of erasability is the *EEPROM*, which can be erased under software control. This is the most versatile type of ROM, and is now commonly used for holding BIOS programs. When you hear reference to a *flash BIOS* or doing a BIOS upgrade by *flashing*, this refers to reprogramming the BIOS EEPROM with a special software program.

Bus Architecture

The bus allows a device to communicate with the motherboard and its underlying circuitry. It is defined by how many data bits can be transmitted at any given instant, such as an 8-bit or 16-bit bus. The size of the bus, known as its width, is the number of wires that make up the bus; the more the better, because this is the amount of data that can be transmitted at one time. This is similar to the lanes on a freeway; the more lanes, the more traffic the freeway can allow.

The modern computer has several different buses providing a wide range of different speeds communicating from the processor, chipset, and various devices within the computer:

■ **The Processor Bus** is the fastest and it is the one used to communicate to the processor.

■ **The Cache Bus** is the bus in which the processor communicates directly with the very fast system cache. Fifth-generation processors, such as all Pentium chips up to but not including the Pentium Pro, use the memory bus to access the system cache.

■ **The Memory Bus** is the bus through which the processor communicates directly with the data placed in memory. The memory bus can also communicate with the chipset.

■ **The Local I/O Bus** is the bus in which performance-oriented peripherals communicate with the processor, memory, and chipset. This includes video cards, disk storage devices, and high-speed network interfaces. The two most common local I/O buses are the VESA Local Bus (VESA) and the Peripheral Component Interconnect (PCI) bus, which will be discussed next.

■ **The Standard I/O Bus** is the bus on which slower devices such as modems, sound cards, and mice communicate. The most common standard I/O bus is the Industry Standard Architecture (ISA) bus.

In general, motherboards have only one or two types of bus architecture on any given board. This is due to the fact that the processor's data bus determines what types of architecture can utilize it. There are several architectures available on the market.

■ **Industry Standard Architecture (ISA)** was introduced after the IBM AT computers were released. AT computers allowed for a 16-bit data bus, but the peripherals at the time were still stuck on the 8-bit bus. To improve the communication speed of the devices, and to provide for an industry standard, several of the larger companies got together and developed ISA technology. This now allows for peripherals to utilize the 16-bit data bus that is available with 286 and 386 processors.

■ **Extended Industry Standard Architecture (EISA)** was introduced to compete against IBM's Micro-Channel Architecture (MCA) devices, which increased their peripheral's bus size from a 16-bit bus to a 32-bit bus. Because MCA was expensive and proprietary, the original companies that developed ISA got together and created a 32-bit card that was not only cheaper, but also retained backward compatibility with the 16-bit ISA cards. This type of bus architecture is used in conjunction with 386 and 486 processors.

■ **Peripheral Component Interconnect (PCI)** was designed in response to the Pentium class processor's utilization of a 64-bit bus. Until the development of the PCI bus, peripherals were tied to the processor architecture as well as the processor data bus. However, PCI buses are designed to be processor independent. They are able to accomplish this by utilizing a special bridge circuit along with a processor-dependent configuration program.

■ **Universal Serial Bus (USB)** is a relatively new bus architecture that is designed to allow for true Plug-and-Play peripherals without your ever having to open the computer case. According to Intel, the USB can handle up to 12 MBps and will accommodate most peripherals utilizing the Plug-and-Play technology. Don't expect any questions on the A+ exam regarding USB, as it was still relatively new during the creation of the A+ exam.

■ **The VESA Local Bus (VL-Bus)** was originally created to address performance issues. One of the problems with earlier bus designs was that they could handle a maximum clock speed of only 8 MHz, while processors could run at much higher clock speeds. The idea was to create a bus that would have the same clock speed as the processor, known as a *local bus*. Components that utilized the local bus increased their performance, and thus several types of components were designed to take advantage of the faster speed.

Table 4-4 illustrates the characteristics of each bus architecture.

exam
ⓦatch
Most new computers come with the AGP bus architecture; however, the A+ exam will not cover the specifics of this bus type.

TABLE 4-4	Characteristics of Each BUS Type

Bus	Width (bits)	Bus Speed (MHz)	Bus Bandwidth (MBps)
8-bit ISA	8	8.3	7.9
16-bit ISA	16	8.3	15.9
EISA	32	8.3	31.8
VL-Bus	32	33	127.2
PCI	32	33	127.2
64-bit PCI 2.1	64	66	508.6

Of the kinds of components that used the new bus architecture—hard drive cards, memory cards, and cache cards—video cards became the most prevalent. However, compatibility issues arose as vendors used proprietary local bus slots and cards. This meant that you had to purchase the vendor's card in order for it to work in the vendor's slot. The Video Electronics Standards Association (VESA) was formed to address this compatibility problem.

VESA created the standards for the local bus architecture that were incorporated into the manufacturer's products. This ensured that a card from one vendor would work in another manufacturer's computer. The VL-Bus used a 32-bit slot and was built upon ISA bus architecture. This meant that the bus was backward compatible with ISA and that configuration would require the old jumper and/or DIP switch configuration methods. The VL-Bus is inherent with the 486 processor, so expect your exposure to VL-Bus to be limited, unless you are supporting older computers.

■ **The Personal Computer Memory Card International Association (PCMCIA)**, or the less hard to remember *PC Card* bus was first created to expand the memory capabilities in small, laptop computers. The bus itself is about the size of a credit card and is only 16-bit. While some computers utilize the PC Card bus, the 16-bit size is somewhat restricting in computers that are capable of handling 64 bits. Therefore, a new standard is currently under construction to increase the PC Card to a 32-bit standard.

exam
Watch

Make sure that you know the difference between each type of bus and what each acronym stands for. While most of the acronyms seem intuitive, the exam will throw in a few that will seem to be just as plausible.

Now that you have seen the various components of the modern computer motherboard, here is a quick reference of possible scenario questions for understanding each of these components and the appropriate answer.

QUESTIONS AND ANSWERS

What is the fastest local I/O bus architecture covered on the A+ exam?	PCI
Name a proprietary bus architecture.	MCA
What is the fastest bus?	Processor bus
What is the type of ROM used when "flashing"?	EEPROM, Electrically Erasable Programmable ROM
What is the most common standard I/O bus?	ISA
Name the most common local I/O buses.	PCI and VL-Bus
What is the type of ROM erased with ultraviolet light?	EPROM, Erasable Programmable ROM
Which level is the cache that is integrated into a processor?	Level 1 cache
Which level is the cache that is integrated onto the motherboard?	Level 2 cache
All Pentium chips up to the Pentium Pro use this type of socket.	Socket 7

Basic Compatibility Guidelines

Whenever you have to determine if an expansion card is compatible with an expansion slot, you should always first refer to the manufacturer's documentation. A good rule of thumb is to remember that an expansion card must be the same type as the expansion slot (e.g. a VL-Bus card can go into only a VL-Bus expansion slot). However, ISA cards are an exception to the rule and can go into an ISA slot, an EISA slot, and a VL-Bus slot.

CMOS (Complementary Metal-Oxide Semiconductor)

The Basic Input/Output System (BIOS) can hold its settings only as long as the power is kept on. Once it loses power, it loses the settings and has to get them again from somewhere. The Complementary Metal-Oxide Semiconductor (CMOS) was designed to store these settings and therefore drastically cut down on the number of times that the user would have to input them. However, the CMOS utilizes a battery that does not have an infinite life, and it is always prudent for you to note the CMOS settings in a safe location in the event that the battery begins to fail.

Basic CMOS Settings

There are several basic CMOS settings that you should familiarize yourself with, as at some point you will have to reconfigure these settings as a result of a dead battery or a system upgrade. Although we discuss these items in the following sections, it is always recommended to consult the manufacturer's documentation in case these settings are slightly different.

Printer Parallel Port

Printer parallel ports come in a few varieties based on their capabilities. Nearly every modern computer supports every type of parallel port listed as follows:

- **Unidirectional** A single directional mode for the parallel port. Data travels only from the computer to the peripheral (usually the printer) in this mode.

- **Bi-directional** A two directional mode for the parallel port. Data travels both from the computer to the peripheral and vice versa.

- **Disable/enable** Enables or disables the parallel port.

- **ECP–Extended Capability Port**   ECP mode offers the same features as bi-directional in addition to the use of a DMA channel for data transfer. This speeds up data transfer rates by bypassing the processor and writing the data directly to memory.

- **EPP–Enhanced Parallel Port**   EPP mode offers the same features as bi-directional and offers an extended control code set.

exam
Watch

Know the different types of parallel ports for the exam, as many people get stuck on this type of question.

Com/Serial Port

Serial ports, also known as communication (COM) ports, are found on every computer today. There are a few settings that you must configure in the BIOS SETUP for serial ports. In some operating systems, such as Windows 95 and Windows 98, you can also configure the serial ports from the System applet in the Control Panel. The following is a list of the items that are configurable for every serial port.

- **Memory address**   All serial ports require a memory address. The memory address is used to receive commands from the processor that are destined for the device attached to the COM port.

- **Interrupt request**   Every COM port must have a unique interrupt. It is through this interrupt that the peripheral attached to the COM port notifies the CPU that there is data available to be retrieved from the peripheral. For example, when the modem receives data, it will fire an interrupt on the COM port, which in turn triggers the CPU to pick up data from the modem. The standard COM1 interrupt address is 4 and the memory address is 03F8. With COM2, the interrupt address is 3 and the memory address is 02F8. This may seem counterintuitive, as COM1 would be listed before COM2.

exam
Watch

Remember the interrupt and memory addresses for both COM1 and COM2 for the A+ Exam.

■ **Enable/disable**   The enable/disable either enables or disables the COM port for use.

on the **Job**

It is important that you memorize standard IRQ and memory address assignments, not just for the A+ exam, but for your real-life experiences. Every technician should have a strong foundation in configuring and troubleshooting resources, such as IRQs and memory addresses. This is especially the case for technicians who upgrade users' computers. They must add additional hardware such as modems, scanners, adapter cards, and mice to the existing computer, and work around the already existing resource assignments. These computers have lots of equipment occupying most of the IRQs, which means you really have to know what you are doing when you are assigning IRQs to devices. If you go in blindly, you will no doubt misconfigure something, and possibly leave the computer in a worse condition than when you arrived. Study and memorize the standard resource assignments, and practice configuring devices to get a good understanding of how to successfully add additional components quickly and effectively.

Hard Drive

There are a number of specifications related to hard drive dimensions and capacity. In older hard drives, you need this information to enter in the system SETUP program when configuring the hard drive. However, nearly every modern hard drive can be automatically detected on system startup. The following is a list of important hard drive settings that will need to be configured:

■ **Size**   The size of the drive is automatically calculated from the number of cylinders, sectors, and heads on the drive. If you need to calculate the size of a drive, use the following formula:

```
(# of cylinders) * (# of sectors) * (# of heads) * 0.5 KB
```

The 0.5KB constant is due to the fact that most hard drives have 512 bytes per sector.

■ **Primary master/secondary slave**   Each hard drive has a controller built into the drive itself that actually controls the drive. When you have more than one hard drive attached to an adapter card, the

FROM THE FIELD

BIOS Fears

Improper handling of the BIOS can cause big headaches and much wasted time. The good news is that the BIOSs are improving over the years. They now autodetect most hardware and set themselves without too much user intervention. The bad news is that most of the BIOSs that you work with will be old.

Over time, batteries become depleted and this resets the BIOS. This causes you to have to replace the battery and reset the settings. You need to choose between all the types of hard drives, or worse, fill in the blank for the cylinder numbers, heads, and so forth. Well, if you have a good hard drive, you can usually find this labeled on the drive. If not, you can always look up this information in a book if you have the manufacturer and the serial number. Eventually, you will come across a hard drive that has none of this information on it. I've seen techs reboot 79 times only to discover that the drive is not one of those preset in the CMOS. Only

third-party software and much time are the answer to this dilemma.

Get a good idea of when these batteries usually die. If you find out that a certain model of computers are losing their batteries after a certain amount of time, make sure you replace the other computers that were bought at about the same time. If the clock starts losing time, you can bet that the battery is to blame. Your best defense, however, is to keep track of the BIOS settings. There are some software programs out there that will save this data and let you print it. Do so, and keep this information with the log for the computer. Not only are hard drives tough to set in the BIOS, but some BIOSs have settings that are very difficult to decipher. With your list, you will never have to guess if you should have a setting activated or not.

—Ted Hamilton, MCSE, MCP, A+ Certified

adapter could get confused as to which controller was in charge. In order to distinguish which controller is actually being used, one of the drives is designated as a master drive and its controller is used to control the other drives, which are called slaves. When you look at the CMOS configuration screen, you will note that you have to fill in the primary master section for the master drive, and the secondary slave section for the slave drive. Please note that even though your hard drive type is automatically configured, you may still have to configure the master and slave drive types; this does not occur automatically.

■ **Tracks**   A hard drive is made up of several disks mounted on a *spindle*. Each disk can be broken down into rings of concentric circles; each ring is called a *track*.

■ **Sectors**   As you can break down a disk into tracks, you can further subdivide the disk into sectors. This is done by *slicing* the disk up as you would a pie. Each piece of that pie is called a *sector*. The number of sectors on a hard drive is usually printed on the outside case of the drive itself.

■ **Cylinder**   When you combine the same tracks on each of the disks in a hard drive, you have what is known as a *cylinder*. The number of cylinders in a hard drive is also printed on the outside case of the drive itself.

■ **Drive type**   Older systems provided a number of cylinder-head-sector configurations associated with a standardized number. Older models' drives could be set up by simply indicating which type of drive it was, for example, a 13 or a 16. For drives that did not fit one of the defined types, you would select "user" and manually enter the number of heads, cylinders, and sectors. Newer systems will automatically detect all of the information needed to set up a hard drive, and also include other drive types, including CD-ROM and removable.

Floppy Drive

The floppy drive, much like the hard drive, requires configuration in the system SETUP program. However, the floppy requires very few settings:

■ **Enable/disable drive**   When installing a floppy drive, you do have the option to disable it. To do this, you must set Drive A to None.

■ **Density**   Drive types are usually defined by the capacity and size of the media. There are five standard types available:

   ■ 5.25" 360KB

- 5.25" 1.2MB
- 3.5" 720KB
- 3.5" 1.44MB
- 3.5" 2.88MB

5.25" drives are rare in today's computers as they are the original floppy drive technology, and purchasing a replacement drive is almost impossible. Most computers today utilize the 3.5" 1.44MB drive even though the 3.5" 2.88MB can hold twice the amount of data. There are several factors that have kept the 3.5" 2.88MB drive from becoming commonplace, but you should familiarize yourself with them for environments that do utilize them.

Boot Sequence

When your computer boots, it has to look for the location of the files and settings that are needed during the boot process. The boot sequence tells the computer where to start looking for these files and in what order to search the various storage devices. For example, if you have the boot sequence set up for floppy drive, hard drive, and CD-ROM, the computer first goes to the floppy drive. If it can't find what it needs on the floppy drive, it then proceeds to the hard drive, and so on.

Although most people have this set up to search for a floppy drive first, you may want to set the machine to look to the hard drive first. Many customers have a tendency to leave their data disk in the drive when they turn their computers off. When they boot, the computer can't find an operating system to load and it produces an error message. You can cut down on the number of calls by setting the boot sequence to check for the hard drive first, and the floppy drive second. However, the drawback to this is that if you do need to boot from a floppy, you will have to reconfigure this setting.

Memory

As mentioned earlier in the "RAM (Random Access Memory)" section of this chapter, memory is the workplace of the computer. When it comes to configuring memory in the CMOS, there is really nothing that you need to be concerned about because memory is automatically detected and configured.

However, there are some cases when you may get a memory error after installing new memory that requires you to enter the CMOS. If this happens, all you need to do is select the EXIT AND SAVE option from the menu and the computer will begin to reboot.

Network Interface Card

Unless you are using a motherboard that has an integrated Network Interface Card (NIC), there is no CMOS setting for this component. If you do work with a computer with an integrated NIC, you must consult the manufacturer's documentation for the correct settings. Integrated NICs are not a common component found in computers. If they are present, you have the ability to boot from the network. You can configure the boot order to include the network card, in addition to the floppy drive, hard drive, and CD-ROM.

Date/Time

The system date and time are stored in the CMOS. This ensures that the user does not have to reenter the date and time every time they boot their computer. This feature is not only convenient for the user; it is used by the operating system and by application software for certain routines that require timing components. The first indication that your CMOS battery is failing is that the system date and time have changed. If you find your system has lost its BIOS settings, you may have to replace the CMOS battery to avoid having to reconfigure the system BIOS settings every time you boot the computer.

Passwords

Most customers do not implement the password feature of CMOS, because they have enough passwords and codes to remember as it is. However, if you work at any high-security sites, they may have the CMOS password feature enabled. To enable it, you will have to type in a password twice, once for the initial setting and a second time for verification. Then, whenever the computer boots, the CMOS will require that password to be entered in order for the computer to complete the boot sequence. You also have the ability on some computers to place a password on the BIOS SETUP program. This will prevent an attempt by a curious novice computer user or experienced hacker from altering the system settings. For example, in the BIOS SETUP program, you can disable the floppy disk drive. A user or hacker may wish to use the floppy drive to copy data to or from the computer, and may try and enter the SETUP program to reconfigure the system to allow use of the floppy drive.

CERTIFICATION SUMMARY

In this chapter, you have learned about the various types of processors that have been used in the computer industry. These chips define the types of memory and peripherals that can be used by the motherboard. We have also discussed the motherboard and its various components, such as memory, communications ports, and CMOS settings. Armed with this knowledge, you should have a good grasp of how these components work together.

TWO-MINUTE DRILL

- ❏ The CPU provides the devices attached to the computer with directives that retrieve, display, manipulate, and store information.
- ❏ Today's Intel Pentium II processors contain 7.5 million transistors and support a 64-bit bus.
- ❏ SIMM stands for Single In-Line Memory Module, which is a type of RAM chip.
- ❏ The Intel 586 (Pentium) chip combined two 486DX chips into one, called the Dual Independent Bus Architecture. This allowed each processor inside the chip to execute instructions simultaneously and independently from each other, which is called parallel processing.
- ❏ The PCI (Peripheral Component Interconnect) was designed in response to the Pentium class processor's utilization of a 64-bit bus. PCI buses are designed to be processor-independent.
- ❏ Review Table 4-2, which provides an overview of the different varieties of processors along with their bus sizes.
- ❏ As a service technician, you should familiarize yourself with each of the motherboard's components and know their functions.

❑ There are three common denotations that are used to represent computer numbers: a kilobyte (KB) is 1,024 bytes; a megabyte (MB) is 1,048,576 bytes; and a gigabyte (GB) is 1,073,741,824 bytes.

❑ DIMM stands for Dual In-Line Module, which is a type of RAM chip.

❑ To ensure that the signals on memory chips are correct, they are constantly updated by a process called refresh.

❑ WRAM, which was design specifically for the Microsoft Windows operating system, utilizes memory that resides on the card itself to perform the Windows-specific functions, and therefore speeds up the OS.

❑ The number of transistors inside a chip helps determine the rate at which a chip can process information.

❑ A memory bank is the actual slot that memory goes into.

❑ There are two basic types of motherboards: AT and ATX.

❑ Industry Standard Architecture (ISA) is an industry standard bus architecture that allows for peripherals to utilize the 16-bit data bus that is available with 286 and 386 processors.

❑ On the AT motherboard, the processor is normally located in the front of the board, which has been an annoyance to many technicians attempting to install a new expansion card.

❑ The communication ports on the system board allow external devices to attach directly to the processor without having to remove the case.

❑ Although SRAM doesn't need a constant update, it does require a periodic update and tends to use excessive amounts of power when it does so.

❑ A serial port transmits data sequentially, bit by bit, over a single conductor and is most commonly used with modems and mice.

❑ A parallel port transmits data over eight conductors at one time and is most commonly used with printers.

❑ The processor socket is the actual socket used to attach the processor to the motherboard.

❏ Cache memory is used to store frequently used instructions and data so that they can be accessed quickly by the computer.

❏ EISA (Extended Industry Standard Architecture) is an industry standard bus architecture that allows for peripherals to utilize the 32-bit data bus that is available with 386 and 486 processors.

❏ Originally created to address performance issues, the VL-Bus was meant to enable earlier bus designs to handle a maximum clock speed equivalent to that of processors.

❏ The Personal Computer Memory Card International Association (PCMCIA), or the less hard to remember PC Card, bus was first created to expand the memory capabilities in small, hand-held computers.

❏ Make sure that you know the difference between each type of bus and what each acronym stands for. While most of the acronyms seem intuitive, the exam will throw in a few that will seem just as plausible.

❏ Know the different types of parallel ports for the exam, as many people get stuck on this type of question.

❏ The memory address is used to receive commands from the processor that are destined for the device attached to the COM port. Each device must have a unique memory address in order to function.

❏ The standard COM1 interrupt address is 4 and the memory address is 03F8.

❏ The standard COM2 interrupt address is 3 and the memory address is 02F8.

❏ Each hard drive has a controller built into the drive itself that actually controls the drive.

❏ The number of heads, sectors, and cylinders on a hard drive is usually printed on the outside of the drive.

❏ Integrated NICs are not a common component found in computers.

SELF TEST

The following Self Test questions will help you measure your understanding of the material presented in this chapter. Read all the choices carefully, as there may be more than one correct answer. Choose all correct answers for each question.

1. Which of the following are true of the Intel 386 processor? (Choose all that apply.)

    A. The chip has a 32-bit address bus.

    B. The chip does not have an internal math coprocessor.

    C. The chip has a 16-bit address bus.

    D. The chip has a 32-bit data bus.

2. Which of the following are true of the Pentium 586 class processors? (Choose all that apply.)

    A. The chip makes use of parallel processing.

    B. The chip has a 64-bit address bus.

    C. The chip has a 64-bit data bus.

    D. The chip has a 32-bit internal Level 1 cache.

3. Which processor featured a register size of 32-bits, a data bus of 16-bits, and an address bus of 24-bits?

    A. 80486DX

    B. 80386DX

    C. 80386SX

    D. 80486SX

4. Of the following, which is the fastest type of RAM?

    A. EDO RAM

    B. DRAM

    C. SRAM

    D. VRAM

5. Which of the following is false concerning WRAM?

    A. It is less expensive than VRAM.

    B. It is dual ported.

    C. It is 25% faster than SRAM.

    D. It is 25% faster than VRAM.

6. What is the most common type of Main RAM?

    A. EDO RAM

    B. SRAM

    C. DRAM

    D. VRAM

7. SIMM memory comes in which of the following sizes? (Choose all that apply.)

    A. 30-pin

    B. 32-pin

    C. 72-pin

    D. 168-pin

8. Which of the following is true about DIMM memory?

    A. DIMMs do not need to be installed in pairs.

B. DIMMs come in only a 64-bit configuration.

C. DIMMs do not use parity.

D. DIMMs come in only 168-pin configuration.

9. Most motherboards manufactured until 1998 were of what form?

A. AT

B. ATX

C. Baby-AT

D. Baby-ATX

10. Which ROM uses an ultraviolet light of a specific frequency to erase the contents of the ROM?

A. PROM

B. EPROM

C. EEPROM

D. EEEPROM

11. Which bus does the Pentium Pro processor use to access the system cache?

A. Processor bus

B. Cache bus

C. Memory bus

D. Local I/O bus

12. What are the two most common local I/O buses? (Choose two from the following.)

A. PCI

B. EISA

C. VL-Bus

D. ISA

13. Which of the following is not true regarding EISA?

A. It is 32 bits.

B. It is less expensive than MCA.

C. It is the bus architecture used in the 386, 486, and Pentium computers.

D. It is backward compatible with ISA.

14. Which bus type has a width of 16 bits, and a speed of 8.3 MHz?

A. EISA

B. 8-bit ISA

C. 32-bit ISA

D. 16-bit ISA

15. What is the bus bandwidth on the PCI bus?

A. 7.9 MBps

B. 127.2 MBps

C. 31.8 MBps

D. 165.2 MBps

16. What is the bus size of the PCMCIA bus on most laptop computers?

A. 8-bit

B. 16-bit

C. 32-bit

D. 64-bit

17. ISA cards can fit into which types of slots? (Choose all that apply.)

A. ISA

B. VL-Bus

C. PCI

D. EISA

18. What does the acronym CMOS stand for?

    A. Conditional Metal-Oxide Semiconductor

    B. Complementary Metal-Oriented Semiconductor

    C. Contemporary Metal-Oriented Semiconductor

    D. Complementary Metal-Oxide Semiconductor

19. Which of the following is not a type of parallel printer port?

    A. ECP

    B. PPL

    C. EPP

    D. Bi-directional

20. What is the standard interrupt and memory address for COM2?

    A. 2 and 02F8

    B. 3 and 03F8

    C. 4 and 03F8

    D. 3 and 02F8

21. Most hard drives have how many bytes per sector?

    A. 128KB

    B. 256KB

    C. 512KB

    D. 1024KB

22. Which of the following is not required when you have to manually enter information for an older hard disk drive in the BIOS SETUP program?

    A. Clusters

    B. Cylinders

    C. Tracks

    D. Sectors

23. How do you disable the floppy disk drive in the BIOS SETUP program?

    A. Set the floppy disk drive to None.

    B. Set the floppy disk drive to something other than the actual type of drive installed.

    C. Set the primary floppy disk drive to Disabled.

    D. You cannot disable the floppy disk drive in the BIOS SETUP program; you must use the operating system to do this.

24. A junior technician calls you with a problem on a user's Windows 95 computer. The computer will not boot to the network floppy disk that he has created. What do you instruct the junior technician to do?

    A. Remove the floppy disk, boot the computer to Windows 95, enter the Control Panel, and enable floppy disk access.

    B. Restart the computer, enter the BIOS setup program, and enable floppy drive access.

    C. Restart the computer, enter the BIOS setup program, and put the floppy drive before the hard drive in the boot order.

D. Restart the computer, and hold down
    the SHIFT key while the memory test
    is being performed.

25. What are two common types of passwords
     on computer systems? (Choose all that
     apply.)

A. Hard drive access password

B. BIOS SETUP password

C. Power-on password

D. ROM shadow password

5

Printers

The business world revolves around paperwork. The need to put data into a tangible, easy-to handle format called a *hard copy* has existed since the early days of computing and will continue to exist for the foreseeable future. It may be quite a while before industries that depend on computer information become totally paperless (if and when that ever occurs). So until then, the need for providing data in printed form will remain. A printer is simply an electromechanical device designed to translate electronic impulses onto a printed page. This chapter reviews the principles of operation, configuration, and maintenance of various printing devices. By the end of this chapter, you should have a working knowledge of what is involved in operating and servicing printers.

CERTIFICATION OBJECTIVE 5.01

Printer Operations and Components

Printers are actually very simple devices. They exist for the sole purpose of taking data from your computer and placing it on a printed page. Printers can be used to print documents from a word processor, create envelopes, banners, labels, full-color photographic-quality images, and T-shirt transfers, just to name a few. This section will deal with common types of printers and their Field-Replaceable Units (FRUs).

Types of Printers

There are many different types of printers available on the market, each having unique advantages and disadvantages. When choosing a printer, it's best to determine what your needs are and select a printer that best meets those needs. It really comes down to what the printer is going to be used for.

Printers can be classified into two major groups: impact and non-impact. *Impact printers*, as the name suggests, require the impact of a print head with an ink ribbon to print characters and images. *Non-impact printers* do not use an ink ribbon, and therefore do not require direct contact with the paper for printing. The easiest way to differentiate between an impact and a non-impact printer is to determine whether it could print multi-part form documents. Images and characters formed on impact printers are actually impressed upon the page, creating copies on all pages, whereas non-impact printers do not.

Daisy-Wheel Printers

Daisy-wheel printers are the first and most archaic type of impact printers. They have a wheel with raised letters and symbols on it that looks like a daisy, which is how the printer got its name. This type of printer is probably the computer peripheral most similar to the typewriter. When the printer receives the command to print a character, it sends a signal to the print head, which, in turn, spins the wheel on the print head until the appropriate character lines up. An electromechanical hammer (also called a *solenoid* or *resistive coil)* is energized, causing it to strike the back of the "petal" containing the character. The character impacts a printer ribbon, which then strikes the paper, leaving the image of the character in its place.

Daisy-wheel printers are not the fastest printers available but they have the advantage of being able to create multi-part forms, which are still used by businesses today. The main disadvantage of this type of printer is the amount of noise it creates from banging the characters against the page. Although measures have been taken to muffle the noise from these machines, they still remain the noisiest printers available.

Dot Matrix Printers

All dot matrix printers form characters and images a few dots at a time. They do this by creating the image or character in a matrix of dots, hence the name *dot matrix.* There are two modes by which these types of printers can operate: font mode, and dot-addressable.

In font mode, the printer already has all the pins programmed for every character in its font set. When the printer receives the message to print the letter "R," for example, it looks up the letter "R" in its character table in ROM and sends the correct pin sequence to the print head. This allows a single input to produce many dots on the page, representing the character desired.

In dot-addressable mode, each printed dot requires an input. This provides for a lot of flexibility to users because they are not limited by the fonts available in the printer's memory. The downside to this mode is that this printing method is much slower than font mode because multiple dots require multiple inputs.

The print head on a dot matrix printer is a series of pins each controlled by its own solenoid (or resistive coil), which is similar in function to the solenoid on a daisy-wheel printer. When the solenoid is energized, the pin is forced away from the print head and impacts the printer ribbon and ultimately the paper, thus impressing the dot on the page. Like the daisy wheel, the advantage of this type of printer is that multiple-page paper may be fed through to create carbon copies. The earliest print heads had 7 pins, whereas dot matrix printers today have up to 24. The print head travels horizontally along the page, striking dots all along the way. It may take several passes to create one line of characters. Some printers are bidirectional, printing both from left to right and from right to left, whereas older dot matrix printers printed in only one direction.

Color of the output is dependent upon the color of the printer ribbon that is installed in the printer. Early dot matrix printers were limited to a single color printer ribbon, but today's models offer ribbons with multiple colors, allowing for color output.

InkJet, BubbleJet, and DeskJet

Unlike daisy wheel and dot matrix printers, where contact with the paper is required, jet-type printers do not require contact with the paper. By use of small nozzles on the print head, a jet-type printer "spray paints" the image onto the page. Jet-type printers are relatively simple devices. They consist of the print-head mechanism, support electronics, and a transfer mechanism that moves the print head across the paper. A paper-feed mechanism is also required to advance the paper through the system, eventually ejecting it.

InkJet is the generic term used to identify a type of printer that deposits tiny drops of ink on a sheet of paper. BubbleJet (Canon) and DeskJet (Hewlett-Packard) are two brands of printers that use this technology. In today's computing environments, all these terms are used interchangeably.

The first InkJet printers used an ink reservoir, pump, and ink nozzle to put the ink on the page. This method was inefficient as well as messy. Today's InkJet printers use a much more efficient and cleaner means by which the ink is propelled towards the page.

BubbleJet printers are actually an advance in technology from the older InkJet printers. BubbleJet printers improved on the InkJet concept by changing the means by which the ink is propelled towards the page.

Every BubbleJet printer operates the same way. BubbleJets are comprised of a disposable ink cartridge that contains the print-head nozzles and ink reservoir. This ink cartridge must be replaced when the ink runs out. Although possible, it is not recommended to have the cartridges refilled with ink. Replacing the cartridges not only provides the printer with a fresh source of ink, but it replaces the nozzles that get worn out by the printing process.

Inside the ink cartridge of a BubbleJet printer are several chambers. At the top of each chamber is a metal plate with a tube leading to the ink supply. The bottom of each chamber contains a single microscopic pinhole used to spray the ink onto the page. The print head passes across the page horizontally, just like a dot matrix, spray-painting each dot along the way

When a chamber receives the command to spray ink, an electrical signal is sent to energize the heating element. The heating element, in contact with the ink, heats up very quickly, causing the ink to vaporize, resulting in a buildup of pressure in the chamber. This pressure forces the ink out the pinhole forming a "bubble" of ink on the page. As the vapor expands, the bubble gets large enough to break off into a droplet. The rest of the ink is drawn back into the chamber due to the surface tension of the ink. This process is repeated for each drop that needs to be sprayed.

One drawback to this type of printer is the tendency for the ink inside the jets to dry and clog the nozzles of the jets. To counter this problem, InkJet and BubbleJet printers move the print-head mechanism to an area known as the *park* or *maintenance* area. In this area, the ink is kept from drying during periods of inactivity.

Laser Printers

Laser printers are an entirely different breed. They are non-impact printers. Using a combination of light, electricity, chemistry, pressure, and heat, they have the ability to create very high-quality images and text on the printed page.

Laser printers are also referred to as *page printers* because they receive their print job instructions one page at a time. Laser printers can perform this feat through use of a *Page-Description Language (PDL)*. Rather than the printer receiving instructions for each dot on the page, the PDL encoded in the printer receives commands from the computer on how to print the page. Using simple line-drawing commands rather than printing each dot along that line greatly simplifies the instructions that must be passed to the printer.

The main components of a laser printer are listed as follows:

- **Cleaning blade**   This rubber blade extends the length of the photosensitive drum. It removes excess toner after the print process has completed and deposits it into a reservoir for re-use.

- **Photosensitive drum**   This light-sensitive drum is the core of the electrophotographic process inside the printer. The cleaning, charging, writing, and transferring processes in the six-step printing process we discuss in detail later in this section affect this drum.

- **Primary corona wire**   This highly negatively-charged wire is responsible for electrically charging the photosensitive drum, thereby preparing it to be written with a new image in the writing stage of the print process.

- **Transfer corona**   This roller contains a positively-charged wire designed to pull the toner off the photosensitive drum and place it on the page.

- **Toner**   Toner is comprised of finely divided particles of plastic resin and organic compounds bonded to iron particles. It is naturally negatively charged, which aids in attracting it to the written areas of the photosensitive drum during the transfer step of the printing process.

■ **Fusing rollers**   These rollers comprise the final stage of the electrophotographic (EP) print process, bonding the toner particles to the page to prevent smearing. The roller on the toner side of the page has a non-stick surface that is heated to a high temperature to permanently bond the toner to the paper.

exam
Ⓦatch   *Understanding the theory of the electrophotographic print process is a key to passing the Printers section of the A+ exam.*

The electrophotographic (EP) print process for putting the image on the page is a six-step process. Though some sources disagree on which step occurs first, the important thing to remember is that this process occurs as a cycle within the printer, and therefore the order of the steps is critical. During this process, the printer cleans and charges the photosensitive drum to prepare it for the image. A laser beam "writes" the data to the drum. Toner is then attracted to the areas of the drum where the laser "wrote" the image. The image is then transferred and bonded to the page for final output. The steps are as follows:

1. **Cleaning**   Before any image formation can occur, the photosensitive drum must be cleaned and electrically erased. For the photosensitive drum to be cleaned, a rubber blade extending the length of the drum gently scrapes away any residual toner left from the previous cycle. If this step were omitted, you would see random specks of black on your printed documents. The toner that is removed is deposited in a debris cavity or recycled in the main toner supply area. Electrical erasure is accomplished by a series of erasure lamps aligned within close proximity of the photosensitive drum. The photosensitive drum is just that—photosensitive. Any light at all will erase the image on the drum. This step ensures that the drum has been electrostatically erased so that it can receive a new image. Now the photosensitive drum is ready for the next step, charging.

2. **Charging**   Charging involves applying a high-voltage negative charge to the photosensitive drum. The voltage can reach as high as −5000Vdc. Because the primary corona wire and the photosensitive

drum share a common ground, applying a large negative charge to the corona wire creates an electrical field between the two. At low voltages, the primary corona would have no effect on the photosensitive drum, but when a high voltage is applied. The air gap between the wire and the drum becomes ionized. This ionization causes negative charges within the drum to migrate to the surface.

3. **Writing**   Now that the photosensitive drum has been prepared, the writing process can begin. A laser sweeps the entire length of the drum, cycling on and off with respect to the image to be created. When the laser is on, it neutralizes the highly negative charge on the drum, making the point where the laser strikes much less negative, almost neutral (approximately -100Vdc). The laser is precisely turned on and off as it sweeps across the drum, optically "writing" the image to the drum.

4. **Developing**   So far, the only evidence of an image in the printer is a series of highly negative and almost neutral charges across the photosensitive drum. The electrostatic image must be converted into a visual image before it can be transferred to the paper. Because the toner is negatively charged by nature, it is attracted to the areas of the photosensitive drum that are less negatively charged. Because the remaining areas of the drum are highly negatively charged, the toner will not be attracted to these areas. Finally, the image is beginning to take form, but we're not there yet.

5. **Transferring**   Once the image has been set in toner on the photosensitive drum, it must be transferred to the print medium, the paper. Because the toner is attracted to the drum, it must be pried away by an even stronger charge to get it onto the paper. A transfer corona is a positively charged wire positioned behind the paper. The transfer corona creates a strong positive charge on the paper sufficient to pull the toner particles from the drum. Once the toner is on the paper, the only force holding it in place is a weak electrostatic charge on the paper and gravity.

6. **Fusing**   Due to the electrostatic properties of toner, it will stick to almost anything. Toner has a negative static charge and the paper has a positive charge. In order to permanently bond the toner particles to the paper, a fusing process must take place. If this step were omitted, the toner would smear and smudge on the page. The paper is pressed firmly between two rollers, one being a non-stick roller. The non-stick roller is heated by a high-intensity lamp, creating the heat necessary to bond the toner to the page.

Thermal Color Printers

Thermal color printers offer a good balance between cost and quality. The quality is high because the inks used in the process don't bleed together or soak into the paper (specially coated paper is required for the best results).

Most color thermal printers have a character-printing thermal head and a half-tone color-image-printing thermal head. The *character-printing thermal head* records a black character on a page by heating the back surface of a black ink film. The *half-tone color-image-printing thermal head* records a color image on the page by heating the back surface of a color ink film having at least cyan, magenta, and yellow ink areas. A heating element of the thermal head of conventional size is used for character printing, and a heating element with a smaller width than that of a conventional thermal head is used for half-tone color image printing.

Alternatively, thermal color printers may use wax inks instead of ink films. This process is similar to the way an InkJet or BubbleJet printer works. Small drops of molten wax are applied to the paper and allowed to cool in order to form the image.

Fonts

All printers work to accomplish the same thing, to put dots on paper. In order for printers and software programs to communicate, there must be a common scheme for deciding where the dots go. An example of one of these schemes is a font. The most common types of fonts are outline and bitmap. Each has its advantages and disadvantages.

Bitmap

Bitmap fonts come in predefined sizes and weights. Think of the size of the font as the height of the font, and the weight as the thickness. A 72-point font is taller (and wider) than a 24-point font. A bold font appears thicker and heavier than a normal font.

Bitmap fonts are usually limited to text and are the fastest way to produce a printed page that uses a small number of typefaces. If your output includes graphics as well as text, then performance will be much slower.

The bitmap is a record of the pattern of dots needed to create a specific character in a certain size with a certain attribute. For example, the bitmaps for a 12-point Times-Roman normal uppercase "A", a 12-point Times-Roman bold uppercase "A", and a 12-point Times-Roman italic uppercase "A" are all different. Multiply all the letters and symbols in the alphabet by the various font sizes, attributes, and typefaces and you can see that storing a wide variety of fonts, sizes, and attributes becomes very costly in terms of space.

Whatever fonts you use to create a document must be stored, at some point, in the printer. Most printers have a few commonly used fonts in firmware. These are fonts like Courier and Line Printer. A printer may also have RAM that can be used for the temporary storage of fonts. If you ever hear someone talking about downloading a font to the printer, you can bet they are talking about moving a copy of that font from the computer to the printer's RAM. Another option for loading fonts into a printer is a font-cartridge. The cartridge contains electronics that store representations of fonts. When you plug the cartridge into the printer, the printer will read the cartridge and use whatever fonts the cartridge contains to create your page.

When the computer has data to send to the printer, the computer first tells the printer which font, size, and attribute to use. This is to make sure the printer uses the right set of bitmaps. The computer then proceeds to send the ASCII code of the characters to be printed. The printer uses the code to look up the bitmap for that character. Once the printer has the bitmap, it can send the needed signals to the print head to recreate the bitmap on the page.

Outline

Outline fonts can be scaled and given attributes. Outline fonts are not limited to specific sizes and attributes. They consist of mathematical descriptions for each character and punctuation mark in the typeface. These types of fonts are called outline fonts because the general outline for a 12-point Times-Roman uppercase "A" is the same for a 72-point Times-Roman uppercase "A."

Consequently, they are commonly used in Page Description Languages (PDL). In a PDL, everything on the page, including text, is treated as a graphic. The printer driver converts the output from text and graphics to a set of commands that can be sent to the printer and used to build the output on the page.

A common PDL that you may have heard of is PostScript. The PostScript language, held in firmware on the printer, receives commands from the PC and converts them into signals that the printer can use to generate the printed page. What the PostScript processor on the printer is actually receiving is a set of mathematical formulas that describe the lines and arcs that make up the characters in the typeface. The commands insert variables into the formulas to change the size and attributes of the outline of the font. For example, a printer might receive the command, "Create a vertical line 6 points wide, which begins at a point 30 dots from the bottom and 20 dots from the right." When commands like this are combined to form a closed character (by creating the outline), then the printer can easily turn on all of the dots inside the outline.

Another major difference between PDLs like PostScript and bitmaps is that a page created using bitmaps is essentially created one character at a time. If an error occurs half-way through the printing of a bitmapped page, chances are that you will get half the page printed at the printer. When using a PDL, an entire page of output is sent to the printer as one large formula (almost like a program). The printer will then process the code and the page will be printed. If an error occurs while the PC is downloading the PDL to the printer, one of two things will happen. Either nothing will print, or page after page of PostScript code will be printed. You will almost be able to read this code, but your page certainly won't look the way you thought it would.

Combining a few typefaces with a few sizes and attributes can create many unique formats. Most printing processes today, including the one used to create this book, use PDLs containing outline fonts. Using a PDL is usually slower than using a bitmap because each individual character on the page is treated as a graphic. However, the system is much more versatile. In order to overcome the performance issues, today's PDL printers are equipped with one or more processors and large amounts of RAM. This allows the printer to receive and process pages of code while it is actually printing a page. The result is a relatively quick, moderately expensive, high-quality printing system.

Common Field Replaceable Units (FRUs)

There are several components that function together to make a printer work. These components make the printer more modular in design. A *modular design* allows components to be easily replaced if they fail. Rather than having to replace the whole printer when it fails, you simply replace the component that failed. As you've read in previous chapters of this book, these components are known as Field-Replaceable Units (FRUs). All printer FRUs are removed and installed differently, so it's important that you consult the manufacturer's guidelines when replacing these components.

Paper-Feed Mechanisms

A paper-feed mechanism is a generic term used to describe the mechanics that move the paper through the printer. There are a variety of paper-feed mechanisms, but most can be classified into one of two categories—continuous form or friction.

CONTINUOUS FORMFEED   Continuous formfeed mechanisms use a continuous piece of paper that has been perforated from the left edge to the right edge, usually at 11-inch intervals. The perforations create the individual sheets of paper. On either side of the paper there is a .5-inch strip of paper that runs the length of the page. There is also perforation between these strips and the print area of the page. Down the middle of each of these strips there is a series of evenly spaced holes. These holes match the pins of either a tractor or sprocket mechanism that is used to advance the paper.

A forms tractor is a belt with stub-shaped pins that push or pull the paper through the printer. The forms-tractor mechanism is often used in printers that print multiple part forms. The holes on the paper are lined up on each of the tractor belts (one on each side of the paper) and a spring-loaded clamp is then snapped into place over each belt. The clamp prevents the paper from lifting off the tractor—particularly useful when using thin multi-part forms.

The sprocket feed is another type of continuous-form paper-feed mechanism. Sprocket feeding is used on most continuous form printers manufactured today. It is less expensive and simpler to build. Sprocket feeding is also referred to as pin feeding. One advantage to pin feeding is that it eliminates paper skew. As we will see in the next section on friction feeding, it is possible to catch one corner of a page slightly before catching the other. The result is that the paper is slightly skewed as it travels through the printer and the print looks as though it were printed at an angle (assuming the paper makes it out of the printer—more often than not, it jams).

The one gotcha to using sprocket feeding is that the paper coming out of the box must be properly aligned with the back of the printer. If the paper box is at an angle, then it is possible to catch the paper on the edges of the box. The paper will either tear at the perforation between sheets, or the sprocket will rip the guide holes. In either case, the paper stops advancing and you have a mess to clean up.

FRICTION FEED   Single-sheet friction feeding has improved greatly over the years. Consequently it is the most popular form of paper-feeding mechanism used today. Friction feeds are used in everything from laser printers to copy machines to fax machines. In the old days, single-sheet friction feeds meant just that—single sheet. You had to feed each sheet into the printer one sheet at a time. Today's modern friction feeds allow you to put multiple sheets of paper in a paper tray and walk away.

A D-shaped roller is used to feed the paper from the top of the stack, and a separator pad or electrostatic bar is used below the paper to prevent more than one page at a time from entering the printer. A series of pressure rollers keep the paper straight and even as it rolls past the printing assembly and is ejected.

Printer Ribbon Types

Although the vast majority of printers sold today are either laser printers or InkJet printers, there are still quite a few dot matrix and even some daisy-wheel printers still being sold. Almost any impact printer (like a dot matrix or daisy wheel) is going to use a print ribbon.

Most ribbons are made from some type of cloth. This isn't the same type of cloth your clothes are made of. This cloth is flexible, durable, and specially designed to hold ink well. The cloth strip is usually between ½-inch and ¾-inch wide and hundreds of inches long. The cloth is fed from one side to the other as the printer is printing. This keeps a fresh piece of cloth in front of the print head at all times. The most common types ribbon feeding mechanisms are reel-to-reel and cartridge.

REEL-TO-REEL   Reel-to-reel mechanisms have been around the longest. They use two separate wheels. One holds the fresh ribbon and the other gathers up the spent ribbon. The wheels are mechanically driven and slowly pull the ribbon from one wheel to the other. When the ribbon reaches the end of one wheel, the wheels reverse direction and the fresh reel becomes the spent wheel and vice versa. This process continues until the ribbon is too depleted to generate quality print.

Two big problems existed with reel-to-reel mechanisms. First, the reels were not encased: they were open to the air. Consequently, they dried out relatively quickly. Second, the reels were often very far apart, sometime as much as twelve inches. Think about two light poles and the lines that run between them. Do they run straight across? They don't. They sag a bit in the center because of the weight of the line. Now, printer ribbons are nowhere near as thick and heavy as power lines, but they obey the same laws of physics. A ribbon that spans a significant distance will sag in the center. Unfortunately, the center is usually exactly where the print head is. What compounds this problem is that after the ribbon has been pulled from one wheel to the next a few times, it becomes a little weaker (the center strip of the ribbon may also have a few hundred thousand minute little holes in it from the print head).

This problem was addressed in a couple of different ways. The first was to increase the tension in the ribbon. That made the mechanisms that drove the wheels work harder, and usually ended up snapping the ribbon when the weakened ribbon was no longer able to support the tension. The second solution was to run the ribbon through a support mechanism (sort of a slot) on either side of the print head. This adequately supported the ribbon, but was a bear for the operator to properly thread, not to mention being very messy. After reading a few thousand complaint letters full on inky finger prints, printer designers went back to the drawing board and came up with the cartridge.

CARTRIDGE   Cartridge ribbons usually have the two ends of the ribbon sewn together to form a continuous loop. Consequently, they have to travel only one direction and require one mechanical drive mechanism. Already the situation has improved by 50%. Another benefit of most cartridge ribbons is that only a tiny piece of the ribbon is exposed at any time. This keeps the ribbon from drying out or picking up dirt.

There are a set of wheels and rollers within the cartridge that keep the ribbon moving smoothly. They are also responsible for collecting the ribbon and packing it inside the cartridge. Some manufacturers put one intentional twist in the ribbon. This twist causes the ribbon to flip once during a full rotation of the ribbon. This allows the print head to hit the ribbon in a slightly different spot on the next pass.

Primary Power Supply Boards or Assemblies

Primary power supply boards provide power to the entire unit. This power is distributed to the various circuits within the printer.

High-Voltage Power Supplies

The EP printing process requires high-voltage electricity. It is the high-voltage power supply that provides this power by stepping up standard AC current (120V and 60 Hz) to the higher voltage required for the printer. This high voltage provides power to the primary corona and the transfer corona.

System (or Main Logic) Boards

The "brain" of the printer is the system board, shown in Figure 5-1. This board houses the Central Processing Unit (CPU), which controls all the input and output within the printer.

Sub Logic Boards

Some printers may contain more than one board in their circuitry. Based on the design of the printer, it may have one or more dependent logic boards, as shown in Figure 5-2, for processing the data.

FIGURE 5-1

Typical printer
system board

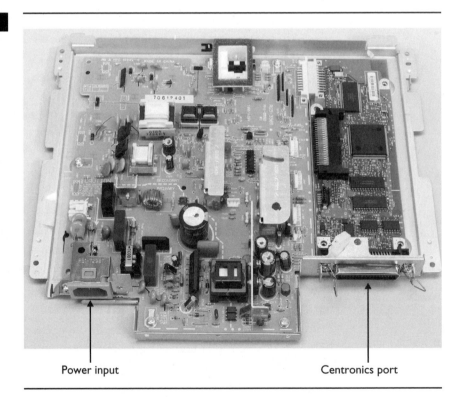

Power input

Centronics port

FIGURE 5-2

A printer's sub logic board

Motors

The voltage is transformed down to approximately 24Vdc to provide power to the various motors used to move the paper through the printer. The main motors that are found within printers are as follows:

- Main drive
- Paper feed
- Transport

Installation of printer motors varies from type to type and model to model, so you must follow the manufacturer's suggested guidelines for installation procedures. Figure 5-3 shows a typical printer motor.

FIGURE 5-3

Typical printer motor

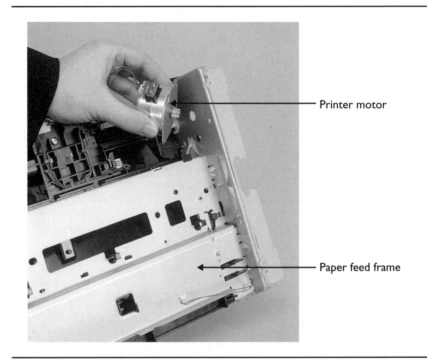

Printer motor

Paper feed frame

Fusers

The fuser consists of three main parts: a halogen heating lamp, a rubberized pressure roller, and a Teflon-coated aluminum fusing roller. The halogen lamp heats the fusing roller to anywhere from 165C to 180C. As the paper passes through the two rollers, the pressure roller forces the paper against the hot fusing roller, bonding the toner to the page.

Rollers

Rollers are located inside the printer to aid in the movement of paper through the printer (see Figures 5-4 and 5-5). There are four main types of rollers: feed, registration, fuser, and exit.

The feed rollers (also known as paper pickup rollers), when activated, rotate against the top page in the paper tray and roll it into the printer. The feed rollers work together with a special rubber pad to prevent more than one sheet from being fed into the printer at a time.

FIGURE 5-4

Printer rollers, front view

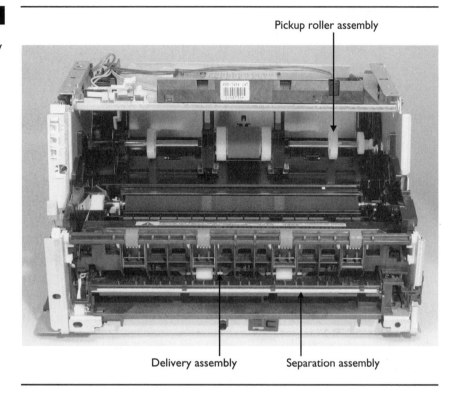

Pickup roller assembly

Delivery assembly   Separation assembly

The registration rollers synchronize the paper movement with the writing process inside the EP printer. The registration rollers do not advance the paper until the EP printer is ready to process the next line of the image.

Fuser rollers, as discussed previously, use a combination of heat and pressure to bond the toner to the paper.

Exit rollers aid in the transfer and control of the paper as it leaves the printer. Depending on the printer type, they direct the paper to a tray where it can be collated, sorted, or even stapled.

Sensors

Sensors may be located in various places within the printer to aid in the paper movement during the printing process. For example, one sensor may detect a paper jam and send a signal to the printer control circuitry to generate an error message.

Printer rollers, side view

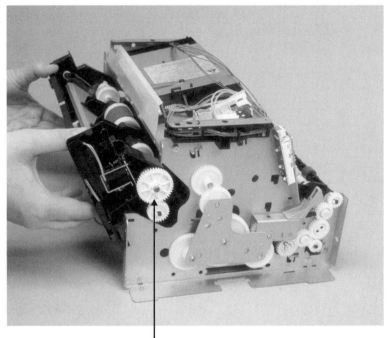

Pickup roller assembly

Switches

Switches (also called DIP switches) provide a means for the user to modify a preset hardware configuration. For example, a DIP switch might control whether the printer defaults to printing in draft mode or letter quality. The use of these switches is diminishing as more and more printers are designed with flashable firmware that allows the printer configuration to be updated with software.

Cables

Cables for the most part are the means of connecting the computer to the printing device. There are normally three separate cable types used to provide the connectivity: parallel, serial, and network.

A parallel cable consists of a male DB-25 connector that plugs into the computer and a male 36-pin Centronics connector that connects to the printer. The recommended length for a parallel cable is ten feet. Lengths any longer than ten feet run the risk of crosstalk, which causes signal degradation and communications to become unreliable.

Serial cables consist of either a DB-9 or DB-25 female connector that plugs into the computer to a DB-25 male connector that plugs into the printer. Because information on a serial cable is traveling along only one wire, serial cables are not as susceptible to crosstalk as are parallel cables, and the cable length can extend up to 25 feet.

Network cables vary from network to network, depending on the media type of the network. Most printers configured with a network interface provide a standard RJ-45 type connector (looks very much like a phone cable). The maximum recommended cable length is specified by the type of network the printer is connected to (for example, a 10BaseT Ethernet network maximum segment length is 100 meters).

Other types of field-replaceable cables may be found inside the printer assembly. These cables may connect power supplies, motors, print heads, and other components to each other as required. The number and type of cables inside the printer can usually be found in the technical manual.

exam
ⓦatch

Minimize your cable lengths for reliable communications. Parallel cables should be limited to 10 feet; serial cables to less than 25 feet.

Print Heads/Toner Cartridges

Print heads and toner cartridges are just about the only FRUs that the printer manufacturer gives the end user responsibility for replacing. Most print quality problems can be remedied by replacement of these components.

RAM SIMMs

Just like a computer, a printer's memory can also be upgraded. Installing additional memory in a printer greatly enhances the amount of information the printer can retain during a print job. This is good news to the computer, because it can resume other applications and processes once the print job has been completely sent to the printer.

Care and Service Techniques

Proper care and service of the printer greatly extends its life and maintains the quality of the documents processed. Like the engine in your car, proper care and maintenance will keep the printer operating and performing like new for many years.

Feed and Output

Most of the problems experienced when operating a printer fall into two major categories: feed and output. Either the printer doesn't properly feed the paper, causing a paper jam, or the quality of the printer output is not as desired. We discuss the common problems experienced in these two areas in the following sections.

Paper Jams

Paper jams are one of the most frequent errors that occur in any machine that processes paper. They occur any time something goes wrong with the paper feeder assembly that would prevent proper feeding of the paper through the printer. They can be caused by the feeder mechanism inadvertently feeding two or more sheets of paper at the same time. Sometimes the paper can be torn and small pieces of paper get lodged in the paper path. Paper jams can happen for a variety of reasons, but are usually easily remedied by opening the printer and removing the faulty page(s). Some printers, especially laser printers, have interactive help that walks you through which compartment or paper tray to open to find the jam.

Print Quality

Print quality is usually affected by the failure of a printing mechanism or from the fact that the printer needs cleaning. Most print-quality issues can

FROM THE FIELD

The Printer Top-10 List

Studies have shown that printer problems account for the most help desk calls. Here are the top ten reasons for these printer calls:

1. Bad driver for the printer installed
2. Dirty rollers
3. Ink or laser cartridges empty
4. Paper jam
5. Bad print job clogging the print queue
6. Poorly formatted document sent to printer
7. Actual mechanical breakage
8. Open paper cabinets, panels, and so forth
9. Network problems (on network printer)
10. Improper media used

Printers can be very confusing for new users. Improper media can practically ruin a printer. Have you ever seen mailing labels sent through an InkJet that rolls the paper instead of keeping it flat? Not a pretty sight or a joy to clean up. The all-too-frequent call about a dead printer that is simply turned off will start to get annoying. Assume nothing when troubleshooting a printer—it could be something really obvious or highly complex. Printer problems may stem from software, network, and cabling problems. There are printer problems that have nothing to do with the printer except for how that particular model of the printer reacts to what is being sent as a print job. Some applications mixed with some operating systems mixed with some network privileges mixed with certain computers mixed with certain printers will have problems. I've seen printer problems so mysterious that all the king's horses and all the king's men and Einstein to boot (plus five MCSEs and TechNet and Microsoft and Hewlett-Packard) could not figure out.

The only solution was to change computers and print the same print job from another computer. Not a total solution but it worked. The more you know about printers and their idiosyncrasies, the more you'll excel in this field.

—*Ted Hamilton, MCSE, MCP, A+ Certified*

be narrowed down to one of these two causes. Print-quality problems vary with each type of printer. Some of the most common ones are covered in the following sections.

Safety Precautions

In addition to observing basic electronic safety precautions, there are a few things to keep in mind when working with printers. All printers are composed of moving parts that advance the paper through the machine. Be sure that you don't have any loose clothing in contact with the parts, or you may find your tie or clothing caught on the plate or other moving parts inside the printer.

Another thing to keep in mind is that components inside a printer can be very dirty. Be careful with your hands around your own clothing and especially around a customer's work area. Everything from ink, toner, and grease is easily spread from one area to another and is difficult to clean.

There are specific tools and measurement equipment provided by the manufacturer for cleaning and to verify proper laser operation. Never take shortcuts with the recommended procedures. Also, some printers have built-in safety interlocks to prevent technicians from injuring themselves. *Never* override an interlocked switch without being advised to do so by the printer service manual.

Preventive Maintenance

One of the easiest ways to ensure trouble-free operation of a printer is by performing periodic preventive maintenance. Although the thought of performing maintenance may not be appealing, taking a few minutes every few months can save you lots of money and unnecessary downtime. Simply put, non-performance of preventive maintenance can lead to expensive, more time-consuming corrective maintenance. As with any piece of equipment you're performing maintenance on, always refer to the procedures outlined in the appropriate user and/or service manuals.

Most printer technical manuals will outline the maintenance that should be performed. The most common types of maintenance include vacuuming, cleaning, lubricating interior components, and general cleanliness of the external case. As you've learned, each printer is designed and put together differently, requiring different methods of cleaning and troubleshooting. Keep this in mind as you work on a printer. When in doubt, follow the manufacturer's recommended procedure.

Laser Printers

Print-quality problems that can occur with laser printers include the following:

- Blank pages
- Speckled pages
- Ghosted images
- Smudged images

Blank Pages

There's nothing more frustrating than sending a print job to a printer and having it spew out page after page of nothing. Most of the time, this is caused by an application on the computer sending corrupt data, but there are other reasons a laser printer may send blank pages:

- **No toner**   If there's no toner in the cartridge, no images will be transferred to the page.

- **Transfer corona failure**   If this wire fails, no toner will be attracted from the photosensitive drum to the paper.

- **HVPS failure**   If the high-voltage power supply isn't providing the voltage necessary to either the primary corona or transfer corona, the printing process will not work correctly.

Speckled Pages

Sometimes a print job may result in little specks of black on the page, random or not. This may be due to a failure of the cleaning step of the EP printing process. Another cause may be a scratch or defect in the EP drum, causing toner to remain in these recesses during the cleaning step.

Ghosted Images

Ghosting occurs when a portion of the image previously printed to the page is printed again, only not as dark. One cause of this is if the erasure lamp fails to operate correctly, not completely erasing the previous image from the EP drum. Another cause of ghosting may be due to a malfunction in the cleaning blade such that it doesn't adequately scrape away the residual toner.

Smudged Images

If an image smudges, then an element of the fusing process has failed. This could be a result of the halogen lamp burning out, failing to melt the toner to the page.

BubbleJet

The majority of problems experienced with BubbleJet printers are print-quality issues. Most of these issues can be resolved by replacing the ink cartridge. If the printer sits idle for a prolonged period of time (a week or more), the ink can dry out in the print-head nozzles and clog them.

A corrective measure for a dry ink cartridge should never be refilling the ink cartridge! Replacing the cartridge not only replenishes the ink, but replaces the old worn-out nozzles with new ones.

Dot Matrix

Dot matrix print-quality issues normally boil down to two things: ribbon replacement or print head replacement. If the output is beginning to fade, it is time to change the ink ribbon. If there are white horizontal streaks on your page, this indicates that a pin is not firing, requiring the print head to be replaced.

CERTIFICATION OBJECTIVE 5.03

Printer Connections and Configurations

There are a variety of ways to provide a connection between your computer and the printing device. Current connections make use of the ports available on the back of your machine, and, if you're on a network, a network connection. There are three major types of connection methods: parallel, serial, and network. A connection method that is not yet as common but has its place in this section is infrared, which is discussed briefly. Other connection methods may be available, but are not as commonly used as the methods discussed here.

Parallel

Most printers are configured to communicate via the parallel port. The parallel port consists of a 25-pin connection that allows transmitting of information along eight different wires (hence parallel). When a printer uses parallel communications, it transmits 1 bit per wire, giving it the ability to transmit 8 bits at a time (1 byte). The parallel port allows for fast communication, which is needed especially when transmitting complex images and graphics to the printer.

Parallel communication is the most common way of getting data from a PC to a printer. In the early days, engineers evaluated the use of serial communication for printing but determined that serial communications would be too slow. *Serial communication* allows only one bit of data to be transferred to the printer at a time.

Parallel communication has remained virtually the same since the early days of PC computing. This is primarily for backward compatibility with old devices. The maximum transmission speed over a parallel port is about 150 kilobytes per second. That's about three times as fast as your 56K modem, a serial device. However, that's not even close to the speed of today's LANs. Another issue with parallel ports that affects speed is the software. Parallel operations require a lot of software support and that software competes with your applications for precious CPU cycles.

Standards are another issue. There are published standards that address parallel operations, but they are not universally accepted and implemented. If you bought parallel cables from two different manufacturers, there would be a good chance that those cables would have different electromagnetic properties. Depending on your environment, one cable might work and the other might not.

Finally, true bidirectional support is lacking in parallel communications. That wasn't much of an issue when all we needed to do was shove data down the pipe to a simple line printer. However, when we start dealing with intelligent devices like scanners, zip drives, and laser printers this lack of good two-way communication becomes a limiting factor that affects what these devices can do.

In the rest of this section we are going to discuss the evolution of parallel communications. We'll define some of the acronyms you might see associated with parallel communication, and we'll take a look at the hardware. We will also address some of the standards.

IEEE 1284 Standard

The IEEE 1284 standard was proposed in 1991 by a group of computer hardware manufacturers and is commonly associated with the bidirectional aspects of parallel communication. The standard attempts to address the issues of performance and compatibility while ensuring backward compatibility.

The requirements set forth by the IEEE 1284 standard are as follows:

- Support for five modes of operation (compatibility mode, nibble mode, byte mode, EPP, and ECP)

- A method of negotiation between PC and device used to determine which modes of operation are supported

- A standard physical interface (for example, cables and connections)

- A standard electrical interface (for example, termination and impedance)

In a parallel cable, there are many data wires. However, all the data wires work together as a set so communications can occur in only one direction at a time. This is often referred to as *half-duplex mode*. The IEEE 1284 standard is a half-duplex standard.

Centronics

Parallel cables are often referred to as Centronics cables. Centronics is a standard that specifies a cable with a DB-25 (25 pins) male connection on one end and a 36-pin female connection on the other end. Eight wires are used as grounds: four for control signals, five for status signals, and eight for data signals. So, out of 25 wires, 8 of them are carrying real data and the other 17 represent overhead. Are you beginning to see the problem?

The advantage to Centronics is backward compatibility. However, the disadvantages are many. Data passes in only one direction, the CPU must constantly poll the status wires, and the entire system is limited to about 150 kilobytes per second.

Some manufacturers have addressed the performance of the original Centronics standard by implementing what is known as Fast Centronics. A Fast Centronics port includes a buffering mechanism implemented in the hardware that receives the data from the PC and then takes over the process of delivering the data to the printer. As far as the PC is concerned the data got there as soon as it reached the buffer. The PC no longer has to manage all the communications overhead. Using Fast Centronics can yield transfer speeds of up to 500 kilobytes per second. When buying equipment, look for parallel ports that support both standard Centronics and Fast Centronics.

Nibble Mode

Nibble mode refers to one process for sending data from a device to a PC. It is the simplest method because it requires no special hardware and can be used with any parallel port. Nibble mode does not require an IEEE 1284 parallel port. Nibble mode uses the five status wires (actually it uses four of the five) to send a byte of data back to the PC in two four-bit chunks called "nibbles."

Nibble mode is very CPU-intensive because of all the interrupts and the need to reassemble the bits into bytes. With all of the additional overhead involved, the realistic transmission rate is about 50 kilobytes per second. This is probably sufficient for most printer operations, but it is a severely limiting factor for any other type of device.

Enhanced Bidirectional Port (Byte Mode)

As higher performance and more powerful peripherals began to hit the market, it was obvious to engineers that a faster bidirectional transfer mechanism was required. PC makers began to add data transfer modes to their parallel communications configurations. Byte mode was one of the first methods.

Byte mode allows reverse direction parallel communication using all eight data wires. Additional hardware is added to the parallel ports of the PC and the device to handle the negotiations. By using Byte mode full parallel communications in either direction can be achieved at the normal 150 kilobyte per second transfer rate.

Byte mode is sometimes referred to as an enhanced bidirectional port. Try not to confuse Byte mode and the more advanced parallel ports that we will discuss in a moment. Byte mode is far less capable than an advanced parallel port, but it may be the only option on older devices that do not support the full IEEE 1284 standard.

Enhanced Parallel Port (EPP)

This mode was designed for devices that need constant two-way communications with the PC. The EPP protocol offers high-speed transfers with relatively low communications overhead. As with earlier modes, handshaking and synchronization (the majority of the overhead) is handled in hardware.

One advantage (or disadvantage depending on your point of view) is that the EPP protocol offers tight control over the communications process. The software program that is using the parallel port must maintain control of the port. This is good for programs that must quickly switch between send and receive modes. The downside is of course the overhead. However, even with a little extra overhead, EPP still achieves transfer rates, similar to an ISA bus—between 500 kilobytes and 2 megabytes per second.

A word of caution: the original EPP parallel port was developed before the IEEE 1284 committee finished defining the standard. As a result, there are minor differences between pre-standard EPP ports and standard EPP ports that can cause communication failures between standard EPP PCs and pre-standard EPP devices.

Extended Capability Port (ECP)

ECP was developed jointly between Microsoft and Hewlett-Packard to address the special needs of devices like high-speed laser printers and scanners. These devices require fast bidirectional communications, but the communication direction is primarily from the device to the PC.

Compared to EPP, ECP transfers are loosely coupled. That means that once the transfer has begun, the software that initiated the transfer does not monitor the transfer. Instead, the software waits for a signal that indicates that the transfer has completed. This reduces the amount of control that the software has over the process, but it also reduces the number of CPU cycles dedicated to moving data. The ECP process is ideal for moving large chunks of data in the background. This makes it ideal for printers and scanners.

ECP ports use a data compression algorithm called *Run-Length-Encoding (RLE)* that can compress data up to 64%. This increases the overall throughput significantly. RLE is not actually part of the IEEE 1284 standard, but it is part of the Microsoft standard for implementing the ECP protocol.

Another feature of ECP ports is the ability to control multifunction devices such as printer/fax or printer/scanner devices. A technique called *channel addressing* is used in conjunction with a Centronics or nibble-mode connection to determine the status of a device. The result is that if one set of functions is busy, other sets are still available. This is how a printer/fax machine can print a document and receive a document at the same time.

Remember that both ECP and EPP are implemented in hardware, which means that hardware manufacturers can implement any performance enhancements they want to as long as they adhere to the protocol standards. ECP and EPP are in many ways a layer of abstraction between hardware manufacturers and software developers.

Connections and Cables

A *standard parallel cable* usually refers to a cable that has a DB-25 male connector on one end and a 36-pin Centronics connector on the other. See Figure 5-6 for examples of cable connectors. The electromagnetic properties of the standard parallel cable are largely undefined. Usually the cable is good for transmissions of up to ten kilobytes per second for up to 6 feet. Good enough for slow dot matrix printers but not even close to being good enough for ECP or EPP operations.

The standard that you want to look for when buying cables is the IEEE 1284-1994 standard. Cables that are compliant with this standard will support data throughput high enough to support ECP and EPP operations. These cables will also support distances of up to ten meters.

FIGURE 5-6

Three types of parallel
cable connectors

Type A DB25   Type B Centronics   Type C
Mini-Centronics

Serial

Some printers can be configured to communicate via the serial port. When
a printer uses serial communication, it transmits one bit at a time along a
single wire. Similarly to modems, the serial port must be configured with
communication parameters (bps, parity, start and stop bits, and so forth)
on both the printer and the computer before communication can occur.

The serial port consists of either a 25-pin or 9-pin connection that allows
transmitting of information along a single wire. The bits are sent one after
another in a single-file line. Because there is only a single wire carrying the
transmission, serial cables are not as susceptible to cross talk as parallel
cables are. Cable lengths for serial cables may extend up to 25 feet with
no signal attenuation.

Network

Some of the newer printers on the market have a network interface that
allows them to be accessed via a network. These printers come equipped
with a Network Interface Card (NIC) that allows them to be plugged
directly into the network. ROM-based software allows the printer to
communicate with the servers and workstations on the network.

Because virtually everyone in an office environment needs access to a
printer, buying a printer for each workstation is not the most economic
solution. Networked environments allow many different users to share

printer resources, saving thousands of dollars on printer costs. Printers can be shared when plugged into a workstation through the parallel or serial port, but this requires that the workstation be up and running in order to share that resource.

Infrared

A recent development in printer technology now allows data communications to exist over a beam of light. Some laptops are equipped with an infrared serial port that allows transmission to any device that has an infrared port just as if you were physically connected. This is a line-of-sight technology, which requires that the transmitting port be directed to the infrared interface on the printer. We will not go into great detail in this method of printer communication but you should know that the method is available.

CERTIFICATION SUMMARY

There are a variety of ways of presenting information on the written page. Having an understanding of the different printing technologies and a logical method of troubleshooting problems when they arise will not only help you out on the A+ examination, but is invaluable information for a technician in the computer industry. The majority of what you will learn about printers will more than likely be from hands-on experience, where the printer's technical manual should be your guide.

 # TWO-MINUTE DRILL

- ❏ A printer is simply an electromechanical device designed to translate electronic impulses into a format that it can understand and transfer to a page.
- ❏ Printers can be classified into two major groups: impact and non-impact.
- ❏ Daisy-wheel printers have a wheel with raised letters and symbols on them that looks like a daisy, which is how the printers got their name.

❑ One advantage of daisy-wheel printers is that they are capable of creating multi-part forms, which are still used by businesses today.

❑ In the font mode of a dot matrix printer, the printer already has all the pins programmed for every character in its font set. In dot-addressable mode, each printed dot requires an input.

❑ The print head on a dot matrix printer is a series of pins each controlled by its own solenoid (or resistive coil), which is similar in function to the solenoid on a daisy-wheel printer.

❑ The earliest dot matrix print heads had 7 pins, whereas printers today have up to 24.

❑ By use of small nozzles on the print head, a BubbleJet printer "spraypaints" the image onto the page.

❑ Replacing the ink cartridges on a BubbleJet printer not only provides the printer with a fresh source of ink, but it replaces the nozzles that get worn out by the BubbleJet process.

❑ Using a combination of light, electricity, chemistry, pressure, and heat, laser printers have the ability to create high-quality images and text on the printed page.

❑ Laser printers are also referred to as page printers because they receive their print job instructions one page at a time.

❑ The main components of a laser printer are cleaning blade, photosensitive drum, primary corona wire, transfer corona, toner, and fusing rollers.

❑ The six-step EP process is as follows: Cleaning, Charging, Writing, Developing, Transferring, and Fusing. Know this process!

❑ During the Cleaning step of the EP process, the toner that is removed is deposited in a debris cavity or recycled in the main toner supply area.

❑ The Charging step of the EP process involves applying a high-voltage negative charge to the photosensitive drum. The voltage can reach as high as −5000Vdc.

❑ In the six-step EP process, an image begins to appear in the Developing step.

❑ In order to permanently bond the toner particles to the paper in the laser printing process, a fusing process must take place.

❑ The main motors that are found within printers are the main drive, paper feed, and transport motors.

❑ The fuser consists of three main parts: a halogen heating lamp, a rubberized pressure roller, and a Teflon-coated aluminum fusing roller.

❑ There are four main types of rollers: feed, registration, fuser, and exit.

❑ Switches (also called DIP switches) provide a means for the user to modify a preset hardware configuration to meet his or her particular needs for the printer.

❑ There are normally three separate cable types used to provide printer connectivity: parallel, serial, and network.

❑ A parallel cable consists of a male DB-25 connector that plugs into the computer and a male 36-pin Centronics connector that connects to the printer.

❑ Minimize your cable lengths for reliable communications. Parallel cables should be limited to ten feet; serial cables to less than 25 feet.

❑ Most print-quality problems can be remedied by replacement of the print head or toner cartridges.

❑ Most of the problems experienced when operating a printer fall into two major categories: feed and output.

❑ Fast Centronics is not part of the IEEE 1284 standard.

❑ An enhanced bidirectional port is only a port that is capable of byte mode. Do not confuse it with an enhanced parallel port (EPP).

❑ IEEE-1284 devices that use EPP might not work with EPP parallel ports produced before the IEEE-1284 standard.

❑ Just because a device supports some of the IEEE-1284 modes of operation, does not mean that it complies with all aspects of the standard.

SELF TEST

The following Self Test questions will help you measure your understanding of the material presented in this chapter. Read all the choices carefully, as there may be more than one correct answer. Choose all correct answers for each question.

1. In the _____ phase of the EP printing process the photosensitive drum is erased.

   A. Charging
   B. Cleaning
   C. Writing
   D. Developing

2. In the _____ phase of the EP printing process a laser sweeps the entire length of the drum, cycling on and off with respect to the image to be printed.

   A. Charging
   B. Cleaning
   C. Writing
   D. Developing

3. In the _____ phase of the EP printing process toner is attracted to the areas of the photosensitive drum that are negatively charged.

   A. Writing
   B. Developing
   C. Fusing
   D. Transferring

4. In the _____ phase of the EP printing process the toner that is on the drum is attracted to the paper with the help of the positively-charged transfer corona.

   A. Writing
   B. Developing
   C. Fusing
   D. Transferring

5. In the _____ phase of the EP printing process the toner is permanently bonded to the paper with intense heat and pressure.

   A. Writing
   B. Developing
   C. Fusing
   D. Transferring

6. Which of the following is the most common interface used for printing?

   A. Parallel
   B. IDE
   C. Serial
   D. Network

7. The most likely cause for random specks of ink on a laser printed page is:

   A. Improper voltage on corona wire
   B. Parallel cable too long
   C. Photosensitive drum dirty
   D. Improper paper type

8. _____ occurs when a portion of the print image from a previous print job is printed again, only not as dark.

   A. Shadowing
   B. Ghosting
   C. Stippling
   D. Image latency

9. _____ is the generic term used to describe a class of printers that squirt ink onto a page in tiny drops.

   A. BubbleJet
   B. DeskJet
   C. InkJet
   D. SquirtJet

10. A _____ cable has a DB-25 male connection on one end and a 36-pin female connection on the other.

    A. Serial
    B. RJ-45
    C. Centronics
    D. Ribbon

11. The _____ mechanism is responsible for moving the paper from the paper tray, through the printer, and into the output tray.

    A. Motor
    B. Paper feed
    C. Logic board
    D. Power supply

12. The _____ consists of three main parts: a halogen heating lamp, a rubberized pressure roller, and a Teflon-coated non-stick roller.

    A. Motor
    B. Fuser
    C. Transformer
    D. Power supply

13. Concerning the EP printing process, the primary corona wire has a _____ charge, the transfer corona has a _____ charge, and toner naturally has a _____ charge.

    A. negative, positive, positive
    B. positive, negative, negative
    C. negative, positive, negative
    D. positive, positive, negative

14. What does PDL stand for?

    A. Printer-Defined Language
    B. Page Description Language
    C. Paper Driver Latch
    D. Printer Device Logic

15. A _____ is used to "fire" each pin in a print head so that the pin will impact with the ribbon and the paper to leave a dot.

    A. Capacitive coil
    B. Resistive coil
    C. Solenoid
    D. Spring coil

16. A(n) _____ is a type of font in which every character in the font-set is predefined. This makes this type of font easy for a printer to process, but limits the user's options.

    A. Bitmap
    B. PDL
    C. Raster
    D. Outline

17. A(n) _____ is a type of font that is defined as a set of mathematical algorithms. This makes this type of font processor intensive, but increases the user's options.

    A. Bitmap
    B. PDL
    C. Raster
    D. Outline

18. Laser printers and jet type printers primarily use a _____ paper feed mechanism to move the paper through the printer.

    A. Tractor feed
    B. Friction feed
    C. Sprocket feed
    D. Continuous form feed

19. A(n) _____ printer is necessary to print multi-part forms.

    A. Laser
    B. Dot matrix
    C. Impact
    D. InkJet

20. _____ is a parallel communications protocol that was developed jointly by Microsoft and Hewlett-Packard to address the special needs of devices like high-speed laser printers and scanners.

    A. EPP
    B. ECP
    C. IEEE-1284
    D. Enhanced parallel

21. _____ is a parallel communications protocol in which the software program that is using a parallel port must maintain control of the port making it ideal for programs that must quickly switch between send and receive modes.

    A. EPP
    B. ECP
    C. IEEE-1284
    D. Enhanced parallel

22. _____ allows reverse direction parallel communication using all eight data wires.

    A. Nibble mode
    B. Byte mode
    C. Data transfer mode
    D. Switching mode

23. _____ allows reverse direction parallel communication using four of the signaling wires to transfer a byte of data in two chunks.

   A. Nibble mode

   B. Byte mode

   C. Data transfer mode

   D. Switching mode

24. A(n) _____ port includes a buffering mechanism implemented in the hardware that receives the data from the PC and then takes over the process of delivering the data to the printer.

   A. Fast Centronics

   B. IEEE-1284

   C. Parallel

   D. Centronics

25. The _____ standard was proposed in 1991 by a group of computer hardware manufacturers and is commonly associated with the bidirectional aspects of parallel communication.

   A. RS-232

   B. RJ-45

   C. IEEE-1284

   D. IEEE-1024

6

Portable Systems

P ortable computing represents a rapidly growing and specialized niche in the computer industry. In many offices today, portable computers are replacing the desktop PC as the computer of choice. Portable systems include any computer that is built with portability in mind. This includes laptops, notebooks, and sub-notebooks. Servicing these unique computers requires a skill set beyond what is necessary to service desktop computers. Each portable computer, even between different models from the same vendor, is slightly different. In this chapter, we discuss some of the many components that are unique to the world of portable computing.

Because manufacturers are constantly driven to make components smaller and smaller, very few standards exist in the world of the portable. As a result, portable computers are all very proprietary. Steps are being taken to make components more interoperable, but we are still a long way from where the desktop PC industry is in terms of standards. Some components are not even compatible between different portable computers from the same vendor. Also, repairs and upgrades to portable computers remain much more expensive compared to desktop PCs.

As with the rest of the computer industry, portable computer technology is rapidly evolving. Almost as soon as one system is released, another is under development to replace it.

CERTIFICATION OBJECTIVE 6.01

Battery Types and Installation

Portable computers need power when a standard AC power source is not available. This power comes from rechargeable batteries. These batteries provide DC power when the portable is not connected to an external AC power source and are recharged when they are connected to an AC source. There are many types of batteries currently used in portable computers.

Nickel cadmium (NiCad) batteries are rarely used in portable computers today. NiCad batteries must be recharged more often than other batteries, and a full recharge can take up to 12 hours. Furthermore, when a NiCad

FROM THE FIELD

Laptop Versus Desktop

If you are contemplating buying a laptop or recommending one to someone else, there are several issues to consider. Laptops have unique repair issues. For one thing, the components are harder to work with because they are smaller. Often, special tools are required. You will not be able to do some of the things that you are used to doing with a desktop PC.

For example, you cannot slave the drive to a desktop, nor swap out any parts to test them unless you have another similar laptop. Consequently, most repairs you will do are on desktops. Finally, because of the expense associated with laptops, it can be tough to find an extra one lying around to use for spare parts.

Pros of a Laptop

- Portable

- All-in-one components

- Ability to use docking stations

- Does not take up much space

- Better resale value

Cons of a Laptop

- Easily dropped or stolen

- Less computing power

- Harder to repair or upgrade

- Components are more expensive

- Screen, mouse, and keyboard not as good

—*Ted Hamilton, MCSE, MCP, A+ Certified*

battery is recharged before it is fully discharged, the battery loses the ability to fully recharge again. This symptom is known as the *memory effect*. Also, NiCad batteries contain cadmium, which is highly toxic. Finally, NiCad batteries are limited to about 1000 recharges.

Nickel/metal hydride (NiMH) batteries offer several advantages over NiCad batteries. Compared to the same size NiCad, a NiMH battery can produce 33-50 percent more power. Advances in NiMH technologies have all but erased the memory effect. NiMH batteries are also more environmentally friendly because they do not contain heavy metals.

Lithium ion (LiIon) is the best computer battery commercially available. LiIon batteries, although slightly more expensive than NiMH batteries, offer many advantages. A smaller, lighter LiIon battery can produce more power than a NiMH battery. LiIon batteries are also becoming available in high-end cellular phones and video camcorders.

exam
Watch

Portable computer batteries must be disposed of properly. Check the label on the battery and then check with local agencies for disposal directions. Do not just throw batteries in the trash!

Installation of batteries in portables is easy for the end user, as demonstrated in Figure 6-1. Many people buy a second battery that they keep charged to use as a spare. Most batteries either install from the bottom or the side. Many have an easy-to-remove plastic cover that must be removed first. Generally, there is a row of contacts on the battery itself that meet with spring-loaded contacts inside the computer. If a battery is not charging properly, it may help to clean these contacts.

If you replace a battery in a portable computer, do not just throw it away! Consult your local waste management company to find out local requirements for battery disposal.

With many different types of batteries available, which one should you use? LiIon is the best choice if it is available, although it is slightly more expensive. NiMH is more common and less expensive, but is slightly heavier and produces less power. Stay away from NiCad batteries if at all possible.

AC Adapter

Each portable computer comes with an AC adapter. This *AC adapter* serves two roles. The first is to convert either 110v-AC or 220v-AC to DC to run the portable computer. The second and equally important role is to recharge the battery. AC adapters come in two types, with either an internal or external power transformer. An internal transformer adds weight and bulk to the portable, but is more convenient than carrying an external transformer.

AC adapters for different models and manufacturers of computers have varying output voltage. Before testing, check with the manufacturer to determine the proper voltage. If a computer is not charging properly, it is easy to replace the AC adapter with another and see if that solves the problem.

FIGURE 6-1

Installing a portable
system battery

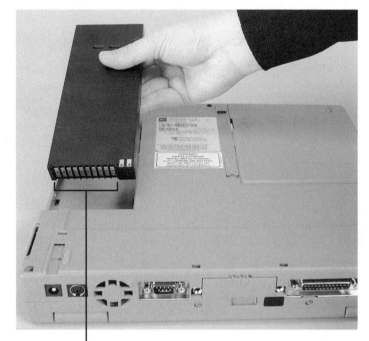

Battery contacts

Portable Displays

Portable displays have come a long way in ten years. Older portable computers actually used a Cathode Ray Tube (CRT) for a display. These behemoths were about the size of a small suitcase! Imagine, having a "portable" computer that is too big to fit in the overhead bin on an airplane. Fortunately, we now have flat *Liquid Crystal Displays (LCD)* that are thinner, lighter, and require much less power than the small CRTs from ten years ago.

Two major types of LCD displays dominate the market in laptop computers today. The major differences between the two are in the quality of the image displayed, the amount of power used, and the cost of manufacturing.

Passive matrix displays used to be the most common form of laptop display. They are cheaper to produce and draw far less power than active matrix displays. Passive matrix displays are easily recognized by poor display quality when viewing the screen from an angle.

Passive matrix displays are made of a grid of horizontal and vertical wires. At the end of each wire is a transistor. In order to light a pixel at (X, Y), a signal is sent to the X and Y transistors. In turn, these transistors then send voltage down the wire, which turns on the LCD at the intersection of the two wires.

Passive matrix screens have problems with images that change quickly. This is very apparent when a mouse pointer is moved quickly across the screen. The cursor will fade from view, and then appear again once the movement has stopped. In fact, Microsoft added the mouse trails option in Windows primarily so people wouldn't lose their cursors on passive matrix displays.

Active matrix displays provide much better image quality at the expense of higher energy consumption and higher cost. Active matrix displays are based on *Thin Film Transistor (TFT)* technology. Instead of having two sets of transistors, active matrix displays have a transistor at every pixel. This allows much quicker display changes and produces display quality comparable to a CRT.

Just like a traditional CRT display, LCD displays need to be cleaned often. This should be done with a damp cloth or a cleaner specifically designed for cleaning computer displays. Be careful not to drip moisture into the keyboard or other parts of the portable when cleaning the display, as it may have undesirable results.

LCD displays are not serviceable. If an LCD display is damaged or broken, it must be replaced. This can be extremely expensive, as the parts will need to come from the original manufacturer. Active matrix screens can easily cost more than $1,000 to replace.

Docking Stations

Docking stations allow users to add desktop-like capabilities to their portable computer. Most people would prefer to use a larger monitor and a full-size keyboard when they are available, especially when in the office or at home. A docking station provides an easy and quick way for people to do this, and at the same time, allows expansion of the portable in ways that would otherwise be impossible, such as adding PCI or ISA slots.

Normally, if a user wanted to use an external monitor, keyboard, or mouse, they would have to plug each one into the portable computer each time that they wished to use it. They would also need to have the appropriate connector available on the portable itself. Then, when they wanted to take the portable computer with them, they would have to unplug all of the peripherals they were using. This is both cumbersome and inconvenient. Over time it may also damage the connectors on the laptop by loosening the pins or creating micro fractures in the circuitry close to the connectors.

A *docking station* allows a user to install their monitor, external keyboard, and mouse to the docking station. Then, whenever they wish to use these peripherals, they can simply connect their portable computer to the docking station. This is a much more convenient way to use full-size peripherals when in the office.

Some operating systems (OSs) automatically detect when the portable computer is installed with a docking station. The OS then uses the appropriate hardware settings and user preferences for your docking station. This is extremely convenient, especially for changing screen resolutions for different displays.

Port replicators are the cheapest and simplest version of the three types of docking stations. Most portable computers have external VGA, keyboard, and serial connections. Port replicators simply provide a copy of the interfaces that already exist on the back of the portable computer. Port replicators often ship with a second power cable so the user can leave it plugged into the port replicator. Port replicators are generally the least expensive way to provide a docking station for your portable, and for most people this is more than enough.

Enhanced port replicators extend the capabilities of port replicators slightly by adding interfaces not available in the portable computer. For example, extended port replicators often add enhanced sound capabilities and more PC Card slots.

A true docking station gives your portable the greatest amount of expandability and power. Docking stations can give your portable all of the same capabilities usually found in a desktop computer. In addition to everything you get with an enhanced port replicator, docking stations may add ISA slots, PCI slots, and SCSI or EIDE capabilities. They may also provide for full-size drive bays for installing full-size hard drives and CD-ROM drives.

A portable computer that has docking capabilities usually does so via a proprietary interface somewhere on the back. Unfortunately, this means that a docking station for one computer will usually not work with a different type of computer, even from the same manufacturer.

Each manufacturer provides slightly different features with their docking stations, and some features available from one manufacturer may not be available from another. Please consult your manufacturer's guidelines for installing a docking station. Figure 6-2 shows what a docking station typically looks like.

Hard Drive

Portable computers employ some of the same standards in hard drives as desktop PCs. Unfortunately, this conformance to standards applies only to the signal, and not the physical interfaces used. Most portable computers at the time of this writing are shipping with 2.5-inch EIDE or UDMA hard drives. Manufacturers use different interfaces and different footprints. To replace a hard drive in a portable computer follow the steps in Exercise 6-1.

FIGURE 6-2

A portable computer and a
docking station

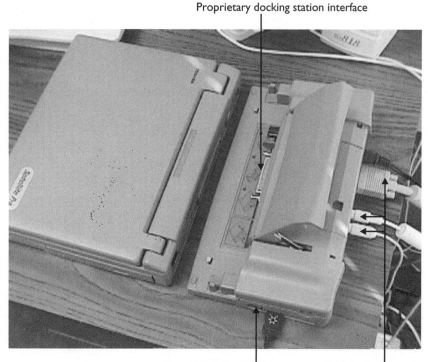

Proprietary docking station interface

Type III PC Card slots

Keyboard, mouse,
VGA connectors

EXERCISE 6-1

Replacing a Hard Drive

1. Usually there is a small plastic cover underneath the computer that
   must be removed.

2. Once the cover has been removed, a few screws usually hold the
   hard drive in place.

3. Be careful not to bend the male connectors when removing the
   hard drive.

4. Insert the new hard drive, again being careful not to bend the
   connectors.

5. Replace the screws.

6. Replace the cover.

Figure 6-3 shows the removal of a typical portable hard drive.

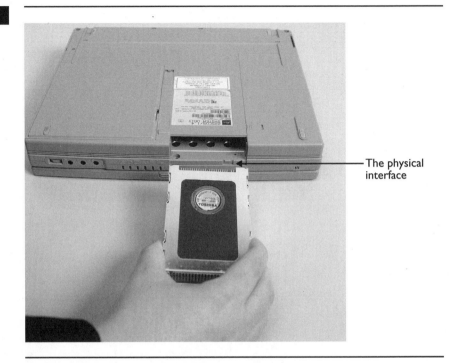

FIGURE 6-3

Removing a hard drive
from a portable system

The physical
interface

CERTIFICATION OBJECTIVE 6.04

PCMCIA and PC Cards

The PCMCIA, or PC Card interface, defines a standard interface to add credit-card-sized peripherals to PCs. *PCMCIA* actually refers to the *Personal Computer Memory Card International Association*, the non-profit organization that defines the specifications for these credit-card-sized peripherals. PCMCIA was founded in 1989 by a consortium of vendors to create and maintain these standards and guarantee interoperability.

The 1.0 version of the PCMCIA specification was released in June 1990, and was originally intended only for memory cards. PCMCIA version 1.0

defined the 68-pin interface that we currently use as well as the physical specifications for the Type I and Type II cards.

The 2.*x* release of the PCMCIA standards expanded the features of the same 68-pin interface and added support for Type III PC Cards. Type III cards are generally reserved for rotating mass storage, such as hard drives. PCMCIA 2.*x* is backward compatible with PCMCIA 1.0 PC Cards.

In 1995, PCMCIA released the latest standard, officially using the name "PC Card." All PCMCIA cards are now referred to as PC Cards. This latest specification added support for DMA, Bus Mastering, Zoomed Video (ZV), and 32-bit CardBus operation. ZV is a direct data connection between a PC Card and host system that allows a PC Card to write video data directly to the video controller. The 32-bit CardBus specification allows speeds of up to 133 Mbps at 33 MHz.

The PC Card specification defines PC Cards as having a length of 85.6 mm and a width of 54.0 mm. Type I cards are the thinnest, measuring only 3.3 mm thick and are generally used only for memory. Type II cards are 5.0 mm thick and are generally used for I/O devices such as modems, network adapters, or SCSI adapters. Type III cards are 10.5 mm thick and are usually used for mass storage devices such as removable hard drives. Most portable computers now come with at least one built-in Type III slot. Some OSs support hot-swapping PC Card devices. This means that you can swap PC Card devices without rebooting your computer.

exam
ⓦatch

All PC Cards are 85.6 mm by 54.0 mm. Type I cards are 3.3 mm thick, Type II are 5.0 mm thick, and Type III are 10.5 mm thick.

Socket Services is a layer of BIOS level software that isolates PC Card software from the computer hardware and detects the insertion or removal of PC Cards. *Card Services* software manages the allocation of system resources such as memory and interrupts automatically once the Socket Services software detects that a card has been inserted in the PC Card slot. If your operating system does not come with support for PC Card services, check with the manufacturer of the hardware for support.

The PCMCIA is continuing to develop new technologies for PC Cards. PC Cards are also useful in other electronic devices besides computers. Many digital cameras now use PC Cards for storage. Figure 6-4 shows the simple installation of a PC Card. Uses for PC Cards today include the following:

- CD-ROM interface
- Cellular phone interface
- Smart Card readers
- Ethernet LAN adapters
- GPS (Global Positioning System) cards
- Hard drives
- ISDN cards
- Memory cards
- Modem/Ethernet combination cards
- Modem cards
- Parallel port interface
- SCSI adapters
- Sound cards, input, and output
- Token ring LAN adapter cards

FIGURE 6-4

Installing a PC Card in a portable system

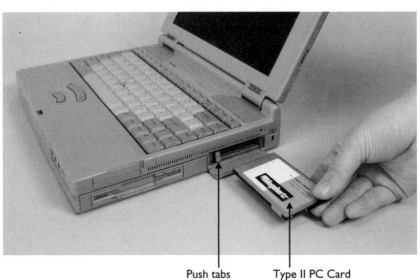

Push tabs   Type II PC Card

Memory Upgrades

One of the most frequently upgraded components in portable computers is memory. Most portables have some RAM on the motherboard. Manufacturers usually provide a proprietary expansion slot for additional RAM. Memory may also be added in the form of a PC Card. The manufacturer should provide documentation on installing additional memory. This is generally a simple task. An example is shown in Figure 6-5. However, should the memory on the motherboard itself go bad, it may be necessary to replace the entire motherboard.

FIGURE 6-5

Installing computer memory

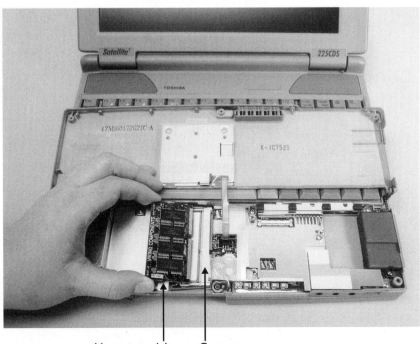

Memory module   Contacts

Pointing Devices

Pointing devices for portable computers differ slightly from their desktop counterparts. Manufacturers have come up with some ingenious ways to provide the same functionality as a desktop mouse, but with a much smaller footprint. We discuss the three most common types of pointing devices, their advantages, disadvantages, and maintenance.

Trackballs

Fewer and fewer trackballs are being produced for portable computers. *Trackballs* are built the same way as an opto-mechanical mouse, except upside-down with the ball up. Trackballs contain the greatest amount of moving parts and require the most maintenance. As the trackball is rotated inside its case, it constantly picks up dust and oils. This dirt and grime builds up inside the rollers and eventually impairs the trackball movement.

To clean a trackball first remove the ring holding the ball. Rotating the ring counter-clockwise usually does this. Once removed, the trackball can be lifted out. Use rubbing alcohol and a Q-tip to swab out the dust and oil from the ball cradle. Then use an alcohol-soaked cloth to wipe down the ball. Be sure to give the cradle and ball time to dry before reassembling them. The worst experience I ever had with a trackball was trying to clean it up in the car, at night, after having foolishly used it following a stop at KFC. My wife can attest that this was probably the longest two-hour trip we have ever taken.

Pointing-Stick

More common than the trackball is the *pointing-stick*. This is a smaller pencil-eraser-sized piece of rubber in the center of the keyboard. One of the best features of the pointing-stick is that your hands never have to leave the keyboard. Maintenance of pointing-stick is usually limited to replacing the rubber cover.

Touch Pads

Touch pads, or scratch pads, are quickly becoming the pointing device of choice for portable computers. The touch pad is a small plastic square usually located near the bottom of the keyboard. To operate the touch pad, place a finger on the surface, and then move in the desired direction. Touch pads require absolutely no maintenance and have no moving parts. The touch pad may also serve as one of the mouse buttons by just tapping on it.

The type of pointing device that you choose comes down to two things: availability and personal preference. I personally prefer the pointing stick, but many people prefer touch pads and trackballs.

CERTIFICATION OBJECTIVE 6.07

Laptop Security and Services

Laptop Security

Laptops are some of the most expensive personal computers manufactured. Unfortunately, because of their size and portability, they are also at the most risk for theft. In order to reduce the risk, manufacturers approach security from a number of perspectives. The first is physical security. Physical security addresses the question, "How do you keep a portable computer from being stolen?" Another type of security is "soft" security. If a computer is stolen, how do you keep someone from accessing the data on that system? In the next few sections we will examine a number of security-related approaches and technologies.

Physical

Physical security also includes protecting your data. This could be protection from theft, or protection from component failures. Notification of component failure, pre-failure alerting on SMART hard disks, and complete notification of system status are all features designed to help maximize the availability of a system and the data on that system. These concepts apply to desktops as well as laptops, but they are particularly relevant for laptops since laptops have a higher risk of theft and damage.

Notebook theft jumped 17 percent over the previous year, according to a 1997 report by Safeware, a Columbus, Ohio-based insurer of computers. The firm says 309,000 portable computers were stolen in 1997, amounting to losses of more than $1 billion.

Soft

Passwords are a major component of software-enabled security. System and hard disk passwords protect the data on the system in the event of system theft. Sensitive internal data remains secure from prying eyes as long as the passwords have been set and are not easily guessed. In some cases the System Administrator is able to remotely enable/disable system passwords and has the ability to reset the system password from a remote site.

Some companies are now implementing mandatory hard drive password. Mandatory passwords enable IT managers to require some or all users to always provide a hard drive password before gaining access to the data on the hard drive, even if that hard drive is moved to another computer.

Many hardware vendors are now offering a registration service to help protect the assets of their clients. One of these companies is Dell Computer Corporation, and their registration service is called DellGuard. For asset protection, DellGuard offers Dell's support in tracking stolen computer systems. If a system is stolen, victims can report their loss by calling a toll-free number. The lost systems tag number is then noted in the Dell product support database. When someone calls Dell seeking support on the stolen computer, the Dell support technician informs the caller that the hardware has been reported stolen and service is denied. The information is then passed on to Dell's Global Security team who will work with the appropriate authorities to assist the owner in retrieving the stolen system.

Asset Management and Fault Management

Asset management is basically accounting. A company needs to know how many computers, monitors, disk drives, CDs, RAM SIMMs, etc. it has purchased. The company also needs to know how many of each kind of thing it owns. With good asset management, a company knows how much to spend for support training for each major component, how much to budget for hardware refresh programs, and which vendors should be targeted for volume purchasing agreements.

Asset management component inventory is made available through standard DMI interfaces. In many cases asset information can be obtained remotely to maintain control of the assets and identify exactly what is deployed in the organization.

Laptop Services

People do things with laptops that they don't normally do with desktop computers. For example, when was the last time you pulled the network card out of your desktop machine while it was powered on? Have you ever tried to use your desktop machine on an airplane or in a car? You probably wouldn't even think twice about doing these things with a laptop.

Many of the capabilities of a laptop that make it portable (and that we take for granted) are implemented as services. These services rely on special hardware and software that doesn't exist on desktop computers.

Docking Services

Docking services provide for swapping of modules (CD-ROM, second hard drive, LS-120, floppy drive, and battery devices), together with hot-docking/undocking capabilities. Docking services can enhance your computer experience by providing the capability to hot-swap devices in either PCMCIA slots or internal bays. Docking services enable a portable computer to undock and dock without having to reboot the system. This functionality now exists for the Windows NT operating system as well as the Windows 9*x* operating systems as long as there is hardware support. The software requires Plug-and-Play BIOS in the portable computer.

Power Management Services

Power management services use software/hardware that is referred to as a *power management controller*. Most controllers are dependent upon a system BIOS that supports power management. However, recently some manufacturers have begun using BIOS-independent power management. Being independent of the BIOS allows the operating system to play a greater role in conserving precious battery power on laptop computers.

Features of power management controllers include an operating system APM-like user interface, support for CPU idle, and the ability to update the system time on a resume from suspend mode. New power management controllers support the Win32 Power Management API. Power-management-aware applications can now "sleep" when there is no activity. This conserves power and provides a way to configure the system to react in a variety of ways to various system events. For example, a laptop could remain in suspend mode until the scheduled time for a disk defragmentation. When the system wakes up, it could then check the amount of remaining power. If there is enough to do the defragmentation, then defragmentation occurs. If there isn't enough power, then the system could write to a log file and go back to suspend mode.

PC Card Services

PC Card services provide a PC Card controller. The controller manages hot-swapping of PC Cards. *Hot-swapping* means that you can remove one PC Card (like a network card) and replace it with another (like a modem) without rebooting the system.

One feature that must be supported for hot-swapping to work correctly is automatic driver installation. In other words, when you add or change a device, the correct device driver must be loaded or installed. Other features that are usually supported include a user interface, socket services, power management support, and PC Card diagnostics. One thing that the PC Card controller must do when you insert a PC Card is to install or load the correct driver for the card. Upon card insertion, the PC Card controller automatically finds the correct driver for card and installs or loads the driver with minimal user interaction. If the user selects an invalid configuration, the error is flagged, and the user can select a valid configuration. The benefit is that this minimizes end-user configuration errors and the resulting technical support inquiries.

CERTIFICATION OBJECTIVE 6.08

Standards and Trends

Standards

Managing computing environments that contain systems from multiple vendors is a difficult task. Many systems have their own management technology and applications for monitoring status and asset information.

This requires many IT groups to install multiple tools and needlessly duplicate the management tasks associated with these systems.

Industry-standard technology is the key to managing mixed computing environments cost effectively. Deploying systems that utilize standard instrumentation enables organizations to quickly determine the status of systems, the inventory of systems, and the components within systems.

Standards help provide a unified approach to:

- Monitor the status of a heterogeneous network and receive notifications of problems
- Retrieve accurate and timely inventory information
- Change large groups of systems in as few operations as possible
- Monitor systems for chassis intrusion to safeguard assets

These four issues are critical because they apply to every system installed. In many cases, these functions have been delivered only by vendor-specific tools, which makes it more difficult for administrators to quickly identify problems in the network or make changes. Standards will help by allowing management application vendors to acquire the information they need from any vendor's machine that supports the standard, and present it from a business point of view, not a vendor point of view.

Which standards help? With so many standards, how can you know which are useful to you? Key management technologies include: the Desktop Management Interface (DMI) and Simple Network Management Protocol (SNMP). DMI is an industry-standard instrumentation agent developed by the Desktop Management Task Force (DMTF), comprised of major computer manufacturers and many computer-related companies. DMI is widely deployed among PC manufacturers for monitoring hardware conditions and hardware asset information.

DMI 2.0 Standard

The Desktop Management Interface (DMI) standard provides consistent information about the system, including asset and fault information. DMI is specifically designed for portable computers. Customers can use a standards-based DMI 2.0 management tool to obtain asset and fault information from all DMI 2.0 compliant systems, thus increasing the consistency of system information even if the systems are from different vendors.

The DMI 2.0 standard provides a consistent way to manage systems. The Desktop Management Interface (DMI) was designed by the Desktop Management Task Force (DMTF) to provide standard definitions for what should be managed in a computer, device, or even software, and how that information should be accessed. An application that supports DMI 2.0 can make a request for information from the DMI on the device in question and receive consistent and meaningful responses, regardless of equipment manufacturer. The DMI can also generate indications of problems to any registered management console, allowing the administrator to take action. Problems might include a system overheating or a disk drive with a pre-failure state. In the former case, the administrator might shut the system down. In the latter case, the administrator could perform a backup and call the vendor for disk service prior to the drive failure.

Using standard technology like DMI allows businesses to manage systems from multiple vendors in the same manner. Management applications should be able to obtain defined, standard information from any system that supports that standard. The administrators will be much more productive when using a single console for managing these systems rather than vendor-specific tools for each platform.

The DMI provides an industry-standard set of OS-independent and protocol-independent application programming interfaces (APIs) for providing manageability through three layers of software. The layers are illustrated in Figure 6-6, which gives a diagram of the DMI architecture. The three layers are as follows:

- **The Service Provider (SP) program**   The SP is responsible for all DMI activities including collecting management information from all products to store in the DMI's database, passing information to management applications as requested, and generating indications to all registered management applications regarding problems as they occur, as opposed to waiting for a request.

- **The Management Interface (MI) API**   The MI provides the interface between the Service Layer and management applications and allows these applications to access, manage, and control desktop systems, servers, components, and peripherals regardless of vendor.

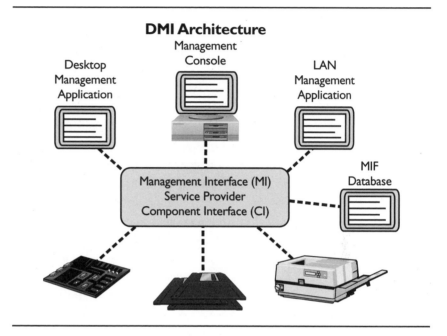

FIGURE 6-6

The DMI architecture

- ■ **The Component Interface (CI) API**   The CI handles communication between manageable elements and the DMI's Service Layer, giving all hardware or software components a common method for describing their management attributes.

The *Management Information Format (MIF)* is an ASCII text file that describes a product's manageable features and attributes. The DMI maintains this information in an MIF database and makes it available to operating systems and management applications.

Users benefit from the availability of highly manageable systems and the opportunity to choose management solutions that best fit their business environment. Systems management vendors benefit because they concentrate on building best-in-class management solutions that assist business control and even reduce costs of deploying systems. Hardware manufacturers benefit because they have a consistent way to instrument systems so they can be managed.

SNMP Standard

SNMP is a time-tested industry management protocol most noted for network management. Management applications like Hewlett-Packard's OpenView Network Node Manager use SNMP to determine the status of computer systems, network devices, and network media.

In an SNMP environment a machine usually plays one of two roles. The simplest role is that of agent. An agent is actually a software program that monitors what is happening on the system. The job of the agent is to report any problems and to fulfill any requests from the management station. The management station is a complex set of applications that receive messages, known as *traps*, from the agents. When a management station receives a trap, it must determine if some action should be taken. If action is required on the agent system, the management station directs the agent to take the action. Rudimentary security is provided in an SNMP environment through the use of *communities*. Only agents and management stations that are in the same community will communicate with each other.

Wired for Management Standard

Other standards to watch out for include Wired for Management (WfM) and Web-Based Enterprise Management. WfM is an initiative from Intel to standardize the management characteristics of all Intel-based systems. These characteristics include DMI instrumentation, remote services, and power management. A consistent managed environment is designed to greatly enhance the opportunity to reduce the systems management portion of the total cost of ownership by providing the same management functions and interfaces for all managed PCs.

Web-Based Enterprise Management Standard

This one is almost too new to be considered a standard. Think of it more as an emerging standard. The *Web-Based Enterprise Management initiative (WBEM)* is one of the newest and most exciting standards efforts. Standards associated with this effort include the PC97 and PC98 specifications for Intel-based clients running Microsoft operating systems.

Anyone interested in PC management standards should watch the *Desktop Management Task Force (DMTF)* very carefully. The DMTF is comprised of committees that cover everything from the development of new technologies to the marketing of existing technologies. For notebook computers, watch for new additions to the Management Information Format (MIF) definitions for managing notebooks and desktops. Standards are also being developed for the SMBIOS reference specification, the pre-boot execution environment specification, and the Advanced Configuration and Power Interface (ACPI) specification. SMBIOS is a hardware-level management interface that complements the new DMI standard by making it easier to obtain system level information.

Portable Trends

Common themes for portable computers are similar to themes for other types of computers. Manufacturers are striving to innovate in areas such as form factor, size, computing power, battery life, and manageability. Consumers want laptops that are smaller, easier to use, and are more powerful. Large companies want systems that are based on industry standards, are interchangeable and upgradeable, and have a low total cost of ownership. You can equate low total cost of ownership to low support cost and little lost productivity due to system failures. To give you a visual example of how laptops have advanced over the last couple of years, Figure 6-7 shows several devices now built into laptops. In addition to these built-in features, laptops now also include the following ports for adding external devices:

- USB
- Parallel
- Serial
- VGA
- Infrared

Besides the standard trends, there are two others that are worth noting. The first is the explosion of the handheld PC market. These little devices are sometimes referred to as *Personal Digital Assistants (PDAs)*. The second trend involves the Windows NT Workstation operating system. Until recently, even Microsoft was reluctant to recommend Windows NT as an OS for laptop computers. That is changing rapidly. In order to lower total cost of ownership companies are trying to standardize on a single OS, and

FIGURE 6-7

Laptops devices are now built-in instead of being attached by cables

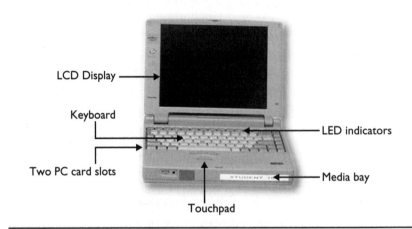

LCD Display

Keyboard

LED indicators

Two PC card slots

Media bay

Touchpad

that OS is Windows NT. Both Microsoft and other companies are demanding that hardware vendors supply laptop computers capable of running Windows NT, and the laptop industry is responding.

Handheld Devices

Personal Digital Assistants are similar to portable computers although they are not nearly as powerful. Some PDAs even run a Microsoft Windows-based operating system known as *Windows CE.* These devices can do some of the same things that your laptop can do. For example, they can synchronize with your e-mail provider, your scheduling service, and your task manager. Most provide the ability to take notes, create files, and record sounds.

Most PDAs also provide a facility for copying files back and forth between the PDA and another computer. They are extremely useful for busy people who do not want to open a laptop every time they want to check their schedule. Some of the more advanced PDAs also provide modems or even wireless communications. These devices can synchronize almost anytime and anywhere. They can send and receive e-mail, faxes, and pages without being physically connected to a network.

Almost all PDAs still use a monochromatic display, but a few advanced models now include color active matrix displays along with stereo recording and playback features. It's like having a multimedia machine in the palm of your hand.

The biggest drawbacks to PDAs at the moment are ease of use, cost, and limited resources. Taking notes on a PDA for an extended period of time can be hard on the eyes as well as hard on the hands. Most PDAs rely on the use of a stylus that traces characters on the screen or is used to tap keys on a miniature keyboard. PDAs do an admirable job of recognizing a variety of writing styles, but they often require a user to write with slightly abnormal strokes. PDAs are also still rather expensive and many vendors do not provide any type of upgrade path. Consequently, you may find yourself spending a lot of money for the latest version of a device, or being stuck with an older version. Finally, most PDAs usually have only eight to sixteen megabytes of memory. That's not a lot to work with considering PDAs do not have hard drives. Luckily all of these issues are being addressed with better technology. As the drawbacks diminish, expect PDAs to become more and more prevalent.

Windows NT Workstation 4.0

Windows NT Workstation has come a long way since its debut in 1993. Windows NT Workstation 4.0 is the latest version of Microsoft's business class 32-bit desktop operating system. Through evolution of its features and the fact that mainstream desktop PCs and laptops now come with Windows NT Workstation preinstalled, it has become a great solution for all business users—not just power users, engineers, and developers. According to Microsoft, Windows NT 4.0:

- Provides the lowest total cost of ownership (TCO)
- Has the highest reliability of any member of the Windows desktop family
- Outperforms the Microsoft Windows 98 operating system on mainstream hardware
- Provides the best security for your desktop from unauthorized use and access to data
- Offers key mobile features for notebooks and laptops
- Provides the easiest upgrade path to Windows 2000 Professional

Service Pack 4 (SP4) is the latest and most comprehensive update for Microsoft Windows NT 4.0. SP4 provides improved management, security, and capabilities that help prepare IT professionals for the Year 2000 and euro currency changes.

An important element in helping to lower total cost of ownership (TCO) in the enterprise environment is the ability to standardize on a single operating system, thus simplifying support, which can help lower support costs. While Windows NT provides many beneficial features for enterprise computing, it has not been traditionally thought of as a strong OS for laptop computers. Consequently, companies have been forced to support at least two operating systems; Windows NT for desktops and Windows 9*x* for laptops.

As a result of customer demand to lower total cost of ownership, hardware manufacturers have begun to provide solutions for optimizing Windows NT for mobile use. Vendors such as Microsoft, Softex, and Dell Computer Corporation have developed Microsoft-verified solutions for adding key mobility features such as advanced power management support, PC Card hot-swap support, and docking services support into notebook computers.

CERTIFICATION SUMMARY

Portable computers represent the most proprietary area of computer hardware. Although the technology between manufacturers is similar, components are not compatible between them. It's important to understand the components that are part of portable systems as well as their capabilities. More and more people are taking advantage of these devices, but their maintenance requires a unique skill set. With the use of docking stations, portable systems are becoming more and more popular with computer users and, in some cases, are even replacing the traditional desktop.

 TWO-MINUTE DRILL

- ❑ Some portable system components are not compatible between different portable computers, even from the same vendor.
- ❑ Type I PC Cards are generally used only for memory.

❑ Port replicators are the cheapest and simplest version of the three types of docking stations.

❑ Portable computer batteries must be disposed of properly. Check the label on the battery and check with local agencies for disposal directions. Do not just throw batteries in the trash.

❑ Passive matrix displays make up the bulk of the laptop displays today.

❑ Most portables have some RAM on the motherboard, but manufacturers usually provide a proprietary expansion slot for additional RAM.

❑ Microsoft added the mouse trails option primarily so people wouldn't lose their cursors on passive matrix displays.

❑ Be careful not to drip moisture into the keyboard or other parts of the portable when cleaning the display, as it may have undesirable results.

❑ A docking station allows a user to install their monitor, external keyboard, and mouse to the docking station rather than to their portable system.

❑ Type III PC Cards are generally reserved for rotating mass storage, such as hard drives.

❑ When a NiCad battery is recharged before it is fully discharged, the battery loses the ability to fully recharge again, which is known as the memory effect.

❑ All PCMCIA cards are now referred to as PC Cards.

❑ All PC Cards are 85.6 mm by 54.0 mm. Type I cards are 3.3 mm thick, Type II are 5.0 mm thick, and Type III are 10.5 mm thick.

❑ Socket Services is a layer of BIOS level software that isolates PC Card software from the computer hardware and detects the insertion or removal of PC Cards.

❑ Touch pads are quickly becoming the pointing device of choice with portable computers.

❑ Type II PC Cards are generally used for I/O devices such as modems, network adapters, or SCSI adapters.

SELF TEST

The following Self Test questions will help you measure your understanding of the material presented in this chapter. Read all the choices carefully, as there may be more than one correct answer. Choose all correct answers for each question.

1. The _____ battery provides the most power with the least amount of weight.

    A. nickel cadmium

    B. lithium ion

    C. nickel/metal hydride

    D. lead acid

2. The _____ effect refers to the tendency of nickel cadmium batteries to lose the ability to fully recharge if they are not completely discharged first.

    A. memory

    B. amnesia

    C. memory leak

    D. flux capacitor

3. The AC adapter on a portable computer changes _____ power to _____ power.

    A. 110v AC to 220v AC

    B. 220v AC to 110v AC

    C. 110v AC or 220v AC to DC

    D. 12v DC to 110v AC

4. The most common display technology used in portable systems is known as _____.

    A. Liquid Crystal

    B. Light Emitting Diode

    C. Cathode Ray Tube

    D. 8514/A

5. A _____ display has a transistor at each pixel.

    A. Passive matrix

    B. 8514/A

    C. Light Emitting Diode

    D. Active matrix

6. Mary says that when she moves her mouse too quickly, her cursor disappears. What suggestion would you have to help?

    A. Change the display mode from Passive to Active.

    B. Set the mouse trails option to On.

    C. Adjust the contrast of the display.

    D. Tell her not to move the mouse so quickly.

7. Most laptops have a limited number of ports, but by using a docking station those ports can be expanded. A docking station can provide which of the following?

    A. PCI slots

    B. ISA slots

    C. Enhanced sound capabilities

    D. All of the above

8. In order to dock a laptop with a docking station, a _____ connector is used.

   A. SCSI

   B. DB-50

   C. DIN

   D. Proprietary

9. PC Cards were originally intended for adding additional _____ to a system.

   A. Hard drives

   B. Hard drive adapters

   C. Memory

   D. Network adapters

10. Type III PC Cards are intended for _____ type devices like hard drives or CD-ROMS.

    A. Modems

    B. LAN cards

    C. Rotating mass storage

    D. Memory

11. PC _____ software manages the allocation of system resources once a PC Card has been inserted.

    A. Card services

    B. Socket services

    C. Windows 95

    D. DOS

12. Uses for PC Cards today include:

    A. Hard drives

    B. Network cards

    C. Memory cards

    D. Global Positioning System cards

    E. All of the above

13. What types of pointing devices are found in portable computers today?

    A. Trackballs

    B. Touch pads

    C. Pointing sticks

    D. All of the above

14. The type of pointing device that has the most moving parts, which in turn makes it the most unreliable is the _____.

    A. Trackball

    B. Touch pad

    C. Pointing stick

    D. VR

15. System and hard drive passwords are an example of _____ security.

    A. Hardware-enabled

    B. Software-enabled

    C. Smart

    D. High-level

16. _____ is basically accounting. If done properly, a company will know how many computers, monitors, disk drives, CDs, RAM SIMMs, etc. it has purchased.

    A. Inventory tracking

    B. FASB

    C. Asset management

    D. Fault tolerance

17. Features of _____ controllers include an operating system APM-like user interface, support for CPU idle, and the ability to update the system time on a resume from suspend mode.

    A. Card Services
    B. Power Management
    C. Docking Services
    D. Socket Services

18. Standards help provide a unified approach to _____.

    A. Monitor the status of a heterogeneous network and receive notifications of problems
    B. Retrieve accurate and timely inventory information
    C. Change large groups of systems with as few operations as possible
    D. Monitor systems for chassis intrusion to safeguard assets
    E. All of the above

19. Customers can use a standards-based _____ management tool to obtain asset and fault information from all compliant systems, thus increasing the consistency of system information even if the systems are from different vendors.

    A. ANSI
    B. SMTP
    C. DMI 2.0
    D. APM

20. _____ is a time-tested industry management protocol most noted for network management.

    A. DMI
    B. SMTP
    C. ANSI
    D. SNMP

21. _____ is an initiative from Intel to standardize the management characteristics of all Intel-based systems. These characteristics include DMI instrumentation, remote services, and power management.

    A. DTMF
    B. WBEM
    C. WfM
    D. DMI

22. Handheld PCs are often referred to as _____.

    A. PDAs
    B. IRDAs
    C. PPCs
    D. UPCs

23. When a PDA _____ with another system, files and other information are automatically copied from one device to the other so that both devices have the exact same information.

    A. Links
    B. Communicates
    C. Synchronizes
    D. Attaches

24. Which of the following operating systems is just now becoming a mainstream operating system for portable computers?

    A. Windows 95
    B. Windows 98
    C. Windows NT Workstation 4.0
    D. Windows NT Server 4.0

25. Which Windows NT Service Pack is required to fully enable the operating system to function with portable computers?

    A. SP1
    B. SP2
    C. SP3
    D. SP4

7

Basic
Networking

N etworking is by far one of the most important fields in the computer industry. For years, companies have used networking to justify the high costs associated with high-end computing devices—such as mainframes, servers, and high-output printers. With the surge in popularity of the Internet in the mid-1990s, a great interest in home and small business networking has developed. Whenever two or more workstations are connected together, a Local Area Network (LAN) is created. At a minimum, nearly every major company has a LAN installed.

There are some basic networking concepts that you will run into time and time again as a technician. Whether or not you have an interest in networking, it is important to be familiar with these basic concepts.

After you have a firm grasp of some basic networking concepts, it is also important to have a general understanding of how to configure a Network Interface Card (NIC). Configuration of a NIC is extraordinarily simple in most cases, and will be useful to you during your career.

CERTIFICATION OBJECTIVE 7.01

Basic Networking Concepts

As a base for your networking abilities, you need to understand some basic networking concepts. Everything in the world of networking revolves around these concepts, and a firm grasp of them is extraordinarily important. These basic concepts include the following:

- Network topologies
- Cabling
- Network Interface Cards
- Network access
- Protocols

Network Topologies

The *network topology* describes a network in terms of physical layout, such as cabling and connected nodes. There are many different topologies available, but only three are of consequence for this exam. The three topologies you will need to focus on are ring, bus, and star topologies. The topology is generally thought of as a conceptual design, developed before cabling is run, to assist in the physical planning of the network. Many networks are designed using a combination of topologies, such as a star-ring or star-bus layout. The following sections discuss the major topologies in greater detail.

Bus

The *bus topology* is the simplest of the three. In a bus topology, computers are connected in a row on the cable. The computers are connected by a coaxial cable, one right after the other, with a terminator at both ends of the network. The coaxial cable in this topology forms the primary data path, known as a *backbone*.

In the bus topology, only one computer at a time can transmit a signal. When one computer is transmitting, all others are listening. This is a *passive* network design, meaning that computers between source and destination computers monitor all data, but if it is not meant for them, they simply pass it down the cable without amplifying the signal. If your network spans a great distance, the signal may become weaker as it travels from one end of your network to the other. This problem is known as *attenuation*. Repeaters can be added to your network at regular intervals to amplify the signal and correct problems with attenuation.

Bus topologies are best suited for small networks with a small number of computers spread out over a minimal distance. Bus topologies are generally the least expensive, as they do not require complex distributed connecting equipment such as hubs. A break in the cable or a cable end without a terminator can cause the entire network to malfunction. If a single computer fails, however, the rest of the network is not affected.

Ring

In a *ring topology*, as the name suggests, all computers are connected along the cable in the form of a closed ring. Because the ring is closed, there is no need for cable termination. Only one computer at a time can transmit a signal to the network. Network signals leave the source computer and travel along the cable in one direction until they find the intended recipient.

The ring topology is an *active* network design, meaning that computers between the source and destination computer accept each network signal, examine it, and, if they are not the intended recipient, regenerate the signal and send it on its way around the ring. Because of the closed ring design, a break in the cable or the failure of a single device on the network will cause the entire ring to fail. For this reason, few networks are implemented in a pure ring topology.

Star

In a *star topology*, the center of your network is a management device called a *hub* (see Figure 7-1). Each computer is connected to the hub by its own cable segment. Only a single computer can transmit at a time, and every computer on the network will examine the data to see if it is meant for them. Because a star network is made up of single devices attached to the ends of single cables, a break in the cable affects only the device attached to that cable. Failure of a single node will not affect the rest of the network. If, however, the central hub fails, the entire network will go down.

The star topology can be implemented as a passive or an active design, depending on the type of hub you select. A passive hub is often utilized for small networks. All data received by a passive hub is passed directly to all computers connected to the hub. An active hub, on the other hand, amplifies incoming signals before transmitting them to the other computers. This amplification will allow a network signal to travel a greater distance without degrading.

Topology Hybrids

As was mentioned, most networks are designed using a combination of topologies, such as a star-ring or star-bus layout. The *star-bus topology* is

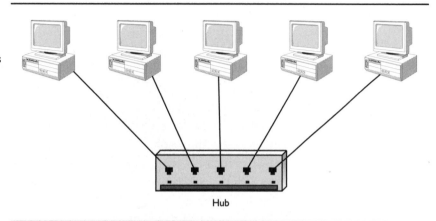

FIGURE 7-1

Each device on a star
topology network connects
to the hub

Hub

made up of a number of hubs connected together by a backbone bus
network. Each hub manages the devices connected to it as a star network.
As the network grows, the bus can be expanded to contain additional hubs.
The *star-ring topology* is similar to a star-bus, but instead of connecting the
hubs over a bus network, the backbone forms a complete ring.

Cabling

Obviously, in order to create a network, you have to somehow physically
connect the devices that will be on the network. This is accomplished using
cables. There are many different types of cables, each with its own
advantages and disadvantages. In the next few sections, we discuss three
types of cabling: twisted pair, coaxial, and fiber optic.

Twisted Pair

Twisted pair is by far the most common type of network cable, primarily
because of its low cost. Physically, in its simplest form twisted-pair cable
consists of a pair of insulated copper wires twisted around each other.
Wrapping the wires in a pair around each other helps reduce interference
from cross-talk and electromagnetic induction (EMI). A single connection
over twisted pair requires both wires. Network standards often call for

multiple connections, so twisted-pair cables are often made up of two or more of twisted pairs enclosed in the same outer insulation.

Twisted-pair cable is considerably less expensive than the other types of cabling. In larger network installations, the lower price of cable offsets the cost of a hub and makes twisted pair a cost-effective networking solution.

There are many different types of twisted-pair cables. Some of these types include unshielded twisted pair (UTP), shielded twisted pair (STP), 10BaseT, and 100BaseT; UTP is the most popular. STP differs from UTP in that, while both contain sets of twisted-pair wires enclosed in a single wire, STP has an outer covering, or shield, between the twisted pair and the outer insulation; this shield acts as a ground.

As shown in Figure 7-2, twisted pair is often configured in a star topology, in which each device is connected to a central device, usually a hub. In the

---

FIGURE 7-2   A twisted-pair Ethernet network is often configured in a star topology

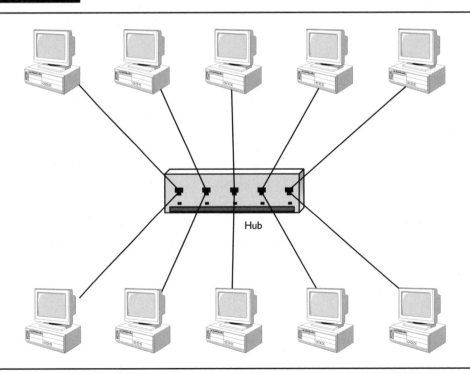

event of a cable being cut or broken, the device that is connected to that cable will no longer be able to communicate on the network, but the broken cable will not affect any other devices on the network.

Coaxial

Coaxial, while not as common as twisted pair, is also a popular type of network cable. Physically, coaxial cable consists of a central wire that is surrounded by a screen of fine wires. Coaxial cable is most common in smaller networks, where it is cheaper to purchase the coaxial cable instead of purchasing both the UTP cabling and hubs. Like twisted pair, coaxial can also be referred to by many names. Some of these names include ThinNet and 10Base2; ThinNet is the most popular. Each device must be connected to a T-connector, shown in Figure 7-3. Each T-connector is connected to the next with a coaxial cable. After all of the devices are connected, the ends of the cable must then be terminated with a 50Ω terminator. As shown in Figure 7-4, a coaxial network is configured in a bus topology. In the event of the cable being cut or broken, the network will cease to operate. To connect two shorter lengths of coaxial cable, you need a BNC (British Naval Connector) barrel connector.

exam
ⓦatch

Coaxial cable requires that each device be connected to a T-connector, which is then connected to the coaxial cable. In addition, each end of the cable must have a 50Ω terminator installed.

FIGURE 7-3

A T-connector is required between each device on a network utilizing coaxial cabling and the coaxial cable

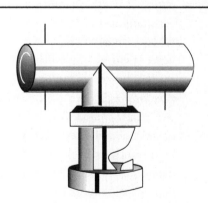

FIGURE 7-4	A coaxial network is usually configured in a bus topology with each device connected to a main cable or bus

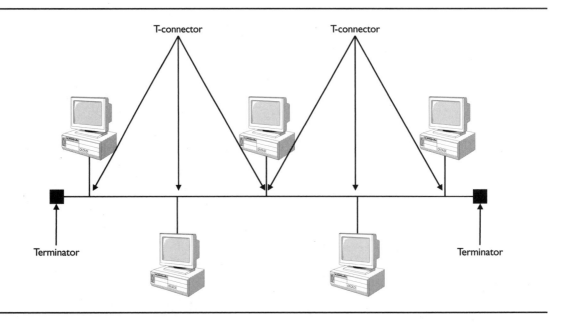

Fiber Optic

Fiber optic (also called *optical fiber*) is the least common of the three types of cabling. Fiber-optic cabling is usually found where long cable lengths are required, where extremely high speed is desired, or where there is high EMI radiation or other environmental difficulties. Traditional copper-based cables such as twisted pair or coaxial cables are susceptible to radiation and other environmental difficulties. Fiber-optic cable is much less susceptible to these environmental difficulties because it uses light impulses along a glass or plastic wire or fiber, rather than electrical signals through an electrically conductive medium. Light signals offer more protection from environmental interferences than electrical signals. Fiber optic is used when long lengths of cable are required because it is able to sustain longer distances without environmental interruption. The light emitting from the end of a fiber-optic cable is a high-density, laser-quality light. Therefore, you should never look directly into the end of a fiber-optic cable or other fiber-optic device, as the light could cause permanent damage to your eye.

Of course, such benefits seldom come without their price, and optical fiber is no exception. Fiber-optic cabling is much more expensive than its copper-based counterparts. The equipment used to connect, transmit, and receive fiber-optic signals is more expensive as well. Fiber-optic connectivity devices, such as hubs or repeaters, are much more sensitive to dust than copper-based devices. While receptors on a twisted-pair hub could be left uncovered, doing the same with a fiber-optic receptor could allow small particles of dust into the receptor. Later, when connecting a fiber cable to the receptor, the small particles of dust could reflect light from the cable, in effect scrambling the data so that it cannot be translated by the data device. Fiber-optic cabling is much more fragile than copper-based solutions, so it will require more protection within an outer cable than would copper. Finally, maintenance of fiber is much more difficult than maintenance of copper. If a copper cable is accidentally cut, it could be quickly spliced back together with tools as simple as a pocketknife and electrical tape. Broken fiber, however, requires special tools to reconnect. The glass or plastic core must be melted back together, and the alignment of the splice must be perfect, or the light signals will be disrupted.

Fiber optic is usually referred to simply as *fiber*. Each segment of fiber-optic cable must be connected at each end with a special fiber-optic connector. Figure 7-5 illustrates a ring topology, the most common configuration used with fiber-optic networks. In this configuration, if the fiber-optic cable is cut or broken, the entire network will cease to operate. Most fiber-optic installations of this type actually include two rings in order to provide redundancy and fault tolerance.

FDDI, or Fiber Distributed-Data Interface, is an example of a fiber-optic network with a ring topology. FDDI networks consist of two token rings. The primary ring offers up to 100 Mbps capacity, and the secondary ring is used for backup. If, however, the secondary ring is not needed for backup, it can also be used to carry data. If this is the case, network capacity reaches an effective 200 Mbps. A single ring can extend a maximum of 200 km (124 miles). A dual ring can extend an additional 100 km (62 miles) for a total of 300 km (186 miles).

FIGURE 7-5   A fiber-optic network is often configured in a ring topology where a token is passed around a ring

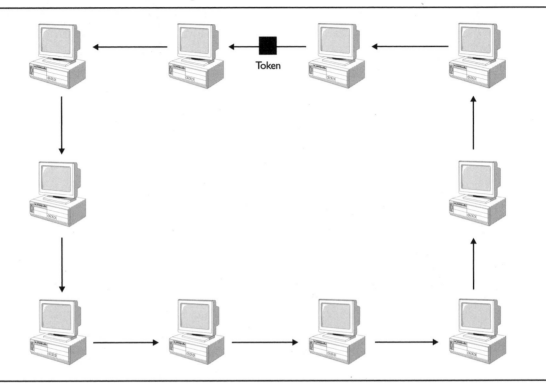

Although it is a less common configuration, fiber-optic technologies can also be used in a star topology, just like twisted pair (as illustrated in Figure 7-2). In this configuration, a broken fiber has the same effect on the network as a broken cable would have in any normal star topology—only the device connected to that cable will no longer be able to communicate on the network, but other network devices will not be affected. Table 7-1 lists and compares each of the cable types discussed in this section.

exam
ⓦatch

Current standards define maximum transmission distances for single, non-repeated lengths of cable as follows: Twisted-pair cable is capable of transmitting a maximum of 100 meters, coaxial is capable of a maximum of 180 meters, and fiber-optic cable standards specify a maximum of more than 2000 meters.

| TABLE 7-1 | | Comparison of Important Characteristics of Cable Types | | |

Cable Type	Topology	Maximum Distance for Single Cable Segment	Transmission Speed	Other Required Devices
Twisted Pair	Star or Ring	100 Meters	10 or 100 Megabits per second	If in a star topology, each networked device must connect to a port on a hub.
Coaxial	Bus	180 Meters	10 Megabits per second	Each networked device must be connected with a T-connector and terminators must be connected to each end.
Fiber Optic	Ring or Star	>2000 Meters	100 Mbps to 2 Gigabits per second with current technology (100 Megabits per second most common)	Each end of a cable segment must have a special fiber-optic transmitter connected.

Network Interface Cards

Network Interface Cards (NICs) connect the PC to the network cable. NICs must be matched to the type of network and the type of network cable that you are using. It is important to choose a NIC that corresponds to your network. Many NIC manufacturers provide models that can connect to multiple network types, such as coaxial networks, or fiber-optic or twisted-pair networks. Figure 7-6 shows an example of an Ethernet NIC than can connect to either an RJ-45 twisted pair cable, or a fiber-optic cable.

Network Communications

Communication sessions on a network take one of three forms: simplex, half-duplex, and full-duplex communications. *Simplex* communications are basic, one-way communications. The easiest way to explain simplex communications is to imagine a television transmission. The data is sent out, and if a device is listening, it will be received and interpreted, but the

An Ethernet NIC with both an RJ-45 twisted-pair connector and a dual-strand fiber-optic connector. The light gray port is the Transmit; the darker gray port is the Receive

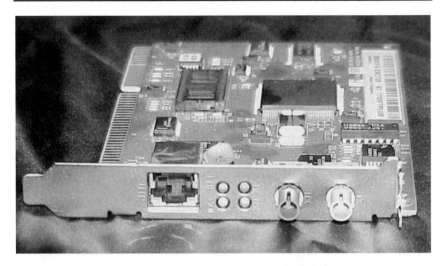

transmitting device has no way of knowing whether the transmission was successful.

Half-duplex communications allow two-way communication, but only one device may transmit at a time. This method could be compared to a CB or walkie-talkie, where one person must wait for the other to finish speaking before responding. If both parties try to talk at the same time, neither will be able to hear the other. *Full-duplex* communications occur when a network device is capable of transmitting in both directions at the same time. In simpler terms, a full-duplex network medium has the capability of sending and receiving simultaneously. You could compare full-duplex networking to a telephone conversation. Both parties are able to speak at the same time, and the communication is not interrupted. Full-duplex networking is often seen in 100 Mbps or higher networks, such as 100BaseT (CAT-5) or 100BaseTX (Fiber).

Network Access

Network access (or *access method* as it is more commonly referred to) is the method by which devices communicate on the network. Without some type of control on the network, any device could transmit at any time, quite possibly at the same time as another device. Just as we have a problem when two people attempt to communicate simultaneously, devices on the network have a similar problem. Network access provides a standard that all devices that wish to communicate on the network must abide by in order to solve this problem. Common types of network access are the following:

- Carrier Sense Multiple Access with Collision Detection
- Carrier Sense Multiple Access with Collision Avoidance
- Demand polling
- Token passing

Carrier Sense Multiple Access with Collision Detection

Carrier Sense Multiple Access with Collision Detection (CSMA/CD) is somewhat similar to how we humans communicate. In the *Carrier Sense* portion of this method, a device listens to the network and waits for a pause in communication, similar to the way we wait for a pause in a conversation before we begin talking. When the network channel is idle, the device transmits data onto the network. Next, the *Collision Detection* portion takes over. If a collision is detected, it means that another device has attempted to transmit onto the network at the same time. In this situation, both devices wait an unspecified random amount of time and attempt to retransmit their data, similar to how we react during the pause in conversation, when two people try to talk simultaneously; both stop talking for a random amount of time, and the first to start talking again is allowed to complete whatever they need to say. CSMA/CD is most commonly found on Ethernet networks. CSMA/CD is one of the faster access methods available, but performance can become an issue on busier networks.

Carrier Sense Multiple Access with Collision Avoidance

With the Carrier Sense Multiple Access with Collision Avoidance (CSMA/CA) media access method, the same principles exist with the carrier sense portion as in CSMA/CD. The difference is, with the Collision Avoidance portion of the communication, after detecting an idle channel, a computer next transmits a signal to the network announcing its intent to transmit data. When the other computers detect the signal, they wait until the signaling computer transmits its data before attempting to transmit data of their own. In this way, data collisions are avoided.

Demand Polling

In demand polling, the hub handles requests for transmission. The hub questions every computer connected to it, looking for a system trying to send data. If the hub finds a computer waiting to send, it opens a connection for that computer, and prevents other computers from transmitting.

Token Passing

Token passing is a bit more organized than CSMA/CD or CSMA/CA. Using token passing, a token is passed from device to device around a virtual (and frequently physical) ring. Whenever a device receives the token, it is then allowed to transmit onto the network. Token passing is most commonly found on fiber-optic and token-ring networks. Token passing, although more organized than other methods, is a bit slower because it requires that devices wait until they hold the token, prior to transmitting onto the network. In the event that the token were lost, the network could be rendered useless until a new token is created, which could take from a few seconds to a few hours. The use of token passing is advantageous where total organization is required, such as in fiber-optic backbones.

Protocols

Data cannot simply be transmitted onto the network. Protocols establish standards for such transmission of data. Both the sending and receiving device must be capable of communicating using the same protocols. Some common protocols are the following:

- TCP/IP
- IPX/SPX
- NetBEUI

Multiple protocols can coexist on one physical network, but only those devices that use a particular protocol are able to communicate with each other. This means that a device running only TCP/IP cannot talk to a device running only IPX/SPX or NetBEUI. Many operating systems, such as Windows, will allow multiple protocols to be installed on a single client.

Suppose your network is comprised of five Windows 95 client machines running IPX/SPX and TCP/IP, a UNIX server running only TCP/IP, and a NetWare server running only IPX/SPX. In this scenario, any of the Windows 95 client machines would be able to communicate with any other device on the network. That is, the clients could communicate with other client machines, with the UNIX server, or with the NetWare server. The UNIX server would be able to communicate with the five Windows 95 clients, but not with the NetWare server. The NetWare server would also be able to communicate with the five Windows 95 clients, but would not be able to see the UNIX server.

Binding protocols to an adapter card is handled through NDIS, the Network Driver Interface Specification, developed by Microsoft and 3Com. NDIS provides a standard Windows driver model interface to allow protocol stacks, such as TCP/IP, NetBEUI, and IPX/SPX, to access various network adapters, such as Ethernet, Token Ring, or FDDI. NDIS standardizes the interface for the protocol stack, the adapter driver, and the protocol manager. The protocol manager facilitates communication between the protocol stack and the adapter driver. NDIS allows any protocol stack to work with any adapter driver. NDIS also makes it possible to bind multiple protocols to a single card, to install multiple cards to a single system, and to assign multiple IP addresses to a single adapter.

TCP/IP

TCP/IP (Transmission Control Protocol/Internet Protocol) is the most common protocol used today; it's the protocol upon which the Internet is built. TCP/IP was originally designed in the 1970s to be used by the Defense Advanced Research Projects Agency (DARPA) and the Department of Defense (DOD) to connect systems across the country. A requirement of this design was the ability to cope with poor network conditions. An advantage of TCP/IP is that it is routable or can be passed beyond a router. A *router* is a network device that connects two or more networks together. The router allows all traffic destined for the network on the other side of the router to cross. TCP/IP's largest disadvantage is that it requires quite a bit of configuration.

IPX/SPX

IPX/SPX (Internetwork Packet Exchange/Sequenced Packet Exchange) is the protocol most commonly used with Novell NetWare. IPX/SPX is a fast, well-established protocol, but is not used on the Internet. Novell developed IPX/SPX for use in NetWare. Like TCP/IP, IPX/SPX is routable and requires some configuration, though nowhere near as much as TCP/IP.

NetBEUI

NetBEUI (NetBIOS Extended User Interface) is a transport protocol that is commonly found in smaller networks. NetBEUI is an extremely fast protocol with very little overhead that was first implemented with LAN Manager products. NetBEUI is not routable and requires little configuration, if any at all. In fact, the only configuration required relates to network planning more than actual client configuration; there is usually no need to configure the protocol itself. Because NetBEUI is not routable, you must have a flat network, and no two systems on your network are allowed to have the same computer name. NetBEUI communicates with other computers on the network by using the NetBIOS computer name. NetBEUI is a very chatty protocol—meaning that it constantly sends a large number of small data packets onto the line—making it an inefficient, collision-prone protocol if used with a large number of clients.

In Windows 95, you can configure the real-mode portion of NetBEUI by selecting the protocol in the network control panel and clicking the Properties button and selecting the Advanced tab. The two configurable options are *Maximum Sessions* and *NCBS (Network Control Blocks)*. Maximum Sessions defines the maximum number of remote connections supported from the NetBEUI redirector. In older versions of Windows, this option would appear in the PROTOCOL.INI file, as the *sessions=* parameter. NCBS defines the maximum number of NetBIOS commands that can be used. Again, in older versions of Windows, this option would appear in the PROTOCOL.INI file, under the *ncbs=* parameter. Remember, these settings only modify the NetBEUI configuration for the *real-mode* NetBEUI, such as when running in Safe mode. Protected-mode NetBEUI (used in a "normal" Windows 95 networking session) dynamically configures these options. For the most part, there is no need to change the default parameters.

Ways to Network a PC

Network standards define the mechanisms by which many computers connect to similar media and operate within a given geographic area. Generally speaking, any network contained in a radius of one mile is a *LAN* (*Local Area Network*). A network spanning from one to ten miles is referred to as a *MAN* (*Metropolitan Area Network*). Anything greater than ten miles is a *WAN* (*Wide Area Network*). This section focuses on some of the technologies that are used to connect systems on your LAN, MAN, or WAN.

Ethernet

Ethernet, the most common architecture for LANs, is perhaps the most popular network architecture in use today. The current standard for Ethernet, as defined by the Institute of Electrical and Electronics Engineers (IEEE), is 802.3. Ethernet supports a variety of topologies, including bus, star, and star-bus.

The 802.3 standard defines the supported topologies, cable types, media access methods, and data frame formats. The current standards support speeds of 10 Mbps (10BaseX) and 100 Mbps (Fast Ethernet, or 100BaseX). The supported media access method is CSMA/CD. Standard Ethernet could use a number of different types of cabling, defined by the 10BaseX standards as follows:

- **10Base2 (ThinNet)**   RG-58 Coaxial cable
- **10Base5 (ThickNet)**   RG-11 or RG-8 Coaxial cable

- **10BaseT (Twisted pair)** CAT-3 or CAT-5 UTP or STP with RJ-45 connectors

- **10BaseFL** 2-strand optical fiber

Fast Ethernet, on the other hand, generally uses either CAT-5 UTP cable, or fiber-optic cable. Fast Ethernet cabling specifications are defined by the 100BaseX standards as follows:

- **100BaseT4** 4-pair CAT-5 UTP

- **100BaseTX** 2-pair CAT-5 UTP or STP with RJ-45 connectors

- **100BaseFX** 2-strand optical fiber

Token Ring

Token ring is a LAN technology that was introduced in the mid-1980s by IBM. Shortly thereafter, the IEEE set the 802.5 token-ring standard. Although not as common as Ethernet, and losing more ground as time goes on, it is still an important standard to be familiar with. Token ring supports only ring or star-ring configuration. Token-ring equipment tends to be more expensive than Ethernet. The IEEE 802.5 standard for token-ring networks defines network transmission speeds of either 4 Mbps or 16 Mbps. Cable types can be shielded twisted pair or unshielded twisted pair cable of IBM Type 1, 2, or 3, although the backbone is often made of Type 5 fiber-optic cabling.

From a logical perspective, token-ring networks meet the qualifications of a ring topology, where data is transmitted from computer to computer in a single direction until it returns to the originating computer. However, given the high risk of complete network failure when a single system in a true-ring topology goes down, the token-ring standard is physically implemented as a star-ring topology. The center of the star, rather than a hub as in a true-star topology, is known as a *MAU* (*multiple access unit*). Many people mistakenly call a MAU a hub, and although they serve similar functions, this would not be a correct representation of the device on a token-ring network.

When a computer on a token-ring network comes online, it generates a network packet known as a *token*. Token ring, as you may have guessed, uses the token-passing media access method. As you will recall from earlier, in this form of network access, a token is passed from device to device around a virtual ring. Whenever a device receives the token, it is then allowed to transmit onto the network. Only one token can exist on a ring at a time. The first computer to come online becomes the token monitor, and will be responsible for regenerating the token if it were to become lost or corrupted.

As you know, a ring topology must make a complete circle to effectively pass the token around the ring. To accomplish this, each MAU has a Ring-Out and a Ring-In port. For a token-ring network with multiple MAUs (there is a maximum of 12 MAU devices), the Ring-Out port on each MAU is connected to the Ring-In port on the next MAU in the ring. At the end, the Ring-Out port of the final MAU is connected to the Ring-In port of the first MAU. This completes the ring, and allows the token to make the full circle of the ring topology.

Remote Networking

So far, all of our discussion has involved using a NIC to connect two or more computers together. If you've ever configured a dial-up connection to the Internet, then you know that you can attach to a network without using a Network Interface Card. In the next few subsections, we will explore some of the methods of remote network connectivity.

Perhaps the most common form of remote connectivity is the use of dial-up networking. Dial-up networking uses a modem to connect two or more workstations together. The majority of people who connect to the Internet from home use dial-up networking on a daily basis. It is considerably slower than using NICs, but can accomplish the same tasks.

The most common form of dial-up networking uses standard analog modems over the *Public Switched Telephone Network (PSTN)*, sometimes referred to as the *Plain Old Telephone Service (POTS)*. The PSTN refers to the global layout of voice-oriented public telephone networks. Today's standards limit your connection speed over the PSTN to around 28.8 to 56.6 Kbps. In the past few years, the *Integrated Services Digital Network (ISDN)* standards have become more prevalent in the area of dial-up networking. ISDN provides for faster digital connections over standard copper telephone cable. ISDN allows for simultaneous voice and digital data communications over the same line, with pure dial-up networking connections reaching speeds of up to 128 Kbps.

High-Speed Remote Networking

As the Internet has developed from a communications medium used by businesses and students for the simple exchange of e-mail to the first truly new communications infrastructure in decades, the bandwidth requirements have steadily increased. With the increase, the demand for inexpensive, high-speed connectivity has been on a steady climb as well. In the past few years, a number of promising technologies have developed that could provide that inexpensive, high-speed connectivity today's Internet users demand. These same technologies that can provide higher-speed Internet access can be used to connect remote users from their homes to their corporate networks. Often, the increase in employee productivity associated with the faster network connectivity can be enough to offset the higher cost associated with the new equipment and communication services required for these technologies.

The first of these technologies is *cable modems*. Cable modems allow you to connect your computer to the Internet through the same coaxial cable over which you might receive cable television. The theoretical maximum connection rate for cable modems is 27 Mbps downstream (from the Internet to your computer), and 2.5 Mbps upstream (from your computer to the Internet). In reality, most cable modems see only a 1.5 Mbps maximum connection speed in either direction—still quite a bit faster than PSTN or ISDN.

Digital Subscriber Line (DSL) is another emerging high-speed remote networking technology. The DSL technologies, which include xDSL, ADSL, RADSL, and HDSL, enable transfer rates of 6.1 Mbps over ordinary copper telephone lines. The theoretical maximum capacity of DSL is 8.448 Mbps, while actual transfer rates will likely average around 1.5 Mbps to 512 Kbps downstream, and 128 Kbps upstream.

Finally, satellite technology provides for a high-speed, wireless downstream connection, while using a standard 28.8 or 56 Kbps modem for the upstream connection. Using equipment and technology similar to

Digital Satellite System (DSS) television, satellite PC connections can provide fast downstream connectivity to areas where other wired solutions may not be available. The downside to this technology is that the satellite can only receive data. The transmission of data, including the data requests sent to the satellite, still requires a connection through a regular modem and PSTN dialup connection.

Direct Cable Connection

A direct cable connection is when two computers are networked using either a serial or parallel cable. Direct cable connections are considerably faster than modem connections, but are still slower than networking using a NIC. Direct cable connections are limited to networking a maximum of two computers and are limited by physical cable restrictions.

Serial cables used for networking computers are known as *null modem* or *cross-over* cables. Null modem cables are limited to 30 feet in length. You cannot connect serial ports with a standard serial extension cable. The parallel cable needed for a direct cable connection is a DB-25M (D-type 25 pin male) connector at both ends. Parallel connections tend to be faster than serial connections.

IrDA (Infrared Data Association) provides a cable-less direct cable connection by sending and receiving data as a modulated ray of infrared light. You can think of IrDA as an invisible null modem cable. IrDA works the same way as a serial port. In fact, the IrDA connector uses the same resources and is addressed as if it were a standard COM port but there is no physical connector. To successfully connect using infrared, you must have a clear line of sight between the two IrDA transceivers.

Although you are unlikely to see questions on your test pertaining to *Universal Serial Bus (USB),* you should be aware that it is possible to network computers using USB. Doing so requires an added USB network adapter or USB network hub. Remember, the USB network hub is *not* the same thing as a normal USB distribution hub. A USB distribution hub simply allows you to connect more USB devices through a single USB connection on your computer, while the USB network hub allows multiple computers to connect and share network resources. The current standards for USB provide slower communications than most network cards, but a faster connection than current serial-, parallel-, or IrDA-based communications.

Configuring Network Interface Cards

Network Interface Cards (NICs) are fairly simple to configure. Most NICs require an IRQ and an IO memory address. Once the resources that the NIC uses have been configured on the NIC (most newer NICs use a software utility rather than the more traditional jumpers or DIP switches; consult your NIC's documentation for exact specifications), the Network Operating System must be configured with the same settings (consult your Network Operating Systems documentation for details, and see Chapter 11 of this book). Configuration will be a less difficult process if the same type of NIC is used in each workstation on your network.

Problems on the Network

As the saying goes, all good things must come to an end. Someday your beautiful network will not continue to operate exactly as it used to. This could be the result of many different things. Some common causes of network problems include the following:

- Physically damaged cable
- Damaged Network Interface Card
- Excessive traffic on the network
- Incorrectly operating hub

■ Missing or incorrectly operating terminator

■ Magnetic fields

■ Incorrectly configured network devices

Reduced Bandwidth

Reduced bandwidth occurs when users' data transmissions across the network begin to take longer, and begin to be timed-out by the applications requesting the transmission. Reduced bandwidth can be caused by any of the common network problems mentioned in the preceding list. The most likely cause of reduced bandwidth is excessive traffic on the network. Excessive traffic usually is not a result of equipment failure, but instead a result of equipment success. The only solution to excessive traffic is to modify the network configuration in order to allow more traffic, or to separate high- and low-traffic users. The most common method of modifying the network configuration to allow more traffic is to upgrade a 10 Mbps LAN to 100 Mbps by replacing hubs, NICs, and possibly the cabling.

Loss of Data

Loss of data can be a result of nearly any of the common network problems mentioned previously. Most methods of data transmission provide some type of assurance that the data has been transmitted successfully. Data loss is therefore usually caused by some type of failure, and not by excessive traffic. In most cases, excessive traffic results in slower delivery of data rather than loss of data.

Network Slowdown

Network slowdown occurs whenever users notice that the network is not operating as quickly as usual. In most cases, this is a sudden change, rather than a gradual change (a more gradual change would be a loss of bandwidth). Because the change appears to be sudden, it is more than likely a result of a hardware problem, rather than a result of excessive traffic.

FROM THE FIELD

A Real-World Networking Lesson

It is very important to understand the limitations of the networks on which you work. Bandwidth costs money, and some corporations try to run their networks on the minimum amount of bandwidth. Once, I was swapping computers for a user and I needed to transfer the user's data to the new computer. Being naïve, I copied all the user data onto a network drive to copy back to the new computer. Because I assumed the network could handle this procedure, I did not ask anyone about bandwidth or server drive size. Well, guess what? My copying took over 25 percent of the network bandwidth and sent all sorts of server alerts to the administrators. Not only was the bandwidth a problem, the network drive I was copying to became totally full. Luckily, everything worked out okay. I deleted the copied data and the network only slowed down a bit rather than coming to a screeching halt. Always find out the capabilities and limitations of a network before doing any kind of work on it. By the way, I

copied the data over by slaving the drives after that and it worked well.

From this example, even if you are on a network that can handle an extra load, you must ask yourself a few questions before doing anything that might strain the network. Are there other people on the network doing something similar to what you want to do? If so, will the combined effect of your collective actions cause network problems? Are there people working on the network who might be slowing things down to a level that would be further aggravated by your actions? Is there another way to do what you are trying to do without using the network? I've seen many techs carry around a portable hard drive with them all day to do data transfers and software installs. Not only are they saving valuable network bandwidth, they are probably getting their data sent faster. In addition, they can carry all the drivers and repair software on this drive.

—*Ted Hamilton, MCSE, MCP, A+ Certified*

CERTIFICATION SUMMARY

This chapter has offered you a general understanding of basic networking concepts, including the various methods by which networks operate and an overview of some of the more common networking problems. A firm grasp of networking fundamentals is becoming an increasing necessity in today's network-oriented computer industry.

As you have learned, Local Area Networks (LANs) are most commonly created by connecting workstations that have Network Interface Cards (NICs). These workstations are usually connected using either twisted-pair, coaxial, or fiber-optic cabling. The physical and logical layout of the LAN is called the topology. The three basic topologies are bus, star, and ring. Communication on the network cable is governed by network access methods such as Carrier Sense Multiple Access/Collision Detection (CSMA/CD) or token passing.

Common network problems can be caused by a number of factors, including physically damaged cable, damaged NICs, excessive traffic on the network, an incorrectly operating hub, missing or incorrectly operating terminator, or magnetic fields. These conditions can result in reduced bandwidth, loss of data, and network slowdown.

 # TWO-MINUTE DRILL

- ❏ A Network Interface Card is more commonly known by its acronym, NIC.
- ❏ Basic networking concepts include topologies, cabling, NICs, network access, and protocols.
- ❏ Common cabling types include twisted pair, coaxial, and fiber optic.
- ❏ Common topologies include star, bus, and ring.
- ❏ A star topology requires that each network device be connected to a port on a hub.
- ❏ In a bus topology, each device is connected to a T-connector that is then connected to the cable that has a 50Ω terminator connected to each end.
- ❏ Fiber-optic cable is often organized in a ring topology, and requires that each end of the cable be connected to a special fiber-optic connector.
- ❏ Twisted-pair cable is capable of transmitting a maximum of 100 meters, coaxial is capable of a maximum of 180 meters, and fiber optic a maximum of 2 kilometers.

❑ Multiple segments of coaxial cable can be connected using a BNC, sometimes called a barrel connector.

❑ Fiber optic is the only type of cable not subject to electromagnetic interference.

❑ When you try to transmit data over too great a distance, the signal degrades in a problem known as attenuation.

❑ NICs are the devices that connect a PC to the network cable. NICs must be matched to the type of network and type of cable that you are using.

❑ Network access defines the method by which devices can communicate across the network.

❑ The two most common network access methods are Carrier Sense Multiple Access/Collision Detection (CSMA/CD), which is commonly used with twisted pair and coaxial cable, and token passing, which is commonly used with fiber optic. Other access methods include Carrier Sense Multiple Access with Collision Avoidance (CSMA/CA) and demand polling.

❑ CSMA/CD is an access method by which a device transmits data onto the network and then detects if any other devices have transmitted onto the network at the same time.

❑ Token passing is an access method by which a token is passed from device to device around a virtual ring, and the device can transmit data only when it receives the token.

❑ Protocols, which ensure that both the receiver and the sender can understand the data that is sent, are used to define how devices communicate with each other.

❑ Some common protocols include Transmission Control Protocol/Internet Protocol (TCP/IP), Internetwork Packet Exchange/Sequenced Packet Exchange (IPX/SPX), and NetBIOS Extended User Interface (NetBEUI).

❑ Most Network Interface Cards require an IRQ address and an IO Memory address in order to operate correctly.

❑ Common network problems can be caused by a physically damaged cable, a damaged NIC, excessive traffic on the network, an incorrectly operating hub, a missing or incorrectly operating terminator, or magnetic fields.

❑ Common results of network problems can include reduced bandwidth, loss of data, or network slowdown.

SELF TEST

The following Self Test questions will help you measure your understanding of the material presented in this chapter. Read all the choices carefully, as there may be more than one correct answer. Choose all correct answers for each question.

1. A coaxial network arranged in a bus topology requires what at both ends?

   A.   BNC

   B.   T-connector

   C.   50W Terminator

   D.   50Ω Terminator

2. Connecting two segments of coaxial cable to make a longer cable must be connected using what?

   A.   BNC

   B.   T-connector

   C.   Hub

   D.   RJ-45

3. A _____ is at the center of a star topology.

   A.   Hub

   B.   Router

   C.   Repeater

   D.   NIC

4. Which of the following are not susceptible to electromagnetic interference? (Choose all that apply.)

   A.   Coaxial cable

   B.   Twisted-pair cable

   C.   Fiber-optic cable

   D.   Telephone cable

5. CAT-5 cable used for IEEE 802.3 Ethernet requires a(n) _____ connector at both ends.

   A.   Fiber optic

   B.   RJ-45

   C.   RJ-11

   D.   T

6. Which cable type transmits and receives data using light signals through a glass or plastic transmission medium?

   A.   Fiber

   B.   Coaxial

   C.   Twisted pair

   D.   Copper

7. Which of the following are types of twisted pair cable? (Choose all that apply.)

   A.   Coaxial

   B.   STP

   C.   UTP

   D.   CAT-5

8. Which of the following are valid topologies for token-ring networks? (Choose all that apply.)

   A.   Bus

   B.   Star

   C.   Ring

   D.   Star-ring

9. What is the maximum transmission speed of Fast Ethernet?

A. 1.45 Mbps

B. 10 Mbps

C. 100 Mbps

D. 1 Gbps

10. What is the maximum transmission speed of standard Ethernet?

A. 1.45 Mbps

B. 10 Mbps

C. 100 Mbps

D. 1 Gbps

11. FDDI runs over what kind of cabling?

A. Coaxial

B. Twisted pair

C. Fiber optic

D. CAT-5

12. The maximum transmission distance of CAT-5 UTP based Ethernet is

_____.

A. 100 meters

B. 180 meters

C. 500 meters

D. 2000 meters

13. The degradation of a network signal when transmitting over a great distance is known as _____?

A. Signaling

B. Attenuation

C. Ringing

D. Beaconing

14. Ethernet uses what access method?

A. CSMA/CD

B. CSMA/CA

C. Demand polling

D. Token passing

15. Token-ring network devices connect to each other through what device?

A. Hub

B. MAU

C. BNC

D. Router

16. Which of the following devices can be used to correct problems with attenuation on a network using a bus topology?

A. Hub

B. BNC

C. Repeater

D. MAU

17. What is the maximum transmission distance of coaxial cable?

A. 100 meters

B. 180 meters

C. 500 meters

D. 2000 meters

18. Which of the following network topologies will always suffer complete failure when a single cable breaks? (Choose all that apply.)

A. Bus

B. Ring

C. Star

D. Star-bus

19. Token ring 802.5 standards specify what transmission speeds? (Choose all that apply.)

    A. 4 Mbps

    B. 10 Mbps

    C. 16 Mbps

    D. 100 Mbps

Scenario for questions 20–23: One of your executive users wants to be able to connect to the corporate network from her home. She is currently using a dial-up connection over a standard telephone line with a 56K modem, but she complains that this connection is too slow. You are asked to evaluate various remote networking options to provide solutions to meet the different requirements as presented in the following four questions.

20. Which solution would provide a data connection of up to 128 Kbps over standard copper phone lines, as well as allowing simultaneous voice and data connections?

    A. ISDN

    B. ADSL

    C. Cable modem

    D. PSTN

21. Which solution would provide a high-speed data connection over coaxial cable?

    A. ISDN

    B. ADSL

    C. Cable modem

    D. PSTN

22. Which solution would provide high-speed downloads, but upload speeds identical to that of the modem?

    A. ISDN

    B. PSTN

    C. Cable modem

    D. Digital satellite

23. Which solution would provide high-speed connectivity up to a theoretical maximum of 8.448 Mbps over standard copper lines?

    A. PSTN

    B. ISDN

    C. DSL

    D. None of the above

24. What is the network protocol used on the Internet?

    A. TCP/IP

    B. IPX/SPX

    C. NetBEUI

    D. AppleTalk

25. What is the device installed in a user's workstation that allows them to connect to the network?

    A. Network Access Card

    B. Network Interface Card

    C. Media Access Card

    D. Hub

8

Customer
Satisfaction

Achieving outstanding customer satisfaction is of paramount importance in the business world. Even though your score on this section of the exam does not affect your overall exam score, it is extremely important to master this subject. Your professional behavior while working with the customer has the potential of boosting your career immensely. There are many aspects to the art of customer satisfaction, which are discussed in this chapter.

CERTIFICATION OBJECTIVE 8.01

Achieving and Maintaining Customer Satisfaction

Achieving and thereafter maintaining customer satisfaction is a complex skill. Once mastered, it can provide you with many benefits. You will probably notice career-enhancing events like pats on the back and phone calls to your boss (and perhaps even your boss's boss) marveling at what a wonderful technician you are. Customer satisfaction may look effortless, but in reality, the art of achieving and maintaining a satisfied customer is as challenging as learning computer technical skills.

Customer satisfaction benefits a business. Smart business people have always known this—that's why customer satisfaction has always been an important aspect in the service industry. If you look at the companies that have stayed in business the longest, chances are they have stressed the importance of customer satisfaction to their employees. Companies are not just interested in computer technicians who will fix their employees' computers. Companies are looking for a worker who is going to make their employees more productive and happy.

Company owners have spent large amounts of money to keep their workers happy. Why would they want to cut corners and send in a bunch of unprofessional computer technicians who would undermine their efforts at employee satisfaction by making the employees frustrated and angry?

What does it take to achieve and maintain customer satisfaction? The first step is to always go the extra mile for the customer. This takes extra time, patience, good listening skills, and the ability to communicate at the user's level of understanding. It also requires the ability to read situations quickly. If you use good professional behavior, listen and communicate well, avoid conflict, and fix the customer's PC, you are on your way to achieving customer satisfaction.

One way of understanding customer satisfaction is to think about a situation when you were a customer. Think back to the last car you purchased. What were you satisfied or dissatisfied with? How did the salesperson present him or herself? Did you receive the attention you expected? These are the elements that make or break an encounter with a customer in any business.

Occasionally customer satisfaction will be measured through the use of a customer satisfaction survey. A survey should include the service performed, timeliness of the service, professionalism of the technician, whether the problem was fixed in one trip, whether the problem recurred, whether the service was done satisfactorily, and if everything worked correctly after the visit. If your company uses these surveys, make sure to look at them frequently.

If a technician fixes a computer, but doesn't have good interpersonal skills, then the technician is not doing the whole job. A technician should always leave customers with the feeling that they have been treated with dignity, respect, and integrity. Many technicians think that if they just fix the machines, then the customer is satisfied. This is rarely the case—most users have no idea what you are doing and the only way that they can judge you is by the way you act and the way they are treated.

Once you have built customer satisfaction, the next step is to maintain it. A good start to maintaining a happy customer is good record keeping. Every time you do anything to the user's PC, you should record exactly what you did. This will be helpful for you or whoever else returns to this PC in the future. Keep these lists in a database. Keep track of what you did, and also what the customer said. Customers appreciate it when you have researched past repairs and are familiar with the situation before you begin working on their machines.

Good records are also helpful if a repair cannot be completed in one visit. It is important to let the user know the status of your work either by visiting, phoning, or e-mailing them. People don't like to be kept in the dark about things.

Communicating and Listening

Communicating and listening is of utmost importance in computer repair. It's about knowing when to listen, when to speak, and what to say. Communication includes e-mail, telephone, notes, and face-to-face conversations. Figure 8-1 shows a typical organization's channels of communication.

Listening

Let's discuss listening first. If nothing else, listening will always bring you more information to think about. Many technicians jump to the conclusion that they can solve the problem before the user has completely discussed the problem. This is a big mistake and the consequences can be tragic.

FIGURE 8-1	Communication channels in a typical organization

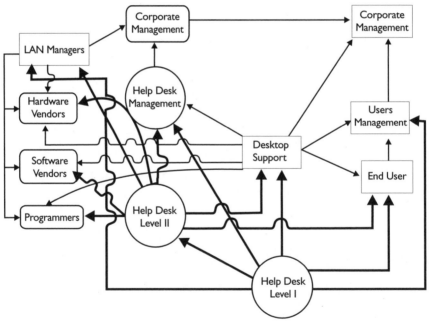

NOTE: Bold lines represent Help Desk level I & II.

Here's an example of a technician coming to a conclusion without fully listening to the customer: A PC is having problems and the technician, without listening to the customer, sees that the network cord is out. Thinking there is a network problem, the technician plugs in the network cord. Unfortunately it was a faulty network card that was causing the problem. Someone had decided to pull it out of the wall so the card would not send out broadcasts, flooding the network. If the technician had only waited to listen to the customer tell them that someone working on the hub had disconnected the cord an hour ago, then a different solution might have been chosen.

Communicating

Along with listening to customers is how you communicate back to them. Knowing when to ask questions is important. The most obvious—and best—approach to communicating with customers is first to ask them what problems are occurring. If a solution is not evident, ask them what had changed on the machine preceding the problem. Don't play the blame game. Just act matter-of-factly and get the information that you need to solve the problem. Try to get the user to remember when and what they were doing when the problem started.

If possible, have the user recreate the problem. If the problem can't be recreated, then give the user your pager number and ask them to page you if the problem occurs again. Speaking of pagers, most companies now provide all their techs with pagers. If you don't have one, get one, and give out the number to those whom you think will use it responsibly. This gives the customer the safe feeling that if there is an emergency, they have a technician they can get in touch with.

When you are done listening to the user and have asked all of your questions, paraphrase what the user has said. Ask them if you "have it right." This can be a question such as, "Just to make sure I understand the problem fully, let me say it back to you"; then state the problem and ask, "Is this what is actually happening?" You are essentially doing two things at once with this technique: The customer is satisfied because they feel you genuinely care about their problem, and you are not on a wild goose chase trying to solve the wrong problem because of miscommunication.

Communicating also involves giving out information about yourself. Always introduce yourself to the user when you first meet. Tell them they can ask for you by name if they run into further problems. Find out the user's name and use it when you meet with them. Many names are difficult to pronounce. Keep a list of the phonetic pronunciation of their names along with their record. If you can't pronounce their name, call them on the phone to let them know you are coming out, and write down the pronunciation at this point. I have found that most people with difficult names respond very well when directly asked, "What is the correct pronunciation of your name?" This removes any guesswork and makes the individual feel like you care about them enough to ask.

One thing that really makes users angry and usually ends up with a call to the help desk (or worse) is when a technician does something to a PC and does not leave a note. Many times, you will be asked to install hardware or software for an entire floor. Let the users know how long it will take you to do each computer. Ask if anyone's computer should be completed first. Work around the user. Save the busiest people for last. Update the users on how long it will take given the current configurations of that particular department's computers.

When approaching a user's desk, always communicate the basic necessities of fixing their PC. Ask the user to clear their desk if necessary, and tell them how long you will need to be there. It is essential that you are polite. I've seen too many techs barge into offices and practically push people out of their seat just to get to their machines. Say things like, "Take your time, make sure you save all you work." The last thing you want is to ruin your first impression with the user by putting them in such a rush that they don't save the important Word documents they have been working on all day.

Communication does not end at the user's desk. Good communication between technicians is also essential. Many companies use pagers, two-way radios, computers, and cell phones so technicians can get in touch with each other throughout the day to troubleshoot problems. Try and eat lunch with the other techs, or at least have a time of day when you can all sit down and pick each other's brains about the problems you are working on. Never be afraid to ask simple questions. Chances are that if you are this far in the A+ certification process, you know a lot about computers, but there is always more to learn. If you don't know what you are doing, ask your peers, and if their answer is not satisfactory find the answer from another source.

Technicians should also be able to quickly discern a user's technical level. You want to use explanations appropriate for a user's level. Explaining the DOS memory model to a non-technical user is probably not the best way to explain the fact that the computer needs more memory to run all of the programs.

Sometimes, technicians have to handle awkward situations. For example, a user may call and ask for access to something that is restricted. They might try to get software and hardware when they haven't received the proper permissions. Other users will try to have someone else's password reset. This is where your communication skills are essential. You want to find out if these are relevant requests, but you do not want to accuse them of anything. Tell the user that it is company policy that so-and-so has to approve certain types of requests.

Interpreting Verbal and Nonverbal Cues

Interpreting both verbal and nonverbal cues when dealing with customers is a must. Verbal cues can be obvious or may be very subtle. Nonverbal cues are even subtler. It is paramount to read all of these cues in order to make sure that things run smoothly.

When you first approach a user, listen to their tone of voice. Are they tense, annoyed, angry, rushed, wanting to talk, or just wanting to do their work while you expeditiously repair the machine? You need to read this and act accordingly. If they are annoyed, let them tell you how annoyed they are. Chances are if they vent all their problems to you about their broken computer, they'll be less likely to tell other people of their frustrations. Even if you don't have a good answer to all their problems, the fact that you are willing to hear them out helps the situation.

Read the mood that they are in. Do they seem like they want to talk about the weather or would they rather just have you fix the problem and be on your merry way? In any corporate climate, moods can vary greatly. Read the cues carefully, because they will indeed dictate the approach that you will use in conversing with the customer.

Verbal cues can contain a plethora of information. Listen very closely to what users say. Sometimes they give away information on how they are feeling with the words that they are using. If they're in a bad mood, chances are they're using a lot of negative words.

Nonverbal cues are quite possibly more important than verbal cues. It is said that 80 percent of all communication is done nonverbally. Nonverbal cues can be seen in the face of the user. If the user looks worried when you are moving things around, take note and be careful. The face can tell a lot.

Look for nonverbal cues to help you know how to handle each situation. For example, if you are in a situation where you've been working on a PC for a long time, the user might just want you to leave and fix it the next day. If they are jingling their car keys, putting on their coat, or packing their briefcase, you want to let the user know that the problem is taking longer than originally planned and ask them if they need to be somewhere else. They may want to go to lunch and don't want to leave you in their office. In this situation, tell the user the status of your repair and let them know how long it will take you to complete it. Be willing to work around their schedule.

Always listen to the hints in the user's voice. If they are stressed, it helps to get the user in a trusting, relaxed, and satisfied mood. Hopefully, you will leave them with a smile on their face when you are done. If you are calm about a situation, it calms the user. Reassure them. If their problem is hardware-related, let the user know that you have a part that you can swap for them and will be back later in the day to swap it. A calm user is a satisfied user.

And when you're thinking about nonverbal cues, don't forget to notice the cues that you are projecting. Are you calm, confident, and collected or are you tense, anxious, and frustrated? The user will be able to sense the kind of mood you are in by your own nonverbal cues. Make sure that you are projecting the type of cues that you want the user to see. If you look anxious, then the user will start to feel anxious. Even if you are frustrated about something not working, don't show it. Realize that it is part of computer repair. Some things are just going to take time and patience. Just stay calm and realize you can't get everything done in a lightning-fast manner. Confidence breeds success in all fields of work; PC repair is no exception.

Responding to the Customer's Technical Level

Responding to the customer's technical level is easy to do, once you get a feel for it. It can save time and help to solve problems. This brings up a very important point. Make sure you are completely up to date with the latest information on computers. You can do this by reading a few of the best computer magazines out there.

You can always ask the user if they are familiar with a certain program. This can save time. Figure out creative ways to determine user abilities. Keep a mental record of the abilities of each user. Never put the user in a situation where they have to admit that they are not as knowledgeable as they could be. Listen to the language that they use when they are describing things. If they are talking about mapping a drive using an UNC path, for example, chances are you're dealing with a technical user. Respect all users regardless of their technical ability. You will always run into a user who is using a PC for the first time in their lives. Treat them kindly, patiently, and with respect.

Most users are casual users. Luckily, the casual and beginning users' problems are the easiest to repair. They get stumped on the same types of problems that you got stuck on eight years ago. Repairing them is second nature to you. Many novice users will act like they understand what you are doing when in reality they have no idea. With these users, it is a good idea to glance over at the notes they are taking and determine if they are getting the gist of what you are telling them.

Always try to put yourself in the customer's shoes. Think of the first time you ever turned on a PC. Think of how confusing everything was. If somebody started talking about EMS or EMM or some other acronym, you would have been lost. A new user often struggles to do what they want to do. Take the extra time and give them hints if time permits. Try to explain the big picture to them. These short lessons can save you and your company time in the long run.

On the other end of the spectrum are the advanced users. It is truly a pleasure to find a user who has a vast knowledge of computers. When this is the case, talk to the user on their level. Let them explain what has been done to the computer. Listening to the user is one of the best troubleshooting techniques. Their help will be key to solving the problem. Even though all of these people may not be total computer wizards, try to let them feel they are. Use comments to show that you realize that they are very good at working with computers.

Being a tech, most people will be in awe of your great computer wisdom. They will take your words as gospel. Please tell them the truth when it comes to computers. Be as knowledgeable as you can about computers and it will be easy to determine the user's abilities with a few questions and observations.

Establishing Personal Rapport with the Customer

Establishing personal rapport with the customer is one of the key elements to maintaining customer satisfaction. Rapport leads to trust, and trust leads to cooperation and a good relationship. Personal rapport includes following up on problems that you judge might end up being a problem again later. It also includes knowing your customers' computer hardware, software, configuration, and history. Finally, it includes knowing your customer on an interpersonal level.

Get to know your users. If you see them in the hall, ask how the last repair you did is working. As is often the case with computers, there will be times when the PC is doing its own thing and there will be dead silence between you and the user. This is the perfect opportunity to get to know them. When the customer views you as a person with whom they have a good rapport, they are less likely to withhold important information from you, and they will be more likely to cooperate with you.

Cooperation is the key to the technician-user relationship. Many times when a PC is messed up, it truly is the user's fault. Never, I repeat, never let them know this. When you have a good rapport with the customer, it is likely that they may actually admit that "somebody" ran FDISK and didn't have the foggiest notion of what they were doing. And being the friendly technician that you are, you buy their story about this "somebody," and gently let them know that this fictitious user should not try to run programs that they are not familiar with.

FROM THE FIELD

Frank Is His Name and Rapport Is His Game

One day I decided to help our lead tech, Frank, do two computer moves. While I was helping him, I noticed how he developed rapport with clients. Frank has been working in this business for over a decade and everyone he runs into thinks that he is a great tech.

After grabbing a pushcart, we started to the first location. Frank, of course, made sure he had his toolkit, extra network cords, safety glasses, and so on. We picked up the first computer from a user's desk; Frank called the user who was to receive the computer to let him know we were coming. He also made sure that this was the right PC and that he did, indeed, want it moved right then. On the way over to another building, Frank greeted about 75 percent of the passersby by their first name. They all smiled broadly and greeted him back. One user walked by and Frank asked him how everything was going. The user replied that his printing was still slow. Frank, knowing each person's particular PC (which amounts to thousands of PCs), told the user that the memory module was being ordered. He then said that he had spoken to the person who ordered it, and they had said that it would be in some time next week. As you can see, Frank lived up to many of the principles set forth in this chapter: communicating with users who needed a service, remembering the problem, following up on the service, and making sure the necessary part is ordered. He was also confident and positive.

When we showed up at our destination, the user was there and we delivered his PC. Frank conversed with this user about non-PC related items. We stayed around long enough for the login to the network just to make sure he could grab a DHCP IP address. Frank then talked to three other people in the department and we left. Everybody was happy.

We then went to our next assignment, which was in the middle of a factory. The person who wanted a PC moved was in the middle of something, so he just gave us directions on how to get to the PC. When we arrived, there was a big argument between two other users about whether this machine should be moved. Frank quickly determined that he would move the computer later. It didn't even faze him that delaying the move would mean trekking the cart all the way out there again later to move it. At this point, he didn't just accept that we'd move it later and walk away. Instead, he turned to the angry user, told him a joke, and had him laughing his head off. I'm sure that user will give him a big hello the next time he sees him in the hall.

Learn from this tech. People like him so much that he has excellent job security and enjoys going to work every day. He has developed these communication skills through years of knowing what people like and what they don't like. The rapport that he has built in all the years is extraordinary.

—*Ted Hamilton, MCSE, MCP, A+ Certified*

Many times, you will find a user for whom you have clearly fixed the problem, but they keep asking about other problems and making requests that are not on the work order. You should use discretion. You might share a story that shows you have to tend to many requests. You might wish to stay on, but your schedule demands you be on to your next repair. Suggest and encourage them to use the help files or whatever else your company has for learning aid.

Good rapport with customers is the patience to stop when they stop you in the hall, and discuss whatever they want to discuss with you. Many times a user will ask about non-company PC issues. Answer them only if you have the time. If you are busy, politely tell them you are busy and will try and get back with them. Invite them to lunch to discuss the matter. Answer their questions to the extent that you can, but make sure that you fully understand the situation that they are facing.

Good rapport with the customer can include keeping up with what they talk to you about on a personal basis. For example, if a user talks to you about his car being in the shop, make sure you ask the next time you see him if the car is fixed. Make the whole PC repair situation as enjoyable as possible. Let users know that you are happy to see them. Even if you do not say this explicitly, make sure that your actions show it. Don't look at problems as a point of frustration. Instead, view them as a learning opportunity. Nothing is more satisfying than learning how to fix a recurring problem on multiple PCs.

Always think of what you are doing as a service-sector job. Think of all the people who are in the service sector that you have dealt with in your life. Think of the ten worst ones and then the ten best ones. What did the ten worst ones do to turn you off? Never do what they did to you. Now think of what the ten best people did. Concentrate on their behavior and act accordingly. What was it that they did right?

Professional Conduct

In the computer services industry, it is essential to understand and practice the concept of professional conduct. This encompasses appearance, attitude, time management, integrity, and competence. All too often in this field there are technicians who don't take professionalism seriously. This can make a department, a company, or even the whole industry look bad. Perception is reality to most people and the way that the customer sees you is how they form opinions about you, your department, and the field in general.

Appearance

Appearance is very important in the business world. The nature of the work of an A+ Certified Professional will often get you into offices that other people will never be able to get into. How often do people get 20 minutes to talk to the true titans of industry in a relaxed atmosphere? Well, when you are fixing their PCs, often they are there and it is your time to shine. In a situation like this, you are going to want to make sure that your appearance is the best it can be. You should wear clothes that match the dress of the corporation and avoid splashing on strong fragrances—some people are allergic to perfume and cologne. Work to achieve an overall neat appearance. The higher up the ladder you go, the more important your appearance.

Attitude

Attitude is important when fixing computers. If you have a good attitude, the user is going to be friendlier and ultimately more satisfied with your work. If you have a lackadaisical attitude about what you are doing, then maybe PC repairs are not for you. Think of your job as fun and be enthusiastic and you will be amazed at how well users treat you.

This brings up the second point on attitude, which is confidence in what you are doing. If you have learned all that you should about computers, then there is no reason not to be confident. This is not being a braggart or cocky, but having an attitude about yourself that makes users understand that you know what you are doing. This instills a sense of trust in them.

Language

Your language is another way people read your attitude. Swearing is unprofessional. We've all seen a frustrated technician swearing at the computer loud enough that the whole department can hear. What this tells people is that the technician has a bad attitude and they assume the technician is incompetent at fixing PCs. Think about it this way: If your physician was swearing and acting frustrated when he was doing a procedure on you, you'd probably be very scared. If you find yourself getting angry on the job and venting, you better ask yourself: Why am I being so negative? The key is to keep your negative emotions contained when you are at the customer's PC. A better place to let out your anger with the machine would be to go back and have a lively discussion with the other techs on what was causing you to be frustrated. PCs inevitably bring you to frustration on occasion. They are not perfect and there will always be problems that make absolutely no sense. Instead of letting the customer know that you have let the machine win, take a breather, do some research, call on your peers, consult TechNet; but don't swear, pout, or do anything that will make the customer think less of the top-notch service that you are capable of providing.

Don't Intrude

Time is a crucial variable that you need to master. It is important to minimize the time spent on each PC. In short, do whatever you can to be respectful of the customer's time.

Sometimes work quarters are tight. Do not barge your way into the user's office and cram them in between the chair and desk. If they are on the phone when you go by to help them, either leave or wait far enough away from them so that they don't think that you are eavesdropping on their conversation. If they are in a meeting, do not interrupt them. You can walk by and gesture that you are there and give them enough time to either stop their conversation and welcome you in or schedule another meeting with you.

Patience

Another tricky problem that constantly happens is that the PC technician shows up but the user is not in. It is common for busy professionals to be pulled away or to forget about a service call. Always ask someone in a neighboring office if it is okay to go into the user's office. If you have not worked with the user or if you have any reservations about entering the workspace, then by all means don't go in—try to contact them another way. Make absolutely sure that you know what the problem is and it is the right

1. DIMM memory sockets
2. Secondary EIDE channel connector
3. Microprocessor
4. Power supply
5. Power input connector
6. Battery socket
7. 3.3-V power input connector
8. Diskette drive interface connector
9. Primary EIDE channel connector
10. Control panel connector
11. System board jumpers
12. ISA expansion-card connectors
13. PCI expansion-card connectors

The inside of the typical IBM personal computer, showing the most vital system components such as the microprocessor, power supply, expansion cards, drive controllers, and memory sockets. Expansion cards, floppy and hard drive cables, as well as the drives themselves have been omitted for a clear view of the motherboard. Every component seen here will be tested on the exam, in addition to other components that are not shown here: hard drives, CD-ROM drives, and tape drives. For the exam, you will be expected to know the characteristics of each component of a standard computer system, and how to diagnose and resolve problems related to each.

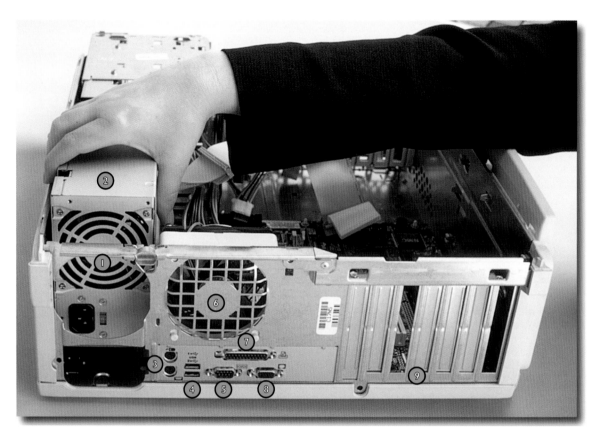

The installation of a power supply in an IBM compatible computer. Most power supplies are removed with four screws on the rear of the power supply. Repair of a power supply should be performed by a skilled technician with the necessary training and equipment to work on power supplies. The replacement of a power supply should occur immediately if the fan stops functioning because the power supply can overheat and destroy the entire computer. For the exam, you will need to understand the symptoms of a failing power supply.

1. Power supply cooling fan
2. Power supply
3. Keyboard and PS/2 mouse connectors
4. USB ports
5. Serial port
6. Cooling fan
7. Parallel port
8. Monitor port
9. Slot covers

1. Cooling fan
2. CPU (processor) central processing unit
3. Processor socket
4. PCI expansion slot
5. 168-Pin DIMM memory
6. Power supply connectors
7. IDE flat data ribbon cable

Installation of a microprocessor in a computer. Notice how the lever in the processor socket is in the raised position. Once the processor is placed in the socket, you then lower the lever to lock the processor in place. To free the processor, you simply raise the lever. This is known as a Zero Insertion Force (ZIF) socket, and not all motherboards are equipped with this type of socket. For the exam, you most likely will not have to worry about the ZIF socket, but you will need to know about the various types of processors on the market. You will need to know the characteristics of each processor, such as the width of the data bus and address bus, and the register size.

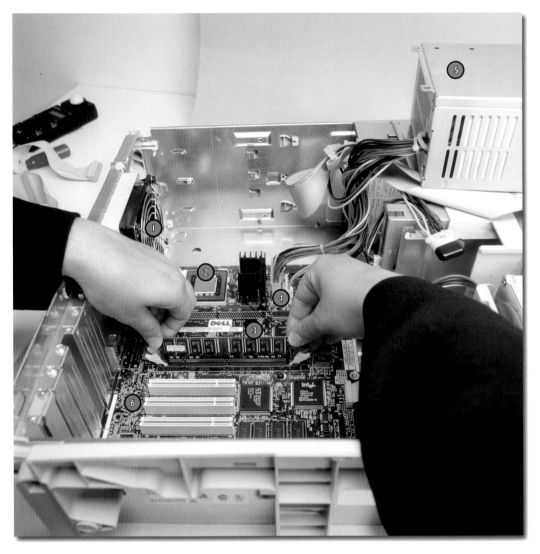

Installation of 168-pin DIMM memory in a computer. With DIMM memory, the module is inserted straight up and down, unlike the insertion method of SIMM memory, which is inserted at a 45 degree angle and then clicked into place when the memory is in the upright position. The notches on the DIMM memory module will lock into place with the keys located on the socket. For the exam, you will need to know the various types of memory available, including ROM, RAM, DRAM, and SRAM, and the characteristics of each.

1. Cooling fan
2. Central processing unit
3. 168-Pin DIMM memory
4. Power supply connectors
5. Power supply
6. PCI expansion slots

Installation of a floppy disk drive in the front bay of an IBM compatible computer. The floppy drive is 3.5 inches in size. Most computers have bays for two 3.5 floppy drives located on the front of the computer. The 5.25-inch bays are used for CD-ROM drives and tape drives. For the exam, you will need to know how to troubleshoot the floppy disk drive subsystem, which includes the media, floppy drive, cable, and the controller.

1. CD-ROM drive
2. Additional CD-ROM or tape drive bay (5.25-inch size)
3. Floppy disk drive bays (3.5-inch size)
4. Floppy disk drive

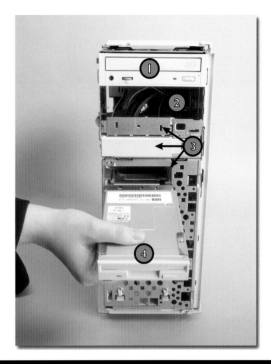

A printer motor used to move the paper through the printer. There are a few motors located in a printer—the main drive, paper feed, and transport motor. Every manufacturer uses different types of motors in varying places throughout the printer, so you must consult your vendor's documentation when replacing or servicing a printer motor. For the exam, you do not need to know about the motor specifically, but you should know what the effect will be on the print quality when a printer motor has failed.

1. Printer motor
2. Paper feed frame

The installation of a CD-ROM drive in an IBM compatible computer. The illustration shows the back of the CD-ROM drive which contains the connector for the 40-pin IDE cable, the power connector, sound card connector, and the master/slave jumpers. You can look down the length of the IDE cable and see another 40-pin connector for attaching another CD-ROM drive or hard drive in a master/slave configuration. For the exam, you should know the connectors and cables used in IDE devices such as hard drives and CD-ROM drives.

1. CMOS battery
2. Master/slave jumpers
3. Sound card connector
4. IDE cable
5. Power cable
6. CD-ROM drive
7. Power supply connectors
8. Additional connector for another IDE device
9. Additional CD-ROM or tape drive bays (5.25-inch size)

An example of replacing an ISA sound card in an IBM compatible computer. Expansion cards are installed with a slight rocking motion with a firm grip on both ends of the card. You can see it is standard for motherboard vendors to color the ISA slots black and the PCI slots white. For the exam, you will need to know the differences between ISA, EISA, MCA, and PCI, and the characteristics of each.

1. Floppy disk drive cable
2. ISA sound card
3. ISA expansion slots
4. PCI expansion slots
5. 168-Pin DIMM memory
6. Additional 168-pin DIMM memory socket

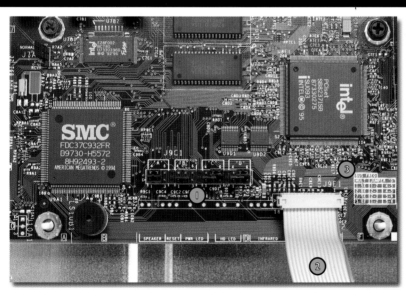

1. Configuration jumpers
2. Floppy disk drive cable
3. Jumper configuration settings

A view of configuration jumpers on a motherboard. Most motherboards have jumpers to configure internal processor speed and external bus speed. These settings are usually stamped on the motherboard in white, as seen in the illustration. If you do not configure these jumpers correctly, you could overclock your processor causing it to burn up; if you underclock the processor, you might not be utilizing the processor to its full potential. For the exam, you probably won't be asked about jumpers on the motherboard, but you will be asked about the data bus, address bus, and register size of the various processors on the market.

Installing an IDE hard drive in an IBM personal computer. From the illustration, you can see the 40-pin IDE connector on the hard drive and the 40-pin ribbon cable. When you are installing a hard drive in a system, you have the ability to make the hard drive the master of its own controller, or to configure the hard drive in a master/slave relationship with another device, such as another hard drive or CD-ROM drive. The exam will test your knowledge of configuring a hard drive using the CMOS SETUP program.

1. ISA expansion slots
2. PCI expansion slots
3. 168-Pin DIMM memory
4. Cooling fan
5. 40-Pin IDE cable
6. 3.5-Inch floppy disk drive
7. 40-Pin IDE connector
8. Power cable
9. Hard disk drive

An internal modem, which has visible jumpers in red for configuring COM port assignments. The illustration also shows a sticker on a chip, which details the various jumper settings to configure the COM port settings. The modem also includes RJ-11 connectors for connecting to the phone line and to the telephone. The exam will test your knowledge of the standard COM ports and IRQs for configuring modems.

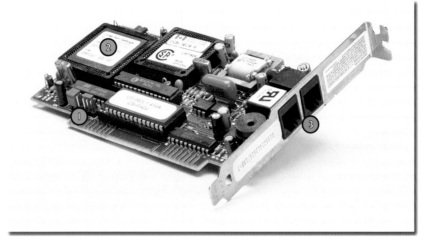

1. Com port setting jumpers
2. Jumper diagram
3. Telephone and phone line connectors

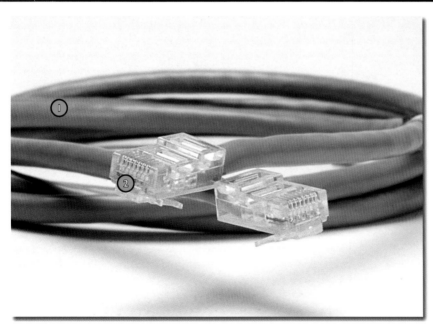

Twisted-pair coaxial cabling with an RJ-45 connector. Coaxial cable is resistant to the interference and signal weakening that other cabling, such as unshielded twisted-pair (UTP) cable, can experience. In general, coax is better than UTP for connecting longer distances and for reliably supporting higher data rates with less sophisticated equipment. For the exam, you should know the type of connector used with UTP cabling.

1. Twisted-Pair cabling
2. RJ-45 connector

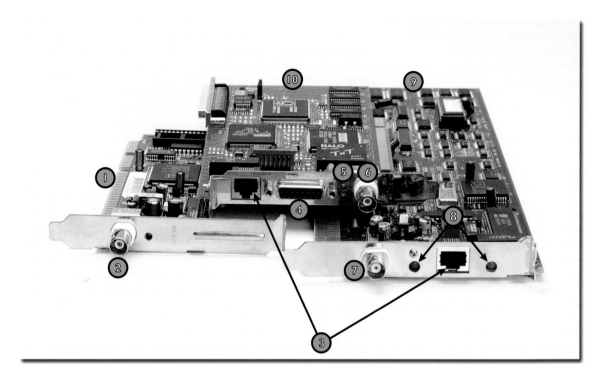

Various network interface cards with support for coax, twisted-pair, and AUI. The network interface card on the left has only one interface for a coax BNC connector. The network interface card on top has an interface for a coax BNC connector, an AUI connector, and a UTP RJ-45 connector. The network interface card on the right has an interface for a coax BNC connector and a UTP RJ-45 connector. Both the top and right network interface cards have power and link lights also. For the exam, you should know what interfaces are available on network interface cards, and the common resources, such as IRQ and I/O address, used for network cards.

1. Coaxial network interface card
2. Coaxial connector
3. Twisted-Pair connectors
4. AUI connector
5. Link and power lights
6. Coaxial connector
7. Coaxial connector
8. Link and power lights
9. Combo network card with twisted-pair and coaxial support
10. Combo network card with twisted-pair, coaxial, and AUI support

A typical printer's system board that consists of the logic required to operate the printer. Every manufacturer uses different types of logic boards in varying places throughout the printer, so you must consult your vendor's documentation when replacing or servicing the logic board. For the exam, you do not need to know about the logic board specifically, but you should know what the affect will be on a printer if the logic board is faulty and needs to be replaced.

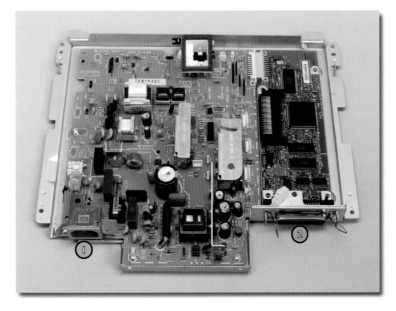

1. Power input
2. Centronics port

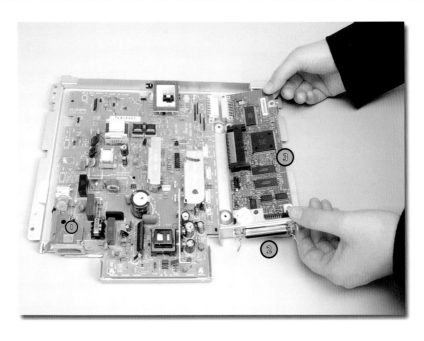

A printer's sublogic board which works in conjunction with the primary printer system board that enables you to replace or upgrade the capability of the sublogic board. Most printer sublogic boards allow you to change the port, such as replacing the Centronics port. For the exam, you should be able to identify the characteristics of parallel ports on a computer, such as ECP, EPP, and Bi Directional printer ports.

1. Power input
2. Centronics port
3. Add-on adapter card with parallel (Centronics) port

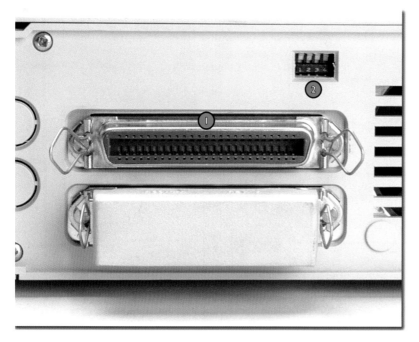

A device with external SCSI interfaces. This particular device uses a 50-pin Centronics SCSI connector, which is nearly identical to the Centronics printer cable connector. Also visible is the SCSI address ID jumper, which enables you to configure a SCSI device for a particular SCSI ID from 1–4. There are eight available addresses for SCSI IDs, with seven usually being reserved for the SCSI adapter itself. The exam will test your knowledge of the various SCSI connectors that are available.

1. Centronics 50-pin SCSI connector
2. SCSI address ID jumpers

SCSI Port

The types of Small Computer Systems Interface (SCSI) connectors available. The top SCSI connector is a 50-pin high-density connector. The middle SCSI connector is a 68-pin high-density connector. The bottom connector is a Centronics 50-pin connector, not to be confused with a Centronics printer connector, which looks almost identical. For the exam, you need to know the types of SCSI connectors presented here.

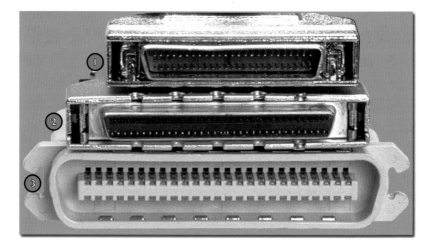

1. 50-Pin high-density SCSI
2. 68-Pin high-density SCSI
3. Centronics 50-pin SCSI

Various SCSI Connectors

A notebook computer combination cable with support for twisted-pair and coaxial cable. This unit plugs into the PCMCIA network interface card located inside the PC card bay of the notebook computer (not shown). As a travelling network technician, it's a good idea to have a combination cable like the one shown so you can connect to both a coaxial or twisted-pair network with the same PCMCIA network card. For the exam, you should know what interfaces are available in a network adapter such as this.

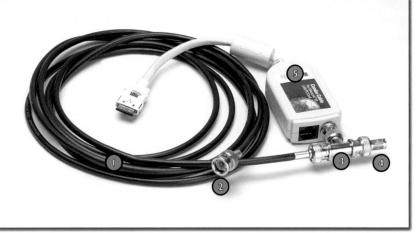

1. Thinwire 10Base2 coaxial cable
2. BNC connector
3. BNC connector
4. Terminator
5. Combination twisted-pair/ coaxial dongle

PCMCIA Ethernet Combo Network Interface Card, with Twisted-Pair and Coax Support

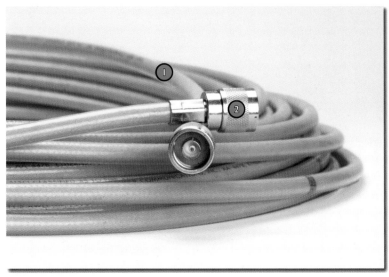

A thickwire (10Base5) cable with a BNC connector. Thicknet is extremely bulky and difficult to work with, therefore it is rarely used. Thickwire cabling is used as a network backbone or a connection between two different hubs or routers. For the exam, you should know the type of connector used with UTP cabling.

1. Thickwire (10Base5) coaxial cable
2. BNC connector

Thickwire Coaxial Cable and the Corresponding BNC Connector

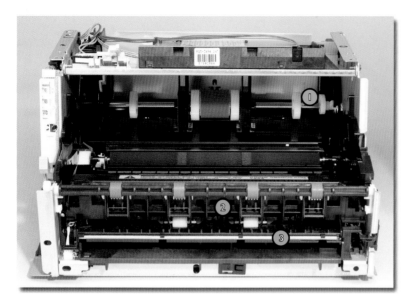

The front view of a printer roller assembly showing the numerous rollers and gears associated with a modern printer. The only internal components of a printer that you will have to be familiar with for the exam is the laser printer and the laser printing process. These components include the primary corona wire, cleaning blade, transfer corona, and the photosensitive drum. Each laser printer component is responsible for a phase during the printing process.

1. Pickup roller assembly
2. Delivery assembly
3. Separation assembly

A side view of the printer roller assembly with a view of the numerous gears involved in the printing process. From the illustration, you can see how the pickup roller assembly is removable and can be replaced in the event it becomes defective. For the exam, the only components of the printing process you should be familiar with are those of the laser printer. In addition, you should know the various phases of the laser printing process, such as the cleaning, charging, writing, developing, transferring, and fusing phase, and what occurs during each of the phases.

1. Pickup roller assembly

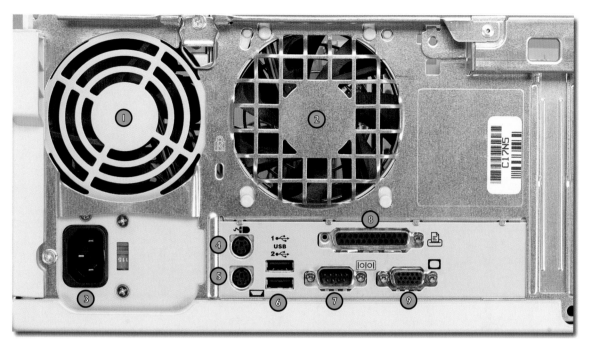

1. Power supply cooling fan
2. Cooling fan
3. Power input
4. PS/2 mouse connector
5. Keyboard connector
6. USB ports
7. Serial port
8. Parallel port
9. Monitor port

The back of a computer, illustrating the power supply and common connectors found on a personal computer. You can see the cooling fan for the power supply in addition to the CPU's cooling fan. The illustration also shows a PS/2 mouse connector, Mini-DIN keyboard connector, two USB ports, and a parallel, serial, and monitor port. For the exam, you should be able identify the physical characteristics of a serial or parallel port.

Installing memory modules in a portable notebook computer. Although most notebook computers are different, the illustration shows one method of upgrading the memory in a notebook computer. For the exam, you will not need to know anything memory-related on a notebook computer. You will need to know about memory in general, including the types of memory chips available, such as the difference between SIMMs and DIMMs.

1. Memory module
2. Contacts

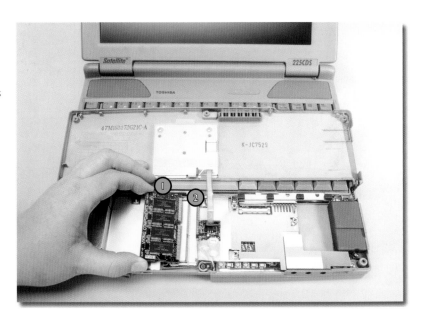

A side view of a printer's rollers and gears. You can see the complex innerworkings of a printer and how you need to provide continual routine preventative maintenance on the printer to keep the rollers and various mechanical devices working correctly. For the exam, you should know how to clean and maintain a dot matrix, ink jet, and laser printer.

computer. It's happened before: A tech fixes the wrong computer, only to find out that it was a laptop that the customer had with them that needed to be repaired. In corporations today, there are so many computers and printers around that if there is any slight chance of ambiguity in the user's complaint, do not proceed. Only proceed if the exact repair is obvious.

Integrity

Integrity goes hand in hand with professionalism. Integrity means that you are not going to compromise yourself or ask others to do so in order to achieve something. Never do anything that even appears to be compromising in terms of integrity. Obey all software copyright laws. Never try to break into anything you should not be getting into. If a person tracks the files that you have opened, and you are going into confidential files, you will not have a fun time explaining yourself. If you need a file with which to experiment, open a new one or ask the user what file it is okay to experiment with. Furthermore, make a copy of any file that you are testing, experimenting with, or modifying.

Integrity needs to be a part of software installation. Many organizations get audited for software compliance, and the penalties for unlicensed software are harsh. Get to know all of the rules for the software in your company. Find out what is site-licensed and what is individually licensed. Follow these rules to a "T." Do not install things that are not licensed. Do not bring in shareware for a user knowing that the trial agreement will be violated. Do not bring in bootleg copies of anything. There is now very sophisticated software that can audit each machine and find what does not belong. You will have a tough time explaining this to the user and your boss when these audits unearth something that should not be there in the first place.

General Professionalism

Business is business, and some things that you would do outside of a company, you would not do inside. Horseplay, pranks, and dirty jokes have no place in most corners of the business world. Stressed executives do not like to see people fooling around. Be aware of the culture in your company and behave accordingly. Some companies are more laid back than others, but be aware of how people act and try to emulate their behavior. Those who don't do this stick out like a sore thumb. These individuals are a definite liability to the corporation. It should go without saying that drugs and alcohol are not part of work life.

In short, professionalism is the image that you want to project. Look in any corporation, and you will soon realize that those who have climbed the ladder of success always act professional and those who can't get there, don't. It is all in how far up in the business world you want to get. If you are not professional, you may end up in an empty room swapping computer boards all day. On the other hand, act professional and you may end up being a leader of some sort.

Conflict Avoidance and Resolution

Conflicts can arise in the PC world for a variety of reasons. Conflicts are a challenge to your job security. A conflict has the potential of harboring bad feelings between the parties for a long period of time. In the extreme, a conflict can get so bad that the users decide to get help elsewhere. Solve all conflicts to the best of your ability, and ask for help if you can't. Do not leave any conflicts unresolved.

Company Policies

One of the most important things to learn as a technician is your company's policies regarding various computer-related topics. For example, there will always be the employees who would like to play solitaire all day. If the management doesn't care, fine. However, if the users are installing video games that affect performance, or if management does not want their employees playing games all day, then you have a situation where you need to figure out how to resolve the problem while letting management and the employees save face. In this particular situation, it is best to ask management about their policy and not give them any names. If the company wants to get rid of games, then simply approach the game players and let them know that management has said that no machines are to have games, and you must remove them.

Other conflicts regarding company policy may arise. One user may get one answer from someone while another user gets another answer. Learn company policies. If you work within the framework of what should be done, it gives you a feeling of confidence in what you say to the users. Users are always happy when you have answers ready to their questions on such items as who to call for passwords, hardware, etc. Once you know these policies, you can solve conflicts between users who are unsure of policy.

Error Between Keyboard and Chair

One problem that every computer technician will eventually face is the EBKAC error. This is usually very easy to fix, but very difficult to explain. EBKAC is an acronym for *Error Between Keyboard and Chair*. This usually entails power cords being unplugged, no paper in the printer, or power switches being turned off. This is usually quite embarrassing for the user, especially if they are watching the repair. In these situations, in order not to cause animosity, conflict, and other negative emotions, do whatever is in your power to allow the user to save face. Say something like, "I see this type of thing all the time, they should have a light on the printer that says 'out of paper'." Or for the power cord, tell them, "The person vacuuming must have dislodged it. I know it is a pain, but if this happens again, could you please look behind the computer and see if the cord has become dislodged?"

Know-It-All User

One challenge that will rear its ugly face every now and again is the know-it-all user. It seems like they must be technician wannabes, and they will try and tell you what you, as a technician, are doing wrong and what should be done. Obviously, they don't know all the answers, or they would not have called you. These people are in need of attention and they must be handled very carefully. Because the customer is always right, never argue with their way of doing things. For example, if they are really convinced that there is not enough RAM and that is why they are getting memory errors in Excel (which you know isn't the case), tell them that you would like to change the memory swap file size. Do not get into the details of how a swap file works. Explain to the user that this may indeed fix their problem and you would like them to try it out for a few days before resorting to buying RAM. Just make sure that you don't look like you are trying to prove a point to the user. Let them understand that this is the departmental policy that software configuration and optimization should be tried before hardware installation.

Angry Users

Another challenge is the angry user who is ready to tell the world about his dissatisfaction. These users generally want to talk to the head honchos and anyone else who will listen about their woes. The key to these users is to resolve their anger before it mounts. Get to them quickly and resolve the problem promptly and professionally. Listen. Show respect for their ideas by giving each one consideration while remaining patient—it can take patience. Users like this generally are satisfied when you go above and beyond the norm to finally solve their problems. Once they have finally expressed their anger, they generally calm down and are willing to sit down and resolve the problem. Don't point fingers at other people; they may just track down the person you are pointing at and chew them out. The key is controlling the situation. These people do not want excuses. They want resolutions. At this point, do whatever you have to do to please this user. Often, these people end up the most satisfied of all. They remember how they felt before you arrived and how they felt after.

Resolving Your Own Errors

Be willing to apologize for any mistake that you make. Nobody is perfect and we all make mistakes. Be prepared to identify, admit, and repair anything you break. Computers can be surprising. You may fix one problem that causes a problem somewhere else. If the user is knowledgeable enough, explain why it was that you did not realize the side effect that resulted. Don't necessarily volunteer the fact that you messed it up, but if asked, admit that what you did caused a problem elsewhere.

Other Types of Conflict

Another form of conflict is the user who will stop you in the hall with many people around and loudly complain that his PC was messed up after you left. Even if you know it is not your fault, never embarrass the user. Tell him that you will take a look at it and make sure it works properly. Many users get a kick out of humiliating the technician in front of their peers and the best defense is to act professionally.

Many times you will find that you step right into the middle of conflict. One user may want you to do one thing and another will want you to do the opposite. For instance, this may involve moving a computer to a different area. Users may even compete at trying to boss you around by telling you not to listen to what the other person is saying. In this kind of situation, never take a side. Tell them politely that you will wait for them to resolve their argument before you will do anything. If necessary, tell them you will come back at a later time when they finally settle their differences. Not taking sides is usually a good idea in most arguments when users try to get you in the middle. For example, when they are arguing if SCSI or non-SCSI is better, tell them the merits of both and the drawbacks, but don't side with any of the arguers. This may result in long-held resentment by the person with whom you did not side.

Measuring the Customer Service Experience

In service industries customer experience will make or break you. Most management teams understand this, so they are very interested in measuring the level of service that their customers are receiving. This section should help to give you a little insight into what management forces are at work, what the goal is, and what the heck they are talking about!

Metrics. That's what we're talking about. When it comes to measuring customer experience (or just about anything these days) the buzzword is "METRICS!" Metrics is just a fancy word for measurement. When people talk about generating metrics, they're just talking about measuring something and reporting what those measurements are.

Now that we know we're supposed to measure something, what do we measure? To answer this question, management might form a focus group that consists of managers, users, and support technicians. The focus group would meet a few times and discuss what is good and bad about technical support at the company (all the while someone is taking notes). Then the managers would get together and form opinions about what needs to be addressed. Eventually, the managers would come up with a set of measurements. A system would then be built, reports would be generated, management would be happy, and the customer experience might just improve.

The most successful customer experience metrics efforts I have been involved with have always been grounded in proven quality management techniques. Total Quality Management (TQM), statistical analysis, and 360-degree communications are quality management tools and techniques that you might be exposed to.

When defining a metrics program, I always work from the top down and from the bottom up looking for the middle ground. By that I mean that I try and understand what the management team is trying to achieve, and I try and understand the work being done from the technicians' perspective. It does no good to try and measure the capital expense of replacement hardware if the technicians don't keep track of replacement hardware and the finance people don't assign a cost to replacement hardware.

Let's look at how we might resolve this apparent disconnect between management's need for the capital cost of replacement hardware and the way that technicians replace hardware. Asking the technicians what the cost is for each piece of hardware probably won't work. They will be quick to tell you that they are technicians, not accountants. Asking the accountants what the cost is for replacement hardware is equally frustrating. After all, they are accountants, not technicians. How should they know how many of one thing or another is replaced? At first it seems easy. The cost of replacement hardware is simply the amount of money the company spends each month buying hardware. Oh but wait, the company is growing, so some of that purchasing is for new equipment related to growth and some is related to equipment replacement.

If the accountants could tell you what the most expensive pieces of hardware are, you could ask the technicians to keep track of just the replacements of those pieces. Then the technicians could tell the accountants how many of those pieces were replaced, the accountants could add, subtract, multiply, and divide, and you could tell management that you can now account for 80 percent of the cost of replacing hardware! Of course management will then ask you to eliminate that cost, but that's another story.

There are a few things I think you should get from the example above. First, if you don't control it you probably can't measure it, and even if you could, so what? You can't do anything about it except keep measuring it. Do technicians control cost? No. They control pieces of hardware. Second, building metrics is an iterative process. Step one of the solution was getting the technicians to routinely and accurately count the hardware, and to do this you had to limit the counting to the 20 percent of the hardware that accounted for 80 percent of the cost. By the way, this is called the 80-20 rule and it is a management favorite. Step two was getting the accountants to assign a cost to hardware. Step three was getting all of this information to management in a format that was useable. The final step, and often the hardest, is to do something with the information. You've gone through all of this work, but unless some meaningful action occurs (like developing a plan for reducing cost) then all of the your work was for nothing.

We'll talk more about using metrics information later. For now, let's talk about some different types of metrics. When measuring customer service, metrics tend to take the form of productivity metrics or quality metrics.

Productivity Metrics

Productivity and efficiency are often used as synonyms. If your productivity is being measured, then the person doing the measuring is interested in how many times you can do something in a given period of time.

Examples of productivity metrics include measuring:

- The number of calls a technician receives at the help desk in an hour
- The number of questions a technician answers from the queue in a shift
- The number of customers a technician visits in a day
- The number of systems a technician installs in a month

Notice that all of these things are quantifiable within a period of time. If you are counting something, you are probably generating a productivity metric.

Quality Metrics

Quality metrics are often referred to as *soft metrics*. They are much harder to define, and data is not easily obtainable. These measurements are subjective. For example, if my question is answered the same day and I perceived it to be a very difficult question, then I would be inclined to say that quality was very high. On the other hand, supposing you had a question that you thought was so easy that the person on the phone should have been able to answer it off the top of their head. On top of that, you needed the answer immediately. It took an hour to get you an answer and now you are inclined to give the same technician a very low quality score.

Great care must be taken when collecting data for quality metrics. You can easily build in biases that adversely affect a particular group of people. If you do that, and personnel decisions are made based on that data, you can expect a call from Human Resources. When attempting to generate quality metrics for individuals, seek professional help.

The instrument of choice for collecting data for quality metrics is the customer satisfaction survey. The process usually goes something like this. When users call the help desk they get an incident number. When the incident is closed, the incident becomes eligible for survey. When it comes time to survey, a random sample of incidents is chosen and those users are sent a survey (usually by e-mail). The survey contains around ten questions that are either true/false, or multiple choice. If the questions are multiple choice, the choices may represent a scale from negative to positive. The user answers the questions in the survey and then e-mails the responses back.

Often, great care is taken to ensure the anonymity of the survey subject. That's good if it helps to get more surveys returned, but it often means that you can't associate a particular survey with the original incident. When that happens, you may miss important trends like, "Customer satisfaction scores are always low for technicians who take calls for the new HR Performance Review program." Is the problem with the technicians (inadequate training), or is the problem that the users hate the program and take it out on the technicians?

Surveys usually try and measure a couple of different dimensions. For example, a quality survey might try and assess the customer's perception of the knowledge level of the technician as well as the customer's perception of how timely the answer was. These dimensions could then be graphed as follows:

Time	High	IV	III
	Low	I	II
		Low	High

Knowledge

If you then plotted all of the scores from all of the surveys, you would hope to see the largest cluster of dots in quadrant III with a few dots in quadrants II and IV and no dots in quadrant I. This would indicate that all of your customers rated you high on at least one dimension, and the majority rated you high on both dimensions.

Trends and Measuring Resolutions

You might be tempted to think that once you have the metrics you're done. Not so! Now the real work begins. Metrics must be analyzed, dissected, and understood by every level of the organization before management will sleep in peace.

Normally the result of generating metrics is a set of corrective action plans. A good corrective action plan will state the problem, the cause, the proposed solution, a set of metrics to measure the effectiveness of the solution, and a set of parameters for those metrics that define what the norm is for future monitoring. For example:

PROBLEM:
Manufacturing line number one is producing too many defective circuits.

CAUSE:
Routine maintenance procedures have been disregarded and the machines are dirty.

SOLUTION:
Reduce the count of dust particles to 5 parts per million through routine maintenance. Develop a maintenance schedule that the line manager must personally verify.

METRICS:
Standard manufacturing particle test administered at the beginning of each shift.

NORMAL RANGE:
3 ppm < Dust Particles < 5 ppm

If you can identify problems and create corrective action plans, you will be speaking a language that management understands. You might even be mistaken for management material!

CERTIFICATION SUMMARY

The A+ exam has a pass/fail grading system. Your customer satisfaction questions will not count towards your results. The score, however, will be reported on the test report. More and more employers are demanding this skill from their technicians. This is a newly added section on the exam and it truly is a call from the employers saying that their technicians are not always treating their customers appropriately. Take this last lesson as more of a way to act than a way to get high scores on the exam. Just because you pass the exam and do your job thereafter does not guarantee you great promotions in the future. Use the following test tips.

Questions on the exam will be mainly aimed at the following concepts:

- Communicating and listening (face-to-face or over the phone)
- Interpreting verbal and nonverbal cues
- Responding appropriately to the customer's technical ability
- Establishing personal rapport with the customer
- Conflict avoidance and resolution

When you are taking the exam, think of how the question is related to these concepts. Many of the answers will look obvious, but when you think about them, most of the obvious answers will have violated one of these principles. Read each question carefully.

In summary, communicating and listening is crucial if you are going to be able to truly understand the clients' wants, needs, and concerns. Interpreting verbal and nonverbal cues is second nature for many and can be learned if you try to pay attention to them. Responding to the customer's level of technical skills is essential. It can save you much time and frustration when you can discern advanced users from novices. Advanced users can relate to information that, to beginners, seems like a bunch of jargon that is useless to them. Establishing rapport with your customer brings a harmony into the workplace that is desirable for both you and the customer.

Professional conduct will always reward you. Too many techs nowadays do not know how to behave as professionally as they could and end up sticking out like a sore thumb. Learn how to conduct yourself professionally with everyone you interact with and they will view you as a professional. Finally, you have learned about conflict avoidance and resolution. You can save your superiors innumerable headaches if you learn how to resolve conflict without it getting out of hand. Because there are so few techs representing such a large number of users, you are in the trenches for achieving overall satisfaction with the customer. Your superiors can promise whatever service they want to the customer on your behalf. The bottom line is that it is up to you to make the customer happy.

 # TWO-MINUTE DRILL

- ❑ Customer satisfaction may look effortless to the inexperienced, but in reality, the art of achieving and maintaining a satisfied customer is as challenging as learning any computer technical skills.

- ❑ When you are done listening to the user and have asked all of your questions, paraphrase what the user has said and say it back to them.

- ❑ One thing that really makes users angry and usually ends up with a call to the help desk or worse, is when a technician does something to a PC and does not leave a note.

- ❑ Companies are not just interested in computer technicians who will fix their employees' computers, but in technicians who exhibit the highest respect for professionalism.

- ❑ When you're thinking about nonverbal cues, don't forget to notice the cues that you are projecting.

- ❑ Communication does not end at the user's desk; good communication between technicians is also essential.

❑ When approaching a user's desk for a repair, make sure they understand what you intend to do and what you expect from them to make the service successful.

❑ It is paramount to read all of a customer's verbal and nonverbal cues in order to make sure that things run smoothly.

❑ Don't assume anything when it comes to a customer's technical level.

❑ Many technicians jump to the conclusion that they can solve the problem before the user has completely discussed the problem. This is a big mistake and the consequences can be tragic.

❑ Nonverbal cues are quite possibly more important than verbal cues.

❑ You will always run into a user who is using a PC for the first time in their lives. Treat them kindly, patiently, and with respect.

❑ Good rapport involves taking the time to talk to the user about what they want to talk about.

❑ Perception is reality to most people and the way that the customer sees you is how they form opinions about you, your department, and the field in general.

❑ When repairing a computer, let the user explain the problem fully before starting to work on it.

❑ Don't go for the misleading answer, which might solve the customer's problem right away; go for the one that maintains the customer satisfaction requirements.

❑ If you have learned all that you should about computers, then there should be no reason not to be confident, which instills a sense of trust in your users.

❑ Integrity means that you are not going to compromise yourself or ask others to in order to achieve something.

❑ The customer is always right!

❑ Solve all conflicts to the best of your ability, and delegate them if you can't.

❑ Avoid taking sides if you get caught in a conflict between two users. Wait for them to settle their differences before you approach the situation again.

SELF TEST

The following Self Test questions will help you measure your understanding of the material presented in this chapter. Read all the choices carefully, as there may be more than one correct answer. Choose all correct answers for each question.

1. Your professional _____ while working with the customer has the potential of boosting your career immensely.

   A. Appearance

   B. Behavior

   C. Personality

   D. Technical skills

2. Which of the following statements is true?

   A. Customer satisfaction is easy to achieve.

   B. Customer satisfaction is not as important as technical skill.

   C. Customer satisfaction is more important than technical skill.

   D. Customer satisfaction is as important as technical skill.

3. A technician should always leave customers with the feeling that they have been treated with _____ .

   A. Dignity

   B. Respect

   C. Integrity

   D. All of the above

4. Customer satisfaction requires _____ .

   A. Time

   B. Patience

   C. Good listening skills

   D. The ability to communicate at the user's level of understanding

   E. All of the above

5. A PC is having problems. To solve the problem, the first thing you should do is:

   A. Ask the customer if they have any ideas about what the problem might be.

   B. Plug in the network cord.

   C. Take the PC back to the repair area.

   D. Reload the operating system.

6. When you are done listening to the user and have asked all of your questions, _____ what the user has said. Ask them if you "have it right."

   A. Write down

   B. Paraphrase

   C. Believe

   D. None of the above

7. Technicians should also be able to quickly discern a user's technical level. You want to use explanations _____ a user's level.

    A. Above

    B. Below

    C. Appropriate to

    D. Don't explain problems to users.

8. Which statement is most true?

    A. Nonverbal communication is not as important as verbal communication.

    B. Nonverbal communication is more important than verbal communication.

    C. Nonverbal communication is as important as verbal communication.

    D. There is no such thing as nonverbal communication.

9. Most users are _____ users.

    A. Super

    B. Power

    C. Casual

    D. Stupid

10. Personal _____ is about bonding with your customers.

    A. Satisfaction

    B. Rapport

    C. Feeling

    D. Relationship

11. Professional conduct is essential to understand and achieve in the computer services industry. This encompasses _____ .

    A. Appearance

    B. Attitude

    C. Time management

    D. Integrity

    E. Competence

    F. All of the above

12. If you have a good _____, the user is going to be friendlier and ultimately more satisfied with your work.

    A. Appearance

    B. Attitude

    C. Concept of time management

    D. Integrity

13. Time is a crucial variable that you need to master. It is important to _____ the time spent on each PC.

    A. Minimize

    B. Maximize

14. If you have not worked with the user or if you have any reservations about entering the workspace, you should _____ .

    A. Try to contact the user.

    B. Enter but leave a note.

    C. Make your repair as soon as possible and leave no trace you were there.

    D. Just come back later.

15. _____ means that you are not going to compromise yourself or ask others to do so in order to achieve something.

   A. Appearance

   B. Attitude

   C. Time management

   D. Integrity

16. Be aware of the_____ in your company and behave accordingly. Some companies are more laid back than others, but be aware of how people act and try to emulate their behavior.

   A. Culture

   B. Opinions

   C. Desires

   D. Environment

17. A _____ has the potential of harboring bad feelings between the parties for a long period of time.

   A. Misunderstanding

   B. Conflict

   C. Communications challenge

   D. Failure

18. The following represent conflicts that you may face as a technician:

   A. Angry users

   B. Your own mistakes

   C. Know-it-all users

   D. All of the above

19. When caught in a conflict between two users, you should_____ .

   A. Side with the user who is correct.

   B. Try to side with both users.

   C. Refuse to participate in the dispute.

   D. Offer unbiased technical information.

20. When it comes to measuring customer experience (or just about anything these days) the buzzword is _____.

   A. Precision

   B. Accuracy

   C. Efficiency

   D. Metrics

21. The following are techniques that may be used to measure customer satisfaction:

   A. Total Quality Management (TQM)

   B. Statistical analysis

   C. 360-degree communications

   D. All of the above

22. The following are examples of productivity metrics:

   A. The number of calls a technician receives at the help desk in an hour

   B. The number of questions a technician answers from the queue in a shift

   C. The number of customers a technician visits in a day

   D. The number of systems a technician installs in a month

   E. All of the above

23. The instrument of choice for collecting data for quality metrics is the

    _____ .

    A. Customer satisfaction survey
    B. Pareto analysis
    C. Trend chart
    D. Histogram

24. Select the truest statement.

    A. Metrics is valuable to managers.
    B. Metrics is valuable to customers.
    C. Metrics is valuable to you.
    D. All of the above

25. Questions on the exam will be mainly aimed at the following concepts:

    A. Communicating and listening (face-to-face or over the phone)
    B. Interpreting verbal and nonverbal cues
    C. Responding appropriately to the customer's technical ability
    D. Establishing personal rapport with the customer
    E. Conflict avoidance and resolution
    F. All of the above

Part II

DOS/Windows
Examination

9

Function, Structure, Operation, and File Management

This chapter introduces you to some of the inner workings of the PC. It provides an overview of the most popular operating systems and explores some of their differences. By the time you complete this chapter, you should be familiar with the basic structure and operation of both DOS and Windows.

Functions of DOS, Windows 3.x, and Windows 95/98

An operating system (OS) is a set of computer instruction codes, usually compiled into executable files, whose purpose is to define input and output devices and connections, and provide instructions for the computer's central processor to operate on to retrieve and display data. The coding is usually broken down into many small, modular component files rather than a few large, complex files.

There have been several competent operating systems developed for the PC (CP/M, QDOS, NDOS, Dr. DOS, Geoworks, and NeXTSTEP, among others), although not all have been commercially successful. At this time however, the PC workstation market belongs primarily to Microsoft, with DOS, Windows, and Windows NT maintaining a healthy market advantage over the various flavors of UNIX and IBM's OS/2. Originally, there were several vendors competing for a share in the "DOS wars," but Microsoft has since dominated the market with its various versions of MS-DOS. MS-DOS reached version 6.22 before being wholly incorporated into Windows 95 as version 7.

DOS is a widely used acronym for Disk Operating System. Microsoft was asked by IBM to develop a disk-based OS for the personal computer, which was still in development. Microsoft accepted this challenge and purchased a precursor to DOS from a Seattle company for $50,000. Microsoft modified this OS and created DOS 1.0. An interesting historical aside, Microsoft had already made the agreement to provide DOS to IBM before fully securing the rights to this initial version.

DOS consists of a set of instruction files that include basic commands and drivers to allow a user to load and execute a set of computer instructions, also known as *software*. These instructions are loaded into the computer through multiple types of hardware devices and storage media.

DOS was created to give PC users easy access to applications and data saved on the PC's storage components. Given the limitations of the then-current hardware, it fulfilled its goal fairly well. It went through several development iterations before reaching a level of adequate device coverage and true stability. Through the use of its internal and external commands placed in scripting or batch files by systems programmers to provide simple task-selection menus, the vagaries of DOS became mostly invisible to the majority of computer users.

At the time DOS was first developed, floppy disks and cassette tapes were the only storage media available for the PC. Hard drives, often known as *Winchesters*, taken from the name of one of the first successful manufacturers, were supported soon after. Modified from their eight-inch size used in the large-system world, hard drives were changed to fit the smaller PC format.

As DOS has evolved over the years, it has grown to support a multitude of other components, such as sound devices, scanners, CD-ROMs, and tape drives. It has also been modified to make provisions for networking activity. While most of that function has been off-loaded by the various vendors whose subsistence is drawn from network development, Microsoft has been a networking player since its inception, and the networking capabilities of both Windows and Windows NT are unmatched in their support for almost every available networking hardware item.

DOS provides a fairly complete set of utilities and commands to perform most computer operations; however, DOS did have two inherent limitations. The first was that DOS was text-based. It required complex strings of commands to be entered to perform the simplest of tasks, which required an in-depth knowledge of the command structure and syntax. The second limitation was that DOS allowed only a single application to be loaded and executed at a time. It was not capable of multitasking, as are most operating systems of today.

Through research done by the XEROX Corporation's Palo Alto Research Center (PARC) on computer usage, it was demonstrated that through the use of a graphical computer environment, users could achieve a much higher level of production due to the enhanced accessibility of an application's components and features. Further enhancement was provided by developing graphical applications with what was to be known as a *common user interface*, where the access to compatible features remained consistent across the various applications.

This idea was seized on by both Apple Computer with its Macintosh computer, unveiled in the mid-1980s and shipped complete with a graphical OS; and Microsoft, who teamed with IBM to develop their own version of a graphical environment. This co-development became Windows. Version 1.0 of Windows hit the streets in 1985, with a resounding thud. While the Macintosh was delivered from the start with hardware capable of supporting the new graphical environment, Microsoft had the baggage of an already-installed user base of millions of computers already geared to text-based computing. Unlike the Macintosh, whose OS was included and preinstalled since its origin, DOS and Windows were additional-cost options, licensed separately from the PC on which they resided. These days, most system vendors preinstall a copy of Windows 98 prior to shipment, and include the cost of the license in their system package. In fact, ordering an Intel-based system without Windows has become increasingly more difficult over the years, as Microsoft sets up pricing agreements with major computer manufacturers with price breaks based in part on the volume and percentage of systems shipped preloaded with a Microsoft operating system.

Unlike the Mac, with its Motorola 680XX series processors, neither the Intel 8088 microprocessor nor the then-current CGA video standard were capable of better than meager support for high-level graphics. It took the development of the 80286 microprocessor and EGA graphics to get Windows off the ground, and the 80386 and VGA to ensure its success.

Continuous improvements in available system horsepower meant that the development of a next-generation OS was needed to take better advantage of the burgeoning hardware and applications that were becoming available for the PC. Microsoft and IBM teamed up to create a new, more powerful version of DOS and Windows to leverage the new hardware. As the size of hard drives, processor speeds, and available RAM started to increase, operating systems started to integrate even more features and include more drivers. Programmers no longer had to worry about streamlining their applications, because machines could handle the extra overhead. The age of *bloatware* was upon us.

DOS was originally developed as a 16-bit application, with its internal code segments written to be accessed 16 bits at a time. This fit the 808X processor and memory format. Once Intel moved on to its 80X86 architecture, the processor and system memory were then able to read and write 32 bits of data per clock cycle. The two giants were determined to develop a completely new 32-bit OS that would take full advantage of this feature, and yet would be backward-compatible with all existing DOS and Windows software. This new OS was to become OS/2.

The Microsoft/IBM alliance ended in 1989, when it was decided by both companies in a much-publicized battle to split their development of OS/2. IBM was to keep all rights to existing and future versions of OS/2, and Microsoft got exclusive rights to Windows and further Windows development, soon to be known as *Windows NT (New Technology)*.

The second limitation of DOS, single-task usage, also was hammered down. While a microprocessor could operate on only a single set of instructions (not true now, because Pentium-class processors can now pipeline up to four concurrent operations) at any given moment, given their speed, task-switching became possible at a rate that produced the effect of multitasking. This ability allowed several applications to be loaded into memory concurrently, and a user could then easily switch between them. Windows, OS/2, and the Macintosh, along with some DOS vendors (notably Quarterdeck with its Deskview software) could not only handle the access, but also provided an easy method to exchange data between the concurrently loaded applications. Known as cut-and-paste, a user could select data, make a copy in memory, and then place the data (usually with its formatting characteristics) into a different application. This made juggling such things as e-mail use, database access, document creation, and event scheduling a snap.

Unlike Windows NT and IBM's OS/2, which are true and complete OSs, Windows (up to Windows 95) is a graphical shell that overlays on DOS, and relies on DOS for its low-level device access. It even requires a separate license from DOS. In order to install Windows (pre-95), a user first had to install a working copy of DOS to the PC. Even though Windows 95 was created to eliminate a requirement for DOS and its reliance on a 16-bit architecture, it still relies on several DOS components, mostly for compatibility reasons. From Windows 95 and on, Microsoft now includes any required DOS components under a single installation and license, and doesn't require a pre-existing copy of DOS. The majority of its internal operations are performed 32 bits wide. Windows 98, the most recent (at the time of this writing, although Windows 2000 is on the visible horizon) metamorphosis of the user-end Windows operating system, takes the entire platform a few steps closer to full 32-bit code. Unfortunately, to maintain backward-compatibility with older applications, quite a bit of the OS is still based on the old 16-bit DOS model.

CERTIFICATION OBJECTIVE 9.02

Operating System Files and Structure

Operating systems provide both system access and a set of utilities. The *core files* are also known as the *system files*.

System Files

System files are responsible for all device access and user interface presentation. While they may require the use of additional device drivers for specific hardware items, by themselves they can start up—boot, or Initial Program Load (IPL)—a computer and give a user the ability to perform some level of system operation.

These core files are listed in the following sections, along with a brief explanation of their function and contents.

DOS System Files

DOS system files include the following:

- AUTOEXEC.BAT
- CONFIG.SYS
- IO.SYS
- MSDOS.SYS
- COMMAND.COM
- HIMEM.SYS
- EMM386.EXE
- ANSI.SYS

AUTOEXEC.BAT is located and automatically executed in the ROOT (C:\) directory at startup. This file contains commands to modify the PC environment (PATH, COMSPEC, and other SET commands), and to execute applications. It can be used to create a menu system, prompt for user input, or call other batch files to maintain a modular structure. By default, it carries no attributes, and is not required for OS startup.

CONFIG.SYS is located in the ROOT directory and loaded by MSDOS.SYS. This file loads low-level device drivers for specific hardware, and adjusts several system parameters for performance tuning and memory usage. By default, it carries no attributes, and is not required for OS startup. Since DOS version 6.*x*, it also may be used in conjunction with an internal menu system to select multiple startup configurations.

IO.SYS is located in the ROOT directory, and defines basic input/output routines for the processor. By default, it carries the hidden, system, and read-only attributes, and is required for OS startup.

MSDOS.SYS is located in the ROOT directory, and defines system file locations. By default, it carries the hidden, system, and read-only attributes, and is required for OS startup.

COMMAND.COM is located and automatically executed in the ROOT directory at startup. This file contains the internal command set and error messages. By default, it carries no attributes and is required for

OS startup. It may be executed from a different location and/or renamed if a SHELL command statement is placed in the CONFIG.SYS file pointing to the correct location and name.

COMMAND.COM displays the DOS prompt.

HIMEM.SYS and EMM386.EXE control memory management and are located in the \DOS directory (\WINDOWS directory in Windows 95 and Windows 98). They are not required for system startup (pre-95) and are explained in detail in Chapter 10.

ANSI.SYS is located in the DOS directory, and can be loaded by CONFIG.SYS if required. This file loads an extended character set for use by DOS and DOS applications that includes basic drawing and color capabilities. ANSI.SYS was often used for drawing and filling different boxes for text-based menu systems, but it is seldom used today. By default, it carries no attributes, and is not required for OS startup.

Windows 3.x System Files

Windows 3.*x* system files include the following:

- WIN.INI
- SYSTEM.INI
- USER.EXE
- GDI.EXE
- KRNLXXX.EXE (KRNL286.EXE for 80286 processors and KRNL386 for 80386)
- WIN.COM

The WIN.INI file contains configuration information for Windows applications. Errors made in this file seldom have global implications to Windows operation, but can cripple specific applications or features. Printing is also controlled by settings in this file. The WIN.INI file is dynamic, and records the way the user configures how the system looks and behaves. The spacing of the icons, the type of wallpaper, screen colors, and other interface features can be customized in the WIN.INI file. This file, as well as the SYSTEM.INI file, are ASCII text files.

The SYSTEM.INI file configures Windows to address specific hardware devices and their associated settings. Errors in this file can and do cause Windows to fail to start, or crash unexpectedly. Both the SYSTEM.INI and the WIN.INI files are automatically modified by applications that require changes to the files. If you need to change information in either file, you do so with either a normal text editor, or the SYSEDIT utility.

The rest of the Windows startup components are explained in detail in the "Components of DOS, Windows 3.*x*, and Windows 95/98" section, later in this chapter.

Windows 95/98 System Files

The Windows 95/98 system files include the following:

- IO.SYS
- MSDOS.SYS
- COMMAND.COM
- WIN.INI
- SYSTEM.INI
- SYSTEM.DAT
- USER.DAT

Because Windows 95 and Windows 98 no longer rely on separate copies of DOS, the fundamentals have changed. While IO.SYS and COMMAND.COM remain for compatibility reasons, MSDOS.SYS no longer contains system code, but allows for special system settings to be user-defined. WIN.INI and SYSTEM.INI are mostly vestigial, allowing for 16-bit (pre-WIN95) applications to still be able to register system variables. The bulk of configuration has now shifted to the SYSTEM.DAT and USER.DAT files. Also, while not listed here, the kernel file, KRNL386.EXE, still teams up with USER.EXE and GDI.EXE to deliver the complete Windows OS.

The MSDOS.SYS, WIN.INI, and SYSTEM.INI files can be edited with any standard text editor. The SYSTEM.DAT and USER.DAT files are part of the Windows Registry. Therefore, changes to these files occur when information in the Registry is changed. The USER.DAT file makes up the part of the Registry known as the HKEY_LOCAL_USER hive. This hive stores data specific to user configurations. Information such as desktop color schemes, screen savers, wallpaper, and user-specific application settings will be in this hive. The SYSTEM.DAT file makes up the part of the Registry known as the HKEY_LOCAL_MACHINE hive. This hive is where information specific to the machine will be stored, such as network settings, hardware drivers, and system-wide software settings.

When configuring the Windows OS, Windows applications, or components in your system, the configuration parameters are stored in the Registry. Usually, it is best to make any changes to your system through the applications provided for that purpose. For example, when changing network settings, you would use the Network Control Panel applet. Any changes you make will be reflected in the registry. If you must manually view or change data stored in the Registry, you must use the REGEDIT or REGEDT32 utility.

You should never change values in your Registry unless you are sure of what effects your modifications will have. While changes to other configuration files can be corrected by booting to a DOS prompt and editing the text files, changes to the Registry can be made only from within Windows. If you can't get Windows to run, you won't be able to fix errors in the Registry. When editing the Registry, keep in mind, there is no "undo" function, and saves are instantaneous upon making any changes. This means that any changes you make will be permanent, unless you manually change them back to prior values.

AUTOEXEC.BAT and CONFIG.SYS are still present in a Windows 95/98 system, but they are not required unless you need to run real-mode DOS drivers. DOS environment variables, real-mode audio drivers, and real-mode CD-ROM drivers are the items most frequently configured through these legacy DOS configuration files.

Components of DOS, Windows 3.*x*, and Windows 95/98

Because DOS and Windows 3.*x* share a common development heritage and supported hardware, it shouldn't come as a surprise that they share much of the same structure.

DOS installs onto a formatted disk by placing its system files in the root directory. Its external command set and device drivers are then, by default, placed in a directory named DOS just off the root. During installation, an alternate path and name can be chosen, but straying from this default often leads to trouble.

WIN.COM is a file created by the Setup program when first installing Windows 3.*x*. You won't find a WIN.COM file on any of the distribution media. During installation, Setup takes three files and combines them together to form the WIN.COM file.

When **WIN** is typed on the command line and the ENTER key is pressed, WIN.COM performs three functions. The first function of the WIN.COM is to ascertain what type of processor is in the computer. The file WIN.CNF, also located in the \WINDOWS\SYSTEM subdirectory, performs this function.

The second function that WIN.COM performs is to switch the computer into the appropriate graphics mode by loading a *.LGO file for the logo display. The *.LGO file is selected based on the type of video card Setup determined was in the computer during installation. Setup selects only one graphics mode and adds it to the WIN.COM file. The following files are used by Windows Setup to create WIN.COM. Note that the file used in the creation of WIN.COM is dependent upon the video driver chosen during the setup process. Windows 95 leaves the logo file out of WIN.COM, and moves it to the root directory as LOGO.SYS.

- VGALOGO.LGO for VGA, Super VGA, or 8514/A displays
- EGALOGO.LGO for EGA color displays
- EGAMONO.LGO for EGA monochrome displays
- CGALOGO.LGO for CGA, EGA B&W (64K), and Plasma displays
- HERCLOGO.LGO for Hercules Monochrome Graphics displays

The third function WIN.COM performs is to load the bitmapped graphic advertisement that Windows displays. The file displayed is in a compressed format with an Run Length Encoded (RLE) extension. Setup selects only one of the following available choices and installs it into the WIN.COM file and into the \WINDOWS\SYSTEM subdirectory:

- VGALOGO.RLE for VGA, Super VGA, or 8514/A displays
- EGALOGO.RLE for EGA color displays
- EGAMONO.RLE for EGA monochrome displays
- CGALOGO.RLE for CGA, EGA B&W (64K), and Plasma displays
- HERCLOGO.RLE for Hercules Monochrome Graphics displays

After the three functions of WIN.COM are completed, WIN.COM hands the control of Windows 3.*x* over to either DOSX.EXE (for Standard mode) or WIN386.EXE (for Enhanced mode). In Windows 95/98, there is no longer any support for Standard mode, so DOSX.EXE has been removed. WIN386.EXE switches the CPU to protected mode, thereby enabling advanced features access to all memory in the computer. Windows then loads its kernel, either KRNL286 or KRNL386, and starts a configuration and initialization process. It reads the values stored in the SYSTEM.INI file, and loads the specified device drivers for the display, keyboard, mouse, and other devices. These files include SYSTEM.DRV, KEYBOARD.DRV, MOUSE.DRV, VGA.DRV, MMSOUND.DRV, and COMM.DRV. Basic screen fonts and fonts for DOS applications are loaded next. If VGA mode is selected, the required fonts loaded are VGASYS.FON and VGAOEM.FON for DOS and FONTS.FON, VGAFIX.FON, and OEMFONTS.FON for Windows. The graphics subsystem is then loaded along with the user interface. These files are GDI.EXE and USER.EXE. The display driver, DISPLAY.DRV (used as a label here; the actual driver name will vary) is then loaded. This allows the other drivers to display an error message on screen if they fail to initialize during the next step. Once the DISPLAY.DRV is in control, messages go through Windows. Windows then initializes all remaining drivers and all true-type fonts.

In the last phase of initialization, Windows 3.*x* starts a desktop manager, usually Program Manager (PROGMAN.EXE), the default shell that Windows uses unless another desktop manager has been selected in the SYSTEM.INI file. PROGMAN.EXE finishes the Windows initialization by running any startup applications specified in the WIN.INI file (these programs can be found in lines starting with either LOAD= or RUN=), and by starting any applications whose icons are stored in the StartUp Group. The last action PROGMAN.EXE takes is to display its own menus and interfaces for use of the system.

Windows 95 and Windows 98 perform many of the same tasks; however, they run only in *protected mode*, so they each have only one kernel. The WIN.COM files no longer support switches for *real* or *standard* mode. They still read the SYSTEM.INI and WIN.INI files, and run whatever applications are listed in the StartUp folder. The big change, though, is the reliance on the system Registry. Windows 3.*x* began the move to a Registry-based startup with a REG.DAT file, mostly used to support individual application parameters for Dynamic Data Exchange (DDE). The dependence on the Registry was greatly expanded in Windows NT, Windows 95, and Windows 98. The Registry is a complex database of settings pertaining to both applications and hardware.

CERTIFICATION OBJECTIVE 9.03

File Allocation Tables, Formatting, and Partitioning

Using the FDISK (for Fixed DISK) and FORMAT utilities provided with DOS, a hard drive is prepared for use through the acts of *partitioning* and *formatting*. A partition is created to separate a single physical drive into multiple logical components. Under DOS, Windows 3.1, and Windows 95/98, a single disk can contain a single primary partition, and a single extended partition. The extended partition can be divided into multiple logical drives. Each partition receives a letter, beginning with C:. If a second drive is installed, it is assigned the letter D: automatically. The third becomes E:, and so forth. So that the computer knows where to start, one of the partitions (typically C:, but there are sometimes reasons to select a different partition) *must* be set as *active* with Fixed FDISK in order to boot from the hard drive.

There are some interesting tricks to the way DOS assigns drive letters to partitions. A single drive installed with multiple partitions will letter the partitions alphabetically. For example, if the drive is divided into three partitions (one primary partition, and one extended partition containing two logical drives) they will be lettered C:, D:, and E:. If a second drive is added and partitioned, however, the partition lettering on the first drive will be reassigned. If you add a second drive with a single partition, the second drive will become the D: drive. The first drive, first partition will still be assigned C:, but the second partition will be E:, and the third will be F:. Drives are lettered in this way because DOS will assign drive letters to all primary partitions before going back and assigning letters to logical drives in extended partitions.

In another drive-lettering example, suppose both the first and the second drive are divided into three partitions. The first drive, first partition will be the C: drive, the second partition will be E:, and the third will be F:. On the second drive, the first partition will be the D: drive, the second partition will be G:, and the third will be H:.

As a final example, suppose we have three drives. The first two are divided into three partitions each. The third is divided into two partitions. In this scenario, the first drive, first partition will be C:. The second drive, first partition will be D:. The third drive, first partition will be E:. Notice how the first active partitions receive priority assignment of drive letters. The first drive, second partition will be F:, and the third partition will be G:. The second drive, second partition is H:, and the third partition is I:. On the third drive, the second partition will be J:. In summary, your partitions will look like Table 9-1.

Under DOS, Windows 3.*x*, and Windows 95/98, each physical drive can have only one primary partition. A primary partition is automatically assigned a drive letter. Each physical drive can also contain a single *extended* partition. An extended partition does not automatically receive a drive

TABLE 9-1		Primary Partition	Extended Partition, Logical Drive 1	Extended Partition, Logical Drive 2
Drive Lettering Under DOS	**Drive 1**	C:	F:	G:
	Drive 2	D:	H:	I:
	Drive 3	E:	J:	—

letter. You must first create *logical* partitions in the extended partition. You can have multiple logical partitions on a single extended partition.

Various versions of DOS have been stretched to their limit by the ever-expanding capacities of hard drives. In the early days of DOS, circa 1981, a large hard drive was 10 megabytes (MB). Today, drives for home computers are expanding beyond 20 Gigabytes (GB) at about the same cost (~$400). Standard versions of DOS—and in fact, the BIOS on many older computers—cannot handle partition sizes beyond 2GB. Until Windows 95 and Windows 98 introduced the FAT32 partitioning scheme, FAT16 had no way of addressing this extended disk space without the use of a *drive overlay,* a piece of software loaded before the OS that made the full disk capacity available to the system.

Once partitioned, a drive must be *formatted.* This process divides the drive logically into groups of sectors and tracks. Sector size is usually set at 512 bytes, and physically varies in size depending on whether the sector's track is located in the inner or outer portion of the drive platter. Hard drives consist of a number of platters rotating on a common spindle, with read/write heads mounted on a pivoting assembly that spans all platters concurrently. The sectors are combined logically into groups called *clusters.* When the partition is formatted, an array of addresses that correspond to the physical starting locations of each cluster is created. Known as the *File Allocation Table (FAT)* it becomes the pointer for DOS to locate information on the drive.

Due to a limitation in DOS's heritage, the FAT on each hard drive partition can catalog 65,535 (roughly 64K) individual addresses. Depending on the size of the partition, the 64K limit dictates the number of sectors, and therefore the size of each cluster. The cluster is the smallest accessible unit to DOS from the FAT of a hard drive. The smallest FAT16 cluster used by DOS contains four 512-byte sectors, or 2048 bytes (2KB). With a partition size of 128MB, the cluster size increases to 4096 (4KB). On a 256MB partition, the cluster size doubles to 8KB; at 512MB, clusters are 16KB; and at 1GB, cluster size is 32KB. Refer to Table 9-2 for clarification.

But what does this expanded cluster size really mean? Suppose you have a text file that requires only 15 bytes of disk space. On a 50MB hard drive with a cluster size of 2KB, that 15-byte file will use 2KB of physical space. On a 1.5GB drive, that same 15-byte text file will receive 32KB of file space! Now, suppose you were saving a 34KB file to the same drive. It would be allocated two full 32KB clusters. One cluster would be completely utilized; the other would have 30KB of unused space. On the average system formatted with a 1.5GB drive formatted to the FAT16 file system, you may see *slack space* between 20% and 30%. *Slack space* refers to the empty cluster space required to store files that do not take up entire multiples of the clusters on the disk.

Because the smallest addressable unit is the cluster, once a file is written to a cluster, the cluster is marked as used and can't have anything else written to it until the file in it is erased or overwritten by another copy of the same file.

When formatting, or afterwards if desired, the partition marked as active must have an operating system installed. In the case of the C: drive, the

TABLE 9-2	Hard Drive Size	FAT Type	Sectors	Cluster Size
Standard DOS Partition Cluster Sizes	0MB–15MB	12-bit	8	4KB
	16MB–127MB	16-bit	4	2KB
	128MB–255MB	16-bit	8	4KB
	256MB–511MB	16-bit	16	8KB
	512MB–1023MB	16-bit	32	16KB
	1024MB–2048MB	16-bit	64	32KB

FORMAT C: /S command formats the C: (boot) drive and puts the DOS system files on the hard drive. At the same time, it puts a pointer in a special location, known as the *boot sector,* which is located in the first cluster on the boot partition. There are two types of boot sectors, a *file system boot sector,* located on the first physical sector on any logical volume, or the *Master Boot Record (MBR),* which is the first physical sector on any physical hard disk. The MBR contains a partition table to describe the layout of the logical volumes on the drive. The pointer referred to above is stored on a file system boot sector. When a machine boots, the BIOS determines which physical device to use as a boot device. The system then checks the first physical sector for the MBR. The MBR tells the system where to find the active primary partition. Once the system finds the active primary partition, it checks the file system boot sector to tell the machine exactly where to find system files required for boot. If for some reason this cluster becomes unusable, the drive can no longer be accessed by DOS. If you choose to add the system files at a later time, the SYS command can be used to reinitialize the boot sector and place the DOS system files in the root directory.

exam
Watch

Keep in mind, formatting or partitioning will wipe out all data on a partition.

Root Directories, Folders, and Subfolders

Each logical drive contains an initial, or root, directory that is created when it is formatted. Each root directory can hold up to 512 files or other (sub)directories. The files and folders combine into a hierarchical tree known as the *directory tree.* In DOS, both file and folder names are limited to eight characters to the left of a period and three characters to the right, also known as *8 dot 3* naming. The total path for locating a file, which includes any subdirectories and the filename, cannot exceed 128 characters in DOS. This is known as the *fully qualified path.* In practice—at least, under DOS—it's best to limit the fully qualified path to less than 60 characters, or else some older applications and utilities can display anomalous behavior.

CERTIFICATION OBJECTIVE 9.04

Managing Files and Directories in DOS/Windows

From the DOS command line, there are several commands used to create and manage files and directories. Table 9-3 shows some of the DOS commands. You can get the information listed here at any time by issuing the command with a /? switch and pressing the ENTER key. First, in order to change from one drive to another, type in the drive letter to change to, followed by a colon (for example, to change to drive D, type D: and press the ENTER key).

e x a m
ⓦ a t c h

Know the command-line switches for the XCOPY command very well.

Command Syntax

As you can see from Table 9-3, most commands include an array of possible options that are accessed by command-line *switches*. These switches are usually preceded by a forward slash (/), although some use a dash (-). It was the reliance on slash-triggered switches that forced the DOS developers to use the backslash character to distinguish subdirectories.

When executing any .BAT, .COM, or .EXE file, the extension may be dropped. Be aware though that there is a hierarchy to execution if multiple files with the same extension are in the same directory (or are executed from a different directory and are in the DOS path). For example, say you issue the NET command from the command line. There may be a NET.COM, NET.BAT, and NET.EXE file all in the path. DOS looks first for .COM files, then .EXE files, then .BAT files. If you ever execute a command and get strange results, be sure and check for the presence of another executable file with the same name, but a different extension.

TABLE 9-3		DOS Command Reference		

Command	Command Type	Action Performed	Available Command-Line Switches	Syntax
CD (or CHDIR)	Internal	Displays the name of the current directory or changes the current directory	Specifies that you want to change to the parent directory. Type CD *drive:* to display the current directory in the specified drive. Type CD without parameters to display the current drive and directory.	CHDIR [*drive:*][*path*] CHDIR[..] CD [*drive:*][*path*] CD[..]
COPY	Internal	Copies one or more files to another location. *Notes:* Does not copy subdirectories. The switch /Y may be preset using the COPYCMD environment variable. This may be overridden with /-Y on the command line. To append files, specify a single file for destination, but multiple files for source (using wildcards or file1+file2+file3 format). (This is also known as *concatenation*.)	*Source:* Specifies the file or files to be copied */A:* indicates an ASCII text file */B:* indicates a binary file Destination: specifies the directory and/or filename for the new file(s) */V:* verifies that new files are written correctly */Y:* suppresses prompting to confirm you want to overwrite an existing destination file */-Y:* causes prompting to confirm you want to overwrite an existing destination file	COPY [/A | /B] source [/A | /B] [+ source [/A | /B] [+ ...]] [destination [/A | /B]] [/V] [/Y | /-Y] *Also, related environment variable, COPYCMD*

TABLE 9-3			DOS Command Reference *(continued)*	

Command	Command Type	Action Performed	Available Command-Line Switches	Syntax
DIR	Internal	Displays a list of files and subdirectories in a directory. *Notes:* Switches may be preset using the DIRCMD environment variable. You may override preset switches by prefixing any switch with - (hyphen)—for example, /-W.	*[drive:][path][filename]:* specifies drive, directory, and/or files to list (Could be enhanced file specification or multiple file specs) */P:* pauses after each screenful of information */W:* uses wide list format */A:* displays files with specified attributes *Attributes:* *D:* Directories *R:* Read-only files *H:* Hidden files *A:* Files ready for archiving *S:* System files -: Prefix meaning not */O:* List by files in sorted order *Sortorder:* *N:* By name (alphabetic) *S:* By size (smallest first) *E:* By extension (alphabetic) *D:* By date & time (earliest first) *G:* Group directories first -: Prefix to reverse order *A:* By Last Access Date (earliest first) */S:* Displays files in specified directory and all subdirectories */B:* uses bare format (no heading information or summary) */L:* uses lowercase */V:* verbose mode */4:* displays year with 4 digits (ignored if /V also given)	*DIR [drive:][path] filename]* *[/P] [/W]* *[/A[[:]attributes]]* *[/O[[:]sortorder]]* *[/S]* *[/B] [/L] [/V] [/4]*

TABLE 9-3 DOS Command Reference *(continued)*

Command	Command Type	Action Performed	Available Command-Line Switches	Syntax
DEL (or ERASE)	Internal	Deletes one or more files	*[drive:][path]filename:* specifies the file(s) to delete. Specify multiple files by using wildcards. */P:* prompts for confirmation before deleting each file.	DEL *[drive:][path] filename* [/P] ERASE *[drive:][path] filename* [/P]
MOVE	External	Moves files and renames files and directories	*[drive:][path]filename1:* specifies the location and name of the file or files you want to move. *Destination:* specifies the new location of the file. Destination can consist of a drive letter and colon, a directory name, or a combination. If you are moving only one file, you can also include a filename if you want to rename the file when you move it. *[drive:][path]dirname1:* specifies the directory you want to rename. *dirname2:* specifies the new name of the directory. */Y:* suppresses prompting to confirm creation of a directory or overwriting of the destination. */-Y:* causes prompting to confirm creation of a directory or overwriting of the destination.	*To move one or more files:* MOVE [/Y | /-Y] *[drive:][path] filename1 [,...] destination* *To rename a directory:* MOVE [/Y | /-Y] *[drive:][path] dirname1 dirname2*
MD or MKDIR	Internal	Creates a directory	None available	MKDIR [drive:]path MD [drive:]path

TABLE 9-3   DOS Command Reference *(continued)*

Command	Command Type	Action Performed	Available Command-Line Switches	Syntax
REN or RENAME	Internal	Renames a file/directory or files/directories	None available	RENAME [drive:][path] [directoryname1 | filename1] [directoryname2 | filename2] REN [drive:][path] [directoryname1 | filename1] [directoryname2 | filename2]
XCOPY	External	Copies files and directory trees	*Source:* specifies the file(s) to copy. *Destination:* specifies the location and/or name of new files. */A:* copies files with the archive attribute set, doesn't change the attribute. */M:* copies files with the archive attribute set, turns off the archive attribute. */D:* date copies files changed on or after the specified date. If no date is given, copies only those files whose source time is newer than the destination time. */P:* prompts you before creating each destination file. */S:* copies directories and subdirectories except empty ones. */E:* copies directories and subdirectories, including empty ones. Same as /S /E. May be used to modify /T. */W:* prompts you to press a key before copying.	XCOPY source [destination] [/A | /M] [/D[:date]] [/P] [/S [/E] [/W] [/C] [/I] [/Q] [/F] [/L] [/H] [/R] [/T] [/U] [/K] [/N]

TABLE 9-3   DOS Command Reference *(continued)*

Command	Command Type	Action Performed	Available Command-Line Switches	Syntax
XCOPY *(continued)*			/C: continues copying even if errors occur.	
			/I: if destination does not exist and copying more than one file, assumes that destination must be a directory.	
			/Q: does not display filenames while copying.	
			/F: displays full source and destination file names while copying.	
			/L: displays files that would be copied.	
			/H: copies hidden and system files also.	
			/R: overwrites read-only files.	
			/T: creates directory structure, but does not copy files. Does not include empty directories or subdirectories.	
			/T /E: includes empty directories and subdirectories.	
			/U: updates the files that already exist in destination.	
			/K: copies attributes. Normal Xcopy will reset read-only attributes.	
			/Y: overwrites existing files without prompting.	
			/-Y: prompts you before overwriting existing files.	
			/N: copy using the generated short names.	

Internal Versus External Commands

The commands shown in Table 9-3 are listed as either internal or external. *Internal commands* are present in the COMMAND. COM shell, and can be executed on the command line at any time from any directory location. *External commands* exist as separate files in the DOS directory. External commands must be executed either from the DOS directory, or from any subdirectory if the DOS directory is included in the DOS path (see PATH command), or by preceding the command with the fully qualified path to the DOS directory (for example, C:\DOS).

File Naming Conventions

File management is crucial for the rapid retrieval of information. One method used to organize data is to use logical filenames within the boundaries set by the operating system.

DOS and Windows 3.1 were limited to what is termed an 8.3 (8 "dot" 3) file naming specification. This meant that no filename could exceed eight characters followed by a period and up to three more characters (that is, FILENAME.EXT). There was also no provision by the operating system for mixed-case names. Everything was in uppercase.

When Windows 95, Windows 98, and Windows NT 4.0 entered the desktop realm, these limitations were eliminated. Windows 95/98 and Windows NT provide long filename support on FAT. This essentially links directory entries within the FAT together to create a long filename (up to 255 characters, counting the fully qualified path) with mixed case and spaces. Windows NT also provides long filename support with its native file system, NT File System (NTFS). In addition, filenames can be mixed-case, although accessing a file is still case-insensitive. If you have a file named Document.doc, you could *not* have another named DOCUMENT.DOC although you could reference the file by either of those names. In most UNIX-based operating systems, DOCUMENT.DOC and Document.doc could coexist in the same directory as separate files.

File Types and Formats

You can save or rename any file to most any combination of eight letters or numbers, a period, and then add a three-letter (or number or combo) extension. DOS performs an action on only certain files based on their three-letter extension. .COM, .EXE, and .BAT files are known as executables. These are the only files that can be executed (or run) by the computer. These executables can then include additional data or functions by loading additional files. Rather than putting all available functions into a single huge executable file, most developers choose to modularize their applications by creating library files that include additional commands and functions. These additional executable enhancement files are usually referred to as *overlays*. These files usually have a .BIN or .OVL extension. Windows took this one step further and developed *Dynamic Linked Libraries (.DLL)* files. These overlays have the additional benefit of being shareable by all of the applications loaded in Windows.

There are additional conventions to file naming, but none that must be adhered to at the OS level. Device drivers usually end in .DRV. You can usually count on .TXT and .DOC files to be documents, .HLP to be help files, and so forth. On the other hand, software applications are usually sticklers at requiring a certain extension to be recognized as a valid file to be opened by the application. Graphics programs, for example, require the proper extension on a file so they will know how the file was encoded. With the wrong extension, the data will appear unusable. Some applications allow the importing of data from several different file types.

Read-Only, Hidden, System, and Archive Attributes

Each file accessible to DOS, regardless of media type, has four attributes that may be associated with it: READ-ONLY, HIDDEN, SYSTEM, and ARCHIVE.

The READ-ONLY attribute prevents a user or application from inadvertently deleting or changing a file. If set, the attribute must be removed before the file can be deleted or overwritten. If the attribute is removed, the file then has READ/WRITE capabilities.

The HIDDEN (H) attribute keeps a file from being displayed when a DIR command is issued. It also prevents the file from being acted upon by standard DOS commands, such as COPY or XCOPY. Some third-party applications ignore the HIDDEN attribute, and will operate on the files regardless, but this is rare.

The SYSTEM attribute is usually set by DOS or Windows, and can be modified using ATTRIB or File Manager. SYSTEM files are hidden by the operating system, which helps prevent accidental deletion.

The ARCHIVE attribute is set automatically when a file is created or modified, and can be switched by backup software when the file is backed up. Not all backup software modifies, or even uses, the ARCHIVE attribute; some applications will instead look at the filename, file size, and file modification date, and compare the date to the last full or incremental backup of the file.

CERTIFICATION OBJECTIVE 9.05

Viewing and Changing File Attributes

File attributes can be viewed from DOS using either the DIR or ATTRIB command. Windows users can use either File Manager (all versions) or Windows Explorer in Windows 95/98 to both view and/or modify the attributes of selected files.

Use ATTRIB.EXE

The ATTRIB command displays or changes file attributes, such as the following:

```
ATTRIB [+R | -R] [+A | -A] [+S | -S] [+H | -H] [[drive:][path]filename] [/S]
```

- ■ + Sets an attribute
- ■ - Clears an attribute
- ■ R Read-only file attribute

- **A**　Archive file attribute
- **S**　System file attribute
- **H**　Hidden file attribute
- **/S**　Processes files in all directories in the specified path

When using the ATTRIB command on a set of files, using the + (plus sign) will add the attribute to the file, and – (minus sign) will subtract that attribute. For example, the ATTRIB –S <path> will remove the SYSTEM attribute from the file specified, including those set by the operating system. The S switch allows a user to reset the SYSTEM attribute on only those files that were previously set on by the user.

There is a specific hierarchy that must be followed to apply the switches, and this hierarchy varies slightly depending on which version of DOS is in use. For example, if a file is hidden, it must be unhidden before the READ-ONLY attribute can be set, but if the file is *already* marked READ-ONLY, it must be set to READ/WRITE (using the –R switch) before it can be hidden. You can also combine multiple attribute changes in a single command. For example, typing "ATTRIB +S +H +R MyFile.DOC" would make the file, MyFile.DOC, a system, hidden, read-only file, with only the single command.

CERTIFICATION OBJECTIVE 9.06

Operating System Navigation

All operating systems provide the user with the ability to manage information. The capabilities vary, but the goal is a common one. Windows, MacOS, OS/2, and other operating systems give the user the ability to easily manage their files and programs. Because everything in most popular operating systems is handled graphically, most functions are present for the user regarding data manipulation, but the features that are present are merely a function of the OS developer's vision of what should be present. In DOS, and other command-line based OSs, ease of use is discarded in favor of power and control. This gap has gradually closed and will continue to do so as the use of the DOS prompt becomes less of a necessity. Keep in mind that a solid grasp of how to accomplish tasks at a DOS prompt will save many hours of frustration when trying to troubleshoot a machine that fails to load Windows.

Navigating Through DOS

Earlier in this chapter, Table 9-3 referenced some of the basic commands used in the DOS environment. Of those commands, the most commonly used for navigating the DOS world are CD (change directory) and the DIR (directory) commands.

The CD command is used in the example shown in Figure 9-1.

The DIR command can be used to search for specific files. This can be accomplished by using the /S (search subdirectories) switch. The DIR /S command, therefore, will display all files in the current directory, as well as all files in all subdirectories. DIR *.TXT /S will display all files with a .TXT extension found in the current directory and in all subdirectories. In most

FIGURE 9-1

Changing directories in DOS

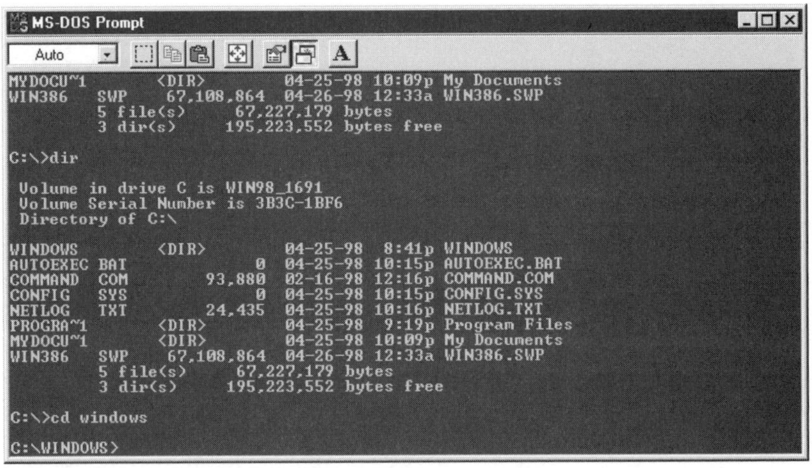

cases, it is best to be in the root, or top, directory of the drive. Figure 9-2 shows an example of this technique.

In addition to command-line utilities, DOS versions 5.*x* and 6.*x* include a somewhat graphical interface to the files and programs on your system. This graphical interface is known as the DOS shell. This utility is installed as part of the full DOS installation; it can be started by typing DOSSHELL from the command line. The DOS shell provides very basic file management functions through an ASCII-type menu system.

Navigating Through Windows 3.*x*/Windows 95/98

Windows pre-95 relies on an application called *File Manager* to navigate through a user's storage devices. Both local and networked drives can be accessed from this single user interface. File Manager helps to organize files and directories. File management can encompass several tasks, such as formatting floppy disks or creating directories, but the primary tasks are storing and searching for files. The WINFILE.INI is the configuration file

FIGURE 9-2

Using the DIR command to perform a file search

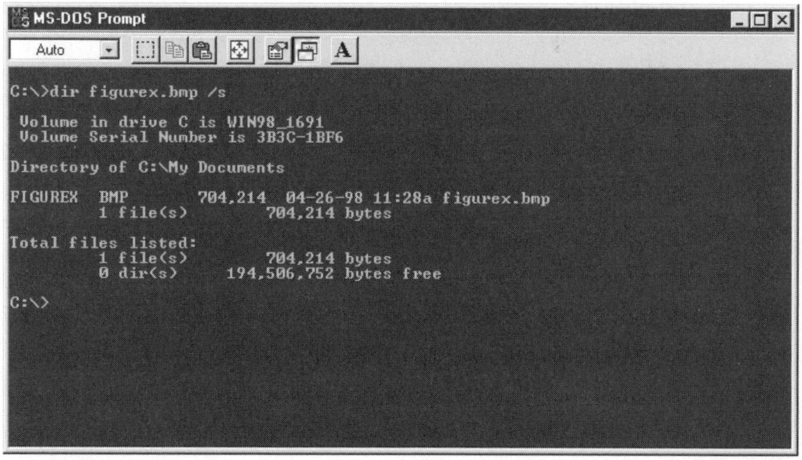

that stores the names of the directories that File Manager displays when starting. File Manager also dynamically tracks all files on the computer. Messages are sent by Windows to File Manager for many operations including file creation and deletion.

File Manager can also be used to start applications. By double-clicking on any document file, Windows automatically tries to find the application that works with that document, and then starts that application. File Manager determines this by the three-character extension of the document file and then consults with the Windows registration database and the [EXTENSIONS] section of the WIN.INI. By selecting a document in the File Manager window and then the File | Run menu option, File Manager also starts the appropriate application. File Manager can also be used to print documents by selecting them in a File Manager window and then using the File | Print menu option. When printing a document in this way, Windows runs the associated application as a background task, prints the document from the native application, and shuts down the application once the print job has been submitted to the queue.

To select a file in File Manager, click on the file's name. To select a range of files in File Manger, click on the first file in the range, and then hold down the SHIFT key when clicking on the last file in the range. File Manager selects the two specified files and all the files in between them. To select multiple files that are not in a contiguous range, hold down the CTRL key while clicking on unselected individual files. If you wish to deselect a single file, you can do so by holding down the CTRL key while clicking on a single selected file.

exam
ⓦatch

Windows 95 includes the File Manager utility, but by default loads a newer utility known as the Windows Explorer.

FROM THE FIELD

Navigating Through an Operating System Can Be Fun

I always enjoy watching a professional technician navigate through an operating system. I can pick up a few shortcuts while I'm watching. Each operating system has its own structure as well as sharing the structure of other operating systems.

I once watched an administrator fix a system problem through DOS commands. He immediately shelled out of the Program Manager and started typing very complex commands. After 26 different commands, the network was up and running. Another tech commented that this particular administrator had the ability to think in DOS.

Because much of the work that you will be doing involves navigating through the operating system, you might as well learn as many shortcuts as you can. Your work will not only be quicker, but those who watch you will be impressed. Furthermore, an in-depth knowledge of DOS commands will enable you to write complex batch files to perform repetitive functions. Below is a list of my favorite Windows 95 shortcuts.

—Ted Hamilton, MCSE, MCP, A+ Certified

Shortcut	Function	Shortcut	Function
Right-click the start button	Launch explorer	CTRL-P	Print
CTRL-ESC	Open the task bar	CTRL-X	Cut
CTRL-TAB	Shuffle Excel windows	CTRL-C	Copy
F5	Update window (good when looking at multiple floppies)	CTRL-V	Paste
CTRL-F	Find	ALT-TAB	Rotate active windows
F1	Help	SHIFT +	Many shortcuts work in reverse with SHIFT +
CTRL-ESC then ALT-M	Minimize all windows	F10	Activate menus
ALT-F4	Close the active window (can be used multiple times to close all windows)		

The Windows Explorer is essentially a turbo-charged version of File Manager. It provides a more solid integration with the Windows 95, Windows 98, and Windows NT environments than File Manager. Another benefit is the fact that Explorer is highly configurable and extensible by third-party software vendors. The entire Windows interface, from the desktop to the file management, now happens through Explorer. There is no need for the separate Program Manager used with Windows 3.1 to arrange program groups and icons. The Windows Explorer handles these tasks by manipulating program groups as folders and program icons as a special type of file called a *shortcut*. Shortcut files end in a .LNK extension.

CERTIFICATION OBJECTIVE 9.07

Disk Management

Due to their capacity to store thousands of files, coupled with the constant creation and modification of data contained therein, several utilities have been created to help manage hard drive real estate. Early versions of DOS came with fairly crude utilities, and many companies made a pretty good living by creating better applications to perform disk management functions.

Beginning with DOS version 5.0, Microsoft included a disk repair tool known as Check Disk. Check Disk could be used to repair basic problems with files, such as lost file clusters. The command for this utility is CHKDSK, and CHKDSK /F indicates that Check Disk should fix any errors it found. Lost clusters repaired by Check Disk are saved to the root directory with .CHK extensions. Usually, these .CHK files contain unrecoverable or incomplete data, and can be deleted without adverse effects.

DOS version 6.0 also included Check Disk, but expanded on its function with two additional utilities, a more advanced disk repair tool (ScanDisk) and a file defragmentation utility (Defrag), which were included out of the box. Windows brought several new utilities into play. These include file management utilities, such as File Manager and Explorer, graphical versions of ScanDisk and Defrag, backup utilities to protect your data, and file-compression utilities to make better use of disk space.

Using Disk Management Utilities

SCANDISK.EXE and DEFRAG.EXE are provided with MS-DOS 6.0 and later, providing many benefits, as mentioned earlier. Similar functionality is provided with Windows 95/98's graphical versions of the programs, which are located in the Programs | Accessories | System Tools program folder.

Using SCANDISK.EXE

The ScanDisk utility provides the ability to scan and correct some data anomalies on a hard drive before they result in data loss. ScanDisk can look for logical or physical file and disk errors. Typically, it moves the data to a non-damaged portion of the disk whenever possible. Table 9-4 lists the valid command-line switches for SCANDISK.EXE.

TABLE 9-4

Command-Line Switches for SCANDISK.EXE

Command Line Switch	Function
/ALL	Scans all local drives for errors
/AUTOFIX	Fixes damage without prompting for user confirmation
/CHECKONLY	Checks drive for damage, but does not repair
/CUSTOM	Forces ScanDisk to read the SCANDISK.INI file for settings
/FRAGMENT	Checks file for fragmentation
/MONO	Causes ScanDisk to use a monochrome display
/NOSAVE	Used with /AUTOFIX. Deletes lost clusters rather than saving them as a file
/NOSUMMARY	Used with /CHECKONLY and /AUTOFIX. Prevents ScanDisk from displaying summary screens
/UNDO	Backs out of previous repairs

Using DEFRAG.EXE

The defragmentation utility included with DOS 6.0 and later provides the ability to rearrange the clusters of data on the hard drive to achieve greater performance by placing all of the clusters for a given file together in a contiguous fashion. One mistake that is commonly made is running Defrag to fix errors. It should be noted that Defrag does *no* repair and will not make any errors disappear. However, with later versions of the utility, such as those included with Windows 95/98, Defrag will automatically run ScanDisk before optimizing your disk.

Typically, the only command-line switch used with Defrag is /FULL. This causes a full defragmentation to take place. The command line would appear as shown in Figure 9-3.

Backing Up

Hard drives are by far the most important part of a computer. That's because they contain the most vital, difficult to replace element: your data. Therefore, it's imperative that the data be kept safe from any failure of the equipment or potential operator error. The best way of doing so is to create

---

FIGURE 9-3

Common DEFRAG.EXE command-line syntax

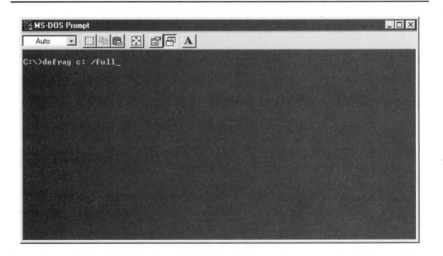

a separate copy of the data, also known as a *backup*. You'd think it would be easy to make copies, because copying files is a feature inherent in DOS, yet this function has perhaps been the most problematic of all.

DOS has included backup utilities since version 2.0. Unfortunately, due to the multitude of problems that have arisen, each succeeding version of DOS came with a backup utility that was incompatible with the previous version. This was by far one of the most difficult limitations to overcome. When installing a newer version of DOS, if problems arose with the new install, the new version would be unable to restore the previous version's data, necessitating a reinstallation of the previous DOS version and then often a complete restore. This could take anywhere from hours to days.

Things have gotten better, but not by much. This version incompatibility still occurs, even using Windows and/or third-party software. Be aware that no backup can be assumed to be complete and restorable, *unless you actually perform a restore operation and it works correctly.* It's a good idea as part of a prudent disaster recovery plan to perform occasional full restorations of a backup set to a *different, similarly configured PC* to be sure that what you thought you saved really was saved.

No amount of preparation or disaster recovery planning is worth the effort if you don't follow the backup plan and make regular backups on a set schedule. If your backup is out of date, being able to recall the data won't be of much help. One of the most common problems with backups is the "it won't happen to me" syndrome. Some of the most computer-savvy people you'll ever meet may never have backed up their personal data. They assume, "I'm good with computers, it will never happen to me." Well, I can tell you from personal experience, technology doesn't care how much you know; when it wants to fail, it will fail. Once you've lost important data, you won't make the mistake of skipping on backups ever again, even if all you ever back up is your data directory.

Defragmenting

Another of the problems inherent in the use of the DOS FAT table is file fragmentation. Because DOS writes files to the hard drive by breaking the file into cluster-sized pieces and then storing each piece in the next available cluster, as files are deleted and then rewritten, they are often written in noncontiguous clusters scattered all over the disk. To access a file, the heads that actually read the data from the platters must traverse to each cluster in sequence. If the clusters are contiguously stored, the read operation is smooth and fast. However, if the file is fragmented, the heads fly wildly across the platters, picking up each scattered cluster one by one. This can slow down access dramatically.

Recognizing this, developers created utilities that reorganize the files back in a proper, contiguous fashion. They do so by moving several of them to an unused portion of the drive, erasing the previous locations in contiguous clusters, then rewriting the cluster back in proper sequence. Performed periodically, *defragmentation* is probably the single best operation a user can perform to maintain a high-performance system. There is both a DOS version and a Windows version of Defrag, as well as third-party versions.

ScanDisk

Besides fragmentation, there are a few other things that can go wrong with a hard drive. Actually, there are two file allocation tables, identical copies, so that in case one FAT gets messed up, there is a built-in backup. Sometimes, the two get out of sync, usually when something unexpected happens. An example might be while saving a file to disk, the power switch is accidentally turned off, or Windows crashes while swapping something to disk. Once this happens, the clusters that are marked in disagreement between the two FATs are considered lost. These lost clusters can be recovered by running the ScanDisk utility.

Also, even though hard drives have become basically bullet-proof, with Mean Time Between Failure (MTBF) readings up in the 100,000 hr + range, occasionally clusters go bad. These clusters must be detected and marked as bad, so that an operating system won't try to write data to them. If data exists there already, some of it may be recoverable. ScanDisk notes any bad clusters, attempts to save any data already present, and flags the cluster as unusable. There is both a DOS version and a Windows version of ScanDisk, as well as third-party versions.

Differences between Windows 3.x and Windows 95

Windows versions prior to 95 were all written as 16-bit extensions to DOS. Windows 95 was written as a full 32-bit OS, but still is stuck with some 16-bit calls to some of the PC's subsystems for legacy support, mostly of existing DOS applications. The 32–bit capability virtually doubled throughput to almost all I/O devices and memory, accelerating access to just about everything. Windows 95 also changed virtually everything else, from its networking capabilities to the user interface itself.

exam
ⓦatch

Familiarize yourself with the networking capabilities of each of the operating systems, as there will be questions about this on the exam. Networking capabilities are explored in other sections of this book.

Again for compatibility purposes, Windows 95 retained the WIN.INI and SYSTEM.INI files, but shifted configuration entries to the SYSTEM.DAT and USER.DAT files. The distinction is fairly clear. The SYSTEM.DAT file resides in the WINDOWS directory, and is loaded at startup to provide specific hardware support. It is common to all users of a particular PC. In contrast, the USER.DAT file contains application and environment preferences specific to each user who *logs on* to the PC. These two files in conjunction are known as the Windows *Registry* database. Windows 95 borrows the Registry concept from Windows NT. Whereas the SYSTEM.INI and WIN.INI files are ASCII text files that are directly editable, the Registry is a compressed database that requires special tools and skills to manipulate.

Fortunately, for the most part, a user usually doesn't need to mess with the Registry. Its entries are handled automatically by Windows when it comes to hardware, and also by the various applications that are installed. The automated handling of hardware devices is called Plug-and-Play. If needed, Windows 95 provides a tool, REGEDIT.EXE, to access and edit the Registry, but again, be aware that any changes made are saved immediately. Any changes or deletions must be carefully considered before they are made.

Older versions of Windows used a shell application known as Program Manager to provide the graphical program menu used to launch application programs. Program Manager organizes applications into groups, with each group displayed in a window that contains a set of application icons. Each group window with individual icons can be viewed, tiled, or cascaded, or the group itself can be minimized to an icon in the Program Manager window. Program Manager stores the information about each group in a .GRP file in the Windows directory.

Major groups (such as Main, Accessories, StartUp, and Games) are formed during installation. The Program Manager File | New menu selection allows creation of new groups. Application installation can also add new groups.

For each of its program icons, Program Manager remembers which *.EXE file should be started when double-clicking on an icon, which directory the *.EXE file resides in, and what title should appear under an icon. The individual groups to be loaded by Program Manager are listed in the PROGMAN.INI file.

Operating systems beyond Windows 95, as mentioned before, now default to a desktop metaphor provided by the Windows Explorer, with a hierarchical menu structure accessed from the Start button on the Task bar. All items in the menu and on the desktop are shortcuts, or link (.LNK) files, stored in subdirectories under Windows. If the PC is configured for use by multiple users and set to maintain individual settings for each, then a PROFILES subdirectory is created in the WINDOWS directory and individual user settings (USER.DAT and Program subdirectories that hold .LNK files) are created for each user. These link files contain either Windows-related information about the to-be-launched application if they pertain to a Windows file, or information about "DOS Box" configuration if it is to launch a DOS application. Again, due to their small size (<2K), link files produce enormous waste of hard drive territory due to slack.

Another change in Windows 95 was to allow file and directory names to have more than the standard 8.3 characters. Filenames can now be up to 255 characters long, although this also must include the fully qualified path in the count. Also, the ability to use spaces between words is now present. This allows a user to save files with a much more descriptive filename to avoid confusion.

Another big change between Windows 3.*x* and Windows 95 pertains to the difference in their multitasking capabilities.

Windows 3.*x* supported 286 and later processors. The 286 had several limitations not present in the 386 and later. The greatest difference is that the 286 supported real and protected modes, but the 386 added virtual *x*86 mode. This limited the 286 considerably because it could not use virtual memory due to a limitation of the Windows architecture. This was also exacerbated because the 286 had only 24 address lines for memory, which translates to a maximum of 16MB. In contrast, the 386 and later have 32 address lines for memory, which is a maximum of 4GB.

Also, due to the virtual *x*86 mode not being present, all DOS applications were task switched, meaning that only one could be executing at a time. This was determined by the selected DOS application in the foreground.

On PCs with 386 and later processors, Windows 3.*x* cooperatively multitasks *all* native Windows applications and preemptively multitasks *all* DOS applications. The older 80286 PCs could load and run only one DOS application at a time.

There are two different types of multitasking: *cooperative* and *preemptive.* Cooperative multitasking means that applications must voluntarily relinquish control of the CPU. When an application relinquishes control of the CPU, Windows then decides which application will execute next. The most common way for an application to relinquish control is by asking Windows if any messages are available.

In preemptive multitasking, control is passed from one program to another automatically by the Windows *process scheduler.* This is accomplished by using specific CPU hardware features of the 386/486/586 processor and the silicon chip timer to tell an application how long the application will be allowed to run. When the preset time expires, the timer interrupts whatever program is running and automatically switches back to the process scheduler. The program is temporarily suspended at this point. Windows is then free to do something else. A very short time later, Windows gives the program another slice of time, then another, and so on. This process of dividing up the time is called *time slicing.* The user perceives all of the running applications to be operating together, when in fact they are actually executing one at a time. Windows uses preemptive multitasking to multitask DOS sessions because DOS programs, unlike Windows programs, were not written to relinquish control of the CPU.

The collection of all the running Windows 3.*x* programs is treated as a single task by the Windows preemptive scheduler. When the collection of Windows programs receives a time slice, the applications multitask cooperatively during that slice of time. This type of "round-robin" scheduling worked pretty well, as long as the running Windows applications were written properly and behaved well, meaning that they would relinquish control correctly. Errant applications, however, would cause Windows to lock up, often forcing a reboot.

For this reason, Windows 95 followed Windows NT into the realm of complete preemptive multitasking. The new task-management structure that allows Windows to take control when an application fails to behave makes Windows 95 much more stable. Poorly written applications sometimes still misbehave, but now a user can force Windows to take control by pressing the CTRL-ALT-DEL key combination, which brings up the running Task List and allows the user to shut down specific running tasks. Errant applications show up in the Task List with a "not responding" entry next to the application's name. Of course, these benefits are only fully realized with 32-bit applications. Older 16-bit applications still have some difficulty playing well with others.

While Windows 3.*x* was fully network-aware, it was geared around a single user. In order to support multiple users on a single PC with independent settings, access to a network server and custom installation procedures were required. Windows 95/98 allows multiple users to retain their own custom settings on the local PC, much like Windows NT. By default, Windows 95 installs for all users to use the same settings. Accessing the Passwords option in the Control Panel lets an administrator configure the PC for multiple user access.

Windows 95 also added a new feature, *System Policies*, to allow a network administrator to more easily configure Windows clients on a network. The System Policy editor, POLEDIT.EXE, while not installed with Windows 3.*x*, is located on the Windows 95 CD-ROM. It is used to set common-denominator defaults for all network users, and add certain restrictions on a global basis if deemed necessary.

Windows 98 provides all of the benefits of Windows 95, with enhanced support for Plug-and-Play, better power management for notebook computers, and enhanced support for Universal Serial Bus (USB) devices. USB was not supported in the original release of Windows 95, but a subsequent Windows 95 update included limited support for USB.

Virtual File Allocation Table (VFAT)

A new *Virtual File Allocation Table (VFAT)* driver is incorporated in Windows 95, and provides a 32-bit protected-mode code path for manipulating the file system stored on a disk. It is *multithreaded,* providing smoother multitasking performance. The 32-bit file access driver is improved over that provided originally with Windows for Workgroups 3.11 and is compatible with more DOS device drivers and hard drive controllers.

Benefits of the 32-bit file access driver over previous DOS-based driver solutions include the following:

- Dramatically improved performance and real-mode disk caching
- No conventional memory used (replacement for real-mode SmartDrive)
- Better multitasking when accessing information on disk
- Dynamic cache support

Using DOS and Windows 3.*x,* manipulation of the FAT and writing to or reading from the disk is handled by the Int 21h MS-DOS function and is 16-bit *real-mode* code. Being able to manipulate the disk file system from *protected mode* removes or reduces the need to transition to real mode in order to write information to the disk through MS-DOS, resulting in a large performance gain while accessing files.

FAT32

FAT32, new to Windows 95 (beginning with the OEM 2 release), provides several enhancements over previous implementations of the FAT file system. While the DOS-standard FAT16 supports drives up to 2GB,

FAT32 can now address drives up to 2TB (terabytes) in size. FAT32 uses smaller clusters (that is, 4K clusters for drives up to 8GB in size), resulting in 10 to 15 percent more efficient use of disk space relative to large standard FAT (FAT16) drives. FAT32 has the ability to relocate the root directory and use the backup copy of the file allocation table instead of the default copy. In addition, the boot record on FAT32 drives has been expanded to include a backup of critical data structures. This means that FAT32 drives are less susceptible to a single point of failure than existing FAT16 volumes.

FAT32 was implemented with as little change as possible to Windows 95's existing architecture, internal data structures, application programming interfaces (APIs), and on-disk format. However, in some cases, existing APIs will not work on FAT32 drives. Most programs are unaffected by these changes, and existing tools and drivers should continue to work on FAT32 drives.

All of Microsoft's bundled disk tools (Format, Fixed DISK, Defrag, and MS-DOS-based and Windows-based ScanDisk) have been revised to work with FAT32. In addition, Microsoft is working with leading device driver and disk tool vendors to support them in revising their products to support FAT32.

For most users, FAT32 has a negligible performance impact. Some programs may see a slight performance gain from FAT32. In other programs, particularly those heavily dependent on large sequential read or write operations, FAT32 may result in a modest performance degradation.

exam
ⓦatch

FAT32 is supported by Windows 95 OEM Release 2 and Windows 98. Windows NT 4.0 does not support FAT32; it supports only FAT16 and NTFS. Windows 2000 will support FAT16, FAT32, and NTFS.

CERTIFICATION SUMMARY

There are several available operating systems for the Intel-based PC. Of the various choices, the marketplace has been dominated by various versions of Microsoft's DOS and Windows. While complex, this OS combination is now well understood, reasonably stable, and well documented. Taking the time to learn the various available commands, their syntax, and correct usage can turn an otherwise daunting occupation into an often fun endeavor. By understanding the inner workings of the various components, you, too, can be the expert.

TWO-MINUTE DRILL

❑ At the time DOS was first developed, floppy disks and cassette tapes were the only storage media available for the PC.

❑ DOS commands can be either internal or external. Internal commands are present in the COMMAND.COM shell, and can be executed on the command line at any time from any directory location. External commands reside in the DOS directory.

❑ CP/M, QDOS, NDOS, Dr. DOS, Geoworks, and NeXT STEP, among others, are all examples of competent PC operating systems. However, the PC market belongs primarily to Microsoft, with DOS, Windows, and Windows NT.

❑ DOS was developed as a 16-bit application, with its internal code segments written to be accessed 16 bits at a time.

❑ Windows (up to Windows 95) is a graphical shell that overlays on DOS, and relies on DOS for its low-level device access.

❑ Because of their small size (<2K), .LNK files produce enormous waste of hard drive territory due to slack space.

❑ System files are responsible for all device access and user interface presentation.

❑ Over the years Windows has evolved to support a multitude of components, such as sound devices, scanners, CD-ROMs, and tape drives.

❑ On the Windows desktop, the spacing of the icons, the type of wallpaper, screen colors, and other interface features can be customized in the Windows WIN.INI file.

❑ The bulk of configuration for Windows 95 has shifted to the SYSTEM.DAT and USER.DAT files.

❑ DOS installs onto a formatted disk by placing its system files in the root directory.

❑ By default, the system files AUTOEXEC.BAT, CONFIG.SYS, and ANSI.SYS carry no attributes, and are not required for OS startup.

❑ The *.LGO file that WIN.COM selects is based on the type of video card setup determined to be in the computer during installation.

❑ Review Table 9-3 for DOS commands.

❑ In Windows 3.x, PROGMAN.EXE finishes the Windows initialization by running any startup applications specified in the WIN.INI file, and by starting any applications whose icons are stored in the StartUp Group.

❑ The Windows 95 Registry is a complex database of settings pertaining to both applications and hardware.

❑ DOS is a widely used acronym for Disk Operating System.

❑ Using the FDISK (for Fixed DISK) utility provided with DOS, a hard drive is prepared for use through partitioning and formatting.

❑ Review Table 9-4 for command-line switches for SCANDISK.EXE.

❑ .COM, .EXE, and .BAT files are known as executables.

❑ Cooperative multitasking means that applications must voluntarily relinquish control of the CPU so that other applications may operate.

❑ Hard drives consist of a number of platters rotating on a common spindle, with read/write heads mounted on a pivoting assembly that spans all platters concurrently.

❑ Up until recently, DOS wouldn't support a partition greater than 2GB.

❑ Because the smallest addressable unit is the cluster, once a file is written to a cluster, the cluster is marked as used and can't have anything else written to it until the file in it is erased or overwritten by another copy of the same file.

❑ When formatting, or afterwards if desired, the partition marked as active must have an operating system installed.

❑ In practice, it's best to limit the fully qualified path to less than 60 characters, or else some older applications and utilities can display anomalous behavior.

❑ Each file accessible to DOS, regardless of media type, has four attributes that may be associated with it: READ-ONLY, HIDDEN, SYSTEM, and ARCHIVE.

❑ With many DOS commands, the /S switch allows a user to process files in all subdirectories in the specified path.

❑ The best way to keep your data safe from any failure of the equipment or potential operator error is to create a separate copy of the data, also known as a backup.

❑ Performed periodically, defragmentation is probably the single best operation a user can perform to maintain a high-performance system.

❑ Windows Registry entries are handled automatically by Windows 95/98 when it comes to hardware, and also by the various applications that are installed. This automation is called Plug-and-Play.

❑ In Windows 95/98, all items in the menu and on the desktop are link (.LNK) files stored in subdirectories under Windows.

❑ Accessing the Passwords option in the Control Panel lets an administrator configure the PC for multiple-user access.

SELF TEST

The following Self Test questions will help you measure your understanding of the material presented in this chapter. Read all the choices carefully, as there may be more than one correct answer. Choose all correct answers for each question.

1. The first step in preparing a new hard drive for an operating system is:

    A. Format

    B. Partition

    C. ScanDisk

    D. Defrag

2. Which of the following do NOT require an initial installation of DOS before they will run? (Choose all that apply.)

    A. Windows 3.1

    B. Windows 95

    C. Windows 98

    D. None of the above

3. Which of these disk utilities finds and corrects problems with the File Allocation Tables such as lost clusters?

    A. ScanDisk

    B. Backup

    C. Fix DISK

    D. Defrag

Scenario for questions 4-10: Suppose you are running a Pentium 90 with 32MB of RAM and two 1.5GB hard drives. The first drive is divided into a 500MB primary partition and a 1GB extended partition, broken into two logical partitions of 512MB each. The second drive is two partitions, a primary of 1250MB, and an extended of 250MB, with all 250MB dedicated to a logical partition. Keep this configuration in mind when answering the following seven questions.

4. The disk partitioning scheme that would be used by DOS on the first partition of the first drive would be:

    A. FAT12

    B. FAT15

    C. FAT16

    D. FAT32

5. The disk partitioning scheme that would be used by Windows 3.1 for the first partition of the first drive would be:

    A. FAT12

    B. FAT16

    C. FAT32

    D. NTFS

6. If you format all of the partitions in the system, how will the drive letters be assigned to the first hard drive?

    A. Primary – C: drive;
       Extended – D: drive

    B. Primary – C: drive;
       Extended – E: drive

C. Primary – C: drive; Logical – D: and E: drives

D. Primary – C: drive; Logical – E: and F: drives

7. If you format all of the partitions in the system, how will the drive letters be assigned to the second hard drive?

A. Primary – D: drive; Extended – G: drive

B. Primary – D: drive; Logical – G: drive

C. Primary – F: drive; Extended – G: drive

D. Primary – F: drive; Logical – G: drive

8. What will be the cluster size on the first drive, first partition formatted with FAT16?

A. 512 bytes

B. 8KB

C. 16KB

D. 32KB

9. What will be the cluster size on the second drive, first partition, formatted with FAT16?

A. 512 bytes

B. 8KB

C. 16KB

D. 32KB

10. How much physical space will a 50-byte text file take up if it is stored on the second partition of the second drive?

A. 50 bytes

B. 512 bytes

C. 4KB

D. 32KB

11. Which of the following technologies are natively supported by Windows 98, but not by Windows 3.*x*? (Choose all that apply.)

A. FAT16

B. FAT32

C. NTFS

D. Plug-and-Play

12. Which of the following files are part of the Windows Registry in Windows 95/98? (Choose all that apply.)

A. AUTOEXEC.BAT

B. SYSTEM.INI

C. USER.DAT

D. SYSTEM.DAT

13. Which of the following utilities will destroy all data on a partition? (Choose all that apply.)

A. FORMAT

B. FDISK

C. DEFRAG

D. PDISK

14. In Windows 95 and beyond, which tool replaces the Windows 3.1 File Manager?

A. Program Manager

B. Windows Explorer

C. Control Panel

D. Windows Browse List

15. Which of the following files is/are required to successfully boot DOS? (Choose all that apply.)

A. AUTOEXEC.BAT

B. CONFIG.SYS

C. COMMAND.COM

D. ANSI.SYS

16. The wasted physical storage space required by a file smaller than the cluster size on the disk is known as what?

A. Slack space

B. Cluster waste

C. Clutter

D. Lost clusters

17. What is the largest partition size supported by native DOS running FAT16?

A. 500MB

B. 2GB

C. 4GB

D. 2TB

18. The first physical sector of any physical hard disk used as a boot device is the:

A. MBR

B. File System Boot Sector

C. System Partition

D. None of the above

19. The first physical sector on any logical volume is known as what?

A. MBR

B. File System Boot Sector

C. System Partition

D. None of the above

20. What is the smallest addressable unit on a hard disk drive?

A. Sector

B. Cluster

C. Partition

D. Byte

21. Under DOS, which of the following attributes can the user set on a given file? (Choose all that apply.)

A. Read-Only

B. Hidden

C. System

D. Archive

22. Which utility helps achieve better disk performance by arranging all clusters for a given file physically closer to each other on a hard disk?

A. Check Disk

B. ScanDisk

C. Defrag

D. DRVSPC

23. Which utility helps you recover from disaster by providing a way to maintain a copy of all of your data files?

A. Scandisk

B. Backup

C. Restore

D. DOSSHELL

24. Which of the following statements are NOT true about the Windows Registry? (Choose all that apply.)

A. It can be easily viewed with a text editor.

B. Any changes made are saved immediately.

C. Incorrectly modifying the Registry can cause your whole system to crash.

D. You can edit the Registry manually through the REGEDIT utility.

25. Under Windows 3.1, which file configures Windows to address specific hardware devices and their associated settings?

A. CONFIG.SYS

B. AUTOEXEC.BAT

C. WIN.INI

D. SYSTEM.INI

10

Memory
Management

Whent contemplating memory, a simple maxim is appropriate: *more is good, less is bad.* While this pretty much sums up the concept of memory management, you need to know some of the details to understand the need for more memory. Over the last fifteen years, the notion of memory and the amount needed in a PC has evolved. In 1983, Peter Norton described the IBM XT, which featured the 8088 processor. He wrote, "So IBM has equipped all XTs with what it considers to be the minimum gear for a serious personal computer. Now the 10-megabyte disk and 128KB [one eighth of a megabyte] of memory are naturals for a serious machine." In today's modern computing world 64MB of RAM is barely enough to run our 3-D games and other resource-intensive applications. While tracking the progression of memory you are likely to be confronted with a barrage of acronyms from ROM and PROM, to SRAM and DRAM, and many others. Sorting out all these acronyms can be quite a chore, so let's get started.

CERTIFICATION OBJECTIVE 10.01

Types of Memory

Physically memory is packaged in many sizes and shapes but a PC's central processing unit (CPU) is able to use only two categories of memory. These are labeled physical memory and virtual memory.

There are several kinds of physical memory. A basic division is between Random Access Memory (RAM), which can be both read by and written to by the CPU, and Programmable Read-Only Memory (PROM a.k.a. ROM). Standard RAM is also known as volatile memory, in that it loses its contents when system power is shut down, while ROM is nonvolatile, its contents remaining unchanged even when power is removed. The primary difference between RAM and ROM is that RAM is readable by any application, while ROM is meant for a specific program.

Physical memory consists of the hardware that handles memory in a PC. This memory is stored in chips that are either ROM (Read-Only Memory chips) or RAM (Random Access Memory).

Types of ROM

ROM began as a write-once chip. Instruction code was electrically fed to the chip and retained there permanently. In order to update this type of ROM, the chip had to be physically replaced by another chip containing upgraded instruction code. This reduced production costs, but installation costs remained high.

Memory developers quickly realized that upgrades would become a fairly regular occurrence, so they came up with the Erasable Programmable Read-Only Memory (EPROM) chip. The EPROM chip was originally developed to be erased by ultraviolet light, and had a small window on the chip itself. The window was taped over with a small metal-foil cover. Removing the cover and exposing the chip window to ultra-violet light would erase it and allow a new instruction set to be loaded. The chips could be changed in this way several times (dozens), but not many (hundreds). Fortunately, ROM is mostly used for specific support of hardware devices, and updates usually are infrequent.

On the heels of the EPROM came the Electrically Erasable Programmable Read-Only Memory (EEPROM), which could be erased by applying a specific voltage to the chip. These chips still usually required removal and insertion into a PROM "burner" to erase and reprogram. Some inventive hardware manufacturers came up with ways of addressing updates onboard their hardware, but these were the exception.

Note: There is a special type of EEPROM that can be erased and reprogrammed in blocks instead of one byte at a time. Many modern PCs have their BIOS stored on a flash memory chip so that it can easily be updated if necessary. Such a BIOS is sometimes called a Flash BIOS.

Most hardware devices now can be updated by running a program from DOS (or some other operating system) that can erase and reprogram their device, usually in conjunction with a small ROM chip onboard. In case the upload fails, the ROM chip is there as a backup to continue to seek an operating code set from a specific source in case one is not present in Flash BIOS.

A primary use of ROM technology is to store system BIOS, also referred to as *firmware.* When a PC is powered off, the information contained in

RAM is dumped, hence the term *volatile memory*. This means we are unable to store information that controls how a PC is to boot up in this type of memory. On the other hand, ROM maintains its data even when the PC is powered off. While ROM works great for things like system BIOS, it isn't designed to handle the demanding read and write requirements placed upon memory to support the operating system and to run applications. For this we need RAM.

SRAM and DRAM

RAM is somewhat of an ambiguous term because there are so many different types of RAM on the market including Static Random Access Memory (SRAM) and the many flavors of Dynamic Random Access Memory (DRAM). RAM has evolved over the years dating back to the first IBM PC, which arrived in 1980. Then, memory was quantified in kilobytes (KB) and a standard memory chip had a whopping 4KB. This small memory chip was considered a marvel, compared to memory modules employed by then-existing systems. Still in use at that time were 4KB memory modules powered by vacuum tubes housed in a 6' × 6' × 6' cube that consumed kilowatts (thousands of watts) of electricity. Today, memory modules come in 2, 4, 8, 16, and 32, 64, and 128 Megabyte (MB) modules, and consume milliwatts (1000th of a watt) of power, allowing huge quantities of RAM to be contained in laptops. To understand RAM, we first need to understand its general relationship to the CPU (central processing unit, also known as the processor). The CPU is responsible for processing data, handling instruction sets from software programs, and interrupts from hardware devices. Working in conjunction with the CPU to store this information is a read/write type of RAM referred to as the *main system memory*. The main system memory is actually comprised of SRAM and DRAM. SRAM deals specifically with the system cache, while DRAM is used as a backup when the information requested by the CPU cannot be fulfilled from the system cache.

When you consider how information is stored in RAM, it is in the most basic sense an electronic impulse. SRAM is a type of Random Access Memory that holds it electrical charge without the need to be refreshed, as long as power is supplied to the circuit. Refreshing is a process of "reminding" or updating the circuit that it contains an electric charge. SRAMs are generally made up of four to six transistors per bit. This is in contrast to DRAM, which is made up of only one transistor per bit and one capacitor. When energized, the capacitor holds an electrical charge if the bit contains a 1 and no charge if the bit contains a 0. The main problem with capacitors is that they can only hold an electrical charge for a short period of time before they discharge. Because the capacitors are very small, the charge fades quickly. For this reason, refresh circuitry is needed to read the value of every cell which in turn refreshes the "charge" before the value fades away and is lost. The term *Dynamic Random Access Memory* comes from the constant process of refreshing, which must be performed hundreds of times per second to maintain the contents stored in memory.

When comparing SRAM to DRAM, which is better? SRAM contains a type of on/off switch to indicate whether an electronic charge is stored. This is in comparison to DRAM, which needs be constantly refreshed. Due to this design, SRAM possesses lightning fast transfer rates of 4 to 10 Ns (a nanosecond is one billionth of a second) compared to DRAM, which ranges from older versions of 120 Ns to modern versions around 60 Ns. A logical question usually comes up about this point. Why would computers depend upon a type of memory that can hold its contents only a fraction of a second and is slow? As with many things, it boils down to a factor of cost. SRAM contains four to six transistors per bit while DRAM contains only one. The smaller size is a big factor in the cost to produce DRAM. Table 10-1 lists the advantages and disadvantages of SRAM and DRAM.

Looking back over the last fifteen years, the personal computer has evolved in many different ways. Take, for example, processors. The 8088 processor ran at 8 MHz compared to the newest Pentium IIIs, which are clocked at 550 MHz. While processor speeds have skyrocketed, memory speed has not kept pace. How do we manage this disparity between the speed of the processor and the speed of memory? One way would be to make all storage devices including memory, hard drives, and CD-ROM drives operate at the same speed as the processor. This would ensure that the processor never has to wait for data. Unfortunately, due to the high cost

TABLE 10-1

A Comparison of SRAM and DRAM

Memory Type	Advantages	Disadvantage
SRAM	**Design:** SRAM doesn't require extra circuitry and constant refreshing to maintain its data. **Speed:** SRAM is much faster than DRAM. Generally 4–10 Ns transfer rates.	**Cost**: Byte for byte, SRAM is more expensive to produce than DRAM. **Size**: SRAM is larger than DRAM.
DRAM	**Size:** DRAM takes up approximately ¼ the size of SRAM. **Cost:** Partly due to the smaller size, DRAM is much cheaper to produce.	**Design:** DRAM requires extra circuitry and constant refreshing in order to maintain its data. **Speed:** DRAM is slower than SRAM. Generally 60–120 Ns transfer rates.

of development and technology limitations, the speed of these devices has not kept pace with the technology of improved processor speeds.

As with most marriages, there must be a compromise if two people, or in our example two components, are going to work together. We've mentioned the high cost of SRAM technology, but instead of building a cost-prohibitive 64MB or 128MB module of SRAM memory, why not build a small 256KB module that is almost as efficient? That sounds like an awfully difficult task, but it has been around since the invention of the 486 processor! How can something like this work? Well, the concept that we're describing is called *caching*. The system cache is based upon a computer science principle called *locality of reference*. Locality of reference states that if the processor recently referenced a location in memory, it is likely that it will refer to it again in the near future. By holding recently used memory values, caching saves the processor from going to main system memory each time to reload them. This provides a significant performance boost, because the main system memory, which is made up of DRAM, is much slower than the processor's system cache, which is comprised of SRAM.

Previously mentioned is the fact that SRAM is more costly to produce than DRAM, yet it offers significantly faster transfer rates. This is the beginning of the compromise that allows us to match a fast processor with slow memory. SRAM is used for a special type of small, fast-access memory called the system cache that works in conjunction with the CPU. Frequently accessed commands and instructions are stored in this special type of on-board SRAM. Because the system cache is actually incorporated into the processor, it is often referred to as an internal cache or L1 cache. This concept of a system cache was unheard of until the arrival of the 486 processor. Since that time, modern processors actually have a small SRAM module built into the processor. To illustrate the smallness of the system cache, the 486 processor featured an 8KB L1 cache, and today's Pentium IIs feature only a 64KB L1 cache.

As processor speeds continued to increase, a secondary type of system cache was developed to bridge the processor /memory performance gap. This second level system cache is called L2 cache. It may also be referenced as external cache because it is physically located outside the processor, that is until the Pentium Pro was introduced. Prior to the Pentium Pro, the L2 cache was an external daughter board that was physically located away from the processor. Intel changed things around when they placed the L2 cache within the same package that housed the processor. While it is still considered external, it is internalized within the processor. To cut down on the confusion, just think of this as L2 cache, and you won't have any problems.

L2 cache is a big reason why Intel sells the Celeron processor for much less than the Pentium II and Pentium III processors. At the time of this writing, the 466 MHz Celeron comes with only 128KB L2 cache in comparison to the Pentium II and Pentium III processors that ship with a standard 512KB L2 cache. Why should this be of concern? To answer that we will examine the process of caching.

When the processor requests information from memory, it goes through a logical progression. First it checks the high-speed L1 cache and L2 cache. If the requested data is found, we have a cache *hit.* If the requested data is not found, we have a cache *miss.* The processor then must access the slower main system memory, which is again comprised of DRAM modules. When considering the size of the system cache you would think that a high percentage of the time the processor would have to access the main system memory, but that isn't the case. For example, the processor experiences a cache hit 90-95 percent of the time with a 512KB L2 cache, caching 64MB of system memory. That is pretty amazing when you stop to consider that the L2 cache is less than 1 percent of the size of the memory it is caching, yet it is able to register a hit on over 90 percent of requests. In light of this high efficiency, a large system cache is very critical to the responsiveness of the applications you work with.

Let's look at a simple example to see how the system cache works with an application. Suppose you start your favorite word processor and open a document. The word processing application reads the contents of the file that you're opening and then displays the contents onto your monitor. From a simplistic programming view, it would look similar to the following:

For each character in the word processing file:

- Read the character.

- Store the character into memory.

- If the user is currently viewing the page this character is on, display it on the screen.

The example above contains approximately 150 characters, which means the application would have looped through the routine 150 times. Imagine how many times the routine would have to be executed for this entire chapter, or better still the entire book! Oblivious to the end user, software programs call thousands of routines like the one described here in the normal everyday use of a program.

So where does memory caching come into play in this scenario? Remember the principle called *locality of reference*. It basically states that even within very large programs like a word processor that contains several megabytes of instructions, only small portions of this code are generally used at any point in time. As in our word processing example, the program would spend a long period of time working in one small area of the code repeating the same task over and over again with slightly different data. Once completed, it would then move on to another area of the program. This repetitive action occurs because of *loops*, which are what programs operate from to accomplish a routine many times in rapid succession. The L1 and L2 system cache allow these loops to be stored in fast access memory. The end result is that your program runs very fast! Now that we have a general understanding of the system cache, we will explore the main system memory.

The Basics of DRAM

Back in the '80s, PCs included RAM in quantities of 64KB, 256KB, 512KB, and finally 1MB. The Commodore 64 was amazing at the time because it featured 64KB RAM!

During the early 1990s, advanced operating systems supporting graphical user interface (GUI), like Windows that required a minimum of 2MB of RAM, appeared on the market. August, 1995 found many avid computer enthusiasts (a.k.a. computer geeks) standing in line at midnight to be the first to purchase Windows 95. Some were shocked to find that they also needed to purchase extra RAM in order to get Windows 95 to run on their systems. Windows 95 requires 4MB RAM, but 8MB is a more realistic minimum requirement. While the need for more RAM has grown through the 1990s, RAM prices have dropped dramatically. Today it would be foolish to consider less than 32MB RAM in a PC. Some power users would consider 128MB to be the minimum for Windows 98 in order to run all of the resource-intensive applications and 3-D games that are being developed.

Before we get into all the different DRAM technologies, we will delve into the basic workings of system memory. All PCs contain a hardware logic circuit called the *memory controller*, which controls the system memory. Whenever memory is read or written to, it is called a *memory access*. In a read access, the memory controller creates the signals to specify which memory location needs to be accessed, and then calls the data up on the data bus to be read by the processor or whatever other device requested it.

To understand how memory is accessed, let's take a look at how memory chips are addressed. For example we will use a 4Mx4 16Mbit chip. This means that there are 4,194,304 different memory locations, or cells, each of which contains 4 bits of data. The memory locations are based upon the binary counting system where 4,194,304 is equal to 2^{22}. This means 22 bits are required to uniquely address each memory location. While in theory 22 address lines are required, memory chips don't have this many address lines. Instead they are logically organized as a "square" of *columns and rows*. The high-order 11 bits are the "column," and the low-order 11 bits are considered the "row." To illustrate, let's say the memory controller needs to access memory location 3,466,201. In binary this is equal to 1101001110001111011001. The first eleven bits, 11010011100, represent the row address and the remaining eleven, 01111011001, represent the column address. This combination allows the memory controller to select the unique location of 3,466,201. To put this into an easier example, if you have worked with a spreadsheet application, you would refer to a cell location by going to row #66 and then looking at column B to find cell B66.

Looking at this mess of rows and columns, it might seem logical to have 22 address pins on each chip. Cost again defies logic. Instead of building 22 address lines, manufacturers consolidate the 22 address lines into 11. This method of locating memory address by row and column allows manufacturers to cut the number of address pins in half on the memory chip. Modern PCs don't have a single memory chip. Rather, most have dozens, depending on total memory capacity and type of DRAMs utilized. The chips are arranged into modules (SIMMs or DIMMs), and then into banks. The memory controller directs which chips are read and accessed for reading or writing data.

The following steps indicate a simplified workflow of how a normal read memory access is performed:

1. The memory controller receives a request from the data bus. It then decodes the memory address and determines which chips are to be accessed.

2. The 11 low-order bits that represent the row address are sent to the chip, and the entire row is read. This process of reading actually refreshes the values in all the cells.

3. The 11 high-order bits that represent the column address are sent to the chips to be read and the selected column is read into the output buffers.

4. The output buffers of all the accessed memory chips feed the data out onto the data bus, where the processor or other device that requested the data can read it.

The time required for memory to produce the required data from the start of the access until when the valid data is available for use, is called the memory's *access time*. This is normally measured in nanoseconds (Ns). Today's memory normally has access time ranging from 5 to 70 nanoseconds. The difference in speed among the various DRAM technologies has more to do with the arrangement and control of the memory chips, rather than the core technology of the DRAM chips themselves.

As described earlier, memory is stored in a format consisting of rows and columns. In order to access it, you must know the cell location. Today, memory isn't read one bit or even one byte at a time; usually, it is read 64 bits at a time on modern PCs. So why is the main system so slow in comparison to the system cache? When we take into account the four steps listed above, the first access to memory takes a long time, usually between 4 to 7 clock cycles. The amount of time required to perform this first access to memory is defined as *memory latency*.

Most of the latency is not a result of actually sending the data, but the process of defining what and how to do the transfer. If we could somehow lower this overhead, we could greatly increase performance. Modern computer systems have done this by accessing memory in four consecutive 64-bit pieces of memory, which are read consecutively (4 x 64 bits = 256 bits or 32 bytes). This is known as *burst mode access* or *bursting*. Because most of the overhead associated with memory transfer is a result of deciphering the request and coordinating the transfer of the first 64-bit chunk, we can cut the time associated to access the other three bits. Instead of taking 4 to 7 clock cycles for each 64-bit chunk, the second, third, and fourth 64-bit chunks take only 1 to 3 clock cycles to access. The system's L2 cache is designed to accommodate 256 bits, allowing it to store all of the 32 bytes read from memory during an access.

The representation of burst mode access is generally stated using the formula: x-y-y-y. The x represents the number of clock cycles to access the first 64-bit read/write. The ys represent how many clock cycles to do the second, third, and fourth reads/writes. An example would be 5-3-3-3, resulting in 14 clock cycles to do the whole burst. (Without burst mode this access would take at least 20 clock cycles: 5-5-5-5.) When comparing the different types of DRAM technologies, it is important to compare the burst mode timing to complete the 256-bit burst.

Hardware Logic Circuit DRAM Technologies

The original IBM PC used *conventional* DRAM. It is said to be *asynchronous* because the memory is not synchronized to the system clock. When a memory access starts, a predetermined wait state occurs before the memory value appears on the bus. The signals required to fulfill the request aren't coordinated with the system clock. This isn't a problem when working with lower-speed memory bus systems, but it is inadequate for high-speed (>66 MHz) Pentium-class memory systems. Asynchronous DRAM is now considered to be obsolete. It isn't used in any modern PCs as it has been replaced with newer DRAM technologies.

FAST PAGE MODE (FPM) DRAM   Fast Page mode (FPM) became the most widely used access method for DRAMs, and is still used on many older systems today. Conventional DRAM requires that a row and column be sent for each access, whereas FPM improved access times by sending the row address only once for accesses to memory in locations near each other. The name Fast Page mode is somewhat deceptive because it the slowest memory technology used in modern PCs today. It is kind of like NT that stands for New Technology. FPM and NT are now considered old technology.

Essentially all PCs that are designed to use conventional asynchronous RAM will support FPM, although it is also not suitable for high-speed memory buses over 66 MHz, because excessive numbers of wait states would have to be added. FPM DRAM typically allows burst system timings as fast as 5-3-3-3 at 66 MHz. You should consider using this type of DRAM only if someone gives it away, or if you have a 486 system that doesn't support any of the later memory types discussed below.

EXTENDED DATA OUT (EDO) DRAM   The last major improvement to asynchronous DRAM came with the Hyperpage mode, or Extended Data Out (EDO). This innovation offers a 25-40% improvement in memory performance while using the same amount of silicon and the same package size as FPM. In a simplistic view, EDO memory modified the timing circuits, allowing subsequent accesses to memory to begin before the last access had completed.

You can use EDO memory only if your motherboard's system chipset supports this type of RAM. EDO found mainstream use in the first Pentium-class systems but it generally isn't recommended for high-speed (75 MHz and higher) memory buses because it isn't that much different than FPM. EDO typically allows burst system timings as fast as 5-2-2-2 at 66 MHz, when using an optimized chipset. EDO provided an improvement to memory access time, but most manufacturers no longer produce it, or offer it in limited production. It is only a matter of time before EDO prices begin to rise, and the equivalent size SDRAM module (described later in this chapter) will be less expensive.

BURST EXTENDED DATA OUT (BEDO) DRAM   Burst EDO (BEDO) was designed to rival the speed promised by SDRAM (described below), but it died before it had a chance to compete with SDRAM. BEDO works with an enhanced burst mode technology that would have provided the 5-1-1-1 access times at 66 MHz that SDRAM promised. The death of BEDO can primarily be attributed to Intel and their decision that EDO was no longer a viable RAM technology. Instead, they focused their motherboard and chipset development to support SDRAM, and they didn't support BEDO on their motherboards.

SYNCHRONOUS DRAM (SDRAM)   As processor speeds continued to skyrocket, it became apparent that bus speeds would need to run faster than 66 MHz, which the original Pentium systems featured. DRAM manufacturers needed to find a way to overcome the momentous processor/memory gap that revolved around latency issues (the processor waiting on memory to access stored data). Prior to the synchronous design, all DRAM technology was asynchronous, which means it was on its own timing mechanism separate from the system clock. The processor had to wait idly for DRAM to complete its internal operations, which could take up to 60 ns. With synchronous control, DRAM transfers information from the processor under control of the system clock. After approximately five clock cycles the data becomes available and the processor can read it from the output lines. When used with a supporting chipset, SDRAM offers 5-1-1-1 system timing.

SDRAM is the current standard for the line of Intel motherboards featuring the 440BX chipset and manufacturers creating Intel compatible motherboards. These motherboards that support 100 MHz memory buses are becoming the mainstream in the modern PC. At the same time, SDRAM is rapidly replacing older technologies because it is designed to work with these high-speed buses, whereas conventional asynchronous DRAM is not.

PROPOSED DRAM TECHNOLOGIES   Just as SDRAM is bringing an end to EDO technology, SDRAM is bound to be replaced by a faster technology. The problem is that SDRAM technology can reach a theoretical memory bus speed of only 133 MHz. In light of our efficient system cache, this limitation is acceptable for the time being, but it will soon be considered too slow as processor speeds continue to increase. In an effort to close the gap between processor and memory performance new DRAM technologies are beginning to emerge, including DDR SDRAM, SLDRAM, and RDRAM.

One of the proposed new standards to replace SDRAM is *Double Data Rate SDRAM (DDR SDRAM)*. DDR SDRAM doubles the bandwidth of the memory by transferring data twice per cycle. It is a technology similar to the one used by AGP that doubles the bandwidth of PCI. Another proposed standard is *SyncLink (SLDRAM)*. SyncLink is based upon a consortium of nine DRAM manufacturers, including Hyundai, IBM, Micron, NEC, and TI, which have proposed a draft standard to the IEEE for uniform memory architecture. The proposal outlines a packet-oriented bus operating at 400 MHz, with a 16-bit-wide data path. The final proposed standard is *Direct Rambus DRAM (DRDRAM)*. It is based upon a proprietary memory channel between DRAM and the processor called the Direct Rambus Channel, a high-speed 16-bit bus running at a clock rate of 400 MHz. DRDRAM is proprietary, and is being designed to use a special type of module called a *Rambus Inline Memory Module (RIMM)*.

Which standard will win out? Initially, DDR SDRAM may go into production, but at best it is a short-term solution. SyncLink DRAM and Direct Rambus DRAM are really the two contenders. SLDRAM has a lot more support from PC and memory manufacturers because they are developing an open standard to be used by all. On the other hand, Intel is banking on Rambus technology, which will be a proprietary model. If it wins out, all manufacturers will have to pay royalties to Intel and Rambus in order to use their design. Generally speaking the word "proprietary" can be the kiss of death when developing new standards. Just ask IBM about their Micro Channel Architecture (MCA) bus standard. The ultimate winner may not be the best technical solution, it may very well come down to economic and political pressure. We'll just have to wait through 1999 and beyond to find out.

Memory Packaging

SIMMs (single in-line memory module) and DIMMs (dual in-line memory modules) are types of memory packages and are explained next.

Dual Inline Packages (DIPs) and Memory Modules

The majority of memory chips come packaged in small plastic or ceramic containers called *dual inline packages (DIPs)*. A DIP is a rectangular-shaped container with rows of pins running along the two longer sides. If you have ever looked at a SIMM or DIMM module, these are the small black boxes mounted on the boards. Since the invention of the original IBM XT-class personal computers, the DIP has been the standard for the packaging of integrated circuits.

Modern PC toolkits still come with a soldering iron which might prove useful if you want to reconnect some DIP memory to your motherboard. Original PCs placed the DIP memory packages directly on the motherboard by soldering them in place or putting them in sockets that were later soldered to the motherboard. Since most systems hold a minute amount of RAM, typically less than one megabyte, this was the easiest way to handle RAM. Unfortunately, this design was problematic, especially when you had to replace an entire motherboard if your memory chips went bad.

Modern systems don't directly use DIP memory packaging. Today, DIPs are soldered onto small circuit boards called *memory modules*. The original design was the *single inline memory module (SIMM)* later followed by the *dual inline memory module (DIMM)*. The SIMM and DIMM design are industry standards that make it very easy to replace and upgrade your main system memory.

Single Inline Memory Modules (SIMMs)

The single inline memory module (SIMM) is by far the most common memory module in use in the PC world today. This is due primarily to the tremendous number of older PCs in use in the world. Newer PCs now use DIMMs, which will eventually overtake the popular SIMM modules. SIMMs were designed in two configurations: 30 pin and 72 pin. The oldest is the 30-pin SIMM that was used in the 386- and some 486-based machines. The newer 72-pin SIMMs are in use in today's 486 and Pentium machines.

SIMMs are either single-sided or double-sided. All 30-pin SIMMs were single-sided, meaning that DRAM chips were found on only one side. 72-pin SIMMs can be single or double. The double-sided variety had DRAM chips soldered on both sides of the circuit board. The 72-pin SIMM provided a 32-bit memory path. Since Pentium-class machines feature a 64-bit data bus, SIMMs must be installed in pairs on Pentium machines.

Dual Inline Memory Modules (DIMMs)

The dual inline memory module (DIMM) is a newer memory module, intended for use in all Pentium-class computer systems. DIMMs have 168 pins, and they provide a 64-bit memory path. Because this matches the Pentium processor data bus, DIMM modules can be individually installed. DIMMs are standard for all new PCs, and they are not used on older motherboards. Therefore, they are not generally available in smaller sizes such as 1MB or 4MB because newer PCs would rarely contain such a small amount of system RAM.

Similar to SIMMs, DIMMs are inserted into special sockets on the motherboard. Generally DIMMs are available in 8MB, 16MB, 32MB, and 64MB sizes. Larger modules can be purchased, but they come at a higher cost per megabyte. While SIMMs are generally used for EDO RAM, DIMMs are the memory module of choice for SDRAM.

CERTIFICATION OBJECTIVE 10.02

Logical Memory Layout

"640KB ought to be enough for anybody." —*Bill Gates, 1981.* It is amazing what a couple of decades can do to our expectations. Because IBM created the first personal computer, their opinion prevailed concerning the PC's operating system logical memory layout. The logical memory layout is the way in which an operating system works with our physical memory, or RAM. As Bill Gates' quote indicates, early presumptions about memory size were just a little off in comparison to today's expectations. Unfortunately, we are bound by the decisions made for the early PC design, and we are stuck with many of the design limitations, which persist to this day. Figure 10-1 illustrates the logical memory model.

Conventional Memory
From its use of segment/offset addressing, the architecture of the 808X processor family used in the PC allowed 1MB (1024KB) of address space for system memory. Of this, 640KB was set aside for the applications and the additional 384KB was reserved for hardware to use.

FIGURE 10-1

Logical memory model

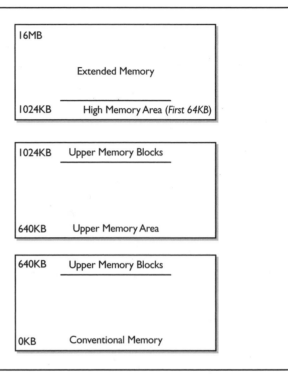

The 640KB of physical memory allocated for the operating system, applications, and data to be loaded in comprises *system memory*. The additional 384KB became *reserved memory*. The 640KB area, while appearing vast at the outset, quickly filled up.

One of the biggest memory consumers was one of the most popular applications at the time: the Lotus 1-2-3 spreadsheet program. 1-2-3 strained the 640KB system memory limit to the breaking point. Lotus realized they had to find a solution that allowed the processor to address more than 640KB of RAM, in order for 1-2-3 to be able to deal with more complex spreadsheets. Lotus teamed up with Intel, the processor maker, and Microsoft, who developed the operating system, and came up with the *Lotus-Intel-Microsoft (LIM)* memory specification. The specification renamed system memory to conventional memory, and defined additional (above the original 1024KB address limit) areas as expanded, extended, and high memory. Even though the 808X processor could address only 1024KB, the newer 80X86 series increased from 16-bit to 32-bit memory addressing, and could use up to 16MB (and soon more) RAM for system memory.

Extended/High Memory

Basically, all memory above the 1024KB line is considered *extended memory*. As we shall see, this area can be used in several ways. The basic division, though, is that 808X processors cannot access extended memory at all, but 80X86 processors can. The first 64KB of extended memory was roped off as a control area, and labeled the *high-memory area (HMA)*. This is the area where HIMEM.SYS loads from DOS. As part of the LIM spec, extended memory is addressed through a standard called *eXtended Memory Specification (XMS)*.

By the time DOS 5.0 rolled out, DOS could also load a portion of itself in the HMA. Originally, use of the HMA was reserved for only a single application. Once an application loaded there, it was "done." Microsoft found a way to load HIMEM.SYS, create the HMA, unload itself, and then place up to 64KB of its system code in its place. To enable this feature, you must include the line **DOS=HIGH** in the CONFIG.SYS file along with the **DEVICE=HIMEM.SYS** line.

Enabling XMS required additional work. Two standards for accessing XMS were developed. While Microsoft and Lotus shook hands to develop the LIM specification, they were at odds as to how to best deal with XMS. Microsoft developed the *DOS Protected Mode Interface (DPMI) specification*, while Lotus embraced a different structure that they inherited from their acquisition of the Phar-Lap Company. Lotus's approach was named *Virtual Control Program Interface (VCPI)*, and was totally incompatible with DPMI. This made for a short-term nightmare, as it became impossible to run Lotus 1-2-3, which used VCPI, under Windows 3.1, which used DPMI. Lotus finally conceded, and DPMI effectively has become the standard.

Upper Memory

The HMA is often confused with upper memory. The 384KB of reserved space (640KB to 1024KB), which became known as *upper memory* (conventional, below 640KB, being *lower memory*), remained scarcely populated by system boards, and allowed much of it to be used as system memory. In order to take advantage of unused upper memory, memory managers, such as EMM386.EXE, were created. Besides the LIM spec, other vendors, notably Quarterdeck with its Quarterdeck Expanded Memory Manager (QEMM) program, developed ways of digging out every unused portion of the reserved area, and converting it to system memory. On 808x processor machines, any additional space was welcome. The addition of this upper memory to the system memory pool increased the usable system (conventional) memory to as much as 720KB. Of course, this "breathing room" lasted about a week. It was clear that something had to be done to allow 808X processors to remain viable until the newer 80X86 processors could dominate. Enter *expanded memory*.

Virtual Memory and Expanded Memory

The LIM specification took into account the 808X processor's inability to address memory beyond 1024KB through the concept of virtualizing RAM. *Virtual memory* is free space located on your hard disk that the processor has been "tricked" into using as if it were actual physical memory. The LIM folks created a "frame" of "pages," each page (also known as a window) being 16KB in size that could be located in free areas of the reserved 384KB hardware address space. Upper memory, remember? The pages could be moved one at a time from the reserved area to either extended memory or the hard drive. A small code segment in lower memory looked at every memory address request made by the processor, and adjusted the requested segment/offset value to match a table it created that redefined the asked-for value into a specific page designation. The processor neither knew nor cared about where it got its code from, that is, whether from extended memory or the hard drive. This new type of memory access became the *Expanded Memory Specification (EMS).*

EMS has a couple of drawbacks when compared to XMS. The paging structure meant that only 64KB could be moved at any one time, and the tabled segment/offset lookups took additional time. What's more, it required that each application be aware that EMS was available to be used. In contrast, XMS was developed for 32-bit processors to access directly, with only a small HMA driver to enable it. Once enabled, the operating system (OS) could then parse out memory as needed to all running applications.

All of this mucking around with the reserved area (a.k.a. upper memory) added to an already existing problem, two devices trying to use the same memory space—a memory conflict.

QUESTIONS AND ANSWERS

When installing new RAM into a 486 PC, the module did not quite fit into the slot. What could be the problem?	Some 486 PCs used 30-pin modules, and newer ones used 72-pin modules. The type of SIMM that was bought for the 486 is the wrong type. The manufacturer should be able to tell you the type of SIMM required for that PC.
When installing a new video adapter card, the PC will no longer boot up into Windows 95. What has occurred?	This is a hard error. The new adapter card has conflicted with an existing card. This is most likely a conflict with the existing video adapter, which may be part of the system board. The video adapter, if a separate card, must be removed from the PC. Or, if it is a video on the system board, it must be disabled—usually through the system BIOS.

Memory Conflicts and Optimization

Confused yet? It was all supposed to work just right. By loading application and system code "low," and device drivers "high," everything was supposed to work perfectly. IBM, with its background in systems hardware, defined specific areas in upper memory to be reserved for specific devices to be accessed by the CPU over the system bus, dubbed the Industry Standard Architecture (ISA) bus. They just didn't foresee how rapidly newer technologies would add a multitude of new devices installed on the bus that would also need to fit into upper memory.

Network Interface Cards (NICs), graphics boards, SCSI adapters, and the like chomped away at already-overloaded upper memory. Worse yet, because there were no defined standards for these new devices, the default settings chosen often overlapped. Installing a new device without knowing how it and already-existing devices were configured to use a "memory footprint" could result in a memory conflict.

Even if you managed to get it to work right, the additional boards ate into those little crannies of memory that were eked out for use by the new memory manager programs. The folks who wrote the memory managers began developing better ways of detecting those areas of upper memory that were free to be used as additional conventional memory.

What Is a Memory Conflict?

A *memory conflict* occurs when a device or program attempts to access a memory location currently in use by another device or program. Memory conflicts usually reveal themselves in one of two ways. If you're lucky, a memory conflict will wait until a specific device driver tries to load, at which time either that device, along with the other conflicting device, ceases to function, or the system will lock up. If you're having a bad day, then you'll install a board that is configured to conflict with something required at startup, such as the display board or hard drive controller, in which case the system will fail to start before the operating system even gets a chance to load. The latter conflicts are usually the easiest to troubleshoot, because they happen immediately upon installation of the offending device, and removal and reconfiguration of it usually meets with success. Conflicts arising from optional devices, such as network cards, can be more difficult to pinpoint.

As long as the boards are populated with switches to make configuration choices, you're home free. Simply by choosing a new switch setting, you can usually resolve conflicts in one or two tries. Newer boards, however, have gotten away from using configuration switches, thanks to the use of EEPROMS or Flash memory, which can be used to store configuration settings. These boards require you to run an installation/configuration program to adjust them, which makes it hard to fix them if you can't start up your computer without it locking up due to a memory or interrupt conflict. Should this occur, if you have another PC available, you can try moving the suspect board to it to see if it will allow the other PC to boot, then use the configuration program to change the settings, and move the board back to the original PC. If you don't happen to have an extra PC lying around, then you're stuck with having to remove all the existing cards (remember, it's not going to work without a display adapter) and/or disabling any onboard hardware and then trying again. As long as you can boot the PC and run the configuration program, you can then try a different setting, then replace/re-enable the stuff you removed and try again.

Memory conflicts have been a burr under a PC user's/administrator's saddle for a long time. IBM tried to address them when they developed the Micro Channel Architecture (MCA) for their next-generation PCs. When installing a new device, a Product Definition File (.PDF) would be included by the device manufacturer that instructed the system as to all of the device's available settings. All MCA machines included a setup program that would read the .PDF files of the installed devices and configure them all to defaults that wouldn't overlap—in theory. It usually worked. Of course, a user was free to specify their own settings, and the setup program would do its utmost to point out any conflicts that the user might have inadvertently chosen.

Competing vendors created a competing bus standard, Extended Industry Standard Architecture (EISA), which had many of the same configuration features as MCA boards, and included a setup program to configure them.

Recently, a majority of vendors have embraced the *Peripheral Component InterConnect (PCI)* bus. Many PCs are distributed with a combination of PCI/ISA bus slots so that both the new and older adapter boards can be used. PCI was developed to increase the speed of data transfer between a peripheral and the processor. As newer technologies increased data transfer speeds, the ISA bus became a bottleneck. This is best represented by the difference between an Ethernet 100BaseT (running at 100 Mbps on the network) PCI network interface card and an Ethernet 100BaseT ISA network interface card. ISA runs at 5 Mbps. PCI runs at 132 Mbps. In the case of an ISA card, a bottleneck exists on the network interface and reduces performance.

PCI supports *bus mastering*. An intelligent peripheral can take control of (master) the bus in order to accelerate a high-priority task. PCI also allows for *concurrency* in bus mastering, where the CPU may operate simultaneously with the bus mastering peripherals. This is illustrated by the ability of the CPU to run a mathematical calculation while, at the same time, a Network Interface Card has control of the bus.

Of greatest interest in memory management, PCI supports Plug-and-Play—a specification for automatic configuration of jumper- and switch-free peripherals designed to avoid conflicting settings.

How Do Memory Conflicts Happen?

Besides conflicting hardware, applications themselves can create memory conflicts. The previously listed problems all arise in the reserved area between conflicting hardware. Applications can reside only in system memory. However, occasionally a device will conflict with a portion of upper memory that is being used by a memory manager as system memory. This usually occurs only with peripheral hardware that loads a driver after the memory manager loads. Fortunately, memory managers can be forced to exclude specific areas to avoid conflicts, and through some careful analysis, a majority of memory conflicts can be resolved.

HIMEM.SYS

The Microsoft driver, HIMEM.SYS, is used to address 80286 and 80386 extended memory, converting it to XMS in accordance with the LIM specification. It also takes the first 64KB of this extended memory area and converts it into the HMA. It is loaded by placing a line—**DEVICE= PATH\HIMEM.SYS**—in the CONFIG.SYS file. Unless you are using a different memory manager, such as QEMM by Quarterdeck, the HIMEM.SYS file must be loaded before EMM386.EXE is loaded so that EMM386 may be used. This also enables an application, or simply the operating system, to access XMS memory.

Use of Expanded Memory Blocks (Using EMM386.EXE)

EMM386.EXE performs two major functions. It enables and controls EMS, if desired, and enables the use of upper memory as system memory. It is generally conservative in its attempts to locate available upper memory. You can force EMM386 to use specific regions of upper memory by using the INCLUDE switch on the command line where it is enabled in CONFIG.SYS, and conversely exclude specific regions using the EXCLUDE switch.

Employing Utilities

As you can see, trying to resolve memory conflicts can be an incredibly difficult endeavor, because they can come from many sources. Also, "failure-mode analysis" often can't be performed because once the offending device is actually loaded in memory, the system will lock up. Third-party vendors, notably Peter Norton with Norton Utilities, concentrated on developing a method of checking and reporting on memory allocation usage. Microsoft followed up with its MEM.EXE, MSD.EXE, and MEMMAKER.EXE utilities.

MEM.EXE is a simple command-line utility that, using various command switches, can display reports of memory usage. If you aren't familiar with it, now is a good time to check it out. MEM.EXE is an external command, and should be present in either your DOS directory, or if running Windows 95, in the WINDOWS directory. The following listing shows switches used with the MEM.EXE command and their definitions.

```
Displays the amount of used and free memory in your system.

MEM [/CLASSIFY | /DEBUG | /FREE | /MODULE modulename] [/PAGE]

  /CLASSIFY or /C  Classifies programs by memory usage. Lists the size of
                   programs, provides a summary of memory in use, and lists
                   largest memory block available.
  /DEBUG or /D     Displays status of all modules in memory, internal drivers,
                   and other information.
  /FREE or /F      Displays information about the amount of free memory left
                   in both conventional and upper memory.
  /MODULE or /M    Displays a detailed listing of a module's memory use.
                   This option must be followed by the name of a module,
                   optionally separated from /M by a colon.
  /PAGE or /P      Pauses after each screenful of information.
```

From a DOS prompt, executing MEM.EXE yields a brief list of total memory usage:

```
Memory Type        Total   =   Used  +   Free
----------------   -------     -------   -------
Conventional        638K        70K       568K
Upper                 0K         0K         0K
Reserved              0K         0K         0K
Extended (XMS)    64,504K        64K    64,440K
----------------   -------     -------   -------
Total memory      65,142K       134K    65,008K

Total under 1 MB    638K        70K       568K

Largest executable program size         568K (581,584 bytes)
Largest free upper memory block           0K       (0 bytes)
MS-DOS is resident in the high memory area.
```

Notice the last line, indicating that DOS has been loaded "high" using the DOS=HIGH setting in the CONFIG.SYS file. Otherwise, it shows a breakdown of memory allocation by area and total. Nice to know, but not particularly helpful if you're in trouble.

Using the /C switch gives you quite a bit more to work with:

```
Modules using memory below 1 MB:

Name           Total       =   Conventional   +   Upper Memory
--------    ----------------    ----------------    ----------------
MSDOS       15,277   (15K)      15,277   (15K)             0   (0K)
SETVER         480   (0K)          480   (0K)             0   (0K)
HIMEM        1,168   (1K)        1,168   (1K)             0   (0K)
MTMCDAI     11,168   (11K)      11,168   (11K)             0   (0K)
COMMAND      2,928   (3K)        2,928   (3K)             0   (0K)
MSCDEX      36,304   (35K)      36,304   (35K)             0   (0K)
DOSKEY       4,144   (4K)        4,144   (4K)             0   (0K)
Free       581,776   (568K)    581,776   (568K)           0   (0K)

Memory Summary:

Type of Memory      Total    =    Used    +    Free
----------------  ----------   ----------   ----------
Conventional         653,312       71,536      581,776
Upper                      0            0            0
Reserved                   0            0            0
Extended (XMS)    66,052,096       65,536   65,986,560
----------------  ----------   ----------   ----------
Total memory      66,705,408      137,072   66,568,336

Total under 1 MB     653,312       71,536      581,776

Largest executable program size        581,584   (568K)
Largest free upper memory block              0   (0K)
MS-DOS is resident in the high memory area.
```

Notice that the summary is included as before, but now all loaded applications and drivers are detailed by name and individual memory usage. You can see immediately any changes that have been made from tweaking load parameters in AUTOEXEC.BAT or CONFIG.SYS. Changing parameters can add or take away free memory, and using MEM.EXE with the /C switch can help diagnose the results.

If you utilize the /C switch, the MEM command will classify all the programs running on your system by the type of memory they utilize. The /C switch also lists the size of the programs, provides a summary of memory in use, and lists the largest memory block available. Because this switch displays a lot of information, the results will most likely span multiple screens. A helpful switch, /P, can be used in conjunction with /C (or any others) to page the results.

Even more details can be obtained by using the /D switch:

```
Conventional Memory Detail:

Segment           Total        Name          Type
-------      ----------------   -----------   --------
00000        1,039     (1K)                   Interrupt Vector
00040          271     (0K)                   ROM Communication Area
00050          527     (1K)                   DOS Communication Area
00070        2,864     (3K)     IO            System Data
                                CON           System Device Driver
                                AUX           System Device Driver
                                PRN           System Device Driver
                                CLOCK$        System Device Driver
                                A: - E:       System Device Driver
                                COM1          System Device Driver
                                LPT1          System Device Driver
                                LPT2          System Device Driver
                                LPT3          System Device Driver
                                COM2          System Device Driver
                                COM3          System Device Driver
                                COM4          System Device Driver
00123        5,136     (5K)     MSDOS         System Data
00264       18,176    (18K)     IO            System Data
               464     (0K)       SETVERXX    Installed Device=SETVER
             1,152     (1K)       XMSXXXX0    Installed Device=HIMEM
            11,152    (11K)       MTMIDE01    Installed Device=MTMCDAI
             1,488     (1K)                   FILES=30
               256     (0K)                   FCBS=4
               512     (1K)                   BUFFERS=15
             1,152     (1K)                   LASTDRIVE=M
             1,856     (2K)                   STACKS=9,128
006D4           80     (0K)     MSDOS         System Program
006D9        2,656     (3K)     COMMAND       Program
0077F           80     (0K)     MSDOS         -- Free --
00784          272     (0K)     COMMAND       Environment
00795           96     (0K)     MSDOS         -- Free --
0079B       36,304    (35K)     MSCDEX        Program
01078          112     (0K)     MEM           Environment
0107F        4,144     (4K)     DOSKEY        Program
01182       88,992    (87K)     MEM           Program
0273C      492,608   (481K)     MSDOS         -- Free --
```

```
Memory Summary:

  Type of Memory        Total   =    Used    +    Free
  ----------------   ----------   ----------   ----------
  Conventional          653,312       71,536      581,776
  Upper                       0            0            0
  Reserved                    0            0            0
  Extended (XMS)     66,052,096       65,536   65,986,560
  ----------------   ----------   ----------   ----------
  Total memory       66,705,408      137,072   66,568,336

  Total under 1 MB      653,312       71,536      581,776

  Memory accessible using Int 15h            0      (0K)
  Largest executable program size      581,584    (568K)
  Largest free upper memory block            0      (0K)
  MS-DOS is resident in the high memory area.

  XMS version  3.00; driver version  3.16
```

This shows not only each loaded application, but also each memory segment and its corresponding location for each piece of each application.

This tool was a major leap forward for Microsoft, allowing a user to visualize changes made in their system. By manually rearranging application and driver loading sequence and related parameters, after much trial and error, you could come up with an optimal configuration that provided the maximum amount of free memory.

Microsoft went one step better when it delivered its MSD.EXE (Microsoft System Diagnostics) program. This little gem roots out almost every conceivable item about your system that you'd ever want to know (and then some!) and displays it in a menu-driven format for you to browse. Conversely, you can run MSD.EXE from the command line, or batch file, and write query results to an output file or printer for a complete analysis using the /P option. An example of the output is included in Appendix G of this book. As you can see, not only is there a full output with statistics equivalent to the MEM.EXE program, but details on the hard drives and their partitioning, and motherboard, video, and networking elements as well. About the only thing missing is the processor speed. Microsoft chose to eliminate MSD.EXE from Windows 95, but in hindsight decided this was a bad idea, and so has posted it as a free download from their Web site.

MemMaker and Other Optimization Utilities

While the MEM.EXE and MSD.EXE programs are excellent tools for memory conflict determination, what was really needed was a tool for problem avoidance. Microsoft delivered this in their MEMMAKER.EXE utility. This program is designed to automatically determine the best possible configuration and load sequence for a given set of applications and drivers. Before using MEMMAKER, the PC should be configured for normal operation (for example, with mouse driver, network operation, and sound support), including any items that are loaded from the AUTOEXEC.BAT and CONFIG.SYS files. MEMMAKER would run through hundreds and sometimes thousands of combinations of command-load sequencing and placement then reboot itself to test its new configuration, and if successful, ask the user to accept its determinations.

MEMMAKER's first version, shipped with DOS version 5.0, was not perfected at its release. Often it required multiple runs to find a setting that would not hang up the PC when it rebooted. By DOS version 6.0, MEMMAKER had smoothed out its rough edges and could be counted on to deliver a clean and lean configuration.

Third-party vendors, notably Quarterdeck with its QEMM suite, continued to deliver slightly better, tighter memory configurations, yielding slightly more deliverable RAM. An added benefit to QEMM was its stealth capabilities that were specifically geared to take advantage of the Micro Channel PC's ability to move its board configurations dynamically, allowing even more available RAM to be recouped.

Windows 95 has now pretty much eliminated the need for memory managers. Previous versions of Windows required that networking elements, often the most memory-hungry components, be loaded in DOS prior to Windows startup. An annoying feature of Windows was that you couldn't have more memory available for DOS applications run from within Windows than an amount that was slightly less than what you had when you started Windows. Windows 95 now loads virtually everything after it starts, freeing up as much as a full 640KB. OS/2 also found a way to deliver as much as 740KB for each DOS session. Although Windows 95 and OS/2 don't require DOS to run, they do provide access to a DOS environment in which to run older DOS applications.

System Monitor

Microsoft Windows 95 includes a utility that can be used to monitor the workstation's hardware, applications, and services. Because Windows systems use a significant amount of hard disk space for memory usage in the swap file, monitoring the disk access can be useful in troubleshooting the errors. The System Monitor can be used from a remote computer over a network if the remote registry service has been installed. When optimizing memory in Windows 95, you should use the System Monitor to see the effect of any changes you have made to the system.

In order to use the System Monitor to track memory, select the Edit menu and choose Add Item. In the Category list window, select the Memory Manager category. Then, in the Item list window, select all the items you wish to monitor.

SmartDrive

SmartDrive is a system utility that creates a disk cache in extended memory. Caching the disk in extended memory can enhance performance. It is not necessary to start SmartDrive in order to run the system, so if there is any need to reduce the utilities in the AUTOEXEC.BAT, SmartDrive can be commented out or deleted. The command for this utility is SMARTDRV.EXE.

Although SmartDrive can significantly boost performance in a DOS/Windows 3.1x system, it should not be used in a Windows 95 system. Windows 95 uses an entirely different method of disk caching that makes SmartDrive unnecessary.

The following is the screen output for the SMARTDRV/? command. It describes the switches that can be used with SMARTDRV.

Installs and configures the SMARTDrive disk-caching utility.

```
SMARTDRV [/X] [[drive[+|-]]...] [/U] [/C | /R] [/F | /N] [/L] [/V | /Q | /S]
[InitCacheSize [WinCacheSize]] [/E:ElementSize] [/B:BufferSize]
/X                Disables write-behind caching for all drives.
drive             Sets caching options on specific drive(s). The specified
                  drive(s) will have write-caching disabled unless you add +.
+                 Enables write-behind caching for the specified drive.
-                 Disables all caching for the specified drive.
/U                Do not load CD-ROM caching module.
/C                Writes all information currently in write-cache to hard disk.
/R                Clears the cache and restarts SMARTDrive.
/F                Writes cached data before command prompt returns (default).
/N                Doesn't write cached data before command prompt returns.
/L                Prevents SMARTDrive from loading itself into upper memory.
/V                Displays SMARTDrive status messages when loading.
/Q                Does not display status information.
/S                Displays additional information about SMARTDrive's
                  status.
InitCacheSize     Specifies XMS memory (KB) for the cache.
WinCacheSize      Specifies XMS memory (KB) for the cache with Windows.
/E:ElementSize    Specifies how many bytes of information to move at one time.
/B:BufferSize     Specifies the size of the read-ahead buffer.
```

Illegal Operation Occurrences

Every now and then, an error pops up on the screen stating that the program you are running caused an illegal operation and will be shut down. Usually, that error is followed by another stating that there has been a page fault or a General Protection Fault (GPF), and then Windows will crash.

What is an *illegal operation*? In this case, illegal does not mean against the law, just not allowed by the processor. The Intel 80x86 (286, 386, 486, Pentium, Pentium Pro, and Pentium II) series of processors are designed to interrupt the execution of a program whenever they detect an abnormal condition. Many times, this abnormal condition is an application trying to access a part of upper memory by mistake. This can be because a conflicting application or device driver that the application did not expect to be using accesses an area of upper memory. Or it can be due to an invalid input from a corrupt file. This type of interrupt is called an *exception*. If you are familiar with Novell's NetWare server operating system, this error is called an *ABEND*, which stands for *abnormal end*—and that pretty much describes what it ends up as.

The operating system normally handles the exception and decides whether to process the exception and return an error, or whether to pass the exception to a handler provided by the application. When the application handles it, you don't see any errors so you never really know when this happens. When the operating system returns an error, the result usually grows to a termination of the application, and many times, of the operating system itself because files are not closed and hardware is not returned to its pre-application state. This, in turn, may lead to lost work and disk errors. Using the DOS CHKDSK command or the SCANDISK command is recommended after an illegal operation to fix the disk errors caused by the files left in an open state. And then, running DEFRAG to defragment the pieces of the files on the hard drive can result in a cleaner FAT table.

Illegal operations can be caused by programs with corrupted files, such as a database program that uses indexes. If you keep getting illegal operations in a database program, find the command that will re-index files or check the database for errors. Bugs in an application can cause illegal operations, too, which can be fixed by applying either operating system or application patches supplied by the manufacturer. And finally, just a glitch in hardware, where a tiny surge in electricity flips a bit or two (changes it from a 1 to a 0 or vice versa), can cause an operation error. If the glitches occur often and there are all sorts of other error messages, and all other routes (such as database index, CHKDSK, DEFRAG, or applying patches) have been exhausted, this may indicate that RAM or the system board may be going bad. Don't assume hardware first, though—these errors are nearly always caused by an application error. Try reinstalling the application.

Conflicts with 16-Bit Applications/Windows 95 Operations

In Windows 3.*x*, people used to get memory errors all the time. The errors would state that either there was no memory, or that you were running out of system resources. The first error—no memory—referred to a problem with the pagefile, which was created for virtual memory.

FROM THE FIELD

Always Check the Swap File Size

Improper swap file size in the real world accounts for a large number of calls to the help desk. Older operating systems, such as Windows 3.1 and Windows for Workgroups, have a horrible problem with memory. The infamous "blue screen of death" was usually attributed to poor memory allocation. Most of the good graphic-intensive programs written for the operating systems would crawl in Windows and you would have to run them straight from DOS. Newer operating systems have improved this memory problem, but it still shows up. On Windows NT, if you open too many applications without a large amount of RAM, you still run into out-of-memory problems.

The swap file that is created can sometimes be the cause of the problem instead of just the size of this file. If there is any question about the integrity of the swap file, delete it and reboot to recreate it. A bug in Windows 3.11 caused, in some instances, a swap file to be put onto a network drive. Imagine this inefficiency: A 10 Mbps line reading and writing on a distant server. Always make sure that your swap file is within the limits of your hard drive's extra memory or you risk your system sending this file to a network drive.

When you look at a personal computer and wonder what is wrong with it, always look for memory swap file relating to signs of trouble, especially if the system is performing poorly compared to other machines that have equal hardware and are running the same software. Memory can also trigger Dr. Watson errors. Even printing errors are suspect. Most memory problems cause the machine to stop responding. Don't be afraid to increase the swap file; it gives your system more virtual RAM. However, actual RAM may end up to be the ultimate solution in some cases. The larger you make your swap file, the more the hard drive is going to thrash in order to access the memory space.

—Ted Hamilton, MCSE, MCP, A+ Certified

In Windows systems, virtual memory is where the operating system allocates more memory than the PC contains, and then pages virtual memory into a file on the hard drive. This means that a PC with 8MB of RAM would look like it had 64MB of RAM if the pagefile was 56MB. The *pagefile*, also called a swap file, would swap pages of RAM to the 56MB file on the hard drive. It would keep the most recently used memory in RAM, so that the current application would be able to run at optimal speed. The system sounds great, but didn't work all that well, because the pagefile was static in size and had to be configured by the user of the PC who might not know off the top of their head what size that file should be.

In Windows 95, 16-bit Windows (Windows 3.*x*) applications run in the System VM (Virtual Machine). The VM is the Windows 95 handler of the pagefile. The VM adjusts the pagefile size to an optimal amount automatically. Because of the way Windows 16-bit applications used to work in Windows 3.1, they must run in the same shared memory space with the core components of Windows 95, and shared DLLs. If there is an error that a Windows 16-bit application causes to virtual memory, it is the most likely cause of a system-wide error. (Windows 32-bit applications each run in a separate private address space within the System VM, yet the address space is totally separate from the shared address space where core components and 16-bit applications reside. Therefore, Windows 32-bit applications don't present the problems that Windows 16-bit applications might. MS-DOS-based applications each run in their own VM, completely separate from the System VM.)

To fix these types of errors, the best course of action is to upgrade the 16-bit application with a 32-bit version, if it exists. If that is not possible, then contact the manufacturer and obtain the latest patches and fixes. If there is any question about the way virtual memory is handled, it can be reviewed in the Control Panel System icon under the Performance tab and adjusted by clicking the Virtual Memory button.

The second error that you used to get in Windows 3.*x* stated that you were running out of system resources. The only way to get rid of the error was to reboot. System resources degraded over time—some programs would not return all the resources even after they closed, and you simply ran out of them. Often.

"System resources" is a rather cryptic term, because system resources refer to small areas of memory called *memory heaps* to be used by the graphics device interface (GDI) and user system components. In Windows 3.*x*, these heaps were 64KB in size and used 16-bit processing. In Windows 95, the heaps became 32-bit, but the 16-bit heaps didn't go away because of the need for backward compatibility.

The errors for running out of system resources are rare under Windows 95 because of the 32-bit heaps. But Windows 16-bit applications using the 16-bit heaps can still cause this error. (Especially when that application was one of the programs that behaved badly and wouldn't give back the system resources when it was done with them.) The only way to fix system resource errors in the short term is to reboot the PC. The best long-term fix is to contact the manufacturer for a patch, or upgrade the application to a 32-bit version.

CERTIFICATION SUMMARY

Memory management is not an easy game to play, nor are resolving memory conflicts and optimization issues. The various flavors of MS-DOS and Windows have each brought with them new concerns with regard to memory management. Hopefully, you leave this chapter with a better understanding of memory placement, how applications and hardware play nicely together, and proper optimization techniques.

 TWO-MINUTE DRILL

❑ Standard RAM is also known as volatile memory, in that it loses its contents when system power is shut down, while ROM is nonvolatile, its contents remaining unchanged even when power is removed.

❑ You can force EMM386 to use specific regions of upper memory by using the Include switch on the command line where it is enabled in CONFIG.SYS, and conversely exclude specific regions using the Exclude switch.

❑ ROM began as a write-once chip. Instruction code was electrically fed to the chip and retained there permanently.

❑ The EEPROM (electrically erasable) chip could be erased by applying a specific voltage to the chip.

❑ DIP chips are physically soldered to a motherboard. SIMMs are chips that are soldered to a small board that is installed into a slot on the motherboard. Using SIMMs allows the memory to be easily replaced.

❑ Be careful in the selection of memory upgrade components. The memory module must match the requirements of the motherboard.

❑ The LIM memory specification renamed system memory to conventional memory, and defined additional (above the original 1024KB-address limit) areas as expanded, extended, and high memory.

❑ Don't assume hardware first when you receive an illegal operation—these errors are nearly always caused by an application error.

❑ Before using MEMMAKER, a PC should be configured for normal operation (for example, contains a mouse driver, network operation, and sound support), including any items that are loaded from the AUTOEXEC.BAT and CONFIG.SYS files.

❑ Virtual memory is memory that the processor has been "tricked" into using as if it were actual physical memory.

❑ Under Windows 95, the only way to fix system resource errors in the short term is to reboot the PC. The best long-term fix is to contact the manufacturer for a patch, or upgrade the application to a 32-bit version.

❑ MSD.EXE roots out almost every conceivable item about your system that you'd ever want to know (and then some!) and displays it in a menu-driven format for you to browse.

❑ Memory conflicts arising from optional devices, such as network cards, can be difficult to pinpoint.

❑ PCI was developed to increase the speed of data transfer between a peripheral and the processor.

- ❏ Windows 32-bit applications don't present the same problems that Windows 16-bit applications might.
- ❏ Memory managers can be forced to exclude specific areas to avoid conflicts, and through some careful analysis, a majority of memory conflicts can be resolved.
- ❏ EMM386.EXE performs two major functions. It enables and controls EMS, if desired, and enables the use of upper memory as system memory.
- ❏ Physical memory consists of the hardware that handles memory in a PC. This memory is stored in chips that are either ROM—read-only memory chips—or RAM—Random Access Memory.
- ❏ MEM.EXE is a simple command-line utility that, using various command switches, can display various reports of memory usage.
- ❏ Windows 95 has now pretty much eliminated the need for memory managers.
- ❏ The Intel 80x86 (286, 386, 486, Pentium, Pentium Pro, and Pentium II) series of processors are designed to interrupt the execution of a program whenever they detect an abnormal condition.

SELF TEST

The following Self Test questions will help you measure your understanding of the material presented in this chapter. Read all the choices carefully, as there may be more than one correct answer. Choose all correct answers for each question.

1. A DIMM memory module would typically have how many pins?

    A. 30

    B. 64

    C. 72

    D. 168

2. Which processor first utilized the Level 1 (L1) system cache?

    A. 8088

    B. 386

    C. 486

    D. Pentium

3. Which processor first combined Level 2 (L2) system cache in the same package as the CPU?

    A. 486

    B. Pentium with MMX

    C. Pentium Pro

    D. Pentium II

4. Which of the following are types of DRAM?

    A. Fast Paged mode

    B. Static Random Access Memory

    C. Enhanced Data Output

    D. Pipeline Cache mode

5. A nanosecond is defined as?

    A. One millionth of a second

    B. One billionth of a second

    C. One trillionth of a second

    D. One zillionth of a second

6. The Level 1 and Level 2 system cache is based upon which computer principle?

    A. Locality of address

    B. Locality of space

    C. Locality of reference

    D. Locality of resource

7. The system BIOS is generally stored on which type of chip?

    A. RAM

    B. DRAM

    C. ROM

    D. SROM

8. Which of the following are advantages of SRAM?

    A. It doesn't require extra circuitry to refresh the data contained in memory.

    B. It is less expensive than DRAM.

    C. It is smaller than DRAM.

    D. It is faster than DRAM.

9. The original IBM PC used which type of DRAM for the main system memory?

A. Basic DRAM

B. Conventional DRAM

C. Paged DRAM

D. Fast Paged mode DRAM

10. On a motherboard that supports a Pentium II Processor, which type of memory module can be installed individually instead of in pairs?

A. Single In-Line Package

B. Dual In-Line Package

C. Single In-Line Memory Module

D. Dual In-Line Memory Module

11. Which type of ROM supported rewrite technology in order to update a device or firmware program?

A. PROM

B. EPROM

C. UPROM

D. CDROM

12. SRAM is typically used for which type of memory?

A. Main system memory

B. Conventional memory

C. System cache

D. L0 cache

13. RAM is typically used for which type of memory?

A. Main system memory

B. Conventional memory

C. System cache

D. L0 cache

14. Another name for L2 cache is?

A. Internal cache

B. Main system cache

C. PII cache

D. External cache

15. Which of the following best describes the Locality of reference principle?

A. If the processor recently referenced a location in memory, it is likely that it will refer to it again in the near future.

B. If the processor writes to a location referenced in memory, it is likely that it will refer to it again in the near future.

C. If an application stores information in a location referenced in memory, it is likely to loop through it again in the near future.

D. None of the above.

16. Which of the following devices is a hardware logic circuit that controls system memory?

A. RAM controller

B. Cache controller

C. Physical memory controller

D. Memory controller

17. Which of the following DRAM technologies was designed to work with 100 MHz memory buses?

A. EDO RAM

B. BEDO RAM

C. FTP RAM

D. SDRAM

18. Which of the following DRAM technologies supports burst mode timings of 5-2-2-2 on a 66 MHz memory bus?

    A. EDO RAM
    B. BEDO RAM
    C. FTP RAM
    D. SDRAM

19. HMA is the first 64KB of?

    A. Convential memory
    B. Expanded memory
    C. Extended memory
    D. Virtual memory

20. Which MS-DOS program can be used to optimize your system's memory?

    A. QEMM
    B. MEMMAKER
    C. MEM
    D. MEMORY

21. Which device is used to manage the upper memory blocks?

    A. HIMEM.SYS
    B. EMM.EXE
    C. EMM386.EXE
    D. MEMMANAGER

22. The Upper Memory Area (UMA) ranges from?

    A. 0–640KB
    B. 0–1024KB
    C. 640–792KB
    D. 640–1024KB

23. Which of the following Windows 95 tools can be used to view memory utilization?

    A. System Monitor
    B. QEMM
    C. Performance Monitor
    D. Task Manager

24. Virtual memory is a combination of which of the following?

    A. Physical memory and conventional memory
    B. SRAM and DRAM
    C. RAM and free hard drive space
    D. System memory and system cache

25. Which of the following statements from the CONIG.SYS file depicts the correct load order?

    A. DEVICE=C:\DOS\EMM386.EXE
       DEVICE=C:\DOS\HIMEM.SYS
    B. DEVICE=C:\DOS\HIMEM.COM
       DEVICE=C:\DOS\EMM386.EXE
    C. DEVICE=C:\DOS\SETVER.EXE
       DEVICE=C:\DOS\EMM386.EXE
    D. DEVICE=C:\DOS\HIMEM.SYS
       DEVICE=C:\DOS\EMM386.EXE

11

Installing, Configuring, and Upgrading

As you've seen throughout this book, a lot of focus has been placed on the hardware in a PC. However, without an operating system (OS), your hardware is simply a collection of plastic and metal. The function of an operating system is to organize the way in which information is processed by the hardware. It is basically an interface between you and the hardware. The OS manages and prioritizes requests made from the applications you work with, whether it is Solitaire or your favorite word processor. All PCs require that some form of operating system be installed on them. Until mid-1996, the most popular operating system was a combination of DOS and Windows 3.*x*. The *x* is used to note that the original Windows 3.1 and later Windows 3.11 are both classified together as offering the same standard features and specifications. Windows 3.11 Windows for Workgroups (WFW) is a networked version of the original Windows 3.1 product. Windows 95 introduced Plug-and-Play (PnP), which provided automatic driver installation and resource distribution. In this chapter, we discuss all of these things and a few more as they relate to DOS, Windows 3.*x*, and Windows 95.

CERTIFICATION OBJECTIVE 11.01

Installing DOS, Windows 3.*x*, and Windows 95

Installation of operating systems such as DOS, Windows 3.*x*, and Windows 95 are all fairly simple; you just follow the screen prompts and you'll have an OS installed. However, there are some further steps required by each of the installation procedures such as creating a partition, formatting the hard drive, and the usage of a setup utility. These are discussed in the sections that follow.

Partition

When you purchase a new hard drive today, it is generally in an unusable condition until you do two things. The first step is partitioning, which entails creating at least one area on your drive in which to store data. The second step is formatting the partition(s) you created. How many partitions can you create? The maximum number of partitions was set in stone by the BIOS and hard drive manufacturers who collaborated together and decided that hard drives will support no more than four partitions. This was back in the days when it was believed nobody would ever need more than four partitions (much like nobody would ever need more than 640KB of memory). Although hard drives can support four partitions, MS-DOS based systems such as MS-DOS, Windows 3.x, and Windows 9x can work with only two partitions, a primary and an extended partition.

The main difference between a primary and an extended partition is that a *primary partition* can be marked *bootable*, meaning that the required boot files for your operating system can be stored on and read from this partition. The process of notifying the system that a partition is bootable is done by marking the partition as Active (see option 2 in Figure 11-1). As mentioned, an MS-DOS based system supports only a single primary partition. This is because nobody ever dreamed of a day when we would be working with multiple-gigabyte hard drives. In order to allow MS-DOS based systems to work with these large drives, the need for an extended partition arose. The *extended partition* supports up to 23 additional logical partitions, also knows as *logical drives*. The only limiting factor is the number of alphabetical characters in the alphabet, 26. Letters C–Z can be used for hard drives, and the primary partition will always be marked as drive C. This is because DOS assigns drive letters to all primary partitions first and then assigns letters to the remaining logical partitions.

Why would you ever need more than one partition? Most likely you are currently running at least Windows 95 or Windows 98 at home. Since you're reading this A+ Certification Guide, there is a good chance that you have or will install Windows NT or Linux in order to learn these newer technologies. If this is the case, you'll definitely want more than one partition because installing two different operating systems on the same partition is inviting trouble. Separate partitions are especially helpful if you ever decide to remove one of the operating systems. To do so, you just delete the partition. (By the way, a sure sign of computer geekdom is when you set up a home network and install NT Server, Novell, Unix, or Linux on one of your home PCs.) Even if you have no desire to learn more about NT, Novell, Unix, or Linux, it is still a good idea to have two partitions: one for your operating system and applications, and the other for your data. That way if you ever need to reinstall your operating system, your data will be intact.

The utility to set up partitions on any MS-DOS based system has, for the most part, remain unchanged for the last ten years. Figure 11-1 illustrates the four options found within FDISK. FDISK is a command-line utility, which means you have to run it from DOS or a Command Prompt window. Technically speaking you could run FDISK within Windows 95 or 98, but it isn't recommended because FDISK is a hard-drive layout utility used to create and delete partitions. You definitely wouldn't want to run the utility within Windows 95 or 98 if you were going to delete the partition the OS is currently loaded on. Listed below are the four things you can do with FDISK:

Create Partitions   FDISK allows you to create a primary DOS partition or an extended partition with logical drives. Before you can create a logical DOS drive, you must first create an extended DOS partition because the logical drives are contained within the extended partition.

Set Active Partition   When you create a primary DOS partition, newer versions of FDISK will allow you to automatically mark the partition as Active. In older versions of FDISK, do this manually. Fortunately, if you say no to the automatic feature or if you have an older version of FDISK, there is a flashing warning message at the bottom of the screen stating that no disk is set Active.

FIGURE 11-1

FDISK is a DOS-based utility that defines the partition structure of a hard drive

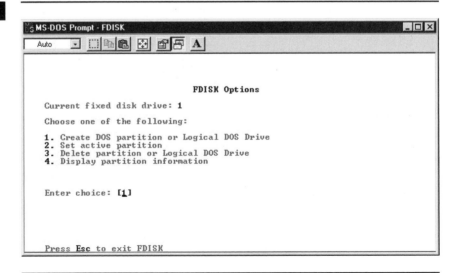

Delete Partitions   FDISK allows you to delete partitions. Unfortunately, the only way to change the size of an existing partition in FDISK is to delete the old one and create a new one with the new size. When deleting extended DOS partitions, you must delete the logical DOS drives first.

Display Partition Information   The fourth option allows you to view partition information for the system. You can view the primary and extended partitions, and as a secondary option, you can view the logical drives within the extended partition. If you want to see some basic information about the partitions on your system without actually going into FDISK, you can use a DOS shortcut by typing FDISK /STATUS from the DOS command line.

On a final note, the versions of FDISK found within DOS systems, Windows 3.*x*, and Windows 95 (version A) support a maximum partition size of only 2048MB (2GB). FDISK that ships with Windows 95 OSR2 (a.k.a. Windows 95 B) and Windows 98 can have larger partitions because of its capability to use the FAT32 file system. The way that you specify if you want to use the FAT32 file system versus the Fat16 file system is by answering Yes to Enable Large Disk Support when you first run the FDISK utility.

Format Drive

Once a partition has been created with FDISK, you must then format the drive (see Figure 11-2). Because you have a brand new partition, it won't contain any data, but you should be aware that if you format an existing drive, all of the existing data on the drive would be lost. As a computer tech this may be the last resort to fixing problems in Windows 3.*x* or Windows 9*x*. Reformatting and reloading an OS should be your last alternative.

Figure 11-2 illustrates the use of the FORMAT command. Like FDISK, it too is a DOS utility that ships with all MS-DOS based systems. To view all of the FORMAT options, type **FORMAT /?** at a DOS prompt. One important option to note is the /s switch that can be used to copy the boot files (IO.SYS, MSDOS.SYS, and COMMAND.COM) after formatting a drive.

FIGURE 11-2

Formatting a drive is a fairly simple process that erases all of the data from a partition

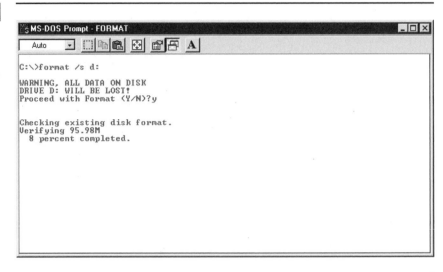

```
MS-DOS Prompt - FORMAT                                    _ □ ✕
Auto    ▼  [ ]  ◱  ◳  ◲  ◰  ◱  A

C:\>format /s d:

WARNING, ALL DATA ON DISK
DRIVE D: WILL BE LOST!
Proceed with Format (Y/N)?y

Checking existing disk format.
Verifying 95.98M
   8 percent completed.
```

exam
ⓦatch

If you want a drive to be bootable, it needs to be formatted with the /s switch. If the drive contains existing data, and you do not want to erase all of the data from the drive, the SYS command can be issued to make the drive bootable. For example, to make drive A: bootable, type "SYS A:" at a DOS prompt. This copies the boot files found on drive C: to the floppy diskette in the A: drive.

Setup Utilities

Prior to Windows, the most common Setup utility was INSTALL.EXE. Windows 3.*x* and Windows 9*x* both use SETUP.EXE as the default installation program file. In any situation, when installing a program or an OS, look for INSTALL.EXE or SETUP.EXE to begin the installation process. DOS, Windows 3.*x*, and Windows 95 all provide fairly intuitive setup utilities. There are a few additional items you need to know before beginning installation. For example, you can expect to be asked for a serial number by the Windows 95 Setup utility, shown in Figure 11-3. In addition, the Windows 95 Setup utility in many cases will ask you to confirm if you have some system devices such as a CD-ROM, sound card, or Network Card.

FIGURE 11-3

The Windows 95 Setup utility provides a graphical user interface that makes the setup process fairly simple

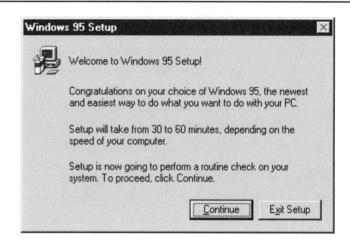

Loading Drivers

Nearly all basic devices require that device drivers be loaded in some shape or form. Most devices, such as Network Interface Cards and sound cards, require that a device driver be loaded.

DOS

DOS does not internally provide any support for loading device drivers. You can, however, install device drivers by adding them to CONFIG.SYS or AUTOEXEC.BAT. We discuss editing CONFIG.SYS and AUTOEXEC.BAT later in the section Editing AUTOEXEC.BAT and CONFIG.SYS Files. The most common devices that would have been installed in this fashion would be sound cards, mice, and CD-ROM drives.

Windows 3.*x*

In Windows 3.*x*, a setup program that is provided by the device manufacturer usually installs device drivers. Some basic drivers such as mouse and video are built into the Windows 3.*x* setup program.

Windows 95

Windows 95 has the capability and requirement of having a device driver loaded for nearly every device in the system. During the setup process, Windows 95 attempts to automatically detect any devices that exist and then load device drivers for those devices. At the time of installation, Windows 95 should automatically load all device drivers that are necessary for the system to be operational.

CERTIFICATION OBJECTIVE 11.02

Upgrading Operating Systems

The process of upgrading operating systems is a rather simple one in most cases. It is a good idea to back up your data prior to any type of upgrade. No matter how well planned and organized an upgrade is, loss of data is always possible.

Upgrading from DOS to Windows 3.x

In the true sense of the word it is impossible to "upgrade" to Windows 3.x because it isn't an operating system. It has been said that Windows 3.x is a clown suit for DOS. It is kind of humorous, but the statement actually has some merit because Windows 3.1 and 3.11 were not operating systems. Rather, they were merely graphical user interfaces (GUIs) that required an underlying operating system (in this case DOS) in order to function. Windows 95 and Windows 98, on the other hand, are operating systems since their GUI interfaces are not add-ons as in Windows 3.x. So when you talk about "upgrading" to Windows 3.x, a better phrase might be "installing" Windows 3.x. Listed below are the minimum system requirements and realistic recommendations to get the full benefit of Windows 3.x:

- 80286 processor (80486 recommended)
- 1MB RAM (8MB recommended)

- MS-DOS 3.1 or higher (MS-DOS 6.0 recommended)
- 5–10MB free hard drive space (30MB recommended)
- VGA graphics adapter supported by Windows
- A mouse

To start the installation of Windows 3.*x* you run SETUP.EXE. After the Welcome screen, you'll be asked to choose Express or Custom installation. If you choose the Express option, Windows makes a lot of installation decisions about your settings and detected hardware. The Express option automatically modifies and saves changes to your AUTOEXEC.BAT and CONFIG.SYS files. It is not a very flexible setup option and it uses a lot of system defaults that may not be optimal for your system.

The Custom installation option requires a more in-depth knowledge of your PC. The Setup utility will ask you to confirm detected hardware such as the mouse and the video adapter. This option also allows you to set up connected printers and other Windows components. If you are installing Windows 3.11 Windows for Workgroups (WFW), you can also configure your network adapter and workgroup settings at this time. The Custom option also allows you to select which DOS programs you would like to set up icons for inside of Windows. While changes are made to the AUTOEXEC.BAT and CONFIG.SYS files, you have a chance to make manual edits prior to saving the changes. The Custom installation allows much greater flexibility and enables a user to install only the components that are needed on the system.

Upgrading from DOS to Windows 95

Upgrading from DOS to Windows 95 is a rather simple process. The first, and most obvious, requirement is that you purchase a copy of Windows 95. If you are going to upgrade from DOS, you need to purchase the Full Version of Windows 95 and not the Upgrade Version. The Upgrade Version requires you to have a licensed copy of Windows 3.*x*. When installing the Upgrade Version, the Windows 95 setup program will actually check your system for an existing copy of Windows. If you do not have it installed, you will need to supply the first setup disk that came with your licensed copy of Windows 3.*x*. On a side note, if you have a system that has DOS installed on it, and is not running Windows 3.*x*, it might be a good idea to consider upgrading hardware prior to installing Windows 95. In most cases, if Windows 3.*x* was not installed on the system, it was because of performance issues, in which case Windows 95 will provide worse performance. The published minimum requirements to run Windows 95 are a 386DX-20 with 4MB of memory. Although this machine is capable of running Windows 95, it will be very slow and incapable of running many applications. A more realistic recommendation would be at least a Pentium processor, with 32MB of RAM.

Upgrading from Win 3.*x* to Windows 95

Upgrading from Windows 3.*x* to Windows 95 is a simple task. Once you have purchased the Windows 95 Upgrade CD, all you need to do is run the Setup utility from the Windows 3.*x* File Manager.

One benefit of upgrading to Windows 95 versus installing from a newly formatted hard drive is that the Setup utility uses the current configuration files (for example, AUTOEXEC.BAT, CONFIG.SYS, WIN.INI, and SYSTEM, INI) from DOS and Windows 3.*x* to help in the hardware-detection process. In addition, all of your software applications and your color preferences are carried over to Windows 95. Furthermore, all the familiar Program Manager groups and icons will be added to the Windows 95 Programs Group under the Start Menu.

Loading Drivers

Once Windows 95 has been installed, nearly all of the necessary device drivers should have been automatically installed for you. If there are any device drivers that were not installed, you can do this by clicking on Add New Hardware. The Add New Hardware Wizard then guides you through the installation process, beginning with scanning the system for new devices.

CERTIFICATION OBJECTIVE 11.03

Boot Sequences for DOS, Windows 3.x, and Windows 95

When a PC first starts up, it goes through a boot sequence. This *boot sequence* is the sequence of events that occur during the bootup process. A PC with a standard configuration usually attempts to boot from a floppy drive first. The PC then attempts to boot the first partition on the master hard drive on the primary drive chain.

Windows 3.x is not automatically started when the system starts. Many users add a line to the end of the AUTOEXEC.BAT file to start Windows 3.x after the AUTOEXEC.BAT has been processed. Windows 95, on the other hand, is automatically started when the system is started.

Booting a System from a Floppy and Hard Drive

In order to boot a system from any type of disk, whether a hard drive or a floppy drive, the partition you wish to boot from must be set as Active (because floppies have only one partition, they are always set as Active), and the system files must be copied to the partition. There are two methods of copying the system files to a partition. One is the FORMAT command with an /s switch (remember, FORMAT will delete all of the data currently on the partition). The second method is using the SYS command, which simply copies the necessary files to the root directory of the partition. On a related note, DOS, Windows 3.x, Windows 95, and Windows 98 require that the system be booted from the first partition of the master drive in the primary drive chain.

Starting DOS

When you push the Power button on a PC, it must go through a series of self-diagnostic tests that check for hardware configuration problems. This process is referred to as *booting*.

The first step involves the activation of the Power On Self-Test (POST). POST is a program, stored on a ROM (BIOS) chip, that instructs the computer to diagnose the hardware. Chapter 2 discussed some of the POST audio messages and errors that can occur during the hardware diagnostic phases. Because POST needs RAM to function, one of the first things it checks is the lower contiguous portions of RAM. If you don't have any RAM on your motherboard, either soldered on the board or in SIMM/DIMM modules, the POST procedure will not continue. Most PCs show you some portion of the POST procedure (a few proprietary systems like Compaq may hide this from your view, but it is still occurring). If your system displays a numeric count on the screen during the boot process, it is the computer testing your installed memory (RAM) chips. Next, POST analyzes the computer's setup information, which is stored in a special kind of chip called the CMOS (Complementary Metal Oxide Semiconductor). The CMOS chip contains your BIOS program, which is also referred to as *firmware*. The BIOS program manages configuration information about your hardware, as well as information such as the system date and time. Table 11-1 indicates the step-by-step process that most BIOS programs follow in order to start DOS.

exam
ⓦatch

Make sure you note the file load order to start DOS (IO.SYS, MSDOS.SYS, CONFIG.SYS COMMAND.COM, and then AUTOEXEC.BAT). The CONFIG.SYS and AUTOEXEC.BAT files are optional to load DOS, whereas the other three are required.

DOS Configuration Files

Once the POST procedure completes and the BIOS program goes through its diagnostic checks, DOS can begin the load procedure. Two important configuration files, the CONFIG.SYS and AUTOEXEC.BAT, are critical to how DOS operates. These files are considered optional because DOS will load without them, but it is very rare that one would actually work in a DOS environment with these configuration files. Both files must be located in the root directory of the bootable hard drive, normally the C: drive, to make sure the OS will locate them. These files are executed in a set order and they each control different portions of DOS.

TABLE 11-1		BIOS Start-Up Procedure
	BIOS Start-Up Steps	**Description**
Step 1	Low Memory Test	If this test fails, it means the lowest bank of RAM has failed.
Step 2	Scan for other BIOS	Some installed boards, like a SCSI adapter, may contain their own ROM BIOS. The system BIOS searches for any additional BIOS.
Step 3	Yield to other BIOS	If the system BIOS detected any other BIOS, it yields to it, allowing it to complete before checking the main system.
Step 4	Inventory the system	Reads the CMOS chip and checks all hardware (such as drives and memory) that it will control. This may take several seconds.
Step 5	Test the system	This is the diagnostic part of the BIOS. Any failed device will generate an error message at this point.
Step 6	Load DOS	Before the BIOS loads the operating system, it first loads DOS. The system looks for a drive that's ready; it's in the boot sequence you set up within your BIOS program. Usually it is set to scan drive A: first, and then to look to drive C: next.
Step 7	DOS loads Master Boot Record (MBR), then loads the DOS Boot Record (DBR)	The DBR contains the hidden files, IO.SYS and MSDOS.SYS.
Step 8	IO.SYS loads CONFIG.SYS, then COMMAND.COM	CONFIG.SYS loads device drivers that can cause a system to hang if you have them incorrectly specified. If COMMAND.COM has been corrupted somehow (such as it's a wrong version or is contaminated by a virus), you'll get a "Bad or Missing COMMAND.COM" error message and your system won't boot.
Step 9	COMMAND.COM loads AUTOEXEC.BAT	Terminate and Stay Resident (TSRs) like virus programs, protocol stacks, and disk caching utilities are loaded by the AUTOEXEC.BAT. Problems with these utilities can cause your system not to boot.

The responsibilities of the CONFIG.SYS file can be broken down into two broad categories: commands and device drivers. Table 11-2 lists several common commands found in the CONFIG.SYS file. Two of the most common are *files* and *buffers*. The *Buffer* statement alerts DOS to the amount of memory to reserve for information transfers to and from the hard drive. The value can be set from 1 to 99, where each buffer takes up approximately 530 bytes. The *Files* command indicates the number of

TABLE 11-2
Common CONFIG.SYS Commands

Command	Description
BUFFERS	Sets the number of disk buffers used by DOS
DEVICE	Loads an installable device driver
DEVICEHIGH	Loads an installable device driver into high (UMB) memory
DOS	Determines whether DOS will use HMA or UMB
FILES	Sets the maximum number of open files DOS will allow
LASTDRIVE	Sets the maximum number of drive letters available to DOS
SET	Sets environment variables
STACKS	Sets the number of stacks set aside for hardware interrupts

concurrent files that can be opened in DOS. The value can be between 8 and 255. The second category of responsibility for the CONFIG.SYS is to govern device drivers and how DOS can work with them. Table 11-3 lists several common devices found in the CONFIG.SYS file. For example, ANSI.SYS expands the ability of DOS to work with advanced video command sets. No longer do you have to work on a black background with

TABLE 11-3
Common CONFIG.SYS Device Drivers

Device Driver	Description
ANSI.SYS	Controls screen colors and the position of the cursor
DRIVER.SYS	Creates drive letters, which are assigned to physical devices
EMM386.EXE	Provides access to the Upper Memory Area and emulates expanded memory
HIMEM.SYS	Manages the Extended Memory area
SETVER.EXE	Manages the DOS version-table
SMARTDRV.EXE	A disk caching system that provides faster access to the data on a hard disk
POWER.EXE	Advanced Power Management (APM) driver that reduces power consumption during system idle time
RAMDRIVE.SYS	Driver that creates a simulated logical drive by using free space from RAM

white letters, you can have a blue background with yellow text if you want!
Two other common device drivers in the CONFIG.SYS that were
mentioned in Chapter 10 are EMM386.EXE and HIMEM.SYS. If you
recall, EMM386.EXE allows access to the upper memory area and
HIMEM.SYS manages the extended memory area.

The AUTOEXEC.BAT file allows a user to customize the DOS
environment. We mentioned the need for ANSI.SYS to be loaded to change
your screen colors, but the *Prompt* command in the AUTOEXEC.BAT is
how you actually specify the settings. The *Path* statement is another
common AUTOEXEC.BAT command. It allows you to set the logical path
to directories that contain executable files. Table 11-4 lists some common
commands found in the AUTOEXEC.BAT file.

In the event you decide to add some more power to your DOS operating
system, it is a good idea to make a backup copy of your AUTOEXEC.BAT
and CONFIG.SYS files. You can "optimize" commands in each of these
files to the point where DOS doesn't function correctly, or you might not
even be able to boot the system! If that happens, DOS provides you with
the ability to bypass these configuration files during the boot process. Once
you've booted the machine, you'll see a text message at the top of the screen
that says "Starting MS-DOS." It is there for only three seconds, but if you
press the F5 key immediately, you can bypass the AUTOEXEC.BAT and

TABLE 11-4		
Common DOS Commands in the AUTOEXEC.BAT File	**Command**	**Description**
	PATH	Sets a logical path to notify DOS of the search order for executable files. For example, path=c:\;c:\dos;\c:\games indicates that DOS should look for executable files first in the ROOT directory, then the \DOS directory, and finally the \GAMES directory.
	SET	Defines DOS Variables. An example would be Set TEMP=C:\temp.
	PROMPT	Establishes and sets the command prompt. The default is PROMPT=PG, which displays the current drive letter and directory followed by the greater-than sign. For example, C:\>.
	@ECHO OFF	Instructs DOS not to display each command as it executes.

CONFIG.SYS files. Alternatively, you can selectively bypass commands in both configuration files if you press the F8 key. You will then be prompted with a message to confirm if each command should be loaded in the AUTOEXEC.BAT and CONFIG.SYS files. The F5 and F8 keys are valuable troubleshooting tools if you ever tweak your DOS configuration files a little too much and you can't boot the system. Hopefully, you made a backup of these files before you started, so fixing the problem won't be that difficult.

Starting Windows 3.x

Windows 3.x can run in two different modes: Standard mode and 386 Enhanced mode. *Standard mode* is used on all 286-based systems and 386-based systems that have 2MB or less of memory. *Enhanced mode* is used on 386 or newer systems that have more than 2MB of memory. The different modes dictate how multiple applications are handled in a Windows 3.x environment. In Standard mode, users are able to switch among multiple applications, but DOS applications won't run unless they are Active (that is, full screen). In Enhanced mode, users are able to run multiple Windows applications, and DOS-based applications that are in the background can continue to run at the same time.

The executable file that starts Windows 3.x is WIN.COM. If this executable is launched on a 286-based system or with the /s switch, then the system starts in Standard mode. If WIN.COM detects a 386 or better processor and no /s switch was used, then the system starts in Enhanced mode. Table 11-5 illustrates the main Windows 3.x operating system files and their functions.

The most common files that you'll have to configure in Windows 3.x are the WIN.INI, SYSTEM.INI, AUTOEXEC.BAT, and CONFIG.SYS. Windows 3.x comes with a utility called *SYSEDIT* that automatically opens all four of these files. SYSEDIT is launched by selecting Run from the File menu in the Program Manager.

TABLE 11-5	File Name	Description
Windows 3.*x* Operating System Files	WIN.COM	Loads the Windows logo and also checks the hardware configuration to determine if Windows should load in Standard or Enhanced mode.
	WIN.INI	Controls Windows environment settings during startup. This file allows you to set up applications that will automatically launch when Windows is started.
	SYSTEM.INI	Controls the system hardware settings and their associated information. This file also contains a list of drivers for the installed hardware.
	CONTROL.INI	Responsible for the color scheme, patterns, printer settings, and installable driver settings.
	WINFILE.INI	Defines the appearance of the File Manager objects and components.
	PROGMAN.EXE	The main organizational tool in Windows 3.*x* where all program groups and program item icons (that is, shortcuts) are created to launch applications. The Start Menu and Desktop in Windows 95 later replaced this.
	PROGMAN.INI	Defines the Program Manager information such as the location of the program group files, their size, and the location of the Program Manager window.
	KRNL286.EXE KRNL386.EXE	Depending on which processor was detected at startup, one of these two files will be loaded. The KRNL*xxx*.EXE file is responsible for memory management, loading, and executing programs at startup.
	USER.EXE	This file controls user interactions with the keyboard and mouse, and the effects on windows, icons, and other user interface items.
	GDI.EXE	The Graphics Device Interface controls the formation of images on the screen and other display devices.

exam
ⓦatch

You will probably want to note for the exam, the four files that are opened with the SYSEDIT program: the WIN.INI, SYSTEM.INI, AUTOEXEC.BAT, and CONFIG.SYS. Also, SYSEDIT doesn't support opening any other files, as there is no File Open command in the SYSEDIT File pull-down menu.

Windows 95 Boot Modes

Windows 95 provides three different modes that the system can be started in: Normal mode, Safe mode, and Command Prompt mode. Whenever you start Windows 95, the computer is automatically booted into Normal mode. To access the other two modes, you need to press the F8 key when you see the text message "Starting Windows 95." The message appears only for a short time, so you have to have your finger poised over the F8 key in order to access the boot menu.

exam
ⓦatch

Make sure you know the difference between MS-DOS and Windows 95 when it comes to pressing the F8 key. Remember that the F8 key in DOS allows you to alternately select which commands to load in the AUTOEXEC.BAT and CONFIG.SYS file, while the F8 key in Windows 95 allows you to access the boot menu.

Normal Mode

Normal mode is the mode in which Windows 95 is started by default. Normal mode provides full functionality of Windows 95. Windows 95 loads all of the drivers that are installed on the system.

Safe Mode

Safe mode is a special diagnostic mode of Windows 95 that starts Windows 95 without any network, CD-ROM, and printer drivers. Only three device drivers are loaded in Safe mode: the standard VGA display, the keyboard, and Microsoft mouse drivers. If you have a Logitech mouse or some other brand that requires special drivers, you should find a standard PS mouse or be very familiar at navigating Windows 95 via the keyboard. The reason is that the standard mouse driver may not work with your mouse and you'll be without the aid of this handy device in Safe mode. The time to use this special mode is when you load some new device and the device drivers aren't working or the driver settings aren't configured correctly. For example, let's say you purchased the newest Voodoo Banshee Video Graphics Accelerator card and rebooted after loading the drivers. Upon reboot you see a blank screen because the card won't work with the drivers or settings you configured. Fortunately, Safe mode loads the standard 16-color VGA drivers and you can change an incorrect setting, which will in most cases allow you to return your abnormally functioning system back to its correct operation.

There is a second type of Safe mode called *Safe mode with Network Support.* This mode loads the drivers for your Network Interface Card and allows you to log onto the network. This can be a valuable help if you need to access additional device drivers or software located on a network share.

Command Prompt

Command Prompt, or DOS Compatibility mode as it is commonly known, allows execution of some older MS-DOS applications that are not capable of running in Windows 95. These applications are primarily applications that attempt to access hardware that Windows 95 controls directly. Applications that require use of MS-DOS mode are usually blocked from operation within Windows 95. The applications that most commonly require the use of MS-DOS Compatibility mode include many graphical games.

A secondary use for Command Prompt mode is the need to run utilities like FDISK, which we discussed in the beginning of this chapter. Another command that should be run in Command Prompt mode and not from within Windows 95, is the Microsoft Diagnostic Program (MSD). It can give incorrect information about your system configuration if it is run within Windows 95. This utility is included on the Windows 95 CD-ROM, but it is not part of a normal installation. If you upgraded from Windows 3.x, you will also be able to access the file as it would be included in the DOS directory. MSD is a useful DOS utility that can provide you with information about what disks are in your system, the amount of memory installed, and system resource usage such as your LPT and COM ports.

Multi-Boot Configurations

It is possible to install more than one operating system on a computer. Configuring a system to have more than one operating system is called a *multi-boot configuration.* The boot options are configured by editing the

MSDOS.SYS file that is located in the root of the system partition on the master drive on the primary drive chain. This file should be edited following procedures detailed in the Windows 95 Resource Kit (this is not something for the faint of heart). Fortunately, if you dual-boot between Windows NT and Windows 95, NT automatically takes care of the multi-boot configuration by providing a boot menu. If you wish to set up a multi-boot configuration, be aware that Windows NT is not compatible with the FAT32 file system. To set up a multi-boot configuration with FAT32 and NTFS partitions, a good bet is a third-party utility called Boot Magic. It comes bundled with Partition Magic, which is a GUI version of FDISK.

CERTIFICATION OBJECTIVE 11.04

Windows 95 Plug-and-Play

Windows 95 Plug-and-Play (PnP) automatically configures the resources that Windows 95 Plug-and-Play-compatible devices use. These resources can include IO memory addresses, IRQ number, and DMA addresses among other things. Nearly all popular devices that are currently manufactured are Windows 95 Plug-and-Play-compatible. Sometimes you may see PnP referenced in a slightly different manner. From time to time, Plug-and-Play fails to live up to its design, and many people affectionately call this technology Plug-and-Pray because sometimes you could use a little extra help when it comes to properly identifying and configuring your devices. Plug-and-Play technology is one of the biggest advantages to the Windows 95 and Windows 98 operating systems compared to Windows NT. In Windows NT you really need to understand I/O port address, IRQs, and DMA channels. Windows 95 makes it a lot easier to install new devices because it "automagically" looks at your system and picks available resource addresses for you. At least that is what's supposed to happen!

exam
ⓦatch

Windows 95 Plug-and-Play automatically configures and tracks resources such as IO Memory Addresses, IRQ Address, and DMA Addresses.

Peripheral Recognition

When Windows 95 is booted for the first time with a particular Windows 95 Plug-and-Play-compatible device installed, the device is automatically recognized by Windows 95.

Loading Appropriate Drivers

When a new device is first detected, Windows 95 attempts to find a driver from its library of drivers. If Windows 95 finds that the driver is in its library and the driver is already installed on the system, Windows 95 continues as normal. If the driver is in the Windows 95 driver library but has not been installed on the system, Windows 95 prompts you to insert the Windows 95 CD and install the drivers. If the driver is not in the library, and has not been installed yet, you are prompted for the disks containing the drivers and the operating system installs them from there.

Assigning System Resources

All system resources are assigned to Plug-and-Play devices automatically using the Plug-and-Play information that Windows 95 has previously gathered. The new devices are given all of the system resources that they request (so long as they are available) and report their usage back to Windows 95.

Plug-and-Play—Working Properly

In proper operation, Windows 95 automatically detects all devices and assigns them the appropriate resources.

Plug-and-Play—Not Working Properly

In the event that devices are not working correctly, a good troubleshooting method is to delete the device from Device Manager and restart the system. This is about the time when you are thinking to yourself that PnP truly stands for Plug-and-Pray. When rebooted, if the device is not redetected and does not work properly, the device is either faulty or Plug-and-Play is not operating correctly. You may have to manually configure your resource settings in Device Manger to get the device working properly.

Loading/Adding Device Drivers

The process of adding device drivers is a rather simple one. It is important that the procedures outlined in your specific operating system's instructions are followed specifically.

DOS

Any device other than video and the keyboard (and including these in special cases) requires that a device driver be installed in the AUTOEXEC.BAT, CONFIG.SYS, or both. Consult the device's documentation for specific instructions.

Most device driver manufacturers provide an installation program that installs whatever lines need to be added to AUTOEXEC.BAT and CONFIG.SYS automatically. If a device driver does not include such an installation program, the drivers need to be copied onto the hard drive, and then AUTOEXEC.BAT and CONFIG.SYS need to be edited according to the device driver's documentation.

Windows 3.x Procedures

Windows 3.x requires the use of DOS device drivers for some devices such as CD-ROM drives and sound cards. In addition to the use of DOS device drivers, nearly all other major devices require that device drivers be installed. Windows 3.x requires device drivers for devices such as video, mice, and many others. Installation of Windows 3.x drivers should be done in accordance with the instructions provided by the driver manufacturer.

Windows 95 Procedures

Windows 95 does not rely on DOS device drivers as Windows 3.*x* does but does support them for backward compatibility. In addition to providing compatibility for DOS device drivers, Windows 95 also provides support for Windows 3.*x* device drivers. If more recent drivers are available, it is highly suggested that you use the Windows 95 driver. To install a device driver in Windows 95, you would simply use the Add New Hardware Wizard shown in Figure 11-4 and follow the directions provided there.

FIGURE 11-4

The Windows 95 Add New Hardware Wizard automatically scans the system for new hardware and installs the appropriate drivers for you

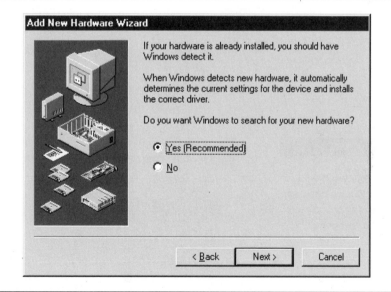

Add New Hardware Wizard

If your hardware is already installed, you should have Windows detect it.

When Windows detects new hardware, it automatically determines the current settings for the device and installs the correct driver.

Do you want Windows to search for your new hardware?

○ Yes (Recommended)
○ No

< Back   Next >   Cancel

Changing Options, Configuring, and Using the Windows Printing Subsystem

The Windows printing system is a well-organized system that simplifies the task of printing. DOS-based programs required that the printer be addressed directly by the application. By using the Windows printing subsystem, applications are required only to submit data to be printed to the standardized subsystem. The subsystem then renders the data, and prints it for you.

The Windows printing subsystem requires very little configuration. To begin to use the subsystem, a printer must first be installed. To install a printer, double-click on Printers from the Control Panel. Click on Add New Printer and select a driver from the list provided. The Add Printer Wizard shown in Figure 11-5 guides you through the process. In some cases (especially with newer printers), Windows 95 may have autodetected the printer at system startup and have already installed the drivers for it.

FIGURE 11-5

The Windows 95 Add Printer Wizard steps you through the process of adding a new printer

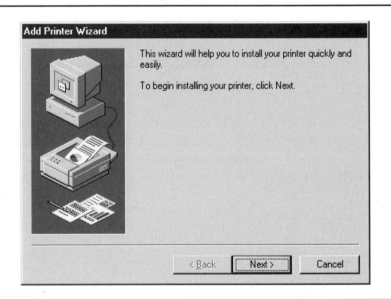

Installing and Launching Windows and Non-Windows Applications

Installation of both Windows and non-Windows applications is a fairly straightforward process. In order to complete the installation, all you need to do is follow the instructions provided by the software manufacturer. Windows-based applications should automatically create a Program Group and Program Item Icon in Program Manager for Windows 3.*x* systems. The process is very similar in Windows 95 in that an Application Group and a shortcut are created in the Start Menu under Programs for your Windows applications.

Non-Windows applications (DOS programs) are controlled via a program information file (PIF) in a Windows 3.*x* environment. A PIF is simply a file that contains information such as memory and video requirements for your DOS application. If you have not specified a PIF, then the default PIF (coincidentally named _DEFAULT.PIF) file will be used. This occurs when you launch the program by double-clicking on the executable file in File Manager. Most DOS applications will work with the default PIF configuration, but you may need to modify some settings to accommodate the particular needs of an application. If that is the case, there are three different ways in Windows 3.*x* to set up a custom PIF:

- The first is during the installation of Windows 3.*x*. The Express option automatically creates Program Item Icons for non-Windows applications. The Custom option allows you to select which non-Windows applications you would like to set up.

- The second option is the *Windows Setup* program. It is a forerunner of the Windows 95 *Add/Remove Programs* applet in Control Panel.

- The third option is to use the PIF Editor located in the Accessories Program Group.

Setting up non-Windows Applications in Windows 95 is done by creating a shortcut to the executable file. When you set up a shortcut to a

DOS-based program, the properties (accessed by right-clicking on the shortcut and selecting Properties) for the shortcut include a Program, Font, Memory, Screen, and Misc tab to control these unique settings for the DOS program. Alternatively, you can also double-click on the executable icon found by browsing to the application's home directory in Windows 95 Explorer. You can also use the RUN command in the Start menu to launch any application whether it is Windows or non-Windows based.

exam
Ⓦatch

For the exam, be sure and note that the PIF Editor allows you to create custom program information files for your DOS applications. Also, remember the _DEFAULT.PIF is used when no PIF is set up for your DOS application.

CERTIFICATION OBJECTIVE 11.08

Editing AUTOEXEC.BAT and CONFIG.SYS Files

AUTOEXEC.BAT and CONFIG.SYS files are two user-editable files. DOS and Windows 95 support a text editor called EDIT.COM. If you are in Windows 95, you can also use Notepad. These are two examples, but any text editor can be used to edit either of these files. As mentioned earlier, it is a good idea to make a backup of these files prior to making modifications. This can save you a lot of time if you ever have to undo a change that you've made. To make a backup of these files, all you have to do is make a copy of the file and put a different extension on the end. A common practice in the DOS days was to use the BAK extension or to use your initials. Windows 95 does not require that any settings are made in either the CONFIG.SYS or AUTOEXEC.BAT file, but they are supported for backward compatibility with older DOS applications. In fact, AUTOEXEC.BAT and CONFIG.SYS do not even have to exist for Windows 95 to function fully. If you find yourself working a lot from a command prompt, you might consider adding the DOSKEY to your AUTOEXEC.BAT. It is an invaluable utility that allows you to access previously typed DOS commands.

FROM THE FIELD

The Fine Art of Editing the System Files

Once you understand the system files, you should have no problem editing them, right? Well, most of the time. However, sooner or later you will run into a file that was previously edited by some other tech who had his or her own ideas of good editing techniques. Often, the way some techs edit them, you'd have better luck deciphering ancient Egyptian hieroglyphics. These files will probably have many added lines and no comments. I saw one so bad that it took me an hour to even start to understand the logic behind the editing. And, to top it all off, the last editor had only placed one remark in the files, written in all caps: "DO NOT CHANGE ANYTHING." Well, it's common that something will need to be changed in these files as hardware and software are installed, and commenting "not to change anything" does nothing more than make a workaround next to impossible. Instead of spending the next week on this PC, I looked at the repair log for that computer and found the previous tech who worked on the machine. Luckily, he was still with the company, so I asked him to edit the file himself.

When you make a change on a computer, always comment what you do and make your changes understandable to the next person. If you use commands that aren't common, make sure you comment on them and explain them. Back up all previous versions before you change them and remark in the file what you have changed and why. All too often, when things are unclear, a tech will resort to using a skeleton or default version of a system file. This may completely reverse any changes that you have made and any hardware or software changes in these files. You may have to end up reinstalling everything, or stitch together the old file and the new file. Of course there is software that can help you do this, but why spend the time?

One last point to ponder on these files: Make sure that when your system boots, you are not getting errors that are on the screen for the user to see. When your operating system boots up, it usually tells you things like "error in config.sys on line 8." Find out why these are happening and fix them. Users don't like to see errors, and furthermore they may be causing other problems. If you know they are not causing problems and are just remnants from an application that was not fully removed, simply REM them out. REMing them out is better, just in case you actually do need them.

—*Ted Hamilton, MCSE, MCP, A+ Certified*

CERTIFICATION SUMMARY

This chapter has offered you a general understanding of installing, configuring, and upgrading the various flavors of Microsoft operating systems and applications. As you have seen in this chapter, these processes are relatively simple and straightforward. There are slight differences between performing these functions on DOS, Windows 3.*x*, and Windows 95 systems—with Windows 95 being the most intelligent in this regard. This chapter has equipped you with the information necessary to be able to perform these functions across the board. Just remember that it's always important to review any specific product's documentation when installing the necessary drivers for it.

 TWO-MINUTE DRILL

❑ This first step in the preparation for using a new disk drive (or an old drive that you want to erase) is to create a partition on the drive using the FDISK utility.

❑ For DOS systems, Windows 3.x, and Windows 95, the maximum size of a partition is 2GB.

❑ If you want a drive to be bootable, it needs to be formatted with the /s switch. If you do not want to erase all of the data from the drive, the SYS command can also be issued to make the drive bootable.

❑ DOS does not internally provide any support for loading device drivers. You can, however, install device drivers by adding them to CONFIG.SYS or AUTOEXEC.BAT.

❑ If you have a system that has DOS installed on it, and is not running Windows 3.x, it is a good idea to upgrade hardware prior to installing Windows 95.

❑ If there are any device drivers that you still need to have installed after you've installed Windows 95, you can do so by clicking on Add New Hardware.

❑ In order to boot a system from any type of disk, be it a hard drive or a floppy drive, the partition you wish to boot off must be set as Active (because floppies only have one partition, they are always set as Active), and the system files must be copied to the partition.

❑ Windows 95 primarily provides three different modes that the system can be started in: Normal mode, Safe mode, and Command Prompt mode.

❑ The Safe mode allows you to change an incorrect setting, which in most cases allows you to return an abnormally functioning system to its correct operation.

❑ Command Prompt mode, or DOS Compatibility mode as it is commonly known, allows execution of some older MS-DOS applications that are not capable of running in Windows 95.

❑ Configuring a system for using more than one operating system is called multi-boot configuration.

❑ Windows 95 Plug-and-Play automatically configures and tracks resources such as IO Memory addresses, IRQ address, and DMA addresses.

❑ In the event that Plug-and-Play devices are not working correctly, a good troubleshooting method is to delete the device from Device Manager and restart the system.

❑ When adding device drivers, it is important that the procedures outlined in your operating system's instructions are followed specifically.

❑ AUTOEXEC.BAT and CONFIG.SYS do not even have to exist for Windows 95 to function fully.

❑ The Windows printing subsystem requires very little configuration. To begin to use the subsystem, a printer must first be installed.

❑ Among other things, CONFIG.SYS provides the ability to install device drivers.

❑ AUTOEXEC.BAT is more commonly used to invoke device drivers for devices such as the mouse and the CD-ROM drive.

SELF TEST

The following Self-Test questions will help you measure your understanding of the material presented in this chapter. Read all the choices carefully, as there may be more than one correct answer. Choose all correct answers for each question.

1. What is the correct load order sequence for the following files?

   A. CONFIG.SYS, AUTOEXEC.BAT

   B. AUTOEXEC.SYS, CONFIG.BAT

   C. ATUOEXEC.BAT, CONFIG.SYS

   D. AUTOEXEC.BAT, COMMAND.COM

2. Which of the following commands will copy the boot files onto a floppy disk without erasing any existing data on the diskette?

   A. SYS A: C:

   B. FORMAT A: /S

   C. COPY BOOTFILES A:\

   D. SYS A:

3. What three files are copied onto a disk after formatting when the /s switch is used?

   A. COMMAND.BAT, IO.SYS, MSDOS.SYS

   B. AUTOEXEC.BAT, CONFIG.SYS, COMMAND.COM

   C. IO.SYS, MSDOS.SYS, COMMAND.COM

   D. IO.SYS, MSDOS.SYS, CONFIG.SYS

4. What key would you press to bypass the CONFIG.SYS and AUTOEXEC.BAT during the DOS boot process?

   A. F3

   B. F5

   C. F6

   D. F8

5. What is a PIF?

   A. Program Initialization File

   B. Program Information File

   C. Permanent Information File

   D. Primary Information File

6. Which of the following files are opened using the SYSEDIT command in Windows 3.x?

   A. WIN.INI

   B. PROGRMAN.INI

   C. AUTOEXEC.BAT

   D. SYSTEM.INI

   E. CONTROL.INI

7. Which DOS 6 driver manages the upper memory area?

   A. EMM387.EXE

   B. EMM386.EXE

   C. HIMEM.SYS

   D. EMM386.COM

8. Which DOS 6 driver manages the extended memory area?

   A. EMM387.EXE

   B. EMM386.EXE

C. HIMEM.SYS

D. EMM386.COM

9. During a Windows 95 upgrade from Windows 3.1, you receive the following error message: "Insert Windows 3.*x* Installation Disk 1." What is the most likely cause of this message?

   A. You are unable to upgrade form Windows 3.1.

   B. Windows 95 couldn't find a current version of DOS.

   C. Windows 95 couldn't find a current version of Windows.

   D. You are installing from a pirated copy of Windows 95.

10. Which of the following initialization files will automatically launch a program when Windows starts?

    A. STARTUP.INI

    B. BOOT.INI

    C. WIN.INI

    D. SYSTEM.INI

11. The <u>BUFFER</u> statement is found in what file?

    A. AUTOEXEC.BAT

    B. CONFIG.SYS

    C. WIN.INI

    D. COMMAND.COM

12. Which file contains system hardware setting specifications?

    A. STARTUP.INI

    B. HARDWARE.INI

C. WIN.INI

D. SYSTEM.INI

13. What file must be loaded in the CONFIG.SYS in order to display color graphics in the DOS environment?

    A. COLOR.SYS

    B. GRAPHICS.SYS

    C. ANSI.SYS

    D. VGA.DRV

14. Windows generates an error message stating it cannot open enough files. Which configuration file needs to be modified?

    A. AUTOEXEC.BAT

    B. WIN.INI

    C. CONFIG.SYS

    D. WINFILE.INI

15. What driver set would be loaded if you booted a Windows 95 machine in safe mode?

    A. Mouse, Keyboard, VGA

    B. Mouse, Keyboard, CD-ROM, VGA

    C. Mouse, Keyboard, SVGA

    D. Keyboard, CD-ROM, SVGA

16. If the Windows 95 Plug-and-Play option is working and if your hardware is PnP compliant, you should expect:

    A. To manually set IRQ settings

    B. That there will be no device conflicts

    C. That you will only have to manually set I/O port addresses

    D. That you will have to allocate resources manually

17. Which of the following are minimum requirements to install Windows 3.x? (Choose all that apply.)

    A. An 80286, 80386, or 80386SX processor

    B. A minimum of 2MB of RAM on an 80386 processor

    C. A hard disk with at least 5MB of storage space

    D. A color graphics display adapter

18. Which of the following files is responsible for loading applications, managing memory, and scheduling task execution?

    A. USER.EXE

    B. MEMMANAGER.EXE

    C. GDI.EXE

    D. KRNL286EXE/KRNL386.EXE

19. Which of the following files displays the Windows logo and determines what mode to start Windows 3.x in?

    A. STARTUP.INI

    B. WIN.INI

    C. WIN.COM

    D. SETUP.EXE

20. In 386 Enhanced mode, Windows 3.x can:

    A. Have both multiple Windows applications and multiple DOS applications active at the same time

    B. Have multiple Windows applications but not multiple DOS applications active at the same time

    C. Have only a single DOS application active at any given time

    D. Have only a single Windows application active when a DOS application is active

21. Which of the following are minimum requirements to install Windows 95? (Choose all that apply.)

    A. 80286 processor

    B. 80386 processor

    C. 80486 processor

    D. 4MB of memory

    E. 8MB of memory

22. Which mode does Windows 95 automatically start up in?

    A. Standard mode

    B. Enhanced mode

    C. Normal mode

    D. Safe mode

23. Which of the following are valid ways to start a DOS application in Windows 95? (Choose all that apply.)

    A. By creating a PIF and double-clicking on it

    B. By using the DEFAULT.PIF if a custom PIF hasn't been created

    C. By creating a shortcut and double-clicking on it

    D. By launching the executable from File Manager

    E. By launching the executable from Windows Explorer

24. Which key do you need to press to access the Windows 95 boot menu?

    A. F3
    B. F5
    C. F6
    D. F8

25. What is the largest partition size found in MS-DOS, Windows 3.x, and Windows 95 (version A)?

    A. 1024MB
    B. 2048MB
    C. 4096MB
    D. 8192MB

12

Diagnosing and Troubleshooting

DOS, Windows 3.*x*, and Windows 95/98 all provide some error messages that can be used to help diagnose common problems, which can be resolved by some common solutions. Whenever you are installing or configuring any type of application, some errors can occur. In this chapter, we discuss some of these common problems and their solutions in addition to some of the tools that can be used to diagnose and fix these problems.

CERTIFICATION OBJECTIVE 12.01

Common Error Codes, Startup Messages, and Icons from the Boot Sequence for DOS, Windows 3.*x*, and Windows 95/98

All operating systems that have ever been produced have provided some type of error codes to alert the operator to troubles. Unfortunately, many of these error codes are a bit difficult to understand. As we progress into the future, these error codes and startup messages have and will continue to become less incomprehensible. In this section, we discuss some of the common error codes and startup messages, and what they really mean.

Post Error Code

As mentioned in Chapter 11, the Power On Self-Test (POST) is a program stored on a ROM (BIOS) chip which instructs the computer to diagnose the hardware. The POST program goes through several diagnostic checks as it verifies the hardware detected during the boot process. If any of the POST diagnostic checks fail, then a POST error message will display on the screen. Table 12-1 lists some of the common POST Diagnostic Error Codes.

TABLE 12-1	Code	Description
POST Diagnostic Error Codes	01	Undetermined problem errors
	02	Power supply errors

Code	Description
System Board Errors	
101–108	Various system board chip failures.
109	Direct memory access test error.
121	Unexpected hardware interrupts occurred.
161	System Options Error.
162	System options not set correctly.
163	Time and date not set.
164	Memory size error.
199	User indicated configuration not correct.
Memory (RAM) errors	
201	Memory test failed.
202	Memory address error.
203	Memory address error.
Keyboard Errors	
301	Keyboard not connected; keyboard did not respond to software reset correctly; or a struck key failure was detected.
302	User indicated error from the keyboard test, or AT systems unit keylock is locked.
303	Keyboard or system unit error.
304	Keyboard or system unit error; CMOS does not match system.
Diskette Drive Errors	
601	Diskette Power on, diagnostics test failed.
602	Diskette test failed; boot record is not valid.
606	Diskette verify function failed.
607	Write protected diskette.
608	Bad command diskette status returned.

exam
ⓦatch

For the exam, you don't need to memorize the entire Table 12-1, but you should note the basic categories for each type of error (e.g. 100's – System Board Errors, 200's – Memory (RAM) errors, etc.). Knowledge of the categories can help you determine where to start diagnosing a POST problem. For example, if you receive a POST 303 error, you should note this falls under the Keyboard category. Often times an object, like a book, can accidentally press a key down on the keyboard, which can cause a POST 303 error. Just move your book or pile of stuff off the keyboard, reboot, and everything will be OK!

DOS

DOS provides three major error messages that are dealt with in this section. These include:

- Incorrect DOS version
- Error in CONFIG.SYS line XX
- Bad or missing COMMAND.COM

Incorrect DOS Version

Whenever a utility is used, it makes some assumptions as to its abilities based on the version of DOS that it is being run on. When the utility first starts, it verifies that it is being run on the version of DOS it was designed for. If the version of DOS is not the version it was created for, the message "Incorrect DOS version" is displayed.

This problem should be fixed by using applications that were created for the version of DOS that you are using. As an alternative, you can also use the SETVER command. SETVER allows you to add or delete entries in the version-table which is a workaround that allows DOS-based applications to function as if they are in the version of DOS the application was designed to use. To prevent the "Incorrect DOS Version" error from occurring, you add the executable file name and the version of DOS the application was designed to work with into the version-table.

SETVER is considered a DOS device driver and as such, it needs to be loaded in the CONFIG.SYS file. To enable SETVER, add the following line to the CONFIG.SYS file: "DEVICE=C:\DOS\SETVER.EXE". Once SETVER is enabled, you can then add or remove applications from the version-table. The required syntax to add and remove programs from the version-table is shown below. Whenever you add or remove applications from the version-table, you need to reboot your system in order for the change to take effect. Also be aware, that if you specify an application that is already in the table, the new entry replaces the existing entry.

Following is the syntax for the SETVER command:

```
C:\>setver /?
Set the version number that MS-DOS reports to a program.

Display current version-table:  SETVER [drive:path]
Add entry:                       SETVER [drive:path] filename n.nn
Delete entry:                    SETVER [drive:path] filename /DELETE [/QUIET]

  [drive:path]    Specifies location of the SETVER.EXE file.
  filename             Specifies the filename of the program.
  n.nn                 Specifies the MS-DOS version to be reported to the program.
  /DELETE or /D        Deletes the version-table entry for the specified program.
  /QUIET             Hides the message typically displayed during deletion of version-table entry.
```

Error in CONFIG.SYS Line XX

The message "Error in CONFIG.SYS line XX" (where XX is a number) indicates there was an error in the CONFIG .SYS file when it was processed. The error can be found by counting the number of lines that are in the CONFIG.SYS file and finding the line number indicated in the error message. This error can appear for a variety of reasons. The most common cause of this error is a device driver file. After determining which driver is creating the error, you should verify that the driver still exists. Another possible cause for this error is an incorrectly typed path statement. DOS is rather particular about spelling. As long as you spell everything correctly there isn't a problem. Accidentally leave out a colon or a backslash, and you'll start seeing "Error in CONFIG.SYS line XX" messages. You may have a legitimate error with a driver for a sound card, a network adapter card, or some other device. You can fix the error by following the instructions provided by the device manufacturer.

Bad or Missing **COMMAND.COM**

Bad or missing COMMAND.COM most commonly occurs when the COMSPEC parameter is set in CONFIG.SYS, and the COMMAND.COM that COMSPEC references does not exist. This error can also occur when starting Windows 95/98.

Windows 3.x

Windows 3.x is a bit more advanced than DOS, so there are more advanced error messages that can be displayed from Windows 3.x. Most of the errors in the following list occur after Windows 3.x has begun to load, but the graphical user interface (GUI) is not displayed. The common error messages discussed here are:

- HIMEM.SYS not loaded
- Unable to Initialize Display Adapter
- Swapfile Corrupt
- A device referenced in the WIN.INI could not be found

HIMEM.SYS Not Loaded

Windows 3.x requires that the HIMEM.SYS driver be loaded in order to access extended memory. Loading HIMEM.SYS allows Windows 3.x to access memory above 1024 KB. This driver should be referenced in the first line in the CONFIG.SYS file. If you receive the missing HIMEM.SYS error, first verify that the first line of CONFIG.SYS is "DEVICE=C:\HIMEM.SYS". If the line is in CONFIG.SYS, you should verify that HIMEM.SYS is in the specified location.

Unable to Initialize Display Adapter

Unlike DOS, Windows 3.x requires that you identify the video adapter that is installed in your system. If Windows gives you an "Unable to initialize display adapter" error, you should use the Windows setup utility to change the adapter type. If you are unsure of the exact model of adapter you have, VGA should always work, although it does not produce the best results. It is important to note that this error could also be the result of a faulty display adapter, but it is less likely.

Swapfile Corrupt

Windows 3.*x* uses a swapfile in order to create virtual memory. When Windows creates a permanent swap file, two hidden files are created on your hard drive. The hidden files are 386SPART.PAR (located in the root directory) and SPART.PAR (located in the Windows directory). In the event that the swapfile becomes corrupted, Windows operates extremely slowly and gives you the message that the swapfile is corrupt. To remedy this problem, you need to delete the swapfile:

1. Open the Control Panel

2. Click on the 386 Enhanced icon.

3. Click the Virtual memory button.

4. Set the swap file type to NONE, and click OK.

5. Click "YES" in the confirmation dialog box, but DO NOT restart Windows.

6. Click the Continue button and exit Windows.

To be sure the file was deleted, from the DOS Prompt, switch to the root directory where Windows is loaded and type the following command: "ATTRIB –r –s –h 386SPART.PAR". The ATTRIB command and the accompanying switches remove the read-only, system, and hidden attributes of the swapfile. In case the file wasn't deleted, you need to remove these attributes in order to even view the file. If the file was successfully deleted by changing the Virtual memory options, you should receive a "File Not Found" error after typing the ATTRIB command. If somehow the file didn't get deleted, simply type **DEL 386SPART.PART**. You will then need to change to the Windows directory and delete the SPART.PAR file if it didn't get deleted earlier.

To ensure your swapfile doesn't continue to corrupt, it is a good idea to defragment your hard disk by running the DOS DEFRAG utility. Defragmenting allows you to free up contiguous space that is needed for a swapfile to work correctly.

A Device Referenced in SYSTEM.INI Could Not Be Found

In the event that a device that is referenced in the SYSTEM.INI file cannot be found, you will receive this error. A device driver that is unable to locate the corresponding hardware can cause this error. Often times this error is generated because a required device driver was deleted from the system. When this occurs, the device driver no longer resides on the system, but the SYSTEM.INI is not aware of this fact, and it continues to reference the missing device.

To eliminate this error message, edit the SYSTEM.INI. You can use any text editor or the SYSEDIT utility included with Windows. Once you have the SYSTEM.INI file open, simply remove the line that is causing the error. You can also "comment" out the line by placing a semicolon in front of the line. The line will remain present in SYSEM.INI, but will not be processed by Windows. You may need to reinstall the device driver software to remedy the problem.

Windows 95/98

Windows 95/98 provides some common error codes that can be used to help troubleshoot a system problem. Knowledge of these error codes can help you in the troubleshooting process. The common error messages discussed here are:

- Missing or Corrupt HIMEM.SYS
- No Operating System Found
- Safe Mode
- VFAT Initialization Failure
- Bad or Missing COMMAND.COM

Missing or Corrupt HIMEM.SYS

Like Windows 3.*x*, Windows 95/98 requires that HIMEM.SYS be loaded for the operating system to function correctly. Windows 95/98 automatically loads HIMEM.SYS from the C:\ directory prior to processing the CONFIG.SYS file. There are two possible problems that could cause you to receive the "Missing or Corrupt HIMEM.SYS" error in Windows 95. First, if the file is actually deleted from the C:\ directory, and second, if there is a line in CONFIG.SYS referencing an incorrect version of HIMEM.SYS. If there is such a line, simply delete it.

No Operating System Found

The message "No Operating System Found" indicates that there are corrupt files (which can be the result of a bad hard drive) or that OS files have been deleted or were never loaded. You should first try booting from a Windows 95 startup disk. If you can successfully boot from the floppy, you should next try running the SYS command to copy the DOS system files from the floppy to the hard disk. If this procedure fails, running the Windows 95 setup program should fix any other problems related to the OS files that could be missing or corrupted. If you are unable to write to the hard drive, the problem could be hardware-related.

Safe Mode

Any time Windows 95 encounters an error in loading, it automatically starts the system in safe mode. Safe mode is a special diagnostic mode that loads minimal drivers and is limited to the keyboard, mouse, and standard VGA drivers. Safe mode provides a method for you to change system settings in many cases where incorrect settings have rendered the system nonfunctional. For example, in the event that an incorrect video driver was installed, safe mode would allow you to correct it, and return the system to its normal functionality. If, for some reason, Windows is not booting into safe mode, you can press F8 when you see the "Starting Windows 95" text message that appears after the system POST. The message only appears for about three seconds, so make sure you have your finger poised over the F8 key. Pressing F8 accesses the Boot Menu, and then you can manually select the Safe mode boot option.

VFAT Initialization Failure

VFAT (Virtual File Allocation Table) initialization failure occurs when the system is unable to initialize the driver that controls the file system on the drive. The first step in attempting to correct this error is to reboot the system, press F8 when the "Starting Windows 95" text message is displayed, and choose "Safe Mode Command Prompt Only" from the list provided. From this command prompt, the ScanDisk utility can be run to attempt to fix physical drive problems. If ScanDisk is unable to fix the error, running Windows 95 setup should correct the problem.

Bad or Missing **COMMAND.COM**

Windows 95/98 expects COMMAND.COM to be installed in the C:\ directory. In the event that COMMAND.COM is not located in the C:\ directory, you should replace it. COMSPEC being set in the CONFIG.SYS file to a directory where COMMAND.COM is not located could also cause the problem. In addition, if a manual path statement has been added to the AUTOEXEC.BAT that does not include the C:\ directory, this could cause the problem.

   If none of these options fix the problem, it is possible that the existing COMMAND.COM file is simply corrupt. If you have a Windows 95/98 system disk (depending on which you are running), booting from the floppy disk and running the SYS command should correct your problem. As a last resort, you can try rerunning Windows 95/98 setup to restore any lost or corrupted files.

CERTIFICATION OBJECTIVE 12.02

Correcting a Startup or Boot Problem

There are many startup or boot problems that can occur. To protect yourself against boot problems, you should always have a boot disk available for your operating system. If your operating system provides the capability to make an Emergency Repair Disk (ERD) or a startup disk, you should take advantage of the feature. The most common and usually easiest solution to startup and boot problems is to boot using the boot disk. If you can successfully boot to the floppy disk, you can use the SYS command to rebuild many of the important system files on your machine. If your machine still refuses to start, you may need to rerun the setup utility that shipped with your operating system. The setup utility should correct any problems you are having that are not related to physical device failure.

CERTIFICATION OBJECTIVE 12.03

Creating an Emergency Boot Disk with Utilities Installed

Creating a DOS boot disk is not a difficult task. It requires a little bit more work than Windows 95 and 98 because you don't have the luxury of clicking on a "create disk" button. Once you have a diskette in the floppy drive, from any DOS prompt you need to type "FORMAT A: /S". This formats the disk and copies the system files (IO.SYS MSDOS.SYS and COMMAND.COM) to the diskette. While you have a bootable diskette it doesn't have any utilities loaded. Technically speaking the AUTOEXEC.BAT and CONFIG.SYS files do not fall under the category of "utilities", but it may be beneficial to include these files on a DOS boot disk. Regardless, you want to copy the following utilities from your DOS directory to the diskette:

- **FDISK.EXE**   Used to create and delete partitions
- **FORMAT.COM**   Used to format a partition or disk
- **SCANDISK.EXE**   Used to check the physical disk for physical errors
- **DEFRAG.EXE**   Used to defragment the hard disk
- **EDIT.COM**   Used to edit or create text files
- **ATTRIB.EXE**   Used to set or modify file attributes
- **XCOPY.EXE**   Used to copy files and folders

Windows 95 and Windows 98 both provide a simple method of creating an emergency boot disk. This diskette will allow you to boot your system with some handy Windows utilities, but you may also want to back up some of your important configuration files like the AUTOEXEC.BAT and CONFIG.SYS. These files are for older 16-bit programs to store their configuration information. Likewise, you might back up the SYSTEM.INI and WIN.INI files because this is where Windows 3.*x* applications stores configuration information. Backing up these files is a good idea, but they can be useless if you can't boot your system. Exercise 12-1 shows you how to create an Emergency Boot Disk in Windows 95 and Windows 98.

| EXERCISE 12-1 | **Creating an Emergency Boot Disk for Windows 95 or Windows 98** |

1. Insert a floppy disk into your floppy drive.
2. Click the Start button and choose Settings | Control Panel.
3. Double-click the Add/Remove Programs icon.
4. Select the Startup Disk tab on the far right.
5. Click the Create Disk button.

Figure 12-1 shows the utility that is used to create the Emergency Boot Disk in Windows 95.

CERTIFICATION OBJECTIVE 12.04

Recognizing Windows-Specific Printing Problems

The Windows printing subsystem simplifies the task of printing for both the user and the applications authors. Unfortunately, with the standardized Windows printing system come some common problems that could occur. These problems are:

- Print spool is stalled.
- Driver is set for bi-directional mode with a uni-directional cable.

FIGURE 12-1

Windows 95 can easily
create a startup disk that
can be used to diagnose
and fix problems in the
event of Windows 95
not working properly

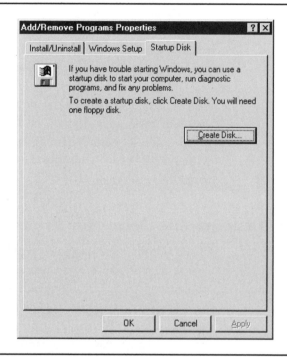

- Incorrect/incompatible driver for printer.
- Printer port not set up correctly in Device Manager.
- Printer is not set to print to correct port.

Print Spool Is Stalled

The print spooler can stall itself in order to hopefully prevent the user from
losing a print job. In the event that the print spooler does become stalled
when it should not be, the problem can be solved by clicking on the File
menu from the Printer Properties and selecting Restart Printing.

Driver Is Set for Bi-Directional Printing/User Is Using a Uni-Directional Cable

Most of the newer and more advanced printers have the capability of using
a bidirectional mode, meaning that the printer is able to talk back to the

computer. This can be extremely useful because it allows the printer to send the user exact error messages that are displayed on the workstation, and helps the spooler to avoid print spooler stalls. In the event that the computer is unable to communicate with a bidirectional printer, your first step should be to turn off bidirectional printing in the Printer Settings tab. If the printer works after bidirectional support is turned off, you can either leave it that way and be happy, or replace the cable with a bidirectional capable cable. Also note that bidirectional support could be turned off in the systems BIOS (consult the system's manual for details on how to correct this problem).

Incorrect/Incompatible Driver for Printer

It is extraordinarily important to verify that the driver that you are using to print to your printer is the correct version for your printer. The driver should either be specifically manufactured for the printer you are using, or should be listed as a compatible driver by the printer manufacturer. If you need to get a new driver for the printer, either visit the manufacturer's Web site or call their technical support team.

Printer Port Is Not Set Up Correctly in Device Manager (ECP, EPP, Standard)

Printers require a properly configured port. Windows 95 usually detects and installs ports correctly, but may install a port as Standard when it should be installed as ECP. To correct this problem, use the Add New Hardware Wizard from the Control Panel to add a new port. If after adding the new port you are still having difficulties, you may want to consult your system's documentation to verify that the port is set in the correct mode in the system's BIOS.

Printer Not Set to Print to Correct Port

Having a printer set to the wrong port is undoubtedly one of the most easily solved printer problems. To change the port that a printer is set to print to, open the Properties dialog box of the printer in question, which is shown in

Figure 12-2. Next, select the Details tab and change the port setting to the correct one.

CERTIFICATION OBJECTIVE 12.05

Common Problems and Causes

There are some common problems that occur frequently on Windows systems. Whenever one of these problems occurs, your system may be left in a less-than-optimal state. Even though the system appears to be functioning properly, it may continue to have difficulties. The best solution for most problems is to simply reboot the system.

FIGURE 12-2

An incorrect port setting can be changed from the Details tab of the Printer Properties dialog box

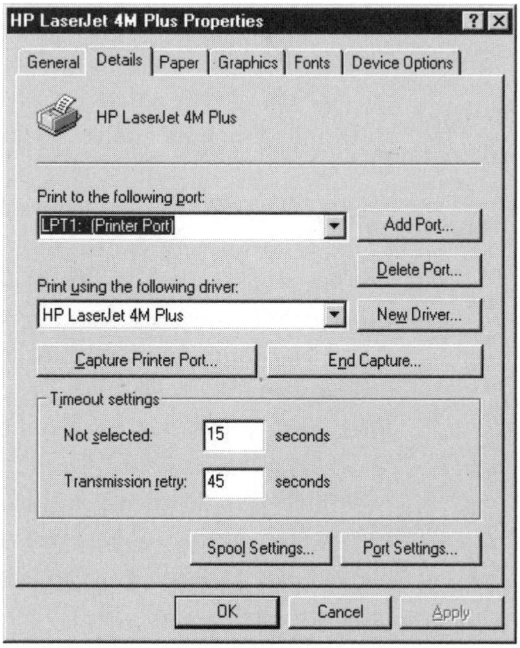

General Protection Faults

General protection faults (GPFs) are often referred to as the "Blue Screen of Death" because of the associated blue screen the error is displayed on. This occurs frequently due to a depletion of memory resources. A GPF can also occur when an application performs an operation that Windows does not normally permit to happen. GPFs can be caused by nearly anything, and can almost be considered a catchall for errors. If an application causes a general protection fault, you should restart the system at your earliest convenience. In many cases, the problem is solved by a simple reboot. In the event that the problem is not solved, you should reinstall the application. If after reinstalling the application the error still continues, it is advisable to contact the program vendor's technical support.

System Lock Up

Applications can easily lock up or hang a system for nearly any reason. In the event that you encounter a lockup, you should simply reboot the system. If lockups continue, you might want to run SCANDISK and DEFRAG on the system. If running SCANDISK and DEFRAG doesn't fix the problem of your system locking up, reinstalling the problematic application can often resolve the problem.

Operating System Will Not Boot

The operating system's failure to boot could be caused by nearly anything, although it is rather rare. You have a couple of troubleshooting options available to you if you're working on Windows 95. One option is to reboot and access the Windows 95 Boot Menu. As a review from Chapter 11, the Boot Menu is displayed when you press F8 after seeing the "Starting Windows 95" text. When you get into the Boot Menu you should try to boot into Safe mode as this only loads the keyboard, mouse, and Standard VGA drivers. If you can boot into Safe mode, you will be able to access Device Manager where you can remove or update devices that may be causing the OS not to load.

A second troubleshooting option in Windows 95 is the special logging feature that records all the devices and drivers that the system attempts to load.

Additionally, it will report a status as to whether the devices and drivers were successfully loaded. The name of the log file is BOOTLOG.TXT and it is automatically created during the installation of Windows 95 in the event you need to troubleshoot installation problems. The log file is only created once after the first successful installation, but you can access the logging feature again via the Windows 95 Boot Menu. A special boot option called Logged (BOOT.TXT) will be available. If you select this boot option, then the BOOTLOG.TXT file will be created on your root drive (usually C:). This file can be opened with any text editor, and you can then determine what devices and drivers the system attempted to load and if there were any failures. If a specific device caused a problem, you could try removing the device and then reinstalling once you're able to get booted into Windows 95.

The final option of rerunning your operating system's setup program (reinstalling your OS) should solve any problems.

Application Will Not Start or Load

In the event that an application does not load, you should first restart the system to attempt to correct the problem. If restarting the system does not solve the problem, reinstalling the application usually does.

Invalid Working Directory

This error is commonly associated with 16-bit applications designed for Windows 3.*x*. The error may also occur today if you're running these older programs in Windows 95 or Windows 98. A common cause of the "Invalid Working Directory" error is specifying a UNC (universal naming convention) name for an application's working directory. A UNC name is a way to reference a network resource. For example, to access the DOCS folder on a server named Kyle, the UNC name would be represented as \\kyle\docs. While a UNC name works great for accessing network resources, it cannot be used for a working directory in the Program Item Properties (Windows 3.*x*) dialog box or in Shortcut (Windows 95/98). This limitation also applies to the startup directory of PIF files for a non-Windows application.

If an application's working or startup directory must point to a network device, then you need to map a network drive to the device. Once you have mapped the network drive to an associated drive letter you'll be able to use the drive letter for the working/startup directory. An example would be to map \\kyle\docs to the F:\ drive. Then specify F:\ as the working/startup directory.

This error can also occur if you have the working directory set incorrectly due to a spelling error or an incorrect path. If at any time the working directory is wrong, it is possible that a program might not function correctly, or at all. If you are receiving errors about an invalid working directory, you should view the settings of the Program Item Properties dialog box (Windows 3.*x*) or Shortcut (Windows 95/98) and then verify that the working directory exists and that it is correct. If the directory does not exist, modify the setting or create the directory.

Option Will Not Function

It is not unusual for a particular option not to function in the manner that you would expect it to. If this occurs, the best solution is to close all programs and shut down the system. After the system is fully shut down, restart it and see if the option functions properly. If the problem is not solved, the best course of action is to uninstall or reinstall the application.

Cannot Log On to Network

In order to logon to a network, a workstation and a server need to be able to communicate with each other. This requires a physical connection comprised of a network adapter card, also referred to as a network interface card (NIC), and some type of network media, usually coax cable, twisted pair cable, or fiber optic cable. The vast majority of network problems are resolved by troubleshooting the physical connection. In addition to the physical connection, you also need a software or logical connection between the network adapter card and your network operating system.

When troubleshooting network problems, you need to determine where the problem exists. One way to begin is by defining who is affected. If the problem exists with only one user, then you most likely have a workstation problem. If the problem exists with a group of users, you may have a problem with either the group of workstations or the server. If everyone is unable to logon, you most likely have a problem on the server side.

If you suspect the problem exists with the workstation, you should check the physical connection first. Be sure the workstation is wired to the network (that is, ensure that the cable is plugged into the network adapter card). Most network adapter cards provide at least one LED light on the back of the card to indicate whether or not it is "linked" to the network. If the LED light is inactive you may want to check the cable connection to be sure it is firmly connected to the card. You may also want to check the operating system to be sure the correct driver for the network adapter card is installed and that there are no resource conflicts (for example, IRQ or I/O address conflicts) with other devices. If the problem is not with the physical connection, you should check the logical connection with the network operating system. The following list contains some common things to check:

- Has the workstation ever logged on to the network? If so, what has changed? If not, continue troubleshooting.

- Do you have the correct protocol installed on the client? The client and server must share a common protocol such as TCP/IP or IPX/SPX.

- Is the workstation logging onto the correct server?

- Be sure to note any error messages that may appear on the screen such as "Invalid password", or "A connection with a Domain controller could not be established." These messages will help you to better determine if there is an error on the workstation or on the server.

If you suspect the problem exists on the server, you need to verify the same physical connections and resource conflicts that were discussed above. Again, you need to ask the question, "Has the server ever worked correctly?" If so, then what has changed on the server? Often when a new device, service, or application is loaded on a server, or any PC for that matter, it can cause conflicts with existing hardware and software. Try to determine if anything has changed on the server. If an individual user is having a problem logging on, you will want to check if the user's account information is correct and that it is enabled for network logon. There are a myriad of other things to check, but many of these are specific to the type of protocol installed on the Server, and the type of Network Operating System in use (i.e. Windows NT, Novell NetWare, AppleTalk, Banyan Vines, Linux, etc.).

DOS- and Windows-Based Utilities and Commands/Switches

There are many different utilities that are provided with both DOS and Windows 3.*x*/Windows 95 that help to diagnose and solve most problems.

DOS

DOS provides some very useful tools that allow us to do anything from gather information about the system to reorganizing the file locations on the hard drive in order to improve performance. The DOS-based tools examined here include:

- MSD.EXE
- SCANDISK.EXE
- DEFRAG.EXE
- MEM.EXE
- EDIT.COM
- FDISK.EXE
- ATTRIB.EXE

MSD.EXE

MSD, Microsoft Diagnostics, is a utility that provides a great deal of information about the system and is shown in Figure 12-3. MSD is useful in determining what resources the system has installed in it, such as memory and hard drives.

The Microsoft Diagnostics utility can be used to provide information about the system. This information can be valuable in determining if a workstation is capable of being upgraded.

SCANDISK.EXE

ScanDisk is a utility that can be used to check disk drives for surface errors. Once completed, the /f switch can be used to fix errors. Running the ScanDisk utility can solve many recurring problems.

DEFRAG.EXE

DEFRAG is a utility that can be used to reorganize a hard disk drive. DEFRAG reorganizes file clusters so that they are contiguous, which usually results in improved system performance.

MEM.EXE

MEM.EXE provides information about the memory that is installed in the system, and what it is being used for. Passing the /c switch displays information on what programs are using the memory, and how much memory they are using. Passing the /f switch provides information about free memory in the

---

FIGURE 12-3

Microsoft Diagnostics provides a good survey of the system's features in one easy-to-read format

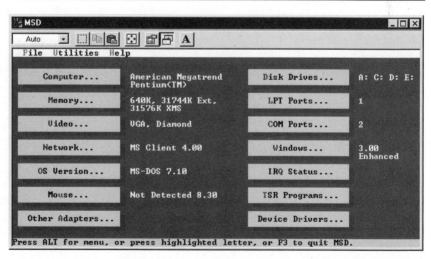

system. Many times there is too much information presented on the screen, and you are unable to read it. To alleviate this problem, passing the /p switch pauses after each page of information is displayed. Simply running MEM.EXE, as Figure 12-4 shows, tells how much memory is installed in the system and how much of that is free.

EDIT.COM

EDIT.COM is a simple ASCII text editor. It can be used to modify system files such as AUTOEXEC.BAT and CONFIG.SYS. It is simple to use and provides a basic GUI and mouse support if a mouse driver is loaded.

FDISK.EXE

FDISK.EXE can be used to create and delete partitions on the system's hard disk drives. Be warned that FDISK.EXE makes changes that are permanent and could easily render the system unbootable and make all data on the hard drives inaccessible. Use FDISK with care and ensure that all your data is backed up. FDISK, as shown in Figure 12-5, provides an easy-to-use menu-driven interface.

FIGURE 12-4

MEM.EXE can be used to provide information on the memory that is installed in the system and how much of it is available

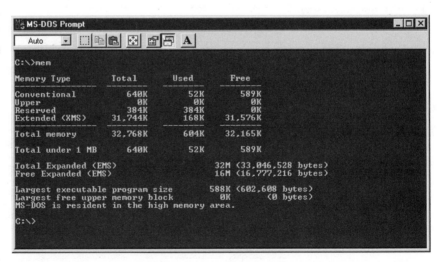

FIGURE 12-5

FDISK.EXE can be used to create and delete partitions on a hard disk drive

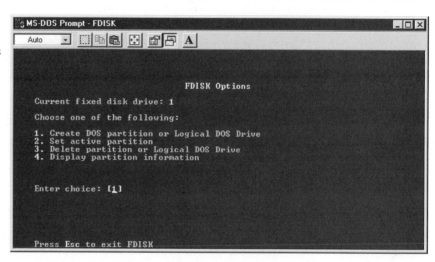

FDISK/MBR can be used to replace the Master Boot Record with a backup copy. This may become necessary if the Master Boot Record becomes infected with a virus. FDISK/MBR is not destructive in any way unless the computer has a third-party boot program installed. These programs are found frequently in older systems with hard drives larger than 540MB installed in them.

ATTRIB.EXE

ATTRIB.EXE is a utility that can be used to change the attributes of a file or group of files. Attributes include Read-Only (r), Archive (a), Hidden (h), and System (s). To apply attributes, add a plus sign in front of the letter corresponding to the attribute. To turn off an attribute, add a minus sign in front of the attribute's letter. To process all of the files in subdirectories, add the /s switch.

An interesting dilemma that you may come across is if you ever try and "unhide" a hidden file that also has the system attribute set. For example, let's say you wanted to remove the hidden attribute to the IO.SYS file (a file required to boot your system in to DOS and Windows 95). You cannot simply type ATTRIB IO.SYS –h. If you do, you'll get an error message stating that you cannot reset a System file. If you try and remove the System attribute first, by typing ATTRIB IO.SYS –s, you'll get an error message that you can't reset a hidden file. It would appear to be impossible to reset a hidden, system file. The trick to this is changing both of the attributes by typing ATTRIB I0.SYS –s –h. This will simultaneously remove both the system and hidden attributes.

Windows-Based Tools

Windows provides some additional tools and some extensions of the DOS-based tools. The tools discussed here are:

- ScanDisk
- Defragmenter
- Device Manager
- System Monitor
- Conflict Troubleshooter
- System Editor
- Control Panel

QUESTIONS AND ANSWERS

To make . . .	Use the command . . .
C:\AUTOEXEC.BAT hidden and read-only	attrib c:\autoexec.bat +h +r
C:\AUTOEXEC.BAT unhidden	attrib c:\autoexec.bat –h
C:\AUTOEXEC.BAT system, read-only, not hidden, and archive	attrib c:\autoexec.bat +s +r -h +a
All files in the root directory with a SYS extension, system, read-only, not hidden, and archive	attrib c:*.sys +s +r -h +a
All files in the C:\INFO directory read only	attrib c:\info +r
All files in the C:\INFO directory and all subdirectories	attrib c:\info+r /s

■ System Applet

■ Registry Editor

ScanDisk

Windows ScanDisk, which is shown in Figure 12-6, is nearly the same as the DOS-based ScanDisk. It is capable of detecting and fixing most drive corruption problems that could exist. ScanDisk is capable of fixing errors that it finds without any special parameters, unlike the DOS-based ScanDisk, which requires a /fix switch in order for it to be able to fix problems it finds. ScanDisk operates more efficiently if you close all applications prior to running it. Clicking on Start, Programs, Accessories, System Tools accesses the ScanDisk utility.

FIGURE 12-6

ScanDisk can be used to detect and fix most drive corruption problems

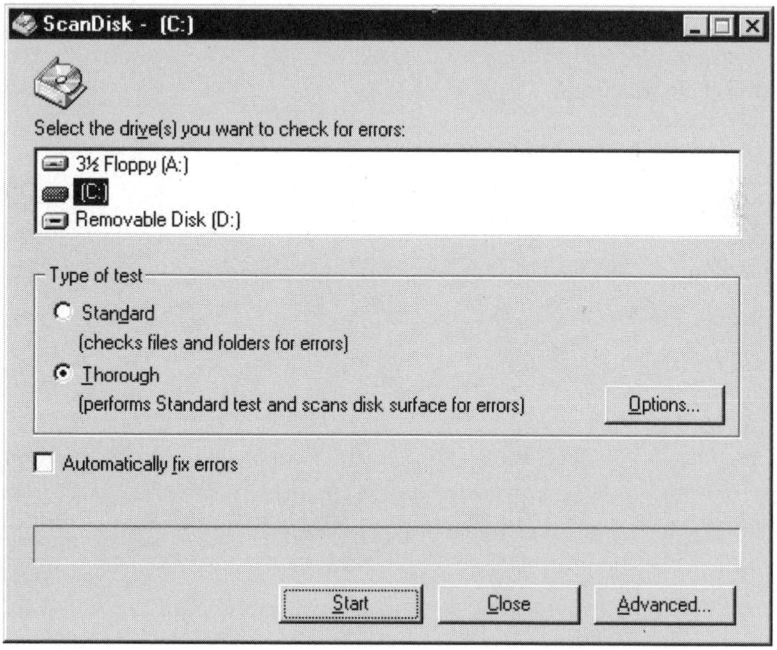

DEFRAG.EXE

Windows DEFRAG is capable of reorganizing the layout of hard disk drives in the same fashion that the DOS-based DEFRAG does. DEFRAG runs more efficiently if all applications are closed prior to running it and after SCANDISK has been run on the drive. The DEFRAG utility is accessed by clicking on Start, Programs, Accessories, System Tools.

Device Manager

Device Manager is a utility that is provided with Windows 95 and Windows 98. Device Manager lists all of the devices that are installed in the system and their properties, as shown in Figure 12-7. You can access Device Manager by double-clicking System in the Windows 95/98 Control Panel and selecting the Device Manager tab.

FIGURE 12-7

Device Manager lists all of the devices that are installed in the system and their properties

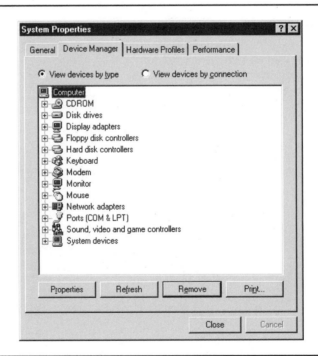

System Monitor

System Monitor is a utility that can be used to track the performance of your Windows 95 or Windows 98 system. Additionally, it can also track your network performance. The utility monitors individual components and resources and displays real-time statistics in a graph format on your screen. The following list shows some of the items that you can track with System Monitor:

- Dial-Up Adapter
- Disk Cache
- File System
- Kernel
- Memory Manager
- Microsoft Network Client
- Microsoft Network Server

Conflict Troubleshooter

Conflict Troubleshooter is a utility that is provided with Windows 95 that can be used to help resolve conflicts between two or more devices. A conflict can occur when two devices attempt to claim the same resource (for example, IRQ Address, I/O Port Address, or DMA Channel). In a perfect world, Plug-and-Play (PnP) is supposed to "automagically" prevent conflicts from occurring. As such, you may need to manually change a resource for a device. Conflict Troubleshooter automatically starts whenever the system starts and aids you in resolving a conflict between devices.

SYSEDIT.EXE

SYSEDIT.EXE, the System Configuration Editor, is a utility that is provided with both Windows 3.x and Windows 95/98. SYSEDIT.EXE, which is shown in Figure 12-8, helps you to easily edit the system configuration files.

FIGURE 12-8

SYSEDIT is a tool that enables you to edit the system configuration files from one easy interface

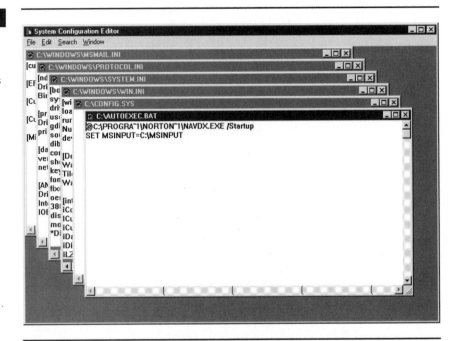

The files that SYSEDIT.EXE enables you to edit are:

- SYSTEM.INI
- WIN.INI
- CONFIG.SYS
- AUTOEXEC.BAT
- PROTOCOL.INI
- MSMAIL.INI

Control Panel

The Control Panel, shown in Figure 12-9, is a utility that can be used to change the settings of the system. By double-clicking any icon that is listed, you can change the properties that are associated with that icon. Note that each system has some core icons such as "Add New Hardware" and

The Control Panel provides
a method of modifying the
configuration of the
computer

"Add/Remove Programs," but icons that are available vary according to
what is installed on the system.

System Applet

The System applet provides information about the computer such as the
version of the operating system, the processor that is installed on the
computer, and the amount of memory that is installed. Also contained
within the System applet is a tab for the Windows 95/98 Device Manager.
Double-clicking the System icon in Control Panel allows access to the
System Properties. Alternatively, you can access the System properties by
right-clicking on My Computer and selecting Properties.

Registry Editor

The Windows 95 Registry Editor, as shown in Figure 12-10, is the most powerful tool in Windows 95. Be extremely careful when using the Registry Editor. Nearly any setting of the system can be changed within the Registry Editor. You will not be warned if a change you are making could negatively affect the system. To access the Registry Editor:

1. Click on the START button.

2. Select the RUN command.

3. Type **REGEDIT** and press ENTER. (Since REGEDIT.EXE is an executable file, you don't have to specify the .EXE on the end of the file name).

FIGURE 12-10

The Windows 95 Registry Editor is capable of changing nearly any setting on the computer

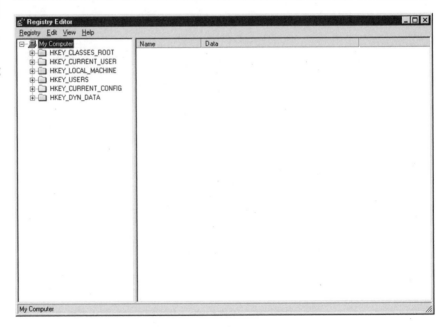

The Windows 95 Registry Editor can be used to change any of the settings of the system that are stored in the registry. The Registry Editor can cause irreparable harm without any warning. Fortunately, if you "tweak" a setting in the registry and your system no longer boots correctly, Windows 95 makes a backup of your current registry every time you successfully boo into Windows 95. The backup files are SYSTEM.DA0 and USER.DA0. Using your Emergency Boot Disk, you can boot to DOS, delete the existing registry files and replace them with the backup files if your system won't start as a result of an incorrect registry setting.

The Windows 95 registry replaces the configuration files found in DOS and Windows 3.*x* such as the AUTOEXEC.BAT, CONFIG.SYS, WIN.INI, and SYSTEM.INI. These files are still supported in Windows 95 for backward compatibility with old DOS and 16-bit Windows applications. The Windows 95 registry is a database of configuration values that is split into two different files. The first is *SYSTEM.DAT* that handles all hardware and software settings. The second is *USER.DAT* that handles user specific settings such as wallpaper settings, color schemes, and profiles. The Windows configuration files (USER.DAT and SYSTEM.DAT) are hidden, read-only files located in the Windows directory. The data from these two files is categorized into sections called *Subtrees* or *Keys*. Table 12-2 illustrates the six registry keys found in Windows 95 and the function of each key.

TABLE 12-2		

Key	Function
Hkey_local_machine	Manages hardware settings
Hkey_current_config	Stores hardware profiles
Hkey_classes_root	Manages file linkings and associations
Hkey_dyn_data	Buffers hardware settings into RAM for faster access
Hkey_current_user	Manages system settings for the current user

Windows 95
Registry Keys

CERTIFICATION OBJECTIVE 12.07

Installing and Configuring DOS Applications, and Potential Problems in Windows 95

Most DOS-based applications can simply be run from within Windows 95 without any difficulties. There are some cases where it is beneficial to make some changes to the configuration of these applications.

Setting Memory

Many DOS programs require that a specific amount of memory be available to the program. Even though there is ample memory available, the programs may attempt to directly access the memory, in which case they can be led to believe there is no memory available. To correct this problem, open the properties for the shortcut to the application that you are dealing with and select the Memory tab, as shown in Figure 12-11. Adjust the memory configuration to the amount the application requires.

Setting Screen Size

Some applications can be difficult to use when they are run in a windowed mode. To change the screen size in which an application is run, select the Screen tab of the Shortcut Properties dialog box, shown in Figure 12-12. From the Screen panel, adjust the initial size to whatever you desire. Remember that a full-screen application can always be forced into windowed mode by pressing ALT-ENTER.

Determine Whether to Display the Win95 Toolbar

Some applications do not perform well when the Windows 95 Toolbar is displayed. In some cases of applications that were not specifically designed for use with Windows 95, the toolbar may cover vital parts of the application. To prevent the toolbar from displaying, uncheck Display Toolbar from the Screen panel of the Shortcut Properties dialog box.

FIGURE 12-11

The Memory tab of the
Shortcut Properties dialog
box can be used to specify
how much memory is given
to an application

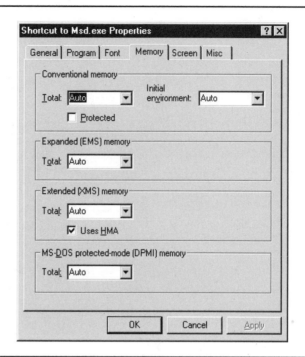

Enable/Disable Dynamic Memory Allocation

Enabling dynamic memory allocation permits Windows 95 to automatically
give an application memory when it needs it and take memory away when
the application is not using it. This is good in most cases, but some older
applications expect a certain amount of memory to be there, and it may
cause problems when it is not. To disable dynamic memory allocation,
uncheck Dynamic Memory Allocation from the Screen panel of the
Shortcut Properties dialog box.

Illegal Operations Error

Illegal operations, in short, occur when an application attempts to access
hardware or memory directly. Windows 95 limits the direct access of any

The Screen tab of the Shortcut Properties dialog box can be used to specify the display mode in which an application starts

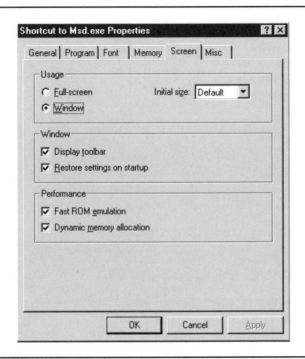

hardware by applications and will repeatedly cause illegal operations in the event that the application attempts this. The best solution to an application that frequently causes illegal operations errors is to force the application to run in MS-DOS mode. Applications can be forced to run in MS-DOS mode by clicking the Advanced button from the Program panel of the Shortcut Properties dialog box, as shown in Figure 12-13. If MS-DOS mode is then checked, the application automatically enters MS-DOS mode (after warning you to save all your work in other applications).

Application May Quit and Windows 95 Stops Functioning

In the event that an application stops functioning, it can frequently hang the entire system and cause the system to appear to be non-functional. Follow the procedures in Exercise 12-2 to remedy this problem.

FIGURE 12-13

The Advanced Program Settings dialog box can be used to force an application to run in MS-DOS mode

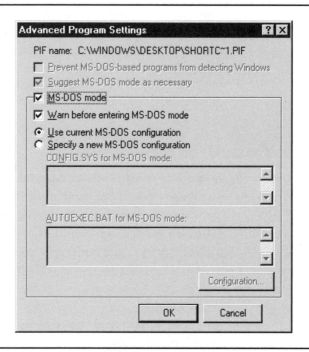

EXERCISE 12-2

Closing a Program That Is Not Responding

1. Press CTRL-ALT-DEL to invoke the Close Program dialog box.

2. Choose the application that is not responding from the list of current applications.

3. Click End Task. This returns the system to a functioning state in many cases.

4. If after a few minutes the system does not return to its previous stability, reboot the system. This should return it to normal operation.

CERTIFICATION OBJECTIVE 12.08

Viruses and Virus Types

Viruses have unfortunately become a part of everyday computer life. Any device that can receive data from another device is susceptible to being infected with a computer virus. Viruses are very dangerous problems that plague computing today. They can cause anything from critical data loss to the annoying message that pops up every few minutes. Viruses can come from nearly anywhere, but are usually created by someone with malicious intentions. Purchasing and installing a good virus scanning/removing application is the best solution to the virus problem.

What are Viruses?

A virus is any program that is designed with the intention of doing harm to a computer. Viruses can result in anything from damaging your computer's hardware to making a siren blare every day or two. The most common result of viruses is a loss of data of some sort. If your system appears to be operating in a manner that you don't expect it to, you should scan it for viruses.

Sources

Viruses are in most cases created by persons with the intention of doing harm to other persons' computers. On some occasions, viruses can be created by an unintentional error of a programmer, although this is extremely unlikely. Viruses can be contracted from a variety of sources including:

- The use of pirated software (something "unheard" of in the computing world, right?)
- Networks
- Shareware and Freeware applications downloaded from the Internet
- Diskettes from untrusted people (such as from a customer sending you information)
- E-mail (The only way to contract a virus from an email message is if you download and open an attached application or executable file.)

FROM THE FIELD

The Cost of Viruses to the World

One can only speculate what goes on in the mind of a demented virus creator. Do they think they are being clever? Funny? Brilliant? What? Perhaps in their own little worlds, they are achieving some kind of goal. But in the real world, they are costing the computing society much more than they can comprehend.

Lost corporate time trying to fix these as well as rebuilding that which they destroy is almost incomprehensible. A destructive virus costs companies collectively more than the biggest armed bank heist in history. I wonder if the creators of these know what their creations are costing people. In the near future, the laws should change on these and make them severe felonies.

Money is not the only factor in this damage. Many users out there are not sophisticated enough to be armed with the absolute latest virus checkers, if they are even armed at all. I think of an 80-year-old who is writing his life story and gets zapped by one of these and Bam!, down the drain. Or even for those who are sophisticated enough to have virus checkers, they may not update them regularly.

Viruses are bad news. They can totally destroy your data as well as hardware. Most of you have probably spent tons of time configuring your system and you would hate to have to re-install everything. The moral: Make sure that you and those whose PCs you work on have the latest patches from a reputable virus prevention software company.

—*Ted Hamilton, MCSE, MCP, A+ Certified*

Spread

Viruses can be spread whenever a computer makes contact with another computer, directly or indirectly. For example, if you download a file from the Internet, the file could be infected with a virus, which could in turn infect your computer. Or, you could infect your computer by opening a file your friend gave you on a floppy disk. Boot sector viruses do not even require that you open a file. If you insert a floppy disk infected with a boot sector virus into your computer and reboot without removing the disk, when the system attempts to boot from the floppy, it will find the boot sector virus and copy it to your local boot device (usually the C: drive).

How To Determine Presence

In most cases, the presence of viruses is fairly difficult to detect without a virus detection application. Virus detection applications are available for sale, and are made by many different software companies. Two of the more popular virus applications are McAfee's VirusScan (http://www.mcafee.com) and Symantec's Norton AntiVirus (http://www.symantec.com).

Removal

Most virus detection packages include the ability to remove the virus from the system. By running the virus removal software, most viruses can be removed. In the event that the software is unable to remove the virus, using the FDISK.EXE and FORMAT.COM utilities from a known virus-free boot disk will remove any viruses.

Prevention

Many of the popular virus detection applications also have the capability to scan the system for viruses and detect/clean any that they find. In addition, some of the more progressive software can automatically check each file as it is opened, and scan any files as they are downloaded. The following list contains several prevention methods to protect against contracting a computer virus:

- Don't use pirated software.
- Don't open or copy a file from a diskette without first scanning the file with a virus protection program.

- Don't download and open attachment(s) you receive via e-mail without first scanning the attachment(s) with a virus protection program.

- Don't leave diskettes in the floppy drive. As mentioned above, a boot sector virus can be transferred from a diskette to your system if you reboot the system with an infected diskette in the floppy drive.

Payload

Payload refers to the effects, either intended or accidental, of a virus. The payload can be benign, meaning it will not cause any harm to your system. Examples of benign payloads include viruses that pop up messages on your computer screen at certain times of the day, or perhaps change the color of your screen once per month. These viruses are more of an annoyance than a threat. Malignant viruses, however, deliver destructive payloads. Examples of malignant payloads span the range from viruses that alter data in a document file to viruses that cause physical damage to your hardware.

Many viruses may first appear to be benign, running quietly in the background causing no problems for an indefinite amount of time. Often, however, they are waiting for a trigger event, such as a certain time of day, or a specific date. When this trigger event occurs, the virus could execute a piece of code that was previously dormant, and that code could act completely different from the original behavior observed before the trigger date. For this reason, it is important to take steps to immediately remove any virus from your system as soon as you detect the virus, no matter how harmless it seems to be.

Types of Viruses

There are many different types of viruses that ultimately cause harm to the overall computer, but all exhibit some individual, specific traits. The virus types discussed here are:

- Boot Sector Virus
- Master Boot Record Virus
- File Virus

- Memory Virus
- Macro Virus
- Hoax Virus

Boot Sector Virus

A boot sector virus stays resident by infecting the boot sector of the computer. Each time the system is booted, it is re-infected from its own boot sector. Any time a floppy disk is inserted into the drive, the floppy's boot sector is infected. If a machine is booted from—or even if an infected floppy disk is left in the floppy drive when the system is rebooted—that computer will then be infected. Since all disks contain a boot sector, the floppy disk does not even have to be a boot disk. A boot sector virus can reside on a data disk just as it could on a boot disk.

Master Boot Record Virus

A Master Boot Record (MBR) virus infects the first physical sector of all affected disks. On a hard disk drive, the MBR—as well as the partition table—is located on Side 0, Track 0, Sector 1. MBR viruses are spread in the same way as a boot sector virus, by booting from an infected floppy. MBR viruses usually cause a loss of files that are on a hard drive, and are usually difficult if not impossible to recover from.

File Virus

A file virus is perhaps the most common type of virus. File viruses either replace or attach themselves to executable files. Most commonly, these files will infect .COM or .EXE files, but they have been known to attach to .DLL, .SYS, .DRV, .BIN, .OVL, and .OVY files as well. Most file viruses spread by loading themselves into memory and attaching to any other files that are executed while the virus is active. Executing any infected program will allow the virus to load itself into memory.

Memory Virus

Memory viruses are viruses that execute and stay resident in memory. Memory viruses usually do not spread themselves, but are carried along with other viruses. Often, these viruses are stand-alone executables, and must be run through some action of the user. To get a user to run such a virus, they are often disguised as useful or entertaining applications. The program that is executed to get a user to install a virus is known as a *Trojan Horse*. Trojan Horse programs usually run an entertaining application in the foreground, while in the background, they are actually loading a virus into memory.

Macro Virus

Macro viruses are viruses that attach themselves to documents in the form of macros. These macros can infect all of the other macros on the system, and all new documents created on the system. Macro viruses most commonly infect Microsoft Word and Microsoft Excel documents, but have the possibility of showing up in any application that includes the ability to create macros.

One of the most widely publicized macro viruses of recent times was the Melissa virus in early 1999. Melissa was a Microsoft Word macro virus, sent as an e-mail attachment. When the attachment was opened, if the user allowed Word to execute the macro, Melissa would automatically send 50 copies of itself out through the user's e-mail program. When recipients of this e-mail opened the document, Melissa would repeat the process. Although Melissa was not a virus that could damage local files or interfere with the operations of the users' computers, the exponential growth of e-mail traffic each time a new set of recipients would run the program caused a severe slowdown in e-mail servers around the world.

Hoax Viruses

Hoax viruses are just that, hoaxes. The most common hoax virus began with the title of "Good Times," and has resurfaced under many other names. These virus hoaxes are usually sent as e-mail warnings not to open any e-mails of these titles. In the event that you receive any e-mail similar to this please notify the sender that it is a hoax, and ignore it. If you question whether or not an e-mail might be a hoax virus, you should check the Symantec AntiVirus Research Center's Hoax Page at http://www.symantec.com/ avcenter/hoax.html, or the McAfee Virus Information Center Hoax Page at http://vil.mcafee.com/ villib/hoax.asp before forwarding on the "warning."

Hybrid Viruses

Some viruses are hybrid combinations of two or more of the virus types listed previously. It is quite common for a boot sector virus to also contain elements of a Master Boot Record virus. Michelangelo is a well-known example of this type of virus. Michelangelo infects the DOS boot sector of floppy disks, and the MBR of the first physical hard drive in a system. Michelangelo spreads from infected floppy disks, and if an infected computer is booted on March 6 of any year, the virus will destroy the first 17 sectors of the first 256 cylinders of the hard drive by overwriting it with random data from memory.

CERTIFICATION SUMMARY

In this chapter, we have examined many of the common errors that you can receive while working on a computer running DOS, Windows 3.*x*, or Windows 95. In addition, we have detailed many of the causes and solutions of these problems and discussed some of the common tools that can be used to repair them.

The information covered in this chapter is vital not only to your successfully navigate the A+ Exams, but also to successfully resolve common errors found in DOS, Windows 3.*x* and Windows 95/98. It would be highly recommended to familiarize yourself with the utilities listed previously, particularly the DOS utilities of FDISK, FORMAT and ATTRIB and the Windows utilities of ScanDisk, DEFRAG, and Device Manager. It may not be a happy realization, but FDISK and FORMAT can, as a last resort, resolve nearly all operating system problems.

✓ TWO-MINUTE DRILL

❑ The SETVER utility can be used to make applications think that they are running on the version of DOS that they want to be running on.

❑ The most common cause of the "Error in CONFIG.SYS line XX" (where XX is a number) error is a missing file.

❑ Both Windows 3.x and Windows 95/98 require that the HIMEM.SYS driver be loaded in order to access High Memory.

❑ If Windows gives you an "Unable to initialize display adapter" error, you should use the Windows setup utility to change the adapter type.

❑ Any time Windows 95 encounters an error, it automatically starts the system in safe mode.

❑ The most common and usually easiest solution to startup or boot problems is to rerun the setup utility that shipped with your operating system.

❑ The message "No Operating System Found" indicates that there is either something wrong with the hard drive of the system or the boot files have been corrupted.

❑ General protection faults (GPFs) can be caused by nearly anything, and can almost be considered a catchall for errors.

❑ The Microsoft Diagnostics utility can be used to provide information about the system. This information can be valuable in determining if a workstation is capable of being upgraded.

❑ DEFRAG is a utility that can be used to reorganize a hard disk drive.

❑ ATTRIB.EXE is a utility that can be used to change the attributes of a file or group of files.

❑ The Windows Device Manager lists all of the devices that are installed in the system and their properties.

❑ Be extremely careful when using the Registry Editor, as nearly any setting of the system can be changed within it and you will never be warned if a change you are making could negatively affect the system.

❑ Enabling dynamic memory allocation permits Windows 95 to automatically give an application memory when it needs it and take memory away when the application is not using it.

❑ Illegal operations, in short, occur when an application attempts to access hardware or memory directly.

❑ The best solution to an application that frequently causes illegal operations errors is to force the application to run in MS-DOS mode.

❑ A virus is any program that is designed with the intention of doing harm to a computer. The best defense against virus infection is to purchase a good virus scanning/removing application.

❑ Memory viruses are viruses that execute and stay resident in memory.

❑ A boot sector virus stays resident by infecting the boot sector of the computer.

❑ MBR viruses are spread in the same manner as boot sector viruses.

❑ Macro viruses are viruses that attach themselves to documents in the form of macros.

❑ The most common hoax virus began with the title of "Good Times," and has resurfaced under many other names.

SELF TEST

The following Self Test questions will help you measure your understanding of the material presented in this chapter. Read all the choices carefully, as there may be more than one correct answer. Choose all correct answers for each question.

1. After upgrading your computer to a newer version of DOS, an older application displays the error message 'Incorrect DOS version.' What should you do to run this application?

    A. Revert to the previous version of DOS.

    B. Add an entry for the application to the application version-table.

    C. Use the SETVER command.

    D. Contact the support line for the application.

2. After clicking on the icon for your word processing application, Windows 3.*x* reports the following error message: 'invalid working directory.' What should you do first?

    A. Check the path statement in the AUTOEXEC.BAT file.

    B. Run SCANDISK.

    C. Check the properties for the program group.

    D. Check the properties for the program item icon.

3. Your PC running Windows 95 cannot connect to the network. You have verified the physical connection is good and the

NIC (network interface card) indicates a link. What should you try next?

    A. Check the version of Windows 95 (version A or version B).

    B. Check the network protocols.

    C. Run the Windows 95 setup utility.

    D. Run the System Monitor utility.

4. You suspect that you have contracted a computer virus. Which will not be affected by the virus?

    A. The System BIOS.

    B. Files stored on a floppy diskette.

    C. Files stored on your hard drive.

    D. The Boot Sector.

5. What log can be used to troubleshoot a Windows 95 installation problem?

    A. DEVICE.LOG

    B. BOOT.LOG

    C. SETUPLOG.TXT

    D. BOOTLOG.TXT

6. Windows 95 automatically creates a backup copy of the Registry files during the boot process. What file extension is used for the backup copies?

    A. DAT

    B. DA0

    C. BAK

    D. REG

7. The majority of the Windows 95 configuration information is stored in:

   A. AUTOEXEC.BAT and CONFIG.SYS

   B. Hkey_localmachine and Hkey_dyn_data

   C. USER.DAT and SYSTEM.DAT

   D. WIN.INI and SYSTEM.INI.

8. To prevent subsequent changes to the file README.TXT, you would run which command?

   A. ATTRIB +A README.TXT

   B. ATTRIB +R README.TXT

   C. ATTRIB –R README.TXT

   D. ATTRIB +H README.TXT

9. What is the most likely cause of POST 201 error?

   A. Memory

   B. Keyboard

   C. Motherboard

   D. Floppy Drive

10. Which of the following memory managers is required for Windows 3.x to access extended memory?

    A. EMM386.EXE

    B. EXTMEM.SYS

    C. HIGHMEM.SYS

    D. HIMEM.SYS

11. What two files comprise a Windows 3.x permanent swap file?

    A. SPART.PAR and SWAP.PAR

    B. 386SPART.PAR and SPART.PAR

    C. 386SPART.PAR and SWAP.PAR

    D. 386SWAP.PAR and SPART.PAR

12. Which applet located in the Windows 95 Control Panel is used to create an Emergency Repair Disk?

    A. FirstAid

    B. System

    C. Add/Remove Programs

    D. Live Update

13. Which Windows 95 utility can be used to scan and repair hard disk surface errors?

    A. SCANDISK

    B. DEFRAG

    C. CHKDISK

    D. FORMAT

14. You suspect your Master Boot Record has been infected with a virus. What utility and switch can be used to restore the Master Boot Record?

    A. FDISK /REPAIR

    B. MBR /REPAIR

    C. FDISK /MBR

    D. FORMAT /MBR

15. Which Windows 95 Control Panel applet contains a tab for Device Manager?

A. Devices

B. System

C. Network

D. Conflict Troubleshooter

16. What is the executable file name that launches the Windows 95 Registry Editor application?

A. REGEDIT32.EXE

B. REGEDIT.COM

C. REGEDT32.COM

D. REGEDIT.EXE

17. What Windows 95 Registry Key is responsible for storing Hardware Profile information?

A. Hkey_Localmachine

B. Hkey_Current_Config

C. Hkey_Hardware_Profiles

D. Hkey_Current_User

18. What term is used to describe the effects of a virus?

A. Payload

B. Load

C. Devastation Factor

D. The Fujitsu Scale

19. Which of the following Windows 95 utilities can be used to track individual system components and resources?

A. Task Manager

B. Network Task Manager

C. System Monitor

D. System Resource Meter

20. Where are the Windows 95 configuration files (SYSTEM.DAT and USER.DAT) stored by default?

A. \WINDOWS\SYSTEM directory

B. \WINDOWS\SYSTEM32 directory

C. \WINDOWS\REGISTRY directory

D. \WINDOWS directory

21. The default Windows 95 location for the Defrag and Scandisk programs is:

A. Control Panel, System, Device Manager

B. Programs, Accessories, System Tools

C. Programs, System Tools

D. Run, Programs, System Tools

22. Which of the following is a new utility included with Windows 95?

A. Print Manager

B. Program Manager

C. Device Manager

D. Control Panel

23. The Windows 95 Registry sections are referred to as what?

A. Classes

B. Subkeys

C. Keys

D. Folders

24. What switch is used with the DOS 6.x version of ScanDisk to automatically fix any errors that are found?

A. /F

B. /FIX

C. /R

D. /REPAIR

25. Which of the following are valid types of viruses? (Choose all that apply.)

    A. Boot Sector Virus

    B. Track Zero Virus

    C. Macro Virus

    D. System Cache Virus

    E. Memory Virus

13

Networks

I n this chapter we will discuss networking capabilities such as the sharing of disk drives as well as print and file services. We will talk about accessing the Internet, its basic functions including downloading files, e-mail, and the Web, and what they can do for you.

CERTIFICATION OBJECTIVE 13.01

Networking Capabilities of DOS and Windows

Both DOS and Windows, with the appropriate networking software installed, are capable of sharing files and printers with other computers on the network. Also, with additional software installed, users can access resources available on other computers in places such as the Internet.

Sharing Disk Drives

The sharing of disk drives is the most basic networking concept. Sharing disk drives is exactly what it sounds like—when drives are shared, other users are given the ability to access the files that you have stored on your drives. Depending on the particular operating system you are using and the permissions you have set on the files, users could read, add, modify, or even delete files located on your drive.

To be able to share printers or folders, or to access shared printers or folders on another Windows operating system, you must have the Microsoft Networking Service installed. In addition, the systems that need to be able to communicate must both be running a common protocol, such as TCP/IP, NetBEUI, or IPX/SPX. These options are all configurable under the Network applet of the Windows Control Panel.

Most users would not want to share out their entire drive. Fortunately, sharing files does not require providing global access to your entire system. In practice, if you choose to share your entire drive, you are actually sharing out the root folder of that drive in the DOS/Windows world. Suppose you wish to share only information found in the DATA directory of your C: drive. You could define a network share, named DATA, that provides access to all files and folders under the C:\DATA directory, without providing access to all other files on your drive.

In both DOS and Windows, adding a $ (dollar sign) to the end of a share name prevents the share name from showing up when users are browsing the network (in Windows 95/98, browsing the network takes place whenever a user clicks on the *Network Neighborhood* icon). If, for example, you renamed your DATA network share to DATA$, the share would be invisible to the casual network browser. To use the hidden share, you would have to tell the user the UNC name.

Network shares in DOS/Windows are accessed through a common naming scheme known as the Universal Naming Convention (UNC), which is formatted as follows:

```
\\servername\sharename
```

Further, using the UNC to locate a file would follow the format:

```
\\servername\sharename\path\filename
```

For example, if you were trying to access the PAYROLL.XLS spreadsheet located on a server named HR, under the DOCUMENTS\SPREADSHEET directory of the share FINANCE$, you would find the file at the following UNC:

\\HR\FINANCE$\DOCUMENTS\SPREADSHEET\PAYROLL.XLS

Sharing Print and File Services

DOS, Windows 3.*x*, and Windows 95/98 are all capable of sharing files and printers with other users on the network. Each operating system has specific methods of sharing these devices. Refer to the operating system's directions for sharing printers and files. Windows 95/98 provides for two different network security schemes, referred to as *user-level* and *share-level* security.

Share-Level Security

Share-level security, also known as password-protected shares, assigns passwords to resources rather than users. Often, there will be multiple passwords for different levels of access. Share-level security assigns a password to a resource, but does not require a specific user account. Depending on the password entered, there may be different levels of access. For example, some users have read-only access to a directory share. They use PASSWORD1 to access that share. Other users need to have full control, so that they can write files as well. They would know the full control password, PASSWORD2. A user's permissions are dependent on which password they use to access a resource.

User-Level Security

User-level security, also referred to as access permissions, provides a mechanism to define different levels of permissions to individual user accounts for various shared resources. Any user who accesses a resource is required to have a unique username and password to access that resource. User-level security is a much more secure model than share-level security. User-level security allows an administrator to track the specific users who access a network resource. With share-level security, you can see that a resource is being used, but there is no easy way to associate the activities with a specific user.

Installing Software

Each workstation that will be communicating on the network must have network software installed on it. This software should include drivers for the NIC, client software that allows the computer to communicate on the network, and software that allows the client software to communicate on the network using the correct protocol.

Network Type and Network Card

DOS, Windows 3.*x*, and Windows 95/98 are capable of communicating on nearly any type of network, so long as the correct network card and drivers are installed. The installation procedures for the network card and drivers provided by the manufacturer should be followed. In Windows 95/98, most network adapters, protocols, and services are installed through the Network applet of the Control Panel (Start | Settings | Control Panel | Network).

You should not install protocols, adapters, or services to your system unless they are in use on the networks you will need to access. Extra network components can slow down the access from your PC to the rest of the network, and in some cases, unused components could cause unwanted network traffic, slowing down your entire corporate network.

Whenever installing network drivers, installing network cards, or configuring file and printer sharing, the manufacturer's procedures should be followed.

CERTIFICATION OBJECTIVE 13.02

The Internet and Setting Up a System for Internet Access

In a period of just a few years, the Internet has been transformed from something that only a select few knew about to something only a select few don't know about. The Internet has become something that many people depend on for their day-to-day work. It is important that you have a good working knowledge of the Internet, some of its most basic functions, and how they apply to you.

TCP/IP

Transmission Control Protocol/Internet Protocol (TCP/IP) is very robust and commonly associated with UNIX systems. It has become the standard for the Internet, as well as the networking industry. TCP/IP is actually a suite of protocols with each protocol in the suite having a specific purpose and function. At the time of its origin, TCP/IP was designed to contend with inferior networking conditions. An ability to reroute packets was therefore built into this protocol. When setting up a system to access the Internet, your only protocol choice is TCP/IP because it is the only protocol that can be used to access the Internet. Networks running IPX/SPX that do not have TCP/IP installed on each client workstation require an IPX to IP gateway to convert IPX packets to IP before they can be sent out to the Internet.

Various services for TCP/IP communicate over *service ports*. TCP/IP client programs connect to TCP/IP server programs using a specific service port. For example, HTTP, the protocol used by Web browsers to connect to Web servers, connects by default through the HTTP service port 80. Table 13-1 is a compilation of common TCP/IP service ports. The complete list of TCP/IP service port standards is available in RFC-1700 from the Internet Engineering Task Force (IETF) home page at http://www.ietf.cnri.reston.va.us/rfc/rfc1700.txt.

TABLE 13-1 Common Service Ports	**Service Name**	**Port Number**	**Purpose**
	FTP	21	File Transfer
	Telnet	23	Telnet Terminal Connection
	SMTP	25	Simple Mail Transport Protocol
	WWW-HTTP	80	World Wide Web Hypertext Transfer Protocol
	POP3	110	Post Office Protocol 3
	NNTP	119	Network News Transfer Protocol
	HTTPS	443	Secure Hypertext Transfer Protocol

FROM THE FIELD

Web Pages for the Professional Upgrade and Repairperson

Here are some great Web pages that have to do with the A+ certification, hardware repair, and upgrades. Take the time to check them out. There is a huge amount of good information on them.

- Where to get a job once you get A+ certified:
http://www.computerjobs.com

- First-rate info on the A+ exam:
http://www.comptia.org

- A great place to find last-minute study tips for many different certifications:
http://www.cramsession.com

- Download an A+ practice test:
http://www.stsware.com/aplus.htm

- Download another A+ practice test:
http://www.aplusexam.com/

- Register for your A+ exam:
http://www.sylvanprometric.com/

- Excellent hardware page:
http://www.tomshardware.com

- A good place to find drivers:
http://www.driverguide.com
(Also, keep in mind, the best place to find drivers is the Web site of the device manufacturer.)

- Many, many downloads of all types:
http://www.download.com/

- The Syngress Media Home Page, with downloadable exam demos:
http://www.syngress.com

—Jeffrey Ferris, MCSE

Downloading

Downloading is the process of transferring a file or files from one computer to another. In every instance where a file is downloaded, the transfer is initiated at the computer that will be receiving the file(s). Any time you click on a link in a Web browser and load a Web page, you are downloading a file. Each Web page is contained within a file that the Web browser understands how to process. Once the file is being downloaded, the browser begins to process the file, and displays the contents of the file.

E-Mail

E-mail (electronic mail) is quickly becoming one of the most popular communication methods within offices and beyond. The concept of e-mail is that people are able to send electronic messages to you that are stored on a server for you until you read them. In fact, e-mail is very similar in concept to traditional mail (commonly referred to these days as "snail-mail"). In both e-mail and snail-mail messages are sent to you and are stored at a post office until you receive them. The major difference is that e-mail is delivered electronically, which in turn allows message delivery to occur within seconds.

Sending e-mail utilizes a protocol known as Simple Mail Transport Protocol (STMP). SMTP runs over TCP/IP port 25. SMTP is limited to sending e-mail, not receiving it, as it has no ability to queue messages on the receiving end. Retrieval of e-mail is handled by Post Office Protocol 3 (POP3). With POP3, e-mail will be received and held by your Internet server. Periodically, your client software, such as Microsoft Outlook, Eudora, or Netscape Mail, will check your mailbox on the server, looking for new messages. Any new mail will be downloaded to your local client.

HTML

Hypertext Markup Language (HTML) is the language in which most Web pages are written. HTML is a modular language that is fairly simple to use, and allows for special formatting to be applied to documents without a great deal of work. HTML is what the World Wide Web is based upon. The majority of pages on the World Wide Web are written strictly in HTML.

Officially, the World Wide Web Consortium (W3C) defines the HTML standards. At the time of this writing, the current W3C HTML standard was HTML 4. In practice, Microsoft and Netscape drive many of the changes to HTML standards as they implement new technologies with each new release of their Web browsing software. Some of the more advanced features of the recent revision of HTML are grouped into a subset known as dynamic HTML (DHTML). Current HTML specifications from the W3C can be found at http://www.w3.org. Microsoft's Web site (http://www.microsoft.com) and Netscape's Web site (http://www.netscape.com) can provide information on the feature sets of their respective browsers.

HTTP

Hypertext Transfer Protocol (HTTP) is the protocol that is most commonly used to transfer information via a Web browser. By default, standard HTTP communications utilize TCP/IP port 80. HTTP was originally used to transfer HTML files to computers, but has been adapted to transfer nearly any type of file. HTTP is the most common transfer protocol on the Internet. HTTP is capable of both downloading and uploading, but is rarely used for uploading.

A more secure version of HTTP, called the Secure Hypertext Transfer Protocol (HTTPS), manages security through the use of a standard developed by Netscape known as the Secure Sockets Layer (SSL). By default, HTTPS communications occur over TCP/IP port 443. SSL allows a Web page to send and receive information over a secure, encrypted communication channel through the use of a public and private key encryption system.

FTP

File Transfer Protocol (FTP) is used to download files from an FTP server to a client computer. FTP is much older than HTTP, and was in use prior to the creation of the World Wide Web. FTP is fairly fast and is connection-oriented, meaning that it attempts to verify that files transferred using FTP have not been corrupted during the transfer. FTP is much faster than HTTP for downloading files.

In addition to downloading files, FTP has the ability to upload files. Uploading is the process of transferring files from one computer to another. Unlike downloading, *uploading* is always initiated from the computer that is sending the files. By default, FTP communicates over TCP/IP port 21.

NNTP

Network News Transfer Protocol (NNTP) is the protocol used on the Internet for posting and reading to Usenet newsgroups. NNTP replaced the original Usenet protocol, called UNIX-to-UNIX Copy Protocol (UUCP) a few years ago. On the backend, NNTP servers, such as those you might find at your ISP, manage the network of collected Usenet newsgroups and postings. On the end-user side, reading and posting to newsgroups requires NNTP client software. Basic client software is often included with Web browsers, such as Netscape and Internet Explorer, but more advanced newsreader software is also available to extend the capabilities beyond that of your Web browser. By default, NNTP communicates over TCP/IP port 119.

DNS

Whenever you are visiting a Web page, or using any other Internet service, for that matter, you can access it by typing in a simple *domain name*. Thinking back to the basics of TCP/IP, you will remember that every computer on the Internet is accessed via a unique, numeric IP address. So how are you able to access these sites with domain names if TCP/IP networks are based on unique numeric identifiers? This is where *Domain Name System (DNS)* comes in to play.

All computers connected to the Internet are required to have a unique IP address in order to be able to communicate on the Internet. DNS is used to resolve the alphanumeric names, known as *Fully Qualified Domain Names (FQDN)*, into the IP addresses that the computer is able to understand. All of this is done behind the scenes without any user intervention required. A good example of this can be seen in Figures 13-1 and 13-2, where we display the Syngress Media, Inc. home page using the domain name and by using the IP address that is assigned to it. As you can see, the pages are identical.

FIGURE 13-1

The Syngress Media, Inc. home page displayed using the domain name

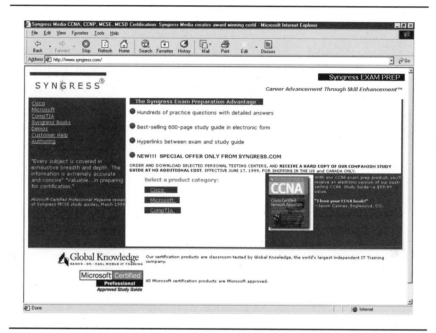

FIGURE 13-2

The Syngress Media, Inc. home page displayed using the IP address

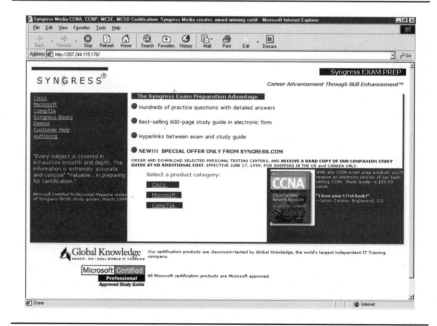

The master database of DNS-to-IP mappings is maintained by the Internic (http://www.networksolutions.com). The Internic registry database assures that multiple organizations cannot register the same domain name. Domain name registrations are handled, for the most part, on a first-come, first-served basis. For example, suppose you own a company in Texas named Track Zero Systems, and someone in Colorado owns a company named Track Zero Technology. You want to register trackzero.com as your domain name, but you discover that Track Zero Technology has already registered that domain name. Since there cannot be a single domain name assigned to two separate organizations, you will have to register a different name, such as track-zero.com or trackzerosystems.com instead.

ISP

An Internet Service Provider (ISP) is a company that provides access to the Internet. Most ISPs provide dial-up access through modems, but in many cases, they also provide access through higher-speed digital leased lines. In general, any company that provides access to the Internet for customers can be considered an ISP. By saying "customers," we mean that the people are paying for the service. A company that gives their employees Internet access through a private bank of modems is usually not considered an ISP.

Dialup Access

An ISP usually provides dialup access to its customers. Dialup access is a method of providing access to the Internet using a phone line and a modem. Windows 95 and Windows 98 both support SLIP and PPP for dialup Internet access. SLIP and PPP are explained in more detail following the installation instructions for Windows 98 Dialup Networking.

Enabling dialup access with Windows 95 and Windows 98 requires the installation of a number of important network components, including the Dialup Networking communications component, a dialup adapter, the TCP/IP protocol, and a modem. Follow the steps of Exercise 13-1 to set up Dialup Networking under Windows 98. The exercise assumes you have already followed the manufacturer's instructions for the successful installation of your modem.

<table>
<tr><td>

</td><td>

Setting up Windows 98 for Dialup Internet Access
Section I: Adding the Dialup Network Communications Component

1. Start the Add/Remove Programs applet from the Control Panel (Start | Settings | Control Panel | Add/Remove Programs).

2. From the Add/Remove Properties window, click the center tab, Windows Setup.

3. In the Components window, highlight Communications and click the Details button.

4. In the resulting Communications box (see Figure 13-3), select the Dialup Networking check box, and click OK.

5. Click OK on the Add/Remove Programs Properties box. You may be prompted to insert your Windows 98 disk. When the system is done copying files, you will need to reboot your computer.

</td></tr>
</table>

FIGURE 13-3

Installing the Dialup
Networking
Communications
Component

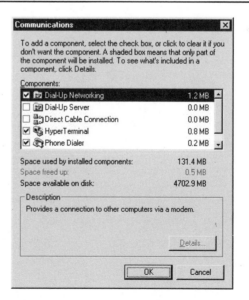

Section II: Configuring the Network Components

1. Start the Network applet from the Control Panel (Start | Settings | Control Panel | Network).

2. On the Configuration tab, you will need the Dialup Adapter and the TCP/IP Protocol, as shown in Figure 13-4. *Note: You may have additional components listed on the configuration tab. Do not delete these components, or you may be removing parts of your system needed for other types of network communication.* If these components are already installed, you may cancel from this box and skip to Section III. If these components are not installed, complete the remainder of this section.

3. To install the Dialup Adapter, click Add. In the resulting Select Network Component Type box, double-click on Adapter.

4. In the Select Network adapters box, choose Microsoft from the Manufacturers column. Next, select Dialup Adapter from the Network Adapters column (see Figure 13-5). Click OK.

FIGURE 13-4

The Windows 98 Network configuration tab after installing the components required for dialup networking

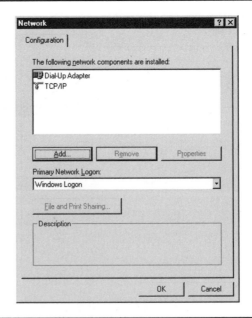

FIGURE 13-5

Installing the Dialup
Adapter

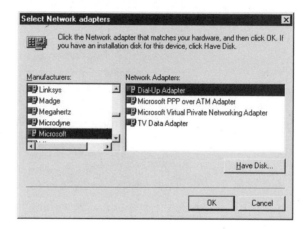

5. You should now be back to the Network Configuration tab. Again, click Add. In the Select Network Component Type box, double-click on Protocol.

6. In the Select Network Protocol box, choose Microsoft from the Manufacturers column. Next, select TCP/IP from the Network Protocols column (see Figure 13-6). Click OK.

FIGURE 13-6

Installing TCP/IP

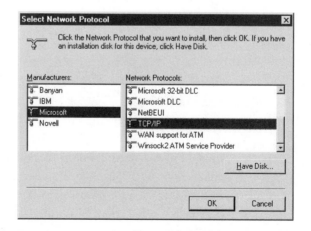

7. You should be back to the Network Configuration tab. The Dialup Adapter and TCP/IP should now appear in the components list, as in Figure 13-4. Click OK. The system may prompt you to insert your Windows 98 disk. When the system is done copying files, you will be prompted to reboot your computer. This completes the configuration of the network components.

Section III: Adding a Dialup Networking Connection

1. Open the Dialup Networking folder under the My Computer icon on your desktop.

2. Double-click the Make New Connection icon.

3. In the first box, type a name for the new connection, such as My ISP. In the Device drop-down box, select the modem you wish to use when making this connection. Click Next.

4. In the next box, enter the area code and phone number of the ISP you wish to dial. Click Next.

5. The next box tells you the name of your new dialup networking connection. Click Finish.

6. The new connection named My ISP, now shows up in the Dialup Networking folder. Double-click the My ISP icon, enter your username and password, and click connect to establish a connection (see Figure 13-7), or right-click and select Properties to explore other settings for this connection.

This completes Exercise 13-1. You should now be able to connect to your ISP using Dialup Networking.

SLIP

Serial Line Internet Protocol (SLIP) was originally designed to provide a dialup connection method for TCP/IP-based UNIX systems. In fact, the only protocol that can run over SLIP is TCP/IP. The phone line, generally thought of as a serial connection, provides the physical media for this IP connection. SLIP, although still used in limited areas, does not have the flexibility of the PPP protocol. SLIP cannot utilize DHCP, nor can it provide error detection. SLIP, therefore, requires more work on the client side for basic configuration. However, because of the limited feature set of SLIP, it requires much less overhead than PPP.

FIGURE 13-7

Connecting to a dialup
network

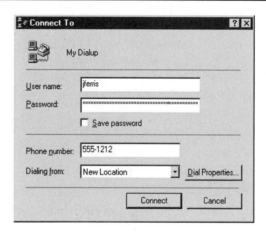

PPP

Point to Point Protocol (PPP) is a serial communication protocol, providing
a communication standard for linking two network devices over a standard
serial link. Typically, this involves connecting a personal computer via
standard phone line to a server in a remote location, such as when
connecting your home computer to your ISP. PPP is a full-duplex protocol
that, while commonly used over standard copper phone lines, can also be
used on other types of physical media including twisted-pair cables or
fiber-optic lines. PPP can even be used for satellite transmission. It uses a
variation of High-Speed Data Link Control (HDLC) for packet
encapsulation.

Even though SLIP requires less overhead, PPP is preferred over the
earlier SLIP connectivity standard because it can handle synchronous as well
as asynchronous communication. PPP can share a line with other users, and
it provides error detection that SLIP lacks. PPP can also provide for
automatic IP addressing, either via the Dynamic Host Configuration
Protocol (DHCP) or through an address pool, whereas SLIP requires
manual entry of an IP address. DHCP can be used to assign a unique IP
address to a TCP/IP client, as well as for setting many other configuration
options, such as the DNS, default gateway, and subnet mask.

Unlike SLIP, which supports only IP, PPP is not limited in protocol
support. PPP provides the flexibility to add support for other protocols

through software upgrades. Even though Microsoft's implementation of PPP includes only native support for TCP/IP, NetBEUI, and IPX, other implementations of PPP make it possible to run additional protocols, such as DECNet or AppleTalk.

PPP can simultaneously transmit multiple protocols across a single serial link, eliminating the need to set up a separate link for each protocol. PPP is ideal for interconnecting dissimilar devices such as hosts, bridges, and routers over serial links.

Configuring a Modem

In order for a computer to have dialup access, a modem must be installed on the system. The modem should be installed according to the modem manufacturer's instructions. After the modem is installed correctly, the dialup connection must be configured according to the specifications your ISP provides for you. Review Section III of Exercise 13-1 for the generic process involved in setting up a new dialup connection to your ISP.

Configuring a Web Browser

When a Web browser is first started, there are some basic configuration steps that should be taken. In most cases, you will not be required to perform these configurations, but they will complement the Web browser and add a great deal of functionality. The settings that should be configured include a default startup Web page, the user's e-mail address, and the user's SMTP server. Figure 13-8 demonstrates some of the common Web browser settings as they would be entered into Microsoft Internet Explorer 4.0.

E-Mail Setup

When configuring an e-mail application, you are usually required to provide some information such as e-mail address, user's full name, POP3 server, and SMTP server. The POP3 and SMTP settings should be provided to you by the ISP. Figure 13-9 provides an example of the Properties dialog box used for Microsoft Outlook Express. Figure 13-10 shows the Servers panel of this dialog box.

FIGURE 13-8

Microsoft Internet Explorer 4.0 provides an easy configuration interface to enter a default startup page

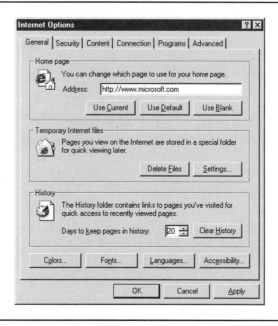

FIGURE 13-9

Microsoft Outlook Express provides a convenient interface to specify the user's full name and e-mail address, in addition to some other optional information

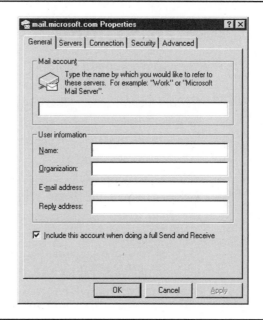

FIGURE 13-10

Microsoft Outlook Express
uses a simple interface to
specify the server
information, such as SMTP
and POP3 servers

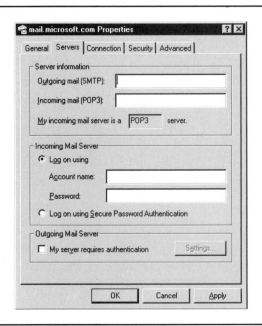

CERTIFICATION SUMMARY

This chapter outlined some of the networking features that can be
integrated with DOS, Windows 3.x, and Windows 95/98. Some of these
features include sharing files and printers, transferring files to and from
remote computers, and viewing Web pages on the World Wide Web.
Network security models supported by Windows 95/98 include user-level
and share-level security.

The Internet provides access to many different types of information,
including e-mail, the World Wide Web, newsgroups, and FTP. Connecting
to various services on the Internet requires the TCP/IP protocol. Client
systems connect to server services over standardized service ports. One of
the ways to connect a computer to the Internet is through dialup
networking. This chapter walked you through setting up a dialup
networking connection under Windows 98.

TWO-MINUTE DRILL

❑ When a Web browser is first started, there are some basic configuration steps that should be taken, including configuring a default startup Web page, the user's e-mail address, and the user's SMTP and POP3 servers.

❑ When folders are shared, other users are given the ability to access the files that you have stored on your drives. Sharing printers allows remote users to print to your printer.

❑ Each workstation that will be communicating on the network must have software installed on it, such as drivers for the NIC, client software that allows the computer to communicate on the network, and software that allows the client software to communicate on the network using the correct protocol.

❑ Whenever installing network drivers, installing network cards, or configuring file and printer sharing, the manufacturer's procedures should be followed.

❑ By definition, each time you load a Web page, you are downloading a file.

❑ In addition to downloading files, the File Transfer Protocol (FTP) has the ability to upload files.

❑ When configuring an e-mail application, you are usually required to provide some information such as e-mail address, user's full name, POP3 server, and SMTP server.

❑ Unlike downloading, uploading is always initiated from the computer that is sending the files.

❑ All computers connected to the Internet are required to have an IP address in order to communicate on the Internet. When using dialup networking, the server computer assigns this IP address to the client workstation.

❑ The Domain Name System (DNS) is used to resolve domain names into the unique IP addresses that the computer needs to locate a host on the Internet.

❑   Most ISPs provide dialup access through modems, but in many cases, they also provide access through high-speed digital leased lines.

❑   Dialup access is defined as access provided to the Internet using a phone line and a modem.

❑   Dialup Internet access through Microsoft Windows 95/98 requires the installation and configuration of a modem, the Dialup Network component, the Dialup Adapter, the TCP/IP protocol, and the definition of a Dialup networking connection.

SELF TEST

The following Self Test questions will help you measure your understanding of the material presented in this chapter. Read all the choices carefully, as there may be more than one correct answer. Choose all correct answers for each question.

1. Which of the following types of network security are supported by Windows 95/98? (Choose all that apply.)

   A. User level

   B. Share level

   C. Password-protected shares

   D. Access permissions

2. TCP/IP clients connect to various services through _____.

   A. Connectors

   B. Protocols

   C. Ports

   D. SOCKS

3. Which of the following is the more secure network security model?

   A. User level

   B. Share level

   C. Password protected shares

   D. All models provide the same level of security

4. What is the standard port used for FTP connections?

   A. 21

   B. 27

   C. 80

   D. 443

5. What is the standard port used for non-secure HTTP connections?

   A. 21

   B. 27

   C. 80

   D. 443

6. You are trying to access a file named CONFIG.DOC on a server named STANDARDS, under the share WORKSTATION, and the directory WINDOWS98. Keeping in mind the UNC standard, what is the proper syntax for accessing this document?

   A. \\STANDARDS\CONFIG.DOC

   B. \\STANDARDS\WORKSTATION\ CONFIG.DOC

   C. \\STANDARDS\WORKSTATION\ WINDOWS98\CONFIG.DOC

   D. \\STANDARDS\WINDOWS98\ WORKSTATION\CONFIG.DOC

7. You have a share named DOCS on a server named HR. How do you make DOCS a hidden share?

   A. Change the share name to DOCS$.

   B. Change the share name to $DOCS.

   C. Change the server name to HR$.

   D. Change the share name to DOCS#.

8. Which of the following components are NOT required to make a dialup Internet connection to an ISP? (Choose all that apply.)

   A. Modem
   B. Dialup Adapter
   C. TCP/IP protocol
   D. None of the above

9. Which of the following protocols can run over SLIP? (Choose all that apply.)

   A. PPP
   B. TCP/IP
   C. IPX
   D. NetBEUI

10. Which of the following protocols can run over PPP? (Choose all that apply.)

    A. SLIP
    B. TCP/IP
    C. IPX
    D. NetBEUI

11. A Fully Qualified Domain Name (FQDN) is translated into an IP address by what service?

    A. SLIP
    B. PPP
    C. DHCP
    D. DNS

12. The Secure Hypertext Transfer Protocol uses what to provide encryption services?

    A. RAS
    B. Certificates
    C. PKI
    D. SSL

13. Which of the following is the protocol required for dialup Internet connectivity?

    A. TCP/IP
    B. Microsoft Dialup Adapter
    C. SLIP
    D. IPX

14. Which of the following protocols are used in sending e-mail? (Choose all that apply.)

    A. POP3
    B. SMTP
    C. SNMP
    D. NNTP

15. Which of the following protocols are used in retrieving e-mail? (Choose all that apply.)

    A. POP3
    B. SMTP
    C. SNMP
    D. NNTP

16. Which of the following protocols is used in posting and reading newsgroup articles?

    A. POP3
    B. SMTP
    C. SNMP
    D. NNTP

17. In Windows 95/98, where do you go to add the TCP/IP protocol?

    A. Add/Remove Programs applet in the Control Panel

    B. System properties

    C. Device manager

    D. Network applet in Control Panel

18. In Windows 95/98, where do you go to add the Dialup Networking component?

    A. Add/Remove Programs applet in the Control Panel

    B. System properties

    C. Device manager

    D. Network applet in Control Panel

19. Which of the following resources can be shared through Windows networking? (Choose all that apply.)

    A. Printers

    B. Folders

    C. Modems

    D. Network connections

20. Which protocol is associated with browsing the Web?

    A. HTML

    B. HTTP

    C. FTP

    D. WWW

    Scenario: You wish to make the DOCUMENTS directory on your C:\ drive available to the other users in your workgroup. Your computer name is WORKSTATION. You are running the Windows 98 operating system. All of the workstations in your organization are running TCP/IP and NetBEUI. The TCP/IP configuration information is statically assigned to each client. The following five questions present additional qualifiers to this scenario.

21. What service would make the TCP/IP client configuration in your organization easier to manage?

    A. SNMP

    B. DHCP

    C. DNS

    D. IPX

22. Which protocol(s) must be installed on your workstation to allow it to communicate with other clients on the network? (Choose the best answer.)

    A. Only TCP/IP

    B. Only NetBEUI

    C. You must have both TCP/IP and NetBEUI installed.

    D. You may have either TCP/IP or NetBEUI installed.

23. If you do not care who is able to access the DOCUMENTS share, and want an easy-to-administer security method, which would be your best choice?

    A. User level

    B. Access permissions

    C. Password-protected shares

    D. None of the above

24. If you want to be able to track which users are accessing your documents share, which network security method should you choose?

   A. User level

   B. Password-protected shares

   C. Share level

   D. None of the above

25. On your computer, you have a file named TIMESHEET.XLS in the PROJECT2 directory under the DOCUMENTS share. How would a user on the network access this file?

   A. \\WORKSTATION\PROJECT2\ TIMESHEET.XLS

   B. \\WORKSTATION\DOCUMENT$ \TIMESHARE.XLS

   C. \\WORKSTATION\DOCUMENTS \PROJECT2\TIMESHEET.XLS

   D. \\WORKSTATION\DOCUMENTS \TIMESHARE.XLS

A

Self Test
Answers

Chapter 1 Answers

1. Which of the following types of system memory is the fastest?

   A. DRAM

   B. ROM

   C. SRAM

   D. WRAM

   C. SRAM. Cache memory is made up of much faster memory called "SRAM" (Static RAM). Starting with the 80386 CPU, DRAM could not work as fast as the CPU and therefore created a bottleneck that slowed down the CPU. SRAM, which runs up to ten times as fast, could not practically replace DRAM since it also costs ten times as much.

2. Which type of floppy disk supported a 1.2MB capacity?

   A. DSDD 3 1/2"

   B. DSDD 5 1/4"

   C. DSHD 3.1/2"

   D. DSHD 5 1/4"

   D. DSHD 5 1/4". The original single-sided 5 1/4" drives had a capacity of only 180 kilobytes. Double-sided drives and disks were later introduced, which increased the storage to 360KB. The 5.25" disks eventually reached a capacity of 1.2MB as technology refined both the accuracy of the drives and the surface of the disk.

3. You have been instructed to install a computer in the library for the new multimedia-based book inventory system. This computer will need to support 256 colors in graphics mode. Which of the following monitor specifications could you use to achieve this? (Choose all that apply.)

   A. SVGA

   B. CGA

   C. EGA

   D. VGA

   A, D. SVGA and VGA. The very first VGA adapter cards were limited to only 16 colors, but competitors quickly designed video adapters to display up to 256 different colors at any given time from a virtually unlimited palette. Resolution was improved to 720 × 400 in text mode and 640 × 480 in graphics mode. Super Virtual Graphics Array (SVGA) hit the market and brought us higher resolution standards of 800 × 600, 1024 × 768 (sometimes known as XGA, or eXtended Graphics Array), 1280 × 1024, and even higher. Depending on the amount of RAM included on the video adapter, the number of colors could be 256 or more.

4. You are watching a junior technician as he prepares to upgrade the modem and video card in a customer's computer. In order to

protect the computer from ESD, he places the computer on the rubber mat and connects one of the two wires to the computer. He then takes the second wire and connects it to the ground pin on the electrical outlet. Next, he puts on his ESD wrist strap and attaches a wire from his strap to the mat. Where did this technician go wrong in protecting the computer from ESD?

A. He should have connected both wires to the ground pin found on any electrical outlet.

B. He should have connected his wrist strap directly to the computer chassis.

C. He should have connected the second wire from the chassis to the ground pin on the power supply.

D. He obeyed all of the recommended ESD prevention practices.
   D. He obeyed all of the recommended ESD prevention practices. In order to properly ground yourself to the computer, you must place the chassis on an ESD mat and connect one of the two wires to the computer. The second wire is connected to a ground pin that can be found on any electrical outlet. To ground yourself, wear an ESD wrist strap and attach the wire from the strap to the mat, or to a common ground.

5. After you have upgraded the processor in a client's computer from a Pentium 75 to a Pentium 166, you notice that the BIOS reports the processor as a Pentium 133.

Which of the following are possible reasons for this? (Choose all that apply.)

A. Misconfigured external speed jumper

B. Improper setting in the SETUP program for the processor

C. Misconfigured CPU clock speed jumper

D. Misconfigured CPU DMA

   A, C. Misconfigured external speed jumper and misconfigured CPU clock speed jumper. Once you have powered your computer on after the processor upgrade, the system BIOS will most likely tell you the speed of the processor. If the reported processor speed is not identical to the actual speed of the processor, you have misconfigured the processor and/or bus settings. Be aware that overclocking a processor can cause system instability and can actually overheat and burn the processor, rendering it useless.

6. What is the physical difference between a SIMM and a DIMM module?

A. A SIMM has 45 pins, whereas a DIMM has 72 pins.

B. A SIMM has two rows of 45 pins, whereas a DIMM has one row of 168 pins.

C. A SIMM has one slot on the bottom, whereas a DIMM has two slots on the bottom.

D. A SIMM has 72 pins, whereas a DIMM has 168 pins.

D. A SIMM has 72 pins, whereas a DIMM has 168 pins. Where the SIMM had a single row of 72 connecting fingers (pins), each making contact on both sides, the DIMM has two rows of connecting fingers, one row on each side, for a total of 168 connections.

7. What type of connector will a VGA or SVGA monitor have?

   A. A male DB-9 connector

   B. A male DB-15 connector

   C. A female DB-9 connector

   D. A female DB-15 connector
   B. A male DB-15 connector. If it is a monochrome, Hercules, CGA, or EGA monitor, it is a digital monitor and will have a male DB-9 connector that plugs into a digital adapter. If it is a VGA or SVGA monitor, it will have a male high-density DB-15 connector that plugs into an analog adapter also located in the back of the computer.

8. DIN-5 connectors are generally found where?

   A. On serial ports

   B. On AT keyboards

   C. On parallel ports

   D. On SCSI ports
   B. On AT keyboards. There are two types of keyboard connectors in use, the DIN-5 connector and the Mini DIN-6 connector. DIN-5s are generally found on AT style keyboards

and have a round port with 5 pins. The Mini DIN-6 came out with the release of IBM's PS/2 machine, and also has a round port but differs in that it has 6 pins with one square plastic positioning pin.

9. What is the Standard Device Assignment for IRQ 6?

   A. Floppy controller

   B. Hard disk controller

   C. COM port 1

   D. Math Co-Processor
   A. Floppy controller. The standard device assignment for IRQ 6 is the floppy disk drive controller. Under most conditions, you will never have a choice to use this IRQ for other devices in your system, as it will be pre-assigned to the floppy controller during operating system install.

10. What is the standard IRQ for Serial port (COM2)?

   A. IRQ 2

   B. IRQ 3

   C. IRQ 4

   D. IRQ 7
   B. IRQ 3. COM2 and COM4 both use IRQ 3. COM1 and COM3 both use IRQ 4. It is imperative that you memorize these standard COM port assignments for the exam. Knowing these standards will also help you in the field as a technician.

11. Which of the following IRQs are cascaded? (Choose all that apply.)

    A. 1

    B. 2

    C. 8

    D. 9

    E. 11

    B, D. 2 and 9. When the AT computer was designed, a second interrupt controller was added to provide 8 more interrupt lines (numbered 8 to 15). This second interrupt controller had to deliver its signal through the primary controller on the motherboard, and IRQ 2 was chosen for this task ("cascade" from second controller). Unfortunately, some earlier cards had already made plans to hook into the IRQ 2 signal wire, so on newer machines with the second controller, that signal wire now leads to IRQ 9 on the second controller.

12. Which of the following is the port address (hex range) for serial port COM2?

    A. 3F8-3FF

    B. 2E8-2FF

    C. 2F8-2FF

    D. 378-37F

    C. 2F8-2FF. In addition to standard IRQ settings, you need to know the standard I/O address settings for the exam. You should have the standard IRQ and I/O port addresses for COM1 – COM4 committed to memory.

13. Which device uses the port address (hex range) of 378-37F?

    A. Serial port COM1

    B. Serial port COM2

    C. Parallel port LPT1

    D. Parallel port LPT2

    C. Parallel port LPT1. This is a common port address that should be memorized for the exam and for real-world experience. Every computer has a parallel port, and by default, you will find this parallel port using the port address of 378-37F.

14. You have been called out to investigate why a user's game can no longer play sounds. The sound card was configured at the factory with standard settings. You are configuring the game to use these same settings. You configure the I/O address of 320, the IRQ of 5, and the DMA channel of 1. Will these settings work correctly?

    A. No, because the I/O address is not the standard sound card I/O address assignment.

    B. No, because the IRQ is not the standard sound card IRQ assignment.

    C. No, because the DMA channel is not the standard sound card DMA channel assignment.

    D. Yes, the sound card should work correctly now.

    A. No, because the I/O address is not the standard sound card I/O address assignment. Creative Labs has been the industry leader in the sound card business, and has set the standard. Typically, sound cards have the following configuration: IRQ 5, DMA 1, and I/O Address 220. These are standard numbers used with SoundBlasters, but as always consult the manufacturer's documentation in case you have one of the esoteric kinds.

15. Which control signal in serial communications tells the receiver that the data terminal (computer) is ready?

    A. TxD

    B. RxD

    C. DSR

    D. DTR

    D. DTR. The Data Terminal Ready control signal is used to tell the receiver that the data terminal (computer) is ready. This is different from the Data Set Ready (DSR) control signal, which is used to tell the receiver that the data communications equipment (usually a modem) is ready.

16. Which type of connector does a video adapter card have?

    A. A socket DB-9 connector

    B. A socket DB-15 connector

    C. A pin DB-9 connector

    D. A pin DB-15 connector

    A. A socket DB-9 connector. DB-9 connectors are distinguished by their trapezoid appearance. There are 9 pins in the connector, 5 pins in the bottom row and 4 pins in the top row. This type of connector is most commonly

used for video display devices and serial ports. Joystick connectors are also trapezoidal in their appearance; however, these connectors are 15-pin DB-15 connectors.

17. Which type of connector is commonly used to attach an unshielded twisted pair (UTP) cable with a network card?

    A. RJ-11

    B. RJ-14

    C. RJ-45

    D. RJ-10

    C. RJ-45. RJ-45 connectors are most commonly used to attach an unshielded twisted pair (UTP) cable with a network card. These connectors have 8 pins, and are similar to the RJ-11 connector. This is the most common connector used on an Ethernet network.

18. What are the characteristics of Wide Fast-20 SCSI? (Choose all that apply.)

    A. Transfer speeds at a maximum of 40 MBps

    B. 16-bit bus

    C. Transfer speeds at a maximum of 20 MBps

    D. 32-bit bus

    A, B. Transfer speeds at a maximum of 40 MBps, and 16-bit bus. SCSI-3 is the latest SCSI standard issued by ANSI. The first variant of SCSI-3 goes by the name Fast-20 SCSI or Ultra SCSI. It was developed for high-performance SCSI devices and comes on an 8-bit bus with a 20 MBps transfer rate. The second variation on a 16-bit bus goes by the labels Wide Fast-20 SCSI and more currently Wide Ultra SCSI. Its characteristics are a 16-bit bus with transfer speeds at a maximum of 40 MBps.

19. How many pins are there on a 16-bit Wide-SCSI connector?

   A. 72 pins

   B. 50 pins

   C. 68 pins

   D. 42 pins
   C. 68 pins. 16-bit Wide-SCSI requires new cabling; either a second 68-pin cable called the B-cable to be used in conjunction with the A-cable, or a newer single cabling method with 68 pins called the P-cable.

20. What do you have to remember when dealing with SCSI termination?

   A. Always terminate the SCSI adapter.

   B. Remove termination from all devices, except the device at the end of the cable.

   C. Terminate the device closest to the SCSI adapter.

   D. Place a terminator at the end of the cable, and a backup terminator on the first device in the chain.
   B. Remove termination from all devices, except the device at the end of the cable. If only one cable is used (either internal or external), the terminator on the adapter itself must be enabled or installed. If both cables are in use, the adapter terminator must be removed or disabled.

21. What do you need to do if you have a bootable SCSI device?

   A. Disable the BIOS on the SCSI adapter.

   B. Disable your system BIOS.

   C. Enable SCSI BIOS shadowing in your system's SETUP utility.

   D. Enable SCSI BIOS on your SCSI adapter.
   D. Enable SCSI BIOS on your SCSI controller. With all of your SCSI devices addressed, installed, terminated, and cabled together, it is time to tell the computer about them. The procedure used depends on whether you have a bootable SCSI device installed. If there is a bootable device, you must enable the BIOS on the adapter card. This is performed through a jumper or DIP switch setting that should be listed in the adapter's documentation.

22. When is the only time you should not wear an ESD wrist strap?

   A. When replacing the power supply

   B. When working on a monitor

   C. When replacing a sensitive IC chip, such as a CPU

   D. When using a multimeter
   B. When working on a monitor. The only time that you would not wear the wrist strap is when you are working

with monitors. Never wear a wrist strap when working on monitors as the high voltage section, even with the power turned off or unplugged, may contain a residual charge that can harm you, or possibly even kill you.

23. Which of the following is a numbering system to denote the size of the blade on a Torx screwdriver?

A. #2

B. R2

C. T2

D. *2

C. T2. Torx screwdrivers also use a numbering system to denote the size of the blade, but are given a *T* instead of the pound (#) sign.

24. Which of the following are common voltages that you will find when testing a computer with a multimeter?

A. +2

B. +5

C. +10

D. +12

B, D. +5 and +12. Testing for proper positive output voltages of the power supply is easy—switch the multimeter to a range that will allow the correct voltage to be displayed without going over full-scale (for instance, if your choices for full-scale are 2, 20, or 200 volts, for measuring +12 or +5 volts, use the 20-volt range).

25. What switch is used with the MEM.EXE command to individually list the programs that use up memory and what type of memory is being used?

A. /L

B. /C

C. /list

D. /A

B. /C. The first step is to actually check the system memory configuration by using a special program called MEM.EXE with the /C switch. The /C tells the memory program *to classify*, or individually list the programs that use up memory and what type of memory is being used.

Chapter 2 Answers

1. Which of the following would indicate a memory error on the POST?

A. 1**

B. 2**

C. 3**

D. 4**

B. 2**. Memory problems are also detected when POST runs at boot time. These types of errors are usually preceded by a 2**, again where the ** can be any set of numbers. Check the descriptive message that comes with the error code and proceed accordingly.

2. You have been called out to diagnose a problem with a user's computer. Whenever they attempt to go online, the mouse no longer functions. What is most likely the cause of this problem?

   A. Conflicting DMA channels

   B. Incorrect DMA channel

   C. Conflicting IRQs

   D. Memory error
   C. Conflicting IRQs. If another device is using the same IRQ or I/O address as the mouse, then it probably won't work at all. This is because the results are being returned to the conflicting device. Try checking IRQs and I/O addresses with diagnostic software to ensure that there is not another device using either of these.

3. What is the most common floppy disk drive-related problem reported?

   A. Bad cable

   B. Loose cable

   C. Media problems

   D. Resource conflicts
   C. Media problems. Commonly, what seems to be a floppy drive error is not actually a drive problem but a media error. Floppy disks are susceptible to physical and magnetic corruption, giving the customer the appearance of a bad drive with "Error reading disk" or "Error writing to disk" messages.

4. You have been called to help a customer who has an important report on a floppy disk that cannot be read. You try reading the floppy disk and discover that Windows 95 is asking to format the floppy disk. The user cannot lose the data and warns you not to format the floppy because it already contains data. What should you do in this case?

   A. The floppy is bad. Format it and start again.

   B. Throw away the floppy disk.

   C. Try the floppy in another computer.

   D. Run SCANDISK on the floppy.
   C. Try the floppy in another computer. Sometimes there are drive incompatibilities so that when one drive writes to a disk, another drive can't read it. This is common, for example, when you copy files from one PC and try to read them on another PC that has an incompatible drive. If you encounter this type of a problem, try reading from another disk, preferably one that was written to by the suspect drive, or writing to a second disk.

5. A junior technician was sent out to replace a floppy disk drive on a customer's computer. The technician has called and cannot figure out why the floppy drive does not work correctly. He tells you the floppy drive activity light stays lit the

entire time when the computer is booting. What would you tell him is the problem?

A. This is normal.

B. Insert a floppy to begin the boot process. The floppy drive is waiting for a disk to be inserted.

C. The floppy drive cable is not connected.

D. The floppy drive cable is on backwards.
    D. The floppy drive cable is on backwards. Cabling can also lead to drive problems. If you have just installed a floppy drive and you are experiencing a problem with the drive, such as the drive light won't go out, you probably have the cable on backwards. This is also the case with the hard disk drive cable.

6. You have been trying to fix a problem with a floppy disk drive on a user's computer. What is the easiest way to determine if the floppy disk controller is the problem?

A. Install the floppy disk controller on another computer.

B. Replace the floppy disk controller in the same computer.

C. Try another floppy disk drive to determine if the problem continues.

D. Run MS-DOS MSD to determine if the controller is having errors.
    C. Try another floppy disk drive to determine if the problem continues. However, if you believe that you have a problem controller card, you can test it by installing a second floppy drive.

If you can successfully use the second drive, then the controller probably isn't the problem. Remember, the components of the floppy disk drive subsystem are the floppy drive itself, the cable, and the disk controller. Replace each component one at a time with known good components to determine where the fault lies.

7. How often should you clean the heads of a tape drive?

A. Every day

B. Every week

C. Every month

D. Depends on how many hours the device is in use
    D. Depends on how many hours the device is in use. Tape drives require cleaning based on the number of hours the drive is used. A cleaning cartridge should be used after the recommended number of hours the drive has been in use. Consult the tape drive manufacturer's recommendations for the amount of time between routine cleanings.

8. Which of the following are required to make a CD-ROM drive accessible in DOS? (Choose all that apply.)

A. A device driver

B. A DMA channel

C. A SET entry in the AUTOEXEC.BAT

D. An MSCDEX.EXE entry in the AUTOEXEC.BAT
    A, D. A device driver and an MSCDEX.EXE entry in the

AUTOEXEC.BAT. For a CD-ROM drive to work, you need the device driver to be loaded from the CONFIG.SYS file, and you also need MSCDEX.EXE to be loaded from the AUTOEXEC.BAT file. MSCDEX.EXE allows a CD-ROM drive to be accessed from the command prompt with a drive designator, just as a partition on a hard drive is capable of being accessed.

9. You think that one of your serial ports is not working correctly because it cannot pass information to a serial port-based device. What is the best way to verify this?

A. Call the manufacturer of the device.

B. Use MSD to determine if there are any resource conflicts.

C. Use a loopback adapter to test.

D. Try opening HyperTerminal and typing ATA to verify connectivity.
C. Use a loopback adapter to test. A hardware loopback adapter is a way to test the serial and parallel ports on a system without having to connect to an external device. For example, you can use a serial loopback adapter to verify that a transmitted signal is leaving your serial port and returning through the loopback adapter, verifying that your serial port is working correctly.

10. Which of the following is the standard configuration for a SoundBlaster compatible sound card?

A. I/O address 220, IRQ 7, DMA 1

B. I/O address 320, IRQ 4, DMA 0

C. I/O address 220, IRQ 5, DMA 1

D. I/O address 240, IRQ 3, DMA 1
C. I/O address 220, IRQ 5, DMA 1. The standard settings for a SoundBlaster compatible sound card is an I/O address of 220, an IRQ of 5, and a DMA channel of 1.

11. Which of the following will most likely be found in an AUTOEXEC.BAT file when a sound card is present?

A. SET SOUND=

B. SET TYPE=

C. SET BLASTER=

D. SET AUTO=
C. SET BLASTER=. Sound cards require an environment setting in the AUTOEXEC.BAT file to work correctly. This variable is set with the SET command. The sound card configuration line will be preceded with the following:

```
SET BLASTER=
```

If your sound card does not work, you should verify that this line is present in your AUTOEXEC.BAT file.

12. If you have a network printer that uses the TCP/IP protocol, what will you have to configure? (Choose all that apply.)

A. DNS name

B. IP address

C. Default gateway

D. Subnet mask
B, C, D. IP address, default gateway, subnet mask. When using TCP/IP, you must configure the IP address, subnet mask, and default gateway; and

improper settings could render the printer unable to communicate on the network.

13. Which of the following can you use to determine the COM port an internal modem is using?

   A. MSD

   B. The MODE command

   C. The DEBUG command

   D. The Modems applet in the Control Panel
   A ,B, C, D. MSD, the MODE command, the DEBUG command, and the Modems applet in the Control Panel. Each of these utilities will enable you to view the COM port settings for modems, in addition to gaining more diagnostic and troubleshooting information.

14. Which of the following methods will cause a POST?

   A. A warm reboot

   B. A cold reboot

   C. Using CTRL-ALT-DEL

   D. Holding the shift key down during a warm reboot
   B. A cold reboot. The Power On Self Test (POST) happens every time you cold-boot the computer. A warm boot (pressing the reset button or using CTRL-ALT-DEL) is not a cold boot, and will not perform the POST test.

15. Which of the following errors would correspond with the 3** error code during a POST test?

   A. Memory error

   B. Keyboard error

   C. Motherboard error

   D. Video error
   B. Keyboard error. Keyboard errors usually generate a 3** error code when POST runs at boot time.

16. Which of the following can cause problems for more than one printer at the same time?

   A. Running out of toner

   B. Print server running out of hard disk space

   C. Misconfigured printer

   D. Slow printer
   B. Print server running out of hard disk space. A print server that has run out of hard disk space will no longer have the ability to queue print jobs for every printer and could crash the server until more hard disk space is free. This can be catastrophic, affecting the entire department or company that depends on this print server.

17. Where is the best place to look for more information on a Windows 95 computer if you feel you have a device conflict with your mouse and another device?

   A. System Admin

   B. WinMSD

C. Device Manager

D. Mouse applet in the Control Panel
C. Device Manager. In Windows 95 and Windows 98, you can use Device Manager, located in the System applet in the Control Panel, to quickly determine if you are having resource conflicts between devices in your system.

18. If you have two hard drives and two hard disk controllers in a system, how could you configure them? (Choose all that apply.)

A. One drive as master on the primary controller, and the other drive as a master on the secondary controller.

B. One drive as the slave on the secondary controller, and the other drive as a slave on the primary controller.

C. One drive as a slave on the primary controller, and the other drive as a master on the primary controller.

D. You cannot have two hard disk controllers in the same system because of IRQ conflicts.
A, C. One drive as master on the primary controller, and the other drive as a master on the secondary controller; and one drive as a slave on the primary controller, and the other drive as a master on the primary controller. If you have more than one hard drive in the computer, verify that

the master/slave configuration is correct. You will need to ensure that both hard drives are configured correctly. One hard drive should be set for master, and the other hard drive should be set for slave. This is the case only for hard drives that are chained to the same controller.

19. Which of the following can reduce the number of paper jams in a printer?

A. Adjusting the brightness/contrast for the computer

B. Cleaning the printer often

C. Replacing the ink cartridge

D. Adjusting the print quality
B. Cleaning the printer often. It only takes a small bit of paper to cause the problem, and usually you have to take the printer apart to find it. If you open the printer and find a lot of paper dust, you need to clean the whole unit to ensure that the dust isn't the cause of the problem as well, as dust and dirt can carry a small charge and cause the paper to stick to metal parts just enough to cause a jam.

20. What should you do when you arrive on the scene and notice a monitor that has a distorted flickering image on the screen?

A. Restart the computer.

B. Swap video cards with a known good card.

C. Try the monitor on another computer.

D. Replace the monitor cable with a known good cable.
C. Try the monitor on another computer. If a monitor swap doesn't do the trick, you may have a problem with the cables or the adapter card. First, check that all of the cables are properly seated before attempting to replace them. This includes the power cable, as the power cord probably connects to a power strip.

21. What is most likely the cause when you see garbled characters across the screen during data communication with another computer?

A. An incorrect video driver

B. Incorrect start or stop bits

C. Incorrect error control

D. Resource conflict
B. Incorrect start or stop bits. Another consideration with modem problems is the communication software itself. Ensure that the baud rate, stop bits, parity bits, and communication protocol used are correct for the session that the customer is attempting to establish. The most common symptom for an incorrect configuration is receiving garbage characters after making a connection.

22. Which of the following are ways to determine if a power supply has gone bad? (Choose all that apply.)

A. The computer will not boot.

B. The POST will give you an error.

C. Windows 95 will give you an error.

D. The fan will stop spinning.
A, D. The computer will not boot, and the fan will stop spinning. If the fan is not moving on the power supply while the computer is running, it is a good bet that it is time to clean it with compressed air or replace it entirely. However, if the system does not boot at all, then the power supply is shot and must be replaced.

23. What can slot covers protect a computer from? (Choose all that apply.)

A. Dust

B. Flourescent interference

C. Heat

D. Magnetic interference
A, C. Dust and heat. Most people do not think that a missing slot cover can cause a problem, but your computer knows better. Computers are designed to allow for proper air flow going into and out of the case. Should the air flow become impeded or its route modified, you run the risk of overheating a component in the computer case. Slot covers also protect a computer from letting excessive dust inside the computer.

24. How do you get a POST memory size error to disappear?

A. Restart the computer.

B. Cold-boot the computer.

C. Enter the SETUP program.

D. Hold down the Shift key while restarting the computer.
C. Enter the SETUP program. The memory size error occurs after a memory upgrade. By entering the SETUP program, you are informing the computer that you are aware of the change in memory.

25. What is the cause if a mouse moves sporadically? (Choose all that apply.)

A. Incorrect driver

B. Incorrectly configured mouse

C. Dirty mouse

D. Memory problem
B, C. Incorrectly configured mouse and a dirty mouse. A dirty mouse is the most common problem reported. The problem is that the roller bars inside of the mouse tend to pick up dust and dirt from the track ball when it rolls over a mouse pad. A misconfigured mouse will also move too fast or too slow on the screen.

Chapter 3 Answers

1. What should be your first source for determining which cleaning products to use on a device?

A. The Internet

B. Phone technical support

C. Manufacturer's documentation

D. Lead technician
C. Manufacturer's documentation. Before beginning any preventive maintenance procedures, it is critical that you consult the manufacturer's documentation. Vendors include the information on the proper cleaning materials to use when cleaning or maintaining their components.

2. Which of the following needs to be cleaned regularly? (Choose all that apply.)

A. Hard drives

B. Floppy drives

C. Printers

D. Tape drives
B, C, D. Floppy drives, printers, and tape drives. Components that require special attention are floppy drives, printers, and tape drives. These mechanical devices are used often and require cleaning in order to perform at their peak.

3. When should you clean the heads in a tape drive?

A. Every ten hours of use

B. Based on the manufacturer's suggested guidelines

C. When the software program informs you

D. When the cleaning LED on the face of the unit illuminates
B. Based on the manufacturer's suggested guidelines. The tape drive, unlike the floppy drive, can inform you when the device needs to be cleaned. However, you should not wait for the blinking LED on the tape drive to clean the device; you should

be cleaning the device on a regular basis based on the manufacturer's suggested guidelines.

4. Which of the following is not a recommended liquid cleaning compound for use with computers and components?

A. Isopropyl alcohol

B. Ammonia

C. Denatured alcohol

D. Mild detergent
   B. Ammonia. Various forms of alcohol are frequently used in cleaning computer components, such as isopropyl alcohol and denatured alcohol. These items are generally used to clean contacts and are applied to special disks used for cleaning floppy drive read/write heads. Mild detergent can be used on the outside of the monitor, the computer case, and on keyboards.

5. Which of the following are recommended methods for cleaning contacts and connectors? (Choose all that apply.)

A. A pencil eraser

B. A cotton swab that has been coated with isopropyl alcohol

C. Tweezers

D. A plastic knife
   A, B. A pencil eraser and a cotton swab that has been coated with isopropyl alcohol. Most components can be cleaned with a cotton swab that has been coated with isopropyl alcohol. However, many

manufacturers recommend that you use a pencil eraser to clean the contacts on expansion cards.

6. When should you use a metal knife when working on a computer?

A. When working on a monitor

B. When working on a power supply

C. When removing chips or adapters

D. You should never use a metal knife when working on a computer.
   D. You should never use a metal knife when working on a computer. When you are called upon to remove hardened residue from metal components, you can use a rubber knife to dislodge particles that the vacuum or dust-free cloth could not remove. Never use a metal knife or other metallic object when cleaning the computer or its components, as you can either damage them or cause injury to yourself through electrostatic discharge (ESD).

7. What two cleaning products should be used when cleaning a mouse?

A. Ammonia and water

B. Isopropyl alcohol and water

C. Soapy water and isopropyl alcohol

D. Soapy water and Windex
   C. Soapy water and isopropyl alcohol. Soapy water should be used to clean the rubber ball, and a cleaning swab with isopropyl alcohol should be used to clean the rollers.

8. How can you tell the difference between a tape-drive cleaning cartridge and a regular cartridge?

    A. Cleaning cartridges are white.

    B. Cleaning cartridges are beige.

    C. Cleaning cartridges are dark brown.

    D. You cannot tell the difference between some cleaning cartridges and regular cartridges.

    D. You cannot tell the difference between some cleaning cartridges and regular cartridges. The cleaning cartridge looks exactly like a normal tape cartridge, although some manufacturers use a different color casing (usually white or beige) around a cleaning cartridge to help differentiate it from a normal cartridge.

9. What is the difference between brownouts and blackouts?

    A. Brownouts cause more damage.

    B. Brownouts are for DC current, and blackouts are for AC current.

    C. Brownouts are decreases in power, and blackouts are huge surges of power.

    D. Blackouts are long-term outages.

    D. Blackouts are long-term outages. Brownouts, which are the momentary lapses in power supply, have become more common. Brownouts can cause problems with computer components that are not designed to withstand these events. Blackouts are similar to brownouts, as they are also lapses in power, but they are long-term power outages.

10. How can you completely eliminate noise from a power line?

    A. Use a surge suppressor.

    B. Use a line conditioner.

    C. Use a noise filter.

    D. You cannot completely eliminate noise from a power line.

    D. You cannot completely eliminate noise from a power line. A UPS contains a special filter, called a *noise filter*, that reduces the amount of noise present in electrical current and eliminates magnetic fields caused by noise, thus providing some protection to the components that utilize the current or are nearby.

11. You are moving a set of servers from one room to another. The new server has a UPS unit that can protect every server in the room from line disturbances and power outages. You need to store the individual UPS units that were in the old server room. What should you do with each UPS before you store it?

    A. Discharge the unit.

    B. Do not discharge the unit.

    C. Remove the battery from the unit.

    D. Remove the charging portion of the unit.

    B. Do not discharge the unit. When you need to store a UPS, you must ensure that is has not been discharged. A discharged UPS that is stored for a long period of time may lose some of its capacity to store power or may become unable to accept a charge at all.

12. What is the best way to protect individual computer components from ESD?

    A. Vacuum them regularly.

    B. Use compressed air on them.

    C. Keep them on a low shelf.

    D. Store them in an anti-static bag.
    D. Store them in an anti-static bag. Computer components are very sensitive to ESD and can even be rendered useless. Whenever you store computer components, you must place them in an anti-static bag to ensure their safety from ESD. Anti-static bags are designed so that static build-up is contained on the outside of the bag rather than on the inside, thus protecting the delicate components.

13. What level are the lasers employed in CD-ROM drives?

    A. Level 1

    B. Level 2

    C. Level 3

    D. Level 4
    C. Level 3. The lasers employed in CD-ROM drives are Level 3 laser beams and are of a significantly lower intensity than those employed in construction or scientific applications. As a result, you will not get a severe burn from them but should nevertheless be cautious when working with them.

14. What are the two types of high-voltage equipment labels? (Choose all that apply.)

    A. Warning

    B. Attention

    C. Danger

    D. Caution
    A, D. Warning and Caution. The first type of label is a Warning label that usually informs you of the potential of equipment damage as well as personal injury. The second type of label is a Caution that tells you of possible personal injuries that can occur.

15. When discharging a monitor, what two parts do you need to make contact with?

    A. The power supply and the electron gun

    B. The anode lead and a jumper wire

    C. The jumper wire and the electron gun

    D. The anode lead and the power supply
    B. The anode lead and a jumper wire. To discharge a monitor, you need to have a jumper wire and a screwdriver with a non-conductive handle. You will need to pry the anode lead, which looks like a small suction cup with a wire connected to it, away from the glass inside the monitor.

16. What does MSDS stand for?

    A. Maintaining Standards Developing Safety

    B. Material Standard Disposal Sheet

C. Material Safety Data Sheets

D. Maintaining Standard Disposal Safety
   C. Material Safety Data Sheets.
   Material Safety Data Sheets (MSDS)
   are white pages that contain
   information on any substance that is
   deemed hazardous, most notably
   cleaning solvents. MSDS is required
   by the United States Department of
   Occupational Safety and Health
   Administration, and must be posted in
   prominent locations.

17. Which of the following are results of ESD?
    (Choose all that apply.)

    A. Downtime

    B. Customer dissatisfaction

    C. Line noise

    D. Damaged components
       A, B, D. Downtime, customer
       dissatisfaction, and damaged
       components. Electrostatic discharge
       can damage computer components
       causing downtime and possibly
       creating customer dissatisfaction as a
       result of this downtime.

18. You have just walked into your shop
    across the carpet and as you sit in your
    chair, you feel a shock, but don't see it as
    you reach for your desk drawer. What is
    the amount of voltage that caused this
    shocking sensation you just felt?

    A. Around 30 volts

    B. Around 500 volts

C. Around 3000 volts

D. Around 20,000 volts
   C. Around 3000 volts. When you
   actually feel the shock caused by ESD,
   that energy transfer is over 3,000 volts.
   Even worse, if you can see a spark
   when ESD occurs, that discharge is in
   the vicinity of 20,000 volts.

19. What is another possible result of ESD on
    a component?

    A. Degradation

    B. Contamination

    C. Transformation

    D. Polarization
       A. Degradation. A component that
       suffers from degradation may continue
       to operate for days, or even months,
       before failing entirely and could
       damage other components while it
       is functioning.

20. A humidity level below what percent tends
    to lead to static electricity?

    A. Below 50 percent

    B. Below 20 percent

    C. Below 30 percent

    D. Below 65 percent
       A. Below 50 percent. A humidity
       level below 50 percent tends to lead to
       static electricity. You will notice this
       especially in the winter months, when
       humidity levels are low naturally.

21. Which of the following will not help minimize the amount of ESD in your work area?

    A. Wear steel-toed shoes.

    B. Use an anti-static spray for the carpet.

    C. Wear a wrist strap.

    D. Use anti-static bags.

    A. Wear steel-toed shoes. It's a better idea to wear shoes that contain a rubber sole so that you do not build up any static electricity between yourself and the carpet as you walk around.

22. Which of the following is not recommended for maintaining a hard disk drive? (Choose all that apply.)

    A. Running a utility such as Scandisk on a regular basis

    B. Low-level formatting the drive once a year

    C. Defragmenting the hard disk often

    D. Partitioning the drive often

    B, D. Low-level formatting the drive once a year and partitioning the drive often. Hard drives have a tendency to become fragmented over a period of time or with excessive use and should be defragmented as a part of normal preventive maintenance. Another problem with hard drives is that the disk surface can become corrupted over time. Use a utility such as Microsoft Scandisk to detect and repair corruption errors.

23. You have been called out to help a small company streamline their computer

processes. You are especially interested in their backup routine, which consists of copying their data to a floppy disk and storing this floppy underneath the counter. The information on this disk is critical, and cannot be lost. The information contained on the floppy is only a few kilobytes worth of service records. How can you help them with their backup process?

A. Have them back up their data to a different area of the hard disk to avoid floppy disk wear and tear.

B. Have them copy their data to numerous floppy disks for each day of the week to avoid wear and tear on the same floppy. Store this floppy somewhere other than underneath the counter, preferably where it is free from dust and debris. Use a cleaning disk several times a month to keep the floppy drive heads clean.

C. Purchase a Zip drive and five disks, one for each day of the week. Have them back up the data to the disks and store them somewhere other than underneath the counter, preferably where it is free from dust and debris.

D. Purchase a tape drive, one cleaning cartridge and five cartridges, one for each day of the week. Have them back up the data to the tape and store them somewhere other than underneath the counter, preferably where it is free from dust and debris.

B. Have them copy their data to numerous floppy disks for each day of the week to avoid wear and tear on the same floppy. Store this floppy somewhere other than underneath the counter, preferably where it is free from dust and debris. Use a cleaning disk several times a month to keep the floppy drive heads clean. Media, such as floppy disks are also susceptible to wear and tear. Continual use of the same floppy disks, tapes, or zip disks will increase your chances of physically wearing out the media. In this particular scenario, there was no need to purchase large-capacity backup devices to back up the company's data.

24. Why is it important to vacuum a computer on a regular basis? (Choose all that apply.)

    A. Because dust and debris can cause components to fail

    B. Because it looks more professional

    C. Because dust and debris can create excessive heat inside the computer

    D. Because you should never use compressed air on the inside of a computer
    A, B, C. Because dust and debris can cause components to fail, because it looks more professional, and because dust and debris can create excessive heat inside the computer. These particles can conduct an electrical charge, resulting in possible damage to the delicate electronic components inside. Any air holes in the case should be vacuumed out to remove dust. Cleaning out a customer's computer always makes a great impression.

25. You have a brand new network server that supports hot-swappable components. Which devices can you remove without damaging the computer?

    A. Hard drives

    B. Hard drives and floppy drives

    C. Hard drives and 16-bit ISA cards

    D. You do not know which devices are hot-swappable without referring to the vendor's documentation.
    D. You do not know which devices are hot-swappable without referring to the vendor's documentation. While the newer computer operating systems, especially network servers, enable you to repair them while the computer is still running, it is extremely important that you follow the manufacturer's guidelines to the letter.

Chapter 4 Answers

1. Which of the following are true of the Intel 386 processor? (Choose all that apply.)

    A. The chip has a 32-bit address bus.

    B. The chip does not have an internal math coprocessor.

    C. The chip has a 16-bit address bus.

    D. The chip has a 32-bit data bus.
    A, B, D. The chip has a 32-bit address bus, does not have an integrated math coprocessor, and has a 32-bit data bus. The 386 processor featured a 32-bit

register size, a 32-bit data bus, and a 32-bit address bus and could handle up to 16MB of memory. However, the 386 did not have an internal math coprocessor and users who required heavy calculations had to purchase one separately.

2. Which of the following are true of the Pentium 586 class processors? (Choose all that apply.)

   A. The chip makes use of parallel processing.

   B. The chip has a 64-bit address bus.

   C. The chip has a 64-bit data bus.

   D. The chip has a 32-bit internal Level 1 cache.
      A, B, C. The chip makes use of parallel processing, has a 64-bit address bus, and has a 64-bit data bus. With the 586 chip, Intel named its chip the Pentium chip and introduced several new features and improvements. The first improvement was in the register size and the data bus size, which was doubled to 64-bit. It also doubled the on-board cache size from 8-bit to 16-bit and increased speeds to a range of 60 MHz up to 200 MHz. The Pentium processor also features parallel processing, which is similar to having two 486 chips in one processor.

3. Which processor featured a register size of 32-bits, a data bus of 16-bits, and an address bus of 24-bits?

   A. 80486DX

   B. 80386DX

   C. 80386SX

   D. 80486SX
      C. 80386SX. The 386 processor was also the first instance where there were two versions of the same basic processor, the SX version and the DX version. The 386SX processor came with a 16-bit data bus, a 24-bit address bus, and a 32-bit register size.

4. Of the following, which is the fastest type of RAM?

   A. EDO RAM

   B. DRAM

   C. SRAM

   D. VRAM
      C. SRAM. SRAM is used for a computer's fast cache memory and is also used as part of the RAMDAC on a video card.

5. Which of the following is false concerning WRAM?

   A. It is less expensive than VRAM.

   B. It is dual ported.

   C. It is 25% faster than SRAM.

   D. It is 25% faster the VRAM.
      D. It is 25% faster than VRAM. WRAM, compared to VRAM, is dual-ported and has about 25% more bandwidth than VRAM but costs less.

6. What is the most common type of Main RAM?

   A. EDO RAM

   B. SRAM

   C. DRAM

   D. VRAM
      A. EDO RAM. Extended Data

Output RAM (EDO RAM) is a DRAM memory chip designed for processor access speeds of approximately 10 to 15 percent above fast-page mode processors and reduces the need for Level-2 cache memory. EDO RAM is the most common type of Main System RAM.

7. SIMM memory comes in which of the following sizes? (Choose all that apply.)

   A. 30-pin

   B. 32-pin

   C. 72-pin

   D. 168-pin
   A, C. 30-pin and 72-pin. SIMMs are available as either 30-pin or 72-pin cards, but each card has a different format. The format is broken down as follows:

   `Capacity of the Chip x Data Bits`

8. Which of the following is true about DIMM memory?

   A. DIMMs do not need to be installed in pairs.

   B. DIMMs come in only a 64-bit configuration.

   C. DIMMs do not use parity.

   D. DIMMs come in only 168-pin configuration.
   A. DIMMs do not need to be installed in pairs. Because the Pentium processor requires a 64-bit path to memory, you need to install SIMMs two at a time. With DIMMs, you can install memory one DIMM at a time.

9. Most motherboards manufactured until 1998 were of what form?

   A. AT

   B. ATX

   C. Baby-AT

   D. Baby-ATX
   C. Baby-AT. Most AT-type motherboards manufactured until 1998 were Baby-ATs.

10. Which ROM uses an ultraviolet light of a specific frequency to erase the contents of the ROM?

    A. PROM

    B. EPROM

    C. EEPROM

    D. EEEPROM
    B. EPROM. Ultraviolet light of a specific frequency can be directed through this window for a specified period of time, which will erase the EPROM and allow it to be reprogrammed.

11. Which bus does the Pentium Pro processor use to access the system cache?

    A. Processor bus

    B. Cache bus

    C. Memory bus

    D. Local I/O bus
    B. Cache bus. The cache bus is the bus in which the processor communicates directly with the very fast system cache. Fifth-generation processors, such as all Pentium chips up to but not including the Pentium Pro, use the memory bus to access the system cache.

12. What are the two most common local I/O buses? (Choose two from the following.)

    A. PCI

    B. EISA

    C. VL-Bus

    D. ISA

    A, C. PCI and VL-Bus. The two most common local I/O buses are the VESA Local Bus (VESA) and the Peripheral Component Interconnect (PCI) bus.

13. Which of the following is not true regarding EISA?

    A. It is 32-bits.

    B. It is less expensive than MCA.

    C. It is the bus architecture used in the 386, 486, and Pentium computers.

    D. It is backward compatible with ISA.

    C. It is the bus architecture used in the 386, 486, and Pentium computers. Because MCA was expensive and proprietary, the original companies that developed ISA got together and created a 32-bit card that was not only cheaper, but retained backward compatibility with the 16-bit ISA cards. This type of bus architecture is used in conjunction with 386 and 486 processors, but not with the Pentium processors.

14. Which bus type has a width of 16 bits, and a speed of 8.3 MHz?

    A. EISA

    B. 8-bit ISA

    C. 32-bit ISA

    D. 16-bit ISA

    D. 16-bit ISA. Although 8-bit ISA, 16-bit ISA, and EISA all have the same bus speed of 8.3 MHz, only the 16-bit ISA has a width of 16 bits.

15. What is the bus bandwidth on the PCI bus?

    A. 7.9 MBps

    B. 127.2 MBps

    C. 31.8 MBps

    D. 165.2 MBps

    B. 127.2 MBps. Both the VL-Bus and first generation PCI bus have a bandwidth of 127.2 MBps. The new 2.1 version of PCI has a bus bandwidth of 508.6 MBps.

16. What is the bus size of the PCMCIA bus on most laptop computers?

    A. 8-bit

    B. 16-bit

    C. 32-bit

    D. 64-bit

    B. 16-bit. The Personal Computer Memory Card International Association (PCMCIA), or the less hard to remember PC Card, bus was first created to expand the memory capabilities in small, hand-held computers. The bus itself is about the size of a credit card and is only 16-bit.

17. ISA cards can fit into which types of slots? (Choose all that apply.)

A. ISA

B. VL-Bus

C. PCI

D. EISA
A, B, D. ISA, VL-Bus, and EISA. ISA cards are an exception to the rule and can go into an ISA slot, an EISA slot, or a VL-Bus slot.

18. What does the acronym CMOS stand for?

A. Conditional Metal-Oxide Semiconductor

B. Complementary Metal-Oriented Semiconductor

C. Contemporary Metal-Oriented Semiconductor

D. Complementary Metal-Oxide Semiconductor
D. Complementary Metal-Oxide Semiconductor. CMOS was designed to store the settings used by the BIOS and therefore drastically cut down on the number of times that the user would have to input them.

19. Which of the following is not a type of parallel printer port?

A. ECP

B. PPL

C. EPP

D. Bi-directional
B. PPL. Parallel printer ports come in Unidirectional, Bi-directional, EPP, and ECP.

20. What is the standard interrupt and memory address for COM2?

A. 2 and 02F8

B. 3 and 03F8

C. 4 and 03F8

D. 3 and 02F8
D. 3 and 02F8. The standard COM1 interrupt address is 4 and the memory address is 03F8. The standard COM2 interrupt address is 3 and the memory address is 02F8.

21. Most hard drives have how many bytes per sector?

A. 128KB

B. 256KB

C. 512KB

D. 1024KB
C. 512KB. If you need to calculate the size of a drive, use the following formula:

```
(# of cylinders) * (# of sectors) * (#
of heads) * 0.5 KB
```

The 0.5KB constant is due to the fact that most hard drives have 512 bytes per sector.

22. Which of the following is not required when you have to manually enter information for an older hard disk drive in the BIOS SETUP program?

A. Clusters

B. Cylinders

C. Tracks

D. Sectors

A. Clusters. With older disk drives and BIOS that does not automatically detect hard drive settings, you will have to manually enter hard drive information, which may consist of entering cylinders, tracks, and sectors, all of which should be labeled on the outside of the hard drive.

23. How do you disable the floppy disk drive in the BIOS SETUP program?

A. Set the floppy disk drive to None.

B. Set the floppy disk drive to something other than the actual type of drive installed.

C. Set the primary floppy disk drive to Disabled.

D. You cannot disable the floppy disk drive in the BIOS SETUP program; you must use the operating system to do this.

A. Set the floppy disk drive to None. When installing a floppy drive, you do have the option to disable it. To do this, you must set Drive A to None.

24. A junior technician calls you with a problem on a user's Windows 95 computer. The computer will not boot to the network floppy disk that he has created. What do you instruct the junior technician to do?

A. Remove the floppy disk, boot the computer to Windows 95, enter the Control Panel, and enable floppy disk access.

B. Restart the computer, enter the BIOS setup program, and enable floppy drive access.

C. Restart the computer, enter the BIOS setup program, and put the floppy drive before the hard drive in the boot order.

D. Restart the computer, and hold down the SHIFT key while the memory test is being performed.

C. Restart the computer, enter the BIOS setup program, and put the floppy drive before the hard drive in the boot order. If you have the boot sequence set up for floppy drive, hard drive, and CD-ROM, the computer first goes to the floppy drive. If it can't find what it needs on the floppy drive, it then proceeds to the hard drive, and so on.

25. What are two common types of passwords on computer systems? (Choose all that apply.)

A. Hard drive access password

B. BIOS SETUP password

C. Power-on password

D. ROM shadow password

B, C. BIOS SETUP password and power-on password. A power-on password will require a password in order to complete the boot process every time you restart the computer. You also have the ability on some computers to place a password on the BIOS SETUP program so users cannot alter the contents of the SETUP program.

Chapter 5 Answers

1. In the _____ phase of the EP printing process the photosensitive drum is erased.

    A. Charging
    B. Cleaning
    C. Writing
    D. Developing
      B. Cleaning. The cleaning process removes left-over toner and erases the drum.

2. In the _____ phase of the EP printing process a laser sweeps the entire length of the drum, cycling on and off with respect to the image to be printed.

    A. Charging
    B. Cleaning
    C. Writing
    D. Developing
      C. Writing. The laser writes the image to the drum.

3. In the _____ phase of the EP printing process toner is attracted to the areas of the photosensitive drum that are negatively charged.

    A. Writing
    B. Developing
    C. Fusing
    D. Transferring
      B. Developing. This is the first visible sign that there is an image on the drum.

4. In the _____ phase of the EP printing process the toner that is on the drum is attracted to the paper with the help of the positively-charged transfer corona.

    A. Writing
    B. Developing
    C. Fusing
    D. Transferring
      D. Transferring. The toner is transferred from the drum to the paper because the transfer corona has such a high positive charge.

5. In the _____ phase of the EP printing process the toner is permanently bonded to the paper with intense heat and pressure.

    A. Writing
    B. Developing
    C. Fusing
    D. Transferring
      C. Fusing. The toner is melted or fused to the paper because of the heat and pressure.

6. Which of the following is the most common interface used for printing?

    A. Parallel
    B. IDE
    C. Serial
    D. Network
      A. Parallel. The other methods are used, and networking is increasing, but parallel is still the most common method of connecting a printer to a PC.

7. The most likely cause for random specks of ink on a laser printed page is:

   A. Improper voltage on corona wire

   B. Parallel cable too long

   C. Photosensitive drum dirty

   D. Improper paper type
   C. Photosensitive drum dirty. If the drum is not properly scraped clean in the cleaning phase, then specks or streaks will result.

8. _____ occurs when a portion of the print image from a previous print job is printed again, only not as dark.

   A. Shadowing

   B. Ghosting

   C. Stippling

   D. Image latency
   B. Ghosting. Another printing defect from the cleaning phase. This one occurs because the erasure lamp is not operating properly.

9. _____ is the generic term used to describe a class of printers that squirt ink onto a page in tiny drops.

   A. BubbleJet

   B. DeskJet

   C. InkJet

   D. SquirtJet
   C. InkJet. BubbleJet and DeskJet are the names that Cannon and HP give to their InkJet printers.

10. A _____ cable has a DB-25 male connection on one end and a 36-pin female connection on the other.

    A. Serial

    B. RJ-45

    C. Centronics

    D. Ribbon
    C. Centronics. The description is for a Centronics cable used in parallel printing.

11. The _____ mechanism is responsible for moving the paper from the paper tray, through the printer, and into the output tray.

    A. Motor

    B. Paper feed

    C. Logic board

    D. Power supply
    B. Paper feed. All parts are indirectly involved, but the paper feed is directly responsible for moving the paper.

12. The _____ consists of three main parts: a halogen heating lamp, a rubberized pressure roller, and a Teflon-coated non-stick roller.

    A. Motor

    B. Fuser

    C. Transformer

    D. Power supply
    B. Fuser. Motors, transformers, and power supplies are usually thought of as single-piece parts.

13. Concerning the EP printing process, the primary corona wire has a _____ charge, the transfer corona has a _____ charge, and toner naturally has a _____ charge.

    A. negative, positive, positive
    B. positive, negative, negative
    C. negative, positive, negative
    D. positive, positive, negative
       C. negative-positive-negative.

14. What does PDL stand for?

    A. Printer-Defined Language
    B. Page Description Language
    C. Paper Driver Latch
    D. Printer Device Logic
       B. Page Description Language. Remember that PostScript is a common example of a PDL.

15. A _____ is used to "fire" each pin in a print head so that the pin will impact with the ribbon and the paper to leave a dot.

    A. Capacitive coil
    B. Resistive coil
    C. Solenoid
    D. Spring coil
       B. Resistive coil.

16. A(n) _____ is a type of font in which every character in the font-set is predefined. This makes this type of font easy for a printer to process, but limits the user's options.

    A. Bitmap
    B. PDL
    C. Raster
    D. Outline
       A. Bitmap. All the characters in a bitmap font are predefined on a grid.

17. A(n) _____ is a type of font that is defined as a set of mathematical algorithms. This makes this type of font processor intensive, but increases the user's options.

    A. Bitmap
    B. PDL
    C. Raster
    D. Outline
       D. Outline. Outline fonts are sets of mathematical algorithms that can be modified to generate characters with different properties.

18. Laser printers and jet type printers primarily use a _____ paper feed mechanism to move the paper through the printer.

    A. Tractor feed
    B. Friction feed
    C. Sprocket feed
    D. Continuous form feed
       B. Friction feed. Laser printers use friction feed, paper feed mechanisms.

19. A(n) _____ printer is necessary to print multi-part forms.

A. Laser

B. Dot matrix

C. Impact

D. InkJet
C. Impact. To print multi-part forms, there must be an impact with the paper (like a typewriter).

20. _____ is a parallel communications protocol that was developed jointly by Microsoft and Hewlett-Packard to address the special needs of devices like high-speed laser printers and scanners.

A. EPP

B. ECP

C. IEEE-1284

D. Enhanced parallel
B. ECP. ECP is ideal for moving large chunks of data primarily in one direction. It is part of the Microsoft standard for implementing parallel ports.

21. _____ is a parallel communications protocol in which the software program that is using a parallel port must maintain control of the port making it ideal for programs that must quickly switch between send and receive modes.

A. EPP

B. ECP

C. IEEE-1284

D. Enhanced parallel
A. EPP. A little older than ECP, EPP is ideal for applications that must quickly switch from send to receive mode and back again, like hard drives.

22. _____ allows reverse direction parallel communication using all eight data wires.

A. Nibble mode

B. Byte mode

C. Data transfer mode

D. Switching mode
B. Byte mode. An entire byte of data can be sent at one time.

23. _____ allows reverse direction parallel communication using four of the signaling wires to transfer a byte of data in two chunks.

A. Nibble mode

B. Byte mode

C. Data transfer mode

D. Switching mode
A. Nibble mode. A byte of data is broken into two four-bit chunks called nibbles.

24. A _____ port includes a buffering mechanism implemented in the hardware that receives the data from the PC and then takes over the process of delivering the data to the printer.

A. Fast Centronics

B. IEEE-1284

C. Parallel

D. Centronics
A. Fast Centronics. With a hardware buffering mechanism and hardware control of the data transfer, data can be transmitted faster and with less overhead affecting the CPU.

25. The _____standard was proposed in 1991 by a group of computer hardware manufacturers and is commonly associated with the bidirectional aspects of parallel communication.

    A. RS-232

    B. RJ-45

    C. IEEE-1284

    D. IEEE-1024

    C. IEEE-1284. Remember this standard when purchasing parallel communications equipment.

Chapter 6 Answers

1. The _____ battery provides the most power with the least amount of weight.

    A. nickel cadmium

    B. lithium ion

    C. nickel/metal hydride

    D. lead acid

    B. Lithium Ion. Lead acid batteries are used in cars. Nickel cadmium and nickel metal hydride batteries are older forms of laptop batteries that do not provide as much power and are usually bulkier.

2. The _____ effect refers to the tendency of nickel cadmium batteries to lose the ability to fully recharge if they are not completely discharged first.

    A. memory

    B. amnesia.

    C. memory leak

    D. flux capacitor

    A. Memory. Nickel cadmium batteries may not fully recharge if they have not been completely discharged. This is known as the memory effect.

3. The AC adapter on a portable computer changes _____ power to _____ power.

    A. 110v AC to 220v AC

    B. 220v AC to 110v AC

    C. 110v AC or 220v AC to DC

    D. 12v DC to 110v AC

    C. 110v AC or 220v AC to DC. It is important to remember that portable computers use DC power regardless of whether the power cord is plugged in. When a portable is not plugged in, the DC power comes from the batteries. When it is plugged in, the AC power coming from standard electrical systems must be transformed to DC power.

4. The most common display technology used in portable systems is known as _____.

    A. Liquid Crystal

    B. Light Emitting Diode

    C. Cathode Ray Tube

    D. 8514/A

    A. Liquid crystal. Older models of laptops used a cathode ray tube (CRT), but CRTs have high power requirements and are very heavy. The type of liquid crystal used in laptop displays is similar to the liquid crystal used in many hand-held calculators and watches.

5. A _____ display has a transistor at each pixel.

   A. Passive matrix

   B. 8514/A

   C. Light Emitting Diode

   D. Active matrix

   D. Active matrix. Active matrix displays require more power and have a much better display because there are so many more transistors. Passive matrix displays have only one transistor per horizontal or vertical line.

6. Mary says that when she moves her mouse too quickly, her cursor disappears. What suggestion would you have to help?

   A. Change the display mode from Passive to Active.

   B. Set the mouse trails option to On.

   C. Adjust the contrast of the display.

   D. Tell her not to move the mouse so quickly.

   B. Set the mouse trails option to On. Microsoft included this feature in order to help users with passive matrix displays keep track of their cursors. One thing that you cannot do is change a laptop display from passive mode to active mode.

7. Most laptops have a limited number of ports, but by using a docking station those ports can be expanded. A docking station can provide which of the following?

   A. PCI slots

   B. ISA slots

   C. Enhanced sound capabilities

   D. All of the above

   D. All of the above. The purpose of a docking station is to convert a laptop into a fully functional PC. Docking stations provide ports for a variety of peripherals including EISA and ISA cards.

8. In order to dock a laptop with a docking station, a _____ connector is used.

   A. SCSI

   B. DB-50

   C. DIN

   D. Proprietary

   D. Proprietary. Unfortunately every hardware manufacturer uses a slightly different configuration for docking ports. This makes one vendor's laptops incompatible with another vendor's docking stations. In some cases even laptops and docking stations from the same vendor can be incompatible if they are different models or versions.

9. PC Cards were originally intended for adding additional _____ to a system.

   A. Hard drives

   B. Hard drive adapters

   C. Memory

   D. Network adapters

   C. Memory. PCMCIA stands for Personal Computer Memory Card International Association. In the early days the most limiting factor for laptop computers was memory.

10. Type III PC Cards are intended for
    _____ type devices like hard
    drives or CD-ROMS.

    A. Modems

    B. LAN cards

    C. Rotating mass storage

    D. Memory
    C. Rotating mass storage devices. In
    1995, PCMCIA released the latest
    standard, officially using the name PC
    Card. All PCMCIA cards are now
    referred to as PC Cards. This latest
    specification added support for DMA,
    Bus Mastering, Zoomed Video (ZV),
    and 32-bit CardBus operation

11. PC _____ software manages the
    allocation of system resources once a PC
    Card has been inserted.

    A. Card services

    B. Socket services

    C. Windows 95

    D. DOS
    A. Card services. PC Card services
    provides a PC Card controller. The
    controller manages hot-swapping of PC
    Cards. Hot-swapping means that you
    can remove one PC Card (like a
    network card) and replace it with
    another (like a modem) without
    rebooting the system.

12. Uses for PC Cards today include:

    A. Hard drives

    B. Network cards

    C. Memory cards

    D. Global Positioning System cards

    E. All of the above
    E. All of the above. Just about
    anything can be implemented as a PC
    Card these days. Some cards are
    completely self-contained like network
    cards and modems while others provide
    the interface for external devices like
    CD-ROMs and GPS locators.

13. What types of pointing devices are found in
    portable computers today?

    A. Trackballs

    B. Touch pads

    C. Pointing sticks

    D. All of the above
    D. All of the above. Trackballs are
    becoming less and less common while
    touch pads seem to be the pointing
    device of choice for most consumers
    and hardware manufacturers. The
    pointing stick is also a very popular
    device.

14. The type of pointing device that has the
    most moving parts, which in turn makes it
    the most unreliable is the _____.

    A. Trackball

    B. Touch pad

    C. Pointing stick

    D. VR
    A. Trackball. A trackball is very much
    like an upside-down mouse. The
    trackball is very susceptible to dirt and
    oils that can foul the device, making it
    necessary to disassemble and clean it.

15. System and hard drive passwords are an example of _____ security.

    A. Hardware-enabled

    B. Software-enabled

    C. Smart

    D. High-level

    B. Software-enabled. An example of hardware-enabled security would be a biometric device, or a cable lock device similar to a bicycle cable lock. A good rule of thumb is that hardware-enabled security requires some kind of physical hardware.

16. _____ is basically accounting. If done properly, a company will know how many computers, monitors, disk drives, CDs, RAM SIMMs, etc. it has purchased.

    A. Inventory tracking

    B. FASB

    C. Asset management

    D. Fault tolerance

    C. Asset Management. Asset management is the process of tracking what hardware and software is being used within the company. There is usually an automated inventory process coupled with an ad hoc reporting tool.

17. Features of _____ controllers include an operating system APM-like user interface, support for CPU idle, and the ability to update the system time on a resume from suspend mode.

    A. Card Services

    B. Power Management

    C. Docking Services

    D. Socket Services

    B. Power Management. New power management controllers also take advantage of the Win32 Advance Power Management API in order to directly interact with the operating system. This allows for more control and flexibility in the area of power management.

18. Standards help provide a unified approach to _____.

    A. Monitor the status of a heterogeneous network and receive notifications of problems

    B. Retrieve accurate and timely inventory information

    C. Change large groups of systems with as few operations as possible

    D. Monitor systems for chassis intrusion to safeguard assets

    E. All of the above

    E. All of the above. Without standards the total cost of ownership for computers would be much higher. Standards allow companies to reduce the amount of hardware they must keep on hand and more importantly define common ways for acquiring and using information.

19. Customers can use a standards-based _____ management tool to obtain asset and fault information from all compliant systems, thus increasing the consistency of system information even if the systems are from different vendors.

A. ANSI

B. SMTP

C. DMI 2.0

D. APM

C. DMI 2.0. The Desktop Management Interface (DMI) 2.0 was designed by the Desktop Management Task Force (DMTF) to provide standard definitions for what should be managed in a computer, device, or even software, and how that information should be accessed.

20. _____ is a time-tested industry management protocol most noted for network management.

A. DMI

B. SMTP

C. ANSI

D. SNMP

D. SNMP. The Simple Network Management Protocol (SNMP) was originally defined as part of the TCP/IP protocol suite. The purpose of SNMP is to provide a way for heterogeneous devices to communicate status information to a more intelligent management device.

21. _____ is an initiative from Intel to standardize the management characteristics of all Intel-based systems. These characteristics include DMI instrumentation, remote services, and power management.

A. DTMF

B. WBEM

C. WfM

D. DMI

C. WfM. The Wired for Management (WfM) standard should provide a consistent managed environment designed to greatly enhance the opportunity to reduce the systems management portion of the total cost of ownership by providing the same management functions and interfaces for all managed PCs.

22. Handheld PCs are often referred to as _____.

A. PDAs

B. IRDAs

C. PPCs

D. UPCs

A. PDAs. Personal Digital Assistants are an emerging technology. Many PDAs are quite powerful and can greatly enhance the productivity of busy professionals. Watch for these devices in your company.

23. When a PDA _____ with another system, files and other information are automatically copied from one device to the other so that both devices have the exact same information.

A. Links

B. Communicates

C. Synchronizes

D. Attaches

C. Synchronizes. Synchronization usually occurs over a serial or infrared communications link. When two devices synchronize, each device requests new information from the other so that they both end up with the same information. This process is mostly automatic, but a user may need to get involved in order to resolve conflicts.

24. Which of the following operating systems is just now becoming a mainstream operating system for portable computers?

    A. Windows 95

    B. Windows 98

    C. Windows NT Workstation 4.0

    D. Windows Nt Server 4.0
       C. Windows NT Workstation 4.0. Windows NT Workstation has come a long way. Through evolution of its features and the fact that mainstream desktop PCs and laptops now come with Windows NT Workstation preinstalled, it is now a great solution for all business users.

25. Which Windows NT Service Pack is required to fully enable the operating system to function with portable computers?

    A. SP1

    B. SP2

    C. SP3

    D. SP4
       D. SP4. Service Pack 4 (SP4) is the latest and most comprehensive update for Microsoft Windows NT 4.0. SP4 provides improved management, security, and capabilities that help prepare IT professionals for the Year 2000 and euro currency changes.

Chapter 7 Answers

1. A coaxial network arranged in a bus topology requires what at both ends?

    A. BNC

    B. T-connector

    C. 50W Terminator

    D. 50Ω Terminator
       D. A 50Ω terminator must be connected to both ends of a coaxial bus network. Without proper termination, the network will not function.

2. Connecting two segments of coaxial cable to make a longer cable must be connected using what?

    A. BNC

    B. T-connector

    C. Hub

    D. RJ-45
       A. A BNC (British Naval Connector) is used to connect two lengths of coaxial cable. T-connectors are used to attach the coaxial cable to the NIC.

3. A _____ is at the center of a star topology.

    A. Hub

    B. Router

    C. Repeater

    D. NIC
       A. Hubs are the center points for star topology networks. If any single device in a star topology fails, the rest of the network is not affected, but if the hub fails, the entire network will go down.

4. Which of the following are not susceptible to electromagnetic interference? (Choose all that apply.)

   A. Coaxial cable

   B. Twisted-pair cable

   C. Fiber-optic cable

   D. Telephone cable
   C. Fiber-optic cable. Fiber uses light signals rather than electrical signals for network communications. Electromagnetic interference does not have an effect on light-based transmissions.

5. CAT-5 cable used for IEEE 802.3 Ethernet requires a(n) _____ connector at both ends.

   A. Fiber optic

   B. RJ-45

   C. RJ-11

   D. T
   B. RJ-45. This is the standard connector as specified by the IEEE 802.3 Ethernet standard.

6. Which cable type transmits and receives data using light signals through a glass or plastic transmission medium?

   A. Fiber

   B. Coaxial

   C. Twisted pair

   D. Copper
   A. Fiber. Coaxial, twisted pair, or any copper-based cable would use electrical signals to transmit data. Fiber might also be called optical-fiber or fiber-optic cable. Specific network specifications for fiber might refer to it as 10BaseFL or 100BaseFX.

7. Which of the following are types of twisted pair cable? (Choose all that apply.)

   A. Coaxial

   B. STP

   C. UTP

   D. CAT-5
   B, C, D. STP (Shielded Twisted Pair), UTP (Unshielded Twisted Pair), and CAT-5 are all types of twisted-pair cable.

8. Which of the following are valid topologies for token-ring networks? (Choose all that apply.)

   A. Bus

   B. Star

   C. Ring

   D. Star-ring
   C, D. Token-ring networks can only be configured with a ring or star-ring topology.

9. What is the maximum transmission speed of Fast Ethernet?

   A. 1.45 Mbps

   B. 10 Mbps

   C. 100 Mbps

   D. 1 Gbps
   C. 100 Mbps. Fast Ethernet, whether fiber or twisted pair, communicates at a maximum speed of 100 Mbps. Standard Ethernet communicates at 10 Mbps.

10. What is the maximum transmission speed of standard Ethernet?

    A. 1.45 Mbps

    B. 10 Mbps

    C. 100 Mbps

    D. 1 Gbps
       B. 10 Mbps. Standard Ethernet, whether fiber or twisted pair, communicates at a maximum speed of 10 Mbps. Fast Ethernet communicates at 100 Mbps.

11. FDDI runs over what kind of cabling?

    A. Coaxial

    B. Twisted pair

    C. Fiber optic

    D. CAT-5
       C. Fiber optic. FDDI stands for Fiber Distributed Data Interface. It generally consists of a redundant ring topology with two rings of dual-strand fiber as the network backbone.

12. The maximum transmission distance of CAT-5 UTP based Ethernet is

    _____.

    A. 100 meters

    B. 180 meters

    C. 500 meters

    D. 2000 meters
       A. 100 meters. CAT-5 UTP is a type of twisted-pair copper cable. Maximum length without a repeater is 100 meters.

13. The degradation of a network signal when transmitting over a great distance is known as _____?

    A. Signaling

    B. Attenuation

    C. Ringing

    D. Beaconing
       B. Attenuation. When a network signal degrades, or weakens, with distance, it is known as attenuation.

14. Ethernet uses what access method?

    A. CSMA/CD

    B. CSMA/CA

    C. Demand polling

    D. Token passing
       A. CSMA/CD. Ethernet uses the Carrier Sense Multiple Access with Collision Detection media access method. With this method, clients attempt to transmit data into the network, and then check the network for collisions. If a collision is detected, the client waits a random amount of time and then attempts to retransmit the data.

15. Token-ring network devices connect to each other through what device?

    A. Hub

    B. MAU

    C. BNC

    D. Router
       B. MAU, or Multiple Access Unit. Many people mistakenly call this device a hub, but a hub is used only for star or star-hybrid networks.

16. Which of the following devices can be used to correct problems with attenuation on a network using a bus topology?

    A. Hub

    B. BNC

    C. Repeater

    D. MAU

    C. Repeater. A repeater accepts an inbound network signal, amplifies it, and regenerates the renewed signal back to the network.

17. What is the maximum transmission distance of coaxial cable?

    A. 100 meters

    B. 180 meters

    C. 500 meters

    D. 2000 meters

    B. 180 meters. Coaxial cable has a range of 180 meters.

18. Which of the following network topologies will always suffer complete failure when a single cable breaks? (Choose all that apply.)

    A. Bus

    B. Ring

    C. Star

    D. Star-bus

    A, B. Pure bus or pure ring-based topologies will fail if a single cable in the network breaks.

19. Token ring 802.5 standards specify what transmission speeds? (Choose all that apply.)

    A. 4 Mbps

    B. 10 Mbps

    C. 16 Mbps

    D. 100 Mbps

    A, C. Token ring 802.5 standards specify transmission speeds of 4 Mbps and 16 Mbps.

Scenario for questions 20–23: One of your executive users wants to be able to connect to the corporate network from her home. She is currently using a dialup connection over a standard telephone line with a 56K modem, but she complains that this connection is too slow. You are asked to evaluate various remote networking options to provide solutions to meet the different requirements as presented in the following four questions.

20. Which solution would provide a data connection of up to 128Kbps over standard copper phone lines, as well as allowing simultaneous voice and data connections?

    A. ISDN

    B. ADSL

    C. Cable modem

    D. PSTN

    A. ISDN uses standard copper phone lines, allows simultaneous voice and data communications, and has a connection speed of up to 128 Kbps.

21. Which solution would provide a high-speed data connection over coaxial cable?

    A. ISDN

    B. ADSL

    C. Cable modem

    D. PSTN

    C. Cable modem. The cable modem is the only one of the listed solutions that uses coaxial cable. The theoretical maximum connection speed for a cable modem is 27 Mbps downstream and 2.5 Mbps upstream.

22. Which solution would provide high-speed downloads, but upload speeds identical to that of the modem?

    A. ISDN

    B. PSTN

    C. Cable modem

    D. Digital satellite

    D. Digital satellite. A digital satellite Internet connection would use the satellite for downstream communications, but would still require the modem for the upstream communication.

23. Which solution would provide high-speed connectivity up to a theoretical maximum of 8.448 Mbps over standard copper lines?

    A. PSTN

    B. ISDN

    C. DSL

    D. None of the above

    C. DSL (Digital Subscriber Lines) provide a theoretical maximum connection speed of 8.448 Mbps over standard copper lines. In practice, the maximum speed is actually 6.1 Mbps.

24. What is the network protocol used on the Internet?

    A. TCP/IP

    B. IPX/SPX

    C. NetBEUI

    D. AppleTalk

    A. TCP/IP, the Transmission Control Protocol/Internet Protocol is used on the Internet. It is also the most common protocol used on corporate networks.

25. What is the device installed in a user's workstation that allows them to connect to the network?

    A. Network Access Card

    B. Network Interface Card

    C. Media Access Card

    D. Hub

    B. A Network Interface Card, or NIC, is the internal device installed in a user's workstation that allows them to connect to a network.

Chapter 8 Answers

1. Your professional _____ while working with the customer has the potential of boosting your career immensely.

   A. Appearance
   B. Behavior
   C. Personality
   D. Technical skills
      B. Behavior. You will be judged as much on your professionalism as you will on your ability. Your behavior in various situations will be used to determine promotions and raises.

2. Which of the following statements is true?

   A. Customer satisfaction is easy to achieve.
   B. Customer satisfaction is not as important as technical skill.
   C. Customer satisfaction is more important than technical skill.
   D. Customer satisfaction is as important as technical skill.
      D. Customer satisfaction is as important as technical skill. Some people make it look easy, but most have to work at attaining high customer satisfaction. It will be difficult for you to be a highly rated technician without both technical skill and the ability to satisfy customers.

3. A technician should always leave customers with the feeling that they have been treated with _____.

   A. Dignity
   B. Respect
   C. Integrity
   D. All of the above
      D. All of the above. If you offend customers by not displaying these characteristics, it won't matter how fast or how well you fixed the problem. You must have people skills.

4. Customer satisfaction requires _____.

   A. Time
   B. Patience
   C. Good listening skills
   D. The ability to communicate at the user's level of understanding
   E. All of the above
      E. All of the above. If you can't effectively communicate with a customer, you will have a difficult time determining what the problem is and what the solution is. In almost every situation, you will need to effectively communicate the solution to a customer before they will be satisfied.

5. A PC is having problems. To solve the problem, the first thing you should do is:

   A. Ask the customer if they have any ideas about what the problem might be.

B. Plug in the network cord.

C. Take the PC back to the repair area.

D. Reload the operating system.
A. Ask the customer. It's always a good idea to start your troubleshooting with a conversation with the user. They may have a vital piece of information that you need and they might not even know it.

6. When you are done listening to the user and have asked all of your questions, _____ what the user has said. Ask them if you "have it right."

A. Write down

B. Paraphrase

C. Believe

D. None of the above
B. Paraphrase. Read your notes back so that the user knows that you understand the problem. A user will be much more at ease if they feel like you were paying attention to them and that you understand their problem.

7. Technicians should also be able to quickly discern a user's technical level. You want to use explanations _____ a user's level.

A. Above

B. Below

C. Appropriate to

D. Don't explain problems to users.
C. Appropriate to. Talking above or below a user's technical understanding will likely result in a frustrated user.

Talk to your users informally as you are working. Try and gauge what they will and will not understand. Plan your explanations accordingly.

8. Which statement is most true?

A. Nonverbal communication is not as important as verbal communication.

B. Nonverbal communication is more important than verbal communication.

C. Nonverbal communication is as important as verbal communication.

D. There is no such thing as nonverbal communication.
C. Nonverbal communication is as important as verbal communication. Eighty percent of communication is nonverbal. Look for body postures and facial expressions that are not consistent with what a user is saying. Be careful if what the user is doing doesn't match what the user is saying.

9. Most users are _____ users.

A. Super

B. Power

C. Casual

D. Stupid
C. Casual. Only a few users will know more about computers than you will. Don't ever refer to "stupid" users. All it takes is one remark like that to get back to a manager or a user, and the next thing you know you are updating your resume.

10. Personal _____ is about bonding with your customers.

    A. Satisfaction
    B. Rapport
    C. Feeling
    D. Relationship
    B. Rapport. Building rapport with your users will result in good communications. If your users trust you, they will be more likely to admit their mistakes and save you considerable troubleshooting time.

11. Professional conduct is essential to understand and achieve in the computer services industry. This encompasses _____.

    A. Appearance
    B. Attitude
    C. Time management
    D. Integrity
    E. Competence
    F. All of the above
    F. All of the above. Try to be a well-rounded individual. Your job as a technician is a service-oriented job. That means that primarily you work with people, not computers. A computer will never give you a compliment, but a satisfied customer will.

12. If you have a good _____, the user is going to be friendlier and ultimately more satisfied with your work.

    A. Appearance
    B. Attitude

C. Concept of time management
D. Integrity
    B. Attitude. Your attitude is reflected in everything you do. Project a positive mental attitude and people will want to be around you. You do not want a user community that dreads your approach.

13. Time is a crucial variable that you need to master. It is important to _____ the time spent on each PC.

    A. Minimize
    B. Maximize
    A. Minimize. You need to learn to juggle. The trick is to spend enough time on a system to adequately repair it and satisfy the user. However, keep in mind that while you are delighting one customer, you may be frustrating another by keeping that person waiting. Best to move on as quickly as possible.

14. If you have not worked with the user or if you have any reservations about entering the workspace, you should _____.

    A. Try to contact the user.
    B. Enter but leave a note.
    C. Make your repair as soon as possible and leave no trace you were there.
    D. Just come back later.
    A. Contact the user. Don't put yourself in an awkward position. Try to avoid being alone in a user's office or cube. If it's an office, try to leave the door open. In today's business

world, it is better to be safe than sorry. Take no unnecessary risks.

15. _____ means that you are not going to compromise yourself or ask others to do so in order to achieve something.

   A. Appearance

   B. Attitude

   C. Time management

   D. Integrity
   D. Integrity. You need trust from your users and your management team to do your job effectively. Your job will be much more enjoyable if you have the freedom to do it. To earn that freedom, you need to have integrity.

16. Be aware of the _____ in your company and behave accordingly. Some companies are more laid back than others, but be aware of how people act and try to emulate their behavior.

   A. Culture

   B. Opinions

   C. Desires

   D. Environment
   A. Culture. You will be evaluated on how well you "fit in." The culture of a company determines what is acceptable and what is not. Often, the culture in a company is very different from the company's rules and regulations. You need to be aware of both to operate effectively.

17. A _____ has the potential of harboring bad feelings between the parties for a long period of time.

   A. Misunderstanding

   B. Conflict

   C. Communications challenge

   D. Failure
   B. Conflict. Always resolve conflicts as soon as possible. Use the two-hour rule. If you can't resolve a conflict in two hours, then get a manager or someone involved who can. Unresolved conflicts tend to grow over time, not shrink.

18. The following represent conflicts that you may face as a technician:

   A. Angry users

   B. Your own mistakes

   C. Know-it-all users

   D. All of the above
   D. All of the above. Watch out for these situations and learn to avoid them. If it can't be avoided, keep your cool and don't let things escalate. Don't hesitate to get a manager involved.

19. When caught in a conflict between two users, you should _____.

   A. Side with the user who is correct.

   B. Try to side with both users.

   C. Refuse to participate in the dispute.

   D. Offer unbiased technical information.
   D. Offer unbiased technical information. Never take sides. In a situation like this you will probably make an ally and an enemy at the same time. People tend to forget their allies much faster than their enemies.

20. When it comes to measuring customer experience (or just about anything these days) the buzzword is _____.

    A. Precision

    B. Accuracy

    C. Efficiency

    D. Metrics
    D. Metrics. It's a buzzword, but metrics are powerful tools for analyzing and improving a business. A robust, relevant set of metrics will lead to a process of continual improvement that will eventually benefit the entire company.

21. The following are techniques that may be used to measure customer satisfaction:

    A. Total Quality Management (TQM)

    B. Statistical analysis

    C. 360-degree communications

    D. All of the above
    D. All of the above. There are many others, but these seem to be the management favorites because they are easily implemented and understood. They also require involvement from all levels of the organization. That means you, too.

22. The following are examples of productivity metrics:

    A. The number of calls a technician receives at the help desk in an hour

    B. The number of questions a technician answers from the queue in a shift

    C. The number of customers a technician visits in a day

    D. The number of systems a technician installs in a month

    E. All of the above
    E. All of the above. Remember that productivity metrics usually focus on a unit of work. A unit of work could be a PC repair or a user support call. If you are counting something, then you're probably generating a productivity metric.

23. The instrument of choice for collecting data for quality metrics is the _____.

    A. Customer satisfactions survey

    B. Pareto analysis

    C. Trend chart

    D. Histogram
    A. Customer satisfaction survey. The other options are statistical analysis techniques. Surveys are usually ten to twenty questions that ask a user to rate a variety of things related to the work being done.

24. Select the truest statment.

    A. Metrics are valuable to managers.

    B. Metrics are valuable to customers.

    C. Metrics are valuable to you.

    D. All of the above
    D. All of the above. A good set of metrics will have something for everyone. The key is to define metrics that allow people to measure

their contributions to an organization. Watching the metrics rise and fall can be almost like playing a game.

25. Questions on the exam will be mainly aimed at the following concepts:

    A. Communicating and listening (face-to-face or over the phone)

    B. Interpreting verbal and nonverbal cues

    C. Responding appropriately to the customer's technical ability

    D. Establishing personal rapport with the customer

    E. Conflict avoidance and resolution

    F. All of the above
       F. All of the above. Remember that this material doesn't directly affect your score on the test, but it will impact your ability to obtain and retain a good job. Don't spend all of your time developing your technical skills. Invest some effort in your people skills if you want to stand out among your peers.

Chapter 9 Answers

1. The first step in preparing a new hard drive for an operating system is:

    A. Format

    B. Partition

    C. ScanDisk

    D. Defrag
       B. Partition. You should first partition, and then format, a new disk when preparing it for an operating system.

2. Which of the following do *not* require an initial installation of DOS before they will run? (Choose all that apply.)

    A. Windows 3.1

    B. Windows 95

    C. Windows 98

    D. None of the above
       B, C. Windows 3.*x* requires an existing installation of DOS before it can be installed. Windows 95 and Windows 98 do away with the requirement for DOS.

3. Which of these disk utilities finds and corrects problems with the File Allocation Tables such as lost clusters?

    A. ScanDisk

    B. Backup

    C. Fix DISK

    D. Defrag
       A. ScanDisk. ScanDisk can be used to repair problems such as lost clusters, and can mark bad sectors on a disk so they will not be used.

Scenario for questions 4–10: Suppose you are running a Pentium 90 with 32MB of RAM and two 1.5GB hard drives. The first drive is divided into a 500MB primary partition and a 1GB extended partition, broken into two logical partitions of 512MB each. The second drive is two partitions, a primary of 1250MB, and an extended of 250MB, with all 250MB dedicated to a logical partition. Keep this configuration in mind when answering the following seven questions.

4. The disk partitioning scheme that would be used by DOS on the first partition of the first drive would be:

   A. FAT12
   B. FAT15
   C. FAT16
   D. FAT32
      C. FAT16. DOS does support FAT12, but it is only for floppy disks or hard drives under 15MB. For everything else, DOS has native support for only FAT16.

5. The disk partitioning scheme that would be used by Windows 3.1 for the first partition of the first drive would be:

   A. FAT12
   B. FAT16
   C. FAT32
   D. NTFS
      B. FAT16. Remember, Windows 3.*x* runs on top of DOS. Therefore, it cannot use a partitioning scheme other than one that DOS would recognize. For this size partition, the only available selection under DOS would be FAT16.

6. If you format all of the partitions in the system, how will the drive letters be assigned to the first hard drive?

   A. Primary – C: drive; Extended – D: drive.
   B. Primary – C: drive; Extended – E: drive.
   C. Primary – C: drive; Logical – D: and E: drives.
   D. Primary – C: drive; Logical – E: and F: drives.

   D. The primary partition will be the C: drive, the second and third partitions (both logical partitions in the one extended partition) will be E and F.

7. If you format all of the partitions in the system, how will the drive letters be assigned to the second hard drive?

   A. Primary – D: drive; Extended – G: drive.
   B. Primary – D: drive; Logical – G: drive.
   C. Primary – F: drive; Extended – G: drive.
   D. Primary – F: drive; Logical – G: drive.
      B. The primary partition of the second disk will be the D: drive. The logical partition, contained by the extended partition, will be the G: drive.

8. What will be the cluster size on the first drive, first partition formatted with FAT16?

   A. 512 bytes
   B. 8KB
   C. 16KB
   D. 32KB
      B. 8KB. The partition size (NOT the disk size) is 500MB. This falls within the range of drives with 8KB cluster sizes.

9. What will be the cluster size on the second drive, first partition, formatted with FAT16?

   A. 512 bytes
   B. 8KB

C. 16KB

D. 32KB

D. 32KB. The partition size (1.25GB) falls within the range of drives with 32KB cluster sizes.

10. How much physical space will a 50-byte text file take up if it is stored on the second partition of the second drive?

A. 50 bytes

B. 512 bytes

C. 4KB

D. 32KB

C. 4KB. The 250MB partition would have 4MB clusters. This means all files must take up physical space in multiples of 4KB. Even though the file is a mere 50 bytes, it will require an entire cluster, or 4KB, of physical disk space.

11. Which of the following technologies is natively supported by Windows 98, but not by Windows 3.*x*? (Choose all that apply.)

A. FAT16

B. FAT32

C. NTFS

D. Plug-and-Play

B, D. Of the listed technologies, Windows 3.1 supports only FAT16. Windows 98 supports all except for NTFS.

12. Which of the following files are part of the Windows Registry in Windows 95/98? (Choose all that apply.)

A. AUTOEXEC.BAT

B. SYSTEM.INI

C. USER.DAT

D. SYSTEM.DAT

C, D. The USER.DAT and SYSTEM.DAT files are part of the Windows Registry for Windows 95 and Windows 98.

13. Which of the following utilities will destroy all data on a partition? (Choose all that apply.)

A. FORMAT

B. FDISK

C. DEFRAG

D. PDISK

A, B. Formatting (FORMAT) or partitioning (FDISK) will both destroy all data on a drive or partition.

14. In Windows 95 and beyond, which tool replaces the Windows 3.1 File Manager?

A. Program Manager

B. Windows Explorer

C. Control Panel

D. Windows Browse List

B. The Windows Explorer. The Windows Explorer replaces both the Windows 3.*x* File Manager and the Windows 3.*x* Program Manager.

15. Which of the following files is required to successfully boot DOS? (Choose all that apply.)

A. AUTOEXEC.BAT

B. CONFIG.SYS

C. COMMAND.COM

D. ANSI.SYS

C. COMMAND.COM is the only one of these files required to boot to DOS.

16. The wasted physical storage space required by a file smaller than the cluster size on the disk is known as what?

A. Slack space

B. Cluster waste

C. Clutter

D. Lost clusters

A. Slack space. The physical space taken up with "empty" data for purposes of making an even cluster multiple is known as slack space.

17. What is the largest partition size supported by native DOS running FAT16?

A. 500MB

B. 2GB

C. 4GB

D. 2TB

B. 2GB. Due to the mathematical limitations of FAT16, the largest supported partition size without an overlay file or special driver is 2GB.

18. The first physical sector of any physical hard disk used as a boot device is the:

A. MBR

B. File System Boot Sector

C. System Partition

D. None of the above

A. The first physical sector of the hard drive used as the boot device contains the Master Boot Record.

19. The first physical sector on any logical volume is known as what?

A. MBR

B. File System Boot Sector

C. System Partition

D. None of the above

B. The File System Boot Sector is the first physical sector on any logical volume. This sector will contain the pointer to the system files required to start your operating system.

20. What is the smallest addressable unit on a hard disk drive?

A. Sector

B. Cluster

C. Partition

D. Byte

B. Cluster. A cluster is the smallest addressable unit on file system.

21. Under DOS, which of the following attributes can the user set on a given file? (Choose all that apply.)

A. Read-Only

B. Hidden

C. System

D. Archive

A, B, C, D. All of these attributes can be set on any given file by a user under DOS, using the ATTRIB command.

22. Which utility helps achieve better disk performance by arranging all clusters for a given file physically closer to each other on a hard disk?

    A. Check Disk

    B. ScanDisk

    C. Defrag

    D. DRVSPC

    C. Defrag. Running Defrag pulls all the clusters of your files over to contiguous physical areas of the disk to optimize read, write, and search times.

23. Which utility helps you recover from disaster by providing a way to maintain a copy of all of your data files?

    A. Scandisk

    B. Backup

    C. Restore

    D. DOSSHELL

    B. Backup. Data is the hardest part of a system to replace. The backup utility provides an easy mechanism by which to ensure the safety of your data. The restore utility brings back information previously saved through the use of the backup utility.

24. Which of the following statements are NOT true about the Windows Registry? (Choose all that apply.)

    A. It can be easily viewed with a text editor.

    B. Any changes made are saved immediately.

    C. Incorrectly modifying the Registry can cause your whole system to crash.

    D. You can edit the Registry manually through the REGEDIT utility.

    A. The Windows Registry cannot be viewed with a text editor. All of the other statements are true.

25. Under Windows 3.1, which file configures Windows to address specific hardware devices and their associated settings?

    A. CONFIG.SYS

    B. AUTOEXEC.BAT

    C. WIN.INI

    D. SYSTEM.INI

    D. SYSTEM.INI. The SYSTEM.INI file is a plain-text file that is used to load and configure hardware devices in Windows 3.*x*.

Chapter 10 Answers

1. A DIMM memory module would typically have how many pins?

    A. 30

    B. 64

    C. 72

    D. 168

    D. 168. The original SIMMs had 30 PINS; newer SIMMs contain 72. DIMMs contain 168 PINS.

2. Which processor first utilized the Level 1 (L1) system cache?

    A. 8088

    B. 386

C. 486

D. Pentium

C. 486. Level 1 (L1) cache can also be referred to as internal cache. Beginning with the 80486 Processor, SRAM was incorporated into the processor to help bridge the memory performance gap.

3. Which processor first combined Level 2 (L2) system cache in the same package as the CPU?

A. 486

B. Pentium with MMX

C. Pentium Pro

D. Pentium II

C. Pentirum Pro. Level 2 (L2) cache can also be referred to as external cache. The Pentium Pro was the first processor to actually integrate this SRAM chip in the same package as the processor. Prior to this, L2 cache was accessed via an external circuit board.

4. Which of the following are types of DRAM?

A. Fast Paged mode

B. Static Random Access Memory

C. Enhanced Data Output

D. Pipeline Cache mode

A, C. Fast Paged mode and Enhanced Data Output. DRAM technologies include conventional, FPM, EDO, and BEDO.

5. A nanosecond is defined as?

A. One millionth of a second

B. One billionth of a second

C. One trillionth of a second

D. One zillionth of a second

B. One billionth of a second. A nanosecond is often used to measure the speed of memory.

6. The Level 1 and Level 2 system cache is based upon which computer principle?

A. Locality of address

B. Locality of space

C. Locality of reference

D. Locality of resource

C. Locality of reference. This principle states that if the processor recently referenced a location in memory, it is likely that it will refer to it again in the near future.

7. The system BIOS is generally stored on which type of chip?

A. RAM

B. DRAM

C. ROM

D. SROM

C. ROM. ROM chips work great for programs like the system BIOS because the contents of a ROM chip are maintained even when the PC is turned off.

8. Which of the following are advantages of SRAM?

A. It doesn't require extra circuitry to refresh the data contained in memory.

B. It is less expensive than DRAM.

C. It is smaller than DRAM.

D. It is faster than DRAM.
   A, D. It doesn't require extra circuitry to refresh the data contained in memory and is faster than DRAM. SRAM chips are faster than DRAM chips and they are primarily used for L1 and L2 cache. Due to the size and higher cost, they are not used for the main system memory.

9. The original IBM PC used which type of DRAM for the main system memory?

   A. Basic DRAM

   B. Conventional DRAM

   C. Paged DRAM

   D. Fast Paged mode DRAM
      B. Conventional DRAM. The first type of DRAM was conventional.

10. On a motherboard that supports a Pentium II Processor, which type of memory module can be installed individually instead of in pairs?

    A. Single In-Line Package

    B. Dual In-Line Package

    C. Single In-Line Memory Module

    D. Dual In-Line Memory Module
       D. Dual In-Line Memory Module. Because a single DIMM module has a 64-bit memory path, DIMMs do not need to be placed in pairs on a PII motherboard. A single SIMM module has only a 32-bit memory path, so they must be placed in pairs in order to match the 64-bit Pentium processor.

11. Which type of ROM supported rewrite technology in order to update a device or firmware program?

    A. PROM

    B. EPROM

    C. UPROM

    D. CDROM
       B. EPROM. It's erasable and can be reprogrammed. A PROM can be programmed only one time.

12. SRAM is typically used for which type of memory?

    A. Main system memory

    B. Conventional memory

    C. System cache

    D. L0 cache
       C. System cache. Due to faster access times, SRAM is typically used for the L1 and L2 system cache.

13. RAM is typically used for which type of memory?

    A. Main system memory

    B. Conventional memory

    C. System cache

    D. L0 cache
       A. Main system memory. DRAM is typically used for the main system memory because the chips are smaller in size and less expensive to produce.

14. Another name for L2 cache is?

    A. Internal cache

    B. Main system cache

C. PII cache

D. External cache

   D. External cache. Because L2 cache is external to the processor it is referred to as external cache. This is in contrast to the L1 cache, internal cache, which is actually incorporated in the processor.

15. Which of the following best describes the Locality of reference principle?

   A. If the processor recently referenced a location in memory, it is likely that it will refer to it again in the near future.

   B. If the processor writes to a location referenced in memory, it is likely that it will refer to it again in the near future.

   C. If an application stores information in a location referenced in memory, it is likely to loop through it again in the near future.

   D. None of the above.

   A. If the processor recently referenced a location in memory, it is likely that it will refer to it again in the near future. Because applications generally work in routine looping sections, if a location in memory is accessed, it is very likely that it will be accessed again. The system cache capitalizes on this principle.

16. Which of the following devices is a hardware logic circuit that controls system memory?

   A. RAM controller

   B. Cache controller

C. Physical memory controller

D. Memory controller

   D. Memory controller. The memory controller controls and manages access system memory.

17. Which of the following DRAM technologies was designed to work with 100 MHz memory buses?

   A. EDO RAM

   B. BEDO RAM

   C. FTP RAM

   D. SDRAM

   D. SDRAM. EDO and BEDO DRAM technologies only work well with the 66 MHz memory bus. SDRAM was designed to capitalize on the 100 MHz memory bus.

18. Which of the following DRAM technologies supports burst mode timings of 5-2-2-2 on a 66 MHz memory bus?

   A. EDO RAM

   B. BEDO RAM

   C. FTP RAM

   D. SDRAM

   A. EDO RAM. EDO was an improvement to FPM DRAM that provided a 25–40% increase in access time.

19. HMA is the first 64KB of?

   A. Convential memory

   B. Expanded memory

   C. Extended memory

D. Virtual memory
C. Extended memory. The first 64KB of extended memory was roped off as a control area, and labeled the high-memory area (HMA). This is the area where HIMEM.SYS loads from DOS.

20. Which MS-DOS program can be used to optimize your system's memory?

A. QEMM

B. MEMMAKER

C. MEM

D. MEMORY
B. MEMMAKER. DOS doesn't automatically manage its own memory, so memory management applications emerged. MEMMAKER was included with DOS 6.0.

21. Which device is used to manage the upper memory blocks?

A. HIMEM.SYS

B. EMM.EXE

C. EMM386.EXE

D. MEMMANAGER
C. EMM386.EXE. It allows access to UMA. The addition of this upper memory to the system memory pool increased the usable system (conventional) memory to as much as 720KB.

22. The Upper Memory Area (UMA) ranges from?

A. 0–640KB

B. 0–1024KB

C. 640–792KB

D. 640–1024KB
D. 640–1024KB. The UMA ranges from 640KB to 1024KB. The 384KB of reserved space became known as upper memory.

23. Which of the following Windows 95 tools can be used to view memory utilization?

A. System Monitor

B. QEMM

C. Performance Monitor

D. Task Manager
A. System Monitor. It is a Microsoft Windows 95 utility that can be used to monitor the workstation's hardware, applications, and services. When optimizing memory in Windows 95, you should use the System Monitor to see the effect of any changes you have made to the system.

24. Virtual memory is a combination of which of the following?

A. Physical memory and conventional memory

B. SRAM and DRAM

C. RAM and free hard drive space

D. System memory and system cache
C. RAM and free hard drive space. Virtual memory is a combination of physical memory (RAM) and free hard drive space.

25. Which of the following statements from the CONIG.SYS file depicts the correct load order?

A. DEVICE=C:\DOS\EMM386.EXE
DEVICE=C:\DOS\HIMEM.SYS

B. DEVICE=C:\DOS\HIMEM.COM
DEVICE=C:\DOS\EMM386.EXE

C. DEVICE=C:\DOS\SETVER.EXE
DEVICE=C:\DOS\EMM386.EXE

D. DEVICE=C:\DOS\HIMEM.SYS
DEVICE=C:\DOS\EMM386.EXE
D. HIMEM.SYS must be loaded
before EMM386.EXE.

Chapter 11 Answers

1. What is the correct load order sequence
for the following files?

A. CONFIG.SYS, AUTOEXEC.BAT

B. AUTOEXEC.SYS, CONFIG.BAT

C. ATUOEXEC.BAT, CONFIG.SYS

D. AUTOEXEC.BAT,
COMMAND.COM
A. CONFIG.SYS,
AUTOEXEC.BAT. When starting
DOS, several files are loaded in the
following order: IO.SYS,
MS.DOS.SYS, CONFIG.SYS,
COMMAND.COM, and lastly the
AUTOEXEC.BAT. For more details,
see the Starting DOS section.

2. Which of the following commands will
copy the boot files onto a floppy disk
without erasing any existing data on
the diskette?

A. SYS A: C:

B. FORMAT A: /S

C. COPY BOOTFILES A:\

D. SYS A:
D. SYS A:. If you have a previously
formatted disk and you want to copy
the system files (IO.SYS, MS.DOS.SYS,
and COMMAND.COM) to it, then
you would run SYS A: (This assumes
the system files are located on the
C: drive.) For more details, refer to the
Exam Watch in the Formatting a
Drive section.

3. What three files are copied onto a disk
after formatting when the /s switch
is used?

A. COMMAND.BAT, IO.SYS,
MSDOS.SYS

B. AUTOEXEC.BAT, CONFIG.SYS,
COMMAND.COM

C. IO.SYS, MSDOS.SYS,
COMMAND.COM

D. IO.SYS, MSDOS.SYS, CONFIG.SYS
C. IO.SYS, MSDOS.SYS,
COMMAND.COM. When you use
the FORMAT command with the /s
switch, this copies IO.SYS,
MS.DOS.SYS, and
COMMAND.COM to the
newly formatted drive. For more
details, refer to the Formatting a
Drive section.

4. What key would you press to bypass the
CONFIG.SYS and AUTOEXEC.BAT
during the DOS boot process?

A. F3

B. F5

C. F6

D. F8

B. F5. When you see the "Starting MS-DOS" text message, you can press F5 to bypass the CONFIG.SYS and AUTOEXEC.BAT files. Pressing F8 allows you to selectively bypass commands in the CONFIG.SYS and AUTOEXEC.BAT. For more details, refer to the DOS Configuration Files section.

5. What is a PIF?

A. Program Initialization File

B. Program Information File

C. Permanent Information File

D. Primary Information File

B. Program Information Files. They provide details for Windows 3.*x* on how to start non-Windows (such as DOS) applications. For more details, refer to the Installing and Launching Windows and Non-Windows Applications section.

6. Which of the following files are opened using the SYSEDIT command in Windows 3.*x*?

A. WIN.INI

B. PROGRMAN.INI

C. AUTOEXEC.BAT

D. SYSTEM.INI

E. CONTROL.INI

A, C, D. WIN.INI, AUTOEXEC.BAT, and SYSTEM.INI. The SYSEDIT program is a utility found in Windows 3.*x.* It opens only four files: WIN.INI, SYSTEM.INI, AUTOEXEC.BAT, and CONFIG.SYS. It cannot be used to open other system files. For more details, refer to the Starting Windows 3.*x* section.

7. Which DOS 6 driver manages the upper memory area?

A. EMM387.EXE

B. EMM386.EXE

C. HIMEM.SYS

D. EMM386.COM

B. EMM386.EXE. This file is a memory manager that allows access to the 384KB of the upper memory area. For more details, refer to the DOS Configuration Files section.

8. Which DOS 6 driver manages the extended memory area?

A. EMM387.EXE

B. EMM386.EXE

C. HIMEM.SYS

D. EMM386.COM

C. HIMEM.SYS. This is a memory manager that allows access to memory above 1024KB (1MB), known as extended memory. For more details, refer to the DOS Configuration Files section.

9. During a Windows 95 upgrade from Windows 3.1, you receive the following error message: "Insert Windows 3.*x* Installation Disk 1." What is the most likely cause of this message?

A. You are unable to upgrade form Windows 3.1.

B. Windows 95 couldn't find a current version of DOS.

C. Windows 95 couldn't find a current version of Windows.

D. You are installing from a pirated copy of Windows 95.
   C. If you are running the Windows 95 upgrade installation, it requires a previous version of Windows 3.*x*. If you don't have Windows 3.*x* loaded on your system, you can insert the Windows 3.*x* Installation Disk 1 and the setup will read a file off the disk and continue the installation. For more details, refer to the Upgrading from Win 3.*x* to Windows 95 section.

10. Which of the following initialization files will automatically launch a program when Windows starts?

A. STARTUP.INI

B. BOOT.INI

C. WIN.INI

D. SYSTEM.INI
   C. The WIN.INI controls how Windows starts up. It can also be used to specify applications that need to launch when Windows is started. This concept is accomplished via the Startup folder in Windows 95. For more details, refer to Table 11-5: Windows 3.*x* Operating System Files.

11. The <u>BUFFER</u> statement is found in what file?

A. AUTOEXEC.BAT

B. CONFIG.SYS

C. WIN.INI

D. COMMAND.COM
   B. CONFIG.SYS. The BUFFER statement alerts DOS to the amount of memory to reserve for information transfers to and from the hard drive. For more details, refer to the DOS Configuration Files section.

12. Which file contains system hardware setting specifications?

A. STARTUP.INI

B. HARDWARE.INI

C. WIN.INI

D. SYSTEM.INI
   D. SYSTEM.INI. This file controls the system hardware settings and their associated information. This file also contains a list of drivers for the installed hardware. For more details, refer to Table 11-5: Windows 3.*x* Operating System Files.

13. What file must be loaded in the CONFIG.SYS in order to display color graphics in the DOS environment?

A. COLOR.SYS

B. GRAPHICS.SYS

C. ANSI.SYS

D. VGA.DRV
   C. ANSI.SYS. This file expands the ability of DOS to work with advanced video command sets. You can change the background and text colors. For more details, refer to the DOS Configuration Files section.

14. Windows generates an error message stating it cannot open enough files. Which configuration file needs to be modified?

    A. AUTOEXEC.BAT
    B. WIN.INI
    C. CONFIG.SYS
    D. WINFILE.INI
    C. CONFIG.SYS. The FILES command in the CONFIG.SYS specifies the number of concurrent files that can be opened in DOS. For more details, refer to the DOS Configuration Files section.

15. What driver set would be loaded if you booted a Windows 95 machine in safe mode?

    A. Mouse, Keyboard, VGA
    B. Mouse, Keyboard, CD-ROM, VGA
    C. Mouse, Keyboard, SVGA
    D. Keyboard, CD-ROM, SVGA
    A. Mouse, Keyboard, VGA. Windows 95 Safe mode loads drivers for the keyboard, mouse, and standard VGA graphics adapter. For more details, refer to the Safe Mode section.

16. If the Windows 95 Plug-and-Play option is working and if your hardware is PnP compliant, you should expect:

    A. To manually set IRQ settings
    B. That there will be no device conflicts
    C. That you will only have to manually set I/O port addresses
    D. That you will have to allocate resources manually

    B. That there will be no device conflicts. When Plug-and-Play (PnP) works correctly, there are no resource conflicts because PnP automatically assigns a PnP compliant device the free resource addresses needed for operation. For more details, refer to the Windows 95 Plug-and-Play section.

17. Which of the following are minimum requirements to install Windows 3.*x*? (Choose all that apply.)

    A. An 80286, 80386, or 80386SX processor
    B. A minimum of 2MB of RAM on an 80386 processor
    C. A hard disk with at least 5MB of storage space
    D. A color graphics display adapter
    A, B, C. An 80286, 80386, or 80386SX processor; a minimum of 2MB of RAM on an 80386 processor; and a hard disk with at least 5MB of storage space. The minimum requirements for Windows 3.*x* are an 80286 processor, 1MB of RAM (however, 2MB is needed for a 386 processor), at least 5MB free hard drive space, and a VGA graphics adapter. For more details, refer to the Upgrading from DOS to Windows 3.*x* section.

18. Which of the following files is responsible for loading applications, managing memory, and scheduling task execution?

    A. USER.EXE
    B. MEMMANAGER.EXE

C. GDI.EXE

D. KRNL286EXE/KRNL386.EXE

D. KRNL286EXE/KRNL386.EXE. The KRNL286.EXE or KRNL386.EXE (depending on which processor is in use) is responsible for loading applications, managing memory, and scheduling task execution. For more details, refer to Table 11-5: Windows 3.*x* Operating System Files.

19. Which of the following files displays the Windows logo and determines what mode to start Windows 3.*x* in?

A. STARTUP.INI

B. WIN.INI

C. WIN.COM

D. SETUP.EXE

C. WIN.COM. This file is the executable file that starts Windows 3.*x*. It displays the Windows logo and determines if the system needs to start in Standard mode or 386 Enhanced mode. For more details, refer to Table 11-5: Windows 3.*x* Operating System Files.

20. In 386 Enhanced mode, Windows 3.*x* can:

A. Have both multiple Windows applications and multiple DOS applications active at the same time

B. Have multiple Windows applications but not multiple DOS applications active at the same time

C. Have only a single DOS application active at any given time

D. Have only a single Windows application active when a DOS application is active

A. Have both multiple Windows applications and multiple DOS applications active at the same time. Enhanced mode allows users to run multiple windows applications and DOS-based applications that are in the background can continue to run at the same time. For more details, refer to the Starting Windows 3.*x* section.

21. Which of the following are minimum requirements to install Windows 95? (Choose all that apply.)

A. 80286 processor

B. 80386 processor

C. 80486 processor

D. 4MB of memory

E. 8MB of memory

B, D. 80386 processor, 4MB of memory. The minimum requirements for Windows 95 are a 386DX-20 with 4MB of memory. To be more realistic, you should have at least a 486 with 32MB of RAM. For more details, refer to the Upgrading from DOS to Windows 95 section.

22. Which mode does Windows 95 automatically start up in?

A. Standard mode

B. Enhanced mode

C. Normal mode

D. Safe mode

C. Normal mode. This mode is the mode in which Windows 95 is started by default. Normal mode provides full functionality of the Windows 95 Explorer, and loads all of the drivers that are installed on the system. For more details, refer to Windows 95 Boot Modes section.

23. Which of the following are valid ways to start a DOS application in Windows 95? (Choose all that apply.)

    A. By creating a PIF and double-clicking on it

    B. By using the DEFAULT.PIF if a custom PIF hasn't been created

    C. By creating a shortcut and double-clicking on it

    D. By launching the executable from File Manager

    E. By launching the executable from Windows Explorer
    C, E. By creating a shortcut and double-clicking on it, and by launching the executable from Windows Explorer. Non-Windows (DOS) applications can be started in Windows 95 by creating a shortcut (this allows configuration similar to the Windows 3.*x* PIF files) or by using Windows Explorer. You can also start DOS applications by using the RUN command found in the START menu. For more details, refer to the Installing and Launching Windows and Non-Windows Applications section.

24. Which key do you need to press to access the Windows 95 boot menu?

    A. F3

    B. F5

    C. F6

    D. F8
    D. F8. To access the Windows 95 boot menu, you need to press F8 when you see the "Starting Windows 95" text message. For more details, refer to the Windows 95 Boot Modes section.

25. What is the largest partition size found in MS-DOS, Windows 3.*x*, and Windows 95 (version A)?

    A. 1024MB

    B. 2048MB

    C. 4096MB

    D. 8192MB
    B. 2048MB. The largest partition size supported on the FAT16 file system is 2048MB (2GB). MS-DOS, Windows 3.*x*, and Windows 95 (version A) all utilize the FAT16 file system. Windows 95 (version B) and Windows 98 can take advantage of the FAT32 file system that allows for partitions greater than 2GB. For more details, refer to the Partition section.

Chapter 12 Answers

1. After upgrading your computer to a newer version of DOS, an older application displays the error message "Incorrect DOS version." What should you do to run this application?

    A. Revert to the previous version of DOS.

    B. Add an entry for the application to the application version-table.

C. Use the SETVER command.

D. Contact the support line for the application.
C. SETVER allows DOS-based applications to function as if they are in the version of DOS the application was design to use. For more details refer to the Incorrect DOS version section.

2. After clicking on the icon for your word processing application, Windows 3.*x* reports the following error message: "Invalid working directory." What should you do first?

   A. Check the path statement in the AUTOEXEC.BAT file.

   B. Run SCANDISK.

   C. Check the properties for the program group.

   D. Check the properties for the program item icon.
   D. Check the properties for the program item icon. If you are receiving errors about an invalid working directory, you should view the settings of the shortcut Program Item Properties (Windows 3.*x*) or Shortcut (Windows 95/98) and then verify that the working directory exists and that it is correct. For more details refer to the Invalid working directory section.

3. Your PC running Windows 95 cannot connect to the network. You have verified the physical connection is good and the

NIC (network interface card) indicates a link. What should you try next?

   A. Check the version of Windows 95 (version A or version B).

   B. Check the network protocols.

   C. Run the Windows 95 setup utility.

   D. Run the System Monitor utility.
   B. Check the network protocols. In order for two networked machines to communicate they must share a common protocol. For more details refer to the Cannot Log On to Network section.

4. You suspect that you have contracted a computer virus. Which will not be affected by the virus?

   A. The System BIOS

   B. Files stored on a floppy diskette

   C. Files stored on your hard drive

   D. The Boot Sector
   A. The System BIOS. BIOS is stored on an EEPROM and it would be impossible for a virus to affect this program. Files stored on a hard drive or floppy drive are the most susceptible, however there are viruses that can infect the boot sector. For more details refer to the Viruses and Virus Types section.

5. What log can be used to troubleshoot a Windows 95 installation problem?

   A. DEVICE.LOG

   B. BOOT.LOG

C. SETUPLOG.TXT

D. BOOTLOG.TXT
   D. BOOTLOG.TXT. This log records all the devices and drivers that the system attempts to load. It reports the status of devices and drivers and if they were successfully loaded. For more details refer to the Operating System Will Not Boot section.

6. Windows 95 automatically creates a backup copy of the Registry files during the boot process. What file extension is used for the backup copies?

   A. DAT

   B. DA0

   C. BAK

   D. REG
      B. DA0. Windows 95 makes a backup of your current registry every time you successfully boot into Windows 95. The backup files are SYSTEM.DA0 and USER.DA0. For more details refer to the Registry Editor section.

7. The majority of the Windows 95 configuration information is stored in:

   A. AUTOEXEC.BAT and CONFIG.SYS

   B. Hkey_localmachine and Hkey_dyn_data

   C. USER.DAT and SYSTEM.DAT

   D. WIN.INI and SYSTEM.INI.
      C. USER.DAT and SYSTEM.DAT. The Windows 95 registry (comprised of SYSTEM.DAT and USER.DAT) replaces the configuration files found in DOS and Windows 3.x such as the AUTOEXEC.BAT, CONFIG.SYS, WIN.INI, and SYSTEM.INI. For more details refer to the Registry Editor section.

8. To prevent subsequent changes to the file README.TXT, you would run which command?

   A. ATTRIB +A README.TXT

   B. ATTRIB +R README.TXT

   C. ATTRIB –R README.TXT

   D. ATTRIB +H README.TXT
      B. ATTRIB +R README.TXT. The ATTRIB command allows you set file attributes to any of the following: Read Only, System, Hidden, and/or Archive. For more details refer to the ATTRIB.EXE section.

9. What is the most likely cause of POST 201 error?

   A. Memory

   B. Keyboard

   C. Motherboard

   D. Floppy Drive
      A. Memory. When a PC boots up, the Power On Self-Test (POST) performs several hardware diagnostic checks. 200 series errors are typically related to memory problems. For more details refer to Table 12-1: POST Diagnostic Error Codes.

10. Which of the following memory managers is required for Windows 3.x to access extended memory?

    A. EMM386.EXE

    B. EXTMEM.SYS

C. HIGHMEM.SYS

D. HIMEM.SYS

D. HIMEM.SYS. Windows 3.*x* requires that the HIMEM.SYS driver be loaded in order to access extended Memory. Loading HIMEM.SYS allows Windows 3.*x* to access memory above 1024KB. For more details refer to the HIMEM.SYS Not Loaded section.

11. What two files comprise a Windows 3.*x* permanent swap file?

A. SPART.PAR and SWAP.PAR

B. 386SPART.PAR and SPART.PAR

C. 386SPART.PAR and SWAP.PAR

D. 386SWAP.PAR and SPART.PAR

B. 386SPART.PAR and SPART.PAR. When Windows creates a Permanent swap file, two hidden files are created on your hard drive. The hidden files are 386SPART.PAR (located in the root directory) and SPART.PAR (located in the Windows directory). For more details refer to the Swapfile Corrupt section.

12. Which applet located in the Windows 95 Control Panel is used to create an Emergency Repair Disk?

A. FirstAid

B. System

C. Add/Remove Programs

D. Live Update

C. Add/Remove Programs. To create an Emergency Boot Disk in Windows 95, you must open the Add/Remove Programs applet in Control Panel, select the Startup Disk tab, and select the "Create Disk" button. For more details refer to Exercise 12-1: Creating an Emergency Boot Disk for Windows 95 or Windows 98.

13. Which Windows 95 utility can be used to scan and repair hard disk surface errors?

A. SCANDISK

B. DEFRAG

C. CHKDISK

D. FORMAT

A. SCANDISK. ScanDisk is a utility that can be used to check disk drives for surface errors and, when passed the /f switch, fix them. Running the ScanDisk utility can solve many reoccurring problems. For more details refer to the SCANDISK.EXE section.

14. You suspect your Master Boot Record has been infected with a virus. What utility and switch can be used to restore the Master Boot Record?

A. FDISK/REPAIR

B. MBR/REPAIR

C. FDISK/MBR

D. FORMAT/MBR

C. FDISK/MBR. FDISK/MBR can be used to replace the Master Boot Record with a backup copy. This may become necessary if the Master Boot Record becomes infected with a virus. For more details refer to the FDISK.EXE section.

15. Which Windows 95 Control Panel applet contains a tab for Device Manager?

    A. Devices

    B. System

    C. Network

    D. Conflict Troubleshooter
       B. System. To access Device Manager, you need to double-click on the System icon in the Control Panel. Alternatively, you can access the System properties by right clicking on My Computer and selecting Properties. For more details refer to the System Applet section.

16. What is the executable file name that launches the Windows 95 Registry Editor application?

    A. REGEDIT32.EXE

    B. REGEDIT.COM

    C. REGEDT32.COM

    D. REGEDIT.EXE
       D. REGEDIT.EXE. The Windows 95 Registry Editor application is launched via the RUN command by typing REGEDIT. Since REGEDIT.EXE is an executable file, you don't have to specify the ".EXE" on the end of the file name. For more details refer to the Registry Editor section.

17. What Windows 95 Registry Key is responsible for storing Hardware Profile information?

    A. Hkey_Localmachine

    B. Hkey_Current_Config

    C. Hkey_Hardware_Profiles

    D. Hkey_Current_User
       B. Hkey_Current_Config. Hkey_Current_Config stores Hardware Profile Information. For more details refer to Table 12.2: Windows 95 Registry Keys.

18. What term is used to describe the effects of a virus?

    A. Payload

    B. Load

    C. Devastation Factor

    D. The Fujitsu Scale
       A. Payload. This term refers to the effects, either intended or accidental, of a virus. The payload can be benign or malignant. For more details refer to the Payload section.

19. Which of the following Windows 95 utilities can be used to track individual system components and resources?

    A. Task Manager

    B. Network Task Manager

    C. System Monitor

    D. System Resource Meter
       C. System Monitor. This utility can be used to track the performance of your Windows 95 or Windows 98 system. For more details refer to the System Monitor section.

20. Where are the Windows 95 configuration files (SYSTEM.DAT and USER.DAT) stored by default?

A. \WINDOWS\SYSTEM directory

B. \WINDOWS\SYSTEM32 directory

C. \WINDOWS\REGISTRY directory

D. \WINDOWS directory
   D. \WINDOWS directory. The Windows configuration files (USER.DAT and SYSTEM.DAT) are hidden, read-only files located in the Windows directory. For more details refer to the Registry Editor section

21. The default Windows 95 location for the Defrag and ScanDisk programs is:

    A. Control Panel, System, Device Manager

    B. Programs, Accessories, System Tools

    C. Programs, System Tools

    D. Run, Programs, System Tools
       B. Programs, Accessories, System Tools. The ScanDisk and DEFRAG utilities are accessed by clicking on Start, Programs, Accessories, System Tools. For more details refer to the Windows-Based Tools section.

22. Which of the following is a new utility included with Windows 95?

    A. Print Manager

    B. Program Manager

    C. Device Manager

    D. Control Panel
       C. Device Manager. This utility is provided with Windows 95 and Windows 98. Device Manager lists all of the devices that are installed in the system and their properties. For more details refer to the Device Manager section.

23. The Windows 95 Registry sections are referred to as what?

    A. Classes

    B. Subkeys

    C. Keys

    D. Folders
       C. Keys. The data from these SYSTEM.DAT and USER.DAT files is categorized into six sections called Keys. For more details refer to the Registry Editor section.

24. What switch is used with the DOS 6.*x* version of ScanDisk to automatically fix any errors that are found?

    A. /F

    B. /FIX

    C. /R

    D. /REPAIR
       B. /FIX. ScanDisk is a utility that can be used to check disk drives for surface errors and, when passed the /fix switch, fix them. For more details refer to the SCANDISK.EXE found under the DOS- and Windows-Based Utilities and Commands/Switches section.

25. Which of the following are valid types of viruses? (Choose all that apply.)

    A. Boot Sector Virus

    B. Track Zero Virus

    C. Macro Virus

    D. System Cache Virus

    E. Memory Virus
       A, C, E. Boot Sector Virus, Macro Virus, and Memory Virus. Common virus types include Boot Sector

Viruses, FAT Master Boot Record Viruses, File Viruses, Memory Viruses, Macro Viruses, and Hoax Viruses. For more details refer to the Types of Viruses section.

Chapter 13 Answers

1. Which of the following types of network security are supported by Windows 95/98? (Choose all that apply.)

   A. User level

   B. Share level

   C. Password-protected shares

   D. Access permissions
   A, B, C, D. User level, share level, password-protected shares, and access permissions. Share level and password-protected shares are the same thing, as are user level and access permissions.

2. TCP/IP clients connect to various services through: _____.

   A. Connectors

   B. Protocols

   C. Ports

   D. SOCKS
   C. Ports. Different TCP/IP services, such as HTTP and FTP, connect over standard ports, defined by the IETF's RFC 1700.

3. Which of the following is the more secure network security model?

   A. User level

   B. Share level

   C. Password protected shares

   D. All models provide the same level of security.
   A. User level. This level of security is more secure. User-level security allows for the definition of rights based on unique usernames and passwords, as opposed to share-level security and password-level security, that assign a single password for each class of users to a specific resource. Any number of users could access the resource through the single share password.

4. What is the standard port used for FTP connections?

   A. 21

   B. 27

   C. 80

   D. 443
   A. Port 21. Services can be configured to use other ports as well, but the default FTP service port is 21.

5. What is the standard port used for non-secure HTTP connections?

   A. 21

   B. 27

   C. 80

   D. 443
   C. Port 80. This is the standard port used by Web browsers and Web servers to provide Web browsing capabilities on the Internet. Port 443 is the port used for secure Web connectivity.

6. You are trying to access a file named CONFIG.DOC on a server named STANDARDS, under the share WORKSTATION, and the directory WINDOWS98. Keeping in mind the UNC standard, what is the proper syntax for accessing this document?

   A. \\STANDARDS\CONFIG.DOC

   B. \\STANDARDS\WORKSTATION\ CONFIG.DOC

   C. \\STANDARDS\WORKSTATION\ WINDOWS98\CONFIG.DOC

   D. \\STANDARDS\WINDOWS98\ WORKSTATION\CONFIG.DOC
   C. \\STANDARDS\WORKSTATION\ WINDOWS98\CONFIG.DOC. The Universal Naming Convention is \\servername\sharename\path\filename.

7. You have a share named DOCS on a server named HR. How do you make DOCS a hidden share?

   A. Change the share name to DOCS$.

   B. Change the share name to $DOCS.

   C. Change the server name to HR$.

   D. Change the share name to DOCS#.
   A. Change the share name to DOCS$. Adding a $ to the end of a share name makes it a hidden share.

8. Which of the following components are NOT required to make a dialup Internet connection to an ISP? (Choose all that apply.)

   A. Modem

   B. Dialup Adapter

   C. TCP/IP protocol

   D. None of the above.
   D. None of the above. All of the listed components are required to make a dial-up Internet connection.

9. Which of the following protocols can run over SLIP? (Choose all that apply.)

   A. PPP

   B. TCP/IP

   C. IPX

   D. NetBEUI
   B. TCP/IP. This is the only protocol that can run over SLIP (Serial Line Internet Protocol).

10. Which of the following protocols can run over PPP? (Choose all that apply.)

    A. SLIP

    B. TCP/IP

    C. IPX

    D. NetBEUI
    B, C, and D. TCP/IP, IPX, and NetBEUI. These protocols can all run over the Point to Point Protocol (PPP). SLIP does not run over PPP; in fact, PPP is the dial-up protocol that has replaced SLIP.

11. A Fully Qualified Domain Name (FQDN) is translated into an IP address by what service?

    A. SLIP

    B. PPP

    C. DHCP

    D. DNS
    D. DNS. Domain Name System provides the service through which a

domain name can be translated to the associated unique IP address.

12. The Secure Hypertext Transfer Protocol uses what to provide encryption services?

    A. RAS
    B. Certificates
    C. PKI
    D. SSL

    D. SSL. Secure Socket Layer, which was developed by Netscape, is used to provide the encryption services over HTTP, setting it up as HTTPS.

13. Which of the following is the protocol required for dialup Internet connectivity?

    A. TCP/IP
    B. Microsoft Dialup Adapter
    C. SLIP
    D. IPX

    A. TCP/IP. This protocol is required for any Internet connectivity. While SLIP can be used for the dial-up connection and PPP could be used in its place, only TCP/IP is a required protocol.

14. Which of the following protocols are used in sending e-mail? (Choose all that apply.)

    A. POP3
    B. SMTP
    C. SNMP
    D. NNTP

    B. SMTP. Simple Mail Transport Protocol is used in sending e-mail. POP3 is used for retrieving e-mail, SNMP (Small Network Management

Protocol) is used for network management, and NNTP is used for communicating with newsgroups.

15. Which of the following protocols are used in retrieving e-mail? (Choose all that apply.)

    A. POP3
    B. SMTP
    C. SNMP
    D. NNTP

    A. POP3. Post Office Protocol, version 3, is used in retrieving e-mail. SMTP (Simple Mail Transport Protocol) is the protocol used in sending e-mail. SNMP (Small Network Management Protocol) is used for network management, and NNTP is used for communicating with newsgroups.

16. Which of the following protocols is used in posting and reading newsgroup articles?

    A. POP3
    B. SMTP
    C. SNMP
    D. NNTP

    D. NNTP. Network News Transport Protocol is used for reading and posting newsgroup articles through a newsreader application.

17. In Windows 95/98, where do you go to add the TCP/IP protocol?

    A. Add/Remove Programs applet in the Control Panel
    B. System properties

C. Device manager

D. Network applet in Control Panel
   D. Network applet in Control Panel. Networking components such as protocols, adapters, and network services are added through the Network applet in Control Panel.

18. In Windows 95/98, where do you go to add the Dialup Networking component?

    A. Add/Remove Programs applet in the Control Panel

    B. System properties

    C. Device manager

    D. Network applet in Control Panel
       A. Add/Remove Programs applet in the Control Panel. The Dial-Up Networking component is installed through the Add/Remove Programs applet in the Control Panel. The Dial-Up adapter and TCP/IP protocol are added through the Network applet in the Control Panel.

19. Which of the following resources can be shared through Windows networking? (Choose all that apply.)

    A. Printers

    B. Folders

    C. Modems

    D. Network connections
       A, B. Printers and folders. These resources are the only items that can be shared through Windows networking.

20. Which protocol is associated with browsing the Web?

A. HTML

B. HTTP

C. FTP

D. WWW
   B. HTTP. Hypertext Transfer Protocol is associated with browsing the Web. HTML is the language used to author Web pages. FTP is the protocol used to transfer files, and WWW, the abbreviation for World Wide Web, is not a protocol.

Scenario for questions 21–25: You wish to make the DOCUMENTS directory on your C: drive available to the other users in your workgroup. Your computer name is WORKSTATION. You are running the Windows 98 operating system. All of the workstations in your organization are running TCP/IP and NetBEUI. The TCP/IP configuration information is statically assigned to each client. The following five questions present additional qualifiers to this scenario.

21. What service would make the TCP/IP client configuration in your organization easier to manage?

    A. SNMP

    B. DHCP

    C. DNS

    D. IPX
       B. DHCP. Dynamic Host Configuration Protocol lets you dynamically assign TCP/IP addresses to clients on the network. In addition, you will be able to assign DNS information, the default gateway, the subnet mask, and a variety of other TCP/IP configuration settings.

22. Which protocol(s) must be installed on your workstation to allow it to communicate with other clients on the network? (Choose the best answer.)

    A. Only TCP/IP

    B. Only NetBEUI

    C. You must have both TCP/IP and NetBEUI installed.

    D. You may have either TCP/IP or NetBEUI installed.
       D. You may have either TCP/IP or NetBEUI installed. Either TCP/IP or NetBEUI will allow you to communicate with other workstations on your network. You could have either or both protocols installed.

23. If you do not care who is able to access the DOCUMENTS share, and want an easy-to-administer security method, which would be your best choice?

    A. User level

    B. Access permissions

    C. Password-protected shares

    D. None of the above
       C. Password-protected shares. Password-protected shares are the easiest to administer, because you simply set an access password, and provide that password to any users who need access to the share. Access permissions and user-level security are the same thing, and both require granting permissions to specific users who need access to the share.

24. If you want to be able to track which users are accessing your documents share, which network security method should you choose?

    A. User level

    B. Password-protected shares

    C. Share level

    D. None of the above
       A. User level. This level of security allows you to assign usernames and passwords for each user who will be given access to your share. Since you assign rights on a user-by-user basis, you would be able to track which users were accessing the share.

25. On your computer, you have a file named TIMESHEET.XLS in the PROJECT2 directory under the DOCUMENTS share. How would a user on the network access this file?

    A. \\WORKSTATION\PROJECT2\ TIMESHEET.XLS

    B. \\WORKSTATION\DOCUMENT$\ TIMESHARE.XLS

    C. \\WORKSTATION\DOCUMENTS\ PROJECT2\TIMESHEET.XLS

    D. \\WORKSTATION\DOCUMENTS\ TIMESHARE.XLS
       C. The file can be accessed through the UNC: \\WORKSTATION\DOCUMENTS\ PROJECT2\TIMESHEET.XLS.

B

About the CD

T

he CD-ROM contains a browser-based testing product, the Personal Testing Center. The Personal Testing Center is easy to install on any Windows 95/98/NT computer.

Installing the Personal Testing Center

Double clicking on the SETUP.HTML file on the CD will cycle you through an introductory page on the *Test Yourself* software. On the second page, you will have to read and accept the license agreement. Once you have read the agreement, click on the Agree icon and you will be brought to the *Personal Testing Center's* main page.

On the main page, you will find links to the Personal Testing Center, to the electronic version of the book, and to other resources you may find helpful. Click on the first link to the Personal Testing Center and you will be brought to the Quick Start page. Here you can choose to run the Personal Testing Center from the CD or install it to your hard drive.

Installing the Personal Testing Center to your hard drive is an easy process. Click on the Install to Hard Drive icon and the procedure will start for you. An instructional box will appear, and walk you through the remainder of the installation. If installed to the hard drive, the Personal Testing Center program group will be created in the Start Programs folder.

Should you wish to run the software from the CD-ROM, the steps are the same as above until you reach the point where you would select the Install to Hard Drive icon. Here, select Run from CD icon and the exam will automatically begin.

To uninstall the program from your hard disk, use the add/remove programs feature in your Windows Control Panel. InstallShield will run uninstall.

Test Type Choices

With the Personal Testing Center, you have three options in which to run the program: Live, Practice, and Review. Each test type will draw from a pool of over 300 potential questions. Your choice of test type will depend on whether you would like to simulate an actual Network+ exam, receive instant feedback on your answer choices, or review concepts using the testing simulator. Note that selecting the Full Screen icon on Internet Explorer's standard toolbar gives you the best display of the Personal Testing Center.

Live

The Live timed test type is meant to reflect the actual exam as closely as possible. You will have 90 minutes in which to complete the exam. You will have the option to skip questions and return to them later, move to the previous question, or end the exam. Once the timer has expired, you will automatically go to the scoring page to review your test results.

Managing Windows

The testing application runs inside an Internet Explorer 4.0 or 5.0 browser window. We recommend that you use the full-screen view to minimize the amount of text scrolling you need to do. However, the application will initiate a second iteration of the browser when you link to an Answer in Depth or a Review Graphic. If you are running in full-screen view, the second iteration of the browser will be covered by the first. You can toggle between the two windows with ALT-TAB, you can click your task bar to maximize the second window, or you can get out of full-screen mode and arrange the two windows so they are both visible on the screen at the same time. The application will not initiate more than two browser windows, so you aren't left with hundreds of open windows for each Answer in Depth or Review Graphic that you view.

Saving Scores as Cookies

Your exam score is stored as a browser cookie. If you've configured your browser to accept cookies, your score will be stored in a cookie named History. If you don't accept cookies, you cannot permanently save your scores. If you delete the History cookie, the scores will be deleted permanently.

Using the Browser Buttons

The test application runs inside the Internet Explorer 4.0 browser. You should navigate from screen to screen by using the application's buttons, not the browser's buttons.

JavaScript Errors

If you encounter a JavaScript error, you should be able to proceed within the application. If you cannot, shut down your Internet Explorer 4.0 browser session and re-launch the testing application.

Practice

When choosing the Practice exam type, you have the option of receiving instant feedback as to whether your selected answer is correct. The questions will be presented to you in numerical order, and you will see every question in the available question pool for each section you chose to be tested on.

As with the Live exam type, you have the option of continuing through the entire exam without seeing the correct answer for each question. The number of questions you answered correctly, along with the percentage of correct answers, will be displayed during the post-exam summary report. Once you have answered a question, click the Answer icon to display the correct answer.

You have the option of ending the Practice exam at any time, but your post-exam summary screen may reflect an incorrect percentage based on the number of questions you failed to answer. Questions that are skipped are counted as incorrect answers on the post-exam summary screen.

Review

During the Review exam type, you will be presented with questions similar to both the Live and Practice exam types. However, the Answer icon is not present, as every question will have the correct answer posted near the bottom of the screen. You have the option of answering the question without looking at the correct answer. In the Review exam type, you can also return to previous questions and skip to the next question, as well as end the exam by clicking the Stop icon.

The Review exam type is recommended when you have already completed the Live exam type once or twice, and would now like to determine which questions you answered correctly.

Questions with Answers

For the Practice and Review exam types, you will have the option of clicking a hyperlink titled Answers in Depth, which will present relevant study material aimed at exposing the logic behind the answer in a separate browser window. By having two browsers open (one for the test engine and one for the review information), you can quickly alternate between the two windows while keeping your place in the exam. You will find that additional windows are not generated as you follow hyperlinks throughout the test engine.

Scoring

The Personal Testing Center post-exam summary screen, called Benchmark Yourself, displays the results for each section you chose to be tested on, including a bar graph similar to the real exam, which displays the percentage of correct answers. You can compare your percentage to the actual passing percentage for each section. The percentage displayed on the post-exam summary screen is not the actual percentage required to pass the exam. You'll see the number of questions you answered correctly compared to the total number of questions you were tested on. If you choose to skip a question, it will be marked as incorrect. Ending the exam by clicking the End button with questions still unanswered lowers your percentage, as these questions will be marked as incorrect.

Clicking the End button and then the Home button allows you to choose another exam type, or test yourself on another section.

C

About the
Web Site

Access Global Knowledge

As you know by now, Global Knowledge is the largest independent IT training company in the world. Just by purchasing this book, you have also secured a free subscription to the Global Knowledge Web site and its many resources. You can find it at:

http://access.globalknowledge.com

You can log on directly at the Global Knowledge site, and you will be e-mailed a new, secure password immediately upon registering.

What You'll Find There. . .

The wealth of useful information at the Global Knowledge site falls into three categories:

Skills Gap Analysis

Global Knowledge offers several ways for you to analyze your networking skills and discover where they may be lacking. Using Global Knowledge's trademarked Competence Key Tool, you can do a skills gap analysis and get recommendations for where you may need to do some more studying. (Sorry, it just might not end with this book!)

Networking

You'll also gain valuable access to another asset: people. At the Access Global site, you'll find threaded discussions, as well as live discussions. Talk to other certification candidates, get advice from folks who have already taken the exams, and get access to instructors.

Product Offerings

Of course, Global Knowledge also offers its products here, and you may find some valuable items for purchase—CBTs, books, or courses. Browse freely and see if there's something that could help you take that next step in career enhancement.

D

DOS Command Reference

ATTRIB

The DOS ATTRIB command can be used to set the attributes of a file. Attributes are properties of a file, such as its ability to be written to. The attributes that can be set are as follows:

- **Read-Only**   When the file can only be read. The read-only attribute keeps important files from being written to.
- **Archive**   Used to mark the archive status of files. In most cases, backup utilities skip files that do not have the archive attribute.
- **System**   Used to mark files that are vital to the system. In most cases, the operating system does not allow files that have the system attribute to be deleted.
- **Hidden**   Used to mark files that are to be hidden. Files are not visible in standard directory listings. (They can, however, be seen using the dir/a command.)

Each attribute can be turned on by placing a + (plus sign) in front of the attribute. In turn, they can be turned off by placing a – (minus sign) in front of the attribute.

Switches

The only switch that the attribute command accepts is /s. The /s switch applies the attributes to the selected directory, and all subdirectories. ATTRIB without any switches is applied only to the particular file or directory. ATTRIB without any attributes specified displays the attributes of the selected file or directory.

Usage

The syntax for the ATTRIB command is as follows:

```
attrib <attributes> <filename and/or path> [/s]
```

CHKDSK

CHKDSK is used to check the integrity of the file system. CHKDSK can fix most of the problems that it encounters. CHKDSK is an older program not found on newer computers (DOS 6.2 and later).

Switches

- **/f** Tells CHKDSK that it is permitted to fix the errors that it encounters
- **/v** Displays the full path of each file as it checks them

Usage

The syntax for the CHKDSK command is as follows:

```
chkdsk <disk and/or path and/or filename> [/f][/v]
```

COPY

The COPY command is used to copy files from one subdirectory to another or from one disk to another. Like the DEL command, wildcard characters can be used, which allows multiple files to be copied with a single command. It is highly recommended that you make a copy of the AUTOEXEC.BAT and CONFIG.SYS files prior to making any changes.

Switches

- **/A** Indicates an ASCII text file
- **/B** Indicates a binary file
- **Destination** Specifies the directory and/or filename for the new file(s)
- **/V** Verifies that new files are written correctly
- **/Y** Suppresses prompting to confirm you want to overwrite an existing destination file
- **/-Y** Causes prompting to confirm you want to overwrite an existing destination file

Usage

The syntax for the COPY command is as follows:

```
copy [/A | /B] source [/A | /B] [+ source [/A | /B] [+
...]] [destination
 [/A | /B]] [/V] [/Y | /-Y]
```

CLS

CLS is a very simple command that clears the screen. This is merely a cosmetic command that allows you to remove from view the results of any previous DOS commands. CLS doesn't support the use of any switches.

Usage

The syntax for the CLS command is as follows:

```
cls
```

DEL

The DEL command is used to delete files from a floppy or hard disk. Wildcard characters can be used with the DEL command to delete multiple files with a single command.

Switches

- ■ /P   Prompts for confirmation before deleting each file
- ■ /F   Forces deleting of read-only files
- ■ /S   Deletes specified files from all subdirectories
- ■ /Q   Quiet mode, does not prompt before deletion on global wildcard
- ■ /A   Selects files to delete based on attributes:

- **R** Read-only files
- **S** System files
- **H** Hidden files
- **A** Files ready for archiving

Usage

The syntax for the DEL command is as follows:

```
del [/P] [/F] [/S] [/Q] [/A[[:]attributes]]
[[drive:][path]filename
```

DELTREE

The DELTREE command is used to delete a tree of files. In other words, DELTREE deletes a directory and all of the subdirectories below it. DELTREE is a powerful tool that can be extremely useful, but it can also cause a great deal of trouble. DELTREE is capable of deleting files with the hidden, system, and read-only attributes without any additional steps.

Switches

The only switch that DELTREE accepts is /y. DELTREE /y is used to delete trees of files without any confirmation. The files are simply deleted. Be warned that this command deletes *everything* below the directory you specify without prompting for confirmation first.

Usage

The syntax for the DELTREE command is as follows:

```
deltree [/y] <directory(s) or filename(s)>
```

DIR

The DIR command is used to display files on different types of storage media including hard disks, floppy disks, and CD-ROMs. Typing DIR at the DOS prompt will display a listing of all the files in the current directory.

Switches

- /P   Pauses after each screenful of information
- /W   Uses wide-list format
- /A   Displays files with specified attributes
- /O   Lists files in sorted order:
    - N   By name (alphabetic)
    - E   By extension (alphabetic)
    - G   Group directories first
    - C   By compression ratio (smallest first)
    - S   By size (smallest first)
    - D   By data and time (earliest first)
- /S   Displays files in specified directory and all subdirectories
- /B   Uses bare format (no heading information or summary)
- /L   Uses lowercase
- /C[H]   Displays file's compression ratio; /CH uses host allocation unit size

Usage

The syntax for the DIR command is as follows:

```
dir [drive:][path][filename] [/P] [/W] [/A[:]attribs]]
[/O[[:]sortord]]
    [/S] [/B] [/L] [/C[H]]
```

DISKCOPY

DISKCOPY copies the contents of one disk onto another. The contents are copied exactly, including any system files. A boot disk can be copied using DISKCOPY, which results in another working boot disk.

Switches

- **/1** Used to specify that only the first disk should be copied (an older switch that is rarely used).

- **/m** Used to specify that the source disk should be copied only to memory. This switch copies as much of the source disk into memory as possible, and then requests that the target disk be put into the drive. The information that was copied into memory is then copied onto the target, and the process is repeated until the entire disk is copied. (This is the default for DOS 6.*x* and earlier.)

- **/v** Used to specify that the copy should be verified after completion.

Usage

The syntax for the DISKCOPY command is as follows:

```
diskcopy <source drive> <destination drive>
```

EDIT

EDIT is a text editor with color pull-down menus and support for the mouse. EDIT can be used to modify text files. EDIT's most common use is to modify system files such as the AUTOEXEC.BAT and the CONFIG.SYS, but it can be used for anything that requires a text editor.

Switches

- **/b**   Forces EDIT to be started in a monochrome mode rather than the standard color VGA mode.

- **/h**   Forces EDIT to be run displaying the maximum number of lines that your computer can use. In most cases, more of a text file is displayed on the screen at one time, making modifications a bit easier.

- **/r**   Forces EDIT to load the file in read-only mode, no matter what the file attributes are.

Usage

The syntax for the EDIT command is as follows:

```
edit [/b][/h][/r] <filename>
```

FDISK

The FDISK command can be used to create and delete partitions on the system's hard drives. Be warned that FDISK.EXE makes changes that are permanent and could easily render the system unbootable and make all data on the hard drives inaccessible. Use FDISK with care and ensure that all your data is backed up.

Switches

- **/status**   Displays information about the current configuration of the drives in the computer. No changes can be made; this is merely for informational purposes.

- **/mbr**   Replaces the Master Boot Record with a backup copy. This is sometimes useful for removing viruses that have become resident in the boot record of a computer.

Usage

The syntax for the FDISK command is as follows:

```
fdisk [/status][/mbr]
```

FORMAT

FORMAT is used to erase all of the data from a partition of a drive. FORMAT is effective and will erase all of the data on the partition it is used on.

Switches

- **/v** Followed by a colon and some text, this switch specifies the volume label that the disk will be given after the format.

- **/q** Forces a quick format. The files are not erased from the partition; the file allocation table is deleted with a new blank one put in its place. This does *not* remove viruses from infected floppy disks.

- **/f** Followed by a colon, this switch specifies the size of floppy disk to format. Possible sizes are: 160, 180, 320, 360, 720, 1.2, 1.44, and 2.88, assuming your hardware supports them.

- **/b** Allocates space on the disk for system files, but does not put them there.

- **/s** Allocates space on the disk for system files and puts them there.

- **/c** Checks all of the clusters on the drive that are marked as bad to verify that they are not recoverable.

Usage

The syntax for the FORMAT command is as follows:

```
format <drive letter> [/V:label][/q][/f:size][/b][/s][/c]
```

LABEL

LABEL changes the disk label of the specified drive. LABEL is not used very frequently, but is useful to be familiar with.

Usage

The syntax for the LABEL command is as follows:

```
label <drive letter>
```

MEM

The MEM command displays information on the programs that are currently in memory and how much memory they are using. In addition MEM tells how much memory the system has installed in it, and how much of that is available.

Switches

- **/c** Displays the amount of memory that is in use by each program
- **/d** Displays the amount of each segment of memory that is used by each program
- **/f** Displays information on the amount of memory that is free
- **/p** Pauses after each full screen of text is displayed

Usage

The syntax for the MEM command is as follows:

```
mem [/c] [/d] [/f] [/p]
```

MORE

MORE displays the contents of a file one page at a time. MORE is very helpful in reading long text files and program documentation.

Usage

The syntax for the MORE command is as follows:

```
more <filename>
```

MOVE

MOVE is a command that moves all of the files and/or directories from one location to another.

Switches

- **/y**   Used to force all files to be moved without prompting for confirmation. Be warned that this could be dangerous.
- **/-y**   Used to force MOVE to prompt you for each file.

Usage

The syntax for the MOVE command is as follows:

```
move [/y] <source file or directory> <destination file or
directory>
```

REN

The REN command allows you to change the name of a file. This
command is useful when you need to update a file while keeping a backup
copy of the original file. While the REN command is used to change the
name of the file, you can't change the location of the file unless you use the
MOVE command. REN doesn't support the use of any switches.

Usage

The syntax for the REN command is as follows:

```
ren [drive:][path]filename1 filename2.
```

SUBST

The SUBST command can be used to substitute a drive letter for another
drive letter or a path on a disk. SUBST cannot be used on network drives.

Switches

- **/d**   Deletes the substituted drive

Usage

The syntax for the SUBST command is as follows:

```
subst <new drive letter> <source drive and path> [/d]
```

SYS

The SYS command copies the system files to a disk and makes the
disk bootable.

Usage

The syntax for the SYS command is as follows:

```
sys <drive letter to which you want the files copied>
```

Obviously, there must be enough free space on the drive for the system files to be copied.

TYPE

The TYPE command is used to display the contents of a text file. This command is not able to read binary files (for example, files with a .COM or .EXE extension). This command is useful when you need to read the contents of a text file, such as a README.TXT file (this is commonly found when in the root directory of an install diskette or CD-ROM for a new application). The TYPE command doesn't support the use of any switches.

Usage

The syntax for the TYPE command is as follows:

```
TYPE [drive:][path]filename
```

XCOPY

XCOPY copies all of the files from one location to another location. XCOPY is extremely sophisticated and is capable of much more than a standard copy of files.

Switches

- **/a** Copies all files with the archive attribute set, and does not modify the archive attribute.
- **/m** Copies all files with the archive attribute set, and turns off the archive attribute.

- **/d** Followed by a colon and a date, this switch copies all files modified after the specified date.

- **/p** Prompts the user prior to creation of each destination file.

- **/s** Copies specified directories, subdirectories, and files except empty subdirectories.

- **/e** Copies specified directories, subdirectories, and files including empty subdirectories.

- **/c** Continues copying even if errors are encountered.

- **/q** Does not display filenames while copying.

- **/f** Displays full source and destination paths and filenames while copying.

- **/h** Copies hidden and system files also.

- **/r** Overwrites read-only files.

- **/t** Copies directory structure but does not copy files. Does not copy empty subdirectories.

- **/t /e** Copies directory structure but does not copy files. Copies empty subdirectories.

- **/u** Updates files that already exist in destination.

- **/k** Copies attributes.

- **/y** Overwrites existing files without prompting the user for input.

- **/-y** Prompts user prior to overwriting existing files.

Usage

The syntax for the XCOPY command is as follows:

```
xcopy <source> <destination>
[/a][/m][/d][/p][/s][/e][/c][/q][/f][/h][/r][/t][/u][/k]
[/y][/-y]
```

E

Network
Troubleshooting
Guide

Networks are an essential part of most corporate computing environments. Unfortunately, they are an enormous hassle when they don't work properly. In the event that your network is not operating as it should, there are some steps you can take to troubleshoot the problem. Because TCP/IP (Transmission Control Protocol/Internet Protocol) networks are most common, we focus on them.

Reboot

Before troubleshooting the problem, reboot the machine to verify that there is an existing problem that you can duplicate, not just something that is user-induced.

Neighborhood Watch

The first step in troubleshooting a network connection problem is to make sure you can duplicate the problem on the initial computer. If you can duplicate it on the initial computer, see if you can duplicate the problem on nearby computers. Are other users able to access information? If they are able to access information, your problem may be isolated to one machine. If all of the machines are having trouble, however, the problem is likely a network outage (keep in mind, depending on your network, this outage could be caused by one computer).

Ping Test

A ping test can be used to verify connectivity. Pinging can be accomplished by typing the command:

```
ping <<destination address>>
```

There are seven destination addresses you should try:

1. **The IP address of the machine on which you are working** This verifies that the machine is able to communicate on the network in the most basic way.

2. **The IP address of the machine's gateway**   This tests communication between the machine and the outside world. If you are unable to ping the gateway, either the machine has a local problem or the entire local network is down. Because you should have already verified that other users are able to connect, the problem is likely to be with this specific machine.

3. **The IP address of a remote host that you should be able to reach**   This verifies that you are able to communicate with a host while knowing its IP address. (I like to test communicating with one of the Internic Web servers at 198.41.0.5.) If your connection to the Internet is behind a firewall, the results of this test could be misleading. Contact your Network Administrator if you think the problem is related to a firewall issue.

4. **The IP address of the machine's name server**   By pinging the name server, you are verifying that the domain name service server is up and that you are able to communicate with it.

5. **The name of a remote host that you should be able to connect to**   This verifies that you are able to communicate with hosts on outside networks. (Again, you may want to use Internic at 198.41.0.5.)

6. **A computer located on the same physical network segment**   This verifies that your problem is with all computers, and not just ones outside your local area.

7. **A computer located on another subnet**   If you are unsure of what to use for this test, contact your Network Administrator.

Trace the Route

You can use the tracert command to trace where your problem is occurring. If the ping test is successful from steps 3 and 5 above, you can skip this step. Type the command:

```
tracert www.internic.net
```

Tracert should tell you where your network trouble is occurring. You can then contact the proper authority to report the outage.

Test the Connection on the Wall (Method 1 *Cheaper)

In many cases, this can be accomplished with a handy 30-foot cable. Simply disconnect your machine from its regular network connection, plug it into a longer network cable, and run that cable to the nearest connection. Repeat the ping tests. If the connection now works, plug the longer network cable into the connection in the wall the machine was originally plugged into. If the machine successfully completes a ping test, trash the old cable and replace it with a new one (of an appropriate length, of course).

Test the Connection on the Wall (Method 2 *Easier)

Disconnect the cable from the machine and plug it into a laptop computer. If the ping test is successful, the problem is with the machine. If the ping test is unsuccessful, replace the cable with a new one and test it again. If the ping test is still unsuccessful, the problem is in the wall and you need to contact the proper authorities; otherwise, the cable was bad.

Workstation Configuration

If you're using DHCP (Dynamic Host Configuration Protocol), re-lease and renew your DHCP lease. With or without DHCP, verify that the IP address, subnet mask, gateway address, and DNS server address are configured correctly. Verify that the correct Network Interface Card drivers are installed. I usually take this a step further and simply delete the drivers for the NIC and re-install it. I then re-enter the information to verify that it is correct.

Bad Ethernet Card?

If all else fails, check the Ethernet card in the workstation. A quick way to test the card is to replace it with another and see if the problem is resolved.

F

Networking
Language

T his appendix presents you with some common networking terminology. You will find more in-depth explanations of some of these technologies in Chapter 7. While most of these terms also appear in the Glossary, some of them do not because of the cryptic nature of the term. You should be familiar with all of these terms.

Topologies

Topology is the physical layout of computers, cables, and other components on a network. Any network design you encounter will be a variation on or combination of the three basic networking topologies:

- Bus
- Ring
- Star

Bus

A bus topology is when all of the devices that are connected to the network are connected to a central line (bus). In most instances of cable breaks, the entire network becomes inoperable.

Ring

A ring topology is when all of the devices are connected to a virtual (and usually physical) ring. A device is not allowed to communicate on the network until a token has been passed around the ring to it. Only a device with a token is allowed to transmit. In most instances of cable breaks, the entire network becomes inoperable.

Star

A star topology is when all of the devices are connected to a central device that allows them to communicate with each other. In most instances of cable breaks, only the machines directly attached to the broken network cable are affected.

Cabling and Physical Connectors

In order to create a network, you must physically connect the devices that will be on the network. This is accomplished using cables. There are many different types of cables, each having advantages and disadvantages.

10BaseT

10BaseT cable is also referred to as Twisted Pair or Unshielded Twisted Pair (UTP). 10BaseT is the most commonly used network cable. 10BaseT is capable of transmitting a maximum of 10 megabits/second at a maximum distance of 100 meters. Networks utilizing 10BaseT can be wired with either Category 3 or Category 5 cabling. 10BaseT is wired in a star topology.

100BaseT

100BaseT cabling has all of the characteristics of 10BaseT except that it is capable of transmitting at a maximum speed of 100 megabits/second and can be wired only with Category 5 cabling.

10Base2

10Base2 cable is also referred to as BNC Coax or Thinwire Coax. 10Base2 is capable of transmitting a maximum of 10 megabits/second at a maximum distance of 180 meters. Networks utilizing 10Base2 are wired in a bus topology.

10Base5

10Base5 cable is also referred to as AUI or Thickwire. 10Base5 is capable of transmitting a maximum of 10 megabits/second at a maximum distance of 500 meters. Networks utilizing 10Base5 are wired in a bus topology.

Category 3 (aka Cat 3)

Category 3 cable, commonly used to wire phones, can be used for 10BaseT networks. However, it is recommended that all new wiring be done using Category 5.

Category 5 (aka Cat 5)

Category 5 cable can be used for both 10BaseT and 100BaseT networks. Category 5 is the preferred cable for new network installations.

T-Adapter

Each device in a 10Base2 network must be connected to a T-adapter, which in turn is connected to the network cable.

Terminator

Each end of the network cable in a 10Base2 network must be connected to a 50 omh terminator.

Connectivity Devices

Network connectivity devices have a wide range of uses, from keeping the network's physical configuration organized, to improving the overall performance of the network.

Hub

A hub is a networking device that takes input from each of its ports and re-transmits it out all of the other ports on the hub. A hub is used in a network of star topology to connect each of the devices on the network.

Repeater

A repeater is a device that allows network cabling to exceed its maximum distances. A repeater simply accepts communication from one side and re-transmits it out the other.

Router

A router is a device that connects two separate networks. The router intercepts traffic and determines if it is destined for the network on the other side of the router. If the traffic is destined for the other side of the router, it is allowed to cross.

Switch

A switch is a device that can be used in place of a hub. A switch allows devices on the network to communicate with each other without transmitting the data over the entire network. A switch determines what devices are on each port, and sends only packets that are destined to one of those devices or that are broadcasts destined for those ports.

G

MSD.EXE
Output

As you saw in Chapter 10, memory conflicts are difficult to diagnose because they can come from many different sources, and are therefore difficult to troubleshoot. One of the most dynamic tools for checking and reporting on memory allocation usage is Microsoft's own MSD.EXE, which is available as a free download at their Web site. This tool provides a full output of every conceivable detail about your system. A sample output follows.

```
Microsoft Diagnostics version 2.13    4/21/98   11:49am   Page   1


=================================================================

-------------------- Summary Information ---------------------

            Computer: Award/Award, Pentium(TM)
              Memory: 640K, 64512K Ext, 64272K XMS
               Video: VGA, Unknown
             Network: Windows 95 Client
          OS Version: MS-DOS 7.10
               Mouse: Not Detected 8.30
      Other Adapters: Game Adapter
         Disk Drives: A: B: C: D: E: F: G: H:
           LPT Ports: 1
           COM Ports: 3
 Windows Information: 4.10, Enhanced

------------------------- Computer -------------------------

       Computer Name: Award
   BIOS Manufacturer: Award
        BIOS Version: Award Modular BIOS v4.50PG
       BIOS Category: IBM PC/AT
       BIOS ID Bytes: FC 01 00
           BIOS Date: 03/14/96
           Processor: Pentium(TM)
     Math Coprocessor: Internal
            Keyboard: Enhanced
            Bus Type: ISA/AT/Classic Bus
      DMA Controller: Yes
        Cascaded IRQ2: Yes
   BIOS Data Segment: None
```

```
Microsoft Diagnostics version 2.13    4/21/98   11:49am   Page  2

=====================================================================

--------------------------- Memory ---------------------------
Legend:  Available " "  RAM "##"  ROM "RR"  Possibly Available ".."
    EMS Page Frame "PP"  Used UMBs "UU"  Free UMBs "FF"
 1024K FC00 RRRRRRRRRRRRRRRR FFFF  Conventional Memory
       F800 RRRRRRRRRRRRRRRR FBFF              Total: 640K
       F400 RRRRRRRRRRRRRRRR F7FF          Available: 580K
  960K F000 RRRRRRRRRRRRRRRR F3FF                     594240
                                                      bytes

       EC00 UUUUUUUUUUUUUUUU EFFF
       E800 UUUUUUUUUUUUUUUU EBFF  Extended Memory
       E400 UUUUUUUUUUUUUUUU E7FF              Total: 64512K
  896K E000 UUUUUUUUUUUUUUUU E3FF
       DC00 UUUUUUUUUUUUUUUU DFFF  MS-DOS Upper Memory Blocks
       D800 UUUUUUUUUUUUUUUU DBFF         Total UMBs: 154K
       D400 UUUUUUUUUUUUUUUU D7FF    Total Free UMBs: 0K
  832K D000 UUUUUUUUUUUUUUUU D3FF  Largest Free Block: 0K
       CC00 UUUUUUUUUUUUUUUU CFFF
       C800 .....UUUUUUUUUUU CBFF  XMS Information
       C400 RRRRRRRRRRRRRRRR C7FF         XMS Version: 3.00
  768K C000 RRRRRRRRRRRRRRRR C3FF      Driver Version: 3.5f
       BC00 ............... BFFF  A20 Address Line: Enabled
       B800 ............... BBFF   High Memory Area: In use
       B400 ............... B7FF          Available: 64272K
  704K B000 ............... B3FF  Largest Free Block: 2048K
       AC00 ............... AFFF     Available SXMS: 64272K
       A800 ............... ABFF  Largest Free SXMS: 2048K
       A400 ............... A7FF
  640K A000 ............... A3FF  DPMI Information
                                      DPMI Detected: Yes
                                            Version: 0.90


--------------------------- Video ---------------------------

           Video Adapter Type: VGA
                 Manufacturer: Unknown
                        Model:
```

```
                      Display Type: VGA Color
                        Video Mode: 3
                  Number of Columns: 80
                     Number of Rows: 50
                Video BIOS Version: S3 86C325 Video BIOS. Version 1.00-10
                  Video BIOS Date: 08/02/96
           VESA Support Installed: Yes
                      VESA Version: 1.02
                    VESA OEM Name: S3 Incorporated. 86C325
                 Secondary Adapter: None


    Microsoft Diagnostics version 2.13    4/21/98   11:49am   Page  3


    =================================================================


    --------------------------- Network ----------------------------

                   Network Running: Yes
                      Network Name: Windows 95 Client
           MS-DOS Network Functions: Supported
                     Computer Name: DA_MACHINE
                   NetBIOS Present: Yes
             NetBIOS INT 5C Address: 0AEE:000F
                      Network Root: C:\WINDOWS
                         User Name: DUDE
           Workgroup: DUDES
    Server Connection: Established
                   Mailslot Support: Yes
                       API Support: Yes
    NetBIOS Card Information:
                 Net01 ID: 0207011BB875
                 Active Sessions for Net01


    ------------------------- OS Version ---------------------------

                  Operating System: MS-DOS 7.10
                  Internal Revision: 00
                 OEM Serial Number: FFH
                 User Serial Number: 000000H
                 OEM Version String: Windows 98 [Version
                                              4.10.1650]
```

```
                    DOS Located in: HMA
                      Boot Drive: C:
                Path to Program: F:\LIBRARY\TEMP\MSD.EXE

                       Environment Strings
---------------------------------------------------------------------
PROMPT=$p$g
winbootdir=C:\WINDOWS
COMSPEC=C:\WINDOWS\COMMAND.COM
SOUND=f:\HARDWARE\CREATI~1
MIDI=SYNTH:1 MAP:E MODE:0
TEMP=G:\temp
TMP=g:\temp
PATH=C:\WINDOWS;C:\WINDOWS\COMMAND;..;F:\DOSUTILS;O:\OFFICE\OFFICE;
windir=C:\WINDOWS
BLASTER=A220 I10 D1 H6 P330 T6
CMDLINE=msd /P test2.txt



  Microsoft Diagnostics version 2.13    4/21/98   11:49am   Page  4


======================================================================


--------------------------- Mouse ---------------------------

                   Mouse Hardware: Not Detected
             Driver Manufacturer: Microsoft
                 DOS Driver Type: Serial Mouse
                Driver File Type: .SYS File
              DOS Driver Version: 8.30
                       Mouse IRQ: 4
                  Mouse COM Port: COM1:
          Mouse COM Port Address: 03F8H
         Number of Mouse Buttons: 2
          Horizontal Sensitivity: 50
            Mouse to Cursor Ratio: 1 : 1
            Vertical Sensitivity: 50
            Mouse to Cursor Ratio: 1 : 1
                  Threshold Speed: 0
                  Mouse Language: English
```

```
----------------------- Other Adapters ------------------------

                        Game Adapter: Detected
                     Joystick A - X: 103
                                  Y: 29
                           Button 1: On
                           Button 2: On
                     Joystick B - X: 0
                                  Y: 141
                           Button 1: On
                           Button 2: On



Microsoft Diagnostics version 2.13    4/21/98   11:49am   Page  5


==================================================================


----------------------- Disk Drives ------------------------
Drive  Type                             Free Space  Total Size
-----  -------------------------------  ----------  ----------
  A:   Floppy Drive, 3.5" 1.44M
          80 Cylinders, 2 Heads
          512 Bytes/Sector, 18 Sectors/Track
  B:   Floppy Drive, 5.25" 1.2M
          80 Cylinders, 2 Heads
          512 Bytes/Sector, 15 Sectors/Track
  C:   Fixed Disk, CMOS Type 46             76M         401M
          102 Cylinders, 128 Heads
          512 Bytes/Sector, 63 Sectors/Track
       CMOS Fixed Disk Parameters
          622 Cylinders, 128 Heads
          63 Sectors/Track
  D:   Fixed Disk, CMOS Type 46            121M         507M
          258 Cylinders, 64 Heads
          512 Bytes/Sector, 63 Sectors/Track
       CMOS Fixed Disk Parameters
          516 Cylinders, 64 Heads
          63 Sectors/Track
  E:   Fixed Disk, CMOS Type 46             68M         495M
          126 Cylinders, 128 Heads
          512 Bytes/Sector, 63 Sectors/Track
       CMOS Fixed Disk Parameters
          516 Cylinders, 64 Heads
          63 Sectors/Track
```

```
F:   Fixed Disk, CMOS Type 46                    26M        495M
        126 Cylinders, 128 Heads
        512 Bytes/Sector, 63 Sectors/Track
     CMOS Fixed Disk Parameters
        516 Cylinders, 64 Heads
        63 Sectors/Track
G:   Fixed Disk, CMOS Type 46                   354M        507M
        129 Cylinders, 128 Heads
        512 Bytes/Sector, 63 Sectors/Track
     CMOS Fixed Disk Parameters
        516 Cylinders, 64 Heads
        63 Sectors/Track
H:   Fixed Disk, CMOS Type 46                    25M        505M
        257 Cylinders, 64 Heads
        512 Bytes/Sector, 63 Sectors/Track
     CMOS Fixed Disk Parameters
        516 Cylinders, 64 Heads
        63 Sectors/Track
I:   CD-ROM Drive
J:   DriveSpace Drive                            71M        563M
        Actual Free Space                        0K
        CVF Filename Is H:\DRVSPACE.001
K:   CD-ROM Drive
L:   CD-ROM Drive
M:   CD-ROM Drive
O:   DriveSpace Drive                            63M        529M
```

Microsoft Diagnostics version 2.13   4/21/98   11:49am   Page 6
==

```
        Actual Free Space                        0K
        CVF Filename Is E:\DRVSPACE.001    U:   DriveSpace Drive
53M     132M            Actual Free Space                        0K
        CVF Filename Is E:\DRVSPACE.002
  SHARE Installed
  MSCDEX Version 2.95 Installed
  LASTDRIVE=Z:
```

------------------------ LPT Ports --------------------------

Port	Port Address	On Line	Paper Out	I/O Error	Time Out	Busy	ACK
LPT1:	0378H	Yes	No	No	No	No	No
LPT2:	-	-	-	-	-	-	-
LPT3:	-	-	-	-	-	-	-

```
-------------------- COM Ports ----------------------

                        COM1:     COM2:     COM3:     COM4:
                        -----     -----     -----     -----
Port Address            03F8H     02F8H     02E8H      N/A
Baud Rate                1200      2400      2400
Parity                   None      None      None
Data Bits                   7         8         8
Stop Bits                   1         1         1
Carrier Detect  (CD)       No        No        No
Ring Indicator  (RI)       No        No        No
Data Set Ready  (DSR)      No       Yes       Yes
Clear To Send   (CTS)      No       Yes       Yes
UART Chip Used           8250      8250   16550AF

--------------- Windows Information -------------------

              Windows version: 4.10
                 Windows mode: Enhanced
            Windows Directory: C:\WINDOWS
             System Directory: C:\WINDOWS\SYSTEM
           Virtual Machine ID: 2
       Display driver version: 0.00
           Display resolution: 1024 x 768
                Bits per pixel: 24
         Number of bit planes: 1

Filename                       Size         Date      Time
----------------------    ---------------   --------  -----
DVA.386                         5195       7/13/96    0:00
BI-DI.386                      26670       6/14/96    4:20
MSMOUSE.VXD                    15809      12/03/97    8:52
VWAVSYN.386                   249144       3/14/97    4:01


Microsoft Diagnostics version 2.13   4/21/98  11:49am
                                                  Page 7


==========================================================
```

```
-------------------- IRQ Status ---------------------

IRQ  Address   Description      Detected         Handled By
---  --------  --------------   --------------  ----------
  0  0AE3:0000 Timer Click      Yes                    (
  1  0920:0028 Keyboard         Yes         Default Handlers
  2  F000:EF6F Second 8259A     Yes                  BIOS
  3  F000:EF6F COM2: COM4:      COM2:                BIOS
  4  F000:EF6F COM1: COM3:      COM1: COM3: Not DeteBIOS
  5  F000:EF6F LPT2:            No                   BIOS
  6  0920:009A Floppy Disk      Yes         Default Handlers
  7  0070:0465 LPT1:            Yes              System Area
  8  0920:0035 Real-Time Clock  Yes         Default Handlers
  9  F000:ECF3 Redirected IRQ2  Yes                  BIOS
 10  F000:EF6F (Reserved)                            BIOS
 11  F000:EF6F (Reserved)                            BIOS
 12  F000:EF6F (Reserved)                            BIOS
 13  F000:F0FC Math Coprocessor Yes                  BIOS
 14  0920:00FA Fixed Disk       Yes         Default Handlers
 15  0920:0112 (Reserved)                   Default Handlers


Microsoft Diagnostics version 2.13    4/21/98    11:49am
Page  8


=============================================================

-------------------- TSR Programs --------------------
Program Name      Address   Size   Command Line Parameters
--------------    -------   ------  ----------------------
  System Data     026C      30512
   HIMEM          026E       1152   XMSXXXX0
   EMM386         02B7       4304   $MMXXXX0
   DBLBUFF        03C5       2960   DblBuff$
   ùË.VSRQP       047F        544   Block Device
   BUFFERS        04A2      16080
Directories       0890       2288
Default Handlers  0920       3072
System Code       09E0         64
```

```
COMMAND.COM          09E5        16
=C:\WIND             09E7       304
WIN                  09FB      3408
(                    0AD1        32
(                    0AD4      8880
???                  0D00       320    /P test2.txt
COMMAND.COM          0D15      5712    /P test2.txt
???                  0E7B      1424    /P test2.txt
MSD.EXE              0ED5       336    /P test2.txt
MSD.EXE              0EEB    335024    /P test2.txt
MSD.EXE              60B7      8192    /P test2.txt
Free Memory          62B8    250976
Excluded UMB Area    9FFF    169408
System Data          C95C    156640
  DRVSPACE           C95E    110576    DBLSYSH$
  OAKCDROM           E45E     36048    MSCD001
  IFSHLP             ED2C      2848    IFS$HLP$
     t.< r$w         EDDF      1200    Block Device
  File Handles       EE2B      5616
  FCBS               EF8B       256
(                    EF9B      1600
```

```
Microsoft Diagnostics version 2.13   4/21/98  11:49am
                                               Page 9


==========================================================

------------------ Device Drivers --------------------

Device        Filename  Units   Header      Attributes
------------  --------  -----   --------    ----------------
NUL                             00C9:0048   1............1..
IFS$HLP$      IFSHLP            ED2C:0000   11.1............
MSCD001       OAKCDROM          E45E:0000   11..1...........
DBLSYSH$      DRVSPACE          C95E:0000   1...............
DblBuff$      DBLBUFF           03C5:0000   11..1....1......
$MMXXXX0      EMM386            02B7:0000   11..............
XMSXXXX0      HIMEM             026E:0000   1.1.............
Block Device  DBLSPACE    18    021E:0000   .11.1....1....1.
CON                             0070:0016   1..........1..11
AUX                             0070:0028   1...............
PRN                             0070:003A   1.1.....11......
```

```
CLOCK$                            0070:004C   1...........1...
Block Device           8          0070:005E   ....1...11....1.
COM1                              0070:006A   1...............
LPT1                              0070:007C   1.1.....11......
LPT2                              0070:008E   1.1.....11......
LPT3                              0070:00A0   1.1.....11......
CONFIG$                           0070:012D   11..............
COM2                              0070:00B8   1...............
COM3                              0070:00CA   1...............
COM4                              0070:00DC   1...............
&MMXXXX0                          0ADE:0000   11..............
mscd$$$$                          0AE6:0000   11..1...........
```

Glossary

Access Method   Also known as *network access,* these are the methods by which a device communicates on a network. Network access provides a standard that all devices that wish to communicate on a network must abide by in order to eliminate communication conflicts. Common types include CSMA/CD and Token Ring.

Active Matrix Display   Active matrix displays are based on Thin Film Transistor technology. Instead of having two rows of transistors, active matrix displays have a transistor at every pixel, which enables much quicker display changes than passive matrix displays and produces display quality comparable to a CRT.

ANSI.SYS   ANSI.SYS is a DOS system file that loads an extended character set for use by DOS and DOS applications that includes basic drawing and color capabilities. Normally used for drawing and filling different boxes for menu systems, it is seldom in use today. By default, it carries no attributes, and is not required for OS startup.

ARCHIVE Attribute   The ARCHIVE attribute is set automatically when a file is created or modified, and is automatically removed by back-up software when the file is backed up.

ATTRIB.EXE   ATTRIB.EXE is a utility that can be used to change the attributes of a file or group of files.

AUTOEXEC.BAT   A user-editable system file, AUTOEXEC.BAT contains commands to modify the PC environment (PATH, COMSPEC, other SET commands), and to execute applications. It can be used to create a menu system, prompt for user input, or *call* other batch files to maintain a modular structure. By default, it carries no attributes, and is not required for OS startup.

Basic Input Output System   See BIOS.

Bi-Directional Print Mode   Most common in some of the newer and more advanced printers, bi-directional print mode means that the printer is able to talk back to the computer, enabling, for example, the printer to send the user exact error messages that are displayed on the workstation. It also helps the spooler to avoid print spooler stalls.

BIOS   Most commonly known as BIOS, Basic Input Output System is a standard set of instructions or programs that handle boot operations. When an application needs to perform an I/O operation on a computer, the operating system makes the request to the system BIOS, which in turn translates the request into the appropriate instruction set used by the hardware device.

Brownout   Momentary lapses in power supply. Brownouts can cause problems with computer components that are not designed to withstand these events.

Bus   A bus is the actual pathway used to transmit electronic signals from one computer device to another.

Bus Topology   In a local area network, a bus topology has each device on the network connected to a central cable, or bus. Most common with coaxial cabling.

Cache Memory   Cache memory is used to store frequently used instructions and data so that they can be accessed quickly by the computer.

Carrier Sense Multiple Access/Collision Detection
See CSMA/CD.

Central Processing Unit   See CPU.

Chip Creep   A phenomenon whereby a computer chip becomes loose within its socket.

Cleaning Blade   This rubber blade inside a laser printer extends the length of the photosensitive drum. It removes excess toner after the print process has completed and deposits it into a reservoir.

CMOS   The Complementary Metal-Oxide Semiconductor (or CMOS) is an integrated circuit composed of a metal oxide that is located directly on the system board. The CMOS, a type of nonvolatile storage, enables a computer to store essential operating parameters after the computer has been turned off, enabling a faster system boot.

Coaxial Cable   A high-bandwidth network cable that consists of a central wire surrounded by a screen of fine wires.

COMMAND.COM   COMMAND.COM is a DOS system file that is automatically executed in the Root directory at startup. This file contains the internal command set and error messages. By default, it carries no attributes, but is required for OS startup.

Complementary Metal-Oxide Semiconductor   See CMOS.

CONFIG.SYS   A user-editable system file that provides the ability to install device drivers.

Cooperative Multitasking   There are two different types of multitasking: cooperative and preemptive. Cooperative multitasking means that applications must voluntarily relinquish control of the CPU. When an application relinquishes control of the CPU, Windows then decides which application will execute next. The most common way for an application to relinquish control is by asking Windows if any messages are available.

CPU   The CPU (Central Processing Unit) is the operations center of a computer. Its job is to provide the devices attached to the computer with directives that retrieve, display, manipulate, and store information.

CSMA/CD   Most commonly found on Ethernet networks, carrier sense multiple access/collision detection (CSMA/CD) is a network access method and operates in much the same way as humans communicate. With CSMA/CD, a device listens to the network for a pause in communication, and attempts to transmit data onto the network during the pause. The device then detects if any other devices have transmitted onto the network at the same time. If it detects that another device has transmitted data onto the network at the same time, the device then waits an unspecified random amount of time and retransmits its data.

Defragmentation   A process that reorganizes fragmented files back in a proper, contiguous fashion. This is done by moving several file clusters to an unused portion of the drive, erasing the previous locations in contiguous clusters, then rewriting the files back in proper sequence. Performed periodically, defragmentation is probably the single best operation a user can perform to maintain a high-performance system.

Device Driver   Device drivers are programs that translate necessary information between the operating system and the specific peripheral device for which they are configured, such as a printer.

Dial-Up Access   Dial-up access is defined as access provided to the Internet, a LAN, or even another computer by using a phone line and a modem. Dial-up access does not have to be a connection to any network.

Dial-Up Networking   Refers to the type of network in which a modem is used to connect two or more workstations.

DIMM   A Dual In-Line Memory Module (DIMM) is very similar to a SIMM; it's a small plug-in circuit board that contains the memory chips that you need to add certain increments of RAM to your computer. Because the memory chips run along both sides of the chip, DIMM chips can hold twice as much memory as SIMM chips.

DIP Switch   Dual in-line package (DIP) switches are very tiny boxes with switches embedded in them. Each switch sets a value of 0 or 1, depending on how they are set. These switches are used to provide user-accessible configuration settings for computers and peripheral devices.

Direct Memory Access   See DMA.

Dirty Current   Noise present on a power line is referred to as dirty current. This noise is caused by *electro-magnetic interference (EMI)* and can stray, or leak, from the current into nearby components. When EMI leaks from power current, it is called a magnetic field and can easily damage computer components.

DMA   Direct memory access (DMA) is a facility by which a peripheral can communicate directly with RAM, without intervention by the CPU.

DNS   Domain Name System (DNS) is the Internet-based system that resolves symbolic names to IP addresses (which are a series of numbers) that the computer is able to understand.

Docking Station   Docking stations allow users to add "desktop-like" capabilities, such as a mouse, monitor, or keyboard, to their portable computer. These components are plugged into a docking station and connect a portable to the docking station, rather than to each individual component.

Domain Name System   See DNS.

DOS Mode   DOS Mode, or DOS Compatibility Mode as it is commonly known, allows execution of some older MS-DOS applications that are not capable of running in Windows 95. Applications that require use of MS-DOS mode are usually blocked from operation within Windows 95.

Download   Downloading refers to the process of transferring a file or files from one computer to another. Unlike uploading, the transfer is always initiated by the computer that will be receiving the file(s).

Downtime   Downtime is the time wasted as a result of a malfunctioning computer or network.

DRAM   Dynamic Random Access Memory (DRAM) chips use small capacitors that could represent 0s and 1s as an electronic charge. This resulted in the ability to store more information on a single chip, but also meant that the chip needed a constant refresh and hence more power.

Dual In-Line Memory Module   See DIMM.

Dual In-Line Package Switch   See DIP Switch.

Dynamic RAM   See DRAM.

EBKAC Error   A common error that most technicians face, the EBKAC error stands for Error Between Keyboard and Chair. As that implies, EBKAC errors are not technical errors, but rather errors on the part of the end user. Common EBKAC errors include power cords being unplugged, no paper in printer, and power switches being turned off.

ECP   ECP (Extended Capability Port) is a parallel port option designed to speed up data transfer rates by bypassing the processor and writing the data directly to memory.

EDO RAM   Extended Data Output RAM (EDO RAM) is a type of DRAM chip designed for processor access speeds of approximately 10 to 15 percent above fast-page mode memory.

EISA   Extended Industry Standard Architecture (EISA) is an industry standard bus architecture that allows for peripherals to utilize the 32-bit data bus that is available with 386 and 486 processors.

Electrophotographic Printing Process   See EP Process.

EMM386.EXE   EMM386.EXE is a DOS system file that, along with HIMEM.SYS, controls memory management. It is not required for system startup in pre-Windows 95 machines. It is an expanded memory emulator that performs two major functions: It enables and controls EMS, if desired, and enables the use of upper memory as system memory.

EMS   Expanded Memory Specification. EMS is an expanded memory standard that allows programs that recognize it to work with more than 1024K of RAM.

Enhanced Parallel Port   See EPP.

EP Process   The EP (Electrophotographic Printing) process is the six-step process that a laser printer uses to put an image on a page. The process follows these six steps: Cleaning, Charging, Writing, Developing, Transferring, and Fusing.

EPP   EPP (Enhanced Parallel Port) is a parallel port option that offers an extended control code set. With EPP mode, data travels both from the computer to the printer and vice versa.

Error Between Keyboard and Chair   See EBKAC Error

Exit Roller   One of four different types of rollers found in laser printers, exit rollers aid in the transfer and control of the paper as it leaves the printer. Depending on the printer type, they direct the paper to a tray where it can be collated, sorted, or even stapled.

Expanded Memory Specification   See EMS.

Extended Capability Port   See ECP.

Extended Data Output RAM   See EDO RAM.

Extended Industry Standard Architecture   See EISA.

eXtended Memory Specification   See XMS.

FDISK   A DOS-based utility program used to create, modify, or delete hard drive partitions.

Feed Roller   One of four different types of rollers found in laser printers. Also known as paper pickup roller, the feed roller, when activated, rotates against the top page in the paper tray and rolls it into the printer. The feed roller works together with a special rubber pad to prevent more than one sheet from being fed into the printer at a time.

Fiber Optic Cable   Extremely high-speed network cable that consists of glass fibers that carry light signals instead of electrical signals. Fiber optic cable is best used for transmission over long distances, and is much less susceptible to environmental difficulties, such as electronic and magnetic interference.

File Transfer Protocol   See FTP.

Flash Memory   A version of EEPROM that, while still basically developed as ROM, can be addressed and loaded *thousands* of times. A type of nonvolatile memory that can be electrically erased and reprogrammed

Fragmentation   Because DOS writes files to the hard disk by breaking the file into cluster-sized pieces and then storing each piece in the next available cluster, as files are deleted and then rewritten, they can be written in noncontiguous clusters scattered all over the disk. This is known as file fragmentation.

FTP Much older than the HTTP protocol, the File Transfer Protocol(FTP) is the protocol used to download files from an FTP server to a client computer. FTP is much faster than HTTP.

Fully Qualified Path A fully qualified path is the entire path of a file, starting from the root of the file system, to the file being referenced.

Fusing Rollers One of four different types of rollers found in laser printers, fusing rollers comprise the final stage of the Electrophotographic Printing (EP) process, bonding the toner particles to the page to prevent smearing. The roller on the toner side of the page has a non-stick surface that is heated to a high temperature to permanently bond the toner to the paper.

Ghosted Image "Ghosting" is what occurs when a portion of an image previously printed to a page is printed again, only not as dark. One cause of this is if the erasure lamp of the laser printer sometimes fails to operate correctly, not completely erasing the previous image from the EP drum. Another cause of ghosting may be due to a malfunction in the cleaning blade such that it doesn't adequately scrape away the residual toner.

Handshaking The process by which two connecting modems agree on the method of communication to be used.

HIDDEN Attribute The Hidden attribute keeps a file from being displayed when a DIR command is issued.

HIMEM.SYS HIMEM.SYS is a DOS system file that, along with EMM386.EXE, controls memory management. It is the Extend Memory Manager, and it creates the high memory area, allowing the computer to recognize and use memory above 1MB (1024K).

Hot Dock Hot docking is the ability of a system to accept new accessories while it is turned on.

HTML Derived from the Standard General Markup Language (SGML), the Hypertext Markup Language(HTML) is the markup language that dictates the layout and design of a Web page.

HTTP Hypertext Transfer Protocol (HTTP) is the TCP/IP-based protocol that is most commonly used for client/server communications on the World Wide Web.

Hub Hubs are common connection points for devices in a star network. Hubs contain multiple ports and are commonly used to connect segments of a LAN.

Hypertext Markup Language See HTML.

Hypertext Transfer Protocol See HTTP.

Impact Printer Impact printers, like the name suggests, require the impact with an ink ribbon to print characters and images. An example of an impact printer is a daisy wheel.

Industry Standard Architecture See ISA.

Input Device Input devices take data from a user, such as the click of a mouse or the typing on a keyboard, and convert that data into electrical signals used by your computer. Several devices that provide input are: keyboards, mice, trackballs, pointing devices, digitized tablets, and touch screens.

Internet Service Provider See ISP.

Internetwork Packet Exchange/Sequenced Packet Exchange See IPX/SPX.

Interrupt Request Line See IRQ.

IO.SYS   IO.SYS is a DOS system file that defines basic input/output routines for the processor. By default, it carries the hidden, system, and read-only attributes, and *is* required for OS startup.

IPX/SPX   Internetwork Packet Exchange/Sequenced Packet Exchange (IPX/SPX) is a very fast and highly established network protocol most commonly used with Novell Netware.

IRQ   Interrupt Request (IRQ) lines are the physical lines over which system components such as modems or printers communicate directly with the CPU.

ISA   Industry Standard Architecture (ISA) is an industry standard bus architecture that allows for peripherals to utilize the 16-bit data bus that is available with 286 and 386 processors.

ISP   An Internet Service Provider (ISP), as its name suggests, is a company that provides computer users with access to the Internet, usually for a fee. On the other hand, a company that gives their employees Internet access through a private bank of modems is usually not considered an ISP.

Jumper   Jumpers, like DIP switches, are used to accomplish configuration manually. Jumpers are actually made of two separate components: a row of metal pins on the hardware itself and a small plastic cap that has a metal insert inside of it. The two parts together form a circuit that sets the configuration. This form of configuration device is only used to set one value for a feature at a time, as opposed to DIP switches, which can handle multiple configurations.

LAN   A local area network (LAN) is created whenever two or more computers in a limited geographic area (within about a two-mile radius) are linked by cables so that users can exchange information, share peripheral devices, or access a common server.

Local Area Network   See LAN.

Material Safety Data Sheets   See MSDS.

MEM.EXE   MEM.EXE is a simple command line utility that, using various command switches, can display various reports of memory usage.

MEMMAKER.EXE   A Microsoft utility that automatically determines the best possible memory configuration and load sequence for a given set of applications and drivers used. Before using MEMMAKER, the PC should be configured for normal operation (for example, mouse driver, network operation, and sound support), including any items that are loaded from the AUTOEXEC.BAT and CONFIG.SYS files.

Memory Address   The memory address is used to receive commands from the processor that are destined for any device attached to a computer. Each device must have a unique memory address in order for it to function.

Memory Bank   A memory bank is the actual slot that memory goes into.

Memory Effect   When a Nickel Cadmium, or NiCad, battery is recharged before it is fully discharged, the battery loses the ability to fully recharge again, which is known as the memory effect.

MSD.EXE   MSD, Microsoft Diagnostics, is a DOS-based utility that provides a great deal of information about the system. It is most useful in determining what the system has installed in it, such as memory and hard drives.

MSDOS.SYS   MSDOS.SYS is a DOS system file that defines system file locations. By default, it carries the hidden, system, and read-only attributes, and is required for OS startup.

MSDS Material Safety Data Sheets (MSDS) are white pages that contain information on any substance that is deemed hazardous, most notably cleaning solvents. The purpose of MSDS is to inform employees about the dangers inherent in hazardous materials and the proper use of these items to prevent potential injuries from occurring.

Multi-Boot Configuration A system that has been configured to allow a user to select one of multiple installed operating systems at boot time.

Multimeter A multimeter is a device that measures current, resistance, or voltage, used to determine whether certain computer components are functioning correctly based on these electrical measurements.

NetBEUI The NetBios Extended User Interface (NetBEUI) is an extremely fast network transport protocol that is most commonly found on smaller networks.

NetBios Extended User Interface See NetBEUI.

Network Interface Card See NIC.

Network Topology The arrangement of cable links in a local area network. There are three principal network topologies: bus, ring, and star.

NIC A network interface card (NIC) is used to connect a PC to a network cable.

Noise Filter UPSs contain a special filter, called a *noise filter*, that reduces the amount of noise present in electrical current and eliminates magnetic fields caused by noise, thus providing some protection to the components that utilize the current or are nearby.

Non-Impact Printer   Non-impact printers do not use an ink ribbon, and therefore do not require direct contact with the paper for printing. An example of a non-impact printer is a laser printer.

Normal Mode   Normal Mode is the mode in which Windows 95 is started by default, which provides full functionality of Windows 95.

Null Modem Cable   A null modem cable is a special cable that has the send and receive lines reversed on the connector. It enables you to connect two computers directly, without using a modem.

Operating System   See OS.

Operator Error   Operator error occurs when the customer inadvertently makes a configuration change.

OS   An Operating System (OS) is a set of computer instruction codes, usually *compiled* into executable files, whose purpose is to define input and output devices and connections, and provide instructions for the computer's central processor to operate on to retrieve and display data.

Output Device   Output devices take electronic signals *from* a computer and convert them into a format that the user can use. Examples of output devices include monitors and printers.

Overlays   Rather than put all available functions into a single huge executable file, most developers choose to modularize their applications by creating library files that include additional commands and functions. These additional executable enhancement files are usually referred to as overlays.

Page Description Language   See PDL.

Parallel Port   One of two types of communication ports found on a motherboard (the other is the serial port), the parallel port is used to connect a peripheral device (most commonly a printer for this type of port) to the computer. A parallel port allows transmission of data over eight conductors at one time. The processor socket is the actual socket used to attach the processor to the motherboard.

Parallel Processing   The Intel 586 (Pentium) chip combined two 486DX chips into one, called the *Dual Independent Bus Architecture*. This allowed each processor inside the chip to execute instructions simultaneously and independently from each other, which is called parallel processing.

Parity   Parity is an error-checking mechanism that enables the device to recognize single-bit errors.

Partition   A section of the storage area on a computer's hard disk. A hard disk must be partitioned and formatted before an operating system can be installed.

Passive Matrix Display   Most common on portable systems, the passive matrix display is made from a grid of horizontal and vertical wires. At the end of each wire is a transistor. In order to light a pixel at (X, Y), a signal is sent to the X and Y transistors. In turn, these transistors then send voltage down the wire, which turns on the LCD at the intersection of the two wires.

PC Card   The PC Card (Personal Computer Memory Card International Association, or PCMCIA) bus was first created to expand the memory capabilities in small, hand-held computers. It is a type of bus used mostly with laptop computers that provides a convenient way to interchange PCMCIA-compatible devices, which are only slightly larger than credit cards.

PCI   The Peripheral Component Interconnect(PCI) was designed in response to the Pentium class processor's utilization of a 64-bit bus. PCI buses are designed to be processor-independent.

PCMCIA   See PC Card.

PDL   Laser printers use a Page Description Language(PDL) to send and receive print job instructions one page at a time, rather than one dot at a time, as with other types of printers.

Peripheral Component Interconnect   See PCI.

Personal Computer Memory Card International Association See PC Card.

Photosensitive Drum   This light-sensitive drum is the core of the electrophotographic process inside the laser printer. This drum is affected by the cleaning, charging, writing, and transferring processes in the six-step laser printing process.

Plug and Play   Plug and Play offers automatic driver installation as soon as hardware or software is "plugged in," or installed. Microsoft first offered PnP support on the PC with Windows 95.

Pointing Stick   One of the three most common types of pointing devices found on portable systems, the pointing stick is a small pencil-eraser-size piece of rubber in the center of the keyboard. The on-screen pointer is controlled by simply pushing the pointing stick in the desired direction.

Point-To-Point Protocol   See PPP.

POLEDIT.EXE   The Windows 95 System Policy feature, POLEDIT.EXE, is used to build a Registry template that will later be used during logon to set common-denominator defaults for all network users, and add certain restrictions on a global basis if deemed necessary.

POP   Post Office Protocol (POP) is a common protocol by which an Internet server lets you receive e-mail and download it from the server to your own machine.

POST   As its name suggests, a Power On Self Test (POST) is a self test performed by the computer that occurs during boot time. It is used to diagnose system-related problems.

Post Office Protocol   See POP.

Power On Self Test   See POST.

Power Spike   When there is a power spike, there is a sudden, huge increase in power that lasts for a split second. Power spikes can literally fry computer components.

PPP   The Point-To-Point protocol, PPP is a serial communications protocol used to connect two computers over a phone line via a modem. SLIP is the alternate protocol that is acceptable to most browsers, though it's not as common as PPP.

Preemptive Multitasking   There are two different types of multitasking: cooperative and preemptive. Preemptive multitasking means that control of system resources is passed from one program to another automatically by the Windows process scheduler.

Primary Corona Wire   This highly negatively charged wire inside a laser printer is responsible for electrically charging the photosensitive drum, preparing it to be written with a new image in the writing stage of the laser print process.

Processor Socket   The processor socket is the actual socket used to attach the processor to the motherboard.

Protocol   A set of communication standards between two computers on a network. Common protocols include TCP/IP, NetBEUI, and IPX/SPX.

READ ONLY Attribute   The READ ONLY attribute prevents a user or application from inadvertently deleting or changing a file.

Refresh   Refresh refers to the automatic process of constantly updating memory chips to ensure that their signals are correct. The refresh rate is the frequency by which chips are refreshed, usually about every 60 to 70 thousandths of a second.

Registration Roller   One of four different types of rollers found in laser printers, the registration roller synchronizes the paper movement with the writing process inside the EP cartridge. Registration rollers do not advance the paper until the EP cartridge is ready to process the next line of the image.

Registry   A complex database used by Windows NT and Windows 95 (and later) pertaining to both application settings and hardware configuration.

Ring Topology   In a local area network, a ring topology has each device arranged around a closed-loop cable. Most common with fiber optic cabling.

Rollers   Rollers are located inside a printer to aid in the movement of paper through the printer. There are four main types of rollers: feed, registration, fuser, and exit.

Safe Mode   Safe Mode is a special diagnostic mode of Windows 95 that starts the operating system without any network, CD-ROM, and printer drivers. This special mode allows you to change an incorrect setting, which will in most cases allow you to return an abnormally functioning system to its correct operation.

Serial Port   One of two types of communication ports found on a motherboard (the other is the parallel port), the serial port connects to a serial line that leads to a computer peripheral—the type most common with modems and mice. The serial port transmits data sequentially, bit by bit over a single conductor.

SIMD   Single Instruction Multiple Data (SIMD) works by allowing a single instruction to operate on multiple pieces of data when an application is performing a repetitive loop.

SIMM   A Single In-Line Memory Module(SIMM) is a small plug-in circuit board that contains the memory chips that allow you to add increments of RAM to your computer. The chips are positioned along one side of the board.

Simple Mail Transfer Protocol   See SMTP.

Single In-Line Memory Module   See SIMM.

Single Instruction Multiple Data   See SIMD.

Slack   Slack is the space left between the end of a file and the end of the cluster in which the file resides.

SLIP   The Serial Line Interface Protocol, SLIP is a protocol used to manage telecommunications between a client and a server over a phone line. PPP is the alternate protocol that is acceptable to most browsers, and is in fact the most common.

SMTP   Simple Mail Transfer Protocol (SMTP) is the underlying protocol for Internet-based e-mail.

Socket Services   Socket Services is a layer of BIOS-level software that isolates PC Card software from the computer hardware and detects the insertion or removal of PC Cards.

Solenoid   The solenoid is a resistive coil found in dot matrix and daisy wheel printers. When the solenoid is energized, the pin is forced away from the printhead and impacts the printer ribbon and ultimately the paper, thus impressing the image on the page.

SRAM   Unlike DRAM, Static RAM (SRAM) retains its value as long as power is supplied. It is not constantly refreshed. However, SRAM does require a periodic update and tends to use excessive amounts of power when it does so.

Star Topology   In a local area network, a star topology has each device on the network connected to a central device, usually a hub. Most common with twisted pair cabling.

Static RAM   See SRAM.

Stylus   Shaped like a pen, a stylus is used to select menu options and the like on a monitor screen or to draw line art on a graphics tablet.

Sync Frequency   Monitors use a *sync frequency* to control the refresh rate, which is the rate at which the display device is repainted. If this setting is incorrect, you get symptoms such as: a "dead" monitor, lines running through the display, a flickering screen, and a reduced or enlarged image.

SYSTEM Attribute   The SYSTEM attribute is usually set by DOS or Windows, and cannot be modified using standard DOS or Windows commands, including the ATTRIB command or File Manager.

SYSTEM.INI   SYSTEM.INI is a Windows 3.*x* system file that configures Windows to address specific hardware devices and their associated settings. Errors in this file can and do cause Windows to fail to start, or crash unexpectedly.

TCP/IP The most common protocol suite in use today, Transmission Control Protocol/Internet Protocol (TCP/IP) is the suite of protocols upon which the Internet is based. It refers to the communication standards for data transmission over the Internet, although TCP/IP can also be used on private networks without Internet connectivity.

Time Slicing The process of the CPU dividing up time between applications for preemptive multitasking is called time slicing.

Token Passing Token passing is a network communication access method by which a token is passed from device to device around a virtual (and frequently physical) ring on a network. Whenever a device receives the token, it is then allowed to transmit onto the network.

Toner Toner is comprised of finely divided particles of plastic resin and organic compounds bonded to iron particles. It is naturally negatively charged, which aids in attracting it to the written areas of the photosensitive drum during the transfer step of the laser printing process.

Touch Pads A touch pad is a stationary pointing device commonly used on laptop computers in place of a mouse or trackball. They are pads that have either thin wires running through them, or specialized surfaces that can sense the pressure of your finger on them. You slide your finger across the touchpad to control the pointer or cursor on the screen.

Trackball Most commonly, trackballs are used in older portable computers in place of a mouse. Trackballs are built the same way as an opto-mechanical mouse, except upside-down with the ball on top.

Transfer Corona This wire inside a laser printer contains a positively charged wire designed to pull the toner off of the photosensitive drum and place it on the page.

Transistor   A transistor is the most fundamental component of electronic circuits. A CPU chip, for example, contains thousands to millions of transistors, which are used to process information in the form of electronic signals. The more transistors a CPU has, the faster it can process data.

Transmission Control Protocol/Internet Protocol   See TCP/IP.

Twisted Pair   By far the most common type of network cable, twisted pair consists of two insulated wires wrapped around each other to help avoid interference from other wires.

Uninterruptible Power Supply   See UPS.

Upload   Uploading is the process of transferring files from one computer to another. Unlike downloading, uploading is always initiated from the computer that is sending the files.

UPS   The uninterruptible power supply (UPS) is a device that was designed to protect your computer and its components from possible injury from the problems that are inherent with today's existing power supply structure, such as noise, blackouts, and power surges.

VESA Local Bus   See VL-Bus.

Virtual Memory   Virtual memory is memory that the processor has been "tricked" into using as if it were actual physical memory.

Virus   Any program that is written with the intent of doing harm to a computer. Viruses have the ability to replicate themselves by attaching themselves to programs or documents. They range in activity from critical data loss to an annoying message that pops up every few minutes.

VL-Bus Originally created to address performance issues, the VESA Local Bus (VL-Bus) was meant to enable earlier bus designs to handle a maximum clock speed equivalent to that of processors.

WAN A wide area network (WAN) is created whenever two or more computers are linked by long-distance communication lines that traverse distances greater than those supported by LANs.

Wide Area Network See WAN.

WIN.INI WIN.INI is a dynamic Windows system file that contains configuration information for Windows 3.*x* applications. Errors made in this file seldom have global implications to Windows' operation, but can cripple specific applications or features. Printing is also controlled by settings in this file.

Windows Accelerator Card RAM See WRAM

WINFILE.INI In Windows 3.*x* systems, this is the configuration file that stores the names of the directories that File Manager displays when starting.

WRAM The Windows Accelerator Card was introduced into the market out of a need to assist some environments with running Microsoft Windows. WRAM utilizes memory that resides on the card itself to perform the Windows-specific functions, and therefore speeds up the OS.

XMS eXtended Memory Specification. XMS is a set of standards that allows applications to access memory above 1024K.

Zoomed Video See ZV.

ZV Zoomed Video (ZV) is a direct data connection between a PC Card and host system that allows a PC Card to write video data directly to the video controller.

INDEX

C

E

F

G

N

O

T

U

Custom Corporate Network Training

Train on Cutting Edge Technology   We can bring the best in skill-based training to your facility to create a real-world hands-on training experience. Global Knowledge has invested millions of dollars in network hardware and software to train our students on the same equipment they will work with on the job. Our relationships with vendors allow us to incorporate the latest equipment and platforms into your on-site labs.

Maximize Your Training Budget   Global Knowledge provides experienced instructors, comprehensive course materials, and all the networking equipment needed to deliver high quality training. You provide the students; we provide the knowledge.

Avoid Travel Expenses   On-site courses allow you to schedule technical training at your convenience, saving time, expense, and the opportunity cost of travel away from the workplace.

Discuss Confidential Topics   Private on-site training permits the open discussion of sensitive issues such as security, access, and network design. We can work with your existing network's proprietary files while demonstrating the latest technologies.

Customize Course Content   Global Knowledge can tailor your courses to include the technologies and the topics which have the greatest impact on your business. We can complement your internal training efforts or provide a total solution to your training needs.

Corporate Pass   The Corporate Pass Discount Program rewards our best network training customers with preferred pricing on public courses, discounts on multimedia training packages, and an array of career planning services.

Global Knowledge Training Lifecycle   Supporting the Dynamic and Specialized Training Requirements of Information Technology Professionals

- Define Profile
- Assess Skills
- Design Training
- Deliver Training
- Test Knowledge
- Update Profile
- Use New Skills

College Credit Recommendation Program   The American Council on Education's CREDIT program recommends 53 Global Knowledge courses for college credit. Now our network training can help you earn your college degree while you learn the technical skills needed for your job. When you attend an ACE-certified Global Knowledge course and pass the associated exam, you earn college credit recommendations for that course. Global Knowledge can establish a transcript record for you with ACE, which you can use to gain credit at a college or as a written record of your professional training that you can attach to your resume.

Registration Information

COURSE FEE: The fee covers course tuition, refreshments, and all course materials. Any parking expenses that may be incurred are not included. Payment or government training form must be received six business days prior to the course date. We will also accept Visa/MasterCard and American Express. For non-U.S. credit card users, charges will be in U.S. funds and will be converted by your credit card company. Checks drawn on Canadian banks in Canadian funds are acceptable.

COURSE SCHEDULE: Registration is at 8:00 a.m. on the first day. The program begins at 8:30 a.m. and concludes at 4:30 p.m. each day.

CANCELLATION POLICY: Cancellation and full refund will be allowed if written cancellation is received in our office at least six business days prior to the course start date. Registrants who do not attend the course or do not cancel more than six business days in advance are responsible for the full registration fee; you may transfer to a later date provided the course fee has been paid in full. Substitutions may be made at any time. If Global Knowledge must cancel a course for any reason, liability is limited to the registration fee only.

GLOBAL KNOWLEDGE: Global Knowledge programs are developed and presented by industry professionals with "real-world" experience. Designed to help professionals meet today's interconnectivity and interoperability challenges, most of our programs feature hands-on labs that incorporate state-of-the-art communication components and equipment.

ON-SITE TEAM TRAINING: Bring Global Knowledge's powerful training programs to your company. At Global Knowledge, we will custom design courses to meet your specific network requirements. Call 1 (919) 461-8686 for more information.

YOUR GUARANTEE: Global Knowledge believes its courses offer the best possible training in this field. If during the first day you are not satisfied and wish to withdraw from the course, simply notify the instructor, return all course materials, and receive a 100% refund.

In the US:

CALL: 1 (888) 762-4442

FAX: 1 (919) 469-7070

VISIT OUR WEBSITE:

www.globalknowledge.com

MAIL CHECK AND THIS FORM TO:

Global Knowledge

Suite 200

114 Edinburgh South

P.O. Box 1187

Cary, NC 27512

In Canada:

CALL: 1 (800) 465-2226

FAX: 1 (613) 567-3899

VISIT OUR WEBSITE:

www.globalknowledge.com.ca

MAIL CHECK AND THIS FORM TO:

Global Knowledge

Suite 1601

393 University Ave.

Toronto, ON M5G 1E6

REGISTRATION INFORMATION:

Course title _____

Course location _____ Course date _____

Name/title _____ Company _____

Name/title _____ Company _____

Name/title _____ Company _____

Address _____ Telephone _____ Fax _____

City _____ State/Province _____ Zip/Postal Code _____

Credit card _____ Card # _____ Expiration date _____

Signature _____